"In *The Notorious Ben Hecht: Iconoclas*  en
Gorbach highlights the character, tl ːnt
of an engaged intellectual, crossing of
assertive advocacy on behalf of a cause deemed too ...... .ieu
in which he was a major element. In focusing on this facet of the life of one
who was a borderline American Jew, Gorbach not only details the personal
biography of Hecht as Hollywood screenwriter, playwright, and novelist,
but in his treatment of Hecht's activities on behalf of the Jewish resistance
in Mandate Palestine against the oppressive British rule, he retrieves that
period of Israel's history shunted aside due to ideological and political bias,
the years of the national liberation struggle prior to the establishment of
the state that have been subjected to a campaign of purposeful neglect and
which affected Hecht as well."

—**Yisrael Medad**, Research Fellow,
Menachem Begin Heritage Center, Jerusalem

"With storytelling skills equal to his subject's, Julien Gorbach shows the
nuance and complexity of Ben Hecht's transformation from secular and
cynical Hollywood script doctor to committed Zionist activist attempting
first to save the Jews of Europe during World War II, and then to found the
state of Israel. Gorbach's deeply researched and vivid depiction of Hecht's
work on behalf of Jewish survival and freedom features a compelling cast
of characters, from stateside intellectuals and entertainers to American
Jewish gangsters and Irgun rebels against British rule. *The Notorious Ben
Hecht* rewards readers as much as Hecht's own films, plays, and novels do."

—**Bill Savage**, Professor of Instruction, Northwestern University

The Notorious Ben Hecht

Cataloging-in-Publication data is on file with the Library of Congress.

Paper: 978-1-55753-865-9
ePDF: 978-1-61249-594-1
ePub: 978-1-61249-595-8

Cover image: Ben Hecht, half-length portrait, facing right, smoking pipe. Photo by George Maillard Kesslere, 1931, courtesy of the Library of Congress (LC-USZ62-111023).

The Notorious Ben Hecht
Iconoclastic Writer and Militant Zionist

Julien Gorbach

Purdue University Press
West Lafayette, Indiana

To say that force is sometimes necessary is not a call to cynicism—it is a recognition of history; the imperfections of man and the limits of reason.

. . . But we do not have to think that human nature is perfect for us to still believe that the human condition can be perfected. We do not have to live in an idealized world to still reach for those ideals that will make it a better place.

. . . For if we lose that faith—if we dismiss it as silly or naïve; if we divorce it from the decisions that we make on issues of war and peace—then we lose what is best about humanity. We lose our sense of possibility. We lose our moral compass.

—President Barack Obama, Nobel Prize for Peace acceptance speech, November 10, 2009

All my life I have been haunted by a phrase read in my youth in one of Joseph Conrad's books—"the soul of man." I grew up with this phrase tugging at my elbow. And I secretly measured literature, people and events by whether or not the "soul of man" was in them.

The "soul of man" meant to me the urgent rivers of emotion on which humans have always traveled—the dark torrents of mania, greed and terror; the bright streams of love and brotherhood. Beyond the monkeyshines of his politics and the inanities of his verbal worlds, this "soul of man" has beckoned my attention, stimulating and horrifying me and occasionally filling me with pride.

—Ben Hecht, *A Child of the Century*, 1954

Contents

Foreword

Any American born after 1900 and before, say, 1960 would have found it difficult to escape the influence of Ben Hecht. For at least half of what has so often been called "the American Century," he must have seemed ubiquitous. Hecht was surely among the most prolific writers of his time; he was unstoppable. He also operated in so many genres that one life—no matter how colorful, no matter how full—barely seems to have encompassed what he achieved, in journalism, in literature, on the screen, and in polemics. Yet until now—that is, until the publication of Julien Gorbach's lively biographical study—Hecht has eluded the grasp of scholarship. Once so pervasive and fertile a figure in the mass media, he has suffered from the neglect that he hardly merited. *The Notorious Ben Hecht* is thus a welcome corrective.

Several reasons for the academic indifference of recent decades can be proposed here. As a writer, Hecht produced his greatest and most enduring work in Hollywood, where scenarists from the birth of the sound era to the death of the studio system were subjected to contempt ("schmucks with Underwoods," in the mogul Jack Warner's famous dismissal). Film credits in the decades when Hecht was producing an endless stream of scripts (Gorbach stopped counting after 140 or so) are quite unreliable, and the retrospective determination of who-did-what in a collective enterprise is often a mug's game. Even Hecht's most famous play, the actor-proof comedy, *The Front Page* (1928), brandished a collaborator (Charles MacArthur). Because Hecht fancied himself writing for the money rather than for posterity, he left a thin paper trail after he'd cashed his checks. He was, moreover, so fluent a storyteller that later researchers may have felt intimidated by the competition; who could match the lip-smacking mirth with which Hecht recalled (or fabricated) the highlights of his own life, especially in *A Child of the Century* (1954)?

A final conjecture for the frustrations in recounting his influence and importance is the enigma of his Jewishness. Until 1939, as Gorbach notes, Hecht came across as the hack who played to popular taste—an extremely skilled and savvy hack, to be sure, but not exactly someone to reach for gravitas. The unprecedented menace of Nazism, and then the struggle for Jewish statehood, made Hecht aware of the pertinence of the Jewish fate to "the soul of man," and turned his life in a direction that could hardly have been foreseen in the raucous days and nights in Chicago and then Hollywood. The two previous books that delve most deeply into Hecht's career (published in 1977 and 1990) are quite inadequate in explaining the forcefulness of his anti-Nazism and his pro-Zionism. The extent to which Gorbach addresses Hecht's politicization in the decade of the 1940s— when it counted—may be the greatest achievement of this book, which is the first that an academic has written and by far the richest that anyone has written. He is now spared the obscurity that he risked falling into, the paradox of a prominence that once was his. The horror of the Holocaust and the rebirth of a sovereign state constitute the two most significant events of modern Jewish history, and Gorbach has entwined Hecht in both of them.

A foreword should not come with a spoiler alert, so I won't dwell on the adroitness with which Gorbach brings to life the career of this amazing litterateur. But I must record the luck of Ben Hecht in having so tenacious a researcher and so elegant a writer in making this bon vivant and provocateur pertinent to a new generation of readers. *The Notorious Ben Hecht* manages both to penetrate a character who was sardonic and sophisticated, and to capture a life that was both flamboyant and mythic. With this book both Julien Gorbach and Purdue University Press rectify the injustice done to Hecht in the academy, and allow readers to see what that child of the century enabled millions of Americans to see.

STEPHEN J. WHITFIELD
Max Richter Chair in American Civilization, Brandeis University

Acknowledgments

"Writing, at its best, is a lonely life," Ernest Hemingway once said, but this book would not have been possible without the help of many wonderful people.

I owe a great debt to my newspaper editors, the redoubtable Bill Decker and Dan Campbell, for the guidance and encouragement they provided me when I was a reporter. They taught me the discipline of daily journalism, conscientiousness, and even some temperance, and went to bat for me on occasions when the targets of my muckraking hollered for my head. Later they wrote the endorsements that launched my career as a scholar.

After nearly a decade in the newsroom, I was welcomed back to academia as an adjunct instructor by the communication faculty of the University of Louisiana at Lafayette. Drs. T. Michael Maher, Lucian Dinu, and Bill Davey mentored me as a novice instructor and urged my pursuit of a doctorate. After I completed my coursework at the University of Missouri, they welcomed my return as if I had never left, now as a visiting lecturer of new media. Dr. Maher was always willing to take a chance with me, while pushing me to achieve further goals.

As a doctoral student, I had the honor of studying under brilliant professors at the University of Missouri in Columbia, the University of Chicago, and Harvard Summer School. In particular, John Frymire, Abdullahi Ibrahim, Elaine Lawless, Glenn Leshner, Earnest L. Perry, Steven Watts, and Betty Winfield in Columbia; Mark Philip Bradley and Paul Mendes-Flohr in Chicago; and Brandeis professor David Engerman in the Harvard summer program opened my eyes to new perspectives and helped me develop the knowledge and skills to become a media historian.

For all his reputed cynicism, Ben Hecht was a great believer in friendship. I am deeply grateful to lifelong friends who have made me a believer as well: Joseph Makkos, Bardia Kohn, Hannah Mackenna, Dave Scott, John Dale, Dave Twidle, Aaron Schindler, Scott Winder, David Briggs, Dane Melancon, and David and Jessica Wiley Leslie. In Columbia, Yusuf Kalyango, Jeffrey Pe-Aguirre, Seth Graves, John Swain, Terra Stephan, and Lekan Oguntoyinbo kept me focused and motivated. Hank Showers, I don't know how I would have made it through the fall of 2010 without your help. During the long slog over the last couple of years in Lafayette, Alfred J. Stahl was a constant supporter and interlocutor. I owe a deep debt of gratitude to Bernard Pearce for reading passages and helping me hash out my ideas through our endless discussions, day after day, month after month, over his marvelous plates of food.

Dr. Margaret Blanchard used to say that a dissertation committee is like a stagecoach journeying on a long and dusty trail, and that it is therefore crucial to embark with the right combination of people. I was blessed to have five extraordinary fellow travelers with me for the seven years that it took to bring the dissertation from inception to completion. They were as honest in their criticism, which I needed and deserved, as they were generous in their praise. For investing so much heart and hard work, far beyond the call of duty, thanks to Drs. Dean Mills, Yong Volz, Carla Klausner, and Stephen J. Whitfield.

Steve, who from the day I called him out of the blue a decade ago has been a stalwart supporter of me and of all things Hecht, has also been gracious enough to write the foreword to this book. I am honored to receive this contribution from such a towering figure in the study of Jewish American culture and politics.

Thanks to the staff of the Newberry Library and to the man who gathered many vital files for me in Chicago, John Montes. Thanks especially to two of the best librarians in the world, Dorothy Carner and Sue Schuermann, who helped me gather and manage a mountain of books.

Thanks to the faculty and staff of the School of Communications at the University of Hawaii at Manoa, who have been the best colleagues I could ask for. They have given me the opportunity to bring this book to fruition and proceed with further scholarship: Gerald Kato, Brett Oppegaard, Ann Auman, Jenifer Sunrise Winter, Wayne Buente, Scott Schimmel, Kelly Bergstrom, Patricia Amaral Buskirk, Ji Yong Kim, Hanae Kramer, Marc Moody, Rachel Neo, Cassandra Tengan, Shellie Kamura, Bernadette Baraquio, Sherrie White, and Dean Denise Konan.

Thanks to Rafael Medoff, executive director of the Wyman Institute, who provided several of the images featured in this book free of charge.

Thanks to Katherine Purple, Bryan Shaffer, and the rest of the staff at Purdue University Press for their incredible work on this book.

Thanks to Buster and Alley for their love, warmth, and fluffiness and to my three young girls, Snowboots, Luna, and Sweetie. Thanks to my noble sister, Roxane Gorbach—would that more people could possess so much goodness—and to my niece and nephew, Camille and Cole Vocelka. I am lucky to have such a great family. Thanks to Carita and Delilah Faul and to the rest of the Faul family, for loving me and being there all along.

And thanks, most of all, to my adviser and mentor Dr. Berkley Hudson, whose gentleness, wisdom, patience, and sense of humor ultimately brought out the best in me. And thanks to my parents, Judith and Sherwood Gorbach, who for fifty years have continued to amaze me with the depth of their love and devotion.

Introduction

This time, people said, Ben Hecht has gone too far.

In the spring of 1947, the American journalist turned screenwriter shocked and outraged newspaper readers across the world with a full-page advertisement that supported terrorist attacks against his country's closest military ally, Great Britain. World War II had cemented America's "special relationship" with Britain, a partnership expected to be the cornerstone of peace and stability in the postwar world. But from 1939 on, British land, sea, and air forces had shut Europe's Jews out of Palestine, effectively clamping Adolf Hitler's trap shut during the war years and, in the aftermath, leaving the survivors to languish as "displaced persons" in the liberated concentration camps. Hecht and the Irgun Zvai Leumi, the faction of Zionist fighters that he championed, believed a guerrilla war was the best way to finally smash the blockade, open the gates to mass immigration by Holocaust survivors, and thus clear a path to Jewish statehood.

Hecht's "Letter to the Terrorists of Palestine," which appeared in more than a dozen newspapers, explained that American support for the Irgun had not been forthcoming because rich and influential American Jews were opposed to the attacks. But speaking for the common person and swearing "on my word as an old reporter," Hecht declared, "Every time you blow up a British arsenal, or wreck a British jail, or send a British railroad train sky high, or let go with your guns and bombs at the British betrayers and invaders of your homeland, the Jews of America make a little holiday in their hearts."[1]

The letter set off a storm of fury that roiled in the international press for months, exposing a deep schism within both Jewish and American life.[2] It was the culmination of Hecht's increasingly inflammatory eight-year propaganda campaign that had generated debate and conflict at every gradation from the private to the public sphere, from bitter arguments in Jewish homes to dueling newspaper editorials to clashes in the streets outside his agitprop theatrical pageants.[3]

Hecht's message, reviled by a liberal elite as populist, tribalistic demagoguery, indeed as Jewish fascism, has resonated ever since. But while Hecht left an indelible mark as a provocateur during the 1940s, he was a remarkably multidimensional figure whose literary talent easily matched his genius for spectacle and controversy. By the time he published his "Letter to the Terrorists of Palestine," he was a prominent writer whose work would remain popular for generations.

From the beginning of his working life, he had established himself as a man with a magical gift for storytelling, a real-life, masculine version of Scheherazade, the tale-spinning heroine of *1001 Arabian Nights*. Having come of age as a young crime reporter in Chicago, he gained national attention with his critically acclaimed first novel, *Erik Dorn* (1921), and a collection of the short sketches he had written for his daily newspaper column, *A Thousand and One Afternoons in Chicago* (1922). He is still best remembered for his first bona fide hit, *The Front Page*, a collaboration with fellow Chicago newsroom veteran Charles MacArthur. Since its sensational 1928 Broadway debut, it has spawned four movies and four television productions, a radio play, and regular revivals on the stage. Walter Kerr praised it as "a watch that laughed" for the clockwork precision of its jokes and twists. *The Front Page* remains cardinal to discussions of journalism in popular culture. With its romantic portrayal of the big-city reporter as rake and rebel, it fired the public imagination of Hecht's day just as *Fear and Loathing in Las Vegas* and *All the President's Men* would for a later generation. "The play has been called the Rosetta stone of journalism, the key to figuring out the hieroglyphics and high jinks of a strange craft," noted journalism scholar Robert Schmuhl.[4]

By 1927 Hecht had already written *Underworld*, the silent film that would launch a gangster movie craze and earn him one of the first Academy Awards. Over the next forty years he spun out blockbusters with a resourcefulness, versatility, and speed that at times resembled sorcery. He justifiably claimed to have "invented the gangster movie," following up *Underworld* with *Scarface*, a 1932 epic produced by millionaire Howard Hughes to be the gangster movie to end all gangster movies. He likewise helped invent the screwball comedy, following *The Front Page* with

Twentieth Century (1934) and *Nothing Sacred* (1937). He penned the final draft of *Gone with the Wind* (1939) in one marathon session with producer David Selznick, and also wrote such classics as *Wuthering Heights* (1939) and Alfred Hitchcock's *Notorious* (1946).[5]

Hecht was the man the studios turned to whenever they were in a jam: he could write well in any genre, at lightning speed. In 1967 *New Yorker* critic Pauline Kael credited him with half the entertaining movies that Hollywood had ever produced.[6] In addition to sixty-five screen credits and contributions to more than 140 films, he authored ten novels, about 250 short stories, a half dozen memoirs, and some twenty Broadway shows, as well as innumerable articles, columns, speeches, wartime propaganda pageants, radio dramas, and television serials.[7]

Yet Hecht's literary achievements have often obscured his historical role as the man who broke the silence about the Nazis' Final Solution to the Jewish Question. Just as Kristallnacht erupted, Hecht wrote the short story "The Little Candle," an uncanny, horrifyingly vivid prophecy of the catastrophe that was about to come. In his younger years, he had epitomized the assimilated "Un-Jewish Jew." But he "turned into a Jew in 1939," he later wrote. "The German mass murder of the Jews, recently begun, brought my Jewishness to the surface."[8]

He became a lone voice in the wilderness, calling out his Jewish movie studio bosses for cowing to the American censorship and Nazi bullying that had kept Hitler's brutal persecution off the silver screen during the 1930s. While the American press remained oblivious to the reports of a German extermination plan that surfaced early in World War II, Hecht launched a massive publicity campaign. He published jolting full-page newspaper advertisements and orchestrated star-studded theatrical spectaculars at Madison Square Garden and the Hollywood Bowl that mobilized public pressure on the Roosevelt administration for an Allied rescue program.

Given the Allied leadership's resistance to his push for rescue, however, he came to view Franklin Delano Roosevelt and Winston Churchill as complicit in the genocide, and as six million perished, his desperation curdled into rage. After the war, he became notorious. He outraged people across the world by partnering with the Jewish gangster Mickey Cohen to arm Jews in Palestine and by calling for terrorism against Britain with his incendiary letter. The letter, with its fierce embrace of Jewish roots and acid rebuke of "respectable" assimilationists, reflected a personal transformation that had been under way since 1939, after he had long dismissed his roots as inconsequential. Hecht may still be known today as "the Shakespeare of Hollywood," the film industry's most legendary screenwriter, but his activism in Jewish politics later in life is equally, if not more, significant.

The Notorious Ben Hecht is the story of how Hecht first earned admiration as a humanitarian and then vilification as an extremist at this pivotal moment in history. By looking at his entire life, the book investigates the origins of his beliefs—rooted in his varied experiences in American media—and the consequences.

The remarkable polemics of Hecht's letter helped shape the public debate about what lessons to draw from the war. On the one side were the humanists, the mainstream Zionists, who envisioned the Jewish state as a liberal democracy and put their faith in diplomacy, multilateralism, and international law. On the other side were Hecht and the Irgun, who believed the Jews could rely on—and could be judged by—no one but themselves. The liberals saw the war as a victory of their ideology over fascism. With the birth of the United Nations, the vote for the partition of Palestine, the Nuremberg trials, the first declaration on human rights, and a convention on genocide, the 1940s were formative years for international law, and Jews could point to these achievements as assurances of their basic rights.[9] Conversely, Hecht and the Irgun read the war as confirmation that the Jews could not survive by the rules the world made for them. While the mainstream Zionists trusted in the United States and Britain, Hecht's faction maintained that even the world's great democracies had failed the Jews in their hour of need. Thus, while both sides vowed "never again," they disagreed about how to guarantee that vow. The liberal Zionists believed in the rule of international law, while Hecht and the Irgun believed in the rule of the gun.

This book attempts to shed light on that argument—which not only was foundational to the birth of the Jewish state but has determined its fate ever since—by examining an underlying question about Hecht's worldview: his concern with what he called "the soul of man."[10] While Hecht's contemporaries in journalism, such as Walter Lippmann and H. L. Mencken, had warned of a public too distracted, ignorant, or dimwitted to understand the complex new problems of the modern world, Hecht always had an even darker take.[11] He saw in humanity a dark sea of savage, primordial currents: the fears and resentments of an innate tribalism that could be churned into hate by the right demagogue. In 1939 his grim view of human nature yielded a kind of second sight, an ability to see, with much greater clarity than most, the horror that was about to unfold in Europe. Yet when the struggle for a Jewish state was under way nearly a decade later, his letter to the terrorists and partnership with Mickey Cohen earned him infamy as a terrorist, gangster, and fascist. Where did this perspective come from, and where did it ultimately lead him?

Differing views about the soul of man have been the basis for a fundamental debate in Western civilization, a debate that connects Hecht's journalism and storytelling to his politics. These differences came to the fore in the clash between Chicago's roguish journalism, portrayed by Hecht in *The Front Page*, and the respectable journalism represented most notably by the *New York Times*, which by the 1920s had embraced fact-based objectivity as a professional standard, in a bid to protect the newspaper as what Lippmann once called "the bible of democracy."[12] This same philosophical schism, within the realm of Jewish politics, separated the Irgun and the mainstream Zionists.

Labels like *conservative* or *right-wing* would be inaccurate for Hecht, particularly given the contemporary connotations of these terms, and simply identifying him as a cynic sheds little light on his worldview. The Zionist leaders who opposed Hecht may indeed fit the liberal label, in the New Dealish center-left or Wilsonian sense. But, more to the point, the followers of Chaim Weizmann and David Ben-Gurion were proponents of liberal humanism, the classic faith of the Enlightenment. The political philosopher Isaiah Berlin has pointed out that while Enlightenment-era thinkers differed in many respects, they shared a basic optimism about human nature and the power of reason.[13] By contrast, Romanticism, a political and cultural reaction to the Enlightenment, reflected a dark view of humanity and its twisted uses of the powers of reason, a view stunningly affirmed by the Great War and the subsequent rise of Nazism. I argue that it is instructive to understand Hecht as a *Romantic*.

While the Enlightenment-Romanticism debate is rooted in Europe, Hecht's story is emphatically an American one. Though he wrote that he "turned into a Jew in 1939," he also explained, "The discovery that I was a Jew did not send me to lighting any Friday night candles, nor did it alter by a phrase any of my attitudes towards life. These are American attitudes, born in America, nurtured in American schools and developed through service in American journalism, literature, drama, and the movies."[14]

From the start, his Jewish activism represented a rebellion within the media, a challenge to the Jewish movie executives—to a system that had long kept the growing menace of Nazism off the theater screens—and to the major, Jewish-owned newspapers, which had similarly kept news of the genocide off their front pages. By aggressively calling attention to his people's plight at a time when so many others were afraid to make waves, Hecht redefined what it meant to be an American Jew, and perhaps even what it meant to be an American.

His propaganda campaign began as an effort to raise a Jewish army that could fight Hitler alongside the Allies, and even during the darkest years of the Holocaust, he was savvy enough to portray the Jews as a shackled force—a "champion in chains"—rather than as victims. He evoked the legends of American Jewish prizefighters—Benny Leonard, Sid Terris, Rube Goldstein, Battling Levinsky, Barney Ross, and Maxie Baer. And he introduced an American image of the "New Jew" of the Middle East: an ancient Hebrew warrior, now resurrected to fight for his people and reclaim his homeland.[15]

But this former Chicago crime reporter and writer of gangster movies ultimately confronted the realities behind his own "tough Jew" myth. His new partner in militant Zionist activities, Mickey Cohen, personified that myth. Cohen, a onetime professional boxer and mob enforcer who rose to replace Bugsy Siegel as king of the West Coast rackets, was a psychopath whom the Federal Bureau of Investigation had directly linked to seven murders; he could smash a magnum of champagne across a stranger's face in a crowded elegant restaurant because of a perceived slight.[16] Cohen's friendship with Hecht during the 1950s—when Hecht's cynical worldview blinded him to the gangster's dark side and manipulations—makes this a cautionary tale about Hecht's legacy.

The political rhetoric of the 1940s linked gangsterism with terrorism, with good reason: the Irgun and its small but highly effective sidekick, the Stern Gang, resorted to extortion and armed robbery to fund their military operations.[17] Hecht's partnership with Cohen and other American underworld figures added another layer to the story of gangsterism and the birth of Israel, raising more questions about the distinctions—then and now—between international lawmaker and lawbreaker.

Supporters of Israel have long been loath to acknowledge that Jewish American mobsters like Cohen and Meyer Lansky made any significant contribution to the Zionist cause through their efforts to smuggle arms and matériel to Palestine. For decades, the involvement of these racketeers and killers has been regarded as a blight on the history of the Jewish state, and, indeed, Israel's enemies have pointed to it as proof of the nation's inherently criminal character and lack of legitimacy. This book investigates the historical evidence, arguing that the importance of the role played by Jewish American gangsters has remained obscured and unrecognized.[18]

Hecht's importance as a multifaceted modern writer does not diminish the role he played in history. He was born shortly before the start of the twentieth century and died just as the 1960s were getting into full swing. He came of age with the advent of mass communication, and his story vividly illustrates how mass media changed the character of our culture. But he was also among the most prominent and influential disputants in a clash of political ideas that came to the fore with the rise of Nazism, the Holocaust, and the birth of Israel. Hecht aptly titled his major autobiography *A Child of the Century*, and his life provides a remarkable window into the times that shaped our world.

The Lost Land of Boyhood

My Jewishness does not belong to any other land. Despite the activities of the back-to-Palestine patriots, the Jew of America has no secondary homeland. . . . As a Jew he is loyal to the same ideas to which he gives his American loyalty. He cries for the rights of man, and for the decent, unperilous operation of government. If he cries more loudly for these than the American next to him, is he not, perhaps, more American?

—BEN HECHT, *A GUIDE FOR THE BEDEVILLED*[1]

Just before America's entry into World War II, Ben Hecht was sitting in a New York City tavern when a chance encounter with an old friend transported him into the past. He and Sherwood Anderson had first met thirty years earlier, just as Anderson was becoming one of the defining voices of the preindustrial American heartland.

Anderson had once written tenderly and deeply of "small towns and small people," Hecht explained in a newspaper column a few days later. His friend had "reinvented the American soul," finding it "in the milking shed, the hardware store, the village meeting hall, in the factory noon-hour, and on the front porch." When Anderson now mentioned that he was about to leave the country, perhaps never to return, Hecht asked why. This "Dostoievsky of the corn belts" invited him to guess.[2]

"I ought to know, and do," Hecht wrote. "Sherwood is off to find something that vanished out of the world he knew and wrote about. It disappeared out of the West and East and even the South, where he went looking for it a few years ago. It was the America he knew—that moody, whimsical, and inarticulate hero of the pre-radio, pre-movie hinterlands."[3]

Hecht thought he understood his friend's plan for self-imposed exile because he too had belonged to that lost America, a world that had been erased by the media, modernization, and war. It was the land of Hecht's boyhood. Although he had been born in New York City on February 28, 1893, his family had settled in Racine, Wisconsin, by about 1903.[4] By all accounts, his adolescence was a Tom Sawyer–like existence, typical of small Midwestern towns before the Great War: idyllic but never-dull days occupied by imaginative schemes drawn from the adventure stories he devoured.

For most of Hecht's life, he had little reason to dwell on the one aspect of his experience that differed from Anderson's, or Mark Twain's: he was the child of Jewish immigrants. "There was no Jewish situation in my world of redskins, buccaneers and acrobats," he later wrote. "Jewish history consisted only of my folks who had, after many hardships, arrived in the U.S.A., and who considered themselves happily to be Americans with a slight accent."[5] Indeed, all that he admired in Jews he also admired in his fellow Americans, and he found so much to celebrate in being American that he saw no reason that his Jewishness even mattered.

Ben's parents, Joseph Hecht and Sarah Swernofsky, had immigrated from Russia in the mid-1880s and settled in the Jewish ghetto on Manhattan's Lower East Side, the primary destination for East European Jews and one of the most densely populated neighborhoods in the world. The couple married in 1892, a year before their son's birth. Reared in this transplanted shtetl, or Jewish village, teeming with pickle vendors, delicatessens, synagogues, union halls, and Yiddish theaters, Ben learned to speak Yiddish almost as fluently as English.[6]

Joseph worked as a cloth cutter in the district's sweating system, a hive of textile production lines crammed into the tenements, where workers often toiled for fourteen hours a day, six days a week. Ben was still a toddler when his father decided to strike out on his own as a clothing designer. The family tried several locations—Boston, Philadelphia, and Chicago, where Joseph had a position as a designer and factory manager—before finally moving to Racine. There Joseph started manufacturing lines of women's clothing, while Sarah operated a store, the Paris Fashion, in the downtown business district.[7]

Once ensconced in pastoral Racine, Ben set roaring autumn-leaf bonfires, shot flaming arrows dipped in kerosene in mock Indian battles, manufactured bottled hydrogen for reasons unknown, hunted frogs, flooded his boardinghouse's backyard to create a skating rink, dug caves in lake banks and built huts in the breakwaters and snow forts in the blizzards, serenaded girls beneath their windows, and nurtured a crush on his Latin teacher. He ran on the track team and played right end for the football team until he was injured, when he became a cheerleader. He went on hayrides, sleigh rides, bicycle rides, train rides, and boat rides.[8]

"I lay dreaming during heavy summer hours on hilltops, staring at cloud galleons, and the sky was part of my flesh," he wrote in his autobiography, *A Child of the Century*.

> The wind blew out of my bones. At night the star clusters were my eyeballs. I was related to everything—to a dead fish, a crushed worm, a wall of green water breaking over my boat. I went leaping after grasshoppers and butterflies, breasts and pelvises, print, and Time itself. I knew no other way to live than to worship each new burst of sun over the horizon. My prayers were yells, my hymns were squeals and curses. I yearned, swelled, wept, ravished, splashed through mud and rolled in flowers—and was never injured, and hurt no one.[9]

There were already hints of the future he would have in the arts and show business. With a box camera as big as a suitcase, he took photos that he tried, unsuccessfully, to sell. He performed shadowgraphs and magic shows, with his younger brother, Peter, as an assistant, who dressed up in a rummaged George Washington outfit. He attended vaudeville shows at the Bijou Theater and dramas at the Opera House.[10]

Despite Hecht's reputation as a firebrand in middle age, teenage peers remembered him as quiet and shy, but they nevertheless remembered him. "Ben was always where the action was and wherever Ben was, there was action," said classmate Grace Miller. "No one seemed to know Ben really well, but everybody certainly liked him. He was really different." He raised money for the school yearbook, *The Comet*, and for a student newspaper by selling advertising copy in verse.[11]

Ben's thirteenth birthday brought a momentous event: the arrival of four crates of books, including a fifteen-volume collection of Shakespeare, thirty-volume sets of Charles Dickens and Mark Twain, and a fifty-two volume History of the World. Joseph, who had little education, had read none of these but had asked a scholar, a brother Elk, to select them. More than forty years later, when he was writing his memoir, Ben still kept the books in his bedroom.[12]

Joseph had also bestowed something else on his son: a natural talent for narrative. "Our father spent many of his evenings talking about his childhood in Russia and composed tales about the country, people, oppression, etc.," recalled Peter. "Dad was a gifted storyteller. He blended the real with unreal—factual with fantasy. This in my opinion was the one real mental quality [Ben] inherited from our father."[13]

But Joseph was a *luftmensch*, to use the Yiddish term for a man lost in reverie. He tried to open another clothing store in Kalamazoo, Michigan, but, according to Peter, was fleeced by his business partner, who absconded with the factory bankroll and as much stock as he could liquidate. "[Dad] was not of the tribe of realists," Hecht related in *A Child of the Century*. "He savored success before it came. He rolled in millions when only pennies were in the safe. The chief and busiest department of his factory was always an air castle. He never had any profits to share with his family, except the happy smile of his daydreams. Tall, lean, straight-backed, child-like, misinformed, his eyes gentle and confused, his wide mouth firm, he retold in miniature the lies of Don Quixote."[14]

As a teenager, Hecht had another opportunity to see dreams collide with reality, in a brief career as a circus trapeze artist. It immersed him in a world equal parts enchanting, melancholy, and surreal, which would thereafter fire his literary imagination. The proprietress of the Hecht family's boardinghouse had once been a bareback-riding beauty married to "Dapper Dan" Castello, a partner of P. T. Barnum and one of the great acrobatic clowns of the American circus. Castello had performed before Queen Victoria and the Prince of Wales, earning the praise of Charles Dickens. Only weeks after the completion of the transcontinental railroad in 1869, his circus and menagerie became the first to complete a coast-to-coast tour, mostly by train. The following year, Castello and business partner W. C. Coup coaxed Barnum out of retirement for what would soon become "the Greatest Show on Earth."[15]

Just after their peak of fortune in 1871, Castello and his wife, Frances, fell on hard times, however. The couple separated, and Castello, who had parted with Barnum by 1875, died a near pauper in 1909. Frances had by then sold the house at 827 Lake Avenue to build the boardinghouse across the street, where the Hechts were given the largest of what Ben described as "a rabbit warren of rooms." The rest were occupied by roughly a dozen transients. "They were circus folk," Hecht recalled, "retired from the sawdust world, but springing constantly out of retirement for lesser roles in smaller and smaller tents."[16]

Hecht described the Castellos' son, Harry, as his first mentor. For about three years, until Hecht was fourteen, the alcoholic former acrobat trained him on the trapeze in the octagonal barn behind the boardinghouse. Whereas once Castello's Egyptian Caravan and Circus had toured the entire Great Lakes and Mississippi River in a 152-foot steamer, Harry and his young apprentice built an eighteen-foot sloop, *The Seabird*, with which Hecht and a handful of friends plied the shoreline of Lake Michigan. And whereas Castello had crossed the mountains and plains with camels and elephants and had ring-mastered Barnum's extravaganza, in 1907 Harry led Hecht and the boardinghouse troupe on a one-ring mud show tour of rural Wisconsin.

The circus was overtaken by bankruptcy after a couple of months. "On the way to Fond du Lac it mysteriously disintegrated," Hecht recalled, "its tent, its blue-painted rows of flap-down seats, its thousands of feet of heavy ropes and various pieces of unsatisfactory equipment, all disappearing along with all my genial and arthritic colleagues of the sawdust."[17]

If the men in Hecht's life had shown him daydreams and their inevitable disappointments, it was two women, his no-nonsense mother and his Tante (Aunt) Chasha, who molded him into a hard-nosed realist and iconoclast. Before her marriage, Sarah had been a showroom model, but for Hecht, "it was her goodness and honor that were her most striking features. They stared out of her a bit fiercely, and gave her a haughty air. With her firm shape and her bold blue eyes she looked, in my youth and hers, a bit more Valkyrie than Venus."[18]

While Joseph blithely accepted his business misfortunes, Sarah apparently made sure the family stayed afloat. She used her savings to buy the Paris Fashion storefront in the choicest location in town because "she didn't care for a position as a housewife," according to Peter. Ben recalled that she was proud and confident despite—or perhaps because of—her hardscrabble beginnings on a farm in southern Russia. But she could also be playful and childlike. She never preached to or harangued her sons, though her interactions with the rest of the world were a different matter. "Among my mother's more disturbing virtues was a passion for truth-telling," Hecht observed. "She was terribly vain of the fact that she couldn't tell a lie. In fact, she was vain of all her virtues and disdainfully conscious of their absence in others."[19]

The cherub-faced Tante Chasha—a "tall, swarthy, fat, and profane" aunt who wore a diamond brooch—was another major influence. She delivered one of her most important lessons when Ben was six years old, during a visit to a Yiddish theater. Caught up in the drama of the play and too young to understand theater etiquette, he had shouted in protest against a gross miscarriage of justice portrayed onstage. Aunt and nephew were brusquely escorted out to the lobby, where a theater manager demanded an apology. Tante Chasha let forth a stream of Yiddish curses as she cracked the manager over the head with her umbrella, sending him backward with a stagger and groan. "Remember what I tell you," she told Hecht, smiling as she whisked him outside. "That's the right way to apologize."[20]

As for the rest of his aunts and uncles, in *A Child of the Century* he paints them in tableau, sketching a portrait of each as he recounts a Fourth of July celebration on the porch in Racine.[21] Uncle Max had a drooping Cossack moustache, Chinese eyes, and a missing finger, deliberately shot off to avoid service in the czar's army. Years after his death, Max's wife, Eta, lavished attention on Hecht, now fully grown, in a tiny Lower East Side restaurant that she owned, her late husband's favorite singer, Caruso, crooning on the phonograph. The struggling widow passed away a few years later, "after many misadventures, including the amputation of a leg."[22]

Uncle Joe had a talent for toil, and his workers cursed him as a slave driver though he labored in their midst, no fewer than twelve hours a day, often all night, and always in his finest attire. His wife, Tante Lubi, hosted all-night poker games for the great Yiddish actors, who would eat from a massive bowl of sauerkraut, goose fat, and onions all diced together.

Tante Millie's husband, Issy, a French Jew, rose from a Bowery pickle peddler to a millionaire clothier, before finally dying destitute.

Most memorable was Uncle Jake, the family hero, Hecht's first model of a tough Jew. Hecht remembered him as a living Samson or Judah Maccabee. Jake was said to be even stronger than the late great Uncle Breitbart, whose favorite stunt—lying on spikes while trucks rode over him—had eventually been his end. In the Russian city of Kremenchug, where the Hechts and Swernofskys hailed from, Uncle Jake had cared little for tending geese, tailoring, and learning about religion. Instead, he stalked the nighttime streets, looking for Jew-hating Cossacks to battle. In America there were no Cossacks, so Jake found a new enemy: capitalism. While the rest of the family plunged into business, he became a socialist and defended downtrodden Jews against strikebreakers. One day a troop of policemen moved to break up a union rally, and Jake stepped into its path. According to the family, it required twenty officers to take him down. He was carried to the hospital with broken bones and was laid up for two months. Jake then retired from fighting and went to work for Uncle Joe.

Having introduced each member of the family, Hecht returned to the scene on the porch that July Fourth. The sun set as the group shared the peppered beef, salami, smoked whitefish, and other delicacies brought along from the ghetto's delis. Once it became dark, they began to sing. "I heard Yiddish songs as I watched the fireworks that celebrated the birth of freedom," Hecht recalled.[23]

The lives of Hecht's aunts and uncles, like those of his native-born neighbors, were hardly trouble-free. They had experienced extreme hardship and tragedy. But dreamers and realists alike were honest and hard-working, and they met their challenges with optimism, and without bitterness or self-pity. Introducing that scene on the porch in *A Child of the Century*, written just a few years after the birth of Israel, Hecht said, "I have believed in a nation of Jews and worked for that belief. But there are moments when I think wistfully of the lost innocence of the Jews, when the only politics they knew was the management of heaven."[24]

Here, preserved in microcosm in Hecht's memory, was the shtetl. Like the youthful America of Sherwood Anderson and Mark Twain, it was a lost world. But the destruction of the shtetl had been deliberate: East European pogroms had killed tens of thousands by 1920, followed by Nazi Germany's "Final Solution to the Jewish Question." In 1946 Hecht reviewed a story collection featuring Tevya the Milkman, the protagonist later popularized for Americans by *Fiddler on the Roof*. Writing for the *New York Times*, Hecht observed:

> "The Old Country," a collection of Sholom Aleichem's tales, is more than a book. It is the epitaph of a vanished world and an almost vanished people. The salty and hilarious folk of whom it tells—the Jews of Europe—are dead. All the Tevyas whose souls and sayings, whose bizarre and tender antics Sholom Aleichem immortalized in the richest

Yiddish prose ever written—were massacred, six million strong, by the Germans. And all the quaint and heartwarming villages in which the Jews of Europe lived are no longer on the map.[25]

Hecht would report that he reached the age of forty without once encountering anti-Semitism or even concerning himself with its existence. Fellow *Daily News* alumnus Meyer Levin found that hard to believe, coming from a Chicago newspaperman with such a Jewish name, and argued that it revealed "Hecht's capacity for attitudinizing and self-deception." By Hecht's lights, however, his sense of belonging in American society had made it easy to live as what he called an "Un-Jewish Jew." The rise of Nazism finally changed that: by 1943 he was witnessing anti-Semitism all over the United States, even among some he had considered friends. It was as if Hitler had spread the disease of Jew hatred around the world.[26]

Hecht said that although he never lived "as a Jew" or even among Jews, "my family remained like a homeland in my heart." Yet one day there would be even more personal reasons driving his turn to activism and embrace of Jewishness. From the circus troupes of his childhood to the reporters, impresarios, militants, and mobsters he knew in succeeding years, Hecht would spend a lifetime attaching himself to various groups, only to drift away. For a man who held the journalistic ethos of objectivity in such disdain, he maintained a curious kind of detachment. The consummate insider, he was also an outsider, like Georg Simmel's *stranger from within*: "he who is far, is actually near."[27]

Having graduated from high school in the spring of 1910, Hecht enrolled that summer at the University of Wisconsin, where he immediately found himself in the uneasy company of fraternity brothers with starched collars. An impulsive comment—that he was not sure what he would learn in the College of Arts and Sciences, since he had already read all the books on the course list—was not well received. His indignant peers demanded an apology. But Hecht, remembering his Tante Chasha's advice about apologies, instead caught a train for Chicago, where he soon joined a new troupe: Chicago newspapermen.

PART I

THE NEWSPAPERMAN
The Chicago School of Journalism

In July 1910, when Ben Hecht was seventeen years old, he ran away by train from the University of Wisconsin in Madison and slept through the night on a bench in the Chicago railroad station. Less than eager to report to his parents, he spent the morning wandering the downtown business loop and was in line for a vaudeville matinee when a distant uncle, long out of touch with his parents, spotted him. Hecht told Uncle Moyses that he was looking for a job. Moyses brought him to *Chicago Daily Journal* publisher John C. Eastman and introduced him as a writer.[1]

Eastman, who was throwing a stag party that evening, promised Hecht a position if he could write a story in verse about a bull who swallowed a bumblebee, defecated it, and got stung in the arse. "I want a moral on the end," Eastman added. Hecht complied. Having passed this test, he was escorted to city editor Ballard Dunne, who told him to report at six the next morning. Incredulous, Hecht pointed out that the next day was the Fourth of July. "There are no holidays in this dreadful profession you have chosen," Mr. Dunne replied.[2]

Over the years that followed, Hecht found fellowship among the tribe of city newsmen. He first emulated and then grew to personify the mix of cynicism, sentimentality, and mischief that he presented in his iconic farce about Chicago reporters, *The Front Page*. In 1919 Hecht spent a grim year as a foreign correspondent, returning to Chicago during the early days of Prohibition and Al Capone. But by then his once-jolly cynicism had soured, and he had grown ambivalent about his old milieu. Over the next decade, he distilled his views of the press and gangsters in works that made him rich and famous: *Underworld* (1927), *The Front Page* (1928), and *Scarface* (1932).

Hildy Johnson, the Faustian protagonist of *The Front Page*, is caught in the spell of his Mephistophelean editor, Walter Burns. Walter sells him on a fantasy of everlasting boyhood deviltry as a newshound, and, thus entranced, Hildy starts to sleepwalk away from his sensible plan to quit journalism, get married, and pursue an advertising career in New York. The devil's bargain that Walter dangles before Hildy evokes Hecht's own proclivities. "Born perversely," Hecht once wrote of himself: a classic Faustian Romantic, he was drawn to the dark, the forbidden, the dangerous, or the just plain wrong, and he found kinship with rebels and renegades.[3] The impulse drove both Hecht's Romanticist approach to storytelling and a fascination with criminals and gangsters that he shared with his fellow newspapermen and women. From the start, he had admired Chicago reporters as a tribe of outlaws, a view encouraged when, in the 1920s, the newspaper industry adopted professional standards that marginalized his city's brand of journalism.[4]

But the link between Chicago's press and outlaws was more than metaphor. In one telling scene in *The Front Page*, reporters greet a gangster named Diamond Louie. Waving off their inquiries about plans to knock off a rival, Louie explains that he is now retired. "Yeah. That's right. I'm a newspaperman . . . working for Walter Burns," he says. "I'm assistant circulation manager for de nort' side."[5]

Perhaps because the epic contest in New York between media titans William Randolph Hearst and Joseph Pulitzer looms so large in American memory, it has overshadowed the dark chapter in journalism that followed, when Hearst shifted his sights to Chicago. Determined to gain an edge on the local competition after the launch of the *Chicago American* in 1900, Hearst hired Max Annenberg, an immigrant from East Prussia and a Chicago West Sider, to organize crews of "sluggers" to strong-arm newsboys into ditching stacks of rival newspapers. The *Tribune* and *Daily News* soon rose to the challenge, and what started with knives and brickbat brawls between gangs of neighborhood toughs evolved into shooting sprees that claimed the lives of newsboys and residents alike.

It became a three-way war, as the top dailies fought each other, and all sides attacked organized labor. Between 1910 and 1913, twenty-seven newsdealers were killed, according to one oft-cited estimate.[6] After that, the killings, beatings, and abductions continued until bootlegging offered the gangs more handsome rewards. By the 1930s, various memoirs and press histories divulged that Chicago's Prohibition-era gangsters had received their training as gunmen in the circulation wars before graduating to organized crime with the passage of the Volstead Act.[7] And it was the alumni of Chicago's newsrooms, Hecht among them, who helped gangsters achieve national celebrity through best-selling books, Broadway hits, and, ultimately, the gangster movie craze.

Despite the carnage of the press's "reign of terror," as one early chronicler called it, the police and the newspapers looked the other way.[8] But this was hardly the only major story they failed to cover. Here was a city crying out for reform. "Chicago is the place to make you appreciate at every turn the absolute opportunity that chaos affords," John Dewey wrote his wife. "Every conceivable thing solicits you; the town seems filled with problems holding out their hands and asking somebody to please solve them—or else dump them in the Lake."[9]

During the same period when Max Annenberg and his brother Moses first signed on with the *American*'s circulation department, the city's *ten* dailies all ignored the fire code violations in the graft-ridden First Ward, which routinely had lethal consequences.[10] Finally, on December 30, 1903, a blaze at the Iroquois Theatre claimed some six hundred lives, mostly children. Over the next three years, it would take a series of exposés in the *Lancet*, a British journal, to break arguably the biggest story in the city's history: the disgusting and dangerous conditions in the stockyards, which became the focus of Upton Sinclair's 1906 novel *The Jungle*.[11]

Chicago's newspapermen reflected the character of the city itself. For a reporter who spent days and nights dashing between crime scenes, trolley car and machinery accidents, and the city morgue, Chicago in the throes of its industrial boom was a raw and brutal place. Doug Fetherling puts it well in his biography of Hecht: "Chicago seemed a prairie Gomorrah where homicide was the logical solution to arguments and chicanery a natural force in the administration of justice. Streets were torn down and new ones erected, gang bosses were murdered to be supplanted by their killers, a dozen railways brought an influx of immigrants never matched

CHAPTER 1

The Chicago School

Journalists! Peeking through keyholes! Running after fire engines like a lot of coach dogs! Waking people up in the middle of the night to ask them what they think of Mussolini. Stealing pictures off old ladies of their daughters that get raped in Oak Park. A lot of lousy, daffy buttinskis swilling around with holes in their pants, borrowing nickels from office boys! And for what? So a million hired girls and motormen's wives will know what's going on. . . . I don't need anybody to tell me about newspapers. I've been a newspaperman for fifteen years. A cross between a bootlegger and a whore. And if you want to know something, you'll all end up on the copy desk—gray-headed, humpbacked slobs, dodging garnishees when you're ninety.

—Hildy Johnson in *The Front Page*[1]

The things we'll do for our papers! We lie, we cheat, we swindle and steal. We break into houses. We almost commit murder for a story. We're a bunch of lice.

—*Herald and Examiner* reporter Sam Blair[2]

There is a rich body of lore about the *Front Page* era of Chicago newspapers, tales reworked over and over in the memoirs of the veterans. Originally swapped in downtown barrooms and greasy spoons, these jumbled yarns, spun by conspicuously unreliable narrators, offer tribute to mischief in the name of journalism.[3] As sources of history, they are a tangle, but though the facts may vary, the essential story remains consistent.

In his own memoir, Hecht recalled that his first job in journalism was to beg, borrow, or (mostly) steal newsworthy photos as a "picture chaser" for the *Journal*. After Tante Chasha sewed large pockets into his jacket to conceal burglary tools and the loot, he "clambered up fire escapes, crawled through windows and transoms, posing when detected as everything from a gas meter inspector to an undertaker's assistant," recalled friend and fellow journalist Charles Samuels. Soon Hecht graduated to working as a reporter and professional hoaxer. Collaborating with photographer Gene Cour, he delivered splashy scoops on police pursuits of riverboat pirates and the Great Chicago Earthquake, which tore a terrific fissure through Lincoln Park.[4]

But our sole source for many of these extraordinary tales is Hecht himself. Samuels was a reporter and did work as a legman for Hecht, but Samuels lived in New York and in 1910 would have been only eight years old.[5] Yet while *A Child of the Century* has been criticized as one of "the less serious books [that] . . . shamelessly fictionalize events," there is a basis of truth to Hecht's newspaper stories.[6] Though they seem fantastic, they explain the traditions of Chicago journalism through a kind of narrative shorthand. It may seem incredible that newspapers paid young men to break into homes and steal photographs, but Theodore Dreiser cites it as common practice in his memoir, *Newspaper Days*. Vincent Starrett, who, like Hecht, started as a picture chaser, describes his own adventures in detail.[7]

Hecht's claim that his promotion to reporter afforded the opportunity for a short-lived career as a hoaxer recalls yet another dubious journalistic sport, one that Chicago reporters adopted and made peculiarly their own. The hoax was a tradition of the nineteenth century: a rash of them had appeared with the advent of New York's penny press in the 1830s, and by the 1850s, variations on the tall tale were a staple of Western newspapers. Mark Twain and Edgar Allan Poe perfected hoaxing as an art, while in more modern times, Orson Welles would leave an indelible mark on mass media history with his *War of the Worlds* broadcast.

But the Chicago hoax went beyond a mere genial prank: it became one more ploy to use in the bare-knuckle fight for scoops. In the 1890s, Finley Peter Dunne of the *Herald* and Charles Dillingham of the *Times* brought it into play against the *Tribune*'s Frank Vanderlip, their competitor on the hotel beat. Vanderlip could not understand how his rivals kept grabbing exclusives with famous and exotic personages who had stopped in town overnight and then vanished without a trace. Vanderlip was fired for incompetence, without ever realizing that these extraordinary hotel guests had never come to town or did not exist. Chicago reporters had put their own spin on the hoax. It was no longer a shared joke but a hustle pulled on the competition and the public alike.[8]

Chicago newspapermen were delinquents and misfits, "part detectives, thieves and con-men who enjoyed prying into the lives and business of others, and a few had the touch of a poet," observed one historian. Hecht's compatriots included an undertaker's assistant, a tramp, an aspiring opera singer, a failed priest, an ex-fighter, a former strong man in the circus, and a crackpot mystic embittered by gonorrhea. "I became a journalist after I had failed at nearly everything else," wrote Starrett.[9]

Oddball quirks, rivalries, and devious tactics all became part of the persona of the modern urban reporter. This identity, which had coalesced by the time Hecht joined the *Journal* in 1910, had its origins in two local institutions of the late nineteenth century, when reporters were developing self-awareness about their profession and were eager to mythologize it.[10] One was Chicago's wire service, the City News Bureau, which functioned as a kind of early journalism school. The other was a fraternity of literary-minded police reporters called the Whitechapel Club, which took its name from the London slum where Jack the Ripper had committed his murders. Hecht evoked both institutions, and their legacies, in his memoirs. All along, he cultivated an image as a Whitechapeler and carried on the spirit of the club.[11]

Home to boisterous rebels and a morbid, bizarre brand of bohemianism, the Whitechapel Club originally convened in the back room of Henry Koster's saloon; the club was established in the summer of 1889 by journalists who found the Press Club of Chicago too stodgy and expensive. It was an alternative to the seamy downtown taverns, a place of refuge at the end of a shift, sometimes late at night, where reporters could discuss their jobs, social issues, and their shared literary ambitions. It served as a forum, wrote Alfred Lawrence Lorenz, "in which they could define themselves as journalists by agreeing on what journalists were, how they should approach their work, and on a set of professional values—in short, what it meant to be a journalist." Although the Whitechapel Club existed for only five years, it became a legend, influencing generations of journalists to follow.[12]

Most memorable was the club's decor. A thick oak door with ornate wrought-iron scrollwork opened to a room dominated by a horse-shoe-shaped bar. Each place was set with a churchwarden's pipe and a tobacco-filled bowl that had once been the brainpan of a skull. The sawed-off lower portions of these skulls served as shades for the club's gas lighting fixtures. Brightly colored glass globes implanted in the eyeholes cast weird, eerie hues. Dr. John C. Spray, a Whitechapel member and superintendent of a hospital for the insane, had donated the skulls, which he had used in a study that purportedly discovered cranial differences between the sound of mind and the mentally ill. The adornments on the walls included a twelve-foot-long snakeskin, skeletons, blades, revolvers, and bullets that had slain famous criminals. The pride of the club, though, was the smaller room upstairs, fitted with a coffin-shaped bar studded with large brass railheads imprinted with the number of each member. Lorenz noted, "The decorations served as symbols of the often-dark world the members covered and the mocking posture they assumed toward it."[13]

Police reporters of the 1890s were exposed to the harshest and most gruesome realities of city life, while under the pressure of intense journalistic competition. The humorist Opie Read recalled that his fellow members sought to produce "photographic exposures of contemporary existence," whereas he wanted his journalism to be more like painting. Whitechapel became a wellspring of the naturalist school that emerged from journalism as a seminal movement in American literature. A hard-bitten, unique literary society, the club contributed to an enduring myth of "men who insisted on talking to one another about the hypocrisy of the social system even while they were being paid to explain it away, . . . who read everything they could get their hands on and fanned one another's literary aspirations as they sat about in the city room on a rainy night," noted journalism historian Larzer Ziff.[14]

The City News Bureau helped to forge another integral element of the Chicago style: the scoop, which, as Martin Mayer explained in *Making News*, "has been cultivated more jealously and single-mindedly in Chicago than anywhere else." A venerable local institution for more than a century, the bureau established itself in the 1890s as a training ground for cub reporters, known for "its iron discipline, its hard-nosed insistence on accuracy and, most of all, its legendary tightfistedness," according to A. A. Dornfeld.[15] In the days before journalism schools, the bureau instilled a code in its graduates and thus in the whole Chicago press—a code shaped by the dictates of free-market competition rather than a sense of civic mission. Speed and accuracy meant survival in a crowded newspaper field. Yet, ironically, the same bottom line that compelled a swarm of young men to get their facts straight also honed their talents for deception and misdirection in the contest for scoops, creating the cutthroat culture portrayed in *The Front Page*.

The City News developed a rather schizophrenic attitude toward the truth. A news service could ill afford mistakes or fabrications, which could damage the reputations of client newspapers or, worse, lead to libel suits. Accuracy thus became the watchword that bureau editors branded on the minds of their young charges. At the same time, *how* reporters got their news was another matter entirely; the papers counted on the City News to be on top of every breaking story. The bureau stretched its budget to the limit to underwrite twenty-four-hour vigils, streetcar fare, legmen, and, most famously, a pneumatic tube system put into use in 1893, which shot dispatches to newsrooms at thirty to seventy miles an hour through an underground labyrinth of pipes. Every reporter knew that the proven ability to produce scoops would be his ticket to his first newspaper job, an end to the grueling hours and pauper's wages of the City News.[16]

"'Get the news! Get the news!'—that was the great cry in the city editorial room," recalled Dreiser, who was struck by the "pagan or unmoral character" of newspaper work.

> Don't worry much over how you get it, but get it, and don't come back without it! Don't fall down! Don't let other newspapers skin us—that is, if you value your job! . . . While a city editor might readily forgive any form of trickery he would never forgive failure. Cheat and win and you were all right; be honest and lose and you were fired. To appear wise when you were ignorant, dull when you were not, disinterested when you were interested, brutal or severe when you might be just the reverse—these were the essential tricks of the trade. . . . And I . . . soon encountered other newspaper men who were as shrewd and wily as ferrets, who had apparently but one motive in life: to trim their fellow newspaper men in the matter of news, or the public which provided the news.[17]

Tales of scooping in the *Front Page* era are legion. Reporters were known to toss false tips that sent the competition on wild goose chases. *Collier's* celebrated Harry Romanoff of the *Herald and Examiner* as

Chicago's greatest telephone reporter because of his talent at impersonations. Once, calling a barroom where a murder had occurred, Romanoff identified himself as Sgt. Donohue of the coroner's office. "That's funny," said the voice on the other end. "So is this." And City News alum and *Herald and Examiner* editor Frank Carson staged a collision of two circulation trucks in front of a police station, a diversion that enabled his operatives to steal the diary of the alluring murderess Ruth Randall out of the evidence room.[18]

Courtroom scoops involved ingenuity and acrobatics. According to one account, City News staffer George Wright enlisted a courthouse janitor to bring a twenty-foot plank into the ceiling crawlspace above grand jury proceedings for the infamous Leopold-Loeb murder case. Wright then drilled a hole and used a stethoscope to listen in, confounding investigators for days. When the jury convened in the famous 1897 case of human remains found in a vat at a sausage factory, Fred A. Smith lowered himself into a courthouse air duct by rope. Hecht's friend Wallace Smith, of the *American*, hung upside down from the eaves of the courthouse roof, fifty feet above the ground, to peer through the windows of the jury room.[19]

Sometimes reporters planted evidence. "If it occurred to us that a janitor's missing mother-in-law might have been lured into the janitor's furnace, and the clues did not fit that attractive hypothesis," wrote Starrett, "we helped the story to headlines by discovering incinerated bones that somehow the police had missed."[20]

Journalism historians have generally contended that by the 1890s all the elements of objectivity had come together. Over the next century, it would become the ideal, or what one media critic in 1996 denounced as "the false god" of the profession. A key element is supposed to be detachment: a textbook from 1911 instructs reporters to "keep yourself out of the story," while one from 2012 explains that journalists "are neutral observers, not advocates or participants."[21] Such admonishments must have struck newshounds of the *Front Page* era as a joke, if not a complete surprise.

When Chicago crime reporters were not breaking into places or pulling a con, they were busy acting as the local law enforcement. "Murder mysteries fascinated readers, and the reporters, not the police, would solve them," wrote John J. McPhaul in *Deadlines and Monkeyshines: The Fabled World of Chicago Journalism*. George Murray, a veteran of William Randolph Hearst's newspaper, argued that the phenomenon of the reporter as supersleuth should not be surprising, since newspapers had far more money and resources for certain investigations than police departments did. Among the most famous newspaper detectives was Buddy McHugh, portrayed in *The Front Page* as "Buddy McCue." When the police hit a dead end interrogating a slow-witted suspect about the fatal beating of a widow, McHugh broke the impasse, asking simply, "Did she scream when you hit her, Eddie?" To elicit the confession of child killer Thomas Richard Fitzgerald, Romanoff presented Fitzgerald with a newly purchased doll that he claimed had belonged to the victim.[22]

In the 1890s the sheriff's department swore in reporters as deputies and allowed them to make their own news by raiding the gambling dens of Michael Cassius McDonald, a Democratic Party boss and the publisher of the *Chicago Globe*. Papers supplied badges that reporters could flash to pass themselves off as detectives or assistant coroners. By the mid-1920s, the police provided press cards inscribed with a note from the chief of police, instructing that journalists be extended all courtesies. But editor Frank Carson, always ready to push things further, invented "muscle journalism," manufacturing phony badges, warrants, and other documents and installing wiretaps. On one occasion, he recruited a bruiser from the Circulation Department to pose as a detective to "arrest" a killer in Adams, Wisconsin.[23]

If the City News was the trade school where journalists learned such arts of manipulation, it was Walter Howey, Carson's mentor and boss, who reigned as master. The managing editor of the *Herald and Examiner*, Howey would become immortalized as the Machiavellian genius Walter Burns of *The Front Page*. *Time* would describe him as "a profane romanticist, ruthless but not cruel, unscrupulous but endowed with a private code of ethics. He was the sort of newsman who managed to have Hell break loose under his feet, expected similar miracles from his underlings, and rewarded them generously." When a staffer named Eddie Doherty produced one "sob story" too many, Howey advised, "This isn't that kind of story, Eddie, it's straight news. And don't try to break my heart. It isn't that kind of heart."[24]

Howey's mild-mannered appearance belied his ferocity as a competitor and power broker.[25] Many of the tales about Howey concerned his journalistic feats, but Howey soon found that his investigative talents were far more useful to newspapers for extortion rather than for journalism. By the time Howey assumed the helm of the *Herald and Examiner*, he had amassed an extensive collection of files on local officials.

Sticking by mayoral candidate William Hale Thompson, when no other paper was willing to support him, proved another winning card. Charlie MacArthur, the coauthor of *The Front Page* with Hecht and a former reporter under Howey for the *Herald and Examiner*, claimed that the police would prevent rival newspapers from taking photographs at crime scenes or would bring perpetrators for interrogation at a hotel near the Hearst headquarters. "The other papers howled with rage, but what could they do?" said MacArthur when interviewed for Howey's obituary. "Walter had the resignations of half a dozen city officials in his desk to be used at his convenience."[26]

Murray explained his editor's view of investigations: "Howey knew that such exposés would do no good, as far as reform is concerned. He was under no illusions about the intelligence of the ordinary citizen, or his capacity to remember from one day to the next which politicians are gypping him and how they are going about it. . . . Howey did not operate his paper by any code of ethics dreamed up at journalism school in an ivory tower full of idealistic professors. He ran it on the same basis as other businesses in the community operated."[27]

☙

While the character of the Chicago news business had taken shape by the 1890s, the arrival of Hearst in 1900—a first step in his national strategy to become president—took things to a new level. That June, Hearst challenged business manager Solomon Carvalho to establish a Chicago paper in time for the Democratic National Convention in Kansas City, just thirty days away.

"It's a tough town," Carvalho had admonished. "We'll have to shoot our way in."

"Take all the ammunition you need," Hearst replied.[28]

His executives and their rivals would soon take those words literally.

Carvalho first deployed the same tactics that had worked so well in New York: he dropped calling cards on all the best editors and writers in the city and lured them in with salary hikes. He also offered the *American* for one penny, while the *Tribune* and the *Daily News* sold for three. The paper retained a network of tipsters that covered the train stations, hotels, hospitals, and police precincts across the city. When a lurid layout, shocking headlines, scoops, and sensationalized copy were deemed insufficient, the editors exhorted legmen and rewrite men to concoct fiction. If a rival paper offered a better piece of fantasy—as in one account that featured firefighters saving lives by forming a human ladder—the reporter was shown the door. The *American* had twenty-seven city editors in its first thirty-seven months, in part because Hearst was using Chicago as a testing ground for talent and would send the best editors on elsewhere.[29]

These efforts represented a good start, but in a city that already had nine daily newspapers, more was needed. The rough handling of newsboys was nothing new; brawls had been common, for example, in the Hearst-Pulitzer contest in New York. Carvalho, however, counted on the shrewd and dangerous Max Annenberg as circulation manager to win his war. Attired in his signature flaming red sweater with a soft cap pulled down over his brow, Annenberg organized crews of goons, many of them broken-down prizefighters, to secure the loyalty of news vendors district by district, using all necessary means of persuasion. In 1902 he was joined by his more sophisticated brother, Moses, who would pursue a lifelong career in newspaper publishing and rackets, the latter with his racetrack wire, the Nationwide News Service.[30]

Though the *Daily News* and the *Tribune* fought back, the violence rarely became lethal until 1910, when the *Tribune* poured a million dollars into a circulation drive, dropped its price to a penny, and, taking a page from Hearst's playbook, poached the Annenberg brothers. They also armed their crews with revolvers. Hearst's lead executive, Andrew Lawrence, responded, and soon gunmen were stalking each other in black circulation trucks, pouring out for firefights in the streets. The *Inter-Ocean* published an editorial demanding indictments, but otherwise news of the bloodshed was suppressed—or falsified as labor troubles—by all of the newspapers except the *Daily Socialist* and the unionized *Daily World*.[31]

The hostilities peaked in 1912. In May the *Daily Socialist* reported the beating and kidnapping of a newsdriver. In June thugs shot a street conductor and then fired wildly through the crowded trolley. In July an assailant blasted bullets into the roof of a streetcar when he found that the passengers were not reading the *American*. Two weeks later, a gang riddled the Wellington Avenue elevated station to intimidate a newsdealer. Circulation crews were spotted wearing special police stars. Attempts to indict Max Annenberg and others ended in acquittals. "Bloody newspapers and bodies were a gruesome but not uncommon sight in the Chicago River," observed crime historian Rose Keefe.[32]

The war began to sputter out by 1913, but incidents of violence continued for years as the circulation departments produced some of the city's most notorious killers, including the infamous Gentelman brothers; labor racketeer Maurice "Mossy" Enright; another of Prohibition's "dean of Chicago gunmen," Walter Stevens; "Big Tim" Murphy; Frank McErlane, described by the *Illinois Crime Survey* as "the most brutal gunman to ever pull a trigger in Chicago"; and James Ragen, who together with another slugger, Mickey McBride, would run childhood friend Moses Annenberg's Nationwide News Service in the 1930s.[33]

"After their honorable discharge from the newspaper wars, all these gunmen and their many pupils opened shop on their own account, having acquired valuable lessons in typical corporation methods," wrote Ferdinand Lundberg in *Imperial Hearst*, his scathing 1936 biography. Most prominent among them was Dean "Deannie" O'Banion, a reigning bootlegger and friend of Hecht and MacArthur who had worked for Hearst until at least 1920, when Prohibition went into effect. In 1925 O'Banion was killed in his flower shop by the Johnny Torrio–Al Capone mob, an event that Hecht depicted in both *Underworld* and *Scarface*.[34]

Though the circulation war was over, the *Front Page* era was still in full steam at the onset of the 1920s, a decade that would deliver unprecedented carnage and bloody spectacle. In 1918 Hearst merged his morning *Herald* with the newly acquired *Examiner* and put Howey in charge to create the paper that would earn a reputation as the most aggressive of the interwar period. "Nobody moved even to the water cooler except at a dead run," reporter Bob Casey said about the Hearst building, which became known as the Madhouse on Madison Street. "The city editor yelled at his copy readers, the copy readers yelled at the copy boys, and the copy boys yelled at each other. Each story, from a triple murder to a purse snatching in the ghetto, was a big story and greeted with quivering excitement by everyone who had anything to do with it." Columnist Arthur James Pegler observed, "A Hearst paper is like a screaming woman running down the street with her throat cut."[35]

CHAPTER 2

Shades of Black: The Stages of Hecht's Cynicism

Some of us guys have more brains on our shoes than we have under our hats.
—CITY NEWS BUREAU REPORTER WILLIS O'ROURKE AT THE
SCENE OF THE SAINT VALENTINE'S DAY MASSACRE[1]

The American expatriate writer Gertrude Stein had heard the owner of a garage lash out at a mechanic, complaining that the employee's whole generation was a useless crop that had been lost to the war. "That's what you all are," Stein later snapped at Ernest Hemingway. "All of you young people who served in the war. You are a lost generation."[2] Hemingway had read something deeper into Stein's griping: not only had the tumult and trauma of the new century buried many sentimental notions of the old world, but it had left its progeny shattered, dazed, and haunted. Hemingway popularized Stein's phrase with his epigraph to *The Sun Also Rises*, reflecting his own shell-shocked malaise. But the phrase was also apt for Ben Hecht, Charles MacArthur, and their fellow crime reporters in Chicago.

Both Hecht and MacArthur would see the carnage in Europe firsthand, but in the years leading up to the conflict, even those who would remain at home got a strong taste of what the war would bring. Hecht recalled reporter Larry Malm, who never took off his overcoat and muffler, even on hot summer days. During coverage of the Iroquois Theatre fire, Malm had found himself buried under a pile of charred corpses and thereafter could never escape the chill in his bones. Vincent Starrett wrote that the first time he was dispatched to steal a photo from a crime scene, he crawled through a window and found himself ankle-deep in blood, alongside the body of a decapitated woman. In St. Louis Theodore Dreiser had rushed to a train wreck where oil tanker cars suddenly exploded, setting a crowd of people on fire before his eyes. Gruesome episodes such as these fill the memoirs of the Chicago press; Hecht offers a long litany in his autobiography *A Child of the Century*.[3]

Like Hemingway, these reporters maintained the stoicism then expected of gentlemen. MacArthur served not only in the Great War but also in the hunt for Pancho Villa in Mexico and later in World War II—an ulcer kept him out of Korea—and despite his best efforts to pretend otherwise, he carried the scars. "This teller of the exuberant anecdote who could talk the night away left behind chiefly a memory of reticence," Hecht wrote in his 1957 biography of MacArthur. "None of the thousand friends, including the women who loved him—except one—knew him deeply. Of our forty years of friendship I can remember hundreds of things he did, but nothing he felt. He never told me."[4]

When Hecht traveled to Germany in December 1918 as a foreign correspondent for the *Chicago Daily News*, he witnessed the devastation and bloody aftermath of the war. Hecht's memoirs trace his own path to disillusionment, from the feigned world-weariness he had adopted as a young reporter to the horror and disgust that would later mark his soul. In the short stories of *Gaily, Gaily*, Hecht portrayed himself as a wide-eyed youth for whom journalism was an initiation into life. Looking back at the things he saw during his year in Germany, Hecht wrote, "They remind me of the darkest fact I have learned in my life—that the decency and sanity of the human race is a small mask."[5]

In the aftermath, Hecht was left to struggle with the question of whether, in the face of the kind of cruelty and injustice he had witnessed in Germany, one could in good conscience remain a journalist-bystander or whether one had an obligation to intervene; it was a dilemma that hinged not so much on journalistic ethics as on Hecht's view of politics as inherently demeaning and soul destroying. His friend and mentor, H. L. Mencken, had advised him that the "leader of every cause was a scoundrel."[6]

ભ

When Hecht started as a crime reporter, his youthful sense of invulnerability had insulated him from the grim realities he witnessed. He was present at some seventeen hangings as a reporter-spectator. Not yet ready to digest the tragic dimensions of such encounters, he focused on their absurdities and ironies. In his *Gaily, Gaily* story "The Fairy," Hecht recalled a closeted homosexual condemned for killing his wife. The man agrees to confess on the condition that he is supplied a woman's vanity case. He walks to the scaffold painted in rouge and lipstick, and in his death rattle, the long, final note that rings from the depths is his true voice—a high-pitched feminine wail. Hecht's lede: "Fred Ludwig lived as a cowardly man but he died a brave woman." Hecht claimed that at another hanging, he and MacArthur pumped a syringe full of adrenaline into a condemned man just after the corpse was pulled from the rope. The two friends believed this would induce a resurrection and thus give them a national exclusive on a scientific marvel.[7]

Hecht and his compatriots knew nothing about public policy and were not much interested in it, but that mattered little: in Chicago in 1910, ward politics was simply crime, and the papers covered it as such. "Election day emptied the Press Room," Hecht recalled in *Gaily, Gaily*. "Even the card-players disappeared. All reporters, regardless of their wiliness, had to take their legs to cover the town's voting centers; not to see who got elected, but to see how many people were slugged, stabbed and shot during the hours in which free men voted."[8]

The "finest political plum" was the First Ward, which had a split personality that made it the most lucrative and powerful territory of the city. Its southern portion was the Levee, a tenderloin of whorehouses, gambling dens, barrelhouses, burlesque theaters, peep shows, Turkish baths, voodoo doctors, and dope dispensaries. Adjoining this to the north was the Loop, the downtown business district. For decades, the First Ward was the domain of two aldermen, "Bathhouse" John Coughlin and "Hinky Dink" Mike Kenna.[9]

Hecht remembered that a few days before each election, every derelict and degenerate of the ward would swarm to the Levee's fleabag hotels. Packed six to a room, these lucky delegates were treated to their fill of free booze, "hop" (heroin), and prostitutes until it was time to cast ballots, when they would gratefully stagger forth to vote multiple times in different precincts under different names. The day after the election, each voter was paid for his service and provided a bonus based on the number of votes cast. Such strategies were evidently so effective that the rule of Bathhouse John and Hinky Dink endured for more than fifty years, from the former's first election to the council in 1892 until the latter stepped down from the post in 1943, five years after Coughlin had died and three years before Kenna's own death.[10]

The most conspicuous symbol of turn-of-the-century Chicago's moral character was the aldermen's annual fund-raiser, the First Ward Ball, also known as the Gangsters' Ball, which Hecht made the centerpiece of his first movie for Hollywood, the silent gangster film *Underworld*. "The guest list included nearly every criminal in town with the price of a shave, and nearly every whore from Englewood to Evanston who had access to a ball gown," Hecht wrote in *Gaily, Gaily*. "Pickpockets, pimps, porch climbers, jack rollers, sluggers, heisters and gunmen I had seen before court judges were on display socially in the Coliseum; and the judges with them. The judges, police officials, bigwigs from the city hall and state capital and every variety of the political genus were intermingled with the agents of crime and vice."[11] This public display of corruption became more brazen each year. Spectacles like the grand march, in which Bathhouse John and Hinky Dink linked arms with bordello madams to parade around the center floor, increasingly drew public ire. After dynamite exploded just before the ball of 1908, and Coughlin's thugs assaulted a newspaper cartoonist and a photographer, the reformers mobilized and put an end to the party.[12]

In 1910 a vice commission appointed by Mayor Fred Busse estimated that there were over a thousand brothels in the Levee, run by nearly two thousand pimps and madams and employing four thousand prostitutes. This generated a gross annual income of some $60 million (equivalent to $1.2 billion today), with $30 million in profits. "The city's courts, police and politicians had been taking bribes for a generation by the time Al Capone began to buy the protection he needed to do business in Chicago and elsewhere," notes historian Michael Lesy in *Murder City: The Bloody History of Chicago in the Twenties*. "By 1929, the parasite that had once been the Levee had begun to consume the city that had once been its host."[13]

Hecht theorized that the "good-citizen majority" remained oblivious because they saw their rogue politicians as a harmless cast of colorful vaudevillians who brought entertainment to their constituents' dull lives.

And though the headlines may have howled in ostentatious outrage, the attitude of Hecht and other rank-and-file newspapermen was actually much the same as that of their readers.[14]

The politicians, the public, and the press all believed that stamping out vice was impossible and not good for business. Instead, it should be strictly relegated to certain districts. This view suited the Romantic journalist, to whom the stern-faced reformers seemed as guilty of Victorian hypocrisy as the grafters. As a youth, Hecht's own idea of reform was to try to make an honest woman out of one of the prostitutes who had introduced him to the joys of sex by convincing the young lady to become his girlfriend; his memoirs suggest that he embarked upon such crusades more than once but that they invariably ended in disappointment.[15]

Political corruption was amusing, but crime reporters like Hecht deemed actual reform to be hopeless, as well as boring. The subject worthy of serious study was the nature of the individual—namely, the criminal. "We were not . . . only scorekeepers of the dead, injured and abused. We were psychologists," Hecht remembered. "We had a great interest in the psychology of everything that came close to us. We sat in saloons, analyzing our fellow humans as people now analyze prime ministers."[16]

Just as Hecht had tried to uplift prostitutes and once rented a room for ten weeks before realizing he was living in a brothel, the young reporter was often taken in by the protestations of innocence and vows of repentance that rang from death row. In *A Child of the Century*, Hecht recounted the case of the brothers Ignace and Manow, caught for killing a farmer in a robbery. At the trial Ignace begs the judge to spare his brother. Hecht believes this touching instance of brotherly sacrifice will make a great newspaper story, but on execution day, when Ignace sees the noose, he can't help but cry out, "Hang Manow!"[17] This came as no surprise to Hecht's more seasoned colleagues. "You'll find that is the easiest thing people can do," remarks Sherman Duffy, Hecht's mentor at the *Journal*. "Change into swine."[18]

Such lessons in life may not have been cheery, but they could not overcome Hecht's youthful exuberance. Amid all the wickedness, Hecht saw journalists as travelers, like Orpheus in the underworld. "There was, I am sure, neither worldliness nor cunning enough among the lot of us to run a candy store," he wrote. "But we had a vantage point. We were not inside the routines of human greed or social pretenses. . . . There was a feast all around us. We attended it as scavengers. . . . Politicians were crooks. The leaders of causes were scoundrels. Morality was a farce full of murders, rapes and love nests. Swindlers ran the world and the Devil sang everywhere. These discoveries filled me with great joy."[19]

Right before the war, however, Hecht discovered that his notion of the journalist's enduring innocence was just one more illusion of youth. And then his mood began to darken, and genuine cynicism set in. "The Negress" in *Gaily, Gaily* is another of Hecht's first-person tales based loosely on fact, in part on the real-life execution of the black activist Grover Cleveland Redding in 1921. In the story, Hecht falls for Dido De Long, a beautiful nightclub singer who has given her heart to the leader of a back-to-Africa movement. But Dido's "Prince Ephraim" kills two policemen when a political rally turns violent, which lands Ephraim on death row. Hecht begs his editors to let him write of Dido's cause, but editor Eddie Mahoney merely jokes that this woman who had dreamed of becoming an African queen has now slept her way through half the capital in a desperate quest for a pardon for her doomed lover.

Editors blocked news of race trouble as a matter of policy, but Mahoney's attitude strikes Hecht like a thunderbolt. "I almost hated Mr. Mahoney," he wrote. "I had never before known anything wrong in the world of myself. Crime, murder, suicide, swindle, and perversion were my daily pickings. But they were outside my world, a storm that blew and rattled wildly beyond its snug windows. Now the storm was inside the windows, the wrong was around me. I had discovered the fact that injustice existed, and that everybody I knew was somehow part of it." If Hecht had struck a devil's bargain the moment he had first become a journalist, he only realized it now.[20]

A tale in *A Child of the Century* titled "The Death of Henry Spencer" catalogs all the discoveries Hecht had made by the eve of war in August 1914. Newly hired as a staffer for the *Daily News*, he is sent to the idyllic small town of Wheaton, Illinois, to cover the hanging of Henry Spencer, condemned for bedding and wedding a wealthy widow and then beating her brains in with a hammer. On the night before the execution, Spencer professes to have found God, impressing Hecht with his aura of total calm. Hecht interprets this conversion as an example of an individual's capacity for change, but reporter Wallace Smith just scoffs. "Nothing can change a man," Smith says. "It's all fake. You are what you are. And you can only pretend to be something else. Henry's a rat and he'll die like a rat."[21]

The sheriff, up for reelection, has built a scaffold and seating area the size of the Coliseum and handed out tickets to every political worker in the county, contracting his brother-in-law for the construction at three times the cost. In the evening, the sheriff's pretty seventeen-year-old daughter greases the noose under pale moonlight. The reporters amuse themselves by betting as to how far Spencer will get up the scaffold stairs before losing his cool and slipping. At dawn, Spencer makes his way up without incident. But after delivering a long homily about God, he loses himself completely and spews out false claims of innocence while crying piteously for mercy.

The dawn, however, has brought more than Spencer's death. It is August 15, and reports have arrived that World War I has begun. "That night is gone," wrote Hecht. "And none like it was ever to be in my time again. For on this August, 1914, night, an innocence was departing from the world. . . . When I look back on that hour, I see more than Henry Spencer dying in the sunlight on the end of a rope, with his immortal soul damned and Hell in his blackening face. A civilization hangs in the Wheaton stockade."[22] Big-city reporters could see that massive changes were already under way, but the war in Europe had yet to unfold, and it would be years before Hecht could appreciate what it had wrought.

ભ

Hecht was twenty years old in 1914 and only beginning to awaken as an iconoclast. By the summer of 1914, Hecht had become a member of the salon around Margaret Anderson's groundbreaking new literary journal, the *Little Review*. He spent the war years as a rising star of both the local press and a historic literary movement, the Chicago Renaissance. In the South Side bohemian community near Jackson Park, Hecht forged friendships with other young talents on their way to national recognition, including Sherwood Anderson, Carl Sandburg, and Max Bodenheim. On November 28, 1915, he married Marie Armstrong, who had briefly worked as a reporter for the *Journal* just before he left. Their child, Edwina, or "Teddy," was born in November 1916.[23]

The couple left Teddy in the care of Marie's mother and traveled to Europe together in the final days of 1918, when the *Daily News* dispatched Hecht there as a foreign correspondent.[24] In retrospect, it seems a curious decision to send a journalist who had never demonstrated any interest in politics, even on the local level, to cover the intrigues, maneuvering, and Byzantine affairs that would shape the postwar world. In *A Child of the Century*, Hecht looks back at the experience as not only prompting the final evolution of his cynicism but also explaining his ability to prophesy the Nazi Holocaust when just about all other American writers remained either unaware or uninterested.

It is reasonable to ask whether Hecht is guilty of reading history backward, of giving himself credit, with the benefit of hindsight, for canny insights into the future that no one else seemed to have. Yet just as Hecht actually predicted the German genocide in a story published in June 1939, his correspondence and published articles from 1919 corroborate his memoir. "Among his reports home he made the prediction that Germany would be at war [again] in 20 years," recalled his brother, Peter Hecht, in a 1976 letter to biographer William MacAdams. "This, nobody believed."[25]

Indeed, unlike most of his peers in the foreign press corps, Hecht understood the game of intrigue that was afoot. Chicago had prepared him well to spot the con games but had not prepared him for the carnage he was about to see. "All the inhumanity that I note today as history, I [first] saw in Germany in 1918 to 1920, except that I saw it then with a youthful delight for the preposterous," he recalled in *A Child of the Century*. ". . . I had no notion that the humorless and macabre atmosphere was to become the air of the world. . . . And I reported them with the enthusiasm I had brought in Chicago to four-eleven fires, basement stabbings, love-nest suicides and all the other hi-de-ho doings outside the norm of living."[26]

Certainly, *Daily News* managing editor Charles H. Dennis regarded Hecht as unprepared. In a letter forwarded Hecht by foreign news chief Edgar Price Bell at the end of January, Dennis made clear that he disagreed with the decision to send Hecht to Berlin in the first place, complained about the time it was taking Hecht to arrive, and worried about expenses. Days later, Hecht responded that he had already submitted eight stories while en route. "I do not understand how it was expected of me to reach Berlin from New York much quicker than I did," he continued, "and in view of that fact I do not understand the office's despair at my general uselessness."[27]

Dennis thought Hecht too superficial for the business of international affairs. In a February 7 letter that critiqued Hecht's interview with the new Weimar chancellor, Philipp Scheidemann, Dennis took him to task for describing the chancellor's surroundings in lush detail and passing over Scheidemann's aims and programs for a new Germany. "Was not there meat in the coconut?" Dennis asked. "Was not this what you went to see him for?" He also chided Hecht for calling Scheidemann an "affable combination of Bismarck and Hinky Dink": "This is playing leapfrog in the presence of a corpse or whistling in church." According to *A Child of the Century*, Bell was so infuriated with the story that he demanded Hecht's removal.[28]

Ensconced at the toney Hotel Adlon, a kind of headquarters and watering hole for foreign correspondents, Hecht found unorthodox local sources who conveyed the sense of impending catastrophe that hung over Berlin. For military gossip, he relied chiefly on a group of homosexual aviators he met at an officers' club:

> These were elegant fellows, perfumed and monocled and usually full of heroin or cocaine. They made love to one another openly, kissing in the café booths and skipping around two a.m. to a mansion owned by one of them. One or two women were usually in the party—wide mouthed, dark-eyed nymphomaniacs with titles to their names but unroyal burns and cuts on their flanks. At times little girls of ten and eleven, recruited from the pavements of Friedrichstrasse, where they paraded after midnight with rouged faces and in shiny boots and in short baby dresses, were added to the mansion parties.[29]

Hecht was no longer the rube once fooled by the cries of innocence or vows of repentance of convicted killers on death row. Indeed, while the foreign press corps and their editors back in the United States hung on every word from official sources, Hecht knew a hustle when he saw one.[30] He understood Scheidemann and his colleagues as pawns in a cynical game, as many historians later would.[31] Behind the scenes, the nation's militarists had set up the Weimar socialists to take the blame for the disastrous outcome of the war, while portraying Germany as weak and wounded, ready prey for the Red Menace of Russia, which strengthened Germany's hand in the Paris peace negotiations.

"What with trying to convince the world that Germany is starving, trying to regain a toehold on the vanishing colonies and trying to persuade German workingmen that Germany is a socialist state, while endeavoring to reassure the outside world that it is not, the present Ebert-Scheidemann government faces difficulties," Hecht reported in the *Daily News* on February 15. In *A Child of the Century*, Hecht recalled, "My knowledge was skimpy, my political insights almost nonexistent and my sources of information limited at the time to drug addicts, nymphomaniacs and a waiter. But the Lie about Russia was as obvious to spot as a sheiss house in a fog." To his astonishment, not only did the priggish foreign correspondents fall for this lie of the impending Russian menace, but Bell and Dennis believed it, too.[32]

Hecht nevertheless still found himself susceptible to a great story that happened not to be true. His front-page article for March 13 startled readers with the revelation that Germany had not actually suffered military defeat but, according to General Max von Hoffmann, chief of staff of the eastern front, had lost as a result of the Russian surrender, which had erased the battle lines that divided the troops and allowed the vaunted German army to become "rotten with Bolshevism."[33]

And yet, days earlier, Hecht had witnessed events that would make him wonder what was really at play. Trailing a small band of doomed Spartacist rebels through the barbed wire and rubble of the Alexanderplatz neighborhood, he had witnessed the final skirmishes that had stamped out the communist revolt known as the January Uprising. On March 11 he had joined a good-natured, well-dressed crowd to watch the army march the rounded-up Spartacists toward Moabit Prison. When the prisoners, handcuffed and herded "like two-legged cattle," approached the gates, a hurdy-gurdy cut its rollicking tunes, and the crowd grew silent. Now the rebels' pleas for mercy could be heard. "Most of them resembled workers in any group to be seen leaving a factory in Chicago at 6 o'clock on a spring day," he reported. "I counted four women. I noticed that six of them were lame and were being dragged along by their upright comrades chained to their wrists."

Ten minutes of silence passed after the last entered the gates. Hecht tried to ask a guard what was happening but was pushed aside. "Suddenly, as I was turning to leave, I heard the sputter of machine guns," he wrote. "They were shooting behind the walls of Moabit. The shooting continued. Above the sound of the guns came the cries of men. I could not distinguish the words. The cries changed to howling. The machine guns continued. I waited till both the howling and the sputtering were over." A white-faced guard turned and told him that all 220 had been cut down.[34]

Once Hecht became convinced that General von Hoffmann's "rotten with Bolshevism" story was a lie, he compiled evidence to correct the record. But these new stories contradicted the analyses of other foreign correspondents. Dennis spiked Hecht's stories and wired: "Your surmises both wild dangerous to President Wilson's work for just peace. Confine yourself solid political facts." Hecht wired back: "All my information solid not surmise."[35]

Decades later, Hecht would recall his differences with the rest of the foreign press corps when asked to write the opening to Alfred Hitchcock's 1940 film *Foreign Correspondent*. Dedicated "to those forthright ones who early saw the clouds of war while many of us at home were seeing rainbows," the story opens in the office of the *New York Morning Globe*'s senior editor. The editor tosses down a cable from Europe in disgust. "'According to a high official, it is believed . . .' Bah! Foreign correspondent! I could get more news out of Europe looking in a crystal ball," the editor rails. "I don't want any more economists, sages or oracles bombinating over our cables! I want a reporter, somebody who doesn't know the difference between an 'ism' and a kangaroo. A good, honest crime reporter. That's what *The Globe* needs. That's what Europe needs. There's a crime hatching on that bedeviled continent!"[36]

With the Munich revolt of April 1919, Hecht came to understand that the grander the game, the bigger the crime, and he discovered how von Hoffmann's tale had been "part of the machinery of the Lie." In *A Child of the Century*, he offered a remarkable tale that, while possibly apocryphal, serves as a vivid allegory that crystallizes how he would always remember his experience of Germany. According to the story, he agreed to offer a well-known Bolshevik agent in Berlin a lift to Munich in an airplane requisitioned with *Daily News* funds. Shortly thereafter, the head of the Anti-Bolshevik League also asked to come along. During the flight, Hecht was shocked to find these two enemies sitting calmly together in the cabin of the bomber, playing poker over a suitcase.[37]

The situation grew even stranger as the plane came in for a landing. In front of the pistol-packing anti-Bolsheviks, the Bolshevik agent asked Hecht to carry his suitcase through customs. It contained a million gold marks, money that would be used to bribe the military garrison to stand down and let the revolutionaries overtake the city. Without a word of protest from the anti-Bolsheviks, who would only have had to draw their guns to end the whole plot, Hecht carried the suitcase through security.

Hecht soon found out why the anti-Bolsheviks had been happy to let their enemies use the money. When the time came, the German army crushed the Munich revolt in a matter of days. The revolutionaries had meanwhile served an important purpose: the headlines they produced scared the world into thinking the Russian threat was real. Hecht wrote that the episode "left me with a permanent cynicism toward history" and that "the cynicism of this action was beyond anything I had yet seen in the world. It said—go hire killers to kill my own people. When the time comes we will kill those killers. And out of all this killing we will win a point. We will convince people that the lie we are telling is the truth."[38]

The Germany Hecht encountered was not altogether devoid of hope, however; along with many dark actors, he found some he considered genuine heroes. One was Count Russworm von Gleichen, who first opened Hecht's eyes to von Hoffmann's lie and the bigger "Lie." Another was Hugo Haase. At the national assembly to draft a new constitution, Haase spoke out against the crimes and deceptions and delivered a brave, impassioned plea for German liberty. These men were defeated in 1919, but to Hecht their conduct was testament to the old adage that war brings out the best and the worst in people: in the face of such inhumanity, they had shown the finest humanity. As he concluded his story about Haase in *A Child of the Century*, Hecht realized that he had neglected to mention that Haase was a Jew.[39]

The lessons that Hecht took from Germany would emerge as recurrent themes in his fiction over the next thirty years and explain, again in narrative shorthand, his own reasons for shifting from a writer to an activist when the Nazis rose to power. In *Foreign Correspondent*, the crime is the rise of Hitler, along with the double-dealing diplomacy that positions him to conquer Europe with a series of lightning strikes. The discovery of this great crime becomes a call to action for the young reporter-hero. As in Hecht's 1937 play *To Quito and Back*, a world-weary reporter is convinced to drop his dime-store cynicism in the face of momentous events and embrace a cause, just as Hecht would do in 1940.

In an essay titled "The Hidden History in Ben Hecht's Suitcase," Ron Rosenbaum explains:

> With his invaluable Chicago newspaperman's instinctual ability to smell a rat, Hecht was soon onto the story that most of the international press was missing: the devious maneuvering by the German General Staff to retain its weapons and its power in German politics. Scheming which gave rise to, among other things, the "Stab in the Back" myth, one of the Big Lies Hitler rode to power.
>
> By maneuvering the hapless socialist government, which had been left holding the bag when the Kaiser fled, into responsibility for signing the onerous armistice (and later, peace treaty) terms with the Allies, the German Army set itself up to claim forever after that it was not

really defeated, but only "stabbed in the back" by the treacherous civilian authorities, the "November Criminals," as Hitler called them (after the November 1918 armistice).

The other aspect of the game the German Army generals were playing—the other rat Hecht smelled—was the way the army seemed to him to be tolerating, if not encouraging, local outbreaks of Red-led revolutionaries, the better to convince the Allies that Germany still needed a well-armed military force to suppress and prevent Bolshevik revolutions from sweeping the nation.[40]

The politics that Hecht encountered in Europe were not fundamentally different from those of Chicago. Before the war he had seen subterfuge as well as brutal violence, but he had never seen such apocalyptic horror, the kinds of scenes that were destined to mark the rest of the twentieth century. The industrial revolution was now mass-producing murder just as it produced the Ford Model T, the tin can, and newspapers. By the time Hecht was writing *Gaily, Gaily* in the early 1960s, he preferred to stay with his memories of the old days of prewar Chicago, "when the stakes were smaller and the Halloween battles for power more fun to watch. . . . I am aware that the political stakes have changed, that human survival is now the name of the game. But I see no alteration in politicians."[41]

In *A Child of the Century*, Hecht concluded, "I was a youth of twenty-four when I entered Germany. When I emerged from it my young cynicism had lost much of its grin."[42] The Chicago he returned to was not the same, either. During his absence the Volstead Act had passed, and the bootlegging wars were now getting under way. The world war was over, but the world had changed for good.

CHAPTER 3

Propagandist in Training

Some little typewriter, eh? I'm gonna to write my name all over this town with it . . . in capital letters!
—Tony Camonte, brandishing a machine gun in *Scarface*[1]

Beginning in April 1924, an odd-looking clock face appeared each day on the front page of the *Tribune*. One of three "Hands of Death" was labeled "Autos" and tracked the new phenomenon of fatal car accidents. The other two were labeled "Moonshine" and "Guns." Other American cities had higher per capita murder rates, but Chicago was the biggest city second to New York and far more violent. While Manhattan was known for bright lights, intellectuals, and artists, Chicago became known for murder.[2] But it wasn't just statistics or a Senate investigation into organized crime that earned the city its reputation. The Chicago press also had a flair for glamorizing bootleggers and violence.

Chicago newspapermen streamed east to invent the lurid style of American tabloids dubbed "jazz journalism," with *Tribune* owner Joseph Medill Patterson launching New York's *Daily News* in 1919, and Howey sent to establish its competitor, the *Daily Mirror*, five years later. A Chicago photographer's hidden camera snapped the iconic image of Ruth Snyder jolted to death in the electric chair. And Chicago became the site of the three Grand Guignols of the jazz age: the Leopold-Loeb murder ("the perfect crime"), the Saint Valentine's Day Massacre, and the killings committed by two young women, Beulah Annan and Belva Gaertner, made famous by the smash Broadway farce *Chicago*, which was written by former *Tribune* reporter Maureen Dallas Watkins.[3]

Mass communication radically changed American culture during the 1920s, and the increasingly shrill sensationalism of jazz journalism—combined with the implication that the press was itself corrupt—raised alarms and prompted calls for reform. "What makes yellow journalism really dangerous," wrote author Frederick L. Allen amid the rising tide of indignation, "is not so much its appetite for scandal as its continual distortion of the news in the interest of undiluted entertainment."[4] Leaders of the news industry felt called on to act, and in February 1922 Hecht's supervisor at the *Daily News*, Charles H. Dennis, joined four other editors at the Blackstone Hotel to found the American Society of Newspaper Editors, drafting a code that demanded "truthfulness, impartiality, fair play and decency."[5] Ultimately, such efforts to establish ethical and professional standards stamped out the hellfire of *Front Page* journalism.

Hecht had returned from Germany in August 1919 with a new awareness of journalism and his place in it. He also had a huge pile of debt.[6] He would no longer work as a reporter but over the next four years would launch a public relations firm; produce a column of daily sketches; publish six novels, several plays, and a collection of short stories; and edit and publish the *Chicago Literary Times*, a prototype of the alternative weekly newspaper. In the next ten years, he would use the skills and knowledge obtained as a reporter—his understanding of public tastes, the tricks he learned as a sketch-hoax literary artisan—to acquire wealth and a modicum of fame. His various roles in the 1920s reflected the changes resulting from the advent of mass media and the early evolution of American mass culture.

In *Erik Dorn*, *The Front Page*, and other works, he would investigate the media and voice many of the major concerns of press critics and scholars of the day. But Hecht was unique in that he effectively combined insights into the media with skills as a practitioner. Just as this earned him fortunes in public relations, theater, and film during the 1920s, it would one day enable him to become a professional propagandist, both for the U.S. War Department and State Department and in his own campaign to rescue Jews and fight for a homeland.

Hecht's evolution from journalist to entertainer to propagandist was a natural consequence of his views. Both in principle and in practice, his Romanticist creed was a rebellion against the lofty Enlightenment ideal of a duty-bound democratic press. The terms *Enlightenment* and *Romanticism* represent opposite ways of seeing the world: reason versus emotion, objectivity versus subjectivity, society versus the individual, and so on.[7] Hecht and his *Front Page* cohort balked at the notion—shared by Thomas Jefferson and his twentieth-century successors, such as the cofounders of the American Society of Newspaper Editors—that the press had a sacrosanct responsibility to inform and engage the public. The Chicago school was skeptical not only about the public—that they could or would listen to reason—but about reason itself.

By 1920 Hecht and his family had adopted a lifestyle far beyond their means, and so he tried his hand at public relations, just as this new field was developing out of the propaganda campaigns of the Great War, which the *New York Times* had called "the first press agents' war." The U.S. and British propaganda bureaus had, from the start of the conflict, relied on the financial support and expertise of Chicago-based military contractors, and these private-public partnerships were instrumental in the burgeoning of publicity in the postwar era.[8] Hecht became a partner in a public relations start-up, soon hiring on his fellow foreign correspondent Richard Little. According to his recollection in *A Child of the Century*, he organized events and campaigns and wrote copy for interests that "came clamoring to our office, which, after the first month, consumed an entire floor in the Francis Willard Building." This would be the first of Hecht's two lucrative forays into the field.[9]

After his brief career in public relations, Hecht conducted an experiment in literary journalism, beginning his One Thousand and One Afternoons column in June 1921. He had envisioned the column as a feat of storytelling, a high-wire act, done just to prove that he could. Every day for more than a year, he produced a different tale about the city. In the fall of 1922, bookstore proprietors Pascal Covici and William McGee published a collection of sixty-four of the columns in book form, interleaving them with expressionistic illustrations in black ink by the artist Herman Rosse. In the book's preface, *Daily News* editor Henry Justin Smith explained Hecht's "Big Idea—the idea that just under the edge of the news as commonly understood, the news often flatly and unimaginatively told[,] lay life. . . . He was going to be its interpreter. His was to be the lens throwing city life into new colors."[10]

Each story, each slice of life, was a shard in the kaleidoscope of modern city life. A great financier finds himself distracted on a rainy day by thoughts about his own insignificance; solitary souls wander through the

mists of a downtown that "is like the exposed mechanism of some monstrous clock"; a poor widow spends so lavishly on her husband's funeral that
she loses her children; a Mr. Prokofieff directs a chaotic, circus-like modernist opera; hundreds of fishermen sit all afternoon along the Municipal
Pier, staring across Lake Michigan at oblivion. There are portraits, ironic
yarns, and mood pieces: "A dark afternoon with summer thunder in the
sky. The fan-shaped skyscrapers spread a checkerboard of window lights
through the gloom." As Smith noted, the stories included "comedies, dia-
logues, homilies, one-act tragedies, storiettes, sepia panels, word-etchings,
satires, tone-poems, fugues, bourrees—something different every day."[11]

Hecht sought to determine the limits of what reporting could offer
the storyteller. His column harkened back to the daily columns of George
Ade and Eugene Field in the Chicago newspapers of the 1890s (possibly
the first signed columns to appear in any American paper) and the Mr.
Dooley stories of Finley Peter Dunne. These were varieties of the newspaper sketch, a broad category that encompassed any report based on personal
observations. Hecht's style most resembled the relatively unmannered realism of Ade's column, "Stories of the Streets and of the Town," which grew
directly out of the latter's reporting experience.[12]

But in the end, Hecht did find the limits of shoe leather, at least for
himself. In the final column of his collection, "Grass Figures," the newspaper reporter opens his notepad at night to find that the "secret of the city"
he had thought he knew during the day has now slipped away from him.
The next day the reporter tries to ferret out the secret by interviewing the
people lying on the grass in Grant Park, staring up at the clouds, but upon
returning home finds that it has eluded him once more.[13]

While the American Society of Newspaper Editors may have been
insisting on objectivity as a standard of professionalism, One Thousand and
One Afternoons reflected the growing acknowledgment of the subjective
nature of journalism. Newspapers were adopting more nuanced notions of
objectivity, distancing themselves from the "naïve empiricism" once understood as realism in the 1890s. Like the debut of the political column, the
more frequent use of bylines, and the emergence of interpretive reporting
(in the form of news summaries and analyses), Hecht's column suggested
that facts and events require interpretation and that every report contains
a point of view. A leading voice of this new skepticism about objectivity was Henry Luce, who worked as a legman for Hecht on the column
(much to Hecht's dissatisfaction) and within two years cofounded *Time*, a

newsweekly full of summaries and analysis. "Show me a man who thinks he's objective," Luce had said, "and I'll show you a man who's deceiving himself."[14]

These doubts about objectivity, the call to regulate journalism, and the birth of an industry of experts who massaged data and carefully calibrated messages coincided with growing pessimism about the notion of a public that was capable of reason and informed decision-making. In *Public Opinion* (1922), Walter Lippmann "had begun to knock the 'public' off the perch that the rhetoric of democracy had built for it," journalism historian Michael Schudson has observed. A spate of writing about crowds and crowd behavior had begun to appear in the late nineteenth century and gained popular attention by the early 1920s, with such works as Everett Dean Martin's *The Behavior of Crowds* (1921). H. L. Mencken, virtually unmatched in his astringency, ridiculed the American middle class as the "Booboisie" (boob-wah-ZEE), dismissed democracy as an "incomparably idiotic" fraud in which political "bugaboos" preyed on the fears and imbecilities of the mob, and maintained that the modest duty of the writer lay in "stirring up the animals." Lippmann wrote in *The Phantom Public* that voters "arrive in the middle of the third act and will leave before the last curtain, having stayed just long enough to decide who is the hero and who is the villain."[15]

Collectively, though, the new attitudes about the press and the public were symptomatic of something deeper. They reflected a legacy of the war: a profound new skepticism about the power of reason and the knowability of truth, a pervasive lack of confidence and sense of distrust. Hecht's search for realism had only affirmed his subjectivity. He had gone off as a reporter seeking facts and found "that the city was nothing more nor less than a vast, broken mirror giving him back garbled images of himself."[16]

Hecht's first novel, *Erik Dorn*, which hit the bookstands in the fall of 1921, offered an inverse perspective to what he provided each day in his column. As the story begins, Dorn is Hecht as he imagines himself six years in the future: no longer a reporter or columnist but now a thirty-four-year-old editor for a newspaper. He has become jaded to the human drama that plays out across the city each day, all the turmoil and tragedy captured and churned out in half a million newspapers a day. Whatever secrets the city holds have been revealed, and he is weary of them all. Walking the streets and scanning the reams of copy that cross his desk, he sees the tumult of human activity like patterns on an anthill. His eyes trace these geometries, but they are meaningless. Newspapers, with their editorial bromides and shrill sensationalism, hold up a carnival mirror to this carnival of life, delivering "a caricature of absurdity itself."[17] Dorn, meanwhile, is captive to the mocking laughter in his own head, his own devastating irony.

"The book as a whole is as beautiful and disturbing as a live thing," wrote a reviewer for *Vanity Fair*. "It remains to consider how far *Erik Dorn* is a brilliantly colored caricature of a generation of disillusionists, a generation which, though still young, can find no reason for its continued existence but that the blood is warm and quick in its veins." Dorn voiced his generation's pessimism, echoing Lippmann's skepticism about the public that same year, lamenting that people "want black and white so they can all mass on the white side and make faces at all the evil-doers who prefer the black. They don't want facts, diagnosis, theories, interpretations, reports."[18]

At the same time, in the character of Dorn, Hecht gave form to a new era's anxieties about corporate efficiency. In an introduction to the 1963 reprint of *Erik Dorn*, Nelson Algren credited Hecht with anticipating the themes of alienation and conformity—the latter personified by the "organization man"—that permeated American literature after World War II. "I'm like men will all be years later," Dorn says, "when their emotions are finally absorbed by the ingenious surfaces they've surrounded themselves with, and life lies forever buried behind the inventions of engineers, scientists and business men."[19] In the early 1920s, efficiency entered the manufacture of everything from tin cans and Ford automobiles to machine guns and bootleg whiskey. It was an efficiency that Hecht and other Chicago newsmen would soon associate with a fresh breed of gangsters, in particular, the cold-blooded Al Capone.

Dorn's cold detachment is not objectivity, however—far from it. Algren suggests that Dorn's cynicism is merely "a hideout from the winds of passion" that blow within him. Biographer Doug Fetherling argues, in turn, that Dorn is a man with more talent, intellect, and promise than he knows what to do with and thus ultimately finds himself dissatisfied and disillusioned.[20] He feels things, even falls in love, but ultimately can't help mocking his own folly. In short, while Hecht's daily experiment with realism in his column had led to a deeper sense of subjectivity, his newspaperman Erik Dorn is his original Romantic egoist, the first of many to follow: a malcontent who is brilliant, coldly rational, and efficient but driven by a mad hidden passion.

With his explosion of output over the next few years, Hecht seemed determined to prove himself a storyteller who could match the Scheherazade of legend. His ability to spin tales at a furious rate had been evident since at least 1917, when, thanks in part to Mencken, who fed him plotlines, he had produced some twenty short stories for the *Smart Set* in a year and a half, contributing as many as eight stories to a single issue. In *A Child of the Century*, he claims that he dictated *The Florentine Dagger* (1923) in thirty-six hours to win a wager: he had bet that he could write a novel within two days that would receive favorable reviews and sell twenty thousand copies.[21] In the years to come, Hecht's ability to produce popular stories in every genre at remarkable speed made him the most sought-after screenwriter in Hollywood; he said that of the more than sixty movies he wrote, over half were written in two weeks or less.[22]

Over the longer term, Hecht's extraordinary output came to be regarded as evidence of shallowness and dissolute talent. *Erik Dorn*, arguably the best of his novels, has on occasion been dismissed as an over-written and plotless mess. And what some admired as Hecht's aptitude for inverting themes and weaving plot variations—a gift that helps account for his productivity—others saw as an endless rehashing of the same material, from *Erik Dorn* to *A Child of the Century*. Such dismissals, however, ignore both the many dimensions of his works and the excellence of a considerable number of them, particularly his best films and books like *A Book of Miracles*, *A Child of the Century*, and *Gaily, Gaily*. Regardless, Hecht's technique of flipping and twisting the tropes of Romantic literature offers a key to understanding his works, individually and holistically, and to understanding the writer himself.

Like his fictional protagonist in *Erik Dorn*, Hecht left his wife for another woman around this time. He had originally met Rose Caylor, a studious, pretty young blonde then working as a City News reporter, just before he departed for Germany with his first wife, Marie. By the time he returned, Rose was working at the *Daily News*, and the two began carrying on an affair. Hecht eventually moved to New York City with her in 1924, and they married in 1926, once he had obtained a divorce.

"She had ash blonde hair, oversized brown eyes, and a lithe, quick-moving body of excellent shape," he wrote in *A Child of the Century*. "When thoughtful she held her chin tucked down and her eyes a bit upturned, like a matador contemplating a bull. When alert she might pass for an Indian uprising." A Jewish woman whose parents had also emigrated from Eastern

Europe, Rose had been active in politics since childhood, when she had grown disillusioned with socialism. Hecht would credit her with his own turn toward politics in 1939. Over thirty-eight years of marriage, during which they often resided on opposite coasts, Hecht would commit many infidelities and maintain two long-term affairs. Nevertheless, for the rest of their lives, Rose would remain his muse, confidante, collaborator, editor, and, on occasion, fierce interlocutor.[23]

"We were all fools to have left Chicago," Hecht would later lament, and in any event he left reluctantly, the last of the Chicago Renaissance writers to move to New York. There Hecht joined a literary society comprising newspaper veterans and magazine writers from the East Coast and elsewhere, including Gene Fowler, Damon Runyon, Dorothy Parker, Herman Mankiewicz, Samson Raphaelson, and George S. Kaufman. Other former reporters from Chicago included sportswriter Ring Lardner, a friend of F. Scott Fitzgerald's who gained acclaim for his short stories; *Tribune* staffer Maurine Watkins, who wrote *Chicago*, which premiered in 1926; and Bartlett Cormack, author of the 1927 Broadway play *The Racket*. In addition to their critical essays, stories, and novels, these writers made a significant contribution to the theater at a peak time for Broadway before the adoption of sound film, when the district was producing some 225 plays a year.[24]

Pauline Kael wrote that they were "ambivalently nostalgic about their youth as reporters, journalists, critics or playwrights, and they glorified the hard-drinking, cynical newspaperman." For many of this group, newspapers had offered both a paycheck and training as writers and storytellers. But quite a few in the press, at the time and since, saw them as daydreamers and partiers who had little commitment to the true mission of journalism in a democratic society. "A lot of the 'reporters' in the 1920s weren't reporters at all," wrote John Justin Smith, a nephew of Hecht's editor at the *Daily News*, in 1974. "They were poets, for heaven's sake. Or playwrights or novelists. . . . They could dance the Charleston, but never heard of investigative reporting."[25]

They nevertheless lampooned and dissected the press onstage and in popular literature, during what has been called "the Golden Age of press criticism." It was, moreover, a golden age of distaste and suspicion of the press. While the American Society of Newspaper Editors struggled to establish a code of ethics, only to find it unenforceable, Upton Sinclair's *The Brass Check* topped a considerable list of radical critiques that denounced the press as captive to big business. While Lippmann and John Dewey disagreed about what could be done to save a democracy from the destruction wrought by urbanization and industrialization, neither held out hope that journalism would come to the rescue.[26]

Meanwhile, scholars at the University of Chicago were laying the groundwork for the study of mass communication as an academic discipline. Harold Lasswell published the seminal *Propaganda Technique in the World War* in 1927, the same year he joined the university's faculty, while another Dewey disciple, Robert Park, helped to lay the foundation of the field in social science.[27]

By 1926 Hecht and Charles MacArthur were expressing their own puckish cynicism about the press. On the payroll of Morrill Goddard's Sunday supplement for Hearst, *The American Weekly*, MacArthur wrote features about the end of the world, spies from Mars, and the accomplishments of fleas. According to Hecht, MacArthur also tried to peddle rejuvenating cream by advertising two lovely young sisters as nonagenarians who had achieved eternal youth.[28] Hecht meanwhile raked in enormous sums in a notorious South Florida real estate scam, his second venture in publicity. He planted news stories across the nation about chests of pirate treasure discovered in Key Largo, inciting a frenzied grab for what was, at the time, a mosquito-infested dump site. Like MacArthur, he had learned to use the hoax not just to earn a scoop but also to gain real dividends.[29]

The two friends soon found another way to profit from Chicago-style subterfuge: by presenting it onstage as farce. They had spent time together as young reporters, and their bond grew tighter when they both moved to New York and began to collaborate on plays. Their first effort was *The Moonshooter*, which they were unsuccessful at selling to Broadway producer Sam Harris.[30] By the time they were both in their thirties, this friendship and collaboration became a way to hold on to the past. "We were both obsessed with our youthful years," Hecht recalled. ". . . We remained newspaper reporters and continued to keep our hats on before the boss, drop ashes on the floor and disdain all practical people."[31] Fresh from writing the treatment for *Underworld*, Hecht spent the summer of 1927 compiling memories of Chicago with MacArthur and weaving them into the script of *The Front Page*.[32]

The play, which opened at the Times Square Theatre on August 14, 1928, ran for 276 performances at a time when 100 was considered successful. Bawdy and raw, the play was Hecht's biggest hit to date and the work he would be most remembered for; the *New York Times* described it as "unfailing entertainment." Canonized by theater critics and scholars as "the best American comedy ever written," it also became the best-known portrayal and critique of journalism from that time.[33]

The action takes place in the pressroom of the Cook County Criminal Courts Building, where reporters are awaiting the execution of Earl Williams, a young radical accused of killing a black police officer. The mayor and Sheriff Hartman are hoping to capitalize on the hanging in an election year in which they are running on a tough-on-crime platform. *Herald and Examiner* managing editor Walter Burns is determined to have star reporter Hildy Johnson cover the story but runs into a problem: Johnson has announced that he is getting married, leaving the news business for good, and taking an advertising job in New York City. He has just dropped by the pressroom to say farewell, when suddenly Williams breaks out of the jail. With a blockbuster story breaking right before his eyes, Johnson finds himself facing "an emergency of spirit."[34]

The Front Page impressed audiences with its gritty, naturalistic portrayal of Chicago journalism; Tennessee Williams would famously praise it as the play that "took the corsets off the American theater."[35] Photographs of the Criminal Courts pressroom show that it closely resembled the sets used in various productions of the play. The action itself is based on two real events. The first was a major story in the city for weeks: "Terrible" Tommy O'Connor's escape from the Cook County jail, with a gun that may have been smuggled to him in a pork chop sandwich, four days before his scheduled execution in December 1921. The second was a practical joke Howey was said to have played on MacArthur when the latter fled to New York to marry fellow staffer Carol Frink: Howey gave MacArthur a pocketwatch as a farewell gift and then arranged to have MacArthur detained on charges of theft when the train stopped in Gary, Indiana. This episode provided the final punch line of the play, delivered by Burns: "The son of a bitch stole my watch!"[36]

The characters of *The Front Page*, with few exceptions, were identifiable as actual people, including the gangster Diamond Louie and the police officer Woodenshoes Eichhorn. The reporters, including McCue, Bensinger, Murphy, and Schwartz, were all recognizable by their names, lines, and idiosyncrasies. Delighted by the casting of the original production, Hecht remarked, "You would have thought you were in Chicago

1917, looking at the real beauties of the Criminal Courts pressroom." The real Hilding Johnson was known for his sartorial elegance and merciless scooping, such as when he pieced together a murder verdict by rummaging through the jury ballots in a wastebasket and then tampered with them so the competition would get the story wrong.[37]

In truth, the Hildy of the play was likely based more on how Hecht and MacArthur preferred to remember themselves. The basic dilemma that Hildy confronts had already appeared in Hecht's novels: "There, the Hechtian man, artist or newsman, is caught between his drive for self-actualization and the demands of the world around him," writes film scholar Jeffrey Brown Martin, "between his work and his home, between his soaring spirit and possibilities and the encroachments of age and the encroachments of a bourgeois civilization that always threatens him."[38]

Once again the style of Hecht's work is realism, but the heart and soul are pure Romanticism. Certainly the opening description of Hildy evokes the figure of Faust—the protagonist of the German legend that Goethe adapted into a classic work of literature. In the legend, Faust is a dying old doctor to whom the devil, Mephistopheles, offers a second chance at life, youth, and romance: a devil's bargain. Hecht and MacArthur introduce Hildy as "a vanishing type—the lusty, hoodlumesque, half-drunken caballero that was the newspaperman of our youth. Schools of journalism and the advertising business have nearly extirpated the species." The description of Burns as a modern, corporate Mephistopheles is explicit: "Beneath a dapper and very citizen-like exterior lurks a hobgoblin, perhaps the Devil himself. But if Mr. Burns is the Devil he is a very naif one. He is a Devil with neither point nor purpose to him—an undignified Devil hatched for a bourgeois Halloween." Will Hildy keep his pact with Burns and stay a vital young caballero, or will he marry and grow old among what Hecht once called "the little greedy half-dead"?[39]

Driving the point home, Burns is jocularly portrayed casting a spell on Hildy ("D'Artagnan never gave Richelieu an ear more startled or more innocent"), convincing Hildy that his story will kick "over the whole City Hall like an applecart." Minutes later, Hildy starts "coming out of the ether: 'You just bitched up my whole life! That's what you've done!'" When the newsmen later find themselves handcuffed and facing criminal charges, Burns tells Hildy not to worry. Arching his eyebrows, he explains, "Something seems to watch over the *Examiner*"—"an unseen power."[40]

The play struck a nerve with defenders of the press. *New York Times* attorney George Gordon Battle blasted it in an editorial: "Managing editors are not all conscienceless and cruel. The standards of all newspaper men are not those of the gutter." When the film version appeared in 1931, along with other movies that showed newspapers in a harsh light, like *Five Star Final* and *The Finger Points*, newspaper editor Stanley Walker warned prospective young journalists against depictions of the reporter who "writes best on twelve Scotch high-balls" and "insults everybody in earshot." Indeed, the image of newsmen as cynical, hard-drinking scoundrels would live on long after the actual era it portrayed, enduring in public memory as "a slick piece of work about very crude people who through constant traffic with corruption, had become ninety-nine percent corrupt themselves," in Fetherling's words.[41]

Yet there was clearly more to the story. In an epilogue included in the third printing of the script in 1928, the authors offer "an apology." They had meant to write a play that "would reflect our intellectual disdain of and superiority to the Newspaper." Instead, they had ended up producing "a Valentine thrown into the past." Burns and Hildy manage to get their scoop and, in the process, save Williams from execution and expose the sinister scheme of the mayor and sheriff. The press comes out the victor in the end, even if "triumph results from a series of comic, cosmic accidents." As media historian Matthew Ehrlich observes, "Hecht and MacArthur—and the seasoned Broadway pros Harris and Kaufman—managed not to stack the deck one way or another. If the play asks not only whether Hildy will leave journalism but also whether he should leave journalism, it very carefully leaves the second question unanswered."[42]

Hecht and MacArthur's comic masterpiece indelibly captured a distinct American newspaper culture and its cynicism about the press in a democracy. But Hecht's ideas about the media were bound up with a broader worldview revealed through his storytelling. His disdain for the public, the mob, matched a fascination with Romantic egoists like Hildy Johnson as well as dark antiheroes. The latter were inspired by the fallen visionaries of Romantic fiction, like Dr. Victor Frankenstein, but expressed a profound distrust of the Enlightenment after the Great War. Rationalism was supposed to have been the key to human progress, tolerance, good governance, and the protection of the "rights of man." Technology, like constitutional democracy, was supposed to improve the human condition.

But it had borne unforeseen fruit: the lethal machinery of tommy guns, mustard gas, tanks, and bombs.

Hecht began to convey his dark conclusions about humankind and the world through screenplays and novels centered around psychopaths. With the character of Erik Dorn, he had begun to imagine the dark side of rationalism, a cold efficiency driven by mad passion. A decade later he would create a more sinister, apocalyptic figure inspired by Al Capone, a figure who at the same time anticipated the emerging technocratic nightmare of Nazi Germany: the celluloid gangster Tony Camonte.

CHAPTER 4

The Journalist and the Gangster

Scarface with Paul Muni was recently barred from Germany when it was discovered that there was an uncommonly close resemblance between some of the gangsters in the picture and certain high Nazi officials.

—FILMFRONT, JANUARY 28, 1935[1]

What're you looking at? You're all a bunch of fucking assholes. You know why? You don't have the guts to be what you want to be. You need people like me. You need people like me so you can point your fucking fingers and say, "That's the bad guy." So what does that make you? Good? You're not good. You just know how to hide, how to lie. Me, I don't have that problem. Me, I always tell the truth. Even when I lie. So say goodnight to the bad guy.

—TONY MONTANA TO A GENTEEL RESTAURANT
CROWD IN THE 1983 REMAKE OF SCARFACE[2]

We live in a depraved and bloodthirsty age, Tony.

—A NOVELIST SPEAKING TO TONY CAMONTE
IN HECHT'S SCRIPT OF SCARFACE[3]

While scoring a hit with *The Front Page*, Hecht used the knowledge he had acquired as a crime reporter to launch the gangster movie craze with his sixty-eight-page treatment for *Underworld*. Films about street gangs dated at least as far back as D. W. Griffith's fifteen-minute one-reeler

The Musketeers of Pig Alley (1912). But *Underworld* is considered the first modern gangster movie. Though it opened with modest hopes, it garnered massive box-office success, and Hecht would receive an Oscar for best original story at the first Academy Awards ceremony, on May 16, 1929. "Here's to crime," wrote a reviewer for *Motion Picture Classic*. "Ever since *Underworld* came through with flying colors, most every producer including its particular sponsor, Paramount, has been trying to duplicate it."[4]

In Hecht's follow-up, *Scarface*, written after the stock market crash, he would push into far darker territory, appealing to a more sophisticated, or more jaundiced, audience.[5] The differences between the two films reflect the contrasts between Hecht's worldview before and after his experience in Germany, as well as the changes wrought by Prohibition in Chicago. While *Underworld* had portrayed the gritty era of the First Ward and the Gangsters' Ball, *Scarface* depicted corporate criminal syndicates that had developed in response to the Volstead Act, engulfing the power structures of the city. The result was a culture and politics suffused with crime. *Scarface* capitalized on the cult of personality around Al Capone, notorious for a ruthlessness that was a mix of icy calculation and ferocity. The film capitalized, as well, on the public's appetite for violence. Its gangsters were not merely thugs but veterans of a world war, armed with its firepower and trained in military tactics.

In short, whether consciously or not, Hecht's terrifying vision of *Scarface* protagonist Tony Camonte and his mob was in many ways suggestive of Hitler and the Nazis, just when Hitler was poised to seize power. Like the Nazis, Camonte was a creature of the world war, born of that combination of mad viciousness and modern efficiency. Like Hitler, Camonte is a media obsession with a genius for manipulating public opinion. But ironically, as a powerful figure who challenges the state, Camonte would also endure as Hecht's iconic outlaw, the fearsome and fearless type Hecht would one day turn to for help when the Jews were in need. In both roles this American movie gangster, like his real-life German counterpart, personified all that had gone wrong in the world.

Underworld had struck a chord because Hecht understood America's fascination with the soul of the racketeer. His own Menckenesque contempt for hypocritical puritan morality had put him at the center of a revolution in morals and manners under way in the 1920s. Gone was the gentility of the Victorian age. After the war, a new, modern urban culture was transforming the nation. In Walter Winchell's gossip column and elsewhere, jazz-age readers were following the love lives of gangsters as closely as their murders and deaths.[6]

"My movies were usually successful because I had a sense of what the public liked," Hecht explained in his unpublished biography of the gangster Mickey Cohen. "I found this out as a newspaperman. It liked hotheaded villains who didn't give a damn for the Commandments or the conventions." When a friend, Herman Mankiewicz, advised that in the movies the villain could have as much sex as he wanted, but heroes and heroines had to be virgins, Hecht recalled, "An idea came to me. The thing to do was to skip the heroes and heroines, to write a movie containing only villains and bawds. I would not have to tell any lies then."[7]

Underworld's director, Josef von Sternberg, who would go on to make the Paramount-UFA coproduction *The Blue Angel*, was the ambassador of German expressionism in Hollywood, and he shot *Underworld*, to Hecht's chagrin, entirely in Paramount's sound stages. This was the Chicago of the auteur's imagination, simply "a great city in the dead of night." The realism that Dreiser, the Whitechapelers, and others had brought to corruption and violence was missing.[8]

The advent of talking pictures in 1927, the year of the *Underworld*'s release, would alter how Americans perceived reality, influencing the public consciousness to a degree comparable to Prohibition and the Great Depression. Hecht would one day tout the gritty truth he had brought to his *Underworld* film treatment, and he blamed Sternberg for adding sentimental touches. But the story itself harkened back to a more innocent time. Comparing it to Hecht's *Scarface* illustrates not just the contrast between silent and sound movies but also that between the days of ward bosses and the modern era of corporatized crime—as well as that between a planet as yet untouched by world war and one shaped by it.[9]

Underworld's release coincided with a wave of successful "fast-talking, liquor-and-crime melodramas" on Broadway, including *Chicago* and Bartlett Cormack's *The Racket*, and with the rise of two Jewish actors. One of the best of the plays was *Four Walls*, in which a young star of the Yiddish theater named Meshilem Meier Weisenfreund played Lower East Side gangster Benny Horowitz. Weisenfruend, who would adopt Paul Muni as his stage name, played Tony Camonte in *Scarface*; he was likely recruited by Hecht after independent producer Howard Hughes and director Howard Hawks were unable to get a studio to lend them one of the stars who were under contract.[10] Muni's cousin, fellow Yiddish-speaking Lower East Sider Emanuel Goldenberg, played the lead that season in *The Racket* under the stage name Edward G. Robinson, before achieving celebrity in MGM's *Little Caesar* (1931). By the late 1930s, Muni and Robinson would take on lead roles as pioneering Hollywood activists seeking to warn America of the Nazi menace. In 1943 they would star together in *We Will Never Die*, Hecht's propaganda pageant meant to raise awareness of the Nazis' Final Solution.

Around this time Capone also rose to fame in books and the press. A smiling portrait of him appeared on the March 24, 1930, cover of *Time* magazine. At a Cubs game, Chicagoans booed President Herbert Hoover but cheered their reigning mobster.[11] "Americans marveled at Capone's wealth and power, built on an empire of prostitution, gambling, racketeering and bootlegging," writes David E. Ruth in *Inventing the Public Enemy: The Gangster in American Culture, 1918–1934.* "In press conferences, interviews with reporters and a highly theatrical social life, Capone worked as hard as any movie star to create a favorable public image."[12]

But it had been the ruthless, calculated efficiency of the 1929 Saint Valentine's Day Massacre that propelled him to national attention. Members of his South Side gang, dressed as police officers, had lured seven of George "Bugs" Moran's rival outfit into a Lincoln Park garage with promises of premium whiskey at a bargain price. When ordered to press their faces up against a wall, Moran's people thought they had been pinched and complied. Capone's hit squad then coolly cut them to pieces with Thompson submachine guns.[13]

In film, a string of crime and gangster movies chased *Underworld*'s success, including a kind of sequel by Sternberg. Moviemakers stumbled, however, in their first efforts at the gangster film in sound, such as *Broadway* and Sternberg's *Thunderbolt*, both released in 1929. By now, audiences had grown too sophisticated for the crime story as Romantic fable. They wanted something that corresponded with the realities they were reading about in the newspaper.[14]

They got it from Darryl F. Zanuck, who in January 1931 was appointed chief executive in charge of all productions for Warner Brothers and its new acquisition, First National. A *Reader's Digest* report that 486 gangsters had been killed on Chicago's streets in 1929 sent Zanuck hunting for Chicago tales. He was not interested, however, in the flock of writers who had written Broadway hits. He wanted journalists, not playwrights.[15] He snatched a Chicago novel syndicated in eighty-two newspapers, *Little*

Caesar, by W. R. Burnett; an unpublished collection of short stories by *Chicago Daily News* reporter John Bright; and an unproduced play by a little-known screenwriter named Rowland Brown. With these, Zanuck turned out three smash hits by the end of that year: *Doorway to Hell*, based on Brown's play; Burnett's *Little Caesar*; and *The Public Enemy*, adapted from Bright's stories. "Zanuck's gambit had paid off," Carlos Clarens notes in *Crime Movies: From Griffith to* The Godfather *and Beyond*. "The Warners' motto proclaimed 'Snatched from Today's Headlines,' and the new vogue was auspiciously launched."[16]

In retrospect, 1931 looms as the year of the gangster film—while none were blockbusters as we understand the term today, they generated the lion's share of attention and discussion. The debut performances of Clark Gable, James Cagney, and Robinson, all playing violent criminals, were cinematic sensations. In response, Hughes was determined to make the gangster film to end all gangster films, surpassing all others "in cost, scope, authenticity, and, needless to say, violence."[17] In choosing to do a thinly disguised biopic of Capone, Hughes also picked the grandest subject.

Hughes, a maverick, was known to spend exorbitantly on his films, with little care for the time and money required. This scared Hollywood, which feared he would break the uneasy truce the studios had maintained with the censors. Indeed, the censorship battles waged over *Scarface* were historic.[18] Seldom has the violence of a film been such an issue.[19]

His crucial production decision was to hire as the principal writers Hecht, Burnett, and Fred Pasley, a Capone biographer and fellow *Chicago Daily News* veteran. Hecht, who later claimed that he had not trusted Hughes, famously insisted on payment of $1,000 at the end of every day of work; he completed his draft in about eleven days in early 1931. Hecht's newspaper experience had taught him not only the public's taste for villains and bawds but also its appetite for mayhem. For a Columbia University oral history project on popular arts, Hecht recalled the pitch he had made to Hughes: that he was not fond of Armitage Trail's novel and would devise his own story instead.[20] When Hughes had asked about the plot, Hecht replied:

> I haven't got any plot, but there have been several gangster pictures made, and I will double the casualty list of any picture to date, and we'll have twice as good a picture. *The Secret Six* killed off about eight people. I will kill off twenty, and we'll have the audience right in our hands.

I killed off anybody I could. I killed as many people as I could shoot down. I shot 'em down because I knew audiences loved that. I always liked to do violent action pictures, because I knew audiences adored disaster, sudden death, explosions, much more than they did ideas, points of view or intelligence of any kind. And the reason I did good pictures was that I stuck to doing things that had no thought in them.[21]

Chicago was a city of extreme wealth and poverty, fantastic energy and growth, disorder and lawlessness. Commentators linked the city's aggressive capitalism with its underworld and with the rise of a new breed of entrepreneur. In pulp stories and popular biographies of Capone, Big Jim Colosimo's pre-Prohibition reign under the sponsorship of Hinky Dink and Bathhouse John was told as a rags-to-riches Horatio Alger story. "His career was built on traditional crimes, limited to a long-standing old vice district, rooted in a village-like community, and supported by patrons reminiscent of a colorful but fading past," explains one cultural historian.[22]

Colosimo's execution, and his replacement by John Torrio, was portrayed as the pushing aside of an old order as Prohibition transformed urban crime into big business. Torrio was the efficient manager, the refined businessman, yet his hold on power was nevertheless short-lived. The various accounts of how Capone replaced Torrio suggest that to be king of the underworld, business acumen was not enough: masculinity—brawn coupled with fearlessness—was also required. The stories of how Capone knocked out his North Side rivals, however, tell us that guts and toughness had to be tempered by cool rationality. Dion O'Banion and Hymie Weiss were bold and clever but fatally hotheaded. In the end, they both failed to play it smart: caught up in their own passion and bluster, they made mistakes.[23]

Scarface was the dark side of Erik Dorn's organization-man efficiency. In his biography of Cohen, Hecht explained:

A new type of industrialist entered American business—the illegal booze maker, and a new type of salesman hit Chicago. They hit it with brass knuckles and Tommy guns in a selling campaign that makes even our present day television commercials seem tame. Rival salesmen operating foolishly for other bosses than Capone were massacred. Customers, café owners and saloon proprietors inclined to shop around for alky products were pistol-whipped and left comatose in their wrecked premises. And the voters of Chicago grinned and drank. Their contempt for the Prohibition law was deeper than their penchant for law and order.[24]

Hecht and others also depicted Capone as a dark reflection of mainstream American culture. Pasley saw him as a self-made man, a heroic figure, like Henry Ford, Charles Lindbergh, and Douglass Fairbanks. In a scene in *Scarface* that mimics *The Great Gatsby*, Camonte piles shirts on his bed to impress his blonde-headed moll, Poppy. Camonte is a postcrash "parody of the American Dream . . . a psychopathic Horatio Alger . . . a reproach to both the principles of the market place and the reigning values of American life," writes Richard Pells. In a seminal essay on early gangster films, Robert Warshow famously asserted, "The gangster is the 'no' to that great American 'yes' which is stamped so large over our official culture."[25]

The talkie-era gangster also appeared as a Frankenstein created by the Great War. Capone claimed that the scars on the left side of his face were from fighting on the Western Front. Pasley believed Capone's service in Europe had introduced him to the machine gun and gave him the upper hand in the bootlegging wars. Zanuck, a veteran himself, wove the war into his films, particularly as the issue that divides brothers Tom and Mike Powers in *The Public Enemy*.

But no film was more packed with war imagery than *Scarface*. After the slaying of the Big Jim Colosimo character, "Costillo," a city editor, presents a dummy of the front page to his managing editor, who tells him it's rotten. "GANG WAR—That's what I want," the managing editor insists. "Costillo's the last of the old-fashioned gang leaders. . . . There's a new crew coming in. . . . They're gonna be shooting each other like rabbits from now till hell freezes for the control of the booze business. It's gonna be like war. Get that in the lead. WAR . . . GANG . . . WAR."[26]

One striking emblem of corporate and military power combined is Camonte's custom-made swivel desk chair, whose tall, bulletproof back is made of a plate of solid steel. But the film's most salient image is the downtown flat Camonte converts into an urban fortress, complete with its own armory and steel window shutters fitted with slots for guns, where Camonte will make his last stand.[27]

While Sternberg may have been the great Hollywood pioneer of expressionism, it would take the advent of sound, and the American director Hawks, to finally capture Hecht's unique blend of realism with

the Romantic themes and phantasmagoria. Departing from the some-
what-stiff, unimaginative filming of *Little Caesar* and *The Public Enemy*,
"Hawks went for violent chiaroscuro, tight grouping within the frame, and
fluid, stalking camera movement," notes Clarens.[28]

Certainly Hawks appreciated Camonte as the "psychopathic Horatio
Alger" of an expressionistic tale. Hawks remembered that what first
attracted him to Capone's legend was a disturbing anecdote about him
hosting a banquet for fellow mobsters. Capone's mood had darkened as
he addressed his dinner companions, until he concluded his speech by
bludgeoning the three guests of honor with a baseball bat.[29]

Hecht had no desire to work on another gangster film, but Hawks
convinced him by suggesting that this one would be different—the story
of the Borgias set down in Chicago. What Hawks likely had in mind was
a twist on the image of domestic bliss that Capone so proudly presented
to the media. Within this context, the incestuous connection between
Camonte and his sister Cesca, written into Hecht's script as a retelling
of Lucrezia Borgia's alleged romance with her brother Cesare, is another
representation of the perversion of the American dream, like Camonte's
tossing of the shirts onto his bed.[30]

The Hays Office censors were determined to suppress the film's suggestions of incest, and little of the Borgia theme in Hecht's original script
survived in the final cut. Just enough remains to sketch the contours that
lead to Camonte's downfall: his jealousy over his sister leads him to kill
the man she has just married, Rinaldo, who is his close friend. At that
point Camonte retreats to his fortress, where he soon finds that the police
have surrounded him. The Camonte siblings reunite "like desperate, guilty
lovers" in a suicidal bid to fend off the invading army of law enforcement.
Cesca, who had come to avenge Rinaldo but cannot bring herself to kill
her brother, now becomes his moll: "I'm like you," she says as she loads
his guns. "You're not afraid, are you?" Her hysterical laughter, rising amid
this "Liebestod of searchlights and gunfire," is cut short by a bullet that
ricochets off one of Camonte's much-vaunted steel shutters, a symbol of
his invulnerability. As she falls, he is suddenly lost.[31]

The room, trembling from explosions, fills with tear gas. He stag-
gers through the smoke—"a mad, disheveled creature"—and then outside,
where he makes one final desperate run, only to be shot down in the
gutter. As the last of his life runs out, flashing neon illuminates his grimy
face. The camera tilts upward to show, through Camonte's gaze, a Cook's

Tours billboard that had been the gangster's lodestar: "THE WORLD IS YOURS."[32]

The ultimate tragedy is Camonte's "terrible innocence," his innate barbarousness, apparent at every turn. He wants to be a respectable member of modern society but seems doomed to be a throwback, a caveman. As a businessman, Camonte wants a secretary, but the thug he chooses for the job fears the telephone, wants to smash or shoot it, and can only grunt and curse into its mouthpiece. Camonte tries to take in a play at the theater with his capos but must leave in the middle of an act to carry out a hit; he later receives a hopelessly garbled report of how the story ends from his lackey Angelo. Camonte goes fishing with a group of sophisticates in Florida, but when he struggles to reel in his line, Angelo ruins things again by blowing the fish apart with a pistol.[33]

In these and other scenes, "we are made to feel the frightening discrepancy between the achievements of civilization and the actual level of culture attained by the individuals who are its by-products," one scholar has observed. It is Camonte's innocence, his lack of awareness, that permits him to kill and ransack, or to murder his sister's husband in a jealous rage. The savage, primitive gangster stands as a reminder of humankind's true nature and the Enlightenment's failure to produce a modern, civilized world.[34]

Camonte's "terrible innocence" is an inversion of Hildy Johnson's Huck Finn–like innocence, just as the gangster's incestuous family life and twisted American dream are an inversion of Johnson's dream of a future in New York with his bride. In Camonte, what seems good, or at least charming or amusing, is really bad, whereas Johnson's wickedness is really his goodness. As opposites, a yin and a yang, Hecht's gangster and reporter are twinned. Their duality, in turn, reflects the dual natures at war within each of them, Camonte's paradoxical "terrible innocence" and Johnson's "lusty, hoodlumesque" yet childlike nature.

Camonte's role as a twentieth-century primordial savage, a Frankenstein's monster borne of the modern era, is as suggestive of Hitler as are the gangster's slick celebrity and ruthless efficiency. Yet there is a crucial difference between the gangster and the dictator. The gangster defies the state, while the Führer embodies it. Camonte is not a politician. He makes no lofty, false claim to be the arbiter of law. He is an outlaw. As such, Hecht regards the gangster as honest and trustworthy. He may reflect an ugly world, but he is a true, honest reflection of it.

And if the gangster is the world's Frankenstein, then he is the perfect devil with whom Hecht can one day strike a bargain on behalf of the Jews, a hunted people who have nowhere else to turn. If this seems upside down, one must consider the fight-fire-with-fire rationale: if the gangster represents the worst of the world, then who better to turn to when the world is at war with you?

PART II

THE WRITER
The Chicago Renaissance
and Hollywood

Dear Ben and Rose:

Thanks very much for the weekly cheque which came this morning. My type-writer rent is now months in arrears and I may lose the machine, but perhaps that will not matter too much since my creations seem to be tacitly rubber-stamped for rejection before they reach the editorial offices. The boys and girls just can't resist the momentum of habit, I suppose. . . . With unrivaled courage and pertinacity, the British government has concentrated five heavy cruisers and an entire division of soldiers to prevent 1500 unarmed, yearning, bedraggled, scarred Jewish refugees from entering Palestine. On our side of the fence, the Mead Investigation drearily nibbles at the fringes of corruption, graft and gorging indulged in by munitions manufacturers and other industrialists while American men were dying and suffering on the battle fronts. As I view the world of reality surrounded by high walls, it seems a bad, corny, utterly unprincipled American dream beneath coats of whitewash and gilding so palpably ridiculous and fraudulent that one wonders why the culprits still bother to wield the paint brushes!

Fond regards to both of you and best wishes to your daughter from a very pessimistic

Bogie[1]

Thus reported Maxwell Bodenheim in one of his epistolary dispatches from a life on the margins in 1947. In these weekly installments to Ben Hecht, the poet telescoped his daily desperation or erupted with the same holy wrath that had once made people take notice. But people had long stopped noticing. His manuscripts were never to be published again, the last of his books being *Selected Poems,* an anthology of old verse issued in 1946. Now he was fighting eviction from his flat in Brooklyn and caring for his sick wife, battles that he was about to lose.[2]

Within a few years, he would hit bottom, peddling his poems for twenty-five cents at the Village Vanguard or Minetta Tavern, his rank smell pushing customers away as he shambled from table to table, a corpse-eyed, toothless scarecrow in dirty pants held up with twine, swollen ankles rising out of laceless shoes. Some believed the poems were worth the quarter, but others bought them solely for the autograph, "for they saw not a besotted bum," explained Greenwich Village chronicler Ross Wetzsteon, "but a defiant spirit, debonair even in his degradation, the poet praised by Pound, the novelist pursued by smut-hounds, the notorious roué of a thousand amours, iconoclast, renegade, scourge of the Philistines, 'unwashed archpriest of Bohemia,' Poet Laureate of Greenwich Village—Maxwell Bodenheim."[3]

Twenty years earlier, Bodenheim had been considered one of the finest poets of his generation, in a class with T. S. Eliot, William Carlos Williams, and Conrad Aiken. Bodenheim and Hecht, the youngest two among the art and literature disciples who would be remembered as the vanguard of the Chicago Renaissance, had once been more than close friends; they were alter egos with a shared sensibility that distinguished them from the rest of their tribe.[4] They grabbed the limelight in the tinseled, cynical era that followed the Great War by savaging their fellow literati in their weekly magazine, the *Chicago Literary Times.* And then, having declared war on everyone and everything else, they declared war on each other. In a well-publicized feud that played off their reputation as a team, Hecht caricatured the poet's flamboyant, caustic egoism in his 1926 novel *Count Bruga,* while Bodenheim, most adept with the counterpunch, lampooned Hecht as a vain and shallow sellout in his 1931 novel *Duke Herring.*[5]

Luminaries of the Chicago Renaissance and, soon thereafter, the New York literary scene of the jazz age, the two rode the crest of modernism, but when the wave broke on the shoals of the Depression, it cast their lives in very different directions. In the 1920s Hecht had reinvented himself as a novelist and playwright before achieving fame and fortune as a Hollywood screenwriter. Bodenheim had become legendary as "a wild-looking Lothario who was relentlessly pursued by women," and he earned a national reputation for his poetry and incisive commentary. His essays appeared regularly in *Poetry* magazine, the *New Republic*, the *Dial*, the *Nation*, *Harper's*, *Bookman*, and the *Yale Review*, and he produced nine books of poems and thirteen novels. But after the crash of 1929, the money and attention evaporated, and during the 1930s his life fell apart. What followed was a long descent into what Hecht called "some private hell."[6]

When a gaunt and shattered Bodenheim had emerged by chance out of the winter rain on Forty-Seventh Street in 1941, Hecht had not seen his old friend in more than a decade. They ducked into a neighborhood bar, where Hecht pored over years' worth of unpublished poems packed into a beat-up briefcase that Bodenheim carried everywhere. When the rain turned into a heavy snowfall, Hecht brought the poet to his home in Nyack, New York, hoping he would stay the night. But a woozy Bodenheim insisted on returning to his dying wife and left before dinner, his overcoat pockets stuffed with socks, shorts, ties, shoes, and pajamas ransacked from Hecht's closets.[7]

His old friend's condition prompted Hecht to make an offer: in exchange for a poem or two pages of prose on any topic every week, he would send Bodenheim a thirty-dollar check. Hecht kept this up for several years. Each week the poet's submission arrived, accompanied by a letter acknowledging receipt of the money or gently noting that it had not yet arrived. "These letters . . . contain one of the most desperate self-portraits I've ever read," Hecht wrote. "The portrait of an unwanted talent; penniless, almost rotted away with liquor and calamities—but still as proud and articulate as any prime minister."[8]

Upon their reunion in 1941, their memories of the Renaissance took on a new significance. Bodenheim was forgotten and penniless, while Hecht had become one of the highest-paid writers on the planet. Yet Hecht had been loudly proclaiming that he felt rudderless and hollow as a mass-media entertainer; as he, too, found himself adrift, the poet's old charge of sellout seemed to stick. Bodenheim needed some way to fit in, somewhere to belong. Hecht needed a sense of meaning and purpose in his life. Both sought something that reminded them of who they had been when they were young, back when they had believed in art and literature and in themselves.

The rising emergency for Europe's Jews thus had a unique effect on Hecht; the more riled he became by the disturbing developments at home and abroad, the more he regained the sense of conviction he had once felt in the confidence of youth. In fact, for a while anyway, he was to discover a truer iconoclasm, a more clear-eyed and authentic banner for his rebelliousness. Over the months and years ahead, the causes of rescuing Jews from the Nazis and supporting militant Zionism would allow him to appreciate his Jewish heritage as a source of self-discovery and renewal. As he later explained of his propaganda, "I did all these things partly out of my own needs."[9] In turn, his activities stirred Bodenheim, whose letters suggest that the poet found in Judaism at least some solace and reassurance—though not, ultimately, a path to redemption.

Hecht's eight-year campaign would become as much an encounter and confrontation with American Jewish writers, actors, publishers, and studio executives as with politicians and the public. Yet although he was rebelling against Hollywood in particular and the culture industry more generally, he nevertheless depended on the studios for a paycheck. The resulting unease about being a sellout was a feud raging within him that echoed his old feud with Bodenheim. During the war years and the aftermath, Bodenheim's plight took on a special significance, which Hecht would continue to write about and wrestle with for the rest of his life.[10]

dim, deep room, if you've ever felt music replacing your shabby soul with a new one of shining gold; if, in the early morning, you've watched a bird with great white wings fly from the edge of the sea straight up into the rose-colored sun—if these things have happened to you and continue to happen till you're left speechless with the wonder of it all, then you'll understand our hope to bring them near to the common experience of the people who read us.[4]

Anderson's *Little Review*, humble and stitched together, heralded Chicago's arrival as an American vanguard of literature and art. By the 1890s the city that poet Carl Sandburg called the "Hog Butcher for the world" had made great strides in establishing institutions of high culture: the University of Chicago, with Thorstein Veblen and John Dewey on the faculty, the Auditorium concert hall designed by the "father of skyscrapers" Henry Louis Sullivan, and, most spectacularly, the World's Columbian Exposition of 1893. Chicago drew writers and artists from small towns across the Midwest, educated them, and thereby gave them things to smash.[5] By 1917 the city's explosion of talent would prompt H. L. Mencken to pronounce in the *Sunday Tribune*: "Find me a writer who is indubitably American and has something new and interesting to say, and who says it with an air, and nine times out of ten . . . he has some sort of connection with that abattoir by the lake—that he was bred there or got his start there, or passed through there during the days when he was tender."[6]

Critic Burton Rascoe has suggested that the Chicago Renaissance started with the 1909 launch of the *Friday Literary Review*, an eight-page book supplement to the *Chicago Evening Post* that, under the farsighted editorial leadership of Francis Hackett, fostered literary culture and promoted local talent. Then, in 1912, Harriet Monroe founded *Poetry* magazine, with Ezra Pound as a foreign correspondent. *Poetry* published T. S. Eliot's first great work, "The Love Song of J. Alfred Prufrock," when Eliot was still an unknown poet, and it became an early outlet for the experimental verse of Hart Crane, Wallace Stevens, William Carlos Williams, Amy Lowell, D. H. Lawrence, and others. Also in 1912, Maurice Browne established the Little Theater, pioneering a new movement of small-scale, semiprofessional productions, which helped to complete the city's emerging bohemian scene.[7]

Yet as Bernard Duffey writes in his incisive account of the Renaissance, "more than either *Poetry* or the *Friday Review*, the first limited by its concentration on verse, the second to what could be smuggled into a book reviewer's columns, the *Little Review* embraced the whole of the Renaissance. Margaret set no limits on the magazine." Assembled according to no principle other than Anderson's inspiration, and printed on wood pulp, rag, or glossy paper depending on what she could afford at the moment, the journal first championed anarchism and socialism before devoting itself to the aesthetic cause of imagism after Pound defected from *Poetry* to become the magazine's foreign editor in 1917. It published W. B. Yeats, Djuna Barnes, and Gertrude Stein; the early stories of Sherwood Anderson; and the first notable vignettes and stories of Ernest Hemingway. But its greatest and boldest contribution was its serialization of James Joyce's *Ulysses* in twenty-three installments from 1918 to 1920, until the Society for the Suppression of Vice charged it with obscenity.[8] "It was Art," Ben Hecht would recall wistfully. "I have met many things in my life that were Art, but they were always Art plus something else—Art plus fame, money, vanity, success, politics, complexes, etc. *The Little Review* was, nakedly and innocently, Art."[9]

This art represented a new consciousness, a new way of looking at and thinking about the world. It is commonly recognized that America experienced a cultural revolution at some point early in the twentieth century. Many believe it happened amid the giddy madness of the jazz age, when a tumult of diversions, lifestyles, and new ideas—from miniature golf and dance marathons to speakeasies and the *Smart Set*—knocked aside old conventions from before the war and forever changed American life. But historians have long argued that the real upheaval had begun before the war, with a transformative burst of creative thought and activity between 1912 and 1917 that Henry Farnham May has called the "Innocent Rebellion."[10]

Hecht, with his journalistic skill for simplicity, put it concretely:

> If you did not believe in God, in the importance of marriage, in the United States Government, in the sanity of politicians, in the necessity of education or in the wisdom of your elders, you automatically believed in art. You did not automatically plunge into the worlds of painting, music and literature. You plunged *out* of worlds, out of family worlds, business worlds, greed and ambition worlds. You did not necessarily stay out of them forever. . . . But as long as you "believed in art" you remained orphaned from the smothering arms of society.[11]

ભ

The Renaissance arose literally out of the ruins of the Columbian Exposition, the epic Chicago world's fair of 1893. The Jackson Park art colony developed at East Fifty-Seventh Street and Stony Island Avenue, in a South Side neighborhood of single-story frame buildings originally constructed for the world's fair as souvenir stands and temporary restaurants. By the spring of 1913, Theodore Dreiser, Sherwood Anderson, Margaret Anderson, Vincent Starrett, Harriet Monroe, and Eunice Tietjens (assistant editor at *Poetry*) had formed a circle that gathered for small parties at the adjoining studio apartments rented by Floyd Dell, who had succeeded Hackett as editor of the *Friday Literary Review*, and Dell's wife, Margery Currey. (The marriage would, however, soon break up, and Dell would move to New York.) At one of their gatherings, Anderson announced her plan to start a magazine and discussed possible titles.[12]

Hecht became acquainted with Anderson and this circle of writers through Currey, hired as a reporter for the *Daily News* in the fall of 1913. Hecht, already rising in the newspaper world, was working on short tales and poems. He was also collaborating on half a dozen short plays produced at Jane Addams's Hull House with Kenneth Sawyer Goodman, an aspiring dramatist and Princeton graduate, the most successful of their later works being *The Wonder Hat* (1916). At some point in early 1914, Currey invited Hecht over to the apartment, and there he found the community that would foster his ambitions as an artist. This "was another world into which I had drifted in my teens," Hecht recalled, "a world unaware of doomed men and 4-11 fires."[13]

Of all the early contributors to the *Little Review*, Hecht was Anderson's favorite. She was charmed by his conversation, and while she rebuffed his advances—she was a lesbian—he appreciated the support and opportunities she offered, and he came to see her purity, devotion, and—most of all—results as a kind of genius. In 1915 the *Little Review* became the first outlet for his creative work, before it began appearing in Mencken's *Smart Set* and elsewhere. When, by 1918, he tired of churning out formulaic fiction for Mencken, he returned to the *Little Review*, contributing some of the best of his early stories; he continued to publish there for the next four years.[14]

Playwright and theater producer Lawrence Langner remembered meeting Hecht during the heyday of the Renaissance. "He expressed his intention of devoting his life entirely to pure literature, as evidenced by certain coruscating stories he had contributed to *The Little Review*," Langner wrote. "These, he said, would win him immortality, though he would undoubtedly die penniless in an attic. Years later I pondered over the evanescent nature of human intentions, as he informed me, with considerable bitterness, that he was then the highest-paid writer in Hollywood."[15]

By the summer of 1914, Hecht had fallen in with another habitué of Currey's studio, Maxwell Bodenheim. Of the young bards now appearing at *Poetry*'s office, "this usually silent figure was perhaps the most unpromising and forlorn," Monroe later wrote. "He was always looked hunted and haunted, as if half-starved and half-ill." But her attitude soon changed when she read Bodenheim's verse. Langner remembered that the poet's arrival sparked a feud between the little magazines. "We have just discovered a new poet," Margaret Anderson had told him breathlessly, "probably one of the greatest in America, and now Harriet is trying to print one of his poems in *Poetry Magazine* so as to claim credit for his discovery before we publish him in *The Little Review*." Years later, at a party in New York given by Bodenheim's publisher, Horace Liveright, Langner heard a loud crash in the hall at two in the morning and inquired timidly what it was. "That," said Liveright with chagrin, "is Maxwell Bodenheim falling downstairs."[16]

Strutting about bohemia like an odd rooster, Bodenheim was shabby but generally clean, often draped in a U.S. Army overcoat in wintertime. He smoked a four-foot-long, malodorous Polynesian pipe with a baby blue ribbon around its stem and was always ready with a lashing remark, a mocking grin, as if privy to a private joke known only to himself, and florid, ornate phrases that many women found beguiling, if also incomprehensible. "Your face is an incense bowl from which a single name arises" was one typical line. "Your hair is a tortured midnight" was another. He was tall, lanky, and handsome, with baby blue eyes that matched the color of his pipe ribbon, and was a gifted if uneven writer, capable of producing fine poetry and compelling essays. Despite his eccentricities, which could be worn as a badge of honor in ever-tolerant bohemia, he looked destined for a brilliant future. "But beneath the surface there lurked a man of acute inner tensions, wracked with self-defeating conflicts," observed one chronicler. "I have a malady of the soul," Bodenheim had begun declaring in Chicago—a line he would often find occasion to repeat thereafter.[17]

Born on May 26, 1892, and raised in Hermanville, Mississippi, Bodenheim had grown up in the shadow of his mother's family's success and his father's failures. Solomon Bodenheimer's shortcomings as a breadwinner were not lost on his domineering wife, who meanwhile saw her brothers and sisters thrive, leading to a home life wracked by bitter quarrels and instability. By the time the family moved to Chicago in 1900, Max had become rebellious; he was later expelled from Hyde Park High School. In 1909 he ran away from home and joined the army.[18]

Hecht reports that Bodenheim was jailed for hitting a lieutenant in the head with his musket after the officer had ridiculed him as a Jew. But according to Bodenheim's first wife, Minna Schein, Bodenheim had tried to desert, only to be recaptured, and then panicked and swallowed lye. He spent the remainder of his duty at Fort Leavenworth. As a result of the lye incident, his teeth began to rot, and his taste buds were destroyed, so that for the rest of his life he dumped bottles of Tabasco and Worcester sauce on everything he ate to give it some taste.[19]

Bodenheim's career was rapidly on the ascent. He had been exchanging poems and letters with Alfred Kreymborg, editor of the poetry magazine *Others*, and at some point—probably in late 1914—traveled out to New York for a stay. Arriving with an old portmanteau in one arm and the other arm in a sling, he had struck his host as "the queerest among the queer." The injury, Bodenheim explained, had occurred when he fell off a streetcar before entraining for the journey—"another of life's little jokes," he had quipped, with the weariness of an old man. "Bogie's poems, mature to the last degree, were frankly admired in the crowd," Kreymborg recalled, "and the poverty-stricken misanthrope, who hated nothing on earth as he hated Chicago and the *Poetry* crowd—the first of an endless series of antipathies—sunned himself in this admiration." William Carlos Williams, who also opened his home to Bodenheim during the monthlong visit, remembered that his guest had arrived with a fake sling in order to avoid assisting with any chores.[20]

With his cackling wit, rakish flair, and literary airs, Bodenheim managed to amuse the likes of Marcel Duchamp, Malcolm Cowley, and Conrad Aiken. He drank at the Hell Hole with Eugene O'Neill, whom he would later profile for the *New Yorker*, and Dorothy Day, composing a long poem with them. As one of the revolving cast of editors for *Others*, he discovered Hart Crane, who related excitedly to his mother in 1917 that "Bodenheim is at the top of American poetry today." When *Others* folded, Williams, who also served as editor, told Amy Lowell that the periodical had been valuable because it had "held the future of such a man as Bodenheim in its palms, even if only for a short while."[21]

In 1920 the *New York Times* spotlighted the publication of Bodenheim's second book of poetry, *Advice*. Critic Herbert S. Gorman announced, "He is a phoenix of strange origin who must have risen from the ashes of some bird . . . bursting upon one from the blue with absolutely no antecedents, no formative guides to point back at. . . . Mr. Bodenheim is a wizard of phrases. He is a master of the elusive word. . . . He peers behind phrases, finding strange lumber there and building up his airy structures with a decisive gesture. 'Advice' is indubitably one of the most important books of the year."[22]

Meanwhile, by the winter of 1915, Hecht was spending time at a Cass Street boardinghouse packed with young bohemians, where Sherwood Anderson rented a third-floor room. Anderson had nicknamed the place, where he reigned as dean, Little Children of the Arts, a joking reference to a nearby Catholic school. He too was a runaway who had landed in bohemia, but of a unique variety. Originally from Ohio, Anderson had owned a manufacturing firm in Elyria, but the business had fallen apart; one morning he had walked out of his office onto the road that led out of town, leaving his wife and three young children behind. His own accounts of what happened over the next four days would always be vague; apparently he became lost in a fugue and suffered amnesia. Finally, he showed up dazed, disheveled, and incoherent at a Cleveland drugstore and was taken to a hospital. The incident ended his marriage and marked the start of a new life and career.[23]

Now thirty-nine years old, Anderson was being hailed by Dell as Chicago's "great unpublished author" for the manuscript he had been writing in his Elyria attic, *Windy McPherson's Son*, and he was well along with two more novels, *Marching Men* and *Winesburg, Ohio*. He found himself among urchins half his age who could talk all night about authors he had never heard of. Despite the insecurity this engendered, he seemed to see his new life in bohemia as a second chance at childhood, and he embraced his newfound sense of innocence and wonder. When his girlfriend, Tennessee Mitchell, brought him to the opera, he remarked that while the music had made no strong impression on him, he found the costumes marvelous. He often lit candles to the gods of inspiration when he read at gatherings or sat down to write at his big table. In the first issue of the *Little Review*, he trumpeted the "new note" entering the world, which owed nothing to what had come before. "If we are a crude and child-like people," he would later assert, "how can our literature hope to escape the influence of that fact? Why indeed should we want it to escape?"[24]

By 1915 Hecht had also befriended Carl Sandburg, when the latter, in his mid-thirties, was working for *The Day Book*, a newspaper that championed the common worker. Hailing from Galesburg, Illinois, Sandburg had been at different times a hobo, a journalist, and a committed activist employed by Wisconsin's Socialist Party. Hecht managed to convince his boss at the *Daily News*, Henry Justin Smith, to hire his new friend, and while the editors found Sandburg infuriating, Hecht and the other reporters were amused by his starry-eyed radicalism and obliviousness to deadlines.[25]

In March 1914 Sandburg's "Chicago Poems" started to appear in *Poetry*. The poems soon earned Sandburg several champions, including Dreiser, Mencken, and Edgar Lee Masters (the latter's *Spoon River Anthology* garnered significant attention after its publication in 1915). Monroe lobbied vociferously for Sandburg, arranging for him to win the 1914 *Poetry* contest.[26]

With the publications of Masters's *Spoon River Anthology*, Sandburg's *Chicago Poems*, and five of Sherwood Anderson's *Winesburg* stories in journals, the Renaissance reached its apex between 1915 and 1916. *Poetry*, the *Little Review*, and the Little Theater had all hit their stride. Anderson and Sandburg would soon soar to fame and literary glory. Anderson's *Windy McPherson's Son* garnered a few exuberant reviews but poor sales in 1916, while his subsequent novel and book of poems both flopped. But his luck changed in the spring of 1919, when publisher Ben Huebsch took a risk with *Winesburg, Ohio*. It became a sensation, and the following year *Poor White* scored another major success. Sandburg earned a Pulitzer Prize for *Corn Huskers* in 1917 and would eventually win two more; his *American Songbag*, printed in 1927, has endured as a seminal compilation of folk songs, while his multivolume biography of Abraham Lincoln is regarded as a masterpiece.[27]

Hecht was furiously producing short stories while continuing to write plays with Goodman. He also partnered with Bodenheim, with whom he wrote *Dregs*, *The Master Poisoner*, and other plays produced by the Players Workshop, a little theater on Fifty-Seventh Street.[28] Reading back over *The Master Poisoner* in the final days of his life, Hecht found it astonishing. The plot and dialogue were both unintelligible. "Yet the printed phrases seemed to spin and leap with some mysterious excitement," he wrote. "Youth in love with words. The embrace may have been a little disorderly, but I have found few things better to love—since then."[29]

CHAPTER 6

Crying in the Wilderness

A process of assortment took place: the Dells and the Cooks left Chicago for New York, while the Hechts and the Bodenheims with their Art-for-Art's sake dictum remained in Chicago for another decade or so, to wait till Greenwich Village was scared by the anti-Red hysteria and lulled by Coolidge Prosperity into a drink-and-sex era, with politics excluded.

—ALBERT PARRY, *GARRETTS AND PRETENDERS*[1]

In the task they perform, modern intellectuals are descendants of the priestly upholders of the sacred tradition, but they are also and at the same time descendants of the biblical prophets, of those inspired madmen who preached in the wilderness far removed from the institutionalized pieties of court and synagogue, castigating men of power for the wickedness of their ways.

—LOUIS A. COSER, *MEN OF IDEAS: A SOCIOLOGIST'S VIEW*[2]

American writers have tended to see themselves as outcasts and isolates, prophets crying in the wilderness.

—SACVAN BERCOVITCH, *THE AMERICAN JEREMAID*[3]

While assembling the third issue of the *Little Review* in May 1914, Margaret Anderson heard anarchist firebrand Emma Goldman lecture and "had just time to turn anarchist before the presses closed." As a result, she lost her funding for the journal. From then on, the poised and gentle lover of art and poetry would draw such notoriety as a seditious firebrand that in 1930 she would title her memoir *My Thirty Years' War*. By the time Wobbly poet Joe Hill was executed by firing squad for the murder of a shopkeeper in November 1915, Anderson had embraced socialism and was now calling the *Little Review* a magazine of "Art and Revolution." In her December editorial, she wondered why the five thousand Chicagoans who marched at Hill's funeral on Thanksgiving Day had not rallied before he was shot. "Incidentally," she added, "why didn't some one shoot the governor of Utah before he could shoot Joe Hill?" For that matter, she suggested, they could now beat up a local police squad on behalf of Chicago's garment strikers, set fire to some of the factories, or sabotage the shops. "For God's sake," she demanded, "why doesn't some one start the revolution?"[4]

On a surface level at least, the Renaissance writers had forged an alliance with Chicago's activists. Hecht, however, stayed true to the creed of newspapermen and maintained a bemused detachment from the radicalism of his friends. Looking back a half century later, he recalled that the public had regarded the true opponents of capitalism, such as Goldman, Bill Haywood, Eugene Debs, Mother Jones, and Jack Reed, "as windy bores, except when they spoke too well. Then they were either run out of town or clapped into jail." In regard to the reporters, Hecht wrote:

> We knew about the sins, about the hungry, jobless poor. And about the arrogant bosses who bilked the workers and called for the state militia to shoot the bohunks down when they became too sassy. . . . But oddly, we young ones who lived on crumbs were ready to defend the feast with our lives—which we were never called on to do. But we showed our metal [sic] in our derision. We sneered at all reformers, including those who worked for improvements among "the great unwashed." Perhaps this was because general poverty and a flourishing few were part of the show we liked.
>
> We who watched the show from our newspaper front seats stood pat against the would-be emancipators of the poor as if we were millionaires all. We were tattered Tories with no more social consciousness than the mooing calves in the Stock Yards. With all the black deeds going on around us, frequently under our noses, we could not imagine a better world.[5]

Hecht's distrust of causes spared him the heartache and misfortune that befell his idealistic friends during the Great War, precipitating an era of disillusionment in which he and Bodenheim would take center stage. In the early 1920s, the pair would fashion their own unique rebellion with a weekly gazette, the *Chicago Literary Times*, which took aim not at capitalism or state power but at the artists—including and especially their own friends—who they felt had strayed from the original ideals of the Renaissance. In targeting their own, Hecht and Bodenheim would emulate the ancient Hebrew prophets, casting themselves ever more radically as outcasts and isolates, their ears tuned to a divine voice only they could hear. It was an iconoclasm that Hecht would later revive during and after World War II, when he would direct his withering gaze on the Allied and Zionist leadership.

But before the *Chicago Literary Times* came the politicization and rapid collapse of the Innocent Rebellion. Renaissance writers and Margaret Anderson herself gradually migrated to New York City, where by 1913 art and revolution had mingled and fallen in love at the Greenwich Village parties of Mabel Dodge, an heiress and patron of the arts.[6] Dodge's apartment was epicenter of the scene in New York, just as Margery Currey's studio had been in Chicago, and it was there that the most dramatic events of the movement—such as it was—began to unfold. "*I* was going to dynamite New York, and nothing would stop me," Dodge recalled in her memoir.[7]

After labor strikes grew increasingly bloody and chaotic, and the United States entered World War I, a reactionary backlash and fierce crackdown followed. Government agents became more numerous than Goldman's followers at her speeches, and just as the post office was poised to ban her magazine *Mother Earth* under the Espionage and Sedition Acts, a U.S. marshal arrested her for conspiring against the draft. The *New York Times* led the call to eject her, and on the freezing morning of December 21, 1919, she and 245 others were shipped out on "the Red Ark" from New York harbor.[8]

When Margaret Anderson moved from Chicago to New York in 1917 after a winter spent in San Francisco, she had trouble fitting in with the East Coast bohemians, and her finances, never steady, became increasingly strained. In 1920 she and her lover and coeditor, Jane Heap, were booked on criminal charges of distributing obscenity through the mails for the publication of *Ulysses*. Though a few years earlier their trial would have been a cause célèbre, the alliance between the literary and political worlds was now long over. The press took little interest in their case, and New York's literary critics, who had never been warm to the book, were mute. At a pretrial hearing, Heap, defying her unhelpful attorney, voiced a lyrical protest that would not soon be forgotten: "Girls lean back everywhere, showing lace and silk stockings, wear low-cut sleeveless blouses, breathless bathing suits; men think thoughts and have emotions about these things everywhere . . . and no one is corrupted." Found guilty of violating the Comstock Act of 1873, the editors incurred a hundred-dollar fine and had to cease the serialization in the *Little Review*. In 1922 Anderson joined the expatriate community in Paris, having concluded that America would neither support nor tolerate her idealism.[9]

The crackdown was just one of the sweeping changes that accompanied the war. The rebels had known change was imminent, but, imbued with the same sunny optimism and confidence as the Victorians, they had been no better prepared for the dark days ahead. For Americans, not only did the war look like the funeral pyre of the old culture, it suggested that this had been the true face of the culture they had inherited from Europe all along. "Is it not a possibility," asked Frank H. Simonds in the *New Republic*, "that what is taking place marks quite as complete a bankruptcy of ideas, systems, society, as did the French Revolution?" Further, the atrocities could appear a vivid repudiation of belief in the basic decency of human nature. The rebels could now feel vindicated in their attacks on the smugness of Victorian society. But there was no joy in the vindication.[10]

ᘓ

By 1920, when the London *Nation* reprinted H. L. Mencken's grand proclamation that Chicago was "The Literary Capital of the United States," most of the principal players of the Renaissance were gone. Theodore Dreiser, Lloyd Dell, Sherwood Anderson, and Margaret Anderson had moved away, while Chicago radicals Eugene Debs and Bill Haywood had been sentenced to jail time in 1918.

That left Hecht, fresh from his return from Germany by the late summer of 1919, to bask with Bodenheim in the limelight of what Dale Kramer called "a new age of cynical glitter" that followed. The two savants held court at the Round Table of Schlogl's, which offered exotic lunchtime fare at equally exotic prices, and became the center of the new scene. Other regulars of this stag club—women and their escorts dined in a dilapidated upstairs room—included newspaper columnists Richard Henry Little and Keith Preston, artist and journalist Wallace Smith, editor Henry Justin Smith, publishers and booksellers Pascal Covici and Billy McGee, physician and medical editor Morris Fishbein, author and literary sage Vincent Starrett, critic Burton Rascoe, and Harry Hansen, whose 1923 book *Midwestern Portraits* focused on Round Table personalities. Of the original Renaissance writers, Dreiser, Sherwood Anderson, and Edgar Lee Masters would occasionally drop by when in town. Other visitors included Vincent Sheean, Ludwig Lewisohn, Louis Untermeyer, Sinclair Lewis, and Charles MacArthur.[11]

"As a matter of fact, the Renaissance became a one-man affair, centering around Hecht," observed the editor and translator Samuel Putnam, the author of a memoir of the lost generation. "It was Hecht who dominated the '*Daily News* School,' the gathering-place of which was Schlogl's Restaurant, with dignified, scholarly Hansen, then literary critic on the *News*, as master of ceremonies. . . . There was good conversation, and it helped to preserve the illusion that Chicago was still the 'capital' it had once been; but it did not require much inspection to discover that this was far from being the case." Hecht would later quip, "Would that our writing had been as fine as our lunches!"[12]

The nighttime hot spot was the Dil Pickle, a kind of vaudeville venue, burlesque club, and carnival freak show rolled into one. What had started as an informal discussion group for the soapbox radicals of "Bughouse Square"—the popular name for Chicago's Washington Square Park—had moved to nearby 18 Tooker Alley by 1917, bordering the northside bohemian community known as Towertown, which had sprung up just before the war.[13] The Dil Pickle offered all-night jazz from the Chicago bands of the early 1920s; Little Theater productions of Henrik Ibsen and August Strindberg starring strippers with stage names like Angela d'Amore and Lucrezia Borgia; and speakers of every stripe, all of whom had to endure the murderous heckling from the Pickle's crowd.

Along with a lecture on a woman's right to live her own life or a heated debate between University of Chicago scientists on the unheard-of topic of atomic energy, "any sensationalist figure of the moment—paroled convict, unwed mother, reformed vegetarian or three-headed guinea pig was apt to appear." A "professor," now graduated to Sirfressor, would rail against socialism, while Triphammer Johnson, a colossal Norwegian with a walrus moustache, expounded on Friedrich Nietzsche and Søren Kierkegaard with the thunder of a Viking. All acts were aggressively promoted by founders Ben Reitman and Jack Jones, the latter an ex-Wobbly whose mangled hand was rumored to have resulted from a nitroglycerin accident while safe cracking, or from a botched sabotage operation during a strike. "I give them the high brow stuff until the crowd begins to grow thin, and then I turn on the sex faucet," Jones told Sherwood Anderson, referring to the club's notorious "sex lectures."[14]

The Pickle's all-inclusiveness stretched well beyond the bounds of Dodge's salon, creating a postwar scene of a different character altogether. It evolved into a speakeasy supplied with gin by gangster George "Bugs" Moran, where hookers blew in from North Clark Street to become the paramours of newspapermen and Wobblies. "A world less like Greenwich Village or Saint Germaine would be hard to imagine," observed Kenneth Rexroth in 1977. "In Paris . . . now that intellectuals are coming back and mixing with the hustlers in cafés . . . there is a kind of ragamuffin bohemia of petty crooks, carnival performers, models and prostitutes, and bad, penniless artists and unprinted poets, which greatly resembles Chicago in the Twenties."[15]

While the Dil Pickle did not rely on Hecht, his regular appearances certainly were good for business. The Picklers welcomed *Dregs*, his seedy one-act play about a derelict, whereas many in the audience at the Players Workshop had stormed out after the opening line, which contained the vulgar oaths "Jesus Christ" and "son of a bitch." On another evening, Hecht and Bodenheim packed the house for a literary debate and then announced the topic: "Resolved, that people who attend literary debates are imbeciles." On this they immediately concurred, declared the debate over, and then fled out the back with the ticket proceeds.[16] That story sums up their attitude in general.

"Around 1920 the audience-change began," Hecht later recalled. "Philistines started turning into aesthetes by the train load. The desire to be peculiar and original was always a part of the artist's ego. It began to become part of the audience's." He attributed this to the ferocious pace of urbanization and industrialization, which made people feel small and insignificant. "Blotted out by the roars and menaces of progress, thrust into anonymity by mob-glutted cities and stuck away in the filing cabinet rash of sky scrapers . . . they shopped for personality among the artists who had continued to flourish under the labels of con men and fakers. Our castaway citizens couldn't join the artists . . . but they could admire the incomprehensible paintings, applaud the headache-inducing symphonies, and even read the incoherent poetry erupting from the art world."[17]

In this world now overrun by boobs and charlatans, Hecht and Bodenheim had at last found their ideal target. To attack "the American Intellectual Establishment" must have appeared, at least intuitively, a deeper and truer form of rebellion than the anarchism and socialism of the prewar set; after all, the ancient Hebrew prophets had directed their challenge not at the pharaohs, Philistines, and sundry other idolaters but at the Chosen People, who had broken their covenant with God. Were today's artists and intelligentsia not the Chosen People of modern times? In 1922 Hecht summoned Bodenheim back from the Village to Chicago: "After seven years you and I are still the best hated men in American literature. Why not pool our persecution mania? . . . I shall be here Monday at 4 with a bottle of gin."[18]

The launchpad for their assault would be the *Chicago Literary Times*, a biweekly riot of absurd, quixotic headlines and snarky commentary printed on tabloid-sized pages of bright pink, yellow, and green, evocatively illustrated by Stanislaus Szukalski, Herman Bosse, Wallace Smith, and George Grosz. Launched on March 1, 1923, with Hecht as editor and Bodenheim hired on a month later as associate editor, this "gazette devoted to the Sacred Ballyhoo" mocked the pretensions of arts and letters, taking aim at any and all targets of opportunity. Local bookshop owner Pascal Covici provided the financing, erroneously believing it would promote his bookselling and publishing concerns. By the time it folded on June 1, 1924, the *Chicago Literary Times* had a circulation of between fifteen thousand and seventeen thousand. Three months after its launch, a *New York Times* editorial headlined "Startling the Radicals" observed, "Shocking the bourgeois has become too stale and tame a sport for Chicago. The game of advanced radicals in that city is now to horrify the radicals of the East. . . . [Hecht and Bodenheim] set themselves up as the real Goths and Vandals of the liberal movement, and have no patience with those 'radical journals' of New York that keep up 'an unceasing caterwauling for justice, heroism, sanity, and beauty of the soul.'"[19]

A favorite practice was to stalk multiple quarries at once, sometimes in juxtaposed left- and righthand columns or other times together in just one. The front page of the premiere issue featured attacks on both Chicago and New York. The lefthand column denounced the "reeking, cinder ridden . . . the chewing gum center of the world, the bleating, slant-headed rendezvous of half-witted newspapers, sociopaths and pants makers," while the polemic on the right, headlined "Concerning the Natl. Cemetery of Arts and Letters," lamented the depressing state of Gotham's magazines. "They seem to be suffering from the lack of a good drink or a good physic," Hecht inveighed. "They are continually talking about Art as if it were their dead grandmother."[20] Two months later, he bashed the lowbrow idiocy of radio broadcasts and, in an adjacent item, derided the pitiful amateurishness of highbrow little magazines. Bodenheim scoffed at the hack writer who every once in a while "sets up a sixteen by fourteen target and calls it Bohemia." In nearly the same breath, the poet ridiculed those deluded downtown poseurs who "have made the word 'Bohemia' to erase the smallness that pervades them during the lulls in their 'artistic' labors."[21]

The literary giants of the day were, with a few notable exceptions, hauled into court and sentenced without mercy. Bodenheim described T. S. Eliot's "The Waste Land" as "Intellect engaging in a drunken commotion, and Erudition prattling with the husky candor of a vagrant in the back-room of a saloon." A review of F. Scott Fitzgerald's play *The Vegetable* asserted that the author, "a ringleader among the class of garrulously obvious writers . . . accomplishes the old trick of swatting hypocrisies and fondling them at the same time." One Bodenheim column offered a round-robin of invective, complaining that the current writers had all become respectable tradespeople who peddled polished and lifeless formulas: "You can be certain that Carl Sandburg will use a bragging slang to persuade people that they are not small and defeated—'what the hell, it'll all come out in the wash'—, that Sherwood Anderson will turn his kindly eye upon the fact that people desire each other's bodies, that D. H. Lawrence will sputter ferociously about the carnal misery of life, . . . that T. S. Eliot and Ezra Pound will run to six languages and certain dry and mirthless tactics to entertain their tired minds."[22]

Each issue was packed with sound and fury, as if the sole objective was to shock readers by dismissing all literature as a grand farce. Headlines were written in a pseudo-news style suggestive of later newspaper parodies like the *Onion*, such as one above a column excoriating critics that announced, "Bodenheim Runs Amuck; 4 Dead, And 3 Wounded."[23] The pair of gadflies received the reaction they hoped for. Anderson wrote to a friend that Hecht's "smartiness" would destroy what little talent he might have had. In a July editorial, Hecht noted the complaints pouring in that the publication seemed to be interested only in irritating people. He responded that however wrongheaded the *Chicago Literary Times* might be, such individuals should be grateful for a periodical that challenged their ideas.[24]

Yet despite the madcap format and tone, the *Chicago Literary Times* served as a forum for Hecht's and Bodenheim's genuine views and criticism. They celebrated Yiddish theater, vaudeville, and Charlie Chaplin. Hecht championed *Ulysses*, albeit by attacking its critics: "We are reminded of the fact that literature is often like a mirror. If an ass looks in, one can hardly expect an apostle to look out." And Bodenheim mourned the closing of the *Little Review* and the departure of its editors to Europe. In the same column, he objected to the decision to award the 1922 Pulitzer Prize for poetry to Edna St. Vincent Millay, passing over such writers as William Carlos Williams and Conrad Aiken. Other items weren't really essays at all but short narrative sketches, like an allegorical lament over the loss of the old, prewar bohemia, or a quick study of tired, disappointed straphangers returning home from Coney Island on a Sunday evening to face another week of drudgery.[25]

Most important, the pair articulated their own aesthetic, social, and political worldview—their creed of individualism. Hecht denounced bolshevism for replacing Christianity as a new magnet for mindless zealotry, asserting:

> Institutions are and always will be a menace to the individual. The battle between rival institutions—between conservatism and radicalism—is an eternally amateur circus. . . . That the progress of man, exciting phrase, does not lie in the substitution of one set of mob notions for another at least a hundred successful "revolutions" have long ago proved. The individual is the only authentic enemy of institutions. And the individual, raised to his highest point—becomes an artist—is the only "hope" for the eventual sanity of existence.[26]

Hecht and Bodenheim had been formulating this code—essentially a reassertion of Romanticism—since their emergence on the literary scene. With the failure of the Innocent Rebellion and the collapse of the war, their ideas seemed borne out by events. Yet Hecht could not wholly embrace the true Renaissance pioneer of apolitical individualism, Sherwood Anderson. When Hecht gave Anderson an early copy of *Erik Dorn*, his old comrade simply cast the book aside. With the friendship turning sour, Hecht described Anderson in the *Chicago Literary Times* as a slick con man with "the mellow garrulity of a small-town barber." Gazing back in the early 1960s, Hecht would recall, "In later years I understood the superiority that Sherwood flaunted over us. We were all buzzing with ego . . . but none of us was full of the magic of self-love." Hecht added, "The only outsiders [Anderson] could love were the characters his pencil created. And these were not outsiders, they were all Sherwoods. He crooned over them and sang like a poet of their big and little troubles."[27]

According to Hecht, Anderson proposed that, as a lark, they cease being friends and assume the roles of enemies in print—although it may have been Hecht who actually proposed the idea, after Anderson's cold reaction to *Erik Dorn*.[28] In one letter Anderson praised Hecht as a talented writer but also cut him down:

> I've always thought Henry Mencken was so nuts on the Puritans . . . because maybe he's afraid that at bottom he's one himself and I'll begin to think that about you and the boobs if you don't quit being so sure everyone in the world but yourself and a few of your special friends are boobs. . . . Just for a kind of vacation consider . . . that you aren't as specialized a thing as you think. . . . The bluff you throw about being so full of energy and being so smart and fast don't bluff me. I've got your number on that because you are so very like myself.[29]

Such words may well have cut deep, because at the time Hecht was struggling, with marginal success, to master the one form of writing that counted most to him and his cohort—the novel. In fairness, this was a literary period of feverish, almost frantic stylistic experimentation. Hecht was particularly influenced by the self-conscious Romanticism of European decadence and the ornate, crystalline imagery of symbolism—by the rococo wordplay of Joris-Karl Huysmans, the depictions of inner torment in Arthur Symons, the eerie tales of Arthur Machen and Oscar Wilde, and the polemics of Edgar Saltus and James B. Huneker. Harry Hansen, who upon their first meeting had found Hecht absorbed in Sir Richard Burton's translation of *The Arabian Nights*, characterized Hecht's fiction as "a fondness for realism, naturalism and iconoclasm; a leaning towards sex psychology and neuropathic and psychopathic studies; a love for glittering phrases . . . ; a dominant preoccupation with the mind and especially psychiatrics."[30]

Although *Erik Dorn* and his other early works received a good deal of praise, even Rascoe, one of Hecht's most stalwart champions, pointed out a characteristic flaw. *Gargoyles* (1922), a stab at social realism loosely patterned after Robert Herrick's *Memoirs of an American Citizen* (1905) and Dreiser's *Financier* (1912), was too watered down with exposition, failing to reveal character through action and dialogue. Others faulted Hecht's constant recycling of material. In a review for the *Dial* titled "Arriviste and Aristocrat" that called *Erik Dorn* "one of the noisiest books ever written," Gilbert Seldes noted that, tellingly, Hecht's admirers often likened his prose to a mechanical marvel. "The rhythm of life, as simple and unpredictable as the pulse beat, has escaped Mr. Hecht entirely. For the most part it has been lost in a torrent of words."[31]

The harshest judge of all, however, turned out to be time. A considerable number of the novelists and poets Hecht and Bodenheim regularly pummeled in their gazette have since been canonized, but within a few years *Erik Dorn*, *Gargoyles*, and *Humpty Dumpty* (1924) ceased to appear as reprints and were soon forgotten. And by the early 1930s Hecht had given up on the novel altogether. The exceptions were a lighthearted toss-off, *I Hate Actors!*, published in 1944, and *The Sensualists*, released by a small press in 1960, which sold poorly and was attacked for its cleverness and thin characterizations, just as his first novels had been nearly forty years earlier.

He would achieve far greater results with his collections of short stories, starting with the tightly constructed tales of *Broken Necks* in 1926, continuing with diverse innovations in styles and themes, from *The Champion from Far Away* (1931) and *Actor's Blood* (1936) to *Gaily, Gaily* in 1963. Arguably his single best book of fiction, and certainly his most extraordinary, was the 1939 *A Book of Miracles*, a sequence of seven novellas. "Reading a volume of stories by Ben Hecht is like walking past a fence covered with brightly colored circus posters," wrote Clinton Simpson for the *Saturday Review*. "You look at the posters, or you read the stories, and are impressed more deeply than you realize at the time."[32]

In the memoirs that he wrote after 1950, his prose achieved the measure and readability that his work as a young man had lacked. But when it came to novels, from the start he had possessed too keen a bead on the critics and public to be unaware of his lack of traction, despite all of his bluff about speed and energy. By the time he had completed *Humpty Dumpty* in 1924, he was tiring of such efforts and abandoned them in favor of exercises in profit making and self-promotion.[33]

The epitome of his literary stunts was *Fantazius Mallare* (1922), published by Covici-McGee in a limited run of two thousand copies that sold for $12.50 apiece, just as Boni & Liveright was issuing *Gargoyles* that September. Intended as bait for the Society for the Suppression of Vice, *Fantazius Mallare* was packed with sadomasochistic sex, though the action is too abstract and indecipherable to be deemed pornographic by contemporary standards. In the plot, which quickly dissolves into a morass of superheated prose, Mallare, a Svengali-like sculptor, seeks to unshackle himself from conventional morality, turns satanic, and spirals into madness when his gypsy love slave, Rita, takes revenge on him by copulating with his hunchbacked golem servant. To ensure the book caught the censors' attention, it included a savage preface "Dedicated to my enemies" and six phantasmagoric illustrations by Wallace Smith in which erect phalluses poke out from nightmarish grotesques.[34]

Hecht's plan had been to retain the great Chicago attorney Clarence Darrow, rally the literati, and reach new heights of fame while achieving a victory for free expression. But he was fired from the *Daily News* because of the book, and no one but Mencken appeared to testify at the trial in February 1924. He and Smith pleaded nolo contendere and were fined $1,000 each. Now finding himself all but alone in Chicago, he prepared to leave with Rose to New York. In a farewell column for the *Chicago Literary Times* in June 1924, titled "My Last Park Bench," he confessed that with the passing of the years, he no longer felt the wonder of the city and the poetry of its streets anymore.[35]

While shifting gears to write plays for Broadway, he churned out the successful potboiler *Florentine Dagger* (1923) and *Kingdom of Evil* (1924), an uninspired sequel to *Mallare*. In his final novelistic effort of the decade, he turned—as if having exhausted all other targets—on Bodenheim. The protagonist of *Count Bruga* (1926) is Jules Ganz, a poet who had once been ushered into New York as a great talent but who had quickly managed to alienate and infuriate everyone he met. Though he had eventually been hounded from the city, Ganz has now returned flush with cash from a rummy game and, having reinvented himself as the noble Count Hippolyt Bruga, invites the newspapers to announce his arrival. Confronted in his room at the Ritz by reporters who have discerned his real identity, he insists that he is an aristocrat who found it necessary to venture into the world as a drunken and buffoonish vagabond poet to develop his genius. The reporters decide to humor him, and in victory the count returns to his garret—above a factory for a snake oil advertised as a love potion.[36]

While written as light comedy, the work rendered Bodenheim as a man hiding beneath layer upon layer of disguise, posturing, and self-delusion. A darker story along similar lines that Hecht related many years later recalls a dinner party during the early days of the Renaissance, at which Bodenheim, finding himself no longer the center of attention, began to chew on a wineglass. "Good God!" someone shouted. "You'll kill yourself swallowing that glass. You're a poet, not a circus freak." Bodenheim had replied, in his typically aloof tone, "Every poet is both."[37]

Deeply wounded by the book, Bodenheim retorted with his 1931 novel *Duke Herring*. It echoes Anderson's suggestion that Hecht was beneath it all a boob. The author of a "thousand-and-one-poses," Duke Arturo Herring "wanted to be an affluent, luxurious, commercial panderer, tossing off flashy bilge with tongue in his cheek, and also an unruly, brilliant, slashing intellect in more serious talk and creations. . . . He wanted to be supreme in both camps, commercial and artistic, without pledging allegiance to either one." A Babbitt at heart, Herring lives in constant fear of "deserting the respectable safeguards and emoluments of his life."[38]

Though the duke makes every effort to find a suitable mistress, he has nowhere to go at night but home or the brothel. He finally finds a mistress and abandons his marriage, only to find himself trapped with a woman who reflects his own vapid cynicism. As for the quality of his work: "His favorite boast was that he intended to accumulate a million dollars in the following year, and though his goal had eluded him so far, he did amass thousands of dollars annually through the sale of meretricious short stories, shallowly clever plays with short runs, and epileptic novels, whose malicious brilliance always held one eye cocked toward the adding machine."[39]

Bodenheim could at least claim that *he* had never been a panderer. When he had traveled to England in 1920, T. S. Eliot had written to his mother: "There is an odd American Jew here named Bodenheim; rather pathetic, although foolish. He is a vagrant poet and man of letters at home, and thought he could pick up work just as easily here. . . . I told him of my history here, and left him to consider whether an American Jew, of only a common school education and no university degree, with no money, no connections, and no polish or experience, could make a living in London."[40]

ଔ

In a 1922 essay for the *Menorah Journal* titled "Jewish Writers in America," Bodenheim observed that each great American iconoclast spawned generations of inferior imitators. He criticized the recent call for a "Wild Whitmanesque" literature that would "express America." The United States was not one thing but many things of different shades and colors, he said, and critics such as Paul Rosenfeld, Waldo Frank, and Louis Untermeyer were calling for something bland and meaningless by comparison. Far from demonstrating the genius of their common heritage, these critics were "exhibiting a surface Jewish tendency—an ability at mimicry and masquerade—a tendency acquired by the Jew of the past for protective reasons." The true genius of Judaism, rather, was a "penetrating tolerance" and flexibility of mind learned by outcasts who, for centuries in which persecution had alternated with indifference to them, had gazed at others from a distance. Jews knew how to blend in, but they had learned more by being outside observers.[41]

Critics and other writers such as Ludwig Lewisohn, Michael Gold, and Samuel Roth refused to remain aloof, Bodenheim continued; they were preoccupied with American rawness and passion and disdained self-detachment. But "the exceptional Jew, who actively reveals the hidden elements of his race, is essentially an aristocrat—an intense individualist who distrusts the lusty mediocrities inherent in democracy and yearns for the distinctive power that life has sought to withhold from him." Such a writer was Hecht, "a combination of street urchin and skeptical intellectual" whose first novel, *Erik Dorn*, had produced an uproar of fearful denunciation and periodic praise. Bodenheim nevertheless faulted Hecht for thus far possessing little interest in Judaism, noting that until such a man of talent shows interest in "the problems and potentialities of his race . . . it will be absurd to claim that Jewish writers in this country form a unit. They may fuse together in the future but at present they are sadly scattered."[42]

Twenty years later, when Hecht wrote about anti-Semitism in the midst of World War II, he would recall that moving to New York City in 1924 had been like arriving in a foreign country full of Jews who were not like his aunts and uncles but were rather "un-Jewish Jews" like himself. These were "writers, publishers, theatrical producers, journalists, wits, actors and mighty drinkers whose only synagogue was Broadway." He confessed that he had been the least Jewish among them, full as he was "of no-man's land iconoclasms." Yet somehow he had found himself drawn to Henry Street in the Jewish immigrant neighborhood of the Lower East Side.[43]

He remembered that he and Rose had been apartment hunting in a taxi with MacArthur, who jumped out at Twenty-Fifth Street, refusing to penetrate any further into the wilds of downtown. As the cab proceeded, Hecht gazed at shabby neighborhoods that brought back memories of his family and of an old rhyme about life going by "gayly gayly" along the riverbank of the ghetto. "I looked out of the cab window and saw sidewalks crawling with infants, push carts hung with ties, alarm clocks and bananas, old gentlemen in linen frock coats smoothing their whiskers, mothers screaming out of windows, little boys and girls playing hide-and-go-seek in refuse barrels," he wrote. "In the midst of all this stood a house to let." He and Rose had stayed there for seven months, but he, unemployed, had withdrawn into himself and missed this opportunity to engage in what was once called "vital contact" with the common people. Driven out at last by the smells that came with summer, he joined the crowd uptown, who regarded this sojourn as a bout of eccentricity.[44]

Several of Hecht's and Bodenheim's uptown Jewish friends and acquaintances had once been guests in Dodge's salon. Dodge never mentioned their heritage in her memoirs, however, which suggests that the "Jewish question" was not a common topic of discussion. When the young radical journalist John Reed brought her to see the conditions of the Lower East Side, she annoyed and embarrassed him by insisting they do the tour in her limousine.[45]

Although the Jewish neighborhood was a world apart from Greenwich Village, its history followed a closely parallel trajectory. During the years in which, as Dodge commented, all the barriers of Victorian society went down and people who had never been in touch were reaching out and finding new ways to communicate, proponents of a Jewish homeland were introducing new concepts and vocabulary—*the melting pot* and *cultural pluralism*. In 1909, three years before everyone became so intertwined at Dodge's apartment, a play titled *The Melting Pot* had opened on Broadway that was written by Israel Zangwill, a "territorialist" who believed in establishing a home for Jews wherever that might turn out to be possible. Hailed as a great work by President Theodore Roosevelt, it offered an assimilationist vision of Americans from all backgrounds shedding their ancient loyalties to form a unified nation.[46] And while art and socialism forged their famous bond in Greenwich Village, union pressure ensuing from a catastrophic 1911 fire in a downtown Jewish factory would push through historic reforms of working conditions for *all* Americans.

In turn, by the time the alliances in Greenwich Village were splintering in 1915, the Zionist philosophy scholar Horace Kallen had repudiated the melting pot ideal in a two-part article for the *Nation*. Instead, he advocated *cultural pluralism*, the proposition that each American should hold fast to his or her distinct heritage while participating in a democratic society, in which tolerance and diversity would be a source of strength.[47]

During the 1920s, cultural pluralism reflected an attitude particularly characteristic of first-generation American Jews like Hecht and Bodenheim. These children of Jewish immigrants were an unwittingly conspicuous group by the time Hecht encountered them in New York. As he would remark, "it had been normal to look on one Jew, myself, and consider him un-Jewish. But it was difficult to look at a swarm of Jews and accept them as similarly un-Jewish." American Jews of Hecht's generation recognized with pride traits of their heritage, namely, a record of struggle against oppression, yet they often refused to regard these traits as uniquely Jewish or to see themselves as exemplary of these qualities because they were Jews.[48]

Cultural pluralism represented a conflicted ethos, the weaknesses of which became more apparent as economic and social pressures made the conflicts more obvious. It was a sense of identity that suffered from a "chronic indistinctness," noted one historian, in the differences between embracing one's heritage, on the one hand, and joining a diverse society in the spirit of cosmopolitanism, on the other. The magazine that explored this most deeply was the *Menorah Journal*, the periodical that had published Bodenheim's essay on Jewish writers, launched in 1916 as the organ of the Menorah Society, which Kallen had helped to establish.[49]

"My colleagues had discarded their Jewishness out of the belief that as Jews they could line up only for a snubbing," Hecht later concluded. "As Americans or, more particularly, as egoists and talents, they could step forth as superiors and even as snobs." During the latter half of the 1920s, Hecht began to notice with pride that New York's Jews ran most of the theaters and publishing houses, composed and sang many of the popular songs, and wrote a sizable portion of the plays and poems. They were also some of the most productive newspaper reporters and columnists. Above all, Hecht was taken by the comedians, "a great Jewish cast of clowns and troubadours." In their clubs and hotel rooms, he joined in their wise-cracking as if they were cousins, these talents who had risen up from the tenements. Among them were three who were to remain lifelong friends—Groucho Marx, Harpo Marx, and Fanny Brice—as well as Jack Benny, Milton Berle, George Burns, Eddie Cantor, George Jessel, and Al Jolson.[50]

The Jazz Singer (Warner Brothers, 1927), starring Jolson, was the first major release to introduce sound—a milestone in Hecht's life because the talking picture created lucrative opportunities for writers in Hollywood. An iconic expression of cultural pluralism, *The Jazz Singer* was the tale of a Jewish cantor's son "whose only synagogue was Broadway," as Hecht put it, who finds himself torn between his roots on the Lower East Side and the bright lights of show business. In the souvenir program for the play, which preceded the movie, author Samson Raphaelson explained that the electrifying spectacle of Jolson performing ragtime had inspired him. Of the man Gilbert Seldes called "the daemonic" Al Jolson, Raphaelson wrote:

> I hear Jazz, and I am given a vision of cathedrals and temples collapsing and, silhouetted against the setting sun, a solitary figure, a lost soul, dancing grotesquely in the ruins. . . . Thus do I see the jazz singer.
>
> Jazz is prayer. It is too passionate to be anything else. It is prayer distorted, sick, unconscious of its destination. The singer of jazz is what Matthew Arnold said of the Jew, "lost between two worlds, one dead, the other powerless to be born." In this, my first play, I have tried to crystallize the ironic truth that one of the Americas of 1927—the one which packs to overflowing our cabarets, musical reviews, and dance halls—is praying with a fervor as intense as that of the America which goes sedately to church and synagogue. The jazz American is different from the dancing dervish, from the Zulu medicine man, from the negro evangelist only in that he doesn't know he is praying.[51]

CHAPTER 7

The Un-Jewish Jew

Samuel Goldwyn, Louis B. Mayer, the Warner Brothers, the Schenk Brothers, Adolph Zukor, Harry Cohn, Irving Thalberg, Carl Laemmle, Jesse Lasky, B. P. Schulberg and their mishpoochas were conducting a Semitic renaissance, sans rabbis and the Talmud. The fact that they were flinging at the world the ancient Greek credo that deluding the mind of the public with tommyrot was better medicine than torturing it with truth (Plato) cut no ice about who was running the renaissance—Greeks or Hebrews. And the first wave of geniuses from Broadway, London, Paris and Berlin was already on hand issuing dinner invitations (black tie), collecting weekly bags of gold and denouncing Hollywood, much as in these pages.

—BEN HECHT, *CHARLIE*[1]

While the rest of the country was plummeting into the Depression, Ben Hecht had reached what he called "the new El Dorado." Hollywood, which asked of writers merely their hearts and souls as the price of admission, would drive the likes of F. Scott Fitzgerald to a "crack-up."[2] But there was a bright side. Hecht was ensconced during those early years on the Youngworth Ranch, a "wooden castle" and avocado farm overlooking MGM's back lots in Culver City, and his guests for a typical night of drinking might include the movie star Jean Harlow, soon-to-be princess of Austria Nora Gregor, director Howard Hawks, Harpo Marx, Dashiell Hammett, composer George Antheil, Charles MacArthur, and other fellow writers.[3]

"The sun shone," Hecht wrote. "The dinner parties looked like stage sets. International beauties sat in candle-lit café nooks, holding hands with undersized magnates. Novelists, poets and playwrights staggered bibulously in and out of swimming pools. Floperoo actors and actresses from New York, ex-waitresses, elevator girls, light o' loves, high school graduates with the right-size boobies all met their Good Fairy and were given seats on the royal bandwagon. And out of the hotel suites, brothels and casinos came a noise of life undaunted such as not been heard since the Forty-niners drank themselves to death looking for nuggets."[4]

On the Hollywood payroll, one joined the most accomplished writers and artists of a generation. But in the heyday of the studio system, writers were paid more money than they had ever seen before to become workers on a factory line. Here perfectionism was anathema, and an author could expect the writing conferences and other machinations of film production to perversely salvage his or her worst ideas while shearing off the best. "Your writing stinks," observed MacArthur, "but you meet the people you want to be in a room with." With fat rolls of cash, studio bosses summoned the highest class of talent if only for the sense of culture it gave them and for the feeling of superiority that came from telling such people what to do.[5]

Hecht had originally been summoned in 1926, by a cable from Herman Mankiewicz that would live on in Hollywood legend: "WILL YOU ACCEPT THREE HUNDRED DOLLARS PER WEEK TO WORK FOR PARAMOUNT PICTURES? ALL EXPENSES PAID. THE THREE HUNDRED IS PEANUTS, MILLIONS ARE TO BE GRABBED OUT HERE AND YOUR ONLY COMPETITION IS IDIOTS. DON'T LET THIS GET AROUND."[6]

Mankiewicz, who would one day script the classic newspaper film *Citizen Kane* (1941), was another half ne'er-do-well, half prodigy within Hecht's close circle of friends in New York. Along with both Hecht and MacArthur, he was by the mid-1920s a member of the Algonquin Round Table, an exclusive clique of newspaper columnists, playwrights, theater producers, and critics who met at least once a week for lunch at New York City's Algonquin Hotel. Forever compensating for his weaknesses for drinking, gambling, and a lack of self-discipline, Mankiewicz possessed a whiplash wit that was a match for even the famously gifted Dorothy Parker.

In 1925 an MGM press agent in New York recruited Mankiewicz for $500 a week to come to Hollywood and write a movie scenario based on his experiences in the Marines. Mankiewicz boasted that he made the scenario up while on the toilet. Shuttling between the coasts over the next two years, he soon achieved a reputation for writing punchy titles for silent films, and producer Walter Wanger helped him obtain a one-year contract with the Famous-Players-Lasky Corporation, shortly before it became Paramount Pictures.

Toward the end of 1926, Mankiewicz marched into the office of production chief B. P. "Ben" Schulberg carrying another contract. This time he insisted that Schulberg hire Hecht. But when Hecht wrote the treatment for *Underworld* within a week and received a $10,000 bonus check, Mankiewicz snatched it out of his hand to pay off gambling debts. Eventually, Hecht grew impatient waiting for reimbursement, so he helped Mankiewicz negotiate a $500-a-week raise and then Hecht took each check directly from Schulberg.[7]

With the advent of sound, Schulberg tasked Mankiewicz with recruiting writers, which he accomplished by drawing from the ranks of streetwise, smart-mouthed big-city newspaper reporters. He found at least one writer other than Hecht who would forever change Hollywood: Nunnally Johnson. While the arrival of New York writers would have been inevitable, Mankiewicz was certainly the catalyst for their migration west.[8] The bait was money, but they were also lured by the camaraderie. By the early 1930s, the crowd included George S. Kaufman; Dorothy Parker and Marc Connelly; Nathanael West and his brother-in-law, S. J. Perelman; Preston Sturges; Arthur Kober; Alice Duer Miller; John O'Hara; Donald Ogden Stewart; Samson Raphaelson; Gene Fowler; and such accomplished playwrights as Philip Barry, S. N. Behrman, Maxwell Anderson, Robert E. Sherwood, and Sidney Howard. Fitzgerald arrived in 1927, and by 1932 William Faulkner was stopping in, as were Ring Lardner and Moss Hart. "In earlier periods, American writers made a living on newspapers and magazines," noted *New Yorker* film critic Pauline Kael. "In the '40s and '50s, they went into the academies (or once they got to college, never left). But in the late '20s and '30s they went to Hollywood."[9]

Hecht, successful in every genre, began to juggle projects furiously, creating some great works along with duds. Between his Broadway hit with MacArthur, *The Front Page*, in 1928 and their experiment with independent filmmaking in 1934, Hecht provided the stories or scripts for twenty films and script-doctored at least another thirteen. "He always had more work than he could cope with," recalled Hugh Gray, a screenwriter and scholar who collaborated with Hecht on the 1954 epic *Ulysses*, starring Kirk

Douglas. "And of course there's nothing so dreadful—it's like an automobile wreck on the freeway, when a producer runs into a tough situation, when his scripts seems to break down for him, and he doesn't know where the hell to go. Where is the automobile club, you know? And of course, here is the doctor! Doctor Hecht."[10]

Gray noted the oft-remarked-on similarities to the other reigning script doctor, Dalton Trumbo, who would manage to survive and even, by some estimates, defeat the Hollywood blacklist. Because of Hecht's militant Zionist activities, he would be driven to the margins as well. "People in trouble, all these producers, no matter how orthodox they were politically, were always appealing to him because he had the touch, as far as they were concerned," Gray said. "Those were the golden boys in Hollywood, the boys who had that. They were all great writers, but these two [also] had the prolific quality. And that was it. They were worth their weight in gold and they were given the gold. It was like bidding for a race horse."[11]

Hecht collaborated with Fowler, Charles Lederer, and Hawks and developed a writing factory, farming out work to Bartlett Cormack, John Lee Mahin, and Johnny Weaver. His own plots included the 1929 horror pictures *The Unholy Night* and *The Great Gabbo*, the Marx Brothers comedy *Monkey Business*, the gangster comedy *Roadhouse Nights*, and *Scarface*.[12] His 1933 film starring Al Jolson, *Hallelujah, I'm a Bum!*, adapted from a story by Floyd Dell, reflected his own insulation from the Depression: it is the lighthearted tale of a carefree "mayor of hobos," too in love with life to be tied down to a job.

Hecht and Hawks were one of the greatest writer-director teams of Hollywood's golden era. "Ben had an instantaneous perception of a good idea," Hawks remembered. After they traveled to Mexico together to gather firsthand information for their biopic of Pancho Villa, *Viva Villa!* (1934), they struggled with how to use an intriguing detail from their research: a woman who lost her man in battle would sometimes take his body home, stick a cigarette in one of his hands and a drink in the other, prop him up, and leave him sitting overnight. The two storytellers mulled this over until, finally, Hawks rushed into Hecht's room at two in the morning with an inspiration: Villa would look up at six corpses in some town, hanging from a scaffolding, and would say, "Cut them down." Then the camera would dissolve, and a new scene would open with the six dead men sitting as a spectral jury, trying the mayor of the town who had murdered them.[13] Hecht stayed up the rest of the night scripting this haunting vision, which he would return to again and again when he wrote of the Holocaust.

Hawks was particularly proud of Villa's death scene: Villa is fatally shot while in a butcher shop, buying a pork chop for his mistress. The dying revolutionary calls to a reporter who has been chronicling the events. What do I say, Johnny? Villa asks. What do great men say, in their final words? Johnny does some quick thinking, then calls out to the local townspeople. As the sun sets, Villa says to the gathering crowd, "Forgive me my Mexico, if I have harmed you it is because I loved you," or something to that effect. Then he turns to Johnny and says, And make sure my wife doesn't find out about the pork chop. Having *now* spoken his last words, Villa passes. Hawks believed his portrait of this strange, half-vicious, half-humorous man could have been one of his best pictures. But after he finished the shooting in Mexico, actor Lee Tracy got drunk and urinated on the Chapultepec Cadets during their Independence Day parade. The ensuing interference by MGM studio head Louis B. Mayer wrecked the film.[14]

Hawks recalled one other incident that typified Hecht's perverse humor. Hecht had ordered some art, but it wasn't finished yet when he returned from Mexico, so he asked Hawks to bring it back for him. At the border, Hawks grew nervous about the suitcase full of art and other items he was carrying, so he ordered some "peon" to take them. Finally, he brought the suitcase out to Nyack, and Hecht opened it. "There were about six boxes of little wax statues that were the dirtiest things I have ever seen in all my life," Hawks said. "I had never seen anything so dirty. They were really horrible, and they were fabulously done, by this erotic, crazy family down there that were great artists who just did things like that. Well, I was going to kill him, because I had cold perspiration just thinking what would have happened if I had gotten caught with these things."[15]

Hecht also continued to write for Broadway, and his best stage works were adapted for the screen. Reviewers bashed his effort with Gene Fowler, *The Great Magoo*, when it premiered in December 1932, but they hailed as genius *Twentieth Century*, his Broadway follow-up with MacArthur to *The Front Page*, when it appeared weeks later. Some fifty years after *Twentieth Century*'s cinematic release (1932), Kael touted the film as "a first-rate hardboiled farce about theatrical personalities," while Andrew Sarris called it one of the era's "maddest and most savage confrontations between the sexes." From the perspective of the late 1970s and early 1980s, both critics regarded the screwball comedies of the 1930s as the wittiest, fiercest, most sophisticated movies to have ever hit the screen, and *Twentieth Century* was the first. Hecht kept going with *Nothing Sacred* in 1937, and Hawks delivered *His Girl Friday* in 1940, the most inspired screen adaptation of *The Front Page*; it recast Hildy Johnson as a fast-talking dame reporter, played by Rosalind Russell.[16]

Within a year, Hecht, MacArthur, and Hawks were collaborating on another comedy for the stage, *Jumbo* (1935), a story of two rival circus families based on Hecht's idea of combining the most spectacular type of theater—the circus—with history's most spectacular plot—*Romeo and Juliet*. Produced by Billy Rose at the old Hippodrome, the musical drama would involve "two acts and eleven scenes with tightrope walkers who worked over an open lion pit, clowns, . . . bareback riders, ax throwers and trained bears." According to one review, it was "a sane and exciting compound of opera, animal show, folk drama, harlequinade, carnival, circus, extravaganza and spectacle."[17]

The blackest mark on Hecht in those years was his latest novel—ironically, the only piece of work he produced that, given the standards of the time, could have established his literary bona fides. Published in 1931, *A Jew in Love* was another dissection of a monstrous egoist, this one a Don Juan. A vulture in both appearance and character, publisher Jo Boshere was a composite of two Jews employed in the arts: Jed Harris, the Broadway producer of *The Front Page* and *Twentieth Century*, and publisher Horace Liveright. The plot consists of Boshere juggling three women with a cruelty that, in the words of one critic, "oscillates between a provocative masochism and relieving sadism." Boshere ships his wife off on ocean liners and torments his mistress while haranguing a third lover, the blond dancer Tillie Marmon, who proves his undoing. When a fourth woman rejects his advances, he destroys her placid marriage just for sport, pitting wife and husband against one another.[18]

Publisher Pascal Covici primed his staff for *A Jew in Love*, announcing it as the best thing Hecht had ever written. But the firm's co-owner, Donald Friede, recalled that shortly after he and three colleagues dove eagerly into its pages, they suddenly stopped and stared at one another as if on cue, realizing that none of them liked it. By then, however, the gears of publishing were already in motion. With the firm's aggressive publicity, the book sold nearly fifty thousand copies, an extraordinary figure at the time and far beyond what any of Hecht's other novels had sold.[19]

"*A Jew in Love* is positively nauseating at times," wrote Bob Stafford of the *Akron Times*. "It is rare that I experience a feeling of revulsion at a book. There were times when I did in this case. And I am not the least squeamish." Some suggested it was obvious from the deep bitterness that the author was settling a personal score. Others were impressed by the sheer brute force of Hecht's prose; a reviewer at Honolulu's *Star Bulletin* observed, for example, that his "almost explosive combinations of words and images have been toned down somewhat, but his style still hammers at the readers with a succession of verbal shocks." Just as often, however, they denounced his novels in general as "disgusting, noisome and thoroughly boresome" (in the words of the critic at the *Milwaukee Journal*), and the most esteemed newspapers dismissed the hullabaloo as another cheap stab at publicity. "Ben Hecht is a man of great talent," observed the *New York Times*. "The talent, however, has never been able to attach itself to ends, and it is continually spending itself in mockery." A critic for the *Wisconsin State Journal* lamented, "I can enjoy his ironic humor, condone his lewdness; it is his sneering hatred of humanity that puts me in a jangle of resentment every time I read one of his books."[20]

While most newspapers either ignored Hecht's treatment of Judaism or dismissed it as incidental, the *Newark News* pointed to it as an example of Jewish anti-Semitism, while the *Buffalo Evening News* asserted that if any gentile had "let loose such a volley of invective," Jews would have every reason to feel themselves victims of bigotry. Outrage cascaded like an avalanche from some quarters of the American Jewish community. Rabbi Louis I. Newman of New York City called the book an "atrocious malignment of the Jew . . . an offense against good taste in general, and a careless, sensational effort to promote sales in the bookshops and stores." The book was banned in Boston, and Springfield, Massachusetts, as well as in Canada. Informed that the largest bookstore in Detroit had refused to sell it on the grounds that it constituted "an unnecessary offensive attack upon the Jewish race," Hecht responded tersely, "The Jewish race will survive."[21]

Passages of the book speak for themselves. The novel begins: "The Jews now and then hatch a face which for Jewishness surpasses the caricature of the entire anti-Semitic press. These Jew faces in which race leers and burns like some biologic disease are rather shocking to a mongrelized world. People dislike being reminded of their origins. They shudder . . . at the sight of anyone who looks too much like a fish, a chimpanzee or a Jew." While Hecht quickly explains that Jo Boshere does not quite look like this, he has burned into the reader's mind an image of a protagonist taken straight from the hate literature of his day. As Leslie A. Fiedler later pointed out, Boshere "is portrayed by Hecht as the caricature of the anti-Semite come to life."[22]

There is a hall-of-mirrors quality to the novel. Hecht, clearly animated by unease with his own background, flays his protagonist as a self-hating Jew who cannot shed his Jewishness. Boshere disdains his sister's Zionism as "raising nickels for a lot of God damn stinking Jews in Palestine," while at the same time claiming that the Zionists are "ashamed of being Jews" and that he has grown beyond both shame and Judaism. In a direct stab at assimilationists, Hecht parodies an Un-Jewish Jew modeled on George Jessel: "Lean, overgroomed, reeking with expensive perfumes, slobbering when he laughed and showing a set of heavy white teeth, Solomon was of the tribe of Jews who dominate the night life of Broadway, who stamp their legendary sophistication as a trademark on American entertainment."[23]

Fiedler called Hecht's novel "a work of inspired self-hatred: a portrait of the Jewish author as his own worst [Jewish] enemy." In suggesting Hecht's unconscious angst, Fiedler noted that Boshere's blond shiksa stands as "an image of a world which all of his assaults and betrayals cannot make his own." In contrast, biographer Doug Fetherling argues that *A Jew in Love* "is a cynical book to no good purpose, redolent of the self-hatred he felt not as a Jew, but as a hostage of show business, as an outsider from Chicago and all that implied." These two interpretations are not mutually exclusive, however. Hecht may have felt alienated both by the commercialism of show business and by a dominant Anglo culture that he believed would never truly accept him.[24]

Hecht told *New York Post* reporter Ruth Seinfel that he was grateful to have recovered his old notoriety as the bad boy of literature—he really couldn't be happy without it. He advised young writers to stay on the losing side of every fight, or they would end up like his friends, Carl Sandburg, Sherwood Anderson, and even Maxwell Bodenheim, who had recently gotten "kudos from all the critics" for *Georgie May*. "When I talk to them now they sound like all the things we used to fight against in the old days," he said.[25]

But to these friends Hecht must have seemed a sellout: he now ascended to wealth and privilege as a lord in philistine movieland, while the vogue of the Don Juan had ended for most people with the crash of 1929. The collapse of the markets, joblessness, and poverty had ignited a new radicalism in the place of jazz-age egoism. As in the old days, both Hecht and his contemporaries saw themselves as rebels, but this time, too, he remained apart. Hecht had much in common with his Jewish contemporaries as well—ironically, in his very rebellion against heritage. But here again, his creed of individualism and egoism set him apart.

The new collectivist uprisings of the 1930s echoed the activism of the Innocent Rebellion and would suffer a similar fate. In 1931 writers for the *Menorah Journal* joined Theodore Dreiser and several of Hecht's old friends and associates from the early days of Greenwich Village and the Renaissance—Floyd Dell, Sherwood Anderson, Alfred Kreymborg, Lincoln Steffens, Waldo Frank, and others—to form an activist vanguard that was an adjunct of the Communist Party. Over the next three years, however, their drift toward Leon Trotsky put them on a collision course with the party, which took its direction from Stalin. In late March 1934, an editorial titled "Unintelligent Fanaticism" in the *New Masses* attacked Dreiser, Anderson, and other writers, along with "the erstwhile *Menorah Journal* group—these loop-de-loopers from Zionism to 'internationalism.'"[26]

As in 1915, the new radicalism collapsed in profound disillusionment, precipitated yet again by the onset of a world war. Lofty principles grew entangled with petty bickering that drained the creative energies of American leftists, as they became sucked into the internecine conflict between the Trotskyites and Stalinists. This time, the disillusionment cut to the core, and the psychic effect on writers was more permanent, part of a sweeping shift from integrationism to egocentrism that emerged after World War II—a shift that Hecht and Bodenheim, as the "best hated men in American literature," had once foreshadowed in the early 1920s.[27]

Hecht would later dismiss the radicalism of the 1930s as group therapy for intellectuals, since none of its firebrands ever led proletarian masses in revolt, nor did they topple any tyrants such as the Russian czar or Chang Kai-shek. While Hecht tended to steer clear of the fights between his Hollywood writer friends over the issue, he later noted that his own "non-communism" never had anything to do with fear of the Soviets or Marxist theory: "It was founded on the simple personal fact that in a Communist state I would be jailed or shot for speaking my mind. I could understand almost anybody espousing Communism except a writing man or a man of active intelligence."[28]

☙

At the 140,000-square-foot Astoria studio in Queens, a marble staircase led up to the grand old office originally built for Paramount Pictures founder Adolph Zukor. Here Hecht and MacArthur installed their producer for a new four-picture deal in 1934: a pinhead named Bippo they had discovered on a visit to Coney Island. They seated Bippo behind a desk and gave him a business suit to replace his old grass skirt from the freak show. "Poor Bippo's head lolled and he drooled a bit," Hecht recalled, "but he was always happy to listen to visitors come with plots, inventions and promotion schemes to sell."[29]

The recruitment of Bippo summed up Hecht and MacArthur's attitude toward the studio bosses, who, in return, handed the two friends enough rope to hang themselves, offering them at least a million dollars to make their own movies at Astoria, a vast and once-lavish outpost for East Coast film production that Paramount had abandoned in 1932. This represented the most significant opportunity for independent filmmakers since the early 1920s. As a dream come true for Hollywood writers, it was a great privilege but also a responsibility: a chance to prove there was a truer and better way to create movies than the corporate compartmentalization of the studio system.[30]

"Neither Charlie nor I had ever spent an hour on a movie set," Hecht boasted. "We knew nothing of casts, budgets, schedules, booms, gobos, unions, scenery, cutting, lighting. Worse, we had barely seen a dozen movies in our lives." They were nevertheless undaunted, certain that they were armed with "the great Secret about movies": that 90 percent of a film's success lay in the script. The rest was up to a handful of competent technicians. All that meddlesome producers and directors contributed was bombast and pretension, which ran up costs and time with the "charging chariots and toppling temples," "clash of extras in togas or tin hats," Mars landings, fistfights, lingering close-ups, and "panoramas showing the littleness of man and the bigness of the director."[31]

An opportunity to strike a blow against corporate schlock while scoring a victory for art, Astoria also represented a shot at personal redemption. Hecht admitted that it wasn't just money and conviviality that drew the talented to Hollywood; it was also weakness—greed, laziness, and fear. The incentives were perverse: an individual could brag of never having written something so lowly as a successful script—which was never a discredit to Fitzgerald or Faulkner, whose work for Hollywood was uneven, at best—while commercial success marked a writer as a literary whore, and good-quality scripts promised neither recognition nor money. Furthermore, Hecht found the work degrading. "Writing cheaply, writing falsely, writing with 'less' than you have, is a painful thing," he wrote. "To betray belief is to feel sinful, guilty—and tastes bad. Nor is movie writing easier than good writing."[32]

In an essay for *Commentary*, Joseph Epstein later noted that, for Hecht, the split between serious art and commercial work first became an issue when he moved from Chicago to New York with old debts and a new wife. Having already produced six novels, he gave up trying to score a best seller and turned to Broadway:

> The issue can be formulated simply enough: was Ben Hecht a sell-out? The term sell-out has a dishonorable history. It originated in the enclosed, always at least slightly paranoid, world of American Communism, where any divergence from the party line sent from Moscow was felt to constitute a desertion, or selling-out, of true principles. Transferred to the realm of art, the term meant betrayal of one's talent for either money or popular success. The assumption was that buyers were everywhere: Hollywood and Henry Luce, the critic Edmund Wilson famously remarked in the 1930s, were the two great enemies of talent in our time.
>
> The notion inevitably lent a strong note of inner drama to artistic careers. Anyone who wrote for the movies, or Broadway, or the news magazines . . . or later television, had to consider the possibility that he was selling out. It was of course also and always a self-congratulatory possibility, implying that one had something high and fine and serious in oneself to sell. . . . But the line between what passed for selling out and what for artistic purity began in time to blur.[33]

Hecht and MacArthur festooned their new offices with thirty-foot banners that proclaimed their mission while simultaneously poking fun at the industry and themselves, bearing slogans like "Better Than Metro Isn't Good Enough" and "When in Doubt Cut to the Chase." The next order of business was to call someone who knew what the hell he was doing and beg for assistance. Hawks recalled Hecht saying over the phone, "For God's sake, will you come back here for a week and help us? We don't know a God damn thing about it." Hawks came for a visit, told them what he would do, and left. His advice may have included hiring Arthur Rosson, who had an excellent record as an assistant director, to handle business and financial issues. Rosson served as general manager on *Crime without Passion* and *The Scoundrel*. On the suggestion of MGM producer David Selznick, they hired cameraman Lee Garmes, who essentially relieved them of the role of director, and avant-garde cinematographer Slavko Vorkapich, whose major contribution was a striking two-minute montage at the beginning of their first film.[34]

Of the four films that Hecht and MacArthur made at Astoria, two, *Crime without Passion* (1934) and *The Scoundrel* (1935), received mostly favorable reviews and were modestly profitable. The other two, *Once in a Blue Moon* (1935) and *Soak the Rich* (1936), were pilloried by the critics and considered disasters by Paramount, which almost refused to release them at all. Film historians like Richard Koszarski, who offers a thorough and unsparing account of the Astoria project in *Hollywood on the Hudson: Film and Television in New York from Griffith to Sarnoff*, have suggested that Astoria did more harm than good for the cause of independent filmmaking in the era.[35]

The Scoundrel was an adaptation of *A Jew in Love* but with virtually all the references to Judaism removed. The most successful of the Astoria films, it illustrates the strengths of Hecht's screenplays. The constraints of writing for a visual medium forced him to stick to dialogue and action, stripping away the exposition that tended to bog down his books. And many of the qualities cited as weaknesses in his novels—the clockwork precision that critics like Gilbert Seldes complained about, the icy darkness of his character portrayals and overall vision—somehow became virtues in the swift, breezy language of film.

The film is elevated by the performance of the multitalented Noel Coward, chillingly convincing as Anthony Mallare, the debonair snake who warns an ingénue that he "always rattles eight times" before he strikes. One quickly gets a sense of Hecht's taste for epigrams. When an assistant asks whether their company's interest is in radical or conservative books, Mallare hisses, "Our firm doesn't care about the battles, it only wants the spoils." Lionel Stander plays the acid-tongued Bodenheim character, Rothenstein, though he seems more of a Colombo-like, wisecracking detective than a poet. Clearly his comments are meant as self-criticisms of Hecht himself. When Mallare says, "I call anyone clever enough to see through me a friend," Rothenstein fires back, "And anyone who doesn't, a sweetheart."[36]

In *A Child of the Century*, Hecht credits Garmes's amazing technical expertise and command of filmmaking: "I would sit by silent and full of admiration as Lee and his magicians prepared the set for my 'direction.' My job seemed little more than putting a frame on a finished canvas."

But as Koszarski points out, Hecht was just admitting what everyone else already knew. Ultimately awarded screen credit as codirector, Garmes marked and lit the scenes, framed the angles, and coached the actors. He kept the Astoria films under budget and on schedule, introducing innovations in efficiency and cost-cutting: he decided to scale down the scenery, fashion it into separate pieces, and set these on wheels for rapid changes. *Time* noted that Garmes might have been more essential to the successes at Astoria than either Hecht or MacArthur.[37]

By the time production had started on Hecht and MacArthur's final movie, rumors were flying that Paramount had called Hecht and MacArthur into conference and warned them to halt playing their backgammon games on the set and their hijinks. *Soak the Rich*—starring Mary "Mimsi" Taylor, a Cecil Beaton model with whom Hecht was having a passionate and increasingly serious affair—was meant to be a lighthearted, wisecracking parody of campus radicalism. As one character puts it: "A few years ago it was the fashion to be Don Juans. Today ideas have taken the place of drink and revolt is the latest form of necking." But by now Garmes, Rosson, and other important members of the Astoria crew had left for other work. The staff who remained seemed weighted down by the effects of the Depression. And two days after production began, Hecht's mother was killed in a car accident on Wilshire Boulevard. The film lacked vitality, and it was obvious. The *New York Sun* concluded, "The Messrs. Hecht and MacArthur prove again, in their *Soak the Rich*, that their gift for writing dialogue and situation is perhaps the most brilliant of all the movie scenarists. They prove, too, in this new film, that they have little talent for directing or producing." In the summer of 1936, when the *Hollywood Reporter* ranked the box-office performance of all 221 features released thus far that year, *Soak the Rich* was at the very bottom.[38]

It is tempting to interpret Hecht and MacArthur's Astoria experiment as damning evidence against the proposition that, in moviemaking, the writer, not the director, is the true author of the film. But Astoria was never a fair testing ground for that argument, which in any case has long been forgotten. "The boys," as Hecht and MacArthur were called by the press, knew absolutely nothing about directing, and the notion that they understood "the great Secret of movies" had been altogether unrealistic in the first place. Rather, Astoria failed because of hubris, or chutzpah, as Hecht might have preferred, which is both ironic and fitting, since the pair's best films were about mad egoists. "Was this to be 'the boys' art now

CHAPTER 8

Return

It has always been the privilege of the Jew to take the measure of the godless and the inhuman. . . . They have a little blindly made us the symbol of the thing they are seeking to overthrow. . . . For do they kill us all, silence us all, and burn all our books, the teachings we have helped give the world will still remain to confront and confound them to the day of their doom.

—BEN HECHT, "FOUR RABBIS SPEAK"[1]

Astoria did not turn out to be a new start for independent filmmaking or for Hecht. Having agreed to be compensated through profit sharing, he and Charles MacArthur had earned little during the first year of the project, so they had to return to Hollywood even before the premier of *The Scoundrel* to write *Barbary Coast* (1935) for producer Samuel Goldwyn. Howard Hawks, who directed it, called it "a lousy picture, a contrived thing done more or less to order." Unlike *Viva Villa!* Hecht could not blame its failure on studio interference. To the extent that the largely autobiographical play he wrote next, *To Quito and Back*, reflected his state of mind in 1936, he was experiencing a general sense of unease, which he also could not altogether blame on Hollywood. His problems lay deeper.[2]

Hecht had long been a serial adulterer, but his affair with Mimsi Taylor was something more. According to director Henry Hathaway, who worked closely with Hecht on *China Girl* (1942) and *Kiss of Death* (1947), the relationship lasted six or seven years, and Mimsi was "the big love of his life." As items about the couple began to appear in newspapers, they traveled to Quito, Ecuador, and their trip became the premise of a new script. His experiences as a war correspondent in Germany also figured in the story, possibly because Hitler's prominence in the news triggered these memories. While *To Quito and Back* is yet another tale of an egoist, Alex Sterns is not a Don Juan but an empty and bewildered middle-aged man.[3]

The play begins with the familiar suitcase full of cash intended to fund a revolution, which Sterns good-naturedly carries past the authorities. His friend Zamiano, the guerrilla leader, talks like one of Hecht's gangsters: "If anybody touch or get fresh—you shoot. I come right away. Understand?" Like Camonte, Zamiano isn't familiar with the word *disillusioned* but understands what it means. Sterns is fond of Zamiano but is unable to buy into the revolution; instead, he dismisses all political beliefs with glib epigrams that he swaps with Frazer, a "hear-all, see-all, do-nothing Newspaper Ned," who once stood by and watched thousands massacred at Moabit Prison in Germany.[4]

As they and fellow sophisticates watch Zamiano's revolution get under way, Frazer recalls his days as a young reporter in Chicago, when radicalism meant a May Day picnic in the park. Now communism is the new religion, laments Sterns, while fascism is communism without the high-minded words, communism minus a soul. Democracy is quaint but relies on the people, a mindless mob. Meanwhile, Sterns is beginning to realize that, having betrayed yet another woman in his life, he can't seem to believe in love anymore, either: "Yes, what I've done has filled me full of distrust. My betrayal of her has taught me not to believe . . . in others, or myself."[5]

With his affair now falling apart, he becomes disgusted most of all by the numb paralysis of his own cynicism, his inability to "get used to the idea of words and actions going together." The repartee of his friends becomes increasingly intolerable: "There's quite a tribe of us at large in the world. Fair-minded citizens who understand the cries of the underdog. . . . We hover on the sidelines of all passionate events, and entertain ourselves with discussion. . . . We're always on the right side of discussions but never on any side of the barricades." Finally, he decides that instead of returning to a life on the treadmill in America, he would rather join Zamiano in hopeless resistance to a fascist counterrevolution. At least dying for a cause might mean something to the poor of Ecuador, who will have to face such oppressors again in the future. In a farewell to his young lover Lola, he explains, "In a world too loud with false gods there is nothing left to serve except the least false of them."[6]

But *To Quito and Back* seems to have only hinted at Hecht's deep malaise—a crisis in which he faced basic questions about his political, artistic, and personal integrity. The swirl of events, from the global to the intimate, was compelling him to make decisions about who he was, decisions he could no longer put off, so he turned to his origins for answers.

In a 1972 interview, Hawks recalled that Hecht was constantly getting into trouble in his marriage. During their 1933 trip to Mexico, Hecht had registered a hotel room with another woman under Mr. and Mrs. Hecht, only to learn that Rose was coming. Begged for advice, Hawks told him, "Christ, you figure it out. You got yourself into it." But Hecht was desperate for some help. "And I said, well, you better be perfectly honest," Hawks recounted. "So the best way to do it—go up and be a reporter and tell her the story about her husband being with another woman, and what is she going to do about it? And he did. And by Christ, he got away with it. Everything was alright. He got out of that in a hurry."[7]

Hawks found that he could at least put Hecht's troubles to good use. "When he got into a real bind," Hawks said, "when he got into trouble with some girl . . . then his mind would really begin to function on the thing he was working on, because that would shut out the other thing." Hawks began to see the affairs as a creative tonic: "God, there were so many of them, I can't remember. I can't remember their names. I used to just laugh about it. Charlie and I would laugh. Charlie would say, he's messed up with another one. And I would say: Let him stay messed up. He writes better when he's messed up. I was never in any hurry to get him out. Because when he was sweating and worried about what Rose was going to do he would write better."[8]

Though absurd and amusing on one level, the effects grew extreme and exacted a toll. Hawks recalled that at one point Rose took boxing lessons and knocked Mimsi out cold. Hecht's affairs also ran up outrageous expenses over the years—keeping the home in Nyack, eventually a new one in Oceanside, California, an apartment in New York City, and whatever other love nests or needs of paramours there happened to be. Hecht was constantly taking on more jobs than he could handle, doing much of the work under the table so that Rose did not find out.

While Hawks believed the pressure brought out the best in his friend, others were less sure. The Austrian director Otto Preminger, with whom Hecht wrote *Where the Sidewalk Ends* (1950), *Whirlpool* (1950), and five other scripts, saw a key similarity to Dalton Trumbo, with whom he also collaborated. Both men were wasting their energies on screenwriting, in Preminger's view, but he thought Hecht's lifestyle and choices, in particular, sapped his extraordinary strength and talent:

> I believe that if Hecht had not been lured by money into the movies, which he always used to call himself—this kind of writing—he called himself prostitution, that he would then have become one of the greatest writers in the theater and in American literature. I mean, he was a great writer. But he would have concentrated far more on what he felt was the more valuable and good writing and not . . . See he did this all somehow almost like a sport, and just to make money. What he did was still better than what most other writers who took picture writing very seriously did. It was still better. But if he had been forced to make a living out of serious writing and literature, novels and plays, and continued with plays particularly, I think he would have written some great, great plays, which unfortunately he didn't after his first plays. He had no time. He always had jobs in Hollywood. And you know, when you look at credits, you probably only see one-tenth, or less than one-tenth of what he really did, because he used to do quick rewrites for people overnight and didn't even really want his name on it.[9]

But as much as Hawks, Preminger, and Hathaway liked and admired Hecht, no one really knew what he felt. Hawks remained convinced that, through it all, Hecht and Rose loved each other deeply. "It's as though other women were appealing to what his imaginative mind would work out and Rose appealed to what he was," Hawks said. "Rose checked him on everything. She took care of him. Otherwise he would've gone to California without any clothes if she didn't pack them. With other women he wasn't trying to make anything that was lasting. Ben had to adore Rose; she was not a nagging person at all. He was a genius in his way and she treated him as one."[10]

Hathaway believed that Hecht and Rose were never suited to each other but that Hecht, like Sterns in *To Quito and Back*, could not leave his wife for his young lover: "He thought that it would be unfair to [Mimsi] anyway, because he didn't think that he could stick with anybody." In any case, Hecht later maintained another years-long relationship, with the Romanian-born model and actress Lisa Ferraday.[11]

Hecht finally ended his affair with Mimsi after writing *To Quito and Back*, patched things up with Rose, and returned to New York to participate in the play's production. He told the *New York Times* that he might be through with pictures for good: "Once in my pristine youth, I wrote books with some mental content. Now I am going back . . . [to] see if it's any fun to be a writer again." But he was soon to find the Theater Guild almost as meddlesome as the studios. Although Hecht probably hadn't consciously created a portrait of appeasement and isolationism in the play, he flew into a rage in the summer of 1937 when "a poor milk soppy looking goon named Maurice Wertheim" suggested that "some of the anti-fascism be cut down because it could outrage Hitler and kill a lot of Jews." The guild watered the play down anyway, and critics saw no connection to the developments in Europe.[12]

Hecht had been paying attention to the plight of German Jews at least since July 31, 1935, when he wrote a guest column on the subject for Walter Winchell, six weeks before Hitler introduced the Nuremberg Laws at the annual Nazi Party rally. During that summer anti-Semitic street violence had become far more virulent. In the column Hecht noted that when the insular religious life of the Jewish ghetto began to dissolve in the early nineteenth century, it was in Germany that Jews first became world citizens. This was unfortunate, he said, because the Germans had the worst inferiority complex in Europe. Now the Jews would be driven back into the ghetto; Germany's desire to rid itself of its own sense of inadequacy would force a sophisticated, metropolitan people to return to an existence they had long outgrown.[13]

Apparently Hecht still believed, as many did, that the current persecution represented just another ugly episode in the long history of German anti-Semitism and that it would ebb again, as it always had in the past. He suggested it would ultimately turn out worse for the persecutors than for the persecuted: "I have a feeling that this Jew consciousness is rather good for the seemingly assimilated Jew. There is a certain strength in shaking hands, however briefly, with so valorous a historic sire as the Jew." The light, even snarky tone of the piece seems jarring in hindsight, and it clearly marks a midway point between the self-hatred of *A Jew in Love* and Hecht's "transformation into a Jew" in 1939. But what is most salient in the column is Hecht's ongoing distaste for assimilation and cosmopolitanism, which he associated with craven conformity and social climbing. Such traits offended the proud individualist who celebrated difference and originality.

Despite his statement that he might be leaving Hollywood for good, he remained a prolific screenwriter in the late 1930s, scripting the screwball comedy *Nothing Sacred* (1937; a savagely funny satire about people's idiocy), the *Goldwyn Follies* (1938), *Gunga Din, Wuthering Heights, Lady of the Tropics, Angels with Dirty Faces, Some Like It Hot, It's a Wonderful World,* and the Marx Brothers' *At the Circus,* all released in 1939, as well as the story lines for John Ford's *Hurricane* (1937) and *Stagecoach* (1939). In his most famous feat as a legendary fix-it man, he produced a down-to-the-wire rewrite of the last nine reels of *Gone with the Wind* for David Selznick.

But Hecht was losing all patience for such work. In 1938 he raged to producer Samuel Goldwyn, "The wanton and amateur rewriting of the last half of the material I gave you, the idiot sabotage played with my lines, scenes and plot points; the total psychopathic mania for change . . . all these items make it impossible for me ever to write anything more for your use or discarding. . . . I am sorry to start rabbit-punching, Sam, because of your lack of respect for my work and your curious urge to change, lessen and debauch it."[14]

At the same time, as he continued to watch events unfold in Europe, he became a changed man. After the Munich Pact was formally issued on September 30, 1938, Hitler invaded the Czechoslovakian Sudetenland in October. On Kristallnacht, "the night of broken glass" on November 9–10, the SA (Sturmabteilung) paramilitary ransacked Jewish homes, businesses, schools, hospitals, and synagogues across Germany, killing ninety-one and arresting some thirty thousand Jews, many of whom were sent to concentration camps.[15] Around this time, Hecht was working on the novella "The Little Candle," his astonishing projection that at the Führer's command, "a great International Pogrom" would slaughter Jews across Europe, leaving those who survived to be hunted down and murdered:

> For when we opened our newspapers we found that the cloud we had watched so long and, in a way, so aloofly, had grown suddenly black and dreadful and immense. It filled all the pages of the journals. The world had made it seem but a single face overnight and this face thrust itself into our breakfast hour, ugly and hellish. Like a monster evoked out of the smoking pages of our history, it confronted us, exultant and with the ancient howl of massacre on its lips.[16]

The story appeared in *A Book of Miracles*, a collection of seven novellas published in June 1939 that he and most critics agreed was the best fiction he ever wrote, although few people read it. Many reviewers were moved by "The Little Candle," but a few remarked that his vision of over half a million people killed seemed farfetched. Hecht's publisher tried to get him "to reduce the dreadful prophecy in 'The Little Candle' to a neat book-keeper's figure of fifty thousand dead," but he refused. Associated Press critic John Selby praised it as "one of the bravest stories the public will see in a long time, and one of the truest," but nevertheless sounded a note of incredulity: "Mr. Hecht imagines that Europe actually decided to kill off the Jews—not many of them but all of them." In a sense, such comments were in line with the remarks he had always received from critics, who were often put off by his contempt for humanity. Only someone with a grim view of the human soul could have imagined that the German people, or any people, would be capable of such a thing.[17]

From late 1938 onward, Hecht seemed to know what was about to happen and was willing to do whatever he could to help stop it. This spirit of activism was altogether new in a forty-four-year-old man who had stood on the sidelines during the Innocent Rebellion and the resurgent radicalism of the early 1930s, who had held all politics in contempt as a cynical journalist, and who had undertaken a two-year party at Astoria during the darkest period of the Depression, as a happily oblivious Hollywood playboy. In his film work, his changed attitude was first evident in *Let Freedom Ring*, released in late February 1939. A western about a young man who enlists workers and the local newspaper to battle a cattle baron, it was a parable for anti-Nazi, antifascist struggles such as the war against Franco, but with jingoistic overtones. Soon thereafter, Rose arranged for him to write a column for *PM*, Ralph Ingersoll's start-up daily newspaper, which could serve as a platform for his views.

Ingersoll could pay only $75 a week for 1001 Afternoons in New York, and the job meant passing up a $7,000-a-week contract with MGM. But Hecht later said he was "grateful for a forum larger than [his] dinner table." In the column, he championed interventionism and criticized powerful American Jews for kowtowing to the isolationists. In one, he relayed the case of Hymie Weinberg, a man who had thousands in the bank but pretended to be a beggar "who couldn't possibly be expected to help anybody." It was a shame that Hymie was so miserly he had died of malnutrition, Hecht remarked, because with a little training he could have become another isolationist congressman or senator. In other columns, Hecht compared the Vichy head of state, Philippe Petain, to a sick, old pelican who drowned in the sea because he lacked the strength and heart to flap his wings; blasted the Hearst newspapers for discouraging American assistance to Britain; and likened the isolationist senator Burton Wheeler to a crackpot who preached that the earth was flat, predicting that in future years Wheeler would remain just as defiantly unrepentant about his folly.[18]

In the spirit of the column of his Chicago days, Hecht captured slices of life in "the addle-headed city of New York—the teeming and invincible citadel of ball games, slum dramas, night life, (and) soap-box revolutions." He wrote of meeting and having drinks with Sherwood Anderson, whom he had not seen since the early 1920s. (Anderson died just a few days after that reunion, on a cruise headed for South America.)[19]

Hecht also related his chance encounter with Maxwell Bodenheim after fifteen years of estrangement, on the occasion when he agreed to pay his friend thirty dollars a week for a poem or two pages of prose. Though Hecht would later offer far less flattering descriptions of how the poet had appeared on that day, in the column he recalled that in his youth Bodenheim had been "a mathematician of words" who "arranged them into acrobatic patterns of cabalistic tenderness." In the corner of a midtown saloon, Hecht had pored over Bodenheim's unpublished work: a record of the calamities and despair wrought by the Depression, but utterly devoid of self-pity. "They were full of love of others," Hecht explained. "They sang of shop girls and laborers and of human gropings for justice. They cried out the immemorial pain of the underdog, and they cast a light."[20]

Hecht's column represented not just a return to younger days in Chicago but also a return to his Jewish roots. "How Do You Do" offered an epitaph for the great Yiddish author and playwright Sholem Aleichem. "It was out of battered and tattered hearts that he wrung his great laughter," Hecht explained, quoting from the author's tombstone: "Here lies a Jew, plain as an old vest, / Who suffered like the devil but wrote comedy the best." In another column Hecht related an impromptu slapstick routine in which Harpo Marx sent a snobbish, anti-Semitic doorman chasing all over the street after a handful of fake jewelry. Groucho Marx praised one of Hecht's pieces ridiculing the Nazis with a brief note: "That's what we need—a little more belligerency professor and not quite so much cringing."[21]

One of Hecht's most important columns, on January 16, 1941, attacked the former ambassador to Britain, Joseph Kennedy, for clandestine meetings in which Kennedy had warned important Jews in Hollywood and New York not to produce anti-Nazi movies and literature. Such propaganda not only would escalate tensions with Germany, Kennedy had advised, but would also make fellow Americans resentful that they were being dragged into "a Jewish war."[22]

Kennedy had made national news two months earlier, on November 10, 1940, when *Boston Daily Globe* reporter Louis Lyons printed off-the-record remarks he had expressed at the Ritz-Carlton. Still ambassador at the time, Kennedy had declared that Britain—having just sustained the German Luftwaffe's bombardment in the Battle of Britain and now enduring the Blitz—was doomed and that "democracy is all done." As for America, "I'm willing to spend all I've got to keep us out of the war," Kennedy had told his three journalist companions before departing. "There's no sense in our getting in. We'll just be holding the bag."[23] A week later Kennedy had delivered "a thundering three-hour monologue" at a luncheon at the Warner Brothers' studio. A former movie executive, Kennedy had been expected to talk about the impediments to exporting movies to Europe during wartime. Instead, he warned that, just as Britain's Jews were being blamed for the war overseas, American and Hollywood Jews would be blamed for whatever suffering the United States incurred should it too join the fight. "He apparently threw the fear of God into many of our producers and executives," Douglas Fairbanks Jr. wrote to Franklin Delano Roosevelt the following day, "by telling them that they should stop making anti-Nazi pictures or using the film medium to promote or show sympathy to the cause of the 'democracies' versus the 'dictators.' . . . He continued to underline the fact that the film business was using its power to influence the public dangerously and that we all, and the Jews in particular, would be in jeopardy, if they continued to abuse that power."[24]

The speech at Warner Brothers was never reported in the newspapers—until Hecht wrote his column in mid-January. Taking aim at Kennedy's core argument, Hecht noted that people never ran out of reasons for hating Jews. Not so long ago, Hollywood Jews had been decried as radical Bolsheviks; now they were accused of being capitalist imperialists intent on bringing the boot down on the workers. "All this is confusing enough to people studying what is known as the Jewish question from the outside," Hecht added. "Studied from the inside it grows a little nightmarish."[25]

When Hecht had been a small boy on the Lower East Side, this Manhattan neighborhood, then home to a half million Jews, had the highest concentration of nickelodeons in America, squeezed in among the tenements, Yiddish theaters, and music halls. On Christmas Eve in 1908, the New York City Police had padlocked the doors of these venues on the grounds that they were unsafe and unsanitary. Six Jewish exhibitors then shifted into film production and joined fellow immigrant Carl Laemmle's exodus to southern California in 1912, successfully defying Thomas Edison's East Coast monopoly on filmmaking. During the 1920s the rise of these "moguls," as they came to be called, prompted xenophobia, a backlash to the era's sudden and dramatic changes. After the lurid trial of silent comedian Fatty Arbuckle and a series of additional scandals early in the decade, the moguls preempted government censorship by recruiting U.S. postmaster general Will Hays, who allied with the Catholic Church to establish the Motion Picture Production Code in 1930.[26]

By then, however, anti-Semitism had begun to blow in from Germany. On December 5 a clutch of burly brownshirts led by Nazi ringleader Paul Joseph Goebbels infiltrated Berlin's Mozart Hall for the second-day screening of the pacifist epic *All Quiet on the Western Front*. As the film began to roll, they unleashed stink bombs, sneezing powder, and white mice into the darkened theater, screaming "Judenfilm!" and other invectives amid the ensuing pandemonium. Members of the audience were savagely beaten as they fled. Over the next several nights, Goebbels followed up with torchlit rallies to protest the film. The German Motion Picture Theater Owners reacted by prohibiting what they now tagged as anti-German propaganda, even though Laemmle published a heartfelt plea to his beloved homeland in a thousand-word newspaper advertisement, written in his native tongue. The Nazis had proven that through violence they could shut down Hollywood's Jews.[27]

And though nobody yet knew it, the Nazis had fired the opening shot in what they understood to be modern war. In *Mein Kampf* Hitler had written that "the picture, in all its forms leading up to the film," far surpassed the power of the written word for whipping people into a fervor and might even one day rival oratory, because with motion pictures "a man needs to use his brains even less." Goebbels explained Nazi propaganda theory on March 28, 1933, inaugurating his Ministry of Public Enlightenment and Propaganda two months after Hitler became chancellor, and he delivered a second diatribe a year later to the Federal Film Corporation at the Kroll

Opera. Gaunt and club footed, with a doctorate in Romantic literature, Goebbels envisioned himself as a maestro playing "upon a vast keyboard" of German media, art, and culture. "We are convinced that the film is one of the most modern and far-reaching means for influencing the masses," he had said in February 1933. "A government can therefore not possibly leave the film world to itself." The leaders of the New Germany, along with Joseph Stalin, viewed the camera as a powerful weapon, and Hollywood as the high ground in a battle.[28]

By 1933 the Reich had maximized pressure within its own borders, enforcing an Aryanization policy that booted out all Jews involved in film production. Meanwhile, the long arm of the German state reached into Hollywood itself, effectively combining forces with the Hays Office and regional American censors. The Nazis capitalized not only on the studios' desire to preserve the lucrative German movie market but also on homegrown American anti-Semitic and isolationist sentiment. By December 1933 the chief censor for the Hays Office was Joseph I. Breen, a lay Catholic and former publicist and reporter, who wrote to a friend the year he was appointed head of the Production Code Administration that the Jews were "probably the scum of the earth." For its part, Germany's most powerful tool was the infamous Article XV of a pre-Nazi censorship law of 1932, which asserted a right to punish the studios for distributing any film, in any country, that was judged offensive to the fatherland. The Nazi consul in Los Angeles, Georg Gyssling, proved remarkably effective at scrubbing Hollywood scripts clean of anything objectionable to Hitler until hostilities escalated in 1939. In this Gyssling was aided by German consular officers across the United States, pro-Nazi groups that protested to mayors and local censor boards, and German-language newspapers that railed against offenses to the Reich.[29]

Organized resistance to the Nazis came from Hecht's close circle of Hollywood friends, so much so, in fact, that his silence during most of the 1930s is conspicuous. In 1933 Herman Mankiewicz outlined *The Mad Dog of Europe*, a tough, unnerving drama about an early friend to Hitler who becomes sucked into the regime's murderous vortex, a plot that aimed squarely at Nazi brutality against the Jews. When the Motion Pictures Producers and Distributors of America told small-time producer Sam Jaffe to back off the project, he sold the script to up-and-coming agent Al Rosen. Hard-nosed and eager to make what he was convinced would be a hit, Rosen was soon showing around a photo of a Hitler lookalike he had cast to play the heavy and boasting that he had collected seven thousand feet of newsreel footage. Mankiewicz was willing to forfeit his job at MGM to make the film. He also planned to take out a full-page advertisement soliciting contributions, with half the profits to go to relief of German Catholics and Jews.[30]

But Breen shut the effort down. Admonishing Rosen that the purpose of Hollywood fare, "primarily, *is to entertain* and *not to propagandize*," he explained, "Because of the large number of Jews active in the motion picture industry in the country, the charge is certain to be made that the Jews, as a class, are behind an anti-Hitler picture and using the entertainment screen for their own personal propaganda purposes. The entire industry, because of this, is likely to be indicted for the action of a mere handful."[31] Breen argued the point to Leon Lewis, a representative of the Anti-Defamation League, who in turn presented the issue to the group's new Los Angeles advisory council. The Anti-Defamation League decided to help block funding for the film, and Rosen found all doors closed to him.[32]

Paul Muni, Edward G. Robinson, and Ernst Lubitsch—later lead participants in Hecht's 1943 pageant for Jewish rescue—were among the most engaged activists in the core organization for resistance, the Hollywood Anti-Nazi League. Launched in 1936 by screenwriter Donald Ogden Stewart and Dorothy Parker, the league pioneered the now-commonplace practice of leveraging star power for progressive activism. The league organized the staged signing of a "Declaration of Democratic Independence," and at least five of the seventeen stars and artists who appear in the photo of the event would later be cheerleaders or activists for Hecht's campaign—Groucho Marx, John Garfield, and Claude Rains, as well as Robinson and Muni.[33]

These two former stars of Yiddish theater and the gangster craze played in key films that tested the boundaries of mainstream anti-Nazi fare. The first was *The Life of Emile Zola* (1937), a man-of-conscience drama starring Muni as the middle-aged writer embroiled in the Dreyfus affair, driven to righteous outrage. Nominated for ten Academy Awards, including best actor, it won best picture for its portrayal of this notorious anti-Semitic episode of the late nineteenth century. Yet the movie illustrates what was so strange and disturbing in the 1930s, for the word *Jew* is never spoken, appearing onscreen only at the end, for about a second and half. All three other references to Jews were cut. Warner Brothers—called by Groucho at the time "the only studio with any guts"—also produced *Juarez* (1939), featuring Muni as the Lincolnesque Latino emancipator in one of the more effective allegorical anti-Nazi movies of the period. Two days later, the studio released the game-changing *Confessions of a Nazi Spy* (1939), starring Robinson—the first explicit, unvarnished attack on Nazism and the first Hollywood movie in which the word *Nazi* appeared since the party had seized power. Protests from Gyssling and a warning from Breen were ignored this time. Picketers rallied at some of the showings, and there were isolated incidents of violence. At one screening in Milwaukee, Nazi sympathizers set fire to the theater.[34]

For his part, Hecht helped bring to the screen a script based on Vincent Sheean's memoir *Personal History* (1935), the story of a foreign correspondent in Hitler's Germany that was to end with the hero rescuing several Jews and marrying a Jewish woman. In June 1938 Breen rejected it, but after Britain went to war, producer Walter Wanger handed the script to Alfred Hitchcock and had it stripped of all direct references to fascism and Jews. Hecht was brought in as a script doctor and framed the new version with an opening drawn from his experiences in Germany: an editor thunders that he has had enough of pretentious foreign correspondents and demands a good old-fashioned crime reporter to cover the great crime that is hatching in central Europe. With thinly veiled references to Nazism and an interventionist story line, *Foreign Correspondent* appeared in theaters in 1940, along with a handful of other anti-Nazi pictures, including the powerful Jimmy Stewart drama *This Mortal Storm*, Charlie Chaplin's *The Great Dictator*, and a Three Stooges' short *You Nazi Spy!*[35]

What distinguished Hecht's entry into the political scene was his undaunted call for American intervention; collectively, the leftist Hollywood activists—despite all their anti-Nazi fervor—remained isolationists through to the end of the decade. The Hollywood Anti-Nazi League was so committed to Soviet dogma that it dutifully snipped "Anti-Nazi" from its name as soon as Stalin signed the Molotov-Ribbentrop Pact, becoming the neutered Hollywood League for Democratic Action. Even as the Germans and Soviets chewed up Poland, and "brave little Finland" stood alone, the league opposed any loans to belligerent nations, including Britain and France, arguing that it would "violate the spirit and essence of our neutrality" and "endanger the peace of this nation." Membership plummeted, and donations evaporated. Mankiewicz never shared the Hollywood Anti-Nazi League's communist sympathies, but he did share their support for isolationism. "I am an ultra-Lindbergh," he announced. "The strength of the Rome-Berlin Axis is so overwhelming as to make the thought of conflict the work of a madman."[36]

In *A Child of the Century*, Hecht wrote that when he "turned into a Jew in 1939" he also became an American. Insofar as he became an ardent interventionist, this was true. In 1940 he joined the advocacy group Fight for Freedom, for which he and MacArthur wrote the stridently patriotic one-act play *Fun to Be Free*. But while Hecht expressed confidence that the United States and its allies would defeat Nazi Germany, he was not optimistic about the fate of Europe's Jews. Moreover, he was deeply disturbed by the silence of the American media regarding the ongoing butchery, and it rankled him that the prominent isolationists muzzled Jews by playing on their fears of appearing un-American. As for the Jews themselves, he was angered to see that even in this time of crisis, social status still counted for so much that the rich and powerful of Hollywood, like the jazz-age Jews of Broadway, "had discarded their Jewishness out of the belief that as Jews they could line up only for a snubbing."[37]

In his 1941 *PM* column about Kennedy's meetings in Hollywood, Hecht wrote that the Nobel Prize–winning French philosopher Henri Bergson had an excellent answer to the former ambassador. The Vichy government had granted Bergson a special exemption so that he would not have to register as a Jew and thus surrender all of his civil rights. In response, the eighty-year-old philosopher had defiantly struggled from his deathbed to join the registration line at the Paris bureau of racial records. He had died a week later.[38]

Hecht did not couch his arguments in terms of the melting pot versus cultural pluralism, but in the 1940s he became one of the first to articulate the more assertive attitudes now associated with identity politics. He may have been unfamiliar with the work of Horace Kallen and Randolph Bourne, but he nevertheless was on intimate terms with cultural pluralism, inasmuch as the phrase reflected the attitude of his generation. He had been rebelling against it at least since *A Jew in Love*, though it had taken him a decade to switch from rejecting his heritage to embracing it. If his mind conflated Israel Zangwill's vision of a melting-pot America with Kallen's vision of a nation that celebrated its diversity, that was because Hecht had seen too many Jews of his generation simply shrug off their Jewishness. Now, in light of the new onslaught against Jews abroad and at home, that was starting to look a lot like cowardice. He took aim at it in an April 15, 1941, column titled "My Tribe Is Called Israel," which also articulated his own new credo.[39]

The column had been prompted by "a barrage of strangely nervous and sadly sensitive letters" criticizing him for addressing the Jewish question openly. Replying to one common objection, he said that he understood very well that Judaism was not a race but that such distinctions hardly mattered to the Nazis and their collaborators. Furthermore, he knew that most Jews were barely Jews at all but citizens of the world, who rarely spoke or even thought about Judaism. He himself had lived as a successful example of this type. Nevertheless, he argued:

> It is the pathetic notion of my critics that the best way to combat this gibbering but powerful attack on the Jews is to stand, anthropology books and citizenship papers in hand, and prove by chapter readings and government stamps that there are no Jews. The thing to do, they say, is to prove by our deeds and words as well as by our great worldliness that we are Americans—fine patriotic Americans first and Jews afterward, if at all. . . . [But] it is back on all the radios of Europe and on an alarming portion of them in the U.S.A. And you won't get very far in your rebuttals by quibbling, Talmudic fashion, as to whether or not you are a Jew. . . . I suggest, too, that you stop wasting your angers on me. I am not attacking you. I am only asking you to fight.[40]

Throughout the 1930s Hecht had been more or less unconsciously folding his critiques of Jewish American culture into his satire of mass media, but after the Kennedy controversy, the connection became explicit. Up until then, he had been writing fiction in the vein of the Hollywood novel, that new literature of alienation and angst in the age of mass culture spawned by the migration of writers to Hollywood, which included such works as *I Should Have Stayed Home* (1938), *Day of the Locust* (1939), *What Makes Sammy Run?* (1941), and *The Last Tycoon* (1941). Hecht's own contributions to this genre, which mainly took the form of short fiction, add up to something significant as a sum total but have been overlooked because they were spread out over so many years and across so many different volumes of his work. In addition to his zany 1944 murder mystery *I Hate Actors!*, they included stories from *The Champion from Far Away* and *Actor's Blood*, as well as the 1943 story "Concerning a Woman of Sin."[41]

Two of the best tales appeared in *A Book of Miracles*. In "The Missing Idol," a frenetic producer named Mr. Kolisher—whose genius is that he knows and understands nothing and, in knowing nothing, understands the people perfectly—becomes inspired to make the most spectacular big-budget passion play of all time. He commissions dozens of screenwriters, biblical savants, and university scholars; buys five hundred camels and one hundred dromedaries; and proceeds to reconstruct ancient Jerusalem. In fact, the thing is so good that God himself grows interested and wants to lend a helping hand. The Lord scoops up the great movie star playing Jesus from the middle of the crucifixion scene and endows him with a small touch of a divine aura. But in a cruel, unforeseen twist of fate, the star can now no longer be captured by a Hollywood movie camera; his career is finished, and he ends up forgotten and bitter.[42]

In "The Heavenly Choir," another story about the relationship between art and media, Hecht considers whether the new medium of commercial radio can bring the beauty of art to the masses. Is this not "the long-awaited liaison between Beauty and the Beast"? No, Hecht concludes, for when the two lie together, "it was not the beast that underwent any marked alterations, but, as always, Beauty. For Beauty lying down with the Beast too often grows a bit cockeyed and contemptible herself."[43]

When Hollywood remained silent about the Nazi massacre of the Jews, Hecht's critique developed from there. In writing *A Guide for the Bedevilled* (1944) during the darkest days of the war, he imagined himself pitching a movie to the studio heads that "had nothing to do with Jews so they need not wince in advance." Instead, it would put "a new villain on the screen . . . a new gangster . . . a new Public Enemy Number One": humanity itself. The story would focus on Ignatz Philip Semmelweis, a Hungarian physician who discovered that doctors could prevent infection and disease by washing their hands before performing medical procedures. Semmelweis's breakthrough could have saved millions of lives, but out of sheer human blindness and callous stupidity, he was ignored. Hecht imagined that in conference a producer would insist on changing the story so that Semmelweis was the villain and the people were the hero. Producer Herbert J. Yates at Republic did indeed turn the idea of the movie down in July 1946.[44]

Hecht noted that in much of what had been written about Hollywood, there was a major lie of omission: the narratives failed to note that it was "an empire of toy-making, invented by Jews, dominated by Jews, and made to flourish like unto the land of Solomon—by Jews, and a few embattled Irishmen." He added that when he was young, the stage was full of Jewish comics and dramas, the magazines "were full of Potashes and Perlmutters," and many popular songs were sung with Jewish inflections: "Don't do dot dance, I tell you, Sadie." Yet "whereupon the two great media of mass entertainment appear—the movies and the radio, both dominated by Jews—and the Jew vanishes."[45]

Nearly a decade later, *Commentary* writer Henry Popkin would build on Hecht's thesis, citing in his essay "The Vanishing Jew of Our Popular Culture: The Little Man Who Is No Longer There" dozens of recognizably Jewish characters who had disappeared from broadcasting and the movies. He credited *A Guide for the Bedevilled* for one of the rare discussions of this during the 1940s. While Popkin neglected to mention that the victims of the Nazi genocide were likewise missing from the airwaves and movie screens, of the missing Jewish characters he wrote, "The source of this phenomenon, as of so many others in Jewish life today, is Hitler. When Hitler forced Americans to take anti-Semitism seriously, it was apparently felt that the most eloquent reply that could be made was a dead silence: the American answer to the banishment of Jews from public life in Germany was the banishment of Jewish figures from the popular arts—in the United States."[46]

Hecht, however, was observing all of this from within the movie industry, and he had a different point to make, both about the character of American mass entertainment and about his powerful Jewish contemporaries in Hollywood. He recalled that when he first came to Hollywood, the Jewish studio executives reminded him not of the smooth sophisticates he had known in New York during the 1920s but of his immigrant aunts and uncles. He had initially assumed that they were crude and simple philistines, but in this he had been quite wrong. In fact, he had found himself in the midst of a great historic current of Jewish genius dating back thousands of years.[47]

Hollywood represented the destiny of a people long pushed to the margins of commerce, "forced to create a world out of their limbo." Jews were accustomed to serving tyrants, but in America the tyrant, in Hecht's view, was the people. And so, years before coming to Hollywood, this "ancient tribe of king-serving and luxury-bringing Jews" had reached to take possession of theaters and amusement parks. "These were naturally theirs," Hecht argued, "for were they not long trained and adept in the business of catering to their masters?" But while such servility may seem the mark of a humble soul, it was really just a mask worn out of necessity. "Under the mask there has remained the gift for loving oneself above one's master," Hecht continued. "In this fact lies the paradox of a servile Hollywood run by the world's most startling collection of egoists." He then linked the movie moguls' fear of standing up for their fellow Jews in Europe and the absence of artistic integrity in Hollywood. "That the great Jews of Hollywood bow to the dictates of Jew haters is only part of their cowardice," he wrote. "It is also the mark of consistency. For the Jew haters are part of the Public, and the servility of Hollywood makes no distinctions in its master."[48]

This was the reasoning of a man not only outraged by the inhumanity of Nazism and the spinelessness of fellow Jews but also saddened by the disappearance of a world he had once known. He was now far from the days of the Jackson Park art colony and young Greenwich Village, from a world where people held readings by candlelight and built temples to art. Hecht had seen art poached by the poseurs, mountebanks, and tourist boobs of the 1920s, before it was then devoured by radio and the movies. By the time television arrived in the early 1950s, Hecht would write:

> Despite the popularity of concerts, exhibitions, ballets and printed matter—or, perhaps, because of it—the artist is a vanishing figure and the arts are becoming a branch of the Advertising Business. Never was the public so "artistic" and never was there so little mystery and magic entering the world.
>
> There are, in fact, no arts. There are only entertainments. Our talents, like our waterfalls, have all been harnessed to make life pleasanter for the Public. The iconoclastic or anti-public artist exists no more than an anti-public traction company.
>
> In Russia all individualism in art has been forbidden by law and is punishable as crime. There are no such laws in the U.S.A. Here our individualism has dried up and blown away by itself. . . .
>
> My announcing the death of American art may be premature. It may be that I am not in touch with its underground. Somewhere beyond my ken possibly there are still candlelit rendezvous in the big and little towns where youth gathers to kick the hell out of syntax and sanity. But I doubt it. Such American revolters as I know in these days are a two-faced lot. They revolt on week ends. The other five days are full of box-office dreams.[49]

ℭ

Hecht may have been noting the conformity or spiritual bankruptcy of the early 1950s, but in the postwar era, individualism—if not actually individuality—was certainly on the upswing. This was as true for average Americans who had returned from the war to settle in the suburbs and pursue the American dream as it was for the nation's cultural elite. "Jewish intellectual life in America since the 1930s has been a mass exodus from the ghettos of revolutionism to the condos of individualism," wrote Mark Shechner in 1987. By the time of Shechner's observation, however, the idea of the late twentieth century as an era of extreme individualism had already become a commonplace, first popularized by Tom Wolfe in his 1976 essay for *New York Magazine* about "the 'Me' Decade," then delineated by Christopher Lasch in his seminal 1979 study *The Culture of Narcissism: American Life in an Age of Diminishing Expectations.*[50]

Although both Hecht and Bodenheim are virtually forgotten as literary figures now, they anticipated this overall trend of the twentieth century and understood their own era's narcissism more clearly than did many of their far more celebrated contemporaries. Their writings touted, dissected, and vilified this narcissism with wit and acumen. Indeed, their very personas augured the often amusingly fraught and imperfect egoism of postwar artist-entertainers. Not only had Hecht and Bodenheim embarked on a quest for self-liberation and self-fulfillment, but they had consequently faced the same internal and external crises. In grappling with popular and commercial success, they displayed the characteristic qualities of artists in the age of mass media—vanity, promiscuity, even cruelty, but also vulnerability and, in Bodenheim's case, self-destructiveness. Moreover, their relationship was uniquely charged by that "strong note of inner drama" that became endemic to artistic careers, particularly as the line between art and entertainment began to blur: the concern over being a sellout.[51]

Bodenheim's novels and poems add up to a significant body of work, one that reveals a writer of extraordinary versatility, honesty, and emotional power. Hecht wasn't interested in psychologizing about his friend, and Hecht saw Bodenheim as Bodenheim saw himself: as a poet, not a novelist. Hecht described Bodenheim's books as "hack work with flashes of tenderness, wit and truth in them, and some verbal fireworks in every chapter." In their time together at the *Chicago Literary Times*, Hecht had seen Bodenheim generate prose of consistent quality and, though always aware of his friend's buffoonery, had observed a slashing wit that put even H. L. Mencken to shame.[52] Hecht was convinced of his friend's innate talent and always saw his sensitivity and depth come through in his writing. Moreover, despite Hecht's preoccupation with cold egoists who found themselves their own best company, his friendships were important to him, and in the 1940s he was saddened to see an old companion plummet so helplessly.[53] For these reasons, and, perhaps most of all, because of Hecht's recognition of his own flaws, what ultimately mattered to him was not what the world did or did not owe his friend but rather what Bodenheim seemed to symbolize.

In youth, Bodenheim had been good theater. In print as in life, he always seemed to be switching between or combining the roles of ragged Baudelarian poet, caustic jester, and fiery rebel with no interest in adjusting to society. But over the years when Bodenheim drifted, sometimes living in cheap rooms and often homeless, it became increasingly obvious that being a misfit had never been a matter of choice—he was not unwilling but *unable* to fit in. As Hecht watched a friend fall apart, and the talent that he had so admired drain away, he could not forget the young man he had once known. Bodenheim illustrated that the rebel poet and tragic outcast could be two sides of the same coin, which made him a uniquely representative and resonant symbol of the artist in Hecht's mind. He was, as Hecht said of Bruga, "a stranger to life."[54]

During the 1940s Bodenheim also gained a new respect and admiration for Judaism, and this at least brought him some consolation. In one of his letters he wrote:

> Frankly, I was never a particularly keen Jewish nationalist in the past, and the fact of my Jewish blood was a matter causing me neither shame (n)or pride—a scarcely noticed, mildly accepted equation. But now, I am beginning to realize that Jewish blood symbolizes innate challenge, defiance, plaintively beset but enormous pride, and a somber breadth of imagination. I have not rushed to the opposite extreme of sublimation. I am simply compelled to recognize the whip-scarred heritage that sets us apart from other people, the heritage we are so prone to forget when we are surrounded by a surface amiability that does not single us out.[55]

Bodenheim could not, however, see a pathway of return to a Promised Land. He was too lost in the wilderness by then. In a room off the Bowery, early on the morning of February 7, 1954, a disturbed twenty-five-year-old dishwasher named Harold Weinberg shot Bodenheim to death and fatally stabbed the poet's third wife, Ruth Fagin. Hecht announced that he was going to pay for the funeral, although it is not clear that he did. In a letter explaining the death to his young daughter, Hecht wrote, "Bogie was my friend and he lived in a sort of doll world surrounded by word-toys—and he never looked up from playing until someone came along to stab, shoot and murder him. He was a young man who lived on top of verbal steeples and walked on sidewalks not visible to other citizens. He was the only poet I ever knew who lived only in the land of poetry and recognized words as the only riches there were."[56]

PART III

THE ZIONIST
From Humanist to Public Enemy

The American press reacted with outrage to Kristallnacht, the giant German pogrom of November 1938. Nearly a thousand editorials ran in metropolitan and small-town newspapers, and firsthand accounts of the brutal violence appeared on front pages for over three weeks. But the Nazis themselves still had no plan for the Jews: their systematic extermination did not start until the invasions of Poland and the Soviet Union, and the Final Solution to the Jewish Question was still some three years away. Although Americans understood November's bloodshed as a portent of things to come, the attitude of the nation, just recovering from nearly ten years of the economic depression, was neatly summed up by the isolationist credo: *America First.*[1]

For the first time, the newspapers linked Germany's treatment of its Jewish citizens to Nazi foreign policy, with one analyst for the *Saturday Evening Post* going as far as to observe, "Hatred of the Jews is the mortar which binds together into one house all the bricks of Hitler's other hatreds." The public outcry prodded President Roosevelt to recall ambassador Hugh Robert Wilson for consultation, and the president joined the choir in expressing his shock: "I myself could scarcely believe that such things could occur in a twentieth century civilization."[2]

But as Deborah Lipstadt has observed, the press "still had difficulty grasping that one of the primary motives for *Kristallnacht* had been to destroy organized Jewish life and to make the Reich *Judenrein.*" The confiscation of Jewish valuables and property was read as a German grab for "easy loot." However, even as American attention flagged, new laws expelled Jews from schools, cabarets, theaters, sports facilities, fairs, city districts, museums, and university libraries; stripped them of their driver's licenses; and prohibited them from all health-related professions.[3]

Gallup polls and the coverage of the day reveal that Americans over-whelmingly opposed immigration by Jewish refugees. In early December 1938, *Time* deferred to the "most statesmanly Jewish pundit in the U.S.," Walter Lippmann, whose "sober and broad-gauge view of the situation" was that the admission of half a million German Jews would not solve Europe's "surplus population" problem. The Poles were already beginning to clamor for entry into the United States as well—where would it end? Lippmann offered that there was enough free space in Africa to dump Europe's excess humanity for years. The *Christian Science Monitor* urged Americans to pray for the Jews. Six months later, when first Cuba and then the United States refused to admit the roughly nine hundred refugees aboard the *St. Louis*, dooming them to return to Europe, the attitude of the press remained much the same.[4]

Thus, Americans were not altogether in the dark about what was hap-pening overseas, but the news coverage in June 1939 had an impassive tone that contrasted sharply with the sense of alarm Ben Hecht telegraphed in *A Book of Miracles*, which hit the bookstores that month. "The Little Candle" prefigured the imminent genocide, depicting the Final Solution well before that plan was unveiled to the various bodies of the Nazi bureaucracy at the Wannsee Conference of January 1942: "This great International Pogrom had taken place under the auspices of the four Nazi-fascist governments and was the flower of a long and careful series of conferences among think-ers of the countries involved. . . . The extirpating of Jews had been carefully planned." Hecht described the fanatic urgency of the killers and the zeal for efficiency—the most salient characteristics, as it would turn out, of the psychology of Wannsee.[5]

But, even more significantly, "The Little Candle" gave readers a vivid look at the horror that was at the world's doorstep, in a narrative so charged that it calls to mind the eyewitness accounts and survivor memoirs of later years: "We learned that overnight some five hundred thousand Jews had been murdered in Germany, Italy, Rumania and Poland. Another million or so had been driven into forests, deserts and mountains. Thousands lay wounded and dying everywhere. More thousands, having seen their loved ones butchered and decapitated under their eyes, had taken leave of their senses and were howling like animals behind the barbed wire of concentration camps into which they had been clubbed."[6]

That summer of 1939—at the cusp of the mechanized war that has dwarfed all others in history—is crowded with stark juxtapositions: dramatic differences, not necessarily in how the various parties saw the future, but in what they were prepared to do about it. That moment revealed both the character of Hecht's soon-to-be allies and opponents and also the ideological lines that would divide them during the war and the battle for Palestine.

Back in February, the Zionist leaders Chaim Weizmann and David Ben-Gurion discovered that they had lost all negotiating power with regard to Palestine, as Britain, girding for battle with Germany, became eager to diffuse Arab unrest throughout North Africa and the Middle East. The British effectively promised Palestine—in the eyes of the Zionists, at least—wholly to the Arabs, drawing to a close the commitments made by the Balfour Declaration, their 1917 pledge to help establish a national home for the Jews. In May, as Nazi terror engulfed Austria and Czechoslovakia, Prime Minister Neville Chamberlain's government announced the White Paper, limiting Jewish immigration to Palestine to seventy-five thousand over the next five years.[7]

"A more evil, foolish and short-sighted policy could not be imagined," Ben-Gurion railed. Weizmann, the architect of the Balfour Declaration and heretofore a devout believer in Britain's benevolence, called it a "death sentence." Now crushed and frazzled, he spoke to the Zionist congress in Geneva that August of "a darkness all around us" but still grasped for hope: "There are some things which cannot fail to pass, things without which the world cannot be imagined." Many of the delegates departed Geneva to face their deaths: less than a week afterward, Germany invaded Poland.[8]

Earlier in the decade, Ben-Gurion had talked of millions immigrating to Palestine, but he had envisioned this as taking place over fifty years. Now faced with an overwhelming catastrophe, his outlook became coldly pragmatic. He famously vowed that the Jews should fight with Great Britain in this war as if there were no White Paper and should fight the White Paper as if there were no war. But it would be inaccurate to say that, particularly in the prewar era, the Zionists devoted themselves to rescue; indeed, they focused emphatically on selectivity—importing the strongest and fittest, those who could best contribute to building a new state. "I was not well-versed on matters of saving the Jews of Nazi-occupied Europe, even though I was chairman of the Jewish Agency," he conceded years later. "The heart of my activity was enlisting Jewry in the demand to establish a Jewish state."[9]

Another contingent was far more engaged in saving the Jews through illegal immigration, and they, impressed with Hecht's columns in *PM*, would ask him in the spring of 1941 to generate publicity for their cause. Peter Bergson and his colleagues represented the Revisionist faction of Zionists, whom Ben-Gurion and the mainstream denounced as fascists. In 1936 Revisionism's founder, Vladimir Jabotinsky, had proposed evacuating a million and a half Jews to Palestine, and a year later the Irgun Zvai Leumi, or National Military Organization, had dispatched Yitshaq Ben-Ami to coordinate illegal immigration from Vienna, Poland, and Prague. Known in Hebrew as Aliyah Bet or Ha'apalah, these Irgun operations from 1937 to 1940 saved somewhere between nine thousand and twenty-four thousand lives. In his memoir, Ben-Ami asserted that the World Zionist Organization, "though it had worldwide Jewish financial resources at its disposal," managed to smuggle only 6,200 Jews to Palestine between 1934 and mid-1940, while the Irgunists moved around twice that many. Although these specific figures are difficult to verify, the two movements made no secret of their respective philosophies; the mainstream Zionists dismissed Jabotinsky's schemes of evacuation as fantasy and, owing to both their ideology and their lack of preparation for the extraordinary catastrophe that was about to occur, pursued immigration in this era with nowhere near as much urgency.[10]

The number of lives saved through the smuggling was minuscule compared to the six million that would be lost, and in any case, the British merely deducted the estimated number of these refugees from the White Paper limit of seventy-five thousand. But the story of illegal immigration nevertheless points to a perverse logic at work during those years. The official Nazi policy was to expel the Jews from Europe, so the allegedly fascist Jewish Irgunists coordinated their rescue efforts with none other than Adolf Eichmann, assigned by the SS (Schutzstaffel) to establish the Central Office for Jewish Emigration in 1938. The Revisionists also developed a close partnership with the anti-Semitic government of Poland, likewise eager to expel its Jewish population, the largest of Europe. According to Ben-Ami, the Irgun's efforts to purchase ships that could have transported up to ten thousand refugees per voyage were thwarted by Weizmann, who in the spring of 1939 advised Robert Rothschild and other Jewish leaders of France, "When you soup with the devil, you've got to have a long spoon."[11]

In America, Zionist and non-Zionist Jewish leaders advised their communities to close their doors to the Revisionists. In February 1940 United Palestine Appeal's executive director, Henry Montor, circulated a letter that stated, "Selectivity is an inescapable factor in dealing with the problem of immigration. . . . Many of those who have been brought into Palestine by the Revisionists have been prostitutes and criminals." Echoing another common complaint, that Ben-Ami and company were cruelly sending the refugees to sea in squalid "death ships," the Emergency Committee for Zionist Affairs, chaired by Rabbi Stephen Wise, issued a twenty-six-page booklet that declared, "The conditions on their boats are revolting. . . . They resemble concentration camps in that passengers are hung to the mast and were refused food in retaliation for criticism or complaints."[12]

It might seem obvious just who distinguished themselves as heroes and who did not during that critical period, but this is hardly the whole story, and the truth is not so simple. The finger-pointing over what could or should have been done to save Europe's Jews has carried on for over seventy years and has significantly shaped the debates over Israel today. In the midst of one particularly venomous round of arguments in the pages of *Commentary* during the early 1980s that involved former partisans and American Jewish scholars, Irving Howe observed, "How various schools of thought responded to the Holocaust and the events leading to it is a question both complex and painful. It needs to be treated sensitively, without polemical coarseness. There are enough failures and mistakes to go around."[13] Indeed, polemics have long distracted from a more holistic assessment of both the wisdom and the errors of each side. If anything is to be learned from this pivotal moment of history, it is necessary to acknowledge that no group had a monopoly on truth and sagacity.

Yitshaq Ben-Ami's son has objected to the frequent denunciations of his father, Hecht, and their colleagues as fascists, right-wing extremists, and terrorists. "I knew these men and women," said Jeremy Ben-Ami, who served as a senior adviser to the Clinton administration and founded J Street, the leading liberal lobby group on American policy toward Israel. "And I read up on what they did in the 1930s and 1940s. Those descriptions were not even close to the truth." He noted that the letterhead of the group's advertisements in American newspapers "reads like a Who's Who of liberal intellectuals and activists." Growing up during the 1970s and 1980s, Jeremy Ben-Ami listened to the ex-Revisionists discuss Israel-related controversies in his living room and found that "some of them leaned to the right, some leaned to the left, and others came down the middle."[14]

Here was another tribe for Hecht, like the circus performers of his childhood, like the Chicago journalists and artists, like the gangsters, like the Don Juans of New York and Hollywood. And like the others, this tribe had a code. But Revisionism, the cause Hecht took up in the 1940s that would change his life and legacy, is challenging to evaluate for several reasons, not the least of which is that, like other movements in Jewish history, it splintered into a multitude of competing factions. Although the disciples Jabotinsky groomed in his youth group Betar adored their leader, fundamental ideological disagreements developed between the "father" and his more radical and militaristic "children." The Irgun itself was an independently formed and operated fighting organization, and disputes over both its direction and its leadership arose between Peter Bergson, who led the six-member delegation to America that partnered with Hecht, and Menachem Begin, who in 1944 became the commander on the ground in Palestine. The Irgun in turn was less radical than the Stern Gang, which, under the leadership of Avraham Stern, split off from the Irgun at the start of the war, when Irgun commander David Raziel called for a unilateral halt to all attacks against Britain.

There were also tensions within the respective groups—between Bergson and Hecht, for example—as well as within the breasts of each of the leaders themselves. Jabotinsky, like Zionism's founder Theodor Herzl, was a humanist whose beliefs were deeply rooted in liberalism and rationalism, yet there are reasons why several of his followers drifted toward fascism. His dream of a Jewish homeland was not in any way eschatological but had developed out of a reasoned analysis of anti-Semitism as a social, political, and economic phenomenon. He was committed to establishing a state that occupied both sides of the Jordan River but emphasized that it could be a nation only when it became populated by a Jewish majority and could thus function as a democracy. "I am just the opposite [of a fascist]: an instinctive hater of all kinds of *Polizei Staat* utterly skeptical of the value of discipline and power and punishment, etc. down to a planned economy," he wrote. At a speech to the Society of History Lovers in Warsaw, he said, "I belong to that old fashioned school who still believe that in every civilized community there must be some respect of man for man, class for class, and race for race."[15]

But as Walter Laqueur has observed,

> The fact that Jews were often the victims of fascism did not necessarily make them immune to fascist influences. Revisionism believed in strength—in a sinful world only the strong were likely to get what was due to them. This manifested itself in the ideology of *Betar*, particularly in the cult of militarism with all its antics—the parades, the stress on uniforms, banners, insignia. To a certain extent all political movements of the 1920s and 1930s were influenced by the *Zeitgeist*. This all too often led to moral relativism, to deriding democracy, to aggression and brutality, and belief in an omnipotent, omniscient leader.

Indeed, by the time Hecht came into contact with Revisionism, it was a broad umbrella covering a variety of individuals and groups, many of whom held reactionary beliefs wholly inconsistent with those of the movement's liberal, pro-British founder.[16]

As a propagandist during the 1940s, Hecht had started out appealing to Americans to buy war bonds, fight for freedom, and support Jewish rescue, but by 1947 he was generating agitprop on behalf of renegades whom he proudly acknowledged to be terrorists and gangsters. He had started as a partner of Bergson, the champion of the great and lonely humanitarian cause of rescue, but ended up touring the country with the mobster Mickey Cohen to raise money and arms for Begin, the Irgun leader described by a British police chief as "a ruthless thug who made Al Capone look like a novice."[17] If one takes into account Hecht's previous odyssey from the self-hatred of *A Jew in Love* to the self-pride of "My Tribe Is Called Israel," his dramatic reversals might even seem a mark of consistency. Alternatively, such apparent contradictions may not be contradictions at all but rather different expressions of a Romanticist philosophy that never changed.

Considered within the context of the competing ideologies that emerged in response to the age of Enlightenment, much of what seems elusive, inconsistent, and even bizarre about both Hecht and the Revisionists begins to make sense. As Jeremy Ben-Ami noted, the narrow right-versus-left terms of today's politics are unhelpful for analysis, because they frame contemporary debates and not the more fundamental disputes of the 1930s and 1940s and afterward.[18] In *The Years of Extermination: Nazi Germany and the Jews, 1939–1945*, Saul Friedländer argues:

> The history we are dealing with is an integral part of the "age of ideology" and, more precisely and decisively, of its late phase: the crisis of liberalism in continental Europe. Between the late nineteenth century and the end of World War II, liberal society was attacked from the left by revolutionary socialism . . . and by a revolutionary right that, on the morrow of World War I, turned into fascism in Italy and elsewhere, and into Nazism in Germany. Throughout Europe the Jews were identified with liberalism and often with the revolutionary brand of socialism. In that sense antiliberal and antisocialist (or anticommunism) ideologies, those of the revolutionary right in all its guises, targeted the Jews as representatives of the worldviews they fought.[19]

It would not be a major stretch to argue that "the crisis of liberalism" precipitated its collapse: while the great liberal powers, America and Britain, emerged victorious, their prosecution of the war—from the White Paper to carpet bombings and Hiroshima—was hardly a resounding affirmation of liberal principles. Moreover, within the new era of the Cold War, the very character of these nations changed forever.

Zionism was simultaneously an outgrowth of the Enlightenment and an indictment of its failures. Herzl and Jabotinsky had both been journalists, fiction writers, and dramatists like Hecht, the type of modern, cosmopolitan Europeans who had proliferated during the nineteenth century thanks to the emancipation of Jewry. They both envisioned a state that would serve as a model of their liberal ideals, and their religion-like devotion to this secular dream was itself characteristic of the post-Enlightenment age. At the same time, the whole idea of Zionism proceeded from an acknowledgment that reason had not proven to be an antidote to humans' primordial prejudices and hatreds. To the contrary, rationalism had made anti-Semitism all the more virulent: Darwinism led to race hatred based on beliefs about superior and inferior bloodlines, while the Final Solution would represent a nightmare scenario of modern technocracy and technology, in all of their awesome efficiency and force, bent to the will of humankind's barbarity.[20]

At the Tenth Zionist Congress, held in 1911, Max Nordau had emphasized the darker side of Zionism, the side that maintained a deep skepticism of the Enlightenment, when he had predicted that millions of European Jews would one day be massacred as a result of emerging political forces. In 1920, while pogroms were slaughtering thousands along the Polish-Russian border, he had first proposed the idea of a mass evacuation of 600,000 Jews within a few months, anticipating that as many as a third would be lost in such a desperate gambit but that many more would be saved. Jabotinsky's Revisionist movement took up Nordau's *catastrophic Zionism*, while the Weizmann–Ben-Gurion mainstream, which envisioned a Jewish utopia, represented Zionism's liberal idealism.[21]

In 1952 the great twentieth-century philosopher and political theorist Isaiah Berlin delivered talks about six thinkers who had been prominent just before and after the French Revolution, whose ideas were "the absolute substance" of the liberal and antidemocratic talk of Berlin's own day. He argued that despite some differences dividing eighteenth-century philosophers, they held shared beliefs that "men were by nature, if not good, at any rate not bad, potentially benevolent, and that each man was the best expert on his own interests and his own values." The prototypical reactionary, Joseph de Maistre, in contrast, had been forever scarred by witnessing the bloody spectacle of the Reign of Terror, which he blamed on the dangerous delusions of his day. Determined to destroy these beliefs, Maistre "defended the importance of mystery, of darkness, almost of ignorance, and above all irrationality, as the basis of social and political life." As for the goodness of humankind, Maistre wrote:

> There are insects of prey, reptiles of prey, birds of prey, fishes of prey, quadrupeds of prey. There is no instant of time when one creature is not being devoured by another. Over all these . . . man is placed, and his destructive hand spares nothing that lives.
>
> Man kills to obtain food and kills to clothe himself. He kills to adorn himself and kills in order to attack. He kills in order to defend himself and he kills in order to instruct himself. He kills to amuse himself and he kills in order to kill. Proud and terrible king, he wants everything and nothing can resist him.[22]

Arguably the grim, antiliberal view of humankind that the Revisionists had in common with Hecht gave them a unique perspective, a different way of seeing the world that enabled many of them to understand what was happening in Germany, to see the future of Nazism even before the Nazis could see it themselves, and to prepare, however inadequately, for the impending catastrophe. This might explain not only why, at one stage of events, the Revisionists seem to have possessed much greater clarity about the future—almost a kind of second sight—and perhaps to have held the moral high ground, but also why, at a later stage, in choosing armed struggle over diplomacy to achieve their ends, they have appeared to many (at the time and ever since) as amoral thugs.

In 1937 Jabotinsky, calling for evacuation, had begged his fellow Jews to heed his warnings. "Jabotinsky," Hecht later wrote, "soldier, hero, and prophet of Jewish doom, had offended Zionism for some years now by riding, riding, like some despairing Paul Revere, through Eastern Europe, warning the poverty laden Jewish communities that they were squatting on a dynamite dump." Jabotinsky had likened European Jews to villagers at the foot of a volcano that was about to erupt. He wrote to the editors of a Jewish newspaper in Warsaw, "I regret that you do not see the dark clouds that are gathering over the heads of the Jews of Europe." The Bergsonite Samuel Merlin explained to Hecht that most Jews had refused to listen because they, like most people in general, honored respectability more than genius, courage, or anything else. Instead, they sided with Weizmann, the eminent Zionist leader who focused on selectivity.[23]

Merlin later wrote that the Jews had suffered from "three fatal weaknesses": "they lacked to an astounding degree a sense and an understanding of the political and social realities around them"; they possessed a misguided faith in "patience to weather the storm"; and they placed too much trust in established leaders, like Roosevelt and Churchill. On this last point, Zionist historians who were not Bergson partisans have agreed: Melvin Urofsky and Henry Feingold both argued that Stephen Wise and other like-minded Jews "labored under the terrible misapprehension . . . that somewhere in the world . . . existed 'a spirit of civilization whose moral concern could be mobilized to save the Jews.'"[24]

Yet there is troubling evidence that everybody had at least some inkling of what was about to happen, including American Jews and even the American public. But then why *would* Weizmann, the liberal idealist, coldly write off some four million Jews as early as 1936 and leave James G.

McDonald, the future U.S. ambassador to Israel, "appalled but not surprised at his ruthless analysis," while the ostensibly cynical Revisionists desperately pursued rescue? Here again, the Bergsonites had an explanation. According to Alexander Rafaeli, the Jews shared with their leadership a "ghetto mentality," a resigned acceptance of their own impotence and victimhood. As he explained in his memoir, "in the U.S. we fought against narrow minds, who saw the Jews as pariahs and small traders incapable of any kind of heroic effort, but the problem was that the Jews themselves felt inferior. They were scared to demand help for European Jews and were frightened to fight against anti-Semitic politicians, primarily in the State Department."[25]

In European culture, various currents of the nineteenth-century backlash against the Enlightenment had revived the medieval mythic ideals of strength, gallantry, and valor. Within Zionism, Nordau had introduced "muscular Judaism" as early as the Second Congress of 1898, an idea that resonated because it supported the goal of Jewish nationalism as a rebirth of body and spirit. The *Muskeljuden* ("muscle Jews"), or the "new Jew," broke from the anti-Semitic stereotype of the scrawny, weak, and inferior Jew. Jabotinsky had embraced this as a guiding principle ever since World War I, when he sought to form a Jewish Legion that would fight together with the Allies. He was described by Weizmann as a man whose honorable qualities were "overlaid with a certain touch of the rather theatrically chivalresque, a certain queer and irrelevant knightliness, which was not at all Jewish."[26]

Hecht's own views had a distinctly American cast, having developed out of his experience as a Chicago crime reporter. He became enamored with the "tough Jew" and thus was rather pleased when he and the Irgun were branded as gangsters. He saw all politics as criminal—the events of the war only deepened this conviction—but the stakes had become too high for him to remain the "hear-all, see-all, do-nothing Newspaper Ned" who had once stood by and watched German troops gun down two thousand people at Moabit Prison. If his efforts to fund and arm the Jews of Palestine required a partnership with a real Jewish gangster like Cohen, that seemed to him only fitting.

The Jews of Europe and Palestine had long found themselves caught in a predicament similar to that of the tragic protagonists of Hecht's *Notorious* (1946) and *Kiss of Death* (1947), which helped usher in the postwar genre of film noir. Cast as criminals and trapped in a shadowy underworld, surrounded by predators in a dark jungle in which no one was who they appeared to be and everybody wanted to do them in, they needed to make deals to survive. Since the days when Herzl had negotiated with the minister of the interior Vyacheslav von Plehve, the arch-butcher of czarist Russia, Zionist leaders had often felt forced into devil's bargains. Weizmann, in contrast, had always objected in principle: "Antisemites are incapable of aiding in the creation of a Jewish homeland; their attitude forbids them to do anything that might really help the Jewish people. Pogroms, yes; repressions, yes; emigration, yes; but nothing that might be conducive to the freedom of the Jews."[27]

For Hecht, engagement in politics was itself a devil's bargain. He took the attitude that all cooperation, with President Roosevelt or the British, for example, depended not on genuine trust and shared values but on mutual interests. As the hoodlum Nick Bianco says when he agrees to squeal for the assistant district attorney in *Kiss of Death*, "Your side of the fence is just as dirty as mine." The public itself was no more trustworthy: in a world in which rational discussion was impossible, benevolent manipulation of the masses was the next-best thing in Hecht's view—the same "science of democracy" strategy, incidentally, that the U.S. Office of War Information adopted from Harold Lasswell and his colleagues in academia. As for the ethics of war, it is true that Palestine often erupted into bloody mayhem and that the Jewish community, known as the Yishuv, had to fight for its life. But while Hecht, like Begin, talked a good deal about scruples and careful moral choices, the actual record of the Irgun tells a different story. Cohen would one day recall that he became "so goddamn excited" when he discovered that "these guys actually fight like racket guys."[28]

Hecht's rhetoric about politics is framed in language about law and authority that seems to draw directly from his experience with crime in Chicago. In *A Child of the Century*, he introduces his own 110-page account of his career with the Bergson Group with an analogy to the criminal court system. He notes that in many of the trials he observed, the accused would begin with the same answer: "Well, your honor, I was just walking down the street, minding my own business, when . . ." Hecht then continues, "It is as a Jewish John Doe under indictment as one of the Palestinian 'Terrorists' who proudly called themselves the *Irgun Zvai Leumi*, that I now speak up. All other witnesses have had their say—the Jewish Zionists, Hebrew statesmen, authors and journalists and the British Empire. I offer my evidence neither as Jew nor propagandist but as an honest writer who was walking down the street one day when he bumped into history."[29]

CHAPTER 9

Jewish Knights: The Bergson Group

At the end of 1935 a group of Zionist activists, members of Beitar, the Revisionist youth movement, traveled to various Jewish communities in Europe to raise money and solicit support. Nothing about this was extraordinary; Zionist activists often took part in such missions. . . . But something about that particular group of Beitarists was unique, for it left a great impression on the different Jewish communities it visited: Its members rode in on motorcycles and dressed in leather jackets.

—Eran Kaplan, *The Jewish Radical Right: Revisionist Zionism and Its Ideological Legacy*[1]

Hecht disliked causes and had scant interest in Peter Bergson's story of a radical Zionist offshoot when the two first met in 1941. Inspired by Hecht's "These Were Once Conquerors" column, the blonde, mustachioed twenty-five-year-old with a voice that tended to squeak when excited had telegrammed Hecht on August 28: "Thanks for giving in Sundays PM magnificent expression to the pride and spiritual heroism which for centuries accumulated in the soul of the genuine and conscious Jew. By creation of a Jewish army we intend to transform this heroic spirit into heroic deeds." Intrigued, Hecht agreed to meet Bergson at the 21 Club in midtown Manhattan, but by the time they were ordering a third round of drinks, he was running out of patience with talk of a leader named Jabotinsky and dreams of a Jewish Renaissance. He was outraged and disgusted by the failure of American Jews to speak out against the massacre in Europe, he explained, but had no interest in Zionist fund-raising. His companion, however, just stared back with a knowing smile—as if Bergson was privy to something that Hecht didn't know about himself.[2]

Over the next few weeks, Hecht became friends with the six delegates of the Irgun who would become known as the Bergson Group. Since the arrival of the first two, Yitshaq Ben-Ami and Arieh Ben-Eliezer, by July 1939, their efforts to raise money for smuggling Jews out of Europe had been a crash course in American culture and the divisive politics of American Jewry. At first they had spoken only basic English—Ben-Eliezer and Alexander Rafaeli could speak none at all. From the start they had a few dedicated supporters, among them the journalists John and Frances Gunther, the book and magazine publisher William Ziff, and the editor and author Harry Louis Selden. But as they traveled to small meetings around the country, the American Zionist organizations sabotaged their efforts at every turn. Rabbi Stephen Wise and his colleagues, who since the early 1930s had labeled Revisionism "a species of fascism," now denounced their fund-raising as illegitimate and unscrupulous. "My pessimism told me that we had already lost the battle," recalled Yitshaq Ben-Ami. "Yet somehow I continued to function, performing to the best of my ability, hoping against hope that some Jews could still be saved. Our small remaining group in the United States did its utmost to raise funds for *Ha'apalah*, but we always came up short."[3]

The delegation would soon find itself the Irgun's "cutoff battalion." Bergson had been the last to arrive in America, disembarking from the SS *Scythia* in July 1940, just three months after Vladimir Jabotinsky, who had come to campaign for a Jewish army. Then in August Jabotinsky unexpectedly died, which left Bergson in sole command of an uncertain mission in a vast, unfamiliar country. Since the outbreak of war, illegal immigration to Palestine had grown increasingly impossible, and with the death of Irgun commander David Raziel in May 1941, their parent organization in Palestine fell into disarray. Hecht recalled in *A Child of the Century* that when he started meeting with the Bergsonites, who were by now shifting to focus on Jabotinsky's plan for a Jewish army, they lacked money for food and were quietly going hungry.[4]

Hecht found little poetry in their speech and in their clunky name for themselves, the Committee for a Jewish Army of Stateless and Palestinian Jews. But there was eloquence in their silent determination. "They sat solemn with energies, like a group of knights dedicated to the rescue of a maiden in distress," he wrote. "Their sense of reality was as deep as their idealism." He told his new friends that, Zionist politics aside, their idea of a Jewish army appealed to him: "I'd like to help do something to bring respect back to the name of the Jew."[5]

But Hecht insisted they make plain that their army was not intended for American Jews; otherwise, their campaign would not only call into question Jewish patriotism but also play into the hands of the isolationists, who were warning Americans against allowing themselves to be dragged into "a Jewish war."[6] As someone already volunteering with the interventionist Fight for Freedom Committee, Hecht saw himself as a Jew but also, by necessity, as an American committed to integration: the specific circumstances of the moment highlighted the need for unity, as well as the dangers of stoking racial divisiveness. Thus, a paradox emerged that was to characterize Hecht's propaganda throughout the war years: the particularism of his newly discovered Jewish pride pushed beyond the boundaries of what American Jews of the era considered acceptable, and yet he himself also appreciated the need for inclusion. That many Americans found the formulation of ethnicity in his propaganda acceptable is evident both in the turnout for the Bergson Group's events and in Hecht's production of remarkably similar content for the U.S. government, right through to the end of the war.

In a radio address during that summer of 1941, the isolationist North Dakota senator Gerald Nye charged that Hollywood was infested with a dangerous "fifth column" of warmongering foreigners. On September 9 Nye appeared as the first witness when a Senate subcommittee of the Interstate Commerce Committee opened hearings on Moving Picture Screen and Radio Propaganda, setting out to investigate foreign infiltration of the mass media industry, just as the House Un-American Activities Committee would probe communist infiltration soon after the war. "Many people seem to assume that our Jewish citizenry would willingly have our country and its sons taken into this foreign war," Nye said at the start of his testimony. "If anti-Semitism exists in America, the Jews have themselves to blame."[7]

The interventionists responded a month later with *Fun to Be Free*, a pageant by Hecht and Charles MacArthur at Madison Square Garden that called for the nation to unite in defeating a threat to the principles that all Americans believed in. On October 5 about seventeen thousand participated in the event, just over half as many as had attended the previous spring's isolationist rally sponsored by the America First Committee, featuring Charles Lindbergh and socialist leader Norman Thomas. *Fun to Be Free*'s chairman was Wendell Willkie, the former Republican presidential candidate who had opposed Roosevelt on a noninterventionist ticket and, to the shock of the isolationists, had turned coat to serve as special counsel defending the movie industry in the Nye hearings. Willkie referred to the recent speeches of Lindbergh, Nye, and others, declaring, "Our opponents were resorting to one of the basest arguments, to divide the United States on the basis of race and religion." In the program guide, journalist Dorothy Thompson denounced the Senate hearings as a Star Chamber inquisition, "the greatest Nazi propaganda stunt ever pulled off in the United States," intended to intimidate Americans into silence. "This fight, therefore, is our fight," she continued. "It is the fight of every human being who believes in freedom of speech, habeas corpus, intellectual integrity, and freedom from intimidation."[8]

Hecht, MacArthur, and their longtime producer Billy Rose were responsible for the "fun" of *Fun to Be Free*, the patriotic ballyhoo, and thanks in large part to producer Rose, there was no shortage of it. "I really fear for the fate of the country . . . ," Hecht wrote his wife days before the performance, "because we may hurl an awful pail of lard at this record-smashing pageant gate."[9] The African American performer Bill "Bojangles" Robinson tap-danced on Hitler's coffin in his flashy gold lamé pants and ermine, Eddie Cantor appeared in a hoopskirt, and Ethel Merman unsuccessfully tried to pick up a five-year-old boy in a sailor suit to help her sing into the microphones, "What Say, Let's Be Buddies." Other stars included Jack Benny, Betty Grable, and George Jessel.

"In addition to comedy, terror and oratory, the rally had considerable emotional appeal," enthused a *New York Times* reviewer. Following the variety show came the pageant written by Hecht and MacArthur, which celebrated the contributions to freedom and the nation made by great Americans from Patrick Henry to Franklin D. Roosevelt. The speeches then faded into a wail of air-raid sirens, as radio announcers barked reports of enemy planes over Laredo, Texas; Los Angeles; and San Francisco, while an air armada approached New York. The lights went dark, searchlights crisscrossed the balconies and vast ceiling, and thousands of parachutists dropped from above, adding the "terror" portion of the evening. The invaders, however, turned out to be tiny cardboard figures. "It is fun to be free," the *New York Herald* proclaimed. "[The show] expresses the native gusto of American life and the characters epitomize America's love of freedom and disposition to fight if necessary."[10]

After the attack on Pearl Harbor two months later, Hecht hailed America's entry into the war with a poem published in *PM*, "Uncle Sam Stands Up." Days later he left for Washington, D.C., where all the officials "cling to me like I was a literary Joe Louis," he wrote Rose. "My reputation as sort of an instantaneous writer seems larger in Washington than it was even in Hollywood." Over the next several years, he would produce propaganda for the Office of War Information, Treasury Bond drives, the Hollywood Victory Committee, and the State Department. He wrote one pageant for the Red Cross, and another as a salute to American labor; patriotic speeches for celebrities like Paul Muni and Frank Sinatra; a comedy for GIs to perform; and a poem and radio play for the war bond campaigns. He also recruited fellow writers, including Clifford Odets, Lillian Helman, Maxwell Anderson, and George S. Kaufman, to write short training films for the public, like one on how to respond to an air raid.[11]

Hecht's newfound patriotism represented a shift in his worldview but not a fundamental change. "I had been no partisan of democracy in my earlier years," he confessed in *A Child of the Century.* "Its sins had seemed to me more prominent than its virtues. But now that it was the potential enemy of the German Police State I was its uncarping disciple. Thus, oddly, in addition to becoming a Jew in 1939 I became also an American—and remained one." He may have remained an American, but he also remained, at heart, a Romanticist. His American and Jewish propaganda shared a fascination with chivalry and its code—with the warrior's oath to protect the innocent and defenseless and a dedication to valor, gallantry, and honor. As Gilad Troy describes it, Hecht's patriotic propaganda was "a curious amalgam of sentiment and cynicism, myth and mysticism."[12]

A Tribute to Gallantry, for example, paid homage both to the civilian victims of the Axis and to the Allied soldiers willing to make the ultimate sacrifice to protect them. In the fall of 1943, performances of this macabre pageant launched the New York War Fund Drive at the Waldorf-Astoria Hotel and at the Madison Square Garden, where it featured a cast of three hundred. The play is set at a gate in "a corner of the sky," where a gatekeeper beckons the dead. They gather and tell their tales—children bombed while playing cards in the British town of Coventry, others while celebrating a confirmation in Luxembourg, dancing in Warsaw, or attending a wedding party in Rotterdam. Each is at one moment full of life and motion, and in the next, with a sudden crash of the orchestra, frozen in a tableau of death.

All have been bombed, shot, or starved: "the killing off of innocent populations has been the new military weapon introduced into war by the Germans and the Japanese," explains a narrator. An old Jew carrying a broken Torah approaches with a child who clings to his coat. They are among three million, they tell the gatekeeper, slaughtered in lime kilns, in gas chambers, and by guns. These victims are joined by Allied soldiers fallen in battle. The gatekeeper promises that once they pass through the gate, all their suffering will be forgotten, but the people quietly insist that they will remain and wait, and the soldiers stand with them. By now a great tide of the dead has formed, and the gatekeeper turns to the audience: "They ask for the sound of victory. They ask that you pour out your energy and your gold, your talent and your valor—as they have poured out their blood."[13]

Miracle on the Pullman, a radio play broadcast over the Blue Network on November 19, 1944, honored the grace of fallen heroes. It begins with "the human hodge-podge that makes up the U.S.A. . . . taking a ride for itself"—heading out on a train from Grand Central Station. The passengers order pillows and highballs, argue politics and play rummy, losing themselves in the petty preoccupations of their comfortable existence. Ordinary mortals, they cannot hear in the high-pitched train whistle the voice of an angel, nor that of another accompanying them: the ghost of a GI named Joe, taking the journey that he had dreamed would one day bring him home. While the passengers snooze and grumble, Joe stares out in wonder at the Hudson River and the land he left behind. Then he begins to weep. They won't remember us, he says. The angel-whistle tries to reassure him: "You're crazy, Joe, to talk like that." No, Joe says, just listen to them. "They don't even look out of the window at the towns goin' by. They don't give a whoop for anything but themselves. Just sit around, very bored with the war, and squawk about their dime a dozen troubles, and how business ain't so good." What do they care about the soldiers, right now in the dark, being blown apart or burned to cinders on the battlefield? "They're dead from the neck up. And they didn't die in any tanks or bombers. They died from sitting in easy chairs."

Then a pretty young woman hears the mournful sound of the whistle and says, "It's funny. I keep thinking about—over there." Her mind is on someone she said goodbye to, but not just on him. She is thinking about all of them, fighting in the war. A farmer says, pardon me, do you know what today is? Why, it's "the day they're opening the War Loan Drive, Number Six. The government's goin' to raise money again—to fight with!" Soon the whole carload is holding an impromptu rally. Urged to give a speech, the young woman says that as she looks out the window, she sees the face of a soldier she knew, and if they will all look out their windows, they will see faces, too. A rummy player volunteers ten grand, and as others up the ante, the sum jumps from one million to two million. Joe stares, slack-jawed. "I told you they'd hear you, Joe," says the whistle. "I told you."[14]

For its part, the Bergson Group's propaganda for a Jewish army, and indeed the Revisionist idealization of the *muskeljuden*, drew from the rich lore of Hebrew history and from recent legend as well. Jabotinsky's great literary effort had been his 1926 novel *Samson*, a somewhat-radical retelling of Samson and Delilah in which Samson is depicted as a political rather than a religious figure. The Revisionists summoned the names of the great ancient rebels: the fierce army of Simon Bar-Kochba that had fought the Roman Empire; and the Maccabees, whose defeat of the Seleucid king Antiochus is celebrated each year at Chanukah. And they drew on the heroes from the pioneering days of Palestine: Yosef Trumpeldor, a leader of the Jewish Legion who died defending the Tel Hai settlement, and Yehiel Michal Halperin, "the Jewish Don Quixote" famous for stepping into the lion's cage at the Jaffa Circus to disprove Arab claims of Jewish cowardice.[15]

The name of Jabotinsky's youth group, *Betar*, also drew on these warrior myths: it was both an acronym for "*brit* Yosef Trumpeldor" (*brit* is Hebrew for "covenant with" or "alliance with") and the name of the city that was the stronghold of the Bar-Kochba revolt. One of the basic principles of the youth group was *Hadar*, a Hebrew word that, as Jabotinsky explained, has no direct translation into other languages but embodies several different concepts: outward beauty, dignity, self-esteem, politeness, faithfulness. While Betar's critics often associated its emphasis on discipline and military strength with fascism, Jabotinsky pointed to progressive, democratic leaders like Giuseppe Garibaldi and Abraham Lincoln.[16]

Hecht translated the case for a Jewish army to his fellow Americans in "Champion in Chains," an October 1942 article for *Esquire*. He explained that he was like many American Jews of late, "a little startled to find themselves Jewish." One day they had felt themselves fully integrated, far away from their Semitism, and then it was as if they had woken up the next morning to a new discovery. It had not happened to everyone at the same time, Hecht explained, and for some of the most comfortable and respectable, it still had not happened at all. But now "the red glare of a new era of Jew persecution" greeted them and returned them to their mostly forgotten identity. Hitler, "for reasons too mystic to determine," had been busy at work for years restoring the consciousness of Judaism. Yet "the discovery that I was a Jew did not set me to lighting any Friday night candles nor did it alter by a phrase any of my attitudes toward life," he wrote. "These are American attitudes, born in America, nurtured in American schools and developed through service in American journalism, literature, drama and the movies."[17]

As he had in *A Book of Miracles* and his columns for *PM*, he expressed the helplessness, rage, and shame felt by American Jews as they witnessed the rise of Nazism. Every time they saw the word *Jew* in the black ink of newsprint, they were reminded of the nightmare into which the world had plunged. "That nightmare has been a butchering block for millions of defenseless people," he wrote. "It has also been a miasma in which the faraway American Jew, however 'emancipated,' however 'assimilated,' has found it hard to breathe." Yet now there was an answer to that nightmare: "He stands in Palestine—the warrior Jew—the descendant of Saul's ancient legions. You've seen him in the prize rings of America often—Benny Leonard, Sid Terris, Rube Goldstein, Battling Levinsky, Barney Ross, Maxie Baer and a horde of others—pugs all, with good jaws, strong hearts and brave fists."[18]

There were some 200,000 Jews of military age in the Middle East who were eager to serve, Hecht continued, and if anyone doubted their courage or abilities, they could look to the record of the November 1941 siege of Tobruk.[19] Thousands of Palestinian Jews had fought along with the British to defend that strategic town and its harbor. Indeed, when the garrison commander had called for volunteers to carry supplies along a heavily bombarded road, so many had come forward and run the gauntlet with such grit that their fellow Irish, Scotch, and Australian soldiers gratefully dubbed it "The Road to Zion." Still, Hecht noted, although the Scotts were permitted to wear their kilts, the Irish their shamrocks and the Australians their native hats, the Jews were forbidden to wear the Star of David.[20]

Finally, there was the heroic example of David Raziel. In May 1941 the British had landed the Irgun commander and a squad of his fighters at Habbaniya, an airfield near Baghdad. According to Nicholas Hammond, a British university lecturer sent to Palestine to train Jewish fighters in explosives, their mission had been to penetrate the capital disguised as Arabs, blow up oil installations, and perhaps even kidnap the Axis-allied Palestinian nationalist leader, the Grand Mufti Haj Amin al-Husseini. On their way to Baghdad, however, Raziel had been killed by a bomb from a lone German aircraft, and the mission was scrapped. Hecht, perhaps relying on an account by Bergson supporter Pierre Van Paassen, reported that before Raziel was killed, his team had accomplished its mission of ambushing 150 German mechanics en route to blow up oil wells that would otherwise go to the British. "There are 200,000 Raziels in Zion today," Hecht declared.[21]

CHAPTER 10

"Champion in Chains"

If you think that there is no other way than for Mr. Begin to offer you weapons—you are committing suicide. If there is no longer conscience in the world—there is the Vistula River.
—Vladimir Jabotinsky, debating Menachem Begin, September 1938[1]

For the land and freedom and government are not given to the weak and are not ever purchased—they have always been conquered by bloodshed and the sword.
—Avraham Stern, "Principles and Conclusions," July 29, 1939[2]

Meyer Levin, a Chicago novelist and onetime feature writer for the *Daily News* who had gotten his start with an endorsement from Hecht, was in New York making documentary films for the Office of War Information when he first met Peter Bergson. At the behest of a colleague, he joined the young Palestinian for lunch and then agreed to attend a small meeting at the apartment of Frances Gunther, an author and one of the original Bergson Group advocates, where supporters were arranging a pageant for Madison Square Garden. Levin had a different perspective from most of Bergson's new American friends; during the 1920s he had lived in Palestine on a kibbutz, where he had become a deeply committed Labor Zionist. As he recalled acidly in his 1950 memoir *In Search*, he did not like what he now saw:

Bergson proved to be a tense little man, almost excessively well controlled. As the luncheon wore on, I began to realize I was in the company of a fanatic.

I couldn't put my finger on anything wrong. His plan for a Jewish army was sound, I felt.

. . . But as Bergson suggested future plans, I realized that he pursued the technique of drawing people in through a project on which there could be little disagreement, and then pushing them into more doubtful territory. His further plans included a Jewish state embracing Trans-Jordan, to be acquired by force if necessary, and there were undertones, suggestions of methods that I felt inadmissible.[3]

Levin could not have known this, but Bergson's edgy demeanor, like the squeak that sometimes crept into his voice, was a sign that for him the bloodletting in Europe was intensely personal. Bergson had been born Hillel Kook in Lithuania in 1915, to a line of eminent scholars and leading rabbis. While his mother was still pregnant with him, his family was among the hundreds of thousands forced to flee when the Russians ordered their expulsion. The Kooks attempted to find shelter in Ukraine but arrived just in time for one of the bloodiest waves of pogroms in history, when four rival armies traversed the battle-scarred landscape, all of them targeting the Jews. During one raid when Bergson was still a small child, his brother was shot multiple times in the chest while he and his mother and sisters hid in a courtyard cellar. "When they emerged, they found Nahum at death's door and the streets of the town literally flowing with blood," explained biographer Louis Rapoport. "The experience was indelibly branded into [Bergson's] soul: His earliest memories were of Jews being shot, or cut down with swords or axes."[4]

As Hecht observed, the Bergson Group believed in action, not words, but therein lay the paradox of their U.S. mission. The ideological offspring of Vladimir Jabotinsky, inured to the violence of Palestine and Europe, they represented a new "maximalist wing" of the party, united in the conviction that the time for speeches had passed. The rising firebrand Menachem Begin, of Jabotinsky's youth group Betar, had, in a famous September 1938 debate with his mentor, "best expressed the increasingly feverish spirit of the Betar ranks in the face of the growing Nazi threat." Zionism, Begin announced, had reached a third stage of evolution: after "practical Zionism" and then "political Zionism," the time had come for "military Zionism"—the time to fight.[5]

In America, however, where Revisionism had never really gotten traction, the "cutoff battalion" was starting from scratch. Hecht was justified in describing the Bergsonites as "Mad Hatters," because in 1941 these six young men who did not even have enough money to feed themselves sought to build an army, rescue an entire people from annihilation, and create a new nation in hostile territory.[6] As if such goals were not farfetched enough, to accomplish all of this they would first have to overcome the vehement opposition of those best positioned to stop them—Stephen Wise and the American Zionist establishment. Clearly they had faith in Theodor Herzl's dictum: "If you will it, it is no dream."[7]

To make any progress, they would need to punch far above their weight, but this had always been both the challenge confronting Zionism and the nature of its genius. Zionist leaders, like Hecht, possessed a talent for theatrics, the only means by which the representatives of a scattered and powerless minority could pursue their goals. Stagecraft had been in evidence ever since Herzl had insisted on formal tails, white ties, and a dignified venue for the First Zionist Congress in 1897; his idea had been to convey "the atmosphere of a State," where the attending delegates would "feel that they were its National Assembly." The Balfour Declaration, the first real achievement of Zionism and indeed a turning point in world history, was arguably accomplished through a similar sleight of hand. Israeli historian Tom Segev contends that Chaim Weizmann had managed to secure sponsorship for a Jewish national home in Palestine by capitalizing on a paranoid, anti-Semitic notion held by the British ruling class: that the Jews wielded a mystic power over the world, that they "turned the wheels of history."[8]

Jabotinsky, a talented essayist and captivating speaker from Odessa who became active in Zionist politics as early as 1902 and rose to membership in the World Zionist Organization's executive for a time, put particular stock in the optics of dignity and power. In successfully lobbying for a Jewish Legion deployed in the Middle East during World War I, he had sought a show of strength that would earn the Jews respect and status. Indeed, since the competing Zionist factions possessed no actual land or power that they could fight over, when Jabotinsky established his Revisionist movement in 1923, he offered only an alternative strategy for diplomacy—a maximalist approach to negotiations with the British over the fate of Palestine, as opposed to the minimalism of Weizmann.[9]

But the disputes over tactics between Jabotinsky and the leaders of the World Zionist Organization represented something more than a clash of egos, competition for power and prestige, and different tastes in rhetoric and symbolism. They reflected a fundamental ideological divide that would harden over time. In this regard, one of the most telling disagreements was over whether to negotiate with anti-Semitic, antidemocratic actors. Since the days of Herzl, Weizmann and others had seen such dealings as both futile and morally indefensible, while Jabotinsky viewed them as realpolitik, often justifiable as the only possible means of saving lives. Beyond competing philosophies of political pragmatism, however, there were basic principles at issue. Jabotinsky was himself a liberal, but as someone relatively sanguine about capitalism and imperialism, he was simply not as averse to right-wing, even fascist regimes as were more liberal colleagues like Weizmann or socialists like David Ben-Gurion.

As the stakes in Jewish lives increased over the years, these disagreements grew deeper and more bitter. When Herzl was roundly attacked for negotiating with the notorious Russian minister of the interior Vyacheslav von Plehve (who in return for vague promises of support for the Zionists wanted them to collaborate with the czar by undermining Jewish revolutionaries), Jabotinsky was Herzl's lone defender. A heated controversy over another devil's bargain ultimately forced Jabotinsky's resignation from the World Zionist Organization executive in 1923: namely, his talks with Simon Petilura, one of the military leaders whose troops had terrorized Ukraine during Bergson's boyhood, killing thousands of Jews in pogroms between 1917 and 1920. Jabotinsky faced scathing criticism at the Twelfth Zionist Congress in 1921, to which he retorted dramatically from the rostrum, "In working for Palestine I would even ally myself with the Devil."[10]

Now no longer a leader in the World Zionist Organization, Jabotinsky set out to build the Revisionist movement, intended as a return to the Herzlian principles from which the mainstream had strayed. In a November 1923 article for the Russian-language exile magazine *Rasswyet* ("Dawn"), he challenged Weizmann's strategy in Palestine. Weizmann had summed up his gradualist approach with the old adage of Lovers of Zion, a coalition of East European proto-Zionist groups, "One more *dunam*, a few more trees, one more cow, one more goat, two more houses in Hadera." He believed that by purchasing land from the Arabs while cooperating with the British, the Jews could minimize resistance and achieve steady progress toward an undefined "national home." Jabotinsky countered that Weizmann grossly underestimated the resolve of the Arabs, dismissing them as a rabble who could be bribed into forgetting their own dream of sovereignty. Only if Arab nationalists were confronted with an "iron wall" of will and might, of either Jewish or British bayonets, could they be expected to make major concessions. In this view, the Palestinian Arabs would capitulate only if cast into implacable darkness, starved of even the faintest glimmer of hope. Since Britain needed a Jewish state as a reliable beachhead for their empire, the Zionists must openly declare their intention of establishing a nation on both sides of the Jordan and then demand the full protection of British arms.[11]

Jabotinsky's new movement grew steadily as the rise of Arab violence and the corresponding British retreat from the pledges of the Balfour Declaration fed discontent with Weizmann. By 1935, when the Revisionists seceded from the World Zionist Organization and founded the New Zionist Organization, they claimed a membership of 713,000, though this figure was undoubtedly exaggerated. But now, with a new generation coming of age, Jabotinsky's overall authority eroded as the ranks swelled, factions developed, and new charismatic leaders emerged. Thousands had joined Jabotinsky's Poland-based Betar, drawn to the myths of strength, discipline, and militarism. Reflecting the radicalism of the era, they increasingly challenged Jabotinsky's more liberal inclinations, particularly his continued preference for diplomacy over armed struggle and his reluctance to turn against Britain. "Revisionist ideology was reminiscent of the European radical right and was accompanied by violence, especially between 1930 and 1938, when Mussolini's racial legislation finally induced Revisionism to discard its pro-Italian orientation," observes Stern Gang chronicler Joseph Heller.[12]

Spearheading the initial confrontation with Jabotinsky and influencing the fights that followed was Abba Achimeir, a journalist and historian. Achimeir was one of the leaders of a group of renegade activists called Brit ha-Biryonim, which took its name from a sect of dagger-wielding Hebrew zealots who had rebelled against the Roman Empire. By 1928 Achimeir had become disillusioned with socialist Zionism and instead embraced the new nationalist movement in Italy, writing a series of eight articles for the daily Doar Hayom ("Daily Mail") titled "From the Notebook of a Fascist." In 1955 he argued in his defense that these had been the incipient days of fascism, when even Winston Churchill had admired Mussolini. Further, Italian fascism was not a fundamentally racist ideology: when Hitler first assumed power, Mussolini sharply criticized Nazi anti-Semitism.

But from the summer of 1932 to late March 1933, Achimeir even praised Hitler, referencing "the glorious names" of nationalist movements, such as "Ataturk, Mussolini, Pilsudski, de Valera, Hitler." Jabotinsky, who had limited control over what young Revisionists said and did in Palestine after he was permanently barred from the country in late 1929, had generally encouraged Achimeir, but now declared that Achimeir would be expelled from the movement if he wrote one more favorable line about Nazism. The increasingly extreme rhetoric reflected the rising tensions between the Revisionists and the Laborites in Palestine, which had led to violent clashes, culminating in the murder in June 1933 of a senior Zionist official, Chaim Arlosoroff. The day he was killed, the Revisionist paper that Achimeir edited had published what many read as a threat against Arlosoroff's life.[13]

Achimeir was charged and tried for conspiracy, along with two other Revisionists. They were acquitted of the killing, but Achimeir was still sentenced to jail for leading a terrorist group. Rage erupted against the Revisionists, from then on branded as fascists and Hitlerites, and against Jabotinsky in particular. "The Arlosoroff affair was to inject further poison into the two wings of Zionism for some time, " Heller observes. "Indeed, both sides perceived it as part of a world struggle between right and left." Recriminations about the murder would persist into the 1980s.[14]

Meanwhile, the early 1930s also saw the emergence of the force that was to become the Irgun. Dissatisfied with the socialist-oriented Jewish militia, the Haganah, Jerusalem commander Avraham Tehomi formed the breakaway unit Haganah Bet in April 1931. About half of the new group was recruited from Betar, and from the start Tehomi appealed to Jabotinsky to be its senior commander. As a clandestine, underground outfit, it hardly fit Jabotinsky's ideal of a Jewish Legion, and he initially demurred; however, he accepted leadership in 1936, realizing that it offered a means of retaining influence over the movement he had started.[15]

In creating Haganah Bet, Tehomi brought along a clique of young nationalists from Jerusalem—Bergson (then still known as Kook) and two Hebrew University students, David Raziel and Avraham Stern. They, among many others, often clashed with a left-leaning faculty that included Judah Magnes and Martin Buber. "The leaders were almost exclusively young intellectuals who had grown up in the Polish revolutionary traditions," writes author and journalist Arthur Koestler, an early Irgun supporter. "This created the peculiar ideological climate of the Irgun—a mixture of that quixotic patriotism and romantic chivalry which characterized Polish student revolutionaries, with the archaic ferocity of the Bible and the Book of the Maccabees."[16]

When the Arab Revolt erupted in 1936, the young commanders decided to fight fire with fire, and their resolve to employ violence transformed Haganah Bet into the Irgun. The storm of Arab rage—largely a reaction to the great surge of Jewish immigration precipitated by Hitler's rise to power—would claim some six thousand lives from the outbreak of unrest that April to its subsidence three years later with the passage of the British White Paper of 1939. Throughout those years, the Haganah maintained a policy of *Havlagah*, or "restraint," refusing to retaliate against the Arab attacks. Many of Haganah Bet's fighters, however, argued that restraint communicated weakness, while the Arabs achieved concessions through violence. Tehomi formally agreed to operate under Jabotinsky's direction in December 1936 but five months later chose to side instead with the Haganah and led about half the force in a return to the fold. The roughly fifteen hundred fighters who remained became the Irgun, with Raziel, Stern, and Bergson assuming leadership.[17]

Jabotinsky vacillated: if he opposed the Irgun's policy of retaliation entirely, he would lose all influence, and yet he objected to the increasingly indiscriminate nature of the attacks, such as terrorist bombings of populated areas that killed women and children. "I can't see much heroism and public good in shooting from the rear an Arab peasant on a donkey, carrying vegetables for sale to Tel Aviv," he told the leaders at a meeting in July 1937. Indeed, at the same time as the Irgun was rescuing lives through illegal immigration, it was also tossing bombs into Arab coffeehouses and marketplaces and shooting up buses. These attacks peaked in midsummer 1938: according to contemporaneous newspaper accounts, on July 6 a milk-can bomb in the Arab market in Haifa claimed twenty-one lives and injured more than sixty; on July 15 an electric mine in the old city of Jerusalem killed ten and wounded twenty-nine; on July 26 another bomb in the Haifa market massacred forty-five civilians and wounded about sixty; and then on August 26 an explosion in Jaffa killed twenty-four and wounded thirty-five. By their own counts, the Irgun claimed to have slaughtered 150 people in July 1938 alone and 130 more between the passage of the White Paper in late May 1939 and the outbreak of war in early September.[18]

These attacks, to be fair, were hardly occurring in a vacuum: Palestine was sinking ever deeper into a bloody morass. Each day brought a new spate of "disorders and disruption—telephones cut, bridges damaged, trains derailed, convoys ambushed and fighting in the hills," recalled one Mandate policeman. The British responded with often-brutal raids on Arab villages, martial law, collective punishment, and torture. From 1936 through 1940, they demolished some two thousand homes, and in the two years following November 1937, they carried out 112 executions, averaging one per week. In much of the violence, however, Arabs targeted other Arabs, either for collaborating or for failing to sufficiently support the insurrection. As a result of the rising toll on Jews, by 1939 the Haganah itself buckled on self-restraint. Caving into pressure from the ranks, Ben-Gurion allowed reprisals through a special operations unit. Other Zionists joined the Special Night Squads, a secret army of vengeance formed by British intelligence officer Orde Charles Wingate. Completing the circle of violence, internecine warfare between the Haganah and the Irgun had also resumed by 1938.[19]

Meanwhile, in Europe, the Revisionists forged devil's bargains that yielded arms and training for their new, maximalist fighting force. Jabotinsky and Betarist leader Jeremiah Halperin had set the precedent in November 1934, when they established a naval academy in fascist Italy's port city of Civitavecchia, with Mussolini's personal approval. Although the Betar leaders ordered their cadets to maintain a distance from the locals, the trainees nevertheless openly expressed support for Mussolini's regime and his war in Ethiopia, marching with Italian soldiers in parade and collecting scraps for munitions.[20]

Jabotinsky was also able to forge an alliance in Poland. Since the Polish citizenry blamed the Jews for the poor national economy, and the government, like the German Reich at this stage, was eager to expel them, Polish officials adopted a pro-Zionist policy. As the American Office of Strategic Services noted in a 1945 report, "The authorities were interested in exploiting the anti-democratic Revisionist party against the democratic Jewish opposition, which fought for equal rights of the Jewish minority."[21] British immigration restrictions and Labor Zionism's noncooperation made the hoped-for partnership in a mass evacuation scheme untenable, but the Poles were happy to provide arms to the Zionist underground in Palestine. According to the recollections of Irgunists, the government stocked a warehouse in Warsaw with twenty thousand rifles and light and heavy automatic weapons, including two hundred Hotchkiss heavy machine guns. But no more than a few hundred of these ever made it to Palestine before Germany's invasion of Poland in September 1939 made further smuggling impossible.[22]

Far more fruitful was the Polish army's four- to six-week training program for the Irgun, conducted during the spring. While only about twenty-five men received training, they would form the core of officers who would later lead the revolt against the British. In addition to being trained in conventional warfare, they were schooled by veterans of Poland's pre–World War I underground army of liberation in "terrorist bombings, conspiracy, secret communications, partisan warfare, and underground planning," according to Irgunist Yaakov Eliav. ". . . Sabotage was taught scientifically."[23]

Stern had arranged the course, and since he scorned Jabotinsky's wavering on restraint and sympathies for England, the father of Revisionism was likely not even aware of the arrangement. Based on the success of this partnership, Stern would later attempt to forge an alliance with the Axis—first with Italy in the fall of 1940, and twice more with the Nazis, late in 1940 and then in December 1941, just weeks before the Wannsee Conference.[24]

While the Irgun challenged Jabotinsky's authority over Revisionism, another challenge arose from within Betar. By 1938 Stern had infiltrated Betar with secret cells, focused not on politics and ideology but on paramilitary training. The young head of Betar's Polish branch, Menachem Begin, articulated the new militancy in a famous debate with Jabotinsky at Betar's third world convention in September. He rose to amend the Betar oath, proposing to change, "I shall not raise my arm except in self-defense," by adding the clause "and for the conquest of my homeland." A world conscience, he argued, was nowhere in evidence, and the League of Nations was about to dissolve. England had ruled in favor of the Arabs because the Arabs had national ambitions and were willing to fight, while only a fraction of the Jewish people were fighting. Echoing Stern, he declared, "We want to fight—to die or to triumph!" While Stern had openly defied Jabotinsky, it was Begin who would later reinterpret the founder's ideas and thus seize control of both his movement and his legacy.[25]

To resolve the question of Jabotinsky's authority, the Irgun leaders convened with the Revisionists in Paris in February 1938, for the meeting that dispatched Yitshaq Ben-Ami and others to United States. Raziel and Bergson attended, but Stern stayed away and a month later convened a press conference where he issued a bellicose warning to the British and Arabs. Even though the "Paris agreement" reasserted Jabotinsky's authority, the aged father nevertheless would fall increasingly out of touch. By the spring Stern was publicly deriding him, lumping him in with the Jewish Agency, the World Zionist Organization's official administrative body in Palestine. Both kowtowed to England, Stern asserted, and both clung to naive delusions about the power of world opinion and the League of Nations. Instead, Stern believed in force, "always decisive in the lives of conquerors and freedom fighters. . . . For the land and freedom are not given the weak and are not ever purchased—they have always been conquered by bloodshed and the sword."[26]

With the publication of White Paper on May 17, 1939, the Irgun announced that "blood and the sword" would decide the outcome in Palestine, and it launched a full-blown rebellion against Britain, blowing up the Palestine Broadcasting Service the same day. For the first time, the Irgunists assassinated a policeman, Arieh Polanski, on May 23. Six days later, Yaakov Eliav put his newly acquired terrorism skills to use, preparing a timed explosive that Irgun fighter Matzliach Nimrodi, a tailor by trade, sewed into a jacket and then wore into Jerusalem's Rex movie theater, where he left it. "I was a man-bomb, like the Arabs who go on suicide missions," Nimrodi later recalled to an Israeli journalist. The explosion killed five Arabs and wounded eighteen. The British responded by clapping Raziel in jail, but the campaign continued, with bombings of phone booths, post offices, and coffeehouses throughout the Mandate. On August 26 an explosion killed Ralph Cairns, the head of the Jewish Department of the Palestine Police, and another officer, Ronald Barker, in retaliation for the torture of Irgun members. Two days later, a British raid netted the entire Irgun command, including Stern.[27]

The Nazis' invasion of Poland and the start of the war on September 1, however, would dramatically change the calculus of the conflict, for both the British and the Revisionists. Jabotinsky immediately declared his allegiance to Britain, and Raziel did the same in a September 5 letter to the commanding officer of the British army in Palestine. He then signed an agreement with the inspector-general of police, Alan Saunders, promising that the Irgun would cease attacks on the British, furnish the Mandate with intelligence, and assist in operations in the Middle East and the Balkans. For their part, the English promised to fund the Irgun, release their imprisoned fighters, and allot them a quarter of the immigration certificates. On October 24, 1939, Raziel was delivered from Sarafend Prison to the King David Hotel, shackled hand and foot: Hecht's "champion in chains."[28]

CHAPTER 11

Campaign for a Jewish Army

My father loved him. The collaboration with Ben Hecht was an incredible collaboration. They together produced amazing—amazing things. They revolutionized political campaigning and lobbying.

   —REBECCA KOOK, DAUGHTER OF PETER BERGSON (HILLEL
   KOOK), SENIOR LECTURER OF POLITICS AND GOVERNMENT
   AT BEN-GURION UNIVERSITY OF THE NEGEV[1]

Fight for the Right to Fight!

   —NEWSPAPER ADVERTISEMENT FOR A JEWISH ARMY[2]

On January 5, 1942, a full-page advertisement in the *New York Times* announced, "Jews Fight for the Right to Fight," beginning the Bergson Group's first full-fledged publicity and fund-raising blitz. Over the next three years, the delegation would publish more than ninety different advertisements in at least forty newspapers in fifteen cities. Many featured dramatic headlines written by Hecht, with evocative, intricate caricatures drawn by the artist Arthur Szyk in the style of illuminated medieval manuscripts and miniature paintings. Other tactics included propaganda leaflets, radio broadcasts, fund-raising dinners, petitions, and relentless door-to-door lobbying in Washington, D.C. According to Hecht, these reflected Peter Bergson's "theory of a hundred guns": "It meant that he would gather cohorts wherever he might find them and shoot in all directions, so that when the day of victory came, no one, not even he, would know which gun had fired the decisive bullet." Bergson thus understood the power of media and American public opinion and knew how to capitalize on it.[3]

The January advertisement included 133 signatures—endorsements from three U.S. senators and fourteen congressmen, eleven rabbis, five clergymen, and numerous authors, journalists, and entertainers—reflecting a basic Bergson strategy. "Putting their hard-won knowledge of the rules for molding American public opinion to use, [Bergson] and delegation members eventually thrashed out a game plan," explains historian Judith Tydor Baumel, "first, convince a qualitative majority of the justice of your cause and the masses will follow suit." The delegation picked many of its first sponsors out of *Who's Who in America*, mailing out a hundred copies of a memorandum that called for a force of Palestinian and stateless Jews to fight alongside the American, British, and other Allied armies, "legally and according to American foreign policy," for the "survival of the Jewish people and the preservation of democracy." Those who offered their support were then listed on the next circular, which went out to another hundred influential people, and so on until hundreds of luminaries had joined the rolls.[4]

For the mainstream Zionists, there was nothing controversial about the Jewish army proposition itself; it had in fact been at the forefront of their agenda since as early as 1938. A Jewish fighting force could not only pursue vengeance against the Nazis but also empower the Yishuv and protect the community against Arab uprisings and invasions, increasingly regarded as an existential threat. But in a meeting with Zionist leaders on a visit to the United States in 1941, David Ben-Gurion had urged the leaders to shut out the Revisionists, and they had sabotaged Vladimir Jabotinsky when he succeeded in obtaining the support of the British ambassador to the United States, Lord Lothian. The Jewish army issue became emblematic of the rancor in Jewish affairs, revealing not only the rising antagonism toward the Revisionists in America but also the widening rift between Ben-Gurion and Chaim Weizmann. While the British did ultimately establish a Jewish Brigade in 1944, scholars have argued that had the Zionists been able to overcome their differences, they could have closed the time gap between England's formal adoption of the plan in October 1940 and its realization four years later.[5]

Bergson undercut the efforts at interference by putting gentiles into leading positions on the Committee for a Jewish Army, as well as his subsequent committees. "The secret was simple," explained Jabotinsky's son, Eri, one of the six members of the Bergson Group. "The Committee for a Jewish Army was a non-sectarian, non-partisan, American organization. It was not a Jewish organisation. The principle was that we, a group of anonymous Palestinians, approached the American public with a request to help us in our enterprise. We didn't pose as the representatives of any movement or any party. We were just representing an idea and asking those who were in accord with our arguments to give us the support of their name."[6]

Over the ensuing years, as the needs kept changing and the group's objectives shifted accordingly, Bergson announced a new committee for each new mission. Hecht found it clumsy to label these as committees and thought that creating so many different titles for essentially the same core of people only sowed confusion. But this obfuscation kept the focus on each specific cause while allowing the delegation to shed the name of Revisionism. This use of aliases was consistent with Hillel Kook's adoption of the pseudonym Peter Bergson, done to insulate his uncle, the chief rabbi of Palestine, Abraham Isaac ha-Kohen Kook, from any association with illegal immigration and other Irgun activities.[7]

The group soon recruited an extraordinary roster of advocates. In addition to John and Frances Gunther, Pierre Van Paassen, and *PM* columnist Max Lerner, they included Lowell Thomas, Dorothy Parker, Upton Sinclair, I. F. Stone, Sinclair Lewis, Langston Hughes, and Paul Robeson. Support reached across the cultural spectrum: on the one hand, the ads ran for free in the blue-collar Hearst scandal sheets that by now had lost much of their old rakish swagger but still yowled just as loudly as in the days of the Chicago *Herald and Examiner.* On the other hand, the group was championed by *PM*, the highbrow, maverick New York daily where Hecht worked as a daily columnist and Dr. Seuss as the chief editorial cartoonist. Hearst and the bombastic Walter Winchell wrote columns trumpeting Bergson's efforts, and so did the erudite theologian Reinhold Niebuhr.[8]

Prominent Americans in the media and in Washington were impressed by the self-confident appeal, not for pity, but for a chance to prove Jewish resilience and strength. In referring to what he called "the Cause," Hecht wrote his longtime close friend and newfound partner on the committee David O. Selznick:

I went into it for the same reason I think that you did. I felt that the Jews have been trying to arouse all kinds of emotions in the world—pity, compassion, horror, guilt,—and that it would do all of us a lot of good if they could, for a change, inspire some other kind of emotions, such as a home run or a successful battle inspires in the Americano. I felt that Jews like ourselves who are a little stronger than most owed it to throw not only a few dimes to the dolor of the Jew but to give him a lift with our strength, to add our voices to his battle cry rather than his moans.[9]

Among the committee's supporters were second- and third-generation assimilated Jews such as Hecht and Lerner, the actor Eddie Cantor, and Alfred Streslin, an advertising magnate Hecht recruited who contributed $5,000. They tended to be attracted to the image of the "new Jew" and to the Revisionists' "*demand* orientation" of defining one's rights and then staking claim to them, as opposed to "the passive *request* orientation then current among other contemporary Jewish organizations," in Baumel's words. The Bergson Group's aggressive rhetoric was virtually unheard of, not only in discussions of the "Jewish problem," but also in American discourse about minorities in general. Although, on Hecht's advice, the committee downplayed its aspirations for statehood, the maximalist Revisionist poet Uriel Helperin had perhaps expressed the spirit best when he announced in 1938, "Our very right to the country is *our own*, and the essence of our power is *our own power*."[10]

Despite Hecht's admonition to keep Zionism out of the equation, the appeal for national liberation gained traction in Congress, where the issue of a Jewish army was raised twenty-four times during 1942. The Bergson Group reached out to other nationalist groups—the Irish, Yugoslavs, Czechs, Polish, Koreans, Chinese, and Free French—and found particularly strong support from the Chicago Czech community and the New York Irish. Congressman Will Rogers Jr., who was part Native American, became an increasingly passionate champion of Jewish rescue, lobbying the Roosevelt administration to establish an agency. Another leading advocate was Representative Andrew Somers, the Brooklyn son of an Irish militant, who compared Britain's policy in Palestine to its handling of Ireland before independence. But their political support only took the Bergsonites so far: Somers's proposal in February for a congressional resolution, the most significant legislative initiative on behalf of the cause, remained bottled up in the Foreign Affairs Committee, blocked by its chairman, Sol Bloom, a representative from New York who was a Zionist.[11]

While the Bergson Group was successful in recruiting some assimilated Jews, it had trouble with those who were, for Hecht at least, closest at hand. In Hollywood, where in early 1942 Hecht's wife, Rose, and committee member Miriam Heyman prepared a fund-raiser for a thousand guests at the Twentieth Century Fox commissary, Hecht realized that he needed a cosponsor for the event, as his name alone would not carry enough weight. Bergson assumed that another sponsor would be easy to find, since Hecht was connected with the twenty most powerful Jews of the film industry. But Hecht recalled that just two years earlier, Louis B. Mayer had served his family's celebrated chicken soup to Nazi editors at a luncheon decorated with swastikas. Even Selznick at first refused to help, on the grounds that he was an American and not a Jew. He finally agreed when Hecht won a bet that if they called any three friends of Selznick's choosing and asked whether he was an American or a Jew, all would identify him as a Jew.[12]

All the careful planning for the evening went awry when Lieutenant Colonel John Patterson, a legendary lion hunter and former Jewish Legion commander, managed to simultaneously bore and offend the diners with a diatribe about British anti-Semitism. As some stormed out while others shouted in protest, gossip columnist Hedda Hopper saved the day by calling above the din with a pledge. Several guests joined in, but of the $130,000 promised, only $9,000 was paid. Hecht later remarked that this fund-raising venture "was a fine success—if you care to overlook its failure." Harry Warner and British film director Victor Saville denounced their hosts to the Federal Bureau of Investigation, and Hecht spent two hours with bureau investigators the next day. Bergson was especially disappointed; the Irgun command had expected to raise millions. Instead, the affair turned out to be another lesson learned. "I don't have to tell you that the only cause such Jews want to hear about are causes which will conceal from them and from the world any hint of their Jewishness," Hecht wrote Selznick. The proceeds, at least, would pay for office rent, a mimeograph machine, and letterhead.[13]

The British War Office finally announced the formation of a Jewish Brigade nearly two years later, on September 20, 1944. This force of 5,500 saw action just weeks before the end of the war, but its soldiers later played a major role in helping survivors emigrate to Palestine. One veteran, Dov Gruner, would become the Irgun's most celebrated martyr in their armed insurgency against the British Mandate.[14]

While there is little evidence that the Committee for a Jewish Army directly influenced the War Office's decision to establish the brigade, the committee could claim credit for a far more enduring, if less concrete, achievement. In Bergson's words: "Until that time Jewish matters appeared on the next to last page of the newspaper. We placed them on the American public agenda, providing momentum for their movement from the dead pages to the news section and even to the front pages. For the first time in the history of the American public, Jewish affairs took up an entire page of the *New York Times*."[15]

Hecht and the committee had shattered the enforced silence in the public sphere. There was an element of truth to the Nazi canard that "the Jews control the U.S. media"—though hardly the worldwide conspiracy that Hitler imagined—and American isolationists had struck preemptively to muzzle them. Charles Lindbergh, Gerald Nye, and others had stoked fears of a Jewish plot to manipulate the masses, while Joseph Kennedy had played on assimilated movie and publishing executives' reluctance to draw attention to themselves as outsiders. Many of the most talented and successful Jewish writers Hecht knew were likewise reluctant to speak out, as were leading representatives of the American Jewish community, who moreover had received explicit instructions from State Department and White House officials not to portray the conflict as "a Jewish war."

To the extent that, as the Bergsonites believed, the collective silence reflected the subconscious self-hatred of diaspora Jewry, the true achievement of the committee lay not in meeting its specific goal but rather in bringing "respect back to the name of the Jew," as Hecht later put it. He and the Bergson Group pulled the legitimate concerns and aspirations of the Jewish people out of the shadows and into the light, making it the prominent topic in American public discourse that it has been ever since. In the process, they raised more than a quarter of a million dollars and drew fifty thousand supporters over the eighteen months of the committee's existence. "In the public relations sphere it was unique on the American scene: militant, but espousing a patriotic aim that was difficult to oppose," notes Baumel, "loud and bombastic, but incorporating these qualities into the American ethos of freedom and minority rights in a way that answered the human, and particularly American need for sensationalism. . . . Hillel Kook [Peter Bergson] filled the vacuum between the distressing reports from Europe and what was seen as contemporary American Jewish organizational impotence. Accordingly, Kook's group enjoyed a positive public image: it had plans, proposals, and noisy protests in comparison to the low-key protests whispered by the Jewish establishment until 1943."[16]

CHAPTER 12

"A Challenge to the Soul of Men"

There were probably those who didn't join [our cause] that we didn't know about because it was known that we were a radical group. If we were radicals we would have thrown bombs. God knows if there was ever a justification to throw bombs, these were the years. We didn't even think about it, because we were not radical. We were humanists.

—Peter Bergson[1]

In the early winter of 1943, Hayim Greenberg, editor of the *Jewish Frontier*, handed Hecht a stack of reports while they were lunching together at a kosher restaurant. Obtained via Switzerland from Nazi-occupied Europe, some were accounts from eyewitnesses, others from sources in the underground. In clipped, factual sentences they described five thousand Jews crammed into freight cars lined with tons of quicklime, rolling to destinations where their partially decomposed corpses were pulled out and tossed into pits; five hundred men, women, and children marched naked into an incinerator; twenty thousand mowed down in a field, target practice for Luftwaffe gunners. At a time when the six Nazi killing centers had not yet come to light, Hecht began to wonder why the Germans were herding all their victims to Poland. Then he realized that the killing of millions would have to be tightly organized, to keep the pileup of the dead from getting out of control.

Hecht told Greenberg that he planned to use the material for an article describing Germany as a nation of murderers. His companion protested: to brand all Germans as killers would be to exhibit the same blanket hatred that the Nazis had for the Jews. "It will be bad for the Jews," the editor said, "if you make the Jews seem as cruel and unthinking as those whom you are trying to attack." Greenberg's thoughtful equanimity in the face of such inhumanity was moving. Hecht thanked him for the help and advice but in parting thought, "His way was not my way. I was unable to answer his philosophical words. My head was full of faraway screams."[2]

Weeks earlier, on November 25, 1942, Peter Bergson had learned from an American news account that the Nazis had slain two million Jews and were carrying out a plan of complete extermination. The article in the *Washington Post* was three inches long and buried on page 6. Rabbi Stephen Wise had delivered the news the previous day at a press conference, announcing that it had been confirmed by the State Department. Bergson ran straight to the office of Assistant Secretary of State Adolf Berle, where he was eventually granted a few minutes' audience between appointments. Years later, he recalled the exchange: "I said, 'What are you going to do about it?' And he says, 'What can we do about it?' And I said, 'Surely you don't say the United States is going to do nothing? I am one individual here, a foreigner, and I *know* I am going to do something.'"[3]

But doing something would turn out to be an extraordinary challenge. The Roosevelt administration maintained that the best and only way to help the Jews was to defeat Hitler as quickly as possible. An effort at rescue would mean a significant shift in Allied war policy, which would require public pressure. Such pressure, however, could proceed only from awareness, yet the public had not even begun to absorb the truth that a modern, civilized world power was systematically eradicating an entire people. Worse, the American press had bungled the story, while the American government had been actively suppressing it. Once again, the Committee for a Jewish Army would have to shatter a wall of silence. Its urgent mission to inform and galvanize the public would involve Hecht in the most significant public relations coup of his life—his 1943 Holocaust pageant, *We Will Never Die*. To succeed, he would have to heed Greenberg's advice: Americans were determined to crush Hitler, but a call for rescue would have to do more than appeal to their hatred of Germany. It would have to inspire their humanity.

Precious time had already been lost. In August the State Department had initially attempted to prevent Wise from receiving a report on the Final Solution from Gerhart Riegner, a representative of the World Jewish Congress in Switzerland. Then Undersecretary of State Sumner Welles had asked Wise to keep the information under wraps until it could be corroborated. More than three months passed before Welles finally confirmed the information, and Wise has been harshly criticized for the delay. "How was he not driven mad by this secret?" wrote Auschwitz survivor Elie Wiesel. "How could other Jewish leaders pledge silence? How is it that they did not cry out in despair?" But defying a State Department request would have meant alienating the one U.S. agency that could help with rescue, and given the general distrust toward reports from Jewish sources, Wise may well have felt he needed "official confirmation" in the first place.[4]

But even Bergson and Samuel Merlin had at first refused to believe the stories, a measure of just how unimaginable the genocide was at that time. News of the extermination of the Jews had in fact been leaking into the mainstream media since the spring, when American journalists who had been held in Germany since Pearl Harbor returned with accounts of mass killings. In June American newspapers had treated with skepticism a report of systematic annihilation because it came from the Jewish socialist organization of Poland, the Bund. Riegner's report had come from a German industrialist with access to classified Nazi files, but since Wise, the chairman of the World Jewish Congress, would be presenting the report to the media, he could not expect to be accorded any better credibility.[5]

In the event, the press buried the story despite Welles's confirmation, and the government offered no support. R. Borden Reams, a specialist on Jewish affairs for the European Division, pressured Wise to "avoid any implications" that the State Department had been his source, and officials were evasive when reached by reporters. When Jewish organizations had held a mass meeting at Madison Square Garden in July, Franklin Delano Roosevelt had sent a message predicting that the Nazis would not succeed in "exterminating their victims any more than they will succeed in enslaving mankind." In August he had warned that the United States and the "United Nations"—the phrase Roosevelt had coined for all countries opposing the Axis—would hold the perpetrators responsible for their crimes, echoing a vow that both he and Winston Churchill had made at the Garden. But although Roosevelt held two press conferences a week, he did not mention the Riegner report to the general public after Wise's press conference and was not asked about it. The Office of War Information likewise refused to publicize the news in early December.[6]

Weeks after Wise's information was published, Hecht wrote a newspaper advertisement criticizing the silence, titled "Ballad of the Doomed Jews of Europe," but Judge Joseph Proskauer of the American Jewish Committee convinced Bergson not to publish it. "Hang and burn but be quiet, Jews!" Hecht had written in his ballad. "The world is busy with other news."[7] As Hecht later explained,

> 1942 went by, with startling news of the rounding up of the Jews of Paris by the Nazis. It was suppressed by the newspapers. The Polish Government-in-Exile found ways to signal its death toll to the world. Seven hundred thousand Jews had already been "resettled" (in Valhalla) since the German occupation of 1939. The news remained buried in the Black Books of Poland mysteriously delivered to my door. The Germans held the Wannsee Conference drawing up the blueprint of their "Final Solution." The Berlin papers proclaimed the completion of their plans. . . . The American newspapers did not pick up these stories from their sources.[8]

The failure to inform the public of the Final Solution amounted to a lapse in journalistic fundamentals. The papers treated the Riegner report as an unimportant development in the old story of Jewish persecution by the Nazis. Though the estimates of the dead during the latter half of 1942 were staggeringly high, such claims made by Jewish sources were given far less prominence than the casualty figures pouring in from Stalingrad and the tallies of U.S. losses during this first year of war, at El Alamein, the Battle of Midway, and Guadalcanal. Over ten million Americans were at arms, and everywhere the war was going badly.

Moreover, the Final Solution failed to register with reporters and editors because the concept made so little sense: why in the midst of this contest of arms would the Germans be so intent on eradicating a minority population of noncombatants? What could possibly be gained? Newspapers offered various explanations—that the deaths were due to the privations of war, that those who died were serving in work battalions, that the Nazis were trying to deal with a potentially troublesome element. Lost amid all of the data and theories was that a genocide was unfolding across Europe, setting a horrific new precedent in modern war. As Deborah Lipstadt put it, a "chasm . . . existed between information and knowledge."[9] When it came to one of the biggest stories of the twentieth century, the American media had—to use the journalistic term—buried the lede.

Hecht had no tolerance for such obliviousness. "Our writers fill their columns daily with intrepid denunciations and exposures of tweedle-dum-tweedledee political confusion in the world," he wrote in February 1943. "But of this overthrow of the basic concept of life, of this plunge into the ways of savagery, of this great backward step into massacre, they speak almost not at all." Years later, in writing about another blunder of the press—their obliviousness of Zionist "perfidy" during the war—he was slightly more understanding: "I have no criticism of these or any other newspapermen. I was once one of them. I remember my own addlehead-edness, blindness toward truth, deafness for its words. My sins were not purposeful. I did not draw my pay as a philosopher or seer. My duties were to report the obvious, to echo the loudest and most important voices. Since these were always the voices of virtue and authority, I was their nimble press agent."[10]

Yet another obstacle confronting the Bergson committee was the attitude of two Jewish publishers of major newspapers: while *New York Times* publisher Arthur Hays Sulzberger refused to treat the extermination of the Jews as a major story, *Washington Post* owner Eugene Meyer staunchly objected to any special effort at rescue and fiercely opposed Bergson and his followers. In early October 1944 the *Post* would run a series of articles attacking the Bergson Group as illegitimate and unscrupulous. The paper admitted error ten days after the first story appeared, publishing a lengthy editorial that retracted most of the allegations and providing Bergson space on page 1 to present his side. But when U.S. solicitor general Fowler Harper sent a personal letter to Meyer objecting to the stories as vicious slander, the publisher replied that the group's demand for rescue constituted "harassment" of a president focused on winning the war. Meyer added that he did not believe "it is necessary for any pressure group, how-ever well meaning, to devote its time and money to the business of 'molding American opinion' on this subject."[11]

Had it not been for Hecht, news of the Final Solution would also have been virtually absent from mainstream American magazines. While the *New Republic* and the *Nation* issued loud protests in December, these liberal publications had relatively small readerships. *Time, Newsweek,* and

Life limited their attention to a brief mention of a UN statement of condemnation, relegated to the back pages. Hecht's "The Extermination of the Jews," which drew from Greenberg's reports and announced that six million would die, appeared in *American Mercury* in February 1943, while a condensed version appeared in *Reader's Digest* that same month under the headline, "Remember Us!" These articles constituted the only substantive coverage to appear in mass-circulation magazines.[12]

Yitshaq Ben-Ami later recalled that during the fall of 1942 there had been heated debates about whether to pull back on the Jewish army campaign and concentrate instead on rescue. But when Wise made his announcement, the committee shifted course. Twelve days later, on the first anniversary of the Pearl Harbor attack, it published "A Proclamation on the Moral Rights of the Stateless and Palestinian Jews," a full-page advertisement in the *New York Times* that publicized the extermination and drew a link to the committee's proposal for a fighting force. Pierre Van Paassen's text was accompanied by 1,500 signatures and an illustration by Arthur Szyk showing a Jewish soldier brandishing a machine gun, rising above a heap of shackled and bleeding victims. On February 8 the committee made the call for rescue explicit with the headline "ACTION—NOT PITY CAN SAVE MILLIONS NOW!"[13]

Newspaper advertisements were a start, but the feeling was that something on a much grander scale would be needed to break the silence. At a strategy meeting in January, Hecht struck on the idea of staging a historical pageant—a form of theater devoted to civic purpose that had been popular with Americans, and American Jews in particular, since the late nineteenth century. In recent years, the flamboyant Zionist impresario Meyer Weisgal had set the standard for spectacle, first with *The Romance of a People*, his 1933 Chicago extravaganza involving some six thousand actors, singers, and dancers. A 1937 follow-up effort, *The Eternal Road*, produced in response to the rise of Nazism, had featured 245 actors and 1,772 costume changes, with a five-tiered stage and a choir six stories above the ground; it required twenty-six miles of electrical cable and $60,000 worth of lighting. The contractors hired to enlarge the space of the New York Opera House had "—like Moses—hit rock and then water," flooding the theater and bringing the already-chaotic rehearsals to a standstill.[14]

Hecht used his Hollywood connections to create a cast-of-thousands aesthetic, reminiscent of Cecil B. DeMille's films, that would top even this. The ninety-minute performance, produced by Billy Rose, directed by

Moss Hart, and scored by Kurt Weill, was a journey from biblical to modern times featuring somber but striking stagecraft. The cast of nearly five hundred included as its narrators, *Scarface*'s Paul Muni and *Little Caesar*'s Edward G. Robinson, as well as Claude Rains, Frank Sinatra, and some three dozen other major and upcoming celebrities. Along with two hundred rabbis and yeshiva students, a choir of fifty cantors, and an equal number of players from the NBC Symphony Orchestra, they performed in front of two forty-foot tablets inscribed with the Ten Commandments and, suspended above, a glowing Star of David. "The aesthetic principle of the spectacle was this: more is more," noted the cultural historian Stephen Whitfield.[15]

The purpose was both to stir the conscience of American Jews and to catalyze public pressure for rescue, but *We Will Never Die* also represented a return volley in the war of propaganda. The Nazis had their own tradition of public mythmaking through spectacle. The Nuremberg Rallies, held from 1933 to 1938, had drawn hundreds of thousands from all parts of Germany and featured sound and lighting effects, martial music, and elaborate presentations of flags and standards. At these and other events, Hitler and minister of propaganda Joseph Goebbels declared "world Jewry" the archenemy of Germany.[16]

While planning the pageant, Hecht saw another opportunity to raise public awareness when he was invited to join thirty famous writers for dinner at the apartment of his friend George Kaufman, the playwright and *New York Times* drama critic. "All had written hit plays or successful novels," he later recounted. "Put their names together and you had the box-office flower of American culture. In addition to success, wit and influence, they had in common the fact that they were all Jews." Together, "they could command the press of the world." With the consent of Kaufman's wife, Beatrice, Hecht addressed the guests as they sat for coffee in the living room. If they all spoke out against this slaughter, he argued, they might make a difference. He was able to recruit Moss Hart and Kurt Weill, but otherwise his speech was met with stony silence. One by one, the guests got up to leave. "I'm sorry it turned out like this," Beatrice said. "But I didn't expect anything much different. You asked them to throw away the most valuable thing they own—the fact that they are Americans."[17]

Because Hecht did not completely grasp Hitler's logic, he could not have fully appreciated the challenge that his own panorama of Jewish history would soon offer to the narrative of hate broadcast by the Nazis. He had told Kaufman's guests that he "felt certain that if we banded together and let loose our talents and our moral passion that we might halt the massacre. . . . Consider what would happen to the Germans if they were to hear that their crime was sickening to the world! If a roar of horror swept the civilized earth and echoed into the land that was once Goethe's and Beethoven's!"[18] This argument might have held true if Hitler's grip on power had been less secure, as it had been in the early 1930s, when he was struggling with the Depression and Jewish activists had organized an anti-Nazi boycott. But now a loud cry of protest could have no such effect, not only because the armies of a newly ascendant Germany were sweeping across Europe, but also for reasons that, at least in the longer run, gave Hecht's pageant resonance. Although Hitler and his inner circle imposed a strict silence about the details of the extermination, the Nazis were not so much denying the Final Solution as weaving their own story, presenting their assault on world Jewry as an integral front in Germany's broader battle. Indeed, after the invasion of the Soviet Union, it became "a means of rallying the German people to continue fighting," observes historian Richard Evans.[19]

On February 24, 1943, Hitler repeated for the sixth time his chilling prophecy of January 1939 to the Reichstag: he warned that should international Jewry plunge the nations yet again into world war, the Jews of Europe would be annihilated. Like other conspiracy theorists, the Führer believed he had uncovered the hidden truth behind world events: that the Jew, a master of mimicry and deception, a wizard of finance and media, was the unseen puppet master controlling Roosevelt, Churchill, and Stalin. Since the summer of 1941, Hitler and Goebbels had spoken of extermination bluntly and often, but as a war of defense against an archenemy bent on global domination. This paranoid fantasy, in which the Nazis viewed themselves as saviors of the world, has been termed "redemptive anti-Semitism" by Saul Friedländer.[20]

In contrast, *We Will Never Die* would make the case for rescue by presenting the Nazi genocide as an assault on humanity itself:

First narrator: There were many civilizations already in the world; many heroes and philosophers had already entered history. But in the record of man's rise out of the fogs of savagery, there was still one page empty. It was on this page that the little tribe of shepherds and farmers beyond the Jordan wrote their creed—the creed that was destined to change the soul of man.

They wrote that the soul of man had not come from the beast, but been given him by God. They wrote that above all the greeds and lusts in the human soul stood goodness, righteousness and justice. They wrote that the destiny of man called him to serve this mighty creed, to serve it above all the other powers on earth. Writing thus on the empty page, this little tribe put down the words of a battlecry that has never ended, and of a dream that has alone survived all the debacles of history. . . .

Second narrator: Today in the dark lands of Europe, the Germans are threatening to destroy the creed written by Abraham, and that now belongs to the whole world.[21]

The pageant thus spun a narrative that would live on in collective memory, portraying the Jewish triumphs of genius and their saga of persecution and survival as a universal history. Once again, Hecht embraced paradox: he did not abandon the themes of strength and gallantry trumpeted in the Jewish army campaign but rather, in three acts, presented the Jew, respectively, as a symbol of the world conscience, as its heroic warrior-defender, and as a martyr. "Our delegation came back to Nyack several times . . . watching in fascination as Hecht's abstract ideas gradually materialized," remembered Ben-Ami. "Hecht immersed himself in research, delving into Jewish history and lore with a vengeance, as if to punish himself for all the years during which he had ignored his heritage."[22]

While rehearsals were under way in mid-February, the *New York Times* reported that the Romanian government had offered to transfer seventy thousand Jews from concentration camps in Transnistria to any place of refuge the Allies chose, in return for the cost of transportation. Hecht seized on the news to unleash his fury at British and American inaction, with an ad three days later that announced, "FOR SALE TO HUMANITY: 70,000 JEWS, Guaranteed Human Beings at $50 a Piece." The ransom—not the first nor the last demanded by an Axis country—was in fact higher; scholars have cited figures of between $350 and $1,300 per refugee. Moreover, the offer had been made by shadowy intermediaries, the Romanian government had made no guarantees, and the Nazis were opposed to any Jewish emigration to Palestine. In any case, the Allies balked. The British Foreign Office expressed deep skepticism that the proposal was genuine, dismissing it as Nazi blackmail. Welles concurred: "The probable actual source is the German propaganda machine which is always ready to use the miseries of the people of occupied Europe in order to attempt to create confusion and doubt within the United Nations."[23]

Along with the oft-cited concern that Axis spies could be slipped in among refugees, the threat of Nazi propaganda had by now become a familiar argument against aid to the Jews: it had served to justify the White Paper as well as its strict enforcement, which sent shiploads of desperate Jewish refugees back to sea. When Merlin announced Hecht's pageant within weeks of the Romanian offer, the State Department's Near East specialist, Wallace Murray, urged his superiors to block the event to prevent its exploitation by the enemy. "Since European Jews were not universally popular," observes historian Richard Breitman, "and since Nazi propaganda featured alleged ties between international Jewry and the Allies, Washington saw little to be gained militarily or politically in assisting the most prominent victims of Nazi persecution. . . . Western humanitarian values were unable to prevail over the anti-Semites and pragmatists who stressed the risks of giving evidence to support German charges. To a remarkable degree, Adolf Hitler had succeeded in devaluing the lives of European Jews in the eyes of the rest of the world." In other words, Hitler was writing the script. As Hecht's narrator would lament in *We Will Never Die*, "it is the cheapness of his death that gives the Jew . . . a bad name."[24]

The furious reaction of American Jews to Hecht's latest newspaper ad—fury not at their government but at *him*—offered yet another vivid display of a characteristic fractiousness. Weeks earlier, Hecht had tried, and failed, to gain the support of nearly three dozen Jewish organizations for the pageant. Meeting with leaders at the Algonquin Hotel, he had read aloud from his script, moving many to tears, but as soon as he had finished and invited a response, old grudges between his guests boiled to the surface. "Within five minutes a free-for-all, bitter as a Kentucky feud, was in full swing," he recalled in *A Child of the Century*. He retreated in disgust to his bedroom, where the antagonists stepped in one by one to bid farewell and wish him luck. This squabbling was an old trouble, they explained apologetically.[25]

To his dismay, the pageant "unleashed a new Jewish battle cry . . . 'Down with Ben Hecht.'" In cities across the nation, he became a target along with rest of Bergson's Committee for a Jewish Army, which was denounced as a Revisionist front with no roots in the American Jewish community, no mandate, and no claim to legitimacy. For the thousands of Jews who belonged to the World Zionist Organization or the American and World Jewish Congresses, the basis for complaint was that they elected their leaders, whereas the Revisionists had eschewed the democratic process since seceding from the World Zionist Organization in 1933. This issue was paramount to Rabbi Wise, David Ben-Gurion, Chaim Weizmann, and their supporters, because it was through elections that such organizations embodied the liberal-democratic principles of modern Jewry. "In whose name do you dare to speak and whom do you represent?" Wise had demanded of Bergson.[26] He and his fellow Irgunists were viewed as irresponsible renegades whose cheap, inflammatory publicity stunts risked scuttling any real chance at rescue. Their efforts to conceal their Revisionist roots only made them seem shadier, because they appeared to be cynically exploiting the cataclysm in Europe for power and financial gain.

The American Jewish Congress had long been planning an event at Madison Square Garden, but it had been postponed several times. Under Wise's leadership, the American Zionist Emergency Council had been exhorting its members to challenge the Bergsonites on the local level since early in the year, and Wise's decision in mid-February to hold the "Stop Hitler Now" rally eight days before *We Will Never Die*'s premiere was likely intended as a preemptive attack against the pageant. The Committee for a Jewish Army tried to proffer a truce, suggesting that the two groups combine forces. Hecht submitted his script to the Congress for objections, and Bergson even offered to drop the committee's name from the billing. But the overture was rejected, and Wise, who according to Hecht had made clear his disapproval of the script, unsuccessfully tried to persuade New York governor Thomas Dewey to postpone an official "Day of Mourning" until after the premiere. The ensuing furor over the show's tour became its own spectacle and seemed to display a sad irony: the Nazis were slaughtering Jews for organizing a worldwide conspiracy, yet American Jews could not even cooperate on an appeal for rescue. "How could Jews," Hecht asked, "under a load of hate in the world, find time to hate each other?"[27]

Wise's tactics in New York, however, did little to dampen public enthusiasm. When fifty thousand people came to buy tickets after the March 9 premiere had already sold out, the committee hastily organized a second, late-night show that evening. Each performance drew a crowd of twenty thousand—a record attendance for the Garden. Loudspeakers accommodated the overflow crowd outside, and the radio carried the broadcast. Weill's mournful overture, based on the Kol Nidre, cut through the chilly darkness to greet the throngs, punctuated by blasts of a shofar and then lilted by cantor and choir. Between the two giant tablets of the Ten Commandments, an actor playing a rabbi emerged. "Almighty God

. . . ," he intoned, "we are here to say our prayers for the two million who have been killed in Europe, because they bear the name of your first children—the Jews." He quoted the prophet Habakkuk: "They shall never die though they were slaughtered with no weapon in their hand."[28]

Muni and Robinson appeared downstage at right- and left-center podiums, on a platform that was likely about sixty feet wide. As they began to speak, the tablets filled with clouds, flames, and shadows. "Roll Call," the first of the pageant's three original parts, offered a recitation of 119 Jews who had made historic contributions to the arts, sciences, philosophy, and politics. As the names were announced, actors in black robes entered carrying candles, while behind them the great faces from across the centuries appeared half visible on the tablets. "Jews in the War," the loudest and most colorful segment, honored those fighting for the eighteen Allied nations, naming the enlisted and the fallen with invocations of Simon Bar-Kochba and Barney Ross. It emphasized that the Jews had no homeland of their own to fight for.[29]

The wrenching final section, "Remember Us," drew from the tragic vignettes Hecht had used in his *Reader's Digest* article. As twenty girls dressed in white emerged from between the tablets, a voice offstage spoke for them:

> The Germans took a hundred and six of us and brought us to a hotel. They gave us perfumes and white robes to put on. They told us that at nightfall they would take us to a brothel and that we were to serve the Germans there. We waited all day. We anointed ourselves with the perfumes and put on the white robes. And when the sun was setting we knelt and prayed and each of us poisoned herself and died. The Germans came but none of us went to the brothel. There were many other thousands like us. Remember us.[30]

The girls were the last to join the scores of actors who had now filled the stage, representing the two million dead. They stood in the shadows, encircling a brightly lit peace table where three Nazis sat beside representatives of the Allied nations. The narrators now reappeared to conclude the performance. If the Germans fulfilled their promise to deliver another four million corpses by Christmas, they explained, there would be no Jews left to sit at this table of judgment. "The massacre of two million Jews is not a Jewish situation," said the narrator. "It is a problem that belongs to humanity. It is a challenge to the soul of man."[31]

We Will Never Die played to packed houses in Philadelphia, Boston, Chicago, and Washington, D.C., with a finale at the Hollywood Bowl in Los Angeles, garnering an estimated total attendance of over a hundred thousand. John Garfield, Burgess Meredith, and Yiddish actor Jacob Ben-Ami performed as the narrators, and the California performance included a fourth scene, "The Battle of the Warsaw Ghetto." It must have been written after the May 19 Chicago show, once the three-week-long uprising had been smashed and the handful of survivors shipped off to camps.

The Washington performance on April 12 was attended by Eleanor Roosevelt, six Supreme Court justices, Cabinet officers, some three hundred members of Congress, top military officials, and a large portion of the foreign diplomatic corps. In her "My Day" column, the First Lady extolled *We Will Never Die* as "one of the most impressive and moving pageants I have ever seen. No one who heard each group come forward and give the story of what happened to it at the hands of the ruthless German military, will ever forget those haunting words: 'Remember Us.'" Yet despite this strong endorsement, the column avoided any mention of the need for an Allied rescue policy.[32]

Her husband similarly remained silent. Billy Rose had asked Roosevelt for a supportive statement to read before the premiere, and Hecht recalled being asked to submit several versions of a brief statement that the president might read. "I toiled all night," Hecht later wrote, "determined to put whatever I had of talent, experience as a newspaperman and writer, and my soul's deep vengeance at the service of my brother Jews." But some time after Hecht had dropped off the pages with presidential aide David Niles, a secretary came out with an answer. "'He said No,' said the secretary and, as in a Chekhov play, burst into tears."[33]

The pageant succeeded in drawing considerable media coverage, but this in turn mobilized the resistance of various Jewish groups. In smaller cities and locales like Buffalo, Niagara Falls, Baltimore, and Gary, Indiana, letter and telephone campaigns vilified the Bergson Group and put local sponsors under pressure. The committee's approach of funding the tour through advance ticket sales became untenable. The result, noted one pundit for the *Jewish Review and Observer*, was that "the most powerful single weapon yet produced to awaken the conscience of America" was stopped cold.[34]

Nevertheless, the committee's bold endeavor was not completely fruitless. Hecht exaggerated when he later claimed that "the news and pictures of the pageant in the press were the first American newspaper reports on the Jewish massacre in Europe," but the sustained attention the show brought to the issue did help to provoke change.[35] While in December the *New York Times* had grieved that nothing could be done for the Jews, a March 3 editorial suggested the United States should "set a good example" for humanity by loosening its immigration laws. *Times* columnist Anne O'Hare McCormick appealed to Christians to do their utmost for rescue, asserting that the Jew is the "symbol of what this war is all about." On the same day, the *New York Herald Tribune* publicized the pageant with an editorial headlined "They Will Never Die."[36] Although the paper had not yet pressed for action, it would do so shortly, as would the *New York Post*, the *New York Sun*, the *Nation*, and others. Meanwhile, a *New York Times* reporter asked Welles at a March 3 press conference what plans the government had in mind "in the light of the mass meeting" held two days earlier. In response, the State Department attempted to show how concerned it had been all along, flourishing a note sent to the British on February 25 that suggested a conference on "the refugee problem."[37]

It soon became clear, however, that despite the glimmers of hope early that spring, the Allies were not going to budge on rescue. In his autobiography, Hecht recalled walking down Fifth Avenue with Weill late one night when the tour was over. "Actually, all we have done is make a lot of Jews cry," Weill had said, "which is not a unique accomplishment."[38]

The shift in public opinion that March may well have given Roosevelt a crucial push to establish the War Refugee Board nine months later, a decision that saved an estimated 200,000 lives.[39] But it would perhaps be too much to argue that Hecht's grand burst of propaganda had succeeded in sparking change and altering history. In the contest against the Nazis, the pageant had never stood a chance; measuring its impact against that of Nazi pageantry, for example, would hardly be fair, since Hitler commanded armies and the Gestapo as well as the vast resources of the Ministry of Popular Enlightenment and Propaganda. The Führer could orchestrate events as well as publicity, applying persuasion hand-in-glove with mass coercion. With blitzkrieg, deportations, and massacres, the Nazis choreographed the fate of whole populations, just as Albert Speer had choreographed the crowds at Nuremberg. Goebbels's ministry laid the groundwork for planned offensives or seized on developments to weave narratives of its choosing.

Even so, such power had its limits. Hitler could achieve nothing unless public sentiment was already in his favor, which is why Goebbels stressed that the ability to control *Haltung*—observable behavior—required a long-term investment in *Stimmung*—sentiment, morale. Although debate continues about the overall effectiveness of the Reich's propaganda, historians broadly agree on its success in stoking racial animosity. The trilogy of infamous films that included *The Eternal Jew* (1941), for instance, was able to exploit the deep-seated *Stimmung* of European anti-Semitism to trigger the *Haltung* of spontaneous pogroms, concurrent to those orchestrated by the regime.[40]

"I knew now that rhetoric was no better than tears for my 'Jewish Problem'—the rescue of the word Jew from the garbage can in which the Germans had dumped it," Hecht later wrote. ". . . I saw that propaganda was incapable of altering anything around it. It might incubate in time, it might mold the future. But it could only confuse the present or irritate it." This was essentially the same conclusion reached by Yale psychologist Carl Hovland, Columbia's Paul Lazarsfeld, and a clique of fellow communication scholars, who were researching media effects at the time for the U.S. Army's Information and Education Division. Their evidence, gathered through newly refined empirical methods, would give rise to a new postwar skepticism about propaganda's power.[41]

Such research, however, did not purport to measure the effect of propaganda on policymakers, who may have already been convinced of its power or—perhaps more often—found the threat of enemy propaganda convenient cover for their own agendas. Regardless of propaganda's actual potency, it became a significant factor, one way or another, in the fate of hundreds of thousands of Jews offered for ransom by the Axis after 1941. Their deaths resulted from what one historian has called "a fatal convergence of preferences: both the Allied governments and Adolf Hitler preferred the extermination of European Jews to any large-scale release of them into Allied hands."[42]

Perhaps *We Will Never Die* is best understood as a valiant effort by a small tribe of hopelessly outmatched underdogs. But while the case can be made that it was largely responsible for the War Refugee Board, what else did it accomplish, if anything? However tempting it is to argue that the pageant set the mold for a postwar Jewish identity, *We Will Never Die* quickly faded from public consciousness once the war ended. Nevertheless, its challenge to the ugly anti-Semitism of the Nazis *at the time* was itself significant. In the darkest hour of Jewish history, at a moment when American Jewry was helpless, fragmented, and bitterly divided, Hecht drew from the past to popularize an affirmative narrative of his people for the generation who lived through the war. Most important, *We Will Never Die* was the first prominent effort to construct collective memory in response to the Holocaust—an event that in recent decades has been as central to the Jewish self-image as it has been controversial. As the first of such efforts, Hecht's portrayal arguably represents an archetype, and so it's worth noting that he presented the Jew not only as a target of persecution but also as the voice and defender of the world's conscience.

Hecht had made an earnest appeal to humanity. This had been Hayim Greenberg's way, and Hecht had tried it. But as he later said, this was not his way. As the months passed and millions more died while his efforts continued in vain, he increasingly came to regard Allied inaction as criminal. By the time military victory had been achieved, the Nazis had slaughtered another four million, effectively erasing the Jewish population of Europe. Hecht's frustration had by then simmered into bitterness and soon thereafter boiled into rage.

CHAPTER 13

"One of the Greatest Crimes in History"

> *Historically, no massacre was ever so unexpected, no act of cruelty ever so great*
> *that it violated the professions of a civilization. . . . But surely there was never so*
> *much self-deception about our essential goodness or our dream of "social security,"*
> *so little philosophic (or moral) searching of the lies our hopes build on our lack*
> *of community, as there is today. . . . Something has already been done, by us the*
> *bystanders and not just the Nazi killers—which can never be undone, except as*
> *we seek to understand it and to grow human again (or expectant or merely wise)*
> *through it.*
>
> —Alfred Kazin, responding to the suicide of Shmuel
> Ziegelboim, "In Every Voice, in Every Ban"[1]

The first half of 1943 was a turning point in the war in more ways than one,
a time of optimism as well as fatalism. The German surrender at Stalingrad
on February 2 ended five grinding months of attrition that had decimated
Hitler's entire Sixth Army and forced an irreversible retreat along the
Eastern Front. By summer, Allied troops had taken Sicily and were poised
to attack the Italian mainland, while rolling, thousand-plane U.S. and
British bombing raids burned Germany's industrial cities to cinders. It
was becoming clear that the defeat of the Thousand-Year Reich was only
a matter of time, but, increasingly, the total liquidation of European Jewry
also seemed inevitable.[2] With each passing week, the Allies grew more
confident of victory while Jews plunged deeper into despair.

As *We Will Never Die* toured the nation, warning that the situation represented "a challenge to the soul of men," Hecht continued to hammer home the message, firing off opinion columns in early March to the *Christian Science Monitor*, the *Los Angeles Times*, and elsewhere. In "Jewish Situation Less Complex," he observed that in solving the "Jewish problem" of Europe, Hitler had created a much bigger problem for the world:

> To date, humanity has done almost nothing. Its indignation has been small. It has raised no sustained official voice. It has shuddered and taken matters for granted. . . . In fact, the German massacre of 2,000,000 human beings without guns or sticks with which to defend themselves has been possible only because humanity has stuck its skull into a fog. Its nerve endings are apparently dead. . . . We who have stood by silently at the overthrow of basic human reason and sensibilities have been honorary members of the German posse. . . . Hitler is a back number—a sort of Typhus Mary. . . . The germs we are combatting are those of spiritual corruption that have burrowed deep into the soul of man. There aren't many Nazis in New York today. But there are a myriad of numb people with hearts deader than doornails. These are the new Jewish situation.[3]

Even many who disagreed with Hecht nevertheless saw the awful events of 1943 as a challenge to the soul of American Jewry. Discourse among Jews had always been rife with storm and stress, but 1943 set a new standard, and though Hecht and his cohort had vowed not to attack their own people, they found themselves the target of increasingly aggressive opposition. Few American Jews had been prepared for the dire choices they would face as a community, choices that would redefine the way they saw themselves and deeply alter their culture and politics. The year was as transformative as it was painful. By its end, with Allied victory all but assured and attention turning to what the world would be like after the war, American Jews had embraced the dream of a homeland as never before. But the fate of their fellow Jews in Europe had by now been sealed; whatever had been done could not be undone, and questions about responsibility would not go away.

In Britain, where public reaction to the Riegner report had been swifter and stronger than in the United States, officials had pressed for a conference on refugees since early winter. With American sentiment stirred by Hecht's pageant and a series of rallies in March, the Allies announced they would convene a meeting to address the crisis within weeks. From the start, however, signs were not auspicious. The choice of Bermuda as a venue meant that wartime restrictions would prevent Jewish groups and journalists from attending. The State Department set ground rules forbidding special attention to the plight of Jews, as well as any talk of using the United States as a haven. Moreover, the conference, which was to begin on April 19 and last two weeks, would have no authority to make decisions; its purpose was purely exploratory.[4]

In the end, the participants suggested that the Intergovernmental Committee on Refugees, dormant since the Evian Conference of 1938, should be reactivated, but it soon became clear that the State Department and British Foreign Office were seeking to sideline rescue proposals. "Young Congressman Will Rogers Jr., one of the Co-Chairman bagged by Peter Bergson, . . . tried to track the commission down," Hecht later recalled. "He quizzed Undersecretary of State Breckinridge Long about it. Alas, the Commission had no office in the United States, and, in England—no address." While the conferees also recommended establishing camps in North Africa to admit three thousand people, overall the experts and officials reaffirmed that the problem of refugees would best be solved by speedy victory in the war. The Jewish representative Sol Bloom, one of two delegates from Congress, argued briefly that the Allies should try to broker deals for the release of Jews, but British and U.S. officials staunchly opposed any negotiations with the enemy. American papers gave cursory attention to the news of these proceedings provided by five wire-service reporters, the only press allowed to attend. The official conference report was classified.[5] Seen by many as a display of utter indifference, the Bermuda conference crushed hopes of rescue.

The conference coincided with the Warsaw ghetto uprising, which broke out the day the conference began. Two days later, a secret Polish transmitter that started to report the battle cut off after four sentences. Its final words: "Save us." Then on May 12 in London, the representative of the Polish Bund, Shmuel Ziegelboim, committed suicide to protest Allied callousness. In a final letter, he wrote that while responsibility for massacring the entire population of Poland lay in the first instance with the perpetrators, it indirectly also fell on the whole of humanity, including the citizens and governments of the Allied nations, "which thus far have made no effort toward concrete action for the purpose of curtailing this crime. By the passive observation of the murder of defenseless millions and of the maltreatment of children, women, and old men, these countries have become the criminals' accomplices."[6]

Hecht later remarked that between the precedence given to the war effort, concerns about floods of refugees, fears of spies and an Arab uprising, and the like, the governments had offered a "deadly alphabet of reasons" for doing nothing in particular to save six million people. While Rabbi Stephen Wise denounced Bermuda as "sad and sordid," and the Jewish press took umbrage after Bloom relayed that he was satisfied with its results, once again it was Bergson's Committee for a Jewish Army that kicked up the most dust. In an advertisement published at the outset of the meeting, the committee called on "the Gentlemen at Bermuda" to take "ACTION—not 'exploratory words.'" Another at the conclusion charged, "To 5,000,000 Jews in the Nazi Death-Trap, Bermuda was a 'Cruel Mockery.'"[7]

This blunt attack sparked outrage on Capitol Hill. Senator Harry Truman promptly quit the Committee for a Jewish Army, incensed that Bergson had used his name on the vituperative ad without his knowledge or approval. The committee had, without checking, imported a list of signatures from a previous proclamation backing the moral rights of stateless Jews and Palestinian Jews. Senator Scott Lucas of Illinois, who had been the other congressional delegate at Bermuda along with Bloom, took the message personally. On the floor of the Senate, he lashed out, emphasizing that Bergson was "not even a citizen of this country." Suspicions that the Irgunists were a group of foreign subversives had already been mounting and would prompt extensive FBI attention over the coming years, as well as efforts to deport Bergson. Weeks before Lucas started raising questions, J. Edgar Hoover had submitted a memorandum to the Justice Department that identified Hecht and the Committee for a Jewish Army as communists involved in political and financial racketeering. The memo cited as its source an executive from the American Jewish Congress, which suggests that Rabbi Wise had been the informant. True to form, Hecht relished the notoriety. "We were creating a new school of Jews in the U.S.," he later wrote, "one which refused to believe blindly in the virtues of their enemies in Democracy's clothing."[8]

Facing this impasse with officialdom and having exhausted—at least temporarily—his enthusiasm for newspaper advertisements, speeches, and pageants, Hecht shifted gears. He spent the next several months writing

A Guide for the Bedevilled, a discursive but "stinging philippic" on anti-Semitism intended to both spread a message and, through its sales, raise additional funds for Bergson's committees. "I wanted to publish 'Guide' the moment I saw it, just on principle, and then very much more after I read it for its fire and power as literature," wrote Maxwell Perkins in January 1944.[9]

Although Perkins, the legendary editor of Ernest Hemingway, F. Scott Fitzgerald, and Thomas Wolfe, assured Hecht that publisher Charles Scribner himself was "greatly taken" by the book, the firm printed such a paltry first run in March and allotted so little for promotion that Rose Hecht later surmised there had been interference by "Rabbi Wise, et al." The Bergsonites were nevertheless determined to make the book a success: Hecht financed additional advertising with his own royalties, while the committee contributed several thousand dollars. Within weeks, *A Guide for the Bedevilled* had reached the top of the nonfiction best-seller list and by September had sold 27,795 copies. Billy Rose, nicknamed the "pint-sized Barnum" and "Midget Maestro" of Broadway by a generally genial press, had taken the reins of publicity and matched dollar for dollar the money raised, so that more than $100,000 poured into Bergson's coffers.[10]

By way of introduction, Hecht argued that the American goons and loons who hated Jews were less harmful than insidious racists full of false talk about tolerance and high ideals. One such, he suggested, was "a woman more famous than intelligent" who in discussing anti-Semitism with him over lunch unconsciously revealed her desire to shift the blame for the murder of millions from the Germans to the Jewish victims themselves—"not all the blame, but enough to remove murder as a political issue." What is it about you Jews, she demanded of Hecht, that makes you so unpopular? "The picture came to me," he recalled, "of an angry policeman badgering a corpse for explanations of the crime committed against it." As she flung about humanitarian phrases, pacing an elegant library stocked with the noblest works of modern civilization, he realized she represented a sickness spreading like the common cold: the quiet acquiescence of high-minded, respectable people everywhere. Upon departing, he resolved to write a book that would contain what little he knew of the Jews and the great deal he knew of their enemies. Many books had been written about the Jews, he said, but the anti-Semite—now here was a far more obscure and elusive topic.[11]

His title was a wry reference to *The Guide for the Perplexed*, the oblique and mystical exegesis on Jewish law by the twelfth-century rabbi Maimonides, exalted by many as the great visionary masterpiece

of the Middle Ages and condemned by others as heresy. Hecht warned
that his "guide" would be an exercise in thinking out loud. Investigating
"twenty-eight hundred years of unreason" would undoubtedly lead down
countless blind alleys and into many thickets of contradictions. At times,
continuity would seem altogether absent. "I may seem to be running backward," he wrote, "or to have stopped moving entirely, or to have vanished
with a squeak down a rat hole." Such confusion, he predicted, will make
excellent fodder for critics.[12]

About this he was not wrong. "It may very well be that what we need
is a good lusty sense of outrage implemented by a vocabulary that could
easily burn the paint off a fire truck passing on the next block," observed
Norman MacDonald of the *Boston Herald*. Although MacDonald and
others gave Hecht high marks for his saucy, entertaining prose, and the
Jewish papers—which viewed the book as a kind of mea culpa for *A Jew in
Love*—were virtually unanimous in their praise, critics were less impressed
by the quality of Hecht's analysis, and *A Guide for the Bedevilled* did nothing to dispel his image as a lowbrow Hollywood hack. In one of the few
unequivocally negative reviews, Selig Greenberg of the *Providence Journal*
wrote, "Mr. Hecht, who is known for his smart-aleck cynicism, here dons
the mantle of the prophet crying in the wilderness. The unwonted attire
fits the repentant cynic poorly, and his peroration is a hodge podge of
vitriolic polemics against anti-Semitism, of autobiography and rambling
philosophizing often bordering closely on the hysterical."[13]

Greenberg's remarks anticipated the reputation Hecht garnered over
the succeeding years—as his rhetoric grew more vitriolic—for radicalism
full of sound and fury and little substance, a reputation that would ultimately doom *A Guide for the Bedevilled* to obscurity. But the book, as the
most complete expression of Hecht's worldview during the 1940s, remains
important: it reflected contemporaneous and future responses to Nazism,
and it drew the contours of American postwar debates about Israel, and
international politics and war more generally.

For the mostly Jewish critics later known as the New York Intellectuals,
little of what Hecht was saying in 1943 was new, and what was new seemed
either half-baked or offensive or more than a bit of both. Several respected
thinkers, among them Rabbi Wise, had already been warning for more
than a decade that the Nazis' attack on Jews represented a threat to modern
civilization. In 1934, while Hecht was still stewing in the self-hatred of *A
Jew in Love*, Wise had written:

The Jew has been a light to the nations, yet he is doomed to darkness. . . . The truth is that Hitlerism is the business of humanity. The truth is inevitably borne upon us who have come to see certain things: . . . what we have cherished as the values and standards of civilization are being broken down [and] . . . the racial fanaticism of the Hitler Reich may be a most immediate and deadly peril to us Jews, but it is no less truly a threat and a danger to all races and to all nations.[14]

What was new in *A Guide for the Bedevilled*, however, was something rooted in a Chicago reporter's cynical view of the human psyche and dark fascination with criminal psychology. What liberals like Wise saw as a mortal threat to civilization, Hecht regarded as symptomatic of human-kind's psychopathology. To make the point, he turned in the first instance to one of the lead architects of the Enlightenment. "Jew hatred was the odd hobby of this Prince of Reason—Voltaire," Hecht observed, "just as a master detective might practice murder on the side." How could such a friend of humanity, such a champion of rational behavior, tolerance, and justice, have harbored such swaggering and irrational hatred? "Where, in God's name," Hecht posited, "was his reason?" The answer, he argued, involved a basic truth about reason that Voltaire never recognized, a point that could be no better illustrated than by Voltaire's own bigotry.[15]

The great French philosopher had failed to understand what Shakespeare and other poets and storytellers had always known: that humans' thinking can never be divorced from their passions—from their loves, jealousies, and hatreds. Voltaire's assertion, for example, that "prejudice is opinion without judgment" revealed not only his own confusion but that which has bedeviled much of the world ever since. "This statement says that our souls can be purged of evil by the attentions of a schoolmaster," Hecht asserted. "It says that we are unreasonable because we have not been exposed to enlightenment. It says that our passions can be arranged into . . . order by the application of external logic—knowledge. It says that error exists because truth has not been offered in exchange. It says that the prejudices which fling us into stupid, silly or barbarous behaviors are no more than an absence of judgment."[16]

Back in the era of *The Front Page*, Hecht had raised similar arguments against the notion of journalistic objectivity, the belief that a reporter need only cast aside personal feelings and biases to attain a higher truth. Such thinking represents an ignorance, Hecht maintained, not only of what literature has to teach but of psychology as well. And without psychology there is no more insight and understanding "than there is history without bloodshed." Voltaire himself had proved that anti-Semitism "can thrive as virulently in the most acute and enlightened mind as it can in the darkened thought of fools."[17]

Hecht did not altogether discount the link between reason and tolerance, but he suggested "true prejudice is an inner unreason as necessary to us as our outer reasonableness." As the externalization of our own weaknesses and sore points, it fulfills a deep need. Projecting blame for our shortcomings onto an invented enemy allows us to excuse and even flatter ourselves. Prejudice empowers us, gives us absolution; "it is our ruse for disliking others rather than ourselves"; it enables us to imagine that we can impose order on forces that would otherwise be out of our control. "It is into this dark place that the word Jew has fallen," Hecht concluded. "It has become a word, not of historical or religious meaning, but a symbol of obsessions—one of the mystic forces by which men are able to outwit their own insufficiencies."[18]

By the same logic, the crime of murdering Jews holds special allure. In visits to the Cook County Jail as a young reporter, Hecht had met many a killer driven by a profound dissatisfaction with his lot in life, by a feeling of defeat that burned deep in the gut like an ulcer. The typical anti-Semite was much the same. "His need is to be lawless," Hecht explained, "to break the laws of logic, sanity, and good behavior, behind which he is hemmed in, bogged down and mousey." Through the act of homicide he shatters these manacles, and in that moment of bloodletting feels free and empowered, "as happy as a felon who has broken jail." But unlike other criminals, such as the thief or gangster, the butcher of Jews need not forfeit social status to experience the thrill of the outlaw. He can remain a respectable citizen. "Anti-Semitism is the one crime for which there is neither a court of law nor bar of human judgment," Hecht asserted. "It is, therefore, the most popular of crimes."[19]

To explain Nazism, he simply attributed this pathology to the whole of Germany, a view reinforced by his own experience there as a foreign correspondent during the grim days of 1919. He had at first found Germans to be polite and cultured, he recalled, but the sight of hundreds of men, women, and children cut down with machine guns in Moabit Prison opened his eyes to "a layer of barbarity in the German soul," a "talent for cruelty" on which they would soon build an empire. Germans were "pig-eyed," "fat-necked," "backward," and slavish, gnawed at by an age-old inferiority complex that had finally turned them into depraved killers. He suggested that upon their defeat in the war, they should be fenced in and declawed, kept in a kind of "Nazi zoo" where they could be studied as criminals for whatever they might teach about abnormal psychology.[20]

This tirade against the Germans, which carried on for forty pages, was what most baffled and repelled the critics. How could an author first announce his book as an attack on prejudice and then exhibit such grotesque prejudice himself? True, he made room for exceptions, noting two Germans who were his heroes—the liberal crusader Hugo Haase and painter George Grosz—and also discussed a self-hating Jew whose anti-Semitism had been as virulent as Voltaire's. He had also warned from the start that he would "blunder into contradictions that a child of four (let alone a critic) will be able to spot in a twinkling." Perhaps he was only illustrating that he was as human as anyone else, and therefore just as governed by unreason. Such considerations, however, hardly mollified the reviewers. Elmer Rice titled his review "A Pitchfork with Prongs at Both Ends." Harold Rosenberg wrote that in Hecht's sweeping condemnation of humankind and of Germany, he solved the murder not by apprehending the perpetrator but by "locking up everybody in the neighborhood."[21]

Hecht boasted that he was first and last a journalist, not a scholar. ("There are too few mariners and too many geographers.") But though his barrage against the Germans may have been crude and intemperate, the question of the average citizen's culpability would endure as a core debate about the Holocaust. Even Wise, the great humanitarian, would write, "No crimes of the men, who later were hanged as criminal war-makers, seemed terrible enough to disturb the . . . conscience of the German people . . . as long as there seemed the faintest hope of winning the war. The penitence that comes after defeat is not penitence." A half century later, historian Daniel Goldhagen reignited the dispute with *Hitler's Willing Executioners: Ordinary Germans and the Holocaust*, creating an extraordinary commotion in Germany just as the nation was adjusting to reunification.[22]

The theories in *A Guide for the Bedevilled* would in fact be examined and hotly contested for decades. Hecht's explanation of Nazism as mass psychosis may have seemed simplistic, phrased as it was in his customary journalese, but it essentially conveyed the premise of Erich Fromm's pioneering 1941 book of political psychology, *Escape from Freedom*. And decades before Americans had heard of Adolf Eichmann, Hecht offered his own version of Hannah Arendt's "banality of evil," imagining what he described as "the little German burgher at his desk, receiving reports of another seven thousand Jews run over by lorries (this money-saving device was thought up by a German general in Romania) . . . and entering [the reports] in a book as fastidiously as any accountant." Like Arendt, Hecht argued that evil need not be committed by raving monsters like Hitler, that it was more often perpetrated, with devastating effect, by ordinary, imbecilic little burghers like Eichmann. He added that it was precisely their ordinariness and imbecility that made them dangerous.[23]

But most important, in terms of Hecht's own subsequent turn toward militancy, was his emphasis on the *criminality* of the Final Solution, which anticipated the coming rhetoric on matters of war and peace—international law, the laws of war, war crimes, and crimes against humanity. He predicted that once peace had been declared, the Allies and Germans would embrace each other like exhausted boxers at the end of a match, and all would be forgiven. His prophecy proved mostly correct: only a small percentage of the top Nazi war criminals were ever prosecuted, and as recently declassified documents have verified, the Central Intelligence Agency recruited some as spies against the communists while keeping quiet about the whereabouts of others, including Eichmann.[24]

While Hecht was writing *A Guide for the Bedevilled* in the summer of 1943, events affirmed his darkest thoughts about the world, except for a major development in his personal life: the birth, on July 30, of his daughter Jenny. Three days later he wrote a poem to her that became the "Dedication and Preface" to his book:

> . . . *What a difference appears to all the world when I look on my daughter, newly born.*
> *Where is the world gone that has lost her face?*[25]

The Bergson Group, meanwhile, spent the early part of the summer organizing the Emergency Conference to Save the Jewish People, a six-day affair attended by fifteen hundred participants that convened on July 20 at New York's Commodore Hotel. The American Jewish Congress and other organizations charged that the conference's goal of formulating a rescue program was redundant: at the March 1 "Stop Hitler Now" rally, on the eve of the Bermuda conference, and again in June, they had presented versions of a plan that called for negotiations with the Axis, liberalization of immigration laws, establishment of safe havens, and other measures that were beginning to gain broad support. The recommendations of the Emergency Conference were indeed similar to those presented in the spring but, along with the proposal in June, differed in one respect: they called for reprisals and punishments for Nazi war criminals.[26]

Moreover, the conference kept the issue of rescue in the headlines and conveyed a pointed message. "We wanted to challenge the 'Let's win the war first' notion," Alexander Rafaeli recalled in his memoir, "as well as the impotence of the Jewish establishment, busily involved in a 'love affair' with the American president." Three major resolutions emerged from the proceedings: first, that the annihilation of Europe's Jews should be considered a separate problem from the general concern about refugees; second, that rescuing four million Jews need not interfere with the war effort; and third, that the Allies should create an independent agency devoted to the purpose.[27]

Now rebranding themselves as the Emergency Committee to Save the Jews of Europe, the Bergsonites were beginning to criticize Roosevelt directly. They were nevertheless surprised by the politically partisan response to their call for a conference, a response that, in any case, far exceeded expectations. "When we approach an honest man, if he is a Republican, he will accept our offer and join us," observed Eri Jabotinsky in an early July report. "If he is a New Dealer, however, he will be sympathetic, but as for joining us and lending us his support, he will first ask 'somebody in Washington,' with the result that we will receive from him a beautiful letter expressing his sentiments and his regrets at not being able to participate because of a sudden trip to the West Coast."[28]

When Max Lerner, who served as cochair of the event, telegraphed Secretary Cordell Hull and Roosevelt for an endorsement, he received a curt reply that the State Department was already doing all that it could. Stung by this rebuke from a president he had staunchly supported, Lerner published a July 22 editorial in *PM* provocatively headlined, "What about the Jews, FDR?" Once again the Bergson Group fared little better with the First Lady, who declined to attend the conference. She encouraged the effort to develop a plan but expressed skepticism that anything more could be done.

Since she nevertheless offered to help in any way she could, Bergson followed up in mid-August with a request for an encouraging message to be broadcast to the Jews of Europe by the Office of War Information. In a brief statement, she extended her sympathies and expressed hope that

the Jewish people would continue to fight for their existence, but reiter-
ated that America could best save lives by winning the war as quickly as
possible. Bergson had also asked her to hand the president a copy of the
conference's findings and recommendations. Days later Roosevelt returned
the document to Eleanor's assistant with a note that said, "I do not think
this needs any answer at this time. FDR."[29]

Hecht later wrote that he had remained an ardent admirer of Roosevelt,
like millions of American Jews, even though Bergson had admonished that
the president had a pact with the British to keep the Jews locked away in
Europe and out of Palestine. Hecht remained loyal despite the government's lack of support for his pageant, its refusal to negotiate over the fate
of the Romanian Jews, and its foot-dragging in general. Nevertheless, he
recalled that he had never felt much affinity for the New Dealers, with
their fine but empty talk about the woes of the common person, lynchings
of Negroes in the South, and other conditions that never seemed to change:

> On the whole, I fear I was a churlish Liberal, to whom all political lead-
> ers of all persuasions seemed no better than gadget peddlers with their
> foot in the door, whining the sale of their wares. With the politician,
> the foot stays longer, the whine is louder and the wares on sale more
> worthless—himself.
>
> Such "Liberals" as myself are apt to be uncomfortable with a friend
> in power. We prefer an enemy on the throne—an arrogant creature
> who despises the rights of man, or some paranoid knight of unreason.[30]

Attacking Roosevelt ran the risk of alienating many American Jews, who
were famously devoted to the president; they had voted for him in greater
proportions than any other ethnic or religious group in the United States.
Roosevelt, formerly governor of New York, had surrounded himself with
Jewish advisers and political allies; testaments to the close bond that Jews felt
with the president were legion, from the well-circulated slur about his "Jew
Deal" to an account of how he was greeted like Moses when campaigning in
Brooklyn. Republican judge Jonah J. Goldstein summed up the sentiment,
lamenting that his coreligionists lived in three *velten* (worlds): *die velt* (this
world), *yene velt* (the next world), and *Roosevelt*. But now that time was running out in Europe, Bergson became convinced that they had to confront
the man they believed to be most responsible for Allied inaction. When the
tensions mounted in the fall, Hecht would eventually jump into the fray.[31]

The escalation began in August and September, when the committee intensified its lobbying and ad blitz, proclaiming that Europe's Jews were still "caught between the hammer of the enemy's brutality and the anvil of democracy's indifference." Among the most caustic was Hecht's "Ballad of the Doomed Jews of Europe," finally published now after having been withheld in late 1942 at Judge Joseph Proskauer's request.[32] At the same time, the group partnered with two ultra-Orthodox organizations, Agudath Israel of America and the Union of Orthodox Rabbis, to organize a demonstration in Washington.

On October 6 five hundred rabbis chanting from the book of Psalms marched to Capitol Hill, where they read a petition for rescue to vice president Henry Wallace and twenty members of Congress. Although coverage of the event was disappointing, it again displayed Bergson's talent for publicity. The striking photo published in *Time* showed the rabbis with their beards and long black coats, staring, tear-streaked, up at the sky in front of Wallace, who "squirmed through a diplomatically minimum answer" to their appeal. From there the rabbis proceeded to the Lincoln Memorial to pray for America's soldiers and a speedy victory, and then on to the White House. Even though the Emergency Committee had tried for weeks to obtain an appointment with the president, Bergson and four leading rabbis were met by his secretary, Marvin McIntyre. Speechwriter and aide Samuel Rosenman had advised that the group behind the petition did not represent "the most thoughtful elements in Jewry," so Roosevelt instead went off to Bolling Field to dedicate Liberator bombers for a Yugoslavian combat unit. "From the president's perspective," noted Richard Breitman in *FDR and the Jews*, "Bergson and his allies gave Jewish issues undue publicity and detached Jewish concerns from broader Allied priorities and principles."[33]

For Hecht, the breaking point came weeks later, with the October 30 "Statement on Atrocities" the president signed with Churchill and Stalin at the Moscow Conference. The declaration vowed punishment for the mass executions in Axis-occupied countries but made no mention of the Jews, although it cited the slaughter of "Polish officers," "French, Dutch, Belgian or Norwegian hostages," and "Cretan peasants." This especially rankled the Bergsonites, and Hecht in particular, given their emphasis on genocide as a war crime.[34]

On November 5, Hecht blasted Roosevelt with a newspaper advertisement that consisted of a fable, "My Uncle Abraham Reports . . ." The tale, which appeared above a reprint of the declaration, told of a ghost of a

Jewish uncle killed by the Nazis, elected by two million fellow ghosts—the "Jewish underground"—to be their world delegate at Allied conferences. Upon returning from the Moscow meeting, Abraham tells his people that they were not named among the Nazi victims the three powers promised to avenge. When a "Ghost from the Lime Kilns of Warsaw" asks why this is so, Abraham cannot say. "We were not allowed by the Germans to stay alive," he replies. "We are not allowed by the Four Freedoms to be dead." Abraham then leaves for the White House to sit on a windowsill two feet from Roosevelt and await justice, but he has left his pencil and notepad at home.[35]

To the great satisfaction of the Emergency Committee, Roosevelt left no doubt that he had felt the blow. Eleanor told Bergson that her husband was very upset by the ad, which he had described as a strike below the belt. Bergson, however, refused to apologize. According to Hecht, the president's financial adviser, Bernard Baruch, telephoned two days after the ad appeared to ask for a halt to such broadsides. Baruch alluded to an important statement Roosevelt was planning to make on a trip to the Middle East, which raised Hecht's hopes for a call to open the ports of Palestine, or something similarly momentous. Bergson, Samuel Merlin, and Yitshaq Ben-Ami were skeptical, but Hecht insisted that the criticism stop immediately. Nothing materialized, however, when Roosevelt traveled to Cairo and Tehran in late November, and for Hecht the amnesty ended when the president returned from a trip to the region in March 1945 singing the praises of Saudi prince Ibn Saud, a vehement anti-Semite and anti-Zionist.[36]

While, to Hecht, Roosevelt was just another duplicitous politician, one can also see him, like Abraham Lincoln, as a man of vision who faced a staggering array of challenges, who had need of all of his considerable charm and political acumen to manage the competing interests and imperatives of the war. In late July the president had reconfirmed his prior promises to mete out justice on behalf of the Jews, when Wise had asked him to threaten reprisals against Nazi satellites such as Romania and Hungary if they continued to cooperate with Germany. "I intend again, on suitable occasions, to revert publicly on this subject, as I am sure the heads of other United Nations Governments will also do," he had advised.[37]

As for Roosevelt's record on Zionism, in May 1942 he had reaffirmed his long-standing support for a Jewish national home and then, in a bid to outdo the Republicans in the 1944 election, ran on a platform that called for a free and independent commonwealth and "unrestricted Jewish immigration and colonization." Yet all along he had approved drafts of anti-Zionist statements from the State Department, and after his reelection he gushed to Congress about his meeting with the Saudi prince, no doubt with America's oil interests and alliance with Great Britain in mind. "Over the course of more than a decade as president," Breitman notes, "Roosevelt sounded at times like a Zionist, at times like a skeptic about Palestine's capacity to absorb new settlers, and at times, when speaking to anti-Semites, like an anti-Semite himself." Nevertheless, Breitman contends, Roosevelt's policies did the Jews more good than harm, despite his dissembling and evasions.[38]

"My Uncle Abraham Reports . . ." hit the newspapers at a crucial time, days before bipartisan rescue resolutions were introduced in the House and Senate on behalf of the Emergency Committee, and just as the conflict between the Bergsonites and the Jewish establishment was coming to a head. Since Bermuda, the Zionists and non-Zionists had shifted away from rescue while stepping up their attacks on the Bergson Group, a course of action that has been a focus of speculation and heated debate ever since. By autumn the Bergsonites were facing the united opposition of the American Jewish Conference, an umbrella organization of more than thirty Jewish groups that had formed in late August when they had gathered to develop a postwar plan for world Jewry.

Rescue had been at the bottom of the agenda in August; as a result, the two Orthodox groups had abstained and joined with Bergson. But the summit turned out to be a watershed event for American Zionism. It exceeded the expectations of Rabbi Wise and other Zionist leaders who, hoping that it might foster a sense of fellowship that would eventually unify support for the Zionist program, had decided not to rush things by pushing a controversial resolution that called for a Jewish commonwealth. This miscalculation gave Wise's chief rival, Rabbi Hillel Silver, an opening to deliver an impassioned and defiant call for statehood. When Silver declared that Jewish homelessness was "the principal source of our millennial tragedy" and had led directly to the Nazi catastrophe, he brought participants to their feet, releasing a flood of pent-up frustration and anguish. Though the speech marked the start of a nasty contest for power between Wise and Silver for leadership of the American Zionist Emergency Council, the movement was energized as never before.[39]

This new coalition mobilized to lift the blockade on Palestine, even as it opposed Bergson's resolutions in Congress. The Emergency Committee was trying to stay focused on the urgent need for rescue and keep the messy politics of Palestine out of the equation. When the Zionists demanded that the rescue resolution include a call to end the White Paper, Bergson was incredulous: "If you were inside a burning house, would you want the people outside to scream 'save them,' or to scream 'save them by taking them to the Waldorf-Astoria?'"[40]

The resolution was sailing through the Senate, but in the House the loyal Zionist congressman Sol Bloom held it up in hearings at the end of November. During the ensuing weeks of contentious testimony, congress-people previously unfamiliar with Jewish factionalism were bewildered by all the sniping. One asked whether he was attending a hearing or an investigation; others questioned the advisability of linking the Palestine issue with "the present and immediate necessity of rescuing the Jews." According to resolution sponsor Guy Gillette, a fellow Senate committee member remarked: "I wish these damned Jews could make up their minds what they want. I could not get inside the committee room without being buttonholed out here in the corridor by representatives who said that the Jewish people of America did not want passage of this resolution."[41]

The American Jewish Conference's opposition culminated in a scathing attack on Hecht and the Bergsonites just before the congressional recess at the end of the year, and weeks before the Senate was expected to vote overwhelmingly in favor of the resolution. Taking aim once again at Hecht's "Guaranteed Human Beings at $50 a Piece" ad, their December 29 press release recited the usual allegations of fraud and declared that Bergson's resolutions had been introduced in "complete disregard of the rescue program which is actively pressed in Washington by representative Jewish agencies." Months later, at a meeting with a State Department official, Zionist leader Nahum Goldmann again demanded the government either draft Bergson into the military or kick him out of the country, describing his efforts as "a gigantic hoax" perpetrated on well-meaning Americans that "had not resulted in the rescue of a single Jew or in the saving of a single Jewish life." Goldmann further relayed that Rabbi Wise regarded Bergson "as equally great an enemy of the Jews as Hitler."[42]

That Jewish organizations united in late 1943 to defeat a congressional rescue proposal has been explained in various ways. According to historian David Wyman, the Zionists reasoned that they would have only one chance to introduce legislation on Palestine, an opportunity that would be squandered by these resolutions. Wise and his allies understood that time was of the essence, that the fluid conditions of the immediate postwar period would afford their best shot at Jewish statehood. Certainly another key factor was a paralyzing despair that gripped American Jews, especially after Bermuda. Historians sympathetic with the Zionists have argued that their actions reflected a tough, realistic assessment of tragic circumstances. They recognized that the hour for wholesale rescue of Jews from the Nazis had passed, if that indeed had ever been possible. What was needed now was a steely focus on the days to come, on securing the survival of Jewry by ensuring that such a catastrophe could never occur again.[43]

In Wise's case in particular, such reasoning becomes more understandable when viewed within the broader context of efforts at rescue that spanned more than a decade with ever-dwindling success, efforts that preceded Hecht's but ironically bore many parallels to them. Biographer Melvin Urofsky called Wise "a voice in the wilderness" during the 1930s, and indeed no American had warned more loudly and consistently about Hitler. Though the rabbi never claimed to have foreseen the full horror that would one day unfold, he cautioned as early as December 1931 that Hitler's threats against the Jews must be taken seriously, while other Americans were dismissing the man as a ridiculous kook. In 1943 Hecht would theorize, incorrectly, that the Nazis might heed an outcry from abroad, but, unfortunately, that had been true during the first couple of years after the Führer first became chancellor in 1933, when Wise had led the American Jewish Congress in organizing two rallies at Madison Square Garden. The first, a March 27 event attended by an overflow crowd of fifty-five thousand, called for an American boycott of German imports. It precipitated a swift backlash: a German boycott of Jewish-owned businesses, as well as a series of laws passed in April and October that forced Jews out of civil service, restricted their professional careers, and imposed quotas in schools. Undeterred, the American Jewish Congress joined with the American Federation of Labor to stage a second rally on March 7, 1934, "The Case of Civilization against Hitlerism," in front of twenty thousand "jurors."[44]

Wise had declared that "the time for caution and prudence has passed," breaking from the Congress's sister defense organizations, the American Jewish Committee and B'nai Brith. These two groups represented a large portion of the Jewish community Wise called the "Sh-Sh Jews," who blanched at such loud protest, and who pleaded instead for quiet, behind-the-scenes appeals to the State Department. During the mid-1930s, he worked to establish the World Jewish Congress, envisioned not only to protect Jews but also to represent their highest ideals. In both campaigns he fought the opposition of those he called the American *Shtadlonim*, or "court Jews," who lacked the mettle to face the crisis of Nazism squarely.[45]

But from the 1940s onward, it was Wise who would be branded "a pitiful *Shtadlan*" by Hecht, the Bergsonites, and later critics, for what they saw as blind obeisance to Roosevelt. Wise's detractors have pointed to the letter he sent to Roosevelt a week after publicizing the Riegner report. "Dear Boss:" he had begun, "I do not wish to add an atom to the awful burden which you are bearing with magic and, as I believe, inspired strength at this point." Even Urofsky, whose reverential biography of Wise is titled *A Voice That Spoke for Justice*, concluded, "His faith in the goodwill of Franklin Roosevelt was not only ill-founded, but would prove disastrous." Urofsky also commented, "If there is one charge that can be sustained against Wise and the others, it is that they placed their trust in Franklin Roosevelt."[46]

There were many differences that divided the Jewish establishment and the Bergsonites—the dispute over the Palestine issue was only the latest—but clearly a key fault line was how to interact with the president at a time when national unity and patriotism were at such a premium. By late 1943 Roosevelt had become the nexus for all points of conflict: who had the right to speak for the Jews, whether Hecht's polemics were hurting or helping chances for rescue, and who could best lead the advance of Jewish statehood. Most significantly, however, the dispute over Roosevelt represented a clash of ideologies.

"It's not a matter of what the Zionists believe," Hecht remembered Merlin explaining. ". . . Stephen Wise will not tolerate any other Jewish organization working for Palestine and stealing honors and publicity from him." While Wise refuted this charge in the autobiography he completed just before his death, his disavowal is not wholly convincing: none of the Jewish leaders could have achieved their positions without highly competitive, egoistic natures. Debating Wise's character and motivation, however, distracts from the core issue: the battle over ideas that makes what would otherwise be just a tragic story of Jewish infighting so important to modern history. Just as the Jews loved Roosevelt, as Hecht observed, "chiefly as the symbol of a new American obsession called 'liberalism,'" Wise—a leading fighter for social justice who cofounded both the National Association for the Advancement of Colored People and the American Civil Liberties Union in 1920—personified the liberalism of American Jews.[47]

Ever since Hecht had started writing for *PM*, he had inveighed against a so-called enlightened worldview shared by many of his fellow Jews that left them paralyzed and uncomprehending prey as the Nazi snake coiled itself around Europe. In 1942 Bergsonite Reinhold Niebuhr argued that some American Jews had refused to face the crisis because they dreaded recognizing "that the solutions provided by the liberal Jewish world have failed to reach the depths of the problem." These assertions suggest a judgment that later became a commonplace: that American Jewish leaders had been psychically unprepared for such an explosion of vicious hatred and a catastrophe of such magnitude that spread so quickly. That it was occurring not in "backwards" czarist Russia but in "cultured" modern Germany had made it all the more difficult to accept. As Roosevelt said in 1938, "I myself could scarcely believe that such things could occur in a twentieth century civilization."[48]

The inadequacy of the liberal response was arguably evident throughout the 1930s in Wise's misplaced faith in a world conscience that could be mobilized to save the Jews; in his ambivalence, as a committed pacifist, toward American military intervention until as late as October 1941;[49] and perhaps also in his failure, as someone so engaged, to see where Nazism was headed. This failure was arguably reflected in what would later seem sluggish, misguided, or even callous about the course pursued by American Jewry during the war. It was a difference in consciousness between those accustomed to the comforts and safety of the United States and the militant young Irgunists who had grown up in Europe during the 1930s. Like Hecht, the latter group saw all of liberal democracy, from the president on down, as criminally responsible for refusing to aid the Jews or even offer them safe harbor. They regarded Wise, the rest of the *Shtadlonim*, and their followers as dupes who clung to respectability, rendered impotent by a fatalistic ghetto mentality.

In his 1949 memoir, Wise himself did not deny the failure of liberalism. He pointed to the *Shtadlonim* of the American Jewish Committee and other "self-appointed protectors of Jewish life" as having been unwilling "to face facts and deal with them aright." Such cowardice, he explained, was "the very saddening confession of the failure of so-called liberalism as the solvent or panacea of human ills." He readily acknowledged this failure in pointing to the anti-Semitism of the State Department and the British. But, in his view, liberalism was not a matter of ideology or of choice. "Jews never were . . . liberals by expediency," he argued. "They understood, as we continue to understand, that Jews . . . have no place or future in an illiberal world." Through the years of genocide and afterward, his refusal to abandon liberal principles took the form of staunch loyalty to Roosevelt.[50]

By the same logic, Wise viewed Revisionism as "a stark surrender to the rightfulness of fascism." For him, the Revisionist movement's undemocratic nature was demonstrated by its 1933 decision to secede from the representative body for Jewish statehood, the World Zionist Organization; by Betar's militarism and the Irgun's use of violence; and, most recently, by the Bergsonites' inflammatory publicity campaign. "They were little more than hoodlums in his eyes," observed Robert Silverberg, author of the Zionist history *If I Forget Thee, O Jerusalem*, "and the fact that they were dedicated hoodlums, pledged to the same sacred cause he served, did not matter."[51]

This clash of ideologies did not simply play out between Jewish leaders. It was waged over kitchen tables, at dinner parties, in restaurants and reception halls, in conference rooms, and on sidewalks outside theaters—everywhere that American Jews gathered. A fellow Bergsonite would later reminisce in a letter to Hecht: "Do you remember the back room of the Penthouse Club and the meetings at homes where the little pip-squeak so-called business tycoons of the ready-to-wear industry proclaimed their loyalty to our Allies the British, whose only intent was to avoid donations to our Cause? And how refreshing it was when you told them point by point the ugly truth of their cowardice and evasions? I remember very well kicking the ass out of one meeting of some 'American patriot' and his silly son." According to pro-Bergson chronicler Louis Rapoport, the questions Hecht and the Emergency Committee raised about loyalty and patriotism touched a nerve for progressives like Wise, who found it difficult to concede that the group might have made any contributions to the cause of rescue. The animosity of the Zionists, Rapoport suggested, revealed "a basic uncertainty about their Jewishness in American life, their simultaneous pursuit of Zionist and assimilationist goals."[52]

CR

Unbeknownst to the Zionists and the Bergsonites, tensions over rescue had been building for months within the Roosevelt administration. The dispute erupted at the end of 1943 in a dramatic confrontation that, on the one hand, seemed to affirm Hecht's worst suspicions about the criminality of government and, on the other, at last produced the policy changes that he and the Emergency Committee had been seeking.

In April Wise had finally obtained a two-page message from World Jewish Congress representative Gerhart Riegner that had been blocked by the State Department, outlining a plan to smuggle Jewish children out of France and Romania with assets that would be frozen in Swiss bank accounts until the end of the war. Despite approvals over the summer from the Treasury Department and the president himself, officials in the State Department and Britain scuttled Riegner's initiative by holding up the transfer of funds for the rest of the year. The obstructionism continued until Secretary of the Treasury Henry Morgenthau wrote to Secretary of State Hull, noting with alarm that three and a half months had passed since Treasury had signed off on "the relatively simple matter of getting our Minister in Switzerland to issue a license." When the British were finally candid about their objections in mid-December, American ambassador John Winant reported that the Foreign Office was "concerned with the difficulties of disposing of any considerable number of Jews should they be rescued from enemy occupied territory." Here, at last, was the truth: British and State Department officials had feared that a rescue plan would in fact *succeed*.[53]

Stunned by the statement from London, Morgenthau's staffers appealed to him to take action. Randolph Paul, one of four attorneys on the staff most engaged in the issue, said: "I don't know how we can blame the Germans for killing them when we are doing this. The law calls it *para-delicto*, of equal guilt." Morgenthau later characterized Winant's statement as "a Satanic combination of British chill and diplomatic double-talk; cold and correct, and adding up to a sentence of death." But he knew he had to tread carefully. The administration's opponents, he explained, would go after him because "I have done something for the Jews because I am a Jew." Before approaching the president, he would have to at least try to confer with Secretary of State Hull and his staff, who were now expecting fallout from Winant's blunt telegram and were hastily backpedaling.[54]

Most nervous among them was Assistant Secretary of State Breckinridge Long, portrayed in many histories of the American response to the Holocaust as an archvillain, the major impediment to Jewish immigration and rescue initiatives. A blue-blooded nativist who served as chief policy-maker on all matters concerning European refugees, Long began in the summer of 1940 to institute a maze of restrictions on visa applications that slowed the flow of immigrants to a trickle, even as thousands clamored for asylum. By mid-December 1943, however, he was already in hot water over his testimony to the House committee on Bergson's rescue resolution. Among the gross inaccuracies and misleading claims now leaking out from his closed-door session, most damaging was his implication that 580,000 Jewish refugees had been admitted to the United States since Hitler took power in 1933, an exaggeration of 250 percent. Moreover, the 165,756 Jews who had immigrated represented only a tenth of those who could legally have been admitted under even the normal quotas.[55]

Meanwhile, the Treasury attorneys were unearthing proof that for a year the State Department had been suppressing all the news it received about extermination. The first piece of intelligence that officials had blocked turned out to be an urgent cable from Riegner in January 1943, which reported that the Germans were killing six thousand Jews a day in Poland and that seventy thousand Romanian Jews who remained alive—half of the original population—were in imminent peril.[56]

Over the Christmas holiday of 1943, Josiah E. DuBois Jr. prepared an eighteen-page document titled "Report to the Secretary on the Acquiescence of This Government in the Murder of the Jews." He detailed the evidence that Long had used the visa application process to shut the door on refugees and then had misrepresented the record in his testimony before the House; that Long and other State Department officials had not only failed to attempt to rescue the Jews or to cooperate with private groups but instead used "government machinery" to prevent such efforts; and that the State Department had also tried to block the flow of information about extermination, engaging in deception to conceal their guilt. "*One of the greatest crimes in history*, the slaughter of the Jewish people in Europe, is continuing unabated," DuBois wrote. ". . . Unless remedial steps of a drastic nature are taken, and taken immediately, I am certain . . . that this government will have to share for all time responsibility for this extermination."[57] When DuBois gave the report to Morgenthau, he said that if the president did not act, he would resign and take his findings to the press.

Morgenthau toned down DuBois's inflammatory title, replacing it with "Personal Report to the President," but retained the assertions that the State Department had earned a reputation for anti-Semitism and that exposure of its conduct would set off a scandal. On January 16, 1944, Morgenthau and two of the attorneys brought it to the president, who asked for an oral summary. Morgenthau added that if Roosevelt did not move ahead with rescue plans, Congress might beat him to the punch by passing Bergson's resolution. The president, however, was well apprised of the political situation and needed little persuasion. He suggested some minor changes and then agreed to sign an executive order after a discussion that lasted only twenty minutes. On January 22, two days before the Senate was scheduled to vote on the rescue resolution, Roosevelt created the War Refugee Board with Treasury attorney John Pehle as executive director.[58]

ও

Hecht saw the liberalism of the "Sensitive Souls" who supported Roosevelt as a kind of moral palsy, "more often an illness than a point of view. It is to goodness what brutality is to strength." Its cravenness seemed apparent to him in the impotency of American Jewry and in Roosevelt's empty promises. Worse, liberal rhetoric often seemed to camouflage anti-Semitism, as it had for Voltaire when he had spoken so eloquently of reason and tolerance. Hecht had seen it in the talk of the chillingly genteel lady whom he met for lunch and in the statements from the "striped pants boys" of the beloved president's own administration. In middle age, Hecht rediscovered the righteous wrath of his youth. Like the Hebrew prophets who had attacked those who should know better—the people of the Covenant— he and Maxwell Bodenheim had once taken aim at the bohemians and intellectuals of the jazz age. Now he chastised the Allies, the liberals, and, indirectly but no less pointedly, the Zionists.

The debates of 1943 have since been rehashed for seventy years, as history has become ideology. After liberal opinion started to turn against Israel in the 1970s, Hecht was championed as the original unapologetic hawk of American Jewry. Yet in Hecht's own view, he never ceased to be a liberal, albeit a churlish one, who had yearned to believe in the president but found him to be just another politician. For a while, the furious quarreling over the Holocaust seemed to blur the old distinctions between right and left, thanks in part to a historian who in later years emerged as Hecht's and Bergson's most formidable critic, Lucy Dawidowicz, a neoconservative contributor to *Commentary* whose positions were as mercurial as they were polemical.[59] Since the 1990s, the original ideological dividing lines have reasserted themselves, particularly as Dawidowicz and others who lived through the turmoil of those years have passed away. All along, however, the arguments over the actual historical record have remained the same. They can be boiled down to three major points of contention: the feasibility of rescue before 1944, the achievements of the War Refugee Board, and the effectiveness of Hecht and the Emergency Committee.

For Dawidowicz, Roosevelt's failings were dwarfed by his achievements in overcoming first the economic collapse of the United States and then the threat to civilization from National Socialism. "No president before or after him ever had to confront responsibilities of such urgency and gravity," she wrote, "whose range and complexity, domestic and foreign, often put them beyond one man's capacity to resolve and, impinging as they did upon one another, beyond any man's capacity to reconcile." Like other interlocutors who followed, Dawidowicz characterized historians critical of Roosevelt and the Allies, like David Wyman, as Holocaust "revisionists" prone to pedantic moralizing, unable to grasp the realities and challenges of the war.[60]

Scholars sympathetic to Roosevelt concede that he might have done more to rein in Long and the State Department but argue he could not have overcome the anti-immigrant sentiment of the American public and a significant bloc in Congress, particularly after the midterm elections of 1942. On Palestine the president was constrained by deep disagreements with the British over war strategy, the military imperative of protecting Middle East oil reserves, the recent record of Arab unrest, and the potential impact of Nazi radio broadcasts to the Arab world. Even the seemingly specious worry that Axis spies might slip in among populations of Jewish refugees may not have been entirely unfounded, at a time when authorities deemed it necessary to warn the public that "loose lips sink ships." Morgenthau reminded the president that only three Jews admitted during the war had raised security concerns,[61] but who really knew how much of a risk tens or hundreds of thousands of new arrivals from Europe would pose?

As for the criticism of mainstream American Jewry, Dawidowicz served up blistering attacks against what she saw as not only gross unfairness and falsehood but as a perversion of history that essentially blamed the victims. In her view, rescuing a significant number of those caught in Hitler's vice had never been possible, but Jewish organizations had nevertheless pushed all they could for a plan to convince the Reich, its allies, and its satellites to allow Jews to emigrate to safe havens. "In effect, they proposed that the Allies beg Hitler to let the Jews go by appealing to his moral sense," she wrote. "They did not have a single bargaining chip to put on the negotiating table. That proposal, conceived in hopelessness and helplessness, was as naïve politically as it was unrealizable logistically."[62]

Regarding the release of seventy thousand Jews from Transnistria, it was never clear that the Romanian government had actually made the offer or that Hitler would have allowed it. But even if the offer had been real, how would Stalin have reacted to ransom payments to the Romanians at a time when their troops were fighting alongside the Germans at Stalingrad? (The Allies would again face this dilemma toward the end of the war, with Eichmann's so-called blood-for-trucks offer for Hungarian Jews.) Yet Hecht and latter-day second-guessers such as Wyman faulted the Allies for not seeing what *might have* happened if the Americans and British had pursued the matter more forcefully. "In Yiddish," Dawidowicz scoffed, "we would say to this: 'If grandma had wheels she'd be a streetcar.'"[63]

Wyman concluded that the success of the War Refugee Board in saving 220,000 lives suggests that many thousands more could have been rescued if the American government had been willing to act fourteen months sooner, when reports of the Final Solution were first confirmed. William D. Rubinstein disputes this, contending in *The Myth of Rescue* that the refugee board saved 20,000 at the most and could not have saved more because Allied forces could not reach the victims until 1944. Underlying such disagreements, however, is the question of whether it matters if "only" hundreds or thousands more could have been rescued. Forty-one years after Riegner sent his famous cable, he weighed in on the verbal crossfire: "Let me say, nobody did enough. In such a situation, nobody does enough."[64]

Finally, the Dawidowicz camp argues that Hecht's and the Bergsonites' publicity did little to influence Roosevelt's decision to establish the War Refugee Board and that the Bergsonites and their advocates have claimed a place in history they don't deserve. But the assessment of Morgenthau and his team, as well as a document in the Hecht archive, suggests otherwise. Morgenthau credited the Emergency Committee resolutions with pushing the president to act, according to records of a March 1944 meeting with DuBois and Pehle. When DuBois praised Morgenthau for the outcome, the secretary responded: "I had something to do with it, granted, but the tide was running with me. . . . I think that six months before I couldn't have done it." He added, "I am just wondering who the crowd is that got the thing this far." Pehle replied that it was the Bergson Group.[65]

While Jewish organizations were incensed that Hecht's newspaper attacks endangered their efforts at quiet diplomacy with the administration, Hecht and Billy Rose may have succeeded in exerting influence through a back channel—likely Bernard Baruch, Rose's close friend and mentor. Eight days after Roosevelt signed the executive order, Rose wrote to Hecht:

> Our tall white haired charmer has evidently gotten part of his job done with the boss. He called me from Washington at the crack of dawn a couple of days before the announcement appeared about the boss's appointment of a Refugee Commission. I have since discussed it with him and the story of how this came about I wouldn't care to entrust to a letter. He is definitely of the belief that something will happen and happen quickly—that this is not merely Bermuda lipservice. . . . He's very insistent that his name never be mentioned in connection with any work he may have done for this cause, because he's afraid it will reduce his effectiveness in the future. I am not under-rating the great contribution made by Peter's organization. I think it helped out plenty but I wouldn't be surprised that our friendship with the old boy helped bring this to a head.[66]

Pehle's record of the meeting with Roosevelt, included in the Morgenthau Diaries, says the president agreed to the executive order right then and there, so were Baruch and Rose merely flattering themselves? Would Roosevelt have signed the order that January had it not been for the Bergson Group? And how many people really were saved as a result? Could Roosevelt have rescued many thousands more by intervening with the State Department, by using the bully pulpit to change immigration policy, or by taking a firm stand with the British? Was a deal on the Romanian Jews, or any subsequent offer, ever viable? How many could have been rescued if America had acted sooner, and does its foot-dragging indeed amount to a colossal moral failure? There are limits to what can be gleaned from the historical evidence, and it may not be possible to ever resolve such questions.

Dawidowicz asserted that while historians can and must make moral judgments, history should be studied on the basis of what it *is*, not what it ought to have been. "We study the history of the murder of European Jews," she wrote in conclusion, "not just to mourn and commemorate them, but to try to understand the past and, if possible, to learn from it."[67] What is clear is that by 1943 Hitler's carnage had concentrated many minds on a fundamental disagreement—on a clash between two worldviews that would be a key legacy of the war. Both sides understood Nazism as a challenge to civilization, even to "the soul of man." On one hand, Hecht, at his most extreme, adopted the position of maximalists like Avraham Stern, espousing the view that National Socialism had exposed an ugly truth, that the great liberal democracies of Churchill and Roosevelt were essentially frauds based on a disingenuous, unreal optimism about human nature. Rabbi Wise and those who shared his views, on the other hand, held that such thinking represented a surrender to fascism.

Ultimately, the conflict came down to the issue of legitimacy—who had the right to speak for the Jews or who could arbitrate the rule of law. To the American Zionists, Bergson and the Irgunists were hooligans, exploiting the Holocaust to perpetrate an egregious hustle. To Hecht and the Bergsonites, the Allied governments had aided and abetted the greatest crime in history. From now on, Hecht would be the mouthpiece for a new American Zionist militancy, engaging the Allies in a war of words about gangsterism, terrorism, and the law while blood spilled in Palestine.

CHAPTER 14

Blood and Fire

For hundreds of years, you have been whipping "natives" in your colonies. . . .
You will not whip Jews in their Homeland. And if British Authorities whip
them—British officers will be whipped publicly in return.
                    —THE IRGUN NEWSPAPER *HERUT*, DECEMBER 1946[1]

If our dreams of Zionism are to end in the smoke of the assassin's pistol and
our labors for the future are to produce a new set of gangsters worthy of Nazi
Germany, then many like myself will have to reconsider the position we have
maintained so consistently and so long in the past.
                    —WINSTON CHURCHILL, NOVEMBER 1944[2]

In blood and fire Judea fell
In blood and fire Judea will rise
              —YAAKOV CAHAN, "HA-BIRYONIM" (THE HOOLIGANS), 1903;
              BETAR YOUTH THEME, BATTLE CRY OF THE STERN GANG[3]

By late 1943 Hecht was sure the Nazis would indeed fulfill their promise
to exterminate all of Europe's Jews, if not by Christmas, then certainly
before the Allies could end the war. Feeling dismal and defeated, he had no
stomach for yet another lost cause when Peter Bergson and Samuel Merlin
approached him about their next quixotic quest—ousting the British and
establishing a Jewish state in Palestine. Hecht told them he would sing no

songs of heroes or martyrs; if his two friends wanted to trumpet a Semitic George Washington or Nathan Hale, they could find someone else to blow the horn. "There are no such characters in Nyack," he said. Besides, what would be the point when almost all of the world's Jews, including the Zionists, were "on their knees to the British? All of them trying to whimper a nation into existence!"[4]

He soon overcame the feeling that "there would remain a small, private area of defeat in me called the Jew," however, deciding that if his fellow underdogs were determined to fight, he could hardly turn his back on them. Stopping by the midtown offices of Bergson's American League for a Free Palestine in early February 1944, he saw "the most glowing-faced and busiest Jews [he] had ever seen," churning out their biweekly magazine, *The Answer*, organizing, and fomenting a nationalist movement.[5]

Menachem Begin, the new commander of the Irgun, had just declared war on the British, and while Hecht was at first unimpressed by unrest in Palestine that seemed no more serious than the daily crime in New York, the attacks quickly grew more frequent and ferocious. "News of every gun [the Irgun] fired, every barrel of dynamite it exploded, of every railroad train it tipped over was brought to me in secret communiqués, some of them hidden in cigarette packages," Hecht wrote in *A Child of the Century*. "I never read news with a more pounding heart. I had had no interest in Palestine ever becoming a homeland for Jews. Now I had, suddenly, interest in little else."[6]

Critics would find Hecht's breathless enthusiasm for bombings and shootings grotesque, but his activism had started with a call for a Jewish army and a pledge to "bring respect back to the name of the Jew."[7] Now he saw a chance to finish what he had started. As for his old reluctance to sully himself with the messy politics of Palestine, he had come too far for such misgivings; this was no longer just politics to him. Like many American Jews, he had not in the past found the arguments and flag-waving for a Jewish homeland compelling, but the experience of the war had changed everything. It had made the logic of Zionism real to him.

From early 1944 onward, Hecht served as propagandist for the Irgun, providing the angry battle cries for the revolt. "Ben Hecht wielded his pen like a drawn sword," proclaimed Begin in 1983, as Israel's prime minister. ". . . He helped shape public opinion, and by doing so, created a defensive shield of public support around the fighters in the field."[8] Hecht's advocacy of armed resistance against Britain, which was radical from the start while the war on Germany was still far from over, would lead him to shift orbits from the moderate Bergson to the militant Begin and then, finally, in the pursuit of money and weapons, to the mobster Mickey Cohen. Hecht felt that Roosevelt and the British leaders made the political criminals of old Chicago seem quaint. If Hinky Dink or Mayor "Big Bill" Thompson had had blood on their hands, this new breed of rogues certainly had far more of it. If the British were going to denounce the Irgun and the Stern Gang as gangsters and terrorists, Hecht would embrace these epithets as badges of honor.

Bergson, by contrast, never really appeared to be a happy warrior, and ultimately tension arose between the two friends over how much of the money Hecht raised should pay for arms versus publicity and diplomacy. Hecht agreed with Begin that America was a sideshow compared to the real battle in Palestine. In his memoirs Hecht never intimates that he grew impatient with Bergson, but the draft of an unsent letter of resignation stored among his papers makes clear that by September 1947 he was getting fed up. In the letter he angrily declared that he no longer wished to finance "foolish Bergsonian high-dee-ho" and demanded that at least half the cash already in the till go to the Irgun.[9]

The Irgun had been in disarray for years after the death of its commander David Raziel in 1941. Whether or not bankrolling armed struggle had originally been the plan in dispatching a delegation to the United States, Bergson later said that he insisted his organization in America keep its nose clean, especially while the Emergency Committee was carrying on its rescue work; the Federal Bureau of Investigation never uncovered any evidence of support for the Irgun, despite investigations that spanned from the war years until 1950. Nevertheless, the Bergsonites were able to provide some level of support, starting early in the fall of 1943, when the original "cutoff battalion" dispatched Arieh Ben-Eliezer to help revive the Irgun, find a new commander, and get things back on track. While the Emergency Committee pressed its rescue resolutions in Congress, Ben-Eliezer was in Palestine recruiting Begin, the former leader of Poland's Betar, who had arrived in the Middle East with the Polish army-in-exile.[10]

The Bergsonites waited until they were confident they had achieved concrete progress toward rescue before announcing their campaign for the liberation of Palestine. Using funds from *A Guide for the Bedevilled*, they purchased the former Iranian embassy in Washington, D.C., for $63,000 and renamed it the Hebrew Embassy. In May 1944 they held a press conference in the thirty-room, unfurnished mansion to unveil the

Hebrew Committee for National Liberation. Five days later they officially announced the creation of the separate committee that Hecht would cochair, the American League for a Free Palestine (the league had actually been organized several months earlier, shortly before Hecht's February visit to its midtown offices).[11]

The press conference on Washington's Embassy Row was a typical Bergson flourish, but his campaign strategy proved a fiasco. He had planned to avoid the problem of "dual loyalty" by distinguishing between Americans of Jewish faith and those he called *Hebrews*—the Palestinian Jews and the stateless Jews of Europe who wished to become members of a new Hebrew state. While *Jewish* described a person's religion, Bergson explained, *Hebrew* would describe a nationality. However farsighted this may have been—anticipating the later distinction between Israeli and non-Israeli Jews—he apparently revealed how poorly he understood American Jews, even as he tried to cater to their sensitivities. He was trying to address uncomfortable questions of ethnic difference in a straightforward manner at a time when many American Jews preferred to gloss over the subject or avoid it altogether.

Once again, American Zionists heaped on the derision. To Meir Grossman, a former confidant of Vladimir Jabotinsky, the Hebrew Committee was "a bunch of clowns"; to Labor Zionist leader Marie Syrkin, they were "charlatans." In the *Washington Post*, Dr. Israel Goldstein described the initiative as "buffoonery" and "comic opera drollery . . . four or five irresponsible young men who have assumed the role of Don Quixote and Pancho setting forth singlehandedly" to resurrect a Hebrew nation. The American Zionist Emergency Council told the press the committee was "made up of a half dozen adventurers" representing "an insignificantly small, pistol-packing group of extremists who are claiming credit for the recent terror outrages." The Revisionist New Zionist Organization itself dismissed the differentiation between Jews and Hebrews as "false and historically groundless." Begin did not approve, and even members of Bergson's core group, including both Yitshaq Ben-Ami and Alexander Rafaeli, never liked the idea. Most important, the concept got no traction with the American Jewish public, which seemed to find it alien and confusing.[12]

Hecht nevertheless gave his full support, perhaps because he had a special place in his heart for ideas that managed to alienate and offend just about everyone. In a message of congratulations on the founding of the Hebrew Committee, he wrote:

Zionism as a political force is as dead as the projects of Montezuma. . . . The Jewish cause has been too long under the domination of Stephen Wise and his fellow Jewish fossils. What the Jews need most is a high wind to blow these ossified politicos out of their places. They are the dust that has gathered over a lost cause. I hope that out of the storm you raise will come the young and noble leadership that Hebrews of Europe deserve.[13]

Representative Richard P. Gale put the note in the *Congressional Record*, along with others sent in support of the committee. As a result, Hecht's disparaging comments about Wise and the Zionists drew fire in Jewish newspapers. While he may not have expected the message to become public, he could not have been surprised. After so many attacks against him and the Bergsonites, he may no longer have felt obligated to hold his tongue against fellow Jews.

The trials of four Stern Gang members that summer proved the ideal forum for challenging Britain's legal authority in Palestine and provided Hecht his first opportunity to put the case for armed rebellion before the American public. Though he had signed on with the Irgun, he served as a propagandist for the fighters of the late Avraham Stern for the rest of the year, unrestrained by the qualms Bergson and Raziel had harbored about the breakaway group. Hecht said little about the Stern Gang in his autobiography but explained, "If I discontinue reference here to the Sternists and write now only of the Irgun, it was not because there was anything less deserving about the Sternists. They were as valorous and nobly inspired a group of human beings as I have ever met in history."[14]

In mid-July he acted as a press agent for the Stern Gang members, writing letters that protested the death sentence of "Palestinian freedom fighter" Matityahu Shmuelevitz to Eleanor Roosevelt, Henry Luce, Eugene Meyer, William Randolph Hearst, Arthur Hays Sulzberger, and a dozen other editors and publishers. The trials, and Shmuelevitz's impending execution in particular, gave the Stern Gang, desperately short on resources, a chance to explain itself to fellow Jews and to the world, courtesy of the British government. Israel Eldad, who became the group's spiritual leader after Stern's demise, characterized the trials as "the first declaration on an official, public platform that the British regime was a foreign and illegal regime."[15]

As Hecht later explained, "American and Jewish newspapers alike chronicled the Irgun's deeds of valor as the scurvy antics of hoodlums and gangsters. . . . The British propagandists hardly needed to bestir themselves." But the tactics and ideology of the Stern Gang, also known as Lehi, had helped earn the Palestinian rebels notoriety as gangsters.

At the start of the war, the Sternists had refused to break off their attacks against British police and soldiers; instead, they had snatched up Irgun arms dumps and turned to bank robbery and, allegedly, extortion to finance their campaign of targeted killings. After a September 1940 "expropriation" of £4,400 from the Anglo-Palestine Bank was quickly used up, they scavenged for cash, guns, matériel, and an underground printing press.[16]

By early 1942 the Sternists had become pariahs within the Yishuv, with few Jews willing to hide them and plenty ready to turn them in. A heist that January had spiraled into disaster when tellers at the Histadrut Bank refused to hand over money and the gang opened fire, killing two Jewish employees. Even more shocking had been Stern's previous radio announcement, on May 10, 1941, that he was pursuing a pact with Hitler. He believed that Rommel would be victorious in the Middle East and that the desire to make Europe "Jew free" put the interests of Nazism in line with Zionism. Championing his scheme as a "revolutionary twist" on the teachings of Jabotinsky, he had sent an emissary to meet with a German official in Beirut in late 1940, and another to Syria in December 1941. With news of these missions beginning to spread, the enmity of fellow Jews reached new heights after the Histadrut Bank killings, and a month later the police finally hunted Stern down and shot him dead, allegedly in cold blood. By mid-May 1942 the rest of his fighters were either in custody or deep underground.[17]

A year later, on October 31, 1943, twenty Sternists tunneled their way out of the Latrun detention camp and resumed operations under new leadership. "Desperate beyond measure, on the far edge of history, despised by their opponents [and] denied by their own," as one chronicler described them, they sought to capitalize on the momentum of the trials of Matityahu Shmuelevitz and three other Stern Gang members in the summer of 1944 with an operation that would change history: the assassination of Lord Walter Moyne, Britain's resident minister for the Middle East. "What was important to us was that he symbolized the British empire in Cairo," reflected Lehi leader Nathan Yellin-Mor. On November 6 two Lehi gunmen fatally wounded Moyne and his driver just outside of his residence.[18]

Churchill threatened that all Jews would be made to pay for Moyne's death. Under the headline "Churchill Warns Jews to Oust Gangs," the *New York Times* reported, "He [Churchill] implied that his own support and that of many others might be withdrawn from the Zionist cause if the gangsterism, which he compared with that of Nazism, were not eliminated from Palestine."[19] Chaim Weizmann and the Jewish Agency vowed immediate action; indeed, the Haganah had for weeks been planning a crackdown, later called the "hunting season," or *saison*, not on Lehi but on the larger Irgun, which had recently reemerged.

"In Tel Aviv the Socialist Jews led by Ben-Gurion, the Zionists and the Jewish Agency-ites, all scampered eagerly to the British headquarters," Hecht later wrote in *A Child of the Century*, "to protest their own innocence, and to prove it by betraying Irgun hiding places to British Intelligence." Mass abductions and brutal interrogations in Haganah safe houses that involved beatings, cigarette burns, broken fingers, and false executions yielded names turned over to the British, effectively crippling Begin's operations for months. But unbeknownst to the Zionists, the die had already been cast: thirty-five years later, historian and British member of Parliament Nicholas Bethell uncovered evidence that Moyne's assassination had prompted Churchill to abandon a partition plan for an independent Jewish state along the lines that Weizmann had advocated just two days earlier.[20]

In response, Hecht fired his opening volley of militant propaganda at Winston Churchill: *A Jewish Fairy Tale*, which premiered at Carnegie Hall on December 4, 1944. The central joke was Churchill's description of himself as a loyal friend to the Jews and "constant architect of their future." (As a rabbi from Yonkers protested in a letter to the *Times*, "we think of the word 'architect' in the expression 'architect of the future of Jews' as spelled with a capital 'A.'"[21]) Hecht performed as the narrator, introducing the play as a fairy tale about a people who had been fond of fairy tales ever since they had heard the one about "a wondrous God who loved them above all His other children." The story features Tevya, Sholem Aleichem's comic-tragic, Job-like dairyman from the bygone world of the Jewish shtetl, in his most familiar role: quibbling with God as if he were kidding with an old friend. This time, however, there was a twist, one that suggested the misfortunes of Aleichem's day were nothing compared to those of 1944.[22]

The action opens with Tevya riding a cloud to the Pearly Gates after his body has been cast in a lime pit with other Jews from Lublin. Upon arriving in heaven, he is surprised to find that God is smoking a cigar and wearing a yachting cap. The Old Man is angry because an Englishman has been killed. Tevya isn't sure he knows the gentleman. "Is his name Itzikle? Lezerel? Jozefle? There were lots of fine people killed—all from different lands." The name is Lord Moyne, thunders God. "Lord Moisha," says Tevya, trying to catch on. He is confused: why should God be upset about this death when so many others have died? "So much excitement over one Englishman in heaven, I didn't expect to find," he complains. Exasperated, the Almighty turns to have these objections stricken from the Book of Fate, which curiously bears the title 10 Downing Street. "How have you rewarded my tireless friendship—my dream of Zionism?" says the Lord. "By producing a new set of gangsters worthy of Nazi Germany. . . . I find it necessary to the architecture of the Jewish future that all Jews must be punished for what these three Jews have done."[23]

God orders Tevya back to inform Europe's Jews that they must now wait another hundred years and pray in their synagogues for "the two percent of the Holy Land which I graciously allotted." Never mind that there may be no Jews left to inform, nor synagogues in which to pray. As Tevya floats toward the smoking graveyard of the continent, he glimpses Palestine for a moment, where a large sign rises up from the soil: "Jews Keep Out—by Order of Their Tireless Friend Winston Churchill." In conclusion, Hecht inserts a version of the customary legal disclaimer: "Any resemblance between the character in our story called God and the true God who presides over the heavens, is purely coincidental." He promises to someday return with another story that has a proper fairy-tale ending, one in which the Jews have a homeland of their own and the Jewish soul "has been given back its good name."[24]

A Jewish Fairy Tale ostensibly satirized Churchill's arrogance and unfairness toward innocent Jews, while affording Hecht the pleasure of playing the heretic once again. Yet by putting his own spin on the events of the day, Hecht served Moyne's assassins as well. His cigar-smoking, finger-wagging God informed the audience that Moyne, "as Secretary of State for the Colonies" in 1942, had "pronounced Jewish immigration into Palestine . . . to be a disastrous mistake." In Boston, Philadelphia, and other major cities, the play thus helped publicize the Stern Gang's deed, while subtly casting what had played in the press as a horrific act of terrorism in a sympathetic light.[25]

Hecht upbraided the British again soon thereafter, in late February 1945, for arresting Eri Jabotinsky, the son of the Revisionists' founder, while he was doing rescue work for the Emergency Committee in Turkey. In an open letter to Britain's ambassador in Washington, Hecht explained that Jabotinsky had recently brought to light that British officials had persuaded the Turks to block the passage of Jewish refugees to Palestine. Jabotinsky had thereby done "a great service to England—at least that part of England which is fighting so valiantly for the sacred rights of man." Now he was in a British concentration camp. "The thousands of Hebrews who have been whisked out of sight without trial or voice to repine behind English barbed wire are as much symbols of British moral collapse as they are of Jewish travail," Hecht charged. ". . . Whisking people off to concentration camps and stuffing gags in their mouths at the same time isn't cricket."[26]

While Hecht was butting heads with the English, he was simultaneously producing propaganda for the Allies with a portly Brit who could have passed for Churchill's twin: Alfred Hitchcock. The two had spent March and April 1944 writing *Spellbound*, and while Hitchcock completed the principal photography in August, they sketched a treatment for *Notorious*. This second collaboration was arguably Hecht's greatest achievement in Hollywood, rivaling even his best work with Charles MacArthur and Howard Hawks. Days after they started writing the script in early December, they were tapped by the State Department and Office of War Information to sell the public on Roosevelt's postwar plans for peace and security. This was remarkable given Hecht's contempt for the administration.[27]

While the department wanted a six- or seven-minute film that wove a speech by Secretary of State Edward Stettinius Jr. together with newsreel footage, "Hitchcock and Hecht preferred to dramatize the need for a world-security organization," explains Hitchcock biographer Patrick McGilligan. After a December 17 brainstorming session before a group of department officials, the pair traveled to Washington the day after Christmas and stayed up most of the night hashing out a script. They suggested presenting "the proposed international organization in dramatic form," according to a Stettinius memo, "by projecting into the future and telling the story of its operations in stopping an unnamed potential aggressor in the year 1960." Their apocalyptic vision, however, alarmed what Hecht called a "vacuous wagonload of politicos . . . not a group of men to stir fear in anyone's heart." Department officials feared the pair were running roughshod over sensitive policy concerns, such as the need to build postwar alliances with former enemies.[28]

Hecht felt little pride in the resulting fifteen-minute short titled *Watchtower over Tomorrow*, for which he "finally put some scraps of information together" and "larded them with rhetoric and war episodes." Directing credit went to John Cromwell and Harold F. Kress. By April he had also written a radio script for ABC's Blue Network, *Watch Tower for Tomorrow*, narrated by Edward G. Robinson, in preparation for the conference in San Francisco to draft the United Nations charter. While the radio program aired during the opening ceremony on April 25, it is unclear whether the film was ever publicly exhibited.[29]

Both the film and the radio script combined stark warnings about future threats with explanations of how a new regime of international law would protect against them. At a time when the atomic bomb appeared to be the stuff of scientific speculation, science fiction, and wartime propaganda, less credible than Goebbels's promise of a "freeze bomb" for the V-3 rocket program, a voice told radio listeners: "You know what will happen in the next war? They'll press a button and blow up whole cities . . . in one smack." The film, in turn, opens with a space-age cannon, launching a warhead into orbit. "Death from the sky," says the famed movie and radio announcer John Nesbitt in a voice-over, "from a bomb fired by an enemy thousands of miles away."

Turning to the explanation of international law, Robinson intones in the radio script that this evening, San Francisco "will become the scene of an international assembly dedicated to the purpose of outlawing war." Doubting Thomases will say "you can't change the face of nations and the soul of man. . . . No? Why not?" Has anybody figured out how they are going to do it? asks an average Joe. "I don't know," replies his buddy Sam. "Going to argue, I guess, and lay down some new laws."[30] The first goal is "to set up a police and justice system to stop and punish the outlaw nations before they can start a war," Commander Harold Stassen, the American delegate, tells radio listeners. The film explains that the effort all started with the international Court of Arbitration in the Hague, followed by the World Court. "This time, thank God, . . . the indifference of 1920 is gone," Nesbitt remarks. At Dumbarton Oaks in Washington, Roosevelt's "Four Policemen"—the Soviet Union, China, England, and America—recently drafted the new plan for future security.[31]

"Sounds okay," says a gum-chewing working stiff on the subway, played by Lionel Stander. "But what happens if some nation won't play ball?" Tense music rises as a future Hitler appears onscreen, standing defiant before the United Nations. Nesbitt explains that in such a situation, the

Security Council, led by its four permanent members, will act to isolate the rogue nation and, if necessary, summon an international force. "I get it!" says Stander. "What happens is like when there's trouble in the neighborhood. Somebody calls the cops, and the riot squad comes and takes care of things before the riot gets started!" We live in a Global Village now, Stassen says, in effect, in the radio script: "The people of the world have found that the earth has grown very small. . . . Science has shrunk the earth and brought every neighbor elbow to elbow."[32]

As soon as Hecht had finished these chores to help ensure the success of the conference, he plotted propaganda to sabotage it. In mid-February Roosevelt had met with the Saudi king and returned to tell Congress on March 2, "I learned more about that whole problem—the Moslem problem, the Jewish problem—by talking with Ibn Saud for five minutes than I could have learned in the exchange of two or three dozen letters." On April 2 Hecht expressed his reaction in a letter to Rose as he prepared to leave for San Francisco. "I am writing today to learn if I am to be barred by the State Dept. from the conference," he said. "I sit sketching out the Jewish 'pageant' I am going to write. As I sketch it, I can understand anything the govt. might do to bar me."[33]

Call the Next Case would portray Roosevelt "brought to trial before the bar of history for his crime on the Jewish question."[34] The scene would be a courtroom with a jury of twelve Jews, sitting motionless and white faced like corpses, representing the millions whom the president could have saved. Here, too, Hecht was framing the issues in terms of the law, but while a vaunted body in San Francisco might sanction a new legal code and court for the world, he suggested, this was only the law of humans and nations. There was a higher authority—"the bar of history"—before which even the great architect of the United Nations would be held to account. "There has been war before," he wrote to Rose,

> but never an extermination of people on such a scale. I am sure history will see Roosevelt and Churchill as workers in the Hitler butcher shop. I see them as representatives of the smallness of the human soul—as part of that decayed pedagogical rubble that piles up in the aging human mind. Both men added together haven't the simple and logical understanding of humanity that you would find in a shepherd boy or a chimney sweep. They can only play politics—as if that sort of playing was a superior thing to life and truth.[35]

Hecht's "grandiose propaganda stroke" was intended to "explode the Jewish issue in the face of the entire world." His play pronouncing Roosevelt guilty of crimes against humanity would appear just blocks from the conference and run as long as the sessions went on. The symbolism was crucial: the context would make the performance an indictment not just of one man but of his whole grand vision for a postwar world. "I grinned at the thought of the State Department attending its opening," Hecht wrote. His cynicism echoed Begin's disdain for the idea of a world conscience and the League of Nations, back when he had debated Jabotinsky in 1938.[36]

This time, however, the power of Hecht's propaganda would not be put to the test. He was writing *Call the Next Case* on April 12, less than two weeks before the opening session of the conference, when news came over the radio that Roosevelt had died. Hecht recalled a national outpouring of grief not seen since the death of Abraham Lincoln; it left him awestruck, and while his own heart remained cold to this "man with the gift for making himself unreasonably loved," he tossed the play into the trash. Had he staged the pageant so soon after the president's death, he could have expected riots in the streets and a backlash that would irreparably damage the cause in Palestine. The music chosen to open the conference, he accurately remembered, was "Lover, Come Back to Me." Staring at the world leaders in the Opera House on April 25, he "knew the show would be a flop. The leading man was missing, the crooning lieutenant in the white pants who gets the girl, for whom the script had been written, had left the cast."[37]

In its first major role on the world stage, the United Nations would be called on to determine the fate of Jewish aspirations in Palestine. Hecht never explained why he agreed to write publicity for an institution that he apparently held in such low regard—whether he did it out of a sense of fellowship with Hitchcock, or whether it was simply good business to lend a hand, or some combination of the two. In the final days of the war with Germany that spring, newspapers and magazines were filled with images of the now-liberated concentration camps, and whatever humanistic idealism once infused Hecht's efforts for rescue had since given way to extreme bitterness. Yet when it came to propaganda, he could be ideologically multilingual. The seemingly glaring contradictions in his propaganda about the United Nations offer yet another indication of a characteristic ambivalence that found its truest expression in art.

Notorious was adapted from a 1921 *Saturday Evening Post* short story, but it was really more based on tales Hitchcock gleaned from friends involved in wartime espionage. Released in August 1946, it starred Cary Grant as T. R. Devlin, an American FBI agent who recruits Alicia Huberman, the daughter of a Nazi, to spy on her late father's associates. A party girl with an untidy past, Alicia is played by Ingrid Bergman, who, as Pauline Kael noted, "is literally ravishing in what is probably her sexiest performance." Devlin falls for her, but his mission is to persuade her to "worm her way into a nest of Nazi spies" by going to bed with one of them. He is forced to choose duty over love. Soon she reports, "You can add Sebastian's name to my list of playmates."[38]

Hitchcock and Hecht packed their film with details that reflected the seaminess and duplicities involved in a conflict that Americans, ironically, would remember as "the good war." Among the wartime particulars that make the film an intriguing historical document, most famous is the MacGuffin, or "pretext for the plot," as Hitchcock explained the term: the uranium ore that the Nazi conspirators have stashed in wine bottles. The atomic bomb was top secret in 1944, and nobody but the experts knew uranium was the key ingredient. Hitchcock later said that he and Hecht became confident they were on to something once they saw the jitters their questions about atom bombs aroused in Dr. Robert A. Milikan, a Nobel Prize–winning physicist at the California Institute of Technology. A detail less remarked on is their prophetic depiction of Nazi war criminals being granted asylum in South America. Ensconced in uranium-rich Brazil, the plotters continue to serve with impunity as executives of IG Farben, the notorious cartel that patented Zyklon B and, as investigations at the time revealed, had tentacles extending deep into American conglomerates.[39] Discussing this spy thriller as Hecht's contribution to a new film genre, Leonard Maltin observes:

> It is far from coincidental that what we now think of as film noir started to take root during World War II, and flourished in the years after the war. There were a lot of people who had gone overseas and came back changed men, not as bright eyed, optimistic, and open-hearted as they once were. And all that is expressed in film noir—that suddenly Hollywood is not focusing on the sun-splashed streets of any town U.S.A., but instead on the dark alleys and the nighttime and the shadows, and the shadowy figures who populate the urban landscape.[40]

CHAPTER 15

Only Thus

Probably Hecht thought he was echoing the brutal warriors and prophets of the early days of our people. But the return to our homeland is not intended to be an atavism. It is not a return to the sometimes primitive morality of our forefathers, whose bloodthirsty battle-cries belonged to the state of society in their time.
— MEYER LEVIN, *IN SEARCH*[1]

If someone makes a law against humanity—who is the law breaker?
— TEVYA, IN BEN HECHT'S *A FLAG IS BORN*[2]

Hecht had taken a brief hiatus from screenwriting during the Jewish emergency in Europe, but now that the war was over, he divided his energies between volunteering for the cause and "beating my way back to solvency" by earning a paycheck in Hollywood. During the latter half of 1945, he was mostly consumed with writing and directing *Specter of the Rose*, a murder mystery set in the world of ballet. Like *The Scoundrel* but not nearly as well received, it featured Lionel Stander as a thinly disguised Maxwell Bodenheim who spat invective while dragging around a tattered sheaf of poems.[3]

Hecht also turned to Hollywood once again for contributions, hosting in August a dinner attended by more than four hundred guests, including producers Samuel Goldwyn, Darryl Zanuck, David O. Selznick, Harry Warner, and Walter Wagner and celebrities Edward G. Robinson and

Frank Sinatra. Weeks later, newspapers reported that Burgess Meredith and his wife, Paulette Goddard, were heading to Palestine to star in a movie Hecht would write about "the heroism of the Jewish self-defense Corps in the war times." Nothing came of this, but the pace and intensity of his propaganda efforts picked up again over the next couple of years. Of the roughly one dozen Hollywood scripts he worked on simultaneously in the mid- to late 1940s, most successful were two well-received collaborations on noir, *Kiss of Death* and *Ride the Pink Horse* in 1947, and his script-doctoring on Selznick's *Duel in the Sun* (1946).[4]

Hecht began to feel reinvigorated, not only because he had shifted from a futile campaign for rescue to an ultimately successful one for liberation, but also because he had new ideas about the usefulness of propaganda and a new confidence in the product he was selling. Previously, he recalled in *A Child of the Century*, "I had come to feel that propaganda was even less than water writing. It was writing traced on the air with a finger." But now

> I knew it was also something else. Propaganda with deeds behind it could echo valor and victory—and raise funds for larger triumphs. It could sustain warriors like a medicine and bewilder their enemy like a plague of locusts. It could confuse the enemy's home front, particularly a British home front as susceptible to phrases as to bombs.
>
> Our Second Front was no longer an impotent yell into a barrel. Propaganda in behalf of dead Jews had been like advertising minus a commodity. In behalf of live men in whose hands flashed the first steel since Bar-Kochba, it was a hell-raising medium. It could sell deeds to the world as lustily as it sold automobiles and hair lotions.[5]

Peter Bergson, however, controlled the money, and he had different priorities. The committee adopted a three-point program dubbed "the three Rs": repatriation of Holocaust survivors, resistance to British occupation, and recognition of the Hebrew Republic of Palestine. Bergson wanted to focus first on smuggling the displaced persons now languishing in the liberated concentration camps through the British blockade.[6] As cochair of the American League for a Free Palestine, Hecht readily agreed, but they soon encountered frustrating obstacles. Talk of financial irregularities and a welter of federal investigations took their toll on the league's credibility. To shore up public trust, on April 13, 1946, Hecht announced the Repatriation Supervisory Board, with prominent individuals such as

Louis Bromfield and Representative Will Rogers guaranteeing that every dollar donated would go exclusively to immigration. A full-page *New York Times* ad on April 17 proclaimed "Give Us the Money . . . We'll Get Them There!," followed by one in the *New York Post* on April 29 that touted "the underground railroad to Palestine." The Zionist mainstream charged that Hecht was an "innocent dupe of a high pressure salesmanship campaign" that was falsely claiming credit for the work of the Jewish Agency. Indeed, the Zionists could legitimately claim to be moving thousands of refugees, while the American League for a Free Palestine and Hebrew Committee for National Liberation never fully made good on their promises.[7]

Meanwhile, Menachem Begin was increasingly frustrated by the lack of support that the Irgun was receiving from its American fund-raising effort. Far more concerned at this stage with action on the ground than with diplomacy and public relations, he did not share Bergson's eagerness to establish a provisional government, which he felt would only bolster the impression that the Revisionists were jockeying for power. He complained about the insufficient funding at an October 1945 meeting in Palestine with Yitshaq Ben-Ami, who found that he could not disagree. "I myself felt that our United States delegation was developing an over-emphasis on the political and symbolic aspects of the struggle," Ben-Ami recounted in his memoir, *Years of Wrath, Days of Glory: Memoirs from the Irgun,* "ironically tilting backwards towards Jabotinsky's old political Zionism when the time for it was past."[8]

The Irgun's fortunes had changed by the fall of 1945. During the "hunting season" in the preceding months, the Jewish Agency had turned over the names of more than a thousand Irgun and Lehi fighters, which ultimately reduced Begin's organization to attacking telegraph poles after its initial sustained burst of fury in 1944. But the rebels had refused to buckle, and their refusal to retaliate against fellow Jews—which Begin described as the real *Havlagah,* or self-restraint—began to earn the grudging respect of the left-leaning Yishuv. By the spring of 1945, the crackdown had become unpopular in the neighborhoods and with the Hebrew press. When Britain's new Labour government proved unwilling to lift the White Paper even after the war was over, and deflected President Harry Truman's call in September for the admission to Palestine of 100,000 displaced persons, calling instead for an Anglo-American Committee of Inquiry, the Jewish Agency could not deny that full-hearted cooperation had been fruitless. The hunting season collapsed altogether, and, reversing

course, the Haganah agreed to a pact of united resistance with the Irgun
and Lehi. The ferocious coordinated attacks of the Tenuat Hameri ("The
Resistance Movement") campaign, as it was called, began to spiral into
violence that would far surpass that of the 1930s, eventually developing
into a three-way all-out war with no front lines.[9]

The Haganah's participation in the resistance ignited fresh debate
in American newspapers about the Jewish gangsters of Palestine. When
reporter Gene Currivan identified them as "an underground gangster
group" in the *New York Times*, one reader wrote to protest. "Underground
it is—the British administration's utter lawlessness is responsible for that,"
he said, "but it is not a gangster group. If expediting the landing and
entry of the so-called 'illegal' immigrants into their national home . . . is a
manifestation of gangsterism, the word obviously needs a new definition."
In the *Nation*, the esteemed journalist I. F. Stone agreed: "The Haganah
are no more gangsters than were the men of Concord and Lexington." He
added that they had "nothing to do with irresponsible terrorist groups like
the Irgun and the Stern Gang." And in June George Nathan Horwitt, a
contributor to the *Answer*, compared the Irgun's female recruits to Molly
Pitcher, after Currivan described them as a "rare breed of teen-age 'gun
molls,' who are far more vicious and blood-thirsty than anything the
United States ever had in real life or on the screen."[10]

Hecht followed the news in Palestine with the relish of a boy reading adventure stories. "No more sizzling battles were ever fought against
towering odds," he later reminisced. ". . . Lion-of-Judea-Begin conducted
the war in the guise of a bearded rabbinical scholar." The Irgun unleashed
a reign of terror that would distinguish them as one of the fathers of
modern guerrilla warfare. They destroyed more than twenty Royal Air
Force bombers and Spitfires, demolished over a dozen railroad bridges and
crippled the Mandate's train system, laid mines that blasted apart armored
trucks, reduced government immigration offices and barracks to rubble,
and launched relentless assaults on police stations. Together with Lehi,
they raided banks, warehouses, arms depots, and a diamond polishing
plant, raking in the £2,000 to £3,000 (between $108,000 and $162,000 in
2018 dollars) required to sustain their operations and propaganda efforts
each month. A combined Jewish underground of about three thousand
pinned down eighty thousand British troops as well as thousands of police,
who cordoned city streets with concertina wire and gun nests and retreated
behind their fortifications. When the British did emerge, they did so en

masse to conduct massive nationwide dragnets. These culminated in late June with Operation Agatha, which rounded up more than a thousand Jews, including senior members of the Jewish Agency.[11]

In response, the Irgun took British officers hostage and demanded prisoner exchanges; further, each detention and prosecution of a fighter became an opportunity to publicly challenge the legitimacy of British authority. "Even more important than military operations, the Irgun exploited the trials of their arrested members," observes historian J. Bowyer Bell. "In June and July the high command devised leveraged tactics to force the British one more step back in public humiliation. From the beginning the Irgun always considered the courts and prisons as their battlegrounds. The courtroom was a public forum, the prison yard a base for confrontation and escape."[12]

Hecht defended the Irgun at the climax of this violence—a massive bombing of British army and civil authority headquarters at the King David Hotel that went horribly awry. As was their practice before every bombing, the Irgun had given warning to minimize the death toll, but either they botched the timing or their phone calls were ignored. The July 22, 1946, blast killed ninety-one people and wounded about forty-five, many of them civilians. It shattered the fragile Tenuat Hameri alliance and might have had a disastrous impact on public support had it not been for General Sir Evelyn Barker's vow to punish the Jews "in a way that the race dislikes as much as any, by striking at their pockets." This eclipsed whatever furor Hecht's comments would otherwise have raised when they appeared in a *New York Times* story headlined "Leading U.S. Jews Denounce Violence." While spokespersons for the American Jewish Committee and the American Zionist Emergency Council condemned the Irgunists as cruel terrorist fanatics, Hecht declared, "The hand which writes British policy in Palestine is directly responsible. . . . Remember this hotel is the nerve center of a regime which uses concentration camps, suppression, terror and torture, which shoots unarmed civilians, and exiles and imprisons without trial."[13]

Hecht recognized that, like early 1943, this was another turning point in history. In April the final report of the Anglo-American Committee had recommended Palestine be handed over to a United Nations trusteeship, which could in turn lead to an independent Jewish state under a negotiated partition plan. The Haganah's withdrawal from the Tenuat Hameri campaign after the bombing presented the Jewish people with a clear choice between two potential paths to statehood: armed struggle, on the one hand, or civil disobedience and diplomacy, on the other. In recommitting to the latter course, the Ben-Gurion camp signaled it would keep faith with Britain, America, and the United Nations, and with the liberal ideals they purported to represent. The militants, on the other hand, presented themselves as the true democrats, since the British were blocking Hebrew rights to self-determination and freedom. The motto of the American League for a Free Palestine was "It is 1776 in Palestine." Hanging in the balance was not only the fate of Europe's displaced persons and the survival of the Yishuv but also the future character of a Jewish state and its position in the world.[14]

After Billy Rose suggested another spectacle on the order of *We Will Never Die*, Hecht spent the early summer of 1946 writing one that would not only draw support for a Jewish homeland but also make the case for armed resistance. *A Flag Is Born* would be another historical pageant, but instead of featuring a "cast of thousands," it would spotlight three Holocaust survivors adrift in Europe and searching for the Promised Land—an especially troubling sight to American audiences in 1946. A vehicle of unvarnished, unapologetic propaganda, the play was crafted by Hecht in partnership with some of the great talents of the Yiddish theater to hit a nerve with Jewish Americans. And it did. Director Luther Adler and his half-sister Celia, the lead actress, were children of the legendary Jacob P. Adler, who had helped establish Yiddish theater in New York City. Celia and Paul Muni played Zelda and Tevya, now rendered as pale apparitions of the once "salty and hilarious folk" who had appeared in Sholem Aleichem's fiction. The doomed couple personified the ghetto mentality of the Jewish Agency yet, paradoxically, also conveyed Hecht's reverence for the world of his parents and grandparents, now lost forever. "All the Tevyas whose souls and sayings, whose bizarre and tender antics Sholem Aleichem immortalized in the richest Yiddish prose ever written—were massacred," Hecht wrote in an essay for the *New York Times* that July. "And all the quaint and heartwarming villages in which the Jews of Europe lived are no longer on the map."[15]

The true star of the show, however, was a disciple of Stella Adler (the sister of Celia and Luther Adler): an eccentric but magnetic twenty-two-year-old actor named Marlon Brando. Stella, a celebrity and drama coach, had groomed Brando's extraordinary natural talent, adopting this boy from Omaha as a member of her own family and introducing him to much of what he now knew of art and culture.[16] The young David who appeared onstage cut a striking figure with his muscular body and stunning good looks: seen from one angle, he was the kind of tousle-headed American youth who had recently beaten Hitler; seen from another, he was the "new Jew" of Palestine.

Brando had already played in three Broadway shows, but his role in *A Flag Is Born* was the first one he was truly excited about. Although Maxwell Anderson's *Truckline Café*, which had opened at the end of February, had been a flop, Brando's performance had generated considerable buzz, which only increased when he rebuffed the efforts of MGM and other studios to get him under contract. Brando was eager to do serious work, and talk of Hecht's new pageant had enthralled Manhattan's progressive community. "I wanted to act in the play because of what we were beginning to learn about the true nature of the killing of the Jews," he later recalled, "and because of the empathy I felt for the Adlers and other Jews who had become my friends and teachers and who told me of their dreams for a Jewish state." The all-star cast agreed to work for the Actor's Equity minimum; technicians gave their services for free, and the set was built at cost. Hecht and composer Kurt Weill donated their royalties.[17]

As rehearsals got under way in August at a West Fifty-Fourth Street studio just above Al and Dick's Restaurant, Muni heard the rumors about this crazy Brando kid who carried around mice and let them run all over the stage. Luther soon became uncomfortable with Brando's tendency to mumble. He discussed his and Muni's concerns with Hecht and suggested they find a safer bet. "Good actors bore me," Hecht replied. "I'm curious to know what this guy Brando is going to do. He intrigues me." Nevertheless, Hecht finally got so fed up that one afternoon he threw down a challenge by acting out a scene himself. Either this provocation or Luther's direction did the trick. "Marlon uncorked," the director recalled. "Muni suddenly thought he had a tiger by the tail. Brando was incredible: flash, violence, electricity. . . . Celia's eyes became soup bowls. Muni turned scarlet. His lips began to tremble; then he got kind of foolish grin of approval on his face." *A Flag Is Born*, preceding *A Streetcar Named Desire*, was Brando's first sensational performance, thus launching the ascent of a cultural icon.[18]

Many postwar American works argued that the Jewish survivors in Europe needed a haven in Palestine,[19] but *A Flag Is Born* challenged the idea that the Jews had to ask Britain or the United Nations for permission to build one. Opening at the Alvin Theater on September 5, the curtain rose to reveal Tevya and Zelda staggering blindly somewhere on a continent that "echoes with the tumult and wail of a rebirth" but is for Jews a realm where the dead hold dominion over the living. "Does one open a shop under the gallows where one's father was hanged?" asks the narrator. "Does one return to picnic near the lime pit where one's children were slain? Europe is a gallows and a lime pit. . . . There are dead people under every road of Europe—dead Jews." Since the Jews have no rights or representatives recognized by any world court, they "can address nothing more official than the world's heart and conscience," explains a brief prologue to the published script. "Are there such things?" The answer, Hecht's play suggested, was no.[20]

Having managed to survive Treblinka, Tevya and Zelda wander like ghosts, stopping to rest in what appears to be a park but turns out to be a Jewish graveyard. There they stumble on eighteen-year-old David, another survivor of Treblinka, stirring from sleep. When Tevya hails the boy's appearance as an answer to their prayers, David mocks his piety, pointing out that God didn't save anyone's sons or daughters in the death camps. The war has seared scorn deep into young David's soul, but he too dreams of the homeland and vows to run the British blockade: "There are three things that British fences can't keep out of Palestine—rain, the wind, and a Jew." He tells of a vision of a nearby bridge to Palestine that has appeared to him in his sleep.[21]

Tevya can't see the bridge, but he is soon overcome by visions of his own—of the Hebrew kings Saul, David, and Solomon. He can no more counsel the angry, suicidal young man than he can provide food and a warm bed to his dying wife, so he appeals to Solomon for guidance. What can we do about a world full of enemies, he asks, who bar us from the one place that offers refuge, our Holy Land? If the world is your enemy, replies the great sage, then you must go to the world, and be not afraid: "In you, Tevya, is the tongue of greatness, the tongue that fashioned the eternal words of justice."[22]

Tevya appears before the Council of the Mighty, a caricature of the United Nations Security Council, where he immediately faces objections. When an English statesman charges that the Jews "have taken up arms against British law and order," Tevya retorts, "If somebody makes a law against humanity—who is the law breaker?" Allowed finally to say his piece, he pours the last of his strength into a soaring plea for a homeland. The delegates cheer and, to his elation, concede that he has convinced them. But when they announce another commission to study the issue, he reaches out pleadingly, and the vision fades. "Look at him!" David spits. "Holding out his heart like a beggar's cap! To whom, Tevya? To the hyenas in the night?"[23]

Tevya has awakened to find Zelda lying motionless at his feet. Overcome by grief, he collapses beside her as the Angel of Death casts its shadow on them. Tevya urges David to continue on, but the young man is now spiraling into despair as well. Just as David raises a knife to kill himself, a light shines, and a voice calls out his name. The envisioned bridge appears, and on it the fighters of the Haganah, the Irgun, and Lehi beckon him to join them. That bridge is in your heart, they tell him; it is a bridge of youth and courage. "Saul and the Maccabees live again in Palestine," says a soldier. ". . . We promise you an end to pleading and proverbs. The manhood the world took from us roars again in Palestine." David takes Tevya's *tallit*, affixes a blue star from his pocket on it, and, holding this flag aloft, runs to the bridge.[24]

New York Times critic Brooks Atkinson praised Muni for one of the great performances of his career, but it was Brando's fiery, accusatory speech about the silence of American Jews that ignited an uproar. "The whole audience sort of rose up, en masse," recalled Brando's friend Jack Bittner. It was "like an electric shock that 'just cut through you with true emotion.'" At some performances, when Brando started to yell, "When the six million were being burned and buried alive in the lime pits, where were you?," Jewish girls got out of their seats and screamed from the aisles, convulsing in anguish and guilt. One woman was so overcome by emotion that she shouted back at him, "Where were *you*?" "At the time there was a great deal of soul-searching within the Jewish community," Brando explained in 1994. When a close friend asked how he had managed to connect on such a personal level, he answered, "I was thinking about the police beating up on Negroes around Times Square."[25]

Louis Kronenberger griped in *PM* about "speeches that are too long, writing that is too purple," and *New Yorker* reviewer Wolcott Gibbs found Hecht's script to be "a combination of dubious poetry and political oversimplification." Yet despite mixed reviews, the public response was overwhelming. The league extended the original four-week run to three months, switching to different Broadway theaters for 120 performances; some shows sold out six weeks in advance. When the cast received a standing ovation on opening night, Luther Adler called out, "If your cheers mean anything, give now before you walk out of the lobby." A member of the production made an appeal after each performance, and the donations exceeded the box-office revenues. *A Flag Is Born* went on to play to packed houses in Boston, Philadelphia, Detroit, and Los Angeles. In Chicago it ran for over a month. The play was banned in England, Canada, and Palestine, but a tour of South America started in the summer of 1947, and refugees performed it in Hebrew at a British internment camp in Cyprus. At the end of the opening season, Luther Adler replaced Muni in the role of Tevya, and later Jacob Ben-Ami took on the role. Brando was eventually replaced by Sidney Lumet, who later gained acclaim as the director of such films as *Dog Day Afternoon* and *Serpico*.[26]

There could be little doubt that Hecht's message was heard by the powers that be. The *New York Times* reported that members of the United Nations had been invited to the premiere and that "there were more than a few of them" who "must have been under the impression that one scene in particular was laid at their doorsteps in Nassau County, in fact right into the chamber of the Security Council." When Whitehall lodged objections with the State Department, Hecht responded, "Britain may be able to patrol the Mediterranean, but she cannot patrol Broadway." The Washington, D.C., performances were diverted to protest racial discrimination at the city's theaters, so the league hired a special train to transport dozens of officials, including foreign diplomats and some eighteen U.S. senators, to the opening night in Baltimore.[27]

The mainstream Zionists mounted as vehement a protest as they had against *We Will Never Die*. Most contentious were the performances in Philadelphia, where the January 27 premiere for a two-week engagement coincided with a Zionist meeting at the Benjamin Franklin Hotel. Local branches and Zionist youth movements organized large street rallies and picketed in front of the Erlanger Theater, holding placards that read: "Do not attend this play!" "Watch your pockets!" and "Do not contribute as the money is being wasted!" A physician named Dr. Bernard Kahn who participated in the conference said that at least a dozen people accosted him in the hotel, appealing for him not to attend the play. He went anyway, saw the pickets, and later conveyed to a local Zionist leader his shock at what met the eyes of many non-Jews that night. "What an impression on them to watch the disgraceful display of disunion among the Jews!" he wrote. "I can hardly express myself adequately the bad taste and disgust I felt . . .

and still do, at this nasty affair perpetuated in the name of the Zionist Organization of America." As for the show itself, he commented, "I have benefited more spiritually by this play than by all the Zionist meetings I have ever attended."[28]

Many critics of the play were appalled by what they saw as salesmanship for terrorism and gangsterism. Remarking that *A Flag Is Born* "overflows with sincere crusading fervor," *Life* observed, "At the end it demands actual physical aid to the Palestine underground." Jewish Agency representative Eliahu Epstein voiced concern that crowds left "the theater excited and impatient with everything that is not based on Irish methods of national struggle." An Americans for Haganah "Sound Truck Project" in Jewish neighborhoods denounced the Irgun and its U.S. publicity campaign, while Zionist youth groups published ads in December 1946 alleging that the money raised by the American League for a Free Palestine would be used by "traitors" to buy "'molotov cocktails, machine guns and home-made flame-throwers to blast the walls of a Labor clubhouse' or rubber hoses with which to beat youths who were reluctant to join the Stern Group."[29]

Perhaps the most incisive retort to the play was an open letter to Eleanor Roosevelt from Judah L. Magnes, the dovish chancellor of the Hebrew University of Jerusalem, criticizing her endorsement of it. Noting that *A Flag Is Born* made "an open appeal . . . for terrorist groups" and talked of speaking "to the English in a new language, the language of guns," Magnes lamented, "This is, indeed: a new Jewish voice, a voice which is opposed to the whole tradition of the Jewish religion. . . . It is but a reflection . . . of the militarism that has seized hold upon the greater part of mankind, and unhappily also part of the Jewish people." A staunch believer in a one-state solution for Arabs and Jews, Magnes decried Hecht's description of the Arabs as "a British lie wearing a tarbush," in one of the few references to them in the script. Finally, Magnes objected to a flyer that asserted that the league's goal was to build a democratic state, with Arabs and Jews sharing the land as equal partners based on the principles of the Four Freedoms and the Atlantic Charter. "It is a profound distortion of the truth to say that those responsible for this play want this," Magnes said. "What they want is a Jewish State, dominated by Jews." A truly democratic state, he explained, would be dominated by the Arabs, since they were in the majority, and in a democracy the majority rules.[30]

Magnes had insinuated that Hecht was peddling fascism, but the play-wright clearly saw himself as a humanist who championed the rights of man, or *human rights*, in the new parlance of the postwar era. Hecht had moved the Washington, D.C., performances of *A Flag Is Born* to Baltimore because he had joined with thirty-two other well-known dramatists to take a stand against racial discrimination. Upon learning that the Maryland Theater in Baltimore restricted blacks to the balcony, which the racists had named "nigger heaven," the league confronted the management hours before the opening curtain. Pointing out that a dustup would draw partic-ular attention since it happened to be Lincoln's birthday, the Bergsonites warned of an angry NAACP picket line and threatened to test the the-ater's policy by having prominent invitees accompany African Americans as their guests. The management relented, and the attendance of ten to twelve black men and women that night scored an important victory for the desegregation of Baltimore venues. "I am proud that it was my play which terminated one of the most disgraceful practices of our country's history," Hecht crowed to the press.[31]

When the *London Evening Standard* expressed alarm that 44,800 people "have already flocked . . . to see the most virulently anti-British play ever staged in the United States," Hecht replied, "I didn't know that backing the rights of people to live peacefully in their own land consti-tuted being anti-British." He added that he expected Britons to like the play, since it protested "concentration camps, book burning and murder." Quentin Reynolds, the famous war correspondent who played the narrator, said that to label Hecht "anti-British" was to dismiss the "great work he did . . . for Britain's cause long before Pearl Harbor."[32]

Indeed, the promotional materials for *A Flag Is Born* were reminiscent of *Fun to Be Free* and Hecht's wartime propaganda and were packed with the same patriotic ballyhoo. Touting him as the Tom Paine or Jefferson of Hebrew liberation, pamphlets distributed at theaters declared, "This is not a Palestinian front or a Hebrew or Jewish front, it is an American front." Democracy is a "cause that is never won but must always be fought for." The play drove home the message with a vignette from the book of Samuel, in which Tevya sees the Hebrews of Jabesh-Gilead awaiting the orders of the great King Saul as they face a siege by Nahash, ruler of the Ammonites. A famous feature of the tale—the Ammonite threat to gouge out the right eye of every Hebrew—suggests that liberty is as dear as an eye, but Hecht also related the more literal explanation provided by the Jewish historian

Josephus: a warrior needs his right eye to see, since his left is hidden behind his shield. The old men of the village implore Saul to surrender, but he commands them to fight or face death by his own hand. "My kingdom is not a matter of flocks and houses and the earnings of careful men," says the great monarch. "It is a matter of the spirit."[33]

Despite the exhortations of Jeffersonian liberalism in the pamphlets and ads for the play, this was the same jingoistic bombast about gallantry that Hecht had provided for the Allies, and it smacked of the same Romanticist sensibility. As Stephen Whitfield noted, "the political signature is easy to identify, since he wished to honor what the reactionary publicist Maurice Barrès called *la terre et les morts* ('the earth and the dead')." Magnes had pointed out the contradictions in Hecht's pageant, which was not the only work by a pro-Irgun writer that was either denounced for its hypocrisy or celebrated for its nuance depending on the commentator's point of view. In fact, *New York Times* critic Richard Watts Jr. contrasted the complexity of Arthur Koestler's novel *Thieves in the Night*, which hit the bookstores while *A Flag Is Born* was on Broadway, with the "simple, primitive, black-and-white propaganda" of Hecht's script. "In the end, though, Koestler is as partisan as Hecht," Watts added, "for all the Hamlet-like qualities he allows his protagonist or the germ of patriotism he permits an occasional Arab or the taciturn decency he concedes to a rare British official."[34]

Brando had believed that he was acting as a militant progressive, just as he would in the 1970s when he supported the American Indian Movement at Wounded Knee, but later in life he had second thoughts about the work he had done for the Irgun. After acting in the play, he had toured as "a kind of traveling salesman" for the cause, speaking at screenings of the eighteen-minute film *Last Night We Attacked*. "That people fresh out of Bergen-Belsen, Dachau and Auschwitz should be stopped on the open sea by British warships and interned again behind barbed wire on Cyprus was enraging," Brando recalled in his 1994 memoir. "I did not know then that Jewish terrorists were indiscriminately killing Arabs and making refugees out of them on their own land. . . . Now I understand much more about the complexity of the situation than I did then."[35]

The American League for a Free Palestine received a total of $742,000 in 1946, overwhelmingly from the ticket sales for *A Flag Is Born* and attendant publicity. How these funds were disbursed remains murky, since support for illegal immigration and the Irgun had to be provided through clandestine methods. Bergson remained in charge of coordinating all efforts, and since he and the rest of the Palestinian Jews of the Hebrew Committee of National Liberation were registered as foreign agents, any assistance they gave to Begin's fighters would violate federal regulations. The Federal Bureau of Investigation wiretapped the group's phones and offices, opened their mail, dug through their trash, raided their offices, and maintained a paid informant, continuing the investigations for years after the state of Israel was established and the group had disbanded. As more than a thousand pages of internal reports released under the Freedom of Information Act reveal, the bureau never uncovered evidence of illegal activity. According to Bergsonite activist Baruch Rabinowitz, however, the group was able to provide support all along while eluding the investigators.[36]

In *A Child of the Century*, Hecht proudly recalled watching in awe as Americans gave "millions" to purchase arms and medical supplies for the Irgun, but this whitewashes the tensions that arose over how much of the money raised actually went to that purpose, and the questions that remain about what happened to the rest. In later years Bergson always maintained that he had opposed direct financing of the Irgun. In his memoir Ben-Ami quotes "a scathing letter" from Begin from July 10, 1947, which complains of receiving "not even a farthing for the battle." Ben-Ami concurred: "All along, not securing sufficient funds had been our greatest failure." Beyond such personal testimony, certain facts are indisputable: Bergson was ousted as chairman of the Hebrew Committee of National Liberation in December 1947—he euphemistically took a leave of absence—and was replaced by Merlin, who agreed to follow Irgun directives. Begin never spoke directly of his conflicts with Bergson, but he barely acknowledges any contributions by the U.S. group in his memoir, *The Revolt*.[37]

Very little of the money seems to have gone to repatriation efforts, either. Funds from the pageant purchased the *Abril*, an eight-hundred-ton yacht that set sail for France as the SS *Ben Hecht* on December 27, 1946. The American League for a Free Palestine told the *New York Times* that it had transferred roughly $300,000 to a repatriation fund in Europe, while a spokesperson for the Maritime Commission reported that the *Abril* had been bought for $36,100. But the European fund evidently did not yield much in the way of results: during the postwar years, Mossad ships transported about seventy thousand refugees to Palestine, including some thirty thousand on nine vessels purchased in America. By contrast, the six hundred refugees aboard the SS *Ben Hecht* appear to have been the total for the Bergson Group. (In any case, the British intercepted all ten American ships, and the refugees were sent to internment camps, mostly in Cyprus.)[38]

So if neither arms nor repatriation can account for a significant portion of the hundreds of thousands that Hecht raised, where did the rest of the funds go? By all accounts, money not reinvested in America went to establishing a provisional Hebrew government in France and to launching a similar publicity campaign there. Using the methods that had proven so effective in United States, Bergson started *La Riposte*, a French version of his magazine the *Answer*, and sought nonpartisan appeal, recruiting leftist intellectuals like Jean-Paul Sartre and Simone de Beauvoir as well as leaders on the extreme right.[39]

A strong believer in the power of media and diplomacy, Bergson appears to have pursued a grand strategy: by gaining recognition for his government-in-exile from France, one of Britain's chief rivals, he could acquire immense quantities of arms, which would dwarf the dribble of American contraband that Begin kept pestering him for. He intimated as much in a letter to Hecht about how he intended to use the windfall from the pageant. "If all this will give us the strength and the means to establish the Provisional government, we are bound to succeed in turning the present tide of defeat, after which the tortuous road to freedom becomes a glorious highway," he wrote in early October 1946. ". . . I know now and I will know then that it was 'The Flag' which provided the Archimedes point and which gave us the lever with which to lift this heavy ballast."[40]

Begin, with his perspective from the front lines, grasped the logic of Bergson's strategy and also understood the dangers. Ben-Ami recalled that when he first relayed the plan for a provisional government during a meeting in Palestine, the Irgun chief became extremely tense. Chopping his hands in the air for emphasis, Begin warned of "a bloody civil war" and later repeated this in his 1947 letter: "To rush with such a decisive political step will be to destroy that edifice before it is built." A year later, one of the most tragic episodes of Israel's early history proved that both leaders, Begin and Bergson, had been right in their own way.[41]

Bergson always adamantly denied that a scheme to overthrow Israel's newly born government was in the works on June 11, 1948, when an Irgun crew set sail from the southern coast of France in a ship called the *Altalena*. But documents from a 1949 French Defense Ministry inquiry reveal that French senior negotiators at least believed a coup was imminent when

Bergson convinced them to ship enough weapons and equipment to supply an entire army. Deputy Chief of Staff Major General Henri Coudraux, put in charge of the operation, stated that there had been "a secret agreement concluded with the Irgun, promising advantages to France if it seized power." In a 2010 study, Israeli historian Meir Zamir suggests that David Ben-Gurion's envoys in France got wind of the agreement, and so, on June 22, 1948, he commanded the Israeli Defense Forces to fire on the ship when it landed in Tel Aviv, killing sixteen Irgunists. Among the dead was Avraham Stavsky, who had been one of the leaders in smuggling refugees during the late 1930s and a personal hero to Hecht. Stavsky had turned his back to the beach when the firing started, Hecht recalled in *A Child of the Century*, and upon learning about the *Altalena* affair, Hecht, too, forever turned his back on the Jewish state.[42]

Whether or not Bergson had been pursuing a grand strategy to gather arms all along, Hecht's papers reveal that he was not made aware of it and had gradually become alienated from his friend. By 1947, as mainstream Zionists and Bergsonites alike began turning to members of the underworld in a scramble to acquire arms, explosives, tanks, planes, and ships, Hecht forged a partnership with the most powerful Jewish gangster of the day: Mickey Cohen. Hecht was in effect now freelancing, going his own way in a departure from the Bergson Group. An angry letter that he drafted shortly after he joined forces with Cohen explains his own politics and priorities at the time. The letter, addressed "Dear Sam"—presumably to Merlin—was written after a September 1947 performance at Carnegie Hall of *The Terrorist*, a salute to the recently martyred Irgun fighter Dov Gruner, which Begin had urged Hecht to write. In a fit of pique after waiting up most of the night for a call or wire that never came, Hecht wrote, "This indifference to me and self-obsession of the League served to wake me up to a number of things that have been on my mind for some time. Here they are."[43]

He objected to the group's continued efforts to outdo the Haganah's repatriation efforts, which he called "absurd and against all propaganda sense. . . . The *Exodus* story can't be topped by a few five-and-ten-cent gestures by the League." He also protested the continued complaints and attacks against the partition plan, which was headed for a vote in the United Nations General Assembly. "The Partition is obviously wrong. But to attack the UN is a thousand times more wrong," he said. "England is the enemy. The UN is a half-fraud." Britain would happily underwrite the league's complaints, because it would provide them an excuse to throw out the whole proposal. "My main point about the League's activities is this—I do not want to further its present policy and expenditures," he continued. "I think all it has done up to two months ago excellent. It was necessary to stir and stir and churn up public emotion—to inspire the Haganah and Zionists to further and bolder action. This the League did."[44]

But now it was frittering away money uselessly on its provisional government adventure and its efforts to compete with the larger organization's repatriation work. He noted that of the $750,000 raised by the league in 1946, only $35,000 went to the Irgun. This year, 50 percent of the earnings should go to the fighters, he argued, instead of less than 5 percent. "I have no wish to finance French junkets and foolish Bergsonian high-dee-ho with my efforts. . . . I have no wish to battle the League—It is only that I wish to withdraw myself from sustaining its (to me) childish and extravagant futility." According to his wife, Hecht never sent the letter; his cooperation with the group continued, but by then Bergson was exiting the scene.[45]

"Only Thus" had been the motto of the resistance, and debate would rage for decades over which course had been more effective in ousting the British—the armed struggle of the Irgun and Lehi or the determined civil disobedience and statecraft of the Jewish Agency. The insurgency came to a climax in the spring and summer of 1947, with the Irgun's spectacular Acre Prison jailbreak and its hanging of two British sergeants, amid a continuing torrent of raids and bombings. That same summer, the saga of the Haganah's refugee ship *Exodus* riveted the world and, at least in popular memory, provided the decisive push for partition when the General Assembly voted on November 29.

In his 1961 book *Perfidy*, Hecht wrote that while on a visit to New York at the end of the 1940s, Churchill met Billy Rose at the home of Bernard Baruch and spoke to him about the recent tumult. "If you were interested in the establishment of an Israeli nation, you were with the right people," Churchill said. "It was the Irgun that made the English quit Palestine." After careful research using archival documents, Israeli historian Aviva Halamish concluded that the *Exodus* did not play the pivotal role at Lake Success it has been assigned in popular memory. Yet as she witnessed the Intifada of the Palestinian Arabs in 1987, she gained a new respect for the restraint that Ben-Gurion's side had exercised decades earlier: "I learned to value even more the illegal immigration as a unique method chosen by the Jewish national liberation movement—Zionism— in its struggle for independence. Not personal or blind terror, nor acts of violence involving physical attacks on the enemy and casualties on the part of the strugglers, but a calculated blend of political and diplomatic activity and a struggle which took advantage of the weakness of the strong and the power of the weak."[46]

It ultimately may have been the combination of Ben-Gurion's tactics and armed resistance that achieved success for the Jews. Regardless, out of the catastrophe of the Holocaust and the ensuing fight for statehood, two distinct perspectives emerged that have defined arguments about Israel ever since.

ଔ

The catastrophe wrought by National Socialism suggested that Hecht had been right to reject the rosy view of humankind and human progress so fundamental to liberalism. Humankind had proven not only flawed but murderous. Like Erich Fromm, Hecht understood Nazism as a case of mass psychopathy, while, in his view, the great governments "of the people," built on the humanistic ideals of the Enlightenment, had been exposed as frauds. At best, Churchill and Roosevelt had responded to the challenge of Hitler by fighting not for ideals but for narrowly defined national interests, even though that had meant forsaking an entire population targeted for annihilation. Hecht had not only predicted the genocide four years before the first news of it arrived but painted a chillingly vivid panorama of what the world could expect. He had cried out for rescue early and often and had kept on doing so even when those cries fell upon deaf ears. History seemed to have proven him right; his so-called cynicism had in fact been realism—even, somehow, a truer humanism. Still, while there could be little confusion about what Hecht did *not* believe, the question remained, what *did* he believe in?

The managing editor of the *Jewish Frontier*, Ben Halpern, offered an answer in a lecture to fellow Labor Zionists of the Pioneer Women's Organization, weeks after Hecht's "Letter to the Terrorists of Palestine" appeared in newspapers. Halpern, a Harvard PhD and deeply engaged Zionist activist, explained Hecht, the Bergson Group, and the Irgun as an "irresponsible, undisciplined opposition" that sought to undermine the Jewish Agency's strategy for statehood and usurp its power. Noting that the Irgunists and Sternists had ambitions to conquer not just Palestine but all of Transjordan and had vowed to resist partition, Halpern warned that the militants were prepared to defy the will of the Jewish majority, by force if necessary. "This is terrorism—terrorism directed against the Jewish community as much as against the British government," he declared. The campaign of violence, he said, went beyond the notorious bombings of British installations: the aim was to rule the Yishuv through intimidation. Citing a recent news article in which the Stern Gang had claimed that "expropriations" accounted for 20 percent of its financing, he charged:

> Whatever the percentage is, they engage in bank robberies and rob businesses in Palestine and they engage in extortions. They threaten people with bombing their business or beating them up if they don't kick in the required sum.
>
> They terrorize the Jewish community in many other ways. They seize taxi cabs and hold drivers prisoners so they can use them in their raids. They terrorize Jewish schoolteachers to force the children in classes to post their bills, to put up their billboards, their posters. They flog young boys for various reasons—sometimes because they have been members of the Stern Group and decided they don't want to be any longer. And cases have been known where they killed young boys in public streets.[47]

Building on this picture, Halpern characterized the Irgun's kidnapping of British officers as a vendetta, intended to instigate a cycle of reprisal that would derail the political process. He argued that a letter from Hecht to a British newspaper that called Britons "the nicest enemies the Jews ever had" amounted to an open invitation to a "game of war." Such a cavalier attitude toward the violence, which Halpern called "Ben Hechtism," put the lives of Jews in peril, he said, because if the British army so chose it could obliterate the entire Yishuv. Halpern's thrust was to explain who the radicals were and what they represented. "These people are fascists," he concluded, "and don't be surprised that there are idealists among them— they are fanatics, devoted to an ideal or ideology, among all fascist groups. As in all fascist groups they are not choosey about their methods. They use lies, use murder, use extortion, they use sympathy of the Jewish community in cases of provocation given by the British." He then offered a definition of the label he had given them: "Fascism in itself is a system for gaining power without any other objectives. . . . This is all a means to gain power;

a sheer power drive." In other words, Hecht's charged rhetoric, theatrics, and contradictions could be understood as pure nihilism, a belief in nothing. Hecht was a huckster for a group of racketeers who valued nothing, understood nothing, except the tactics of grabbing money and power.[48]

Was Hecht a fascist? Halpern's definition of fascism was common in his day, but by the 1960s scholars began to challenge the contention that it was indeed an ideology devoid of content. On the one hand, fascism had been a political movement that emerged in Italy in 1919 and came to the fore when Mussolini took power in 1922. On the other hand, after World War II the term become *the* epithet hurled at anyone whom people—mostly on the left—didn't like, the unanswerable, capping insult to any argument. "While in our political vocabulary there are not many terms that have enjoyed such a considerable vogue as the word *fascism*, there are equally not many concepts in contemporary political terminology so notoriously blurred and imprecise," wrote Israeli political scientist Ze'ev Sternhell in 1976, expressing the view of his peers. Much of the confusion stemmed from the fact that the original Italian fascists had never clearly delineated their core principles in the first place.[49]

In more recent years, scholars have offered explanations based on identifying the characteristics common to various fascist movements. One early point of agreement was that Italian fascism could easily be distinguished from National Socialism, since the latter was rooted in a virulent racism, a war against the Jews that was even more defining than its opposition to Marxism. Another was that fascism should be understood as something more than a set of negatives, a consensus that emerged largely in response to one of the great first works about fascism, by the German philosopher and historian Ernst Nolte. Nolte had argued that fascism was the great *anti-* ideology: antiliberal, anti-Marxist, antibourgeois, in short, a rejection of everything modern.[50]

Had Hecht heard the more recent explanations of fascism, he might have been reluctant to admit how much they fit with ideas he had professed since his days as a young rebel. In *The Birth of Fascist Ideology: From Cultural Rebellion to Political Revolution*, Sternhell, for instance, describes an early twentieth-century cultural and intellectual movement that started as "a rejection of the heritage of the Enlightenment and French Revolution." In seeking to synthesize "an organic, tribal nationalism," it "wished to rectify the most disastrous consequences of modernization," namely, pervasive alienation in a new urban, industrialized world, the dehumanization of the individual in an increasingly fragmented society. Sternhell could just as well have been discussing Hecht's commentary on Voltaire when he observed that many writers of the era "constantly attacked the critical spirit and its products, opposing them to instinct, intuitive and irrational sentiment, emotion and enthusiasm—those deep impulses which determine human behavior and which constitute the reality and truth of things as well as their beauty."[51]

One such progenitor of fascism was Maurice Barrès, who believed that "to ensure the welfare of the nation, one had to turn to the people and exalt the primitive force, vigor and vitality that emanated from the people, uncontaminated by the rationalist and individualist virus."[52] This is reminiscent, for the most part, of Hecht's cheerleading for the tough "new Jew." He was certainly fond of tribes, having been as loyal to the Irgun and to the Jews as he had been in the past to journalists, artists, and circus troupes. But Hecht was neither the kind of nationalist nor the anti-individualist that Sternhell goes on to discuss, and the analysis offers nothing that would explain or account for Hecht's campaign for rescue. Hecht was as much a liberal as was Jabotinsky, and his advocacy for individual and minority human rights had been in no way insincere.

However unsatisfying Halpern's explanation of fascism might be for later generations of scholars, he had been on to something in suggesting that Hecht and the Revisionists were defined by an *absence* of belief. After all, a deep and abiding faith in the democratic process—in the face of so much evidence to the contrary—was what kept the Ben-Gurion camp from violently resisting British policy and underpinned their policy of restraint. By the same token, the Irgun's rejection of restraint resulted in the slaughter of civilians, in their reprisals against the Arab Revolt, their bombing of the King David Hotel, and their killing of over a hundred Arabs in the village of Deir Yassin in 1948.

The marketplace bombings of the 1930s had been loudly condemned, Ben-Ami recalled in his memoir, but something had to be done to stop the Arabs from smuggling weapons in on vegetable trucks while the Mandate police looked the other way. Irgunists involved in the King David Hotel explosion swore that they had given sufficient warnings; the British had simply chosen to ignore them. As for Deir Yassin, Irgun and Stern Gang veterans always described what happened as a ferocious house-to-house battle to clear a village that had been a staging ground for Arab attacks during the siege of Jerusalem. Women and children were killed because the fighters had been forced to toss grenades into each home. But in the aftermath Haganah and British commanders circulated allegations of a massacre, mass rapes, and prisoners paraded through the streets of Jerusalem, while lurid accounts of atrocities broadcast in Arabic were remembered as having sparked the panicked flight that created the Palestinian refugee crisis. Many of the most damning reports about Deir Yassin have not held up to scrutiny, but the episode seared the infamy of the Irgun and the Stern Gang into the collective memory.[53]

Latter-day defenders point out that the Jewish militants were allegedly committing these crimes at the same time as Jews were being persecuted, hunted, and exterminated by the millions. Who has the right to judge the measures taken by people fighting for their lives during such desperate times? No one, however, has condemned the militants more harshly than their Jewish contemporaries did at the time. Regardless of the justifications they provided for each individual incident, by the time the rumors were spreading about Deir Yassin, the Irgun and the Stern Gang had a record of civilian casualties clearly distinguishing them from the Haganah. It would forever be part of their legacy to the Jewish state.[54]

Hecht never expressed any regrets, but for the rest of his life, he brooded over the choices he had made. After the British Cinematograph Exhibitors' Association announced a boycott of Hecht's films in October 1948, he shifted from screenwriting to introspective autobiography. The book about Mickey Cohen that he started in the late 1950s turned out to be less biography than self-reflective inquiry into questions from the previous decade that still preoccupied him. Cohen's odyssey from a pint-sized Boyle Heights boxer with the Star of David stitched into his trunks—"that wild, hot-headed Jew kid with the lean face and Indian hair-do"—to the King of the Sunset Strip resonated as myth as well as farce, and Hecht could not resist finding ways to link the gangster's ongoing war against law, order, and respectability with yesteryear's Jewish rebellion in Palestine.[55] As Hecht delved deeper into the story—until Cohen double-crossed him by peddling it to others—his drafts and correspondence betray an uncertainty about whether he had been serving as a proud troubadour of the "tough Jew" or a friend of the devil. Perhaps he was both.

Sarah Hecht with Ben, top, and his brother, Peter, on her lap (BHNL).

Joseph Hecht with Peter, left, and Ben, right (BHNL).

Edwina "Teddy" Hecht, born in November 1916, was Ben's daughter with his first wife, Marie Armstrong.

Rose Caylor Hecht, Ben's second wife, was born in Lithuania in 1898 and arrived in America in 1907. A University of Chicago graduate, she met Ben while working as a reporter for the *Daily News*. She was as passionate in her politics as she was erudite.

Ben with his daughter, Jenny, whose life came to an early, tragic end. After her father's death in 1964, Jenny became a member of The Living Theater, the long-standing experimental drama group. In 1971, she appeared in the low-budget biker movie *The Jesus Trip*. She died of a drug overdose later that year in her downtown Los Angeles hotel room. It is unknown whether her death was accidental or a suicide (BHNL).

Rose and Ben. Despite his infidelities, their love for one another endured (BHNL).

Young Ben in Racine (BHNL).

Ben as an adolescent (BHNL). Hecht with a rooster in 1911 (BHNL).

Hecht circa 1920 (BHNL).

A Cubist portrait of Hecht from a 1922 issue of *Milwaukee Arts Monthly* (courtesy of Brian Levine, Mt. Gothic Tomes).

A portrait of Hecht for the back panel of the dust jacket for the first edition of *Count Bruga*, 1926 (courtesy of Brian Levine, Mt. Gothic Tomes).

A rendering of Hecht by *Chicago Daily News* reporter Gene Markey, included in his collection of caricatures of writers, *Literary Lights* (Knopf, 1923).

Hecht in Quito, Ecuador, during the fateful trip with paramour Mary "Mimsi" Taylor that inspired his play *To Quito and Back* (BHNL).

Hecht speaking, circa 1948 (BHNL).

Hecht with his signature writing board, in which he carved the titles of many of his works. Those who collaborated with Hecht recounted the intense focus and discipline of his writing routine (BHNL).

Margaret Anderson. "First there was Mrs. O'Leary's cow," Hecht once observed, referencing the alleged instigator of the Great Chicago Fire of 1871. "Then there was Margaret."

Hecht with Sherwood Anderson, on the right. "It is a fact that every time I am with you I feel you liking me OK but at the same time I feel antagonism," Anderson once wrote to Hecht. "Let's disarm. There aren't such a hell of a lot of people a man can talk to. If I am like another side of you perhaps you are like another side of me too."

Three-time Pulitzer Prize recipient Carl Sandburg (Chicago History Museum, ICHi-065379; Jun Fujita, photographer).

Maxwell Bodenheim in 1919.

Dutch-born artist Herman Rosse contributed moody evocations of Chicago for Hecht's *Chicago Literary Times* and *A Thousand and One Afternoons in Chicago* collection (BHNL).

Back cover of the April 1, 1923 issue of the *Chicago Literary Times*, which played the role of carnival barker for the modernist arts and literary scene. The drawing is by Wallace Smith, Hecht's friend and a reporter for William Randolph Hearst's *Chicago American* (BHNL).

A portrait of Hecht for the *Chicago Literary Times* by Wallace Smith (BHNL).

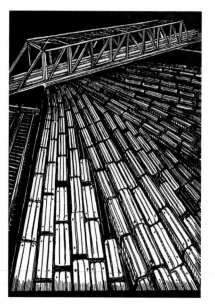

Another Rosse rendering of modern urban life, for the March 1, 1923 issue of the *Chicago Literary Times*.

More Herman Rosse drawings for *A Thousand and One Afternoons in Chicago* (1922).

More Rosse drawings for *A Thousand and One Afternoons in Chicago* (1922).

Wallace Smith's illustrations for *Fantazius Mallare* (1922) succeeded in landing him, Hecht, and publisher Pascal Covici in court for distributing "lewd, lascivious and obscene" literature through the United States mail. Artist and writer were fined $1,000 each for their offense.

The seventh of Wallace Smith's drawings for *Fantazius Mallare*.

A publicity still for *His Girl Friday* (1940), Howard Hawks' electric adaptation of *The Front Page*, starring Rosalind Russell and Cary Grant (Sony Pictures).

Hecht and his best writing partner, Charles MacArthur, during their heyday (BHNL).

The dust jacket for the first edition of *The Front Page* (1928) (courtesy of Brian Levine, Mt. Gothic Tomes).

Howard Hawks, the legendary director who was Hecht's close friend and long-time collaborator.

Herman Mankiewicz, left, plays a klutzy waiter in *More Soup,* a ribald short silent movie that he and Hecht made as a birthday present for Paramount producer B. P. "Ben" Schulberg.

Hecht with his "favorite Hollywood boss," producer David O. Selznick, during the filming of *A Farewell to Arms* (1957) (BHNL).

Mary "Mimsi" Taylor, who was the "big love" of Hecht's life, according to director Henry Hathaway (Getty Images).

Carole Lombard with John Barrymore, the hard-drinking, incandescent actor, in the Hecht-MacArthur hit, *Twentieth Century* (1934) (Sony Pictures/Getty Images).

Criterion Theatre movie marquee and billboard advertising *Viva Villa* (1934). (Irving Browning/The New York Historical Society/Getty Images)

Cary Grant and Ingrid Bergman as Agent Devlin and Alicia Huberman in the Hecht-Hitchcock masterpiece, *Notorious* (1946) (Getty Images).

Billy Rose, the talented Broadway impresario who was a crucial ally to Hecht in his propaganda efforts.

Peter Bergson with his deputy, Samuel Merlin, also a close friend of Hecht (courtesy of the Wyman Institute).

Yitshaq "Mike" Ben-Ami, one of the five leaders of the Bergson Group, and author of the memoir *Years of Wrath, Days of Glory* (1982).

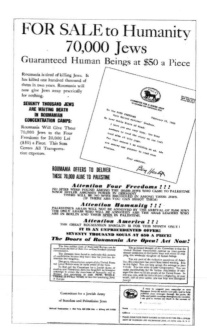

The *Chicago Sun*, Monday, November 29, 1943, page 9 (courtesy of the Wyman Institute).

When Hecht penned his "For Sale to Humanity" ad about the Nazis' ransom offer for Romanian Jews, many American Jews responded with fury . . . at Hecht. *New York Times*, Tuesday, February 16, 1943, page 11 (courtesy of the Wyman Institute).

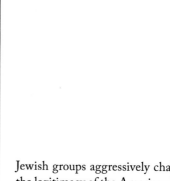

Jewish groups aggressively challenged the legitimacy of the American League for a Free Palestine, and other incarnations of the Bergson Group (PSCP).

In late 1942, the Bergson Group withheld Hecht's caustic poem, "Ballad of the Doomed Jews of Europe," at the request of Judge Joseph Proskauer, president of the American Jewish Committee. The committee did run the ad nearly a year later, in September 1943 (The Taube Family Arthur Szyk Collection, The Magnes Collection of Jewish Art and Life, University of California, Berkeley).

An image from the Jewish Army campaign: "This painting depicts the defense by Jewish settlers of the colony of Tel Hei in Palestine. Headed by Captain Joseph Trumpeldor, who was killed by the Arab bands attacking the settlement, the subject, in the words of Mr. Szyk, illustrates the 'physical resistance' by Jewish people in modern times." Advertisement from the *Jewish Record* of Elizabeth, New Jersey, September 10, 1942 (PSCP).

We Will Never Die debuted on March 9, 1943 (PSCP).

We Will Never Die program cover (PSCP).

Hecht's "My Uncle Abraham Reports" advertisement, which appeared in the *New York Times* on Friday, November 5, 1943, page 14, got the attention of President Roosevelt (courtesy of the Wyman Institute).

A Szyk illustration from the program for the Emergency Committee to Save the Jews of Europe's Madison Square Garden "Show of Shows," on March 13, 1944. It featured performances by Bob Hope, Milton Berle, Paul Robeson, the Count Basie Band, and others (PSCP).

The *Washington Post*, Tuesday, January 18, 1944, page 11 (PSCP).

Marlon Brando, Paul Muni, and Celia Adler in *A Flag is Born* (Getty Images).

World champion and Silver Star war hero Barney Ross became a military recruiter for the Bergson Group (Getty Images).

This April 9, 1947, *New York Post* ad appeared less than two weeks before the British hanged Dov Gruner and three other Irgun fighters. Gruner called the British Army and administration "criminal organizations" (PSCP).

Two young passengers among over six hundred Holocaust survivors aboard the SS *Ben Hecht* in March 1946 (Wyman Institute).

A 1947 issue of *The Answer*, the newspaper of the American League for a Free Palestine (PSCP).

Who is the lawmaker and lawbreaker? An advertisement from PM, Tuesday, December 10, 1946 (PSCP).

An advertisement for the George Washington Legion boxer Barney Ross' outfit of American volunteers who planned to fight in the Israeli War of Independence, but was ultimately blocked by the United States government (PSCP).

"The California Wildcat" featherweight Mickey Cohen in 1928, with the Star of David on his blue satin trunks.

Cohen doing his obsessive handwashing at his income tax trial hearing in 1951. To quote Shakespeare's *Macbeth*: "Will all great Neptune's ocean wash this blood from my hand?" (*Los Angeles Examiner* negatives collection, USC).

Cohen convicted of income tax evasion, June 20, 1951 (*Los Angeles Examiner* negatives collection, USC).

Mickey Cohen signing an autograph for a boy (Ed Clark/the *LIFE* Picture Collection/Getty Images).

A photo of Cohen that appeared in the Hecht biography excerpt published in the first issue of *Scanlan's*, March 1970, page 67.

Mickey Cohen, king of publicity (Ed Clark/the *LIFE* Picture Collection/ Getty Images).

Mickey Cohen off to meet Ben Hecht in La Paz, Mexico, 1958 (*Los Angeles Examiner* negatives collection, USC).

Agent Devlin (Cary Grant) and Alicia Huberman (Ingrid Bergman) sneak a meeting at a crowded racetrack in *Notorious*: "Dry your eyes, baby. It's out of character. It's a tough job you're on." (Getty Images).

The Screenwriter & the Hoodlums

Hecht's 1948 fund-raising speech to the underworld at Slapsy Maxie's has become the stuff of legend, recounted in countless articles, books, and academic studies. This depiction, by illustrator Mark Anderson, appeared on the spring 2014 cover of the *Jewish Review of Books*.

PART IV

THE MEMOIRIST
Writing about L.A.'s Al Capone

On May 24, 1948, in the midst of the Arab-Israeli War, Ben Hecht arrived at an Irgun fund-raiser at Slapsy Maxie's, a popular Hollywood nightspot, to find the gala attended by some of the most powerful mobsters in the country and hundreds of their underworld associates. Mickey Cohen, who had recently become king of the West Coast rackets, had taken care of the invitations. Hecht was delighted to address "a thousand bookies, ex-prize fighters, gamblers, jockeys, touts and all sorts of lawless and semi-lawless characters; and their womenfolk." He was sure the audience would be receptive to his message.[1]

He spoke about the 1943 Warsaw ghetto uprising, when thirty thousand Jews with "pike poles, old guns and bombs made out of tin cans" withstood the full might of the Nazi war machine. They held out for twenty days, praying for supplies from the Allies, but no help ever came. Now that the war was over, the survivors of that European slaughter were once again fighting alone, this time in Palestine, in their "desperate hour of rebirth." Would the Jews of America continue to turn their backs or finally reach out and help?[2]

When Hecht finished, Cohen dealt him a stinging blow to the arm. "Make another speech and hit 'em again," Cohen said. Still weak from a recent gallbladder operation, Hecht begged off, so his host pushed Mike Howard, "manager and bodyguard," onto the stage. Hecht later recounted:

"You tell 'em," Mickey ordered grimly. "Tell 'em they're a lot o' cheap crumbs and they gotta give double." Mickey pointed to me and his eyes filmed. "You heard what he said. It's for Jews ready to knock hell out of all the bums in the world who don't like them. Go on—tell 'em."

Mr. Howard roared inarticulately into the microphone. When he had done, Mickey came to the edge of the stage and stood in the floodlights. He said nothing. Man by man, the "underworld" stood up and doubled the ante for the Irgun.[3]

Over a year earlier, Mickey Cohen had been wary when a man appeared at his headquarters in Hollywood and asked for help in arming the Jews of Palestine. "He tells me especially about the Irgun and the type of war they're fighting against the British and the type of guys they are and all this," Cohen remembered. "And I got high on him. But you know when *you're* kinky, your mind runs kinky." Still, the visitor's claim to represent the screenwriter Ben Hecht had impressed business manager Mike Howard. Urged to take the request seriously, Cohen accepted an invitation to meet Hecht face-to-face and find out what this was all about.[4] At Hecht's home down the coast in Oceanside, California, Howard initially did the talking, explaining that his boss wanted to make sure the appeal was on the level. Cohen had just been sold a phony bronze plaque from Palestine for $200 by a Chicago grifter posing as a Jewish patriot. "As soon as Mr. Cohen's friends catch this thief," Howard went on, "they will break his head. In the meantime, we would like to be of some help to the Jewish situation—if we can be assured we are not going to be trimmed. So Mr. Cohen would be obliged if you told him what's with the Jews who are fighting in Palestine. Mr. Cohen is sorry for the dead Jews in Europe but is not interested in helping them."[5]

Hecht could be reasonably confident about winning his guests over, despite their leeriness, because he was familiar with the gangster code. He knew Cohen professed a deep sense of duty to his people, like Meyer Lansky, whose East Coast "Combination" had ordered Cohen back home to assist fellow Jew Benjamin "Bugsy" Siegel a decade earlier, and like Siegel himself, for whom Cohen, as a young gunman, had served as chief enforcer, bodyguard, and apprentice. All had received the same street-corner schooling in their youth, which for Cohen had taken place in Boyle Heights, the West Coast version of the Lower East Side. In such neighborhoods throughout the country, the rules were the same, for the Italians, Irish, and everyone else: Don't show weakness. When someone shoves you, shove back. Be loyal to your blood—your family and your kind, the ones you can count on in a fight. And last but not least, a blow against one is a blow against all.

For Jews, this creed dated back to the early twentieth century, when Samuel "Nails" Morton had organized a defense group to fight off Polish gangs marauding in Chicago's "Jewtown" along Maxwell Street. On New York's East Side, Big Jack Zelig had defended his community against Italian toughs seeking to rob businesses and lure Jewish girls into prostitution. "It was not simply an aspect of protecting one's turf against rivals," observed Jewish mob historian Robert Rockaway, "but a deeper commitment to the safety of one's people."[6]

As Hecht likely knew, Jewish mobsters had waged war against the Nazis in their own way since Hitler first took power, often through personal campaigns that revealed much about a gangster's character. Cohen boasted that during a short stint in the Los Angeles county jail, he was delighted to find himself sharing a holding cell with two well-known Nazi numbskulls, radio propagandist Robert Noble and Ellis O. Jones, codirector of Friends of Progress. Seizing the opportunity, Cohen bashed their heads together, then left them climbing the bars and screaming for the guards while he calmly returned to reading his newspaper. FBI records show that Cohen was indeed serving time for bookmaking when the pair was arrested for libel in April 1942, a charge for which they received five-year sentences. They later faced federal prosecution, along with twenty-six other Nazi sympathizers, in the Great Sedition Trial of 1944.[7]

Whatever personal satisfaction Cohen may have gained from the alleged thumping, it hardly could have added much to the measures already undertaken by state and federal law enforcement against the conspirators—and such conspirators turned out to be far more effective at stirring debates about civil liberties than at threatening national security. Still, word of the assault brought requests: the Writer's Guild asked for help dealing with harassment by Nazi sympathizers, and a judge wanted a German Bund meeting busted up. "So we went over there and grabbed everything in sight—all their bullshit signs—and smacked the shit out of them," said Cohen, hardly a civil libertarian himself. "Don't forget we had to fight the coppers too, because a lot of the coppers were Nazis themselves in those days."[8]

Siegel's most legendary exploit is memorable not only for its signature razzle-dazzle but also for the intriguing possibility that he could have changed the course of history. According to a dishy 1967 biography by mob reporter Dean Jennings, who also wrote a *Saturday Evening Post* series that would seal the fate of Hecht's unpublished manuscript on Cohen, Siegel traveled to Italy in 1938 as "Sir Bart" Siegel, a baronet from an old English line, to pursue a get-rich-quick scheme with his paramour, a real Italian countess named Dorothy di Frasso. The lovers planned to sell Mussolini a powerful new explosive compound called Atomite, but their demonstration flopped. This angered Mussolini, who in addition to demanding the full return of his $40,000 advance, expropriated the countess's Villa Madama and installed two unwelcome guests: Joseph Goebbels and Hermann Goering.[9]

The Nazis' arrival forced the countess and her boyfriend into living quarters in the stable. Siegel, who was familiar with Goebbels, became "apoplectic every time he saw the German rolling up the Villa driveway in his bullet-proof Mercedes." Further incensed that the countess would allow the propaganda minister and "that fat bastard Goering" into the stable for a social call, Siegel let slip that he planned to kill them—hardly an idle threat, considering the source. But when she begged him to consider the consequences, self-interest won out over homicidal impulse—Siegel had, after all, originally come to sell munitions to a Nazi ally—and he promptly dropped the idea.[10]

By contrast, Lansky's well-documented private wars had both more serious impacts and deeper implications. After German U-boats had sunk 272 merchant ships within six months of America's entry into the war, in 1942 he brokered and oversaw a pact between U.S. Naval Intelligence and an incarcerated Charles "Lucky" Luciano. In exchange for commutation of his sentence, Luciano issued orders from jail for the Mafia to clear out infiltrators along New York's waterfront and keep watch over the nearby restaurants, hotels, bars, and brothels, where loose lips could sink ships. When a U-boat delivered eight Nazi saboteurs to American shores in June 1942, the underworld got a fix on the Long Island landing point for four of them and traced them to New York City. Luciano's contacts also furnished topographical details for the July 1943 Allied invasion of Sicily and divulged the secret location of the Italian Naval Command, which in turn yielded an intelligence bonanza.[11]

Lansky was thus not referring to razzle-dazzle when he later told a trio of Israeli biographers: "I want to make my situation clear. The reason I cooperated was because of strong personal convictions. I wanted the Nazis beaten. I made this my number one priority even before the United States got into the war. I was a Jew and I felt for those Jews in Europe who were suffering. They were my brothers." Then, having paused for thought, he added: "I've never got used to the idea of being called a criminal, and I'd like to tell you how and when this label was first put on me."[12] After Hitler took power, he explained, the rise of Nazi sympathizers in America alarmed Jewish leaders, including the most respected of all, Rabbi Stephen Wise. The rabbi sent Lansky a message urging him to do something about this dangerous trend. In 1935 Republican New York judge Nathan Perlman also asked him "to take action" against meetings of the German American Bund. Flattered to be of service, Lansky refused the judge's offer of money and legal assistance but did request one thing: insulation from criticism in the Jewish press. Perlman promised to try, and Lansky got his campaign under way.[13]

Long forgotten now, the ensuing clashes between the Bundists and the Jews in New York and New Jersey lasted for more than a year on a surprising scale. Estimates of the Bund's national strength vary, from a Justice Department figure of 8,500 at its peak in 1938 to a tally of 22,000 reported after a six-month investigation by the *Chicago Daily Times* in 1937. The Bund published newspapers, ran a network of Hitler Youth summer camps, and held a Madison Square Garden rally in February 1939, attended by some twenty-two thousand people. To beat back this rising tide, Lansky brought in Siegel and other members of the Brooklyn hit squad Murder Incorporated, at the same time that he was quietly approached by Jews of various ages and occupations. "We taught them how to use their fists and handle themselves in fights, and we didn't behave like gents," Lansky said.[14]

Since he had begrudgingly promised Perlman not to kill anyone, his crew broke Nazi arms, legs, and ribs with practiced efficiency. While some Bund leaders and brash anti-Semites earned themselves special treatment, "the main point was just to teach them that Jews couldn't be kicked around." At first Lansky understood Perlman and Rabbi Wise to be pleased with the results. But as the clashes grew more intense, so did the publicity. In April 1938 the *New York Herald Tribune* reported a bloody three-way melee at the uptown Yorkville Casino between several hundred brown-shirts, a crowd of Jews, and some seventy-five policemen.[15]

To Lansky's surprise, condemnations rang forth from the Yiddish *Morgen Journal* of New York and other Jewish newspapers. The judge had not kept his word. "When they reported our anti-Bund activities they referred to us as 'the Jewish gangsters,'" he recalled bitterly. ". . . In fact the Jewish newspapers were the first to call us the 'mob of Lansky and Bugsy Siegel.' This was the first time I was ever publicly mentioned as a gangster." Soon the label stuck in the mainstream newspapers and on the radio. When Lansky tried to protest, he could hardly argue with the reply: his own people were already describing him that way.[16]

Rabbi Wise and other leaders now decried the violence. "They wanted the Nazis taken care of but were afraid to do the job themselves," Lansky complained to Rockaway. "I did it for them. And when it was over they called me a gangster." To his Israeli biographers, he allowed that there were groups who became known as Murder Incorporated and by other sensational titles. "Of course there were criminals, but I had nothing to do with that kind of criminal violence," he insisted. "But as the years went on, people confused the issues."[17]

To a similar protestation of innocence from Cohen, Hecht once conceded, "It's a point." After all, in the postwar years, Hecht had aided the Irgun and the Stern Gang by challenging the distinctions between lawmaker and lawbreaker. In this he had merely been following the playbook: everyone engaged in the armed struggle against British rule, from former law student Menachem Begin and scholarly Lehi sage Israel Eldad to the average fighter on the street, understood the rebellion in such terms. Moreover, Hecht and the Bergson Group had charged the U.S. government and the Allies with aiding and abetting "one of the greatest crimes in history." They had issued some of the earliest and most strident calls for holding German authorities accountable as war criminals, going so far as to urge the use of chemical weapons in reprisal for the Nazi war crime of gassing Jewish civilians.[18]

But although Hecht was an expert at "simple, primitive, black-and-white propaganda," he was at heart a Hamlet type, a writer whose inclination to mix up villains with heroes had made him the bane of Hollywood censors since the days of *Scarface*, who had often left even those closest to him wondering whether he held any true convictions at all. For a man so adept at twisting tropes and themes, who had made a career out of embracing various points of view, the propaganda wars of the 1940s had put certain intriguing perplexities into focus. He began to realize that he had always accepted the same "relaxing bed-time story" as the rest of society. "How cozy to imagine still that the law-breakers are our greatest danger, and not the law-makers," he wrote in the introduction to his Cohen biography.[19]

During the latter half of the 1950s, the Cohen project became Hecht's means of addressing questions that had lingered for more than a decade. If society did indeed have it wrong, then where *should* the lines be drawn between law and lawlessness? Where lay the true differences between the cop and the criminal, between the civilized and the savage, between good and evil? What was the difference anymore, in a world full of governments and corporations far more powerful and rapacious than any crime syndicate, in a world where poison gas, firebombs, atom bombs, and even the Irgun's terrorist bombs had become necessary to protect the innocent?

The 1940s had been a long journey for Hecht, from a studiously apolitical Hollywood writer to a volunteer propagandist to a militant who had partnered with an outlaw in arming a guerrilla underground. Now he wanted to retrace his steps. "My friend, Mr. Cohen, one-time underworld potentate who has cajoled me into being his official biographer, is likely to gnash his teeth off and on as his reads, for I am loud with data only vaguely related to him," Hecht wrote. "And though I shall write fully about this erstwhile industrious law-breaker, he shall be missing from many of my pages. In his place will be musings and recollections he has unwittingly aroused in me. *For Mickey is as much a point of view as a character*" (italics added).[20]

Turning biography into autobiography was nothing new for Hecht. Beginning with *A Guide for the Bedevilled*, he had been writing books that wove together facts and discussion of his purported subject with personal tales that sometimes took him far astray. Early in Hecht's 1957 book about Charles MacArthur he would drop the pretense that he was writing a biography, describing it instead as "a letter about a friend who has died." Though he had tried to capture MacArthur's spirit, *Charlie* ended up revealing far more about the author than about the dearly departed. Hecht also attempted to summon the late Maxwell Bodenheim's spirit the following year, in 1958, with his off-Broadway play *Winkelberg*, but he used his own words for the poet's speech and verse. In an article for the *New York Times*, he explained that his friend's words were "a bit too fragile for public ken." This outraged some old-time Greenwich Villagers loyal to Bodenheim, and they picketed the performances.[21]

Hecht's editor at Doubleday, Margaret Cousins, recalled fondly, "When I knew him he found it absolutely necessary to devote his time to telling the world about his friends and what had happened to them, and the only way he could do it was to write." In writing of them, he transformed each friend into an archetype—Charlie, the comedian who laughed in the face of tragedy; Bogie, the tormented, uncompromising poet; and, finally, Mickey, the outlaw, the tough Jew. As one old friend after another now passed away in the 1950s, each became, "in a sense, a collaborator in the myth of Hecht's own past," explained biographer Doug Fetherling.[22]

Though Rose Hecht had always been a supportive wife and even at times Hecht's collaborator, the book on Cohen rankled her. She shared her concerns with her sister, the respected psychiatrist Minna Emch, who in early July 1958 wrote a letter that posed a question to her brother-in-law: Just whose idea had it been to write this book? Was this something Hecht had felt compelled to do . . . or was it possible that he was subtly being used? This gave him pause, for it had already begun to dawn on him that inevitably the book, provisionally titled *The Soul of a Gunman*, would become not just an investigation of ideas but of Cohen. The choices he faced about how to present Cohen's story were forcing him to arrive at a judgment about the man.[23]

Hecht's book about Cohen is revealing in part because in finding out more about the gangster, the author had to delve deeper into his own assertions, namely, the myth of the tough Jew that he had offered to the American public. As he admitted, the book was at least as much autobiography as biography, and confronting the realities of his mobster-collaborator turned out to be a test of his own ideas and character as well. Having agreed to split the profits fifty-fifty with Cohen, he had embarked on a project that revealed itself to be his own devil's bargain. Indeed, it was one of the truest tests he ever faced, precisely because he never saw it coming . . .

CHAPTER 16

"Some Kind of Strength"

In his eyes we Israelis had been molded by blood, violence, and a struggle for survival and power in the sands of the Middle East. Meyer perceived his background on New York's Lower East Side as similar, though in a different setting. He felt a kinship with me that transcended generations, cultures and continents.
—URI DAN, INTRODUCTION TO *MEYER LANSKY: MOGUL TO THE MOB*[1]

Interviewer: Mr. Hecht, do you think that murder is ever justified?
Hecht: I think valor is always justified.
—BEN HECHT, INTERVIEW WITH A BRITISH NEWSMAN, CA. MAY 1947[2]

By the spring of 1947, Hecht was long past making appeals to world conscience and, in the face of increasingly shrill vilification, no longer felt obliged to hold his tongue against his Jewish detractors. "I had been promoted from a wanton, publicity-seeking racketeer to a Fascist out to plunge the surviving Jews into a blood bath," he later recalled. He answered his critics in April, with a speech at a Hotel Astor banquet for the crew of the refugee ship the SS *Ben Hecht*. There had until recently been "fifty-seven varieties of Palestinian strategists, Zionist Palaverers, and Hebrew disputants," he told the dinner guests. "Today there are only two Jewish parties left in the field—the Terrorists and the Terrified." In other words, Jews faced a stark choice in the Middle East: inflict terror or be its victims.[3]

Two weeks later his "Letter to the Terrorists of Palestine," alienated even some close friends, including actor Edward G. Robinson, one of his staunchest allies on the Emergency Committee. "His comments about his delight at the death of every English soldier sickened me," Robinson wrote in a memoir. "I thought him, at the very least, irrational. I never acknowledged him again." Among Peter Bergson's delegation, his chief deputy, Samuel Merlin, was disturbed by the tone and opposed publishing the ad. Bergson did not see a problem, though he later felt it should not have been run because it was "bad propaganda."[4]

Responding to furious protests from the British government, President Truman demanded an end to incitement. "Despite the fact that he is president," Hecht remarked blandly, "Mr. Truman is still entitled to his opinion." American newspapers roundly condemned him as a warmongering extremist, including his old employer, the *Chicago Daily News*, which scolded, "This white-hot inspiration to hatred is a sad disservice both to the cause of Zionism and to the hopes of world peace. Mr. Hecht in effect joins Hitler in preaching that the issue cannot be resolved peacefully." The *New York Herald Tribune* warned that in all probability "more terror will produce only more bitter and violent reactions everywhere and that the fugitive chance of a reasonable settlement will in the end be lost." In a letters column filled entirely with denunciations, reader William A. Kirk expressed disbelief that the *Herald Tribune* would dare to run a full-page ad "to aid and abet crime and violence" against "a nation friendly to the United States." Others cautioned that the sympathy of Americans would soon evaporate if the Jews carried on this way.[5]

Jewish groups rushed to distance themselves from Hecht's claim that American Jews—except, he had stipulated, the rich and respectable—had "a holiday in their hearts" when British blood was spilled. "Terrorism is hostile to Jewish religion and tradition," explained the American Jewish Committee. Another *Herald Tribune* reader pointed out that "to call the activities of the extremists Zionist policy is simply to confuse two entirely opposite views and principles." The British *Daily Express* opined that Hecht had encouraged anti-Semitism, while the *Daily Mail* published a response by *Palestine Post* editor Gershon Agronsky that called Hecht responsible "for a criminal insanity that is killing Jews as well as Britons." An editorial in the *Palestine Post* complained that Lord Beaverbrook's *Mail* and *Daily Express* were using Hecht to tar Zionism with one brush and vent their own anti-Semitic rage.[6]

Among the lone voices speaking out in his defense were columnists Walter Winchell, who relished jousting with British journalists, and Leonard Lyons. In addition, *Daily News* reader J. M. Winnetka wrote that while people accused Hecht of hurting rather than helping the Zionist cause, "I see no evidence that anyone is helping the Jews but themselves. A national home for the Jews is not only desirable from a symbolic point of view, it is an immediate necessity." Marion Kuhn argued in the *Herald Tribune*, "The admission of 100,000 displaced persons is a matter which transcends all considerations of politics and power. These people have been through hell on earth. They have waited for eight tortured years. Is there to be no end to the waiting?"[7]

Hecht had packed his letter with references to freedom fighters and 1776, but liberal contemporaries like Robinson heard only a bizarre and disturbing call for more bloodshed. Amid such an uproar, one could be forgiven for either missing or dismissing his point: that among the parties in Palestine, the Irgun were in fact the true champions of liberal-humanist ideals. In his view, they were defending the rights of man, not only as the vanguard of a national liberation movement, but also as the front line in a war for survival. He saw nothing fascist or antidemocratic in their pessimism about Britain's good faith, about the moral authority of the United Nations, or, for that matter, about the existence of a world conscience; that was merely clear-eyed recognition of the realities borne out by the war and the situation in Palestine.

"For however stupid and wry-headed the world may seem when studied from headline to headline," he had said at the Astor, "there is one flag it flies that has never been lowered. This is the flag of moral justice and human rights." By contrast, the battle cry of "the loquacious Zionists and Tweedledum Knights of the Jewish Agency"—"Whatever happens, let us stay in the good graces of our enemy"—"seemed a peculiar technique for a revolution."[8] This myopia and cowardice, he asserted, was the real threat to the aspirations of the Jews, and to all human aspiration. "There will always be Jews who imagine that if they are seen crawling on their bellies among their enemies they will be mistaken for non-Jews or at least for high-class Jews," he admonished. "I'm thinking of a white Christmas named Arthur Sulzberger, owner of the *New York Times*. Mr. Sulzberger's stomach-tour among Anglo-Saxons is not a new spectacle in Jewish history. It is one of the few authentic bases for anti-Semitism. Looking on the immemorial Sulzbergers the anti-Semite says, 'If a Jew is so ashamed of his cause and his people, what a shameful cause and people they must be.'"[9]

The return of the nineteen crewmen honored that evening, most of them American, represented another coup for the Bergson Group. The American League for a Free Palestine had sent the *Ben Hecht* on a kind of Trojan-horse mission, expecting that the arrest and imprisonment of U.S. citizens would embarrass England. It did. After intercepting the ship on March 8, 1947, British destroyers transported the six hundred refugees to an internment camp in Cyprus and the crew to Acre Prison, where many Irgun and Lehi fighters were jailed. In response, the league rallied the American public with a flurry of ads and press releases, the mother of one crewman launched a grassroots campaign, and the league's members in Congress demanded the crew's release. "The British can capture ships to their hearts' content," Hecht proclaimed, "but there are many more where they came from." One advertisement noted, "The British in Palestine are democratic with respect to prisons—they'll jail anyone; Hebrews, Arabs— AND NOW AMERICANS. . . . The only 'law' in Palestine is British might." After the House of Representatives condemned the seizure, the British released the crew, and they arrived home to a cheering crowd at City Hill on April 17.[10]

Bergson had left for Paris months earlier, in late 1946, to establish a provisional government, while in America the league's activists had shifted their focus from repatriation to armed struggle. Hecht underwent surgery for peritonitis in mid-June 1947; he was discharged from the hospital on June 24 but had to undergo a second surgery three weeks later. He was still recovering at Roosevelt Hospital in New York when he was asked to compose another appeal for funds. Members of the committee smoked and paced around his highly flammable oxygen tent as he wrote on the back of his X-ray chart, penning a paean to three Irgun fighters hanged by the British on July 29. "Requiem for Three" vowed that their deaths would be answered by "the roar of guns, motors and bombs." Three weeks later, Menachem Begin cabled to suggest a play about Dov Gruner—who had been hanged with three others on April 16—and to offer praise for Hecht's "readiness to take the stones hurled at you from all sides."[11]

By September 1947 Hecht's *The Terrorist* appeared at Carnegie Hall. Set on the morning of Gruner's hanging, it opens with Tevya once again, this time accompanied by Judah Halevy, a twelfth-century poet, philosopher, and proto-Zionist. The two are angels, and they stand above the fighter as he awaits execution.

Halevy: . . . It is his good name the English hang—so that he shall seem a criminal instead of a Hebrew soldier who fought to free his homeland of an invader.

Tevya: To hang a soldier—this is against the law! And the English—they are in Palestine against the law. The whole thing is against the law, Reb Halevy!

Halevy: Nothing that is done to Jews is against the law—if it is done by a nation. A nation can only commit a crime against another nation. And the Jew, however numerous he be, is forever outside the law, because he belongs nowhere.[12]

In this play, Hecht returned to the questions raised in *A Flag Is Born* about who were the lawmakers and who the lawbreakers, this time within the context of the armed revolt. A Scottish sergeant calls Gruner a traitor upon learning that he is a fellow British war veteran who had also fought at Alamein. Gruner replies that he still serves the same cause, the struggle against tyranny. "A fine cause it is," the sergeant scoffs, "when your own Jewish people call ye a lawbreaker and a terrorist!" My people have lived like an unwelcome guest for so long, Gruner says, that they don't know how to fight for themselves. When guards arrive to march him to the scaffold, Gruner asks whether he will die in prison garb. "Gangsters and hoodlums are not entitled to military dress," an officer spits back. Gruner points out that he was arrested in military uniform. In reality, he had been disguised as either a British policeman or an Arab prisoner in a raid on a police armory, but that would muddle Hecht's point: a prisoner of war cannot be executed under the Geneva Conventions, whereas a criminal has no such rights.[13]

Yet when the guards start to beat their condemned prisoner for refusing an order to stand, the Scottish sergeant decides he has heard and seen enough. A furious officer barks at him to remember his duty as he rushes to Gruner's defense, but he has been roused by a more personal sense of duty. "I'm a Scotchman, not an Englishman!" he yells. "I'm a man! And as a man I ask ye to stop what you're doin'!"[14]

The final gallows scene echoes the macabre tableaux of Hecht's wartime pageants and their sometimes-overwrought symbolism. In chorus, ghostly victims tell Gruner they have dreamed that one day he would come, to stand up for them all. He drops into the noose as the lights go out. When they come on again, Gruner is gone, and the flag of Israel hangs from the rope.[15]

In Palestine Gruner's execution had ignited a chain of reprisals that brought the revolt to a fever pitch, and a direct appeal from Irgun chief Begin may have prompted Hecht to approach Mickey Cohen. On June 10 Begin had sent "a scathing letter" to the Hebrew Committee, furious that thousands had been spent on the *Ben Hecht* while fighters were dying in the field. Despite some optimism about cooperation in March 1947, the high command had lost patience with Bergson. All along, Hecht had maintained direct contact with the Irgun. "Around me in Nyack the Palestinian underground crackled constantly," he later wrote. "Russian and British spies pattered through the house and eavesdropped at the swimming pool where the Irgun captains were wont to gather for disputation."[16]

By all accounts, he first met Cohen at Oceanside, California, late that summer. Twenty years later, the gangster recalled the encounter: "Ben had somebody else with him from Israel, from the Irgun. This guy got me so goddamn excited. He started telling me how these guys actually fight like racket guys would. They didn't ask for quarter and they gave no quarter. And I got pretty well enthused with them. And then I could see and sense that's what Ben wanted me to do."[17]

Yitshaq Ben-Ami later explained that the Irgun had always drawn support from lower-income and first-generation American Jews, but the spectacular Acre Prison jailbreak after Gruner's death and the execution of British soldiers in the summer of 1947 captured the attention of another subgroup: the Jewish mob. Decades later, Cohen had vivid memories of the events:

> I started to have relationships with Irgun members back in Israel. They got to understand me better and I got to understand them better, and this was when the English hung those three Jewish kids.
>
> I had pretty near got blowed up with the Irgun about this. I even had a beef with Ben Hecht. I told him and the Irgun, "Lookit, everything from this part of the country is going to stop cold if you don't get hold of some top English officers and hang them up in the same public square. If you don't, that's going to be the end of my involvement with it."
>
> And they done it. They hung some British officers right in the middle of the goddamn public square.[18]

Ben-Ami acknowledged Cohen's contributions but said another key figure was "Uncle Joe," a Cockney and dabbler in sentimental poetry who was particularly disturbed by his native land's conduct. Uncle Joe set up meetings in New York, Chicago, Detroit, and Los Angeles where Hecht and other Irgun representatives spoke. A lunch in Detroit attended by twenty-five people, for example, raised $30,000. "The respectable Jews did very little to help," wrote Ben-Ami, echoing Hecht. "The 'Jewish rejects' did come across—as did the Jewish-speaking ones from the Lower East Side of New York and the Jewish ghettoes in Philadelphia, Boston and Chicago." Altogether, "the Jewish underworld" gave about $120,000, most of which went to outfitting and arming the *Altalena*, he said, although some was transferred to an account in Switzerland.[19]

The Yishuv was outnumbered and desperate for weapons by late fall, when Palestine erupted into a chaotic civil war. Arab gunmen fired the opening rounds, attacking two Jewish buses near Petah Tikva on November 30, a day after the United Nations General Assembly passed the partition resolution. Within days, it was obvious the clashes were escalating into a full-scale conflict, despite the continued presence of British troops. Thousands of foreign fighters poured in to reinforce the militias of the eight hundred Arab villages: hundreds of Muslim Brotherhood volunteers and the relatively well-equipped Arab Liberation Army, a force of between four thousand and seven thousand. More ominous, from the Jewish perspective, were the armies of Egypt, Syria, Transjordan, Iraq, Lebanon, and Saudi Arabia, which stood waiting on the sidelines, poised to attack with their air force, tanks, and modern artillery as soon as the British left in mid-May.

"We need war material and the means to make war," Merlin wrote Hecht from Palestine on December 30, 1947. ". . . Precisely now we face a war of life or death. Expressis verbis: life or death." Between the Haganah's core strike force, the Palmach, and the fighters of the Irgun and Lehi, the Jews had seven thousand troops at most. In theory, the Haganah could also call up its militia of thirty-five thousand. But there were not even enough guns for half of them.[20]

"I guess [Ben] thought I was some kind of strength," Cohen explained, "that could help certain people." Cohen said the mob smuggled weapons along the East Coast waterfront, a role that would have been an easy transition from its cooperation with Naval Intelligence during the war, as Meyer Lansky also claimed. Overseeing operations were Albert Anastasia, acting chief of the Combination's killing machine, Murder Incorporated, and Charlie "the Jew" Yanowsky. "Charlie had the docks in New Jersey," Cohen explained, "and Albert had them in New York." Their web of control over longshoreman unions, stevedore firms, police, and politicians had been spun long back, in the days of Prohibition. Another important player on the docks was Newark's Longy Zwillman, whose Minutemen had also fought the Nazi Bund in the 1930s. "We knew he not only ran the rackets, he elected mayors and governors," recalled journalist and New Jersey native Sidney Zion. "We knew he was running guns to the Irgun when they were fighting the Arabs with matzo balls. . . . I knew plenty of guys in Newark who were saved by him from anti-Semitic hoods."[21]

The mob tracked and sabotaged shipments going to the Arabs, ensured security for crates delivered to the docks for the Jews, and stole U.S. military surplus arriving on ships. "I had access to all that stuff on the docks," Cohen said. "Some of the stuff and equipment like machine guns that we got back to Israel had never got a chance to be used in the Second World War. They weren't even put together. They were still in the cases, in the straw, in the oil and everything. We shipped them right over." Many Irish longshoremen had gained expertise in arms and explosives fighting the British and felt solidarity with the Jews. Cohen said he convinced a New Jersey dockworker named "Chopsie" to join the fight in Palestine.[22]

Contraband came in regularly from local Revisionists like Abraham and Sylvia Zweibon, who had been gathering arms for the Irgun since late 1945. The Zweibons received a steady stream of packages, mostly from army veterans, at their floor-covering store in Brooklyn. Donations of guns and matériel piled so high that the couple ran out of space even after opening a second store nearby, and they soon filled up the basement of their upstate vacation home. Lower East Side funeral home owner Lawrence Schwartz drove a hearse with weapons-filled coffins to warehouses around the city, and then on to Marine Terminal in Hoboken, New Jersey (Yanowsky's turf), or Bush Terminal in Brooklyn. "I watched with awe as they rose out of their stores and work shops and came to our side," Hecht recalled. "Jewish clerks and salesladies, garage workers, plasterers, elevator boys, Yeshiva students, policemen, garment workers, prize fighters, housewives, Jewish sailors and soldiers still in their uniforms, Jews from night clubs, tenements, farm lands, synagogues and even penthouses came boldly to the Irgun banner."[23]

Cohen said he organized league fund-raisers in Boston, Philadelphia, Miami, and elsewhere, which seems consistent with Ben-Ami's account. A group of Jewish mobsters in St. Louis agreed to host a dinner if former world champion boxer Barney Ross would give the keynote speech.

The event raised over $100,000, according to an unpublished memoir by old-guard Revisionist Rabbi Baruch Rabinowitz. Another league activist, Paul Gropman, remembered Cohen's muscle at a league meeting in Los Angeles. "You can always spot these guys," he said. "They keep their right hand in their pocket if they're right-handed, because that's where the gun is. . . . He sent these guys there, I think there were two of them, and he probably said, 'Hey, I don't want the meeting disrupted.' It was a Jewish meeting. These guys weren't Jews, or they didn't look like Jews to me. These guys were hoods. What the hell were they doing at this Jewish nationalism meeting?"[24]

With Cohen and Ross as league advocates, Hecht's activism continued beyond May 14, 1948, when David Ben-Gurion declared Israel's independence. The day before, Hecht staged a final pageant at Madison Square Garden, *The End of Silence*, drawing a crowd of twenty thousand with yet another a roster of celebrities: Sid Ceasar, Hazel Scott, Dean Martin, and Jerry Lewis, among others. It was in part a benefit for the George Washington Legion, Ross's force of American volunteers seeking to fight in Israel, just as the Abraham Lincoln Brigade had once fought in Spain. Ross, a two-division boxing titleholder and Marine Corps war hero wounded at Guadalcanal, had recruited 2,500 volunteers by the end of March, but the U.S. government had refused to issue them passports. In April and again in May, he and over four hundred recruits marched on Washington to protest the travel prohibition.[25]

Then, on May 24 Cohen held a major fund-raiser at Slapsy Maxie's, a swanky nightclub on Wilshire Boulevard. It was an apt locale: its namesake, Maxie Rosenbloom, was another world champion Jewish boxer, and he had earned the nickname "Slapsy" because of his unique style of offense—open-handed cuffs thrown in lightning flurries. An actor in more than sixty films, including Hecht's *Nothing Sacred*, he played either the punch-drunk boxer or "the comic tough guy, the B-movie gangster, saying 'dese,' 'dem' and 'dose' in his heavy New York accent."[26]

Hecht's account of that evening in *A Child of the Century* has become iconic, a romantic folktale about the Jewish mob saluting Israel that has been quoted and recounted in countless books, articles, and academic papers. But Hecht's story may be misleading in certain particulars. There were indeed plenty of "lawless and semi-lawless characters" present, but the crowd of 1,500 also included so many high officials that the scene might have reminded Hecht of aldermen Hinky Dink and Bathhouse John's

Gangsters' Ball in Chicago's First Ward back in the days of his youth. One guest struck by the mix of personalities was Lieutenant Rudy Wellpott, head of the Vice Squad—later "Administrative Vice"—for the Los Angeles Police Department. "It was interesting to notice who some of the people were that were present," he told a prosecutor at a 1949 grand jury investigation. "There were some judges, Assemblymen, Congressmen, some people from your office." Then again, Wellpott could have been lying: he had already been indicted for bribery and perjury, in a scandal orchestrated by Cohen that would soon turn Los Angeles upside down.[27]

Although Hecht's reference to a recent hospital stay and Ben-Ami's account would place the event around the late summer of 1947, club owner Charles DeVore dated the event to May 1948 when he testified at Cohen's tax trial three years later. Further, the text of Hecht's speech, stored among his papers, clearly suggests that time frame. (Charles, the official owner of the club along with his brothers, Al and Sy, recalled being so inspired by the speech that when Cohen was about to pay the club $5,000 cash for the event, Charles asked the gangster to keep half as a donation.[28])

Hecht told the crowd that he had come on behalf of Begin. "He asks that I do what I can to arouse among the Jews who are not fighting in the Holy Land, the knowledge that without them the Holy Land will be lost. . . . 'We are fighting against great odds,' the Irgun commander says. 'The enemy outnumbers us and is better equipped. His resources are unlimited. Great Britain is supplying him with its millions, its munitions and its manpower. We have only ourselves.'" Hecht invoked the memory of the Warsaw ghetto uprising, when thirty thousand Jews with only junk-yard scrap for weapons, "outnumbered as in a nightmare," had held out against the German *Wehrmacht* for twenty days. The Allies hadn't provided arms or any other support, he said, because of Britain's "shabby little plan to steal Palestine for themselves." Now, with money from American loans, Britain was pouring arms and expertise into Transjordan's Arab Legion and the other Arab armies, hoping to install a puppet regime. "A champion stands in Palestine," Hecht concluded. "He will not surrender. But he calls on us. He needs us. If he loses, he will lose because we did not put a gun in his hand."[29]

Decades later, in early 1981, a shocking tale aired on *60 Minutes* about what happened to over $750,000 raised that evening. Cleveland mobster-turned-informant Jimmy "the Weasel" Fratianno repeated for host Mike Wallace the allegations he had made in the newly released biography about him, *The Last Mafioso: The Treacherous World of Jimmy Fratianno*. Cohen had scammed the money, Fratianno claimed, by handing it to a trusted "rabbi" and then planting a *Los Angeles Herald-Examiner* article about a ship loaded with arms for Israel that sank somewhere at sea. "He's tapping his finger against the newspaper," Fratianno said in the book, "and looking at me with his hound-dog eyes, not a fucking expression on his face, and he keeps repeating, 'Oh, terrible, terrible. What a tragedy.'"[30]

Immediately after the *60 Minutes* episode, Ben-Ami tried to correct the record, providing his account of Uncle Joe, the Irgun's mysterious guide in the American underworld, and the fund-raisers held for the Irgun by the mob. Cohen's event at the nightclub, Ben-Ami wrote, had raised only $50,000–$60,000, and the money was given to Hecht, who passed it directly to representatives of the league and the Irgun. Fratianno's figures of $750,000 and up were "sheer fantasy," and none of the money was stolen. Ben-Ami also had an explanation for the origins of the tale about the alleged *Herald-Examiner* article: after the *Altalena* was shelled, he said, Cohen's enemies had circulated the story that the ship never existed and that it was all a con.[31]

The mob's intrigue with the Irgun had a fitting coda in June 1948. Weeks after the benefit at Slapsy Maxie's, Ben-Ami phoned fellow Bergsonite Alex Rafaeli in Europe and asked him to fly to Palermo on an unspecified mission. Escorted upon arrival to the Las Palmas Hotel, Rafaeli cooled his heels for two days before finally being summoned to the dining room, where he was met by a pale, haggard-looking Lucky Luciano. The Mafia don had been released from prison in exchange for his aid to Naval Intelligence but then deported. Now he wanted to return to America and knew the Bergsonites were friendly with Henry Morgenthau. "If you can help get me back to America," he told Rafaeli, "I'll get you all the boats you need." Rafaeli said that he would pass on the proposal as soon as he returned to Rome. By the time he had arrived in the Italian capital, however, various arms pipelines were already flowing to Israel, and there was no need for Luciano's fishing boats.[32]

It is impossible to know how important the underworld's assistance was to the Jewish state—an issue that remains shrouded in controversy. During the critical early months of the civil war, the only large arms shipments came from Europe, particularly from Czechoslovakia. These deliveries finally arrived on March 31 and April 2, 1948, totaling 4,700 rifles, 240 medium machine guns, and five million rounds of ammunition, and they reached Palestine just in time for the Haganah to break the siege on Jerusalem. By May years of planning at last began to fall into place, and the Haganah's hauls of fighter planes, B-17 Flying Fortress heavy bombers, armor, jeeps, munitions, and matériel dwarfed what the Irgun had accrued. The story is told in Leonard Slater's 1970 book *The Pledge*, which downplays the notion that the mob played any meaningful role.[33] But the exclusion of American Jewish gangsters from Israel's history may have parallels to Lansky's experience with Rabbi Stephen Wise in the 1930s: many supporters would have regarded the help of organized crime as a terrible blight on the Jewish state, and its enemies would have seen it as further evidence of Israel's illegitimacy.

Many firsthand accounts acknowledge the role of the mob. The headquarters of the Haganah's vast smuggling scheme was the seedy Hotel Fourteen at 14 East Sixtieth Street, where chief operative Yehuda Arazi crafted deals and Teddy Kollek coordinated the flow of goods. Right downstairs was the glitzy Copacabana Club, the favorite haunt of the New York underworld. "In my business . . . we can't be too fussy about who we do business with," Slater quotes Arazi as saying after he met with two hoods from Murder Incorporated. But none of Arazi's deals with the underworld amounted to anything, Slater maintains, because the offers were either fake or overpriced. Kollek, however, recounted in his memoir that his work touched on "liaisons with spies, mobsters, movie moguls, statesmen, bankers, professors, industrialists, and newspaper men; and no lack of illegalities, from petty to international." Reuven Dafni, another Haganah agent, said he had accepted a total of $50,000 in donations from Bugsy Siegel, and he credited Miami gangster Sam Kay with providing the connection to the president of Panama, which allowed the Jews to register ships under the Panamanian flag.[34]

Smuggling the goods through the ports became the responsibility of twenty-two-year-old Elie Schalit, who set up an array of shell companies with the aid of New York attorney Nahum Bernstein. But given the thousands of tons of contraband that began to move to Israel over the summer and fall, it is hard to believe help from the mob on the waterfront was not necessary. If Naval Intelligence had to rely on the active assistance of the mob to secure U.S. shipping, wouldn't such assistance have been necessary to secure so much illegal shipping? According to Lansky, Arazi summoned him to Hotel Fourteen and said, "I know the mafia, or whatever you want to call it, controls the Port of New York." When Arazi then asked Lansky to intercept a shipment going to the Arabs and divert it to Haifa, the cooperation with Luciano partner Joe Adonis, Anastasia, and the longshoremen began.[35]

Regardless of how important such aid turned out to be, *everyone* involved in the arms smuggling was violating the U.S. embargo act of December 5, 1947. "Here was an opportunity that happened maybe once in a lifetime, maybe not even once in a lifetime," said Al Robison, a textile manufacturer who was among the prominent U.S. Jewish businessmen backing the cause. "That we could be cloak-and-dagger people, that we could live dangerously and feel highly virtuous about it." The government itself was looking the other way. When the New York City police received a tip from a building superintendent in April 1948, they discovered hundreds of rifles and pistols in a loft on West Twenty-Eighth Street. At a pretrial hearing a month later, Judge Frederick Strong dismissed the case against two young men discovered at the scene, arguing that their mere presence in the loft did not prove they were in sole possession of the contraband. A New Jersey case stemming from an arrest in late November was similarly dismissed. Even the discovery of some 250 tons of TNT that crashed off a waterfront crane on a rainy January night did not result in a single day of jail time (though it was still a serious setback for the Haganah).[36]

Disregard for the embargo act may have reached all the way to the president. "It was only God's will that Harry Truman was president," said Cohen. "He couldn't openly allow it to be known that he was okaying the stuff to be shipped back there or that stuff was being stolen from the ships that were coming back from the Second World War. But it was only with Truman looking the other way, or with his being in favor, that it was done." The embargo may have been a sop to the Arabs and a way of appeasing the many officials in Truman's administration who strongly favored taking their side in the conflict. But senior adviser Clark Clifford had persuasively argued that the Arab states depended on the United States for 90 percent of their oil revenue—"their need of us is greater than our need of them." And while "the Jewish vote" and campaign finance must have been factors in Truman's decision-making, so were his personal friendships with Jews, as well as his sympathy for their plight.[37]

This rampant flouting of the law has, of course, led to some sore feelings. In the *Journal of Palestine Studies*, Ricky Dale-Calhoun noted derisively that oil magnate Rudolf Sonneborn and the seventeen business-men who started to develop the smuggling plan with Ben-Gurion weeks before the end of World War II "took maximum advantage of a number of conditions," seizing on "corruption, malfeasance, and dereliction of duty on the part of local officials; connections with the American criminal underworld; and legal expertise to exploit the weaknesses and loopholes in U.S. law." As a result, he huffed, "despite the heroic myth in which it has previously been cloaked, the Jewish Agency's U.S. arms procurement effort amounted to a highly effective criminal conspiracy."[38]

In the final days of the American League for a Free Palestine, Hecht ignited yet another controversy, one that exacted a personal toll. Amid continuing Israeli victories in the fall, United Nations mediator Count Folke Bernadotte had proposed a peace plan that would give the Negev Desert to the Arabs and internationalize Jerusalem. When four members of Lehi assassinated Bernadotte on September 17, 1948, Hecht told the press he was "an ass not worthy of so fine a death." Hecht added, "He was not sharp enough to be the villain of the piece. He was a professional cat's paw, hired to pull the chestnuts out of the fire for the British." Hecht, who still held to Vladimir Jabotinsky's dream of a Greater Israel spanning both sides of the Jordan River, argued that if Bernadotte's plan was adopted, "Israel would be reduced to a Miami Beach." Weeks later, the Council of Britain's Cinematograph Exhibitors' Association announced a boycott of his films, citing Hecht's holiday-in-his-heart remark. Though the ban was finally lifted in 1952, as late as 1956 he was denied credit for *The Iron Petticoat* out of fear of losing the British market.[39]

More than a year of Zionist gun-running, and Begin's transition from Irgun commander to political leader, had done nothing to alter the rhetoric of previous days. When Begin visited America at the end of November, the league wished him luck at a banquet in the Waldorf-Astoria, which was also a farewell ceremony. Tonight, Hecht said, "we go back to smaller things. . . . My interest in the land of Israel lies only in this deeper knowledge—that if Israel is beaten down, it will not be a nation alone that is beaten. . . . It will be Truth and the unending cry of the human soul for freedom that will be conquered."[40]

Days later, Albert Einstein, Hannah Arendt, and Sidney Hook were among the signatories of a letter in the *New York Times* that likened Begin's new Herut, or Freedom Party, to "Nazi and Fascist Parties," formed, as it was, out of the terrorist Irgun. "Today they speak of freedom, democracy and anti-imperialism, whereas until recently they openly preached the doctrine of the Fascist state," the letter asserted. "It is in its actions that the terrorist party betrays its real character." The authors cited the massacre of 240 civilians in the peaceful village of Deir Yassin, which was "not a military objective"—allegations that would not prove to be entirely accurate. "The IZL and Stern groups inaugurated a reign of terror in the Palestine Jewish community," they continued. "Teachers were beaten up for speaking against them, adults were shot for not letting their children join them. By gangster methods, beatings, window-smashing, and widespread robberies, the terrorists intimidated the population and exacted a heavy tribute."[41]

Hecht's career as an activist was over, but he would long remain rankled by what he saw as the hypocrisy of those who had labeled him a terrorist and gangster, of those who professed to speak in the name of law and order, of the distinctions they drew between lawmaker and lawbreaker.

CHAPTER 17

Champion in Chains, Revisited

Organized gangsterism is returning—a new kind of gangsterism, combining the ruthlessness of the Prohibition Era with the scientific tactics and strategy used by the underground in World War II.

—Movie trailer for *A Street with No Name*[1]

Hecht once told a colleague about the day Mickey Cohen's bulletproof limousine first pulled up to the house in Oceanside, California. Throughout the whole visit, the gangster and his two burly bodyguards never took their hats off.

"They acted like people I made up," Hecht said.[2]

Indeed, even the voluble author never quite articulated the uncanny degree to which his visitor was a composite of the characters he had known in youth and the ones who populated his own imagination. For decades, Hecht been spinning tales about them in prose, plays, and movies and, finally, in the myth of the tough Jew in his propaganda. In some ways, Cohen appeared a funhouse-mirror reflection of Chicago hoods like Nails Morton and the public relations–savvy Al Capone, or Hecht's own Diamond Louie and Tony Camonte. A simian figure with pouty lips and a scar curling under one eye, standing five-foot-five in elevator shoes, "the Mick" resembled "the fifth banana in a B-fight picture . . . a dark cupid." His cream-colored and pastel suits draped a once-sinewy pugilist's body gone soft from pastries and ice cream.[3]

Yet Cohen was something other than a pug-faced, pint-sized parody who posed for magazine covers in front of his spectacular clothing closet and the monogrammed bed of his dog, Tuffy. Friends such as Hecht understood that his compulsive habit of washing his hands fifty to sixty times a day was simply germ phobia. Others in Hollywood found it eerily reminiscent of crazy Lady Macbeth's vain attempts to scrub out that damn spot, recalling the line from the great bard: "Will all great Neptune's ocean wash this blood clean from my hand?"[4] And Cohen was also something far more than comic relief: by the late 1940s, he had amassed a vast empire.

Groomed by Benjamin "Bugsy" Siegel and a debonair gambler known as Nick the Greek, Cohen had graduated from a gun thug "going on the heavy"—pulling heists—to "a bookie's bookie" who ran a network of six to eight spots that offered under-the-table off-track betting, each raking in anywhere between $30,000 and $150,000 daily. He also opened exclusive gambling clubs that catered to the Hollywood elite. With these revenue streams, by 1945 he had expanded into protection, extortion, loan sharking, strikebreaking, slot and pinball machine concessions, and, though he denied it, prostitution and narcotics. He had "his finger in every pie, his hand in every wallet," noted biographer Tere Tereba, and his dominion stretched across Southern California and down to Mexico. It was rumored to reach up to San Francisco and as far out as Honolulu and Manila.[5]

Cohen was Tony Camonte on steroids, a Jewish Scarface for the atomic age, a "miniature colossus" equipped on a scale far beyond what Hecht and Howard Hawks had imagined in their early talkie. Among the legitimate businesses that served as Cohen's fronts, Michael's Exclusive Haberdashery at 8804 Sunset Boulevard was his headquarters, a fortress that put Camonte's steel shutters and bulletproof desk chair to shame. By the time of the Slapsy Maxie's fund-raiser, "any appearance he made in Hollywood was sure to draw gunfire," Hecht recalled. Beneath the walnut-walled showroom filled with imported gabardine suits, camel-hair coats, finely woven shirts, and smoking jackets, Cohen protected his private office with an electronically operated, triple-layered mesh steel door, reinforced with wrought iron. As a final redoubt for the hoods who sometimes doubled as clothing salesmen, he installed a secret chamber wired to observe the store and office, soundproofed and comfortably accoutered with a radio and fully stocked fridge. Around the corner was a chop shop where a Ford sedan could be rapidly rebuilt into a replica of a Los Angeles Police Department (LAPD) squad car.[6]

By the time his enemies launched an all-out onslaught of shotgun blasts, machine-gun strafings, and bombings—what the newspapers called "the Battle of the Sunset Strip"—Cohen had brought West some twenty "ex-convicts, muscle guys, bust-out gamblers and killers." In addition to his soon-to-be-deceased right hand, Hooky Rothman, "built like a bull," and his "left arm," Neddie Herbert, the weapons expert and court jester, there was Johnny Stompanato, a twenty-two-year-old ex-Marine ladykiller reputedly charged with watching over the beautiful women Cohen used for blackmail. Soon they were joined by the lethal "Happy" Harold Meltzer from the East Coast, where he was liked for the recent icepick murder of Charlie "the Jew" Yanowsky.[7]

Cohen's troops drove a fleet of navy blue Cadillacs with torpedo fins and shining chrome, bulletproofed, souped up for speed, and outfitted with secret weapons stashes, as well-suited for the Strip's poshest clubs as for boulevard firefights. The crew, decked out in finery from Michael's, was undoubtedly one of the nattiest armies in history. "If he had a coat of arms," quipped bookmaker George Redston, "it probably would have shown $100 bills rampant on a field of double-crosses."[8]

In one of a dozen assassination attempts, gunmen opened fire from both sides of Cohen's street as he was pulling into his Brentwood home, forcing him to duck below window level and drive blindly backward for two blocks. After that, he purchased a 4,400-pound Cadillac Fleetwood that could roll through the next barrage on its Goodrich Silvertown Seal-o-Matic tires. It was armored in eight-inch-thick high-carbon steel that could resist anything short of a direct hit from a bazooka, lined with bulletproof fiberglass, and had inch-thick window glass with a beveled windshield and slits to allow for outgoing fire. Unfortunately, once the $7,000 worth of modifications had been made, a judge would agree to issue a road permit only if Cohen would tell who had permitted testing of the vehicle at the LAPD gun range. According to Cohen, he tried to sell the Cadillac to Emperor Haile Selassie, Juan Perón, and a Latin American dictator, who was indeed interested but was killed before he could make the purchase. The car sat in storage for a long time before it was finally sold, for a pittance, to a car museum in Texas.[9]

☙

The son of Russian immigrants from Kiev, Meyer Harris Cohen—called Mickey—was born in Brownsville, Brooklyn, in 1913. His devout, ortho-dox father, Max, who "was in some kind of import business to do with Jewish fishes," died when Mickey was only weeks old, leaving his mother, Fannie, with little money to raise her six children. In 1915 she brought Mickey and his three brothers and two sisters out to Los Angeles and opened a small grocery in Boyle Heights, which Hecht called "the toughest and grittiest area of the city." It was an immigrant district full of Italians, Jews, Mexicans, and a dozen other ethnicities, like the slums of the East Coast, or Maxwell Street and the Near West Side in Chicago.[10]

During the years when the circulation wars were honing the skills of young thugs in Chicago, little Mickey was learning to scrap and hustle as a newsboy on the West Coast. He was three when he first sat on a pile of newspapers and found that he could furtively swap copies of the *Los Angeles Record* for hot dogs and candy. "I was really looking to make a buck at a very early age," he told Hecht. As a boy he would sleep in the men's room of the *Examiner*, help city editor Jim Richardson sober up, and, in return, be the first to grab a hot edition to sell, "say the Dempsey-Firpo fight," as it rolled off the presses. "I hung around the Newsboys Club at Spring and Court streets, and during these days became rather adept at whipping other newsboys who challenged my rights to profitable corners," he related.[11]

Never much for school, he loitered in pool halls, ran numbers and bottles of whiskey, hired himself out for protection, and soon got into trouble with the authorities. He was nine when police found a still behind his brothers' drugstore, and after he hit an officer with a hot plate of food, he was booked for bootlegging. One incident followed another: he was nabbed stealing a crate of Abba-Zaba from a candy factory; was kicked out of Hebrew school for flicking the lights on and off during an assembly and hitting another kid in the mouth; and was caught trying to hold up a downtown movie theater with a baseball bat. "He took to burglary as a duckling takes to water," Hecht observed. "No Jewish morality, nor family decency touched his spirit."[12]

He had done two spells in reform schools and was on probation when local boxing referee Abe Roth, volunteering as his big brother, helped channel all that aggression into the ring. At twelve, Cohen began to fight four-rounders across the city several nights a week, showing promise. A year later he won the flyweight title at the American Legion Newsboy's Championship. "I won the fight, but my real pleasure was putting money together," he said. "Of course, if there was any way to steal money, I'd steal it, too." His early victories inspired confidence that he could go pro, and so at fifteen, with truant officers on his tail, Mickey hoboed out to Cleveland to see his brother Harry, who agreed to act as his manager.[13]

Through boxing Cohen then became acquainted with the underworld. Cleveland was a booming industrial hub, and its proximity to Canada made it an important bootlegging link for the Combination, the East Coast organization controlled by Meyer Lansky, Lucky Luciano, and Frank Costello. The local powers were the Italian Mafia of Murray Hill and Mayfield Road, which Hecht referred to as "the Hill Mob." Soon to establish themselves (by 1926) were the Cleveland Four, a quartet of Jewish rumrunners that included Lou Rothkopf, later a major player in Las Vegas, and former Detroit Purple Gang member Moe Dalitz. But when Cohen arrived in 1928, the Italians ran the rackets, unlike in New York, where various ethnic groups were wedded in "a happy marriage of convenience," as New York Police Department investigator Ralph F. Salerno described it: "The Jews supply the moxie. The Italians take care of the muscle. And they split the money between them."[14]

Cohen, like others of his ilk, would shrug off the various names given to each gang; to him, they were simply "the people." "It is a bashful synonym for the word society or the word government," Hecht explained. "The real gangster offers it almost mystic allegiance. Young Cohen was gangster from his toes up. No glimmerings of other codes disturbed him. He accepted the people, as a stray dog, destined for the dog pound, accepts a hearth studded with meat bones."[15]

Cohen's talents in the ring attracted such attention that within a year his managers sent him to train at the legendary Stillman's Gym, located on West Fifty-Fourth Street in Manhattan, the nexus of the boxing universe and the Combination. Amid the crowds and smoke, "the people" sat ringside and did business. "The place is one of the centralizing institutions of the underworld," observed Alva Johnston in the *New Yorker*. "Rival low-life factions meet here casually under a flag of truce, as the rival financial and social mobs fraternize at the opera." Cohen started to get to know Damon Runyon, the boxing reporter and great underworld chronicler who gave Slapsy Maxie his nickname, and met famous fight enthusiasts like Al Jolson. Cohen's managers introduced him around, promoted him, and lined up bouts for "the California Wildcat," the new featherweight with a white Star of David and monogram emblazoned on his blue satin trunks.[16]

As a writer who had often eulogized fighters—Jewish ones, in particular—Hecht must have been eager to learn about his friend's past career. Enthusiasm for the sport had prompted Hecht to briefly return to journalism in the late 1920s: he covered half a dozen Madison Square Garden bouts for the New York *Morning Telegraph* and wrote an essay about the Garden crowds for the *New Yorker*. Ten years later, a lyrical final column for *1001 Afternoons in New York* began, "I saw Jack Dempsey knocked out of the ring at Atlantic City and come back to win. / I saw Ben Jeby, knocked down three times, climb back on his feet and land a haymaker."[17]

Hecht's rhapsodies about Jewish pugilists became a hallmark of his propaganda. In his "Letter to the Terrorists of Palestine," he recalled sitting ringside at the Max Schmelling–Max Baer fight with one of Hollywood's "respectable Jews," who had been unable to bear the sight of the German Schmelling beating the Jewish Baer. For the first nine rounds, Hecht's companion kept his head down, then cheered himself hoarse in the tenth, when Baer finally knocked Schmelling onto the canvas. Among the many in Hollywood who shared Hecht's enthusiasm, the Jewish screenwriter Budd Schulberg, the author of *On the Waterfront* (1954), used to talk boxing with Cohen and regularly attended fights at Hollywood Legion Stadium. "I must confess we had a special *kvell* [delight] for the exploits of our Jewish boxers," Schulberg remarked. Immigrants of his father's generation, like Adolf Zukor, had boxed to survive, earning a dollar per round in back alleys. The American-born boys of Schulberg's and Hecht's generation saw boxing, like show business, as a path to fame and fortune. A Jewish champion, Schulberg said, was "a repudiation of the stereotype of Jews being afraid to fight back."[18]

Cohen, however, was no champion like Barney Ross or Benny Leonard. "I fought with the best of them," he explained to Hecht. "I wasn't the worst. Neither was I the tops." He claimed to have participated in thirty-two main events, a figure he later doubled to seventy-nine. One credible source suggests he had seven wins and two losses when he went up against his first major competitor, Tommy Paul, who had forty-seven wins and six losses. The pummeling Paul delivered shattered Cohen's confidence and his dreams: "I began to see that I really didn't have it to be great in the ring." After that, the young fighter lost nine of his next ten matches before quitting the game for good.[19]

Hecht might have considered casting Cohen as a heroic underdog—the David-with-a-slingshot type—but the young featherweight did not quite fit that mold either. The classic journeyman fighter of lore is a brawler who makes up in heart for what he lacks in skills and conditioning. He can't beat a champion, but he can give as good as he gets long enough to give the crowd its money's worth. But Paul had knocked Cohen bleeding and senseless two minutes into the first round, spinning Cohen into a two-year losing streak. "A man who fought Baby Arizmendi may boast," Hecht ventured. Cohen had indeed fought the Mexican champion, as well as the equally legendary Chalky Wright, but by these final fights he was out of shape and hadn't lasted three rounds. "Nowadays Mickey likes to reminisce about his record as a gladiator," wrote magazine writer Dean Jennings, who in 1958 handed out a journalistic bashing. "Actually he was a second-rater with a glass chin and was knocked out in most of his bouts."[20]

The stories that Cohen shared with Hecht revealed him to be a different sort of fighter altogether. "I must have been a real crazy punk," he confessed.

> For example, one night I'm fighting a pretty good man named Carpenter, and the fight was on the belly [the bout wasn't fixed]. It's a very important fight for me because a lot of the people are at ringside. And I'm eager to make a good impression. So from the first bell I climb all over my opponent and punch the hell out of him. By the third round he's got glass eyes and his arms are hangin'. I belt him and knock him down. He gets up. I knock him down again. I keep knockin' him down five, six times in a row and he keeps gettin' up every time. I finally get so upset by his not stayin' down that I jump in and start biting his ear off. So help me, I nearly got it bitten off before the referee can pry us apart. My opponent runs around hollerin' with a glove over his bloody ear. The referee hangs on me. "You got him dead," he says. "What do you want to do—eat him?"[21]

The ring had rewarded Cohen with years of sweat and dirt, lousy money, disfiguring scars under his eyes, and a broken nose. His true passion had always been crime anyway, and during his rise and fall as the California Wildcat, he had launched a career in armed robbery. With a black bandanna and a tommy gun—or pistol or shotgun, whatever was handy—he and a crew of Italians robbed establishments all over Cleveland, three to four times a week. "It made me equal to everybody," he said. "Even as small as I was, when I whipped out that big .38 it made me as big as a guy six foot ten."[22]

Cohen estimated that he pulled two hundred stickups, which would have made him a major contender even then, when the most notorious crime wave in American history was hammering the nation's midsection. During 1933 and 1934, Bonnie and Clyde were swapping headlines with John Dillinger, Pretty Boy Floyd, Ma Barker and the Barker-Karpis Gang, Machine Gun Kelly, Baby Face Nelson, and dozens of other brigands. So adroit was Cohen that he never got arrested. The Hill Mob did catch up with him, though, since his crew specialized in gambling joints, cafés, and whorehouses. Fortunately, the old Italian bosses had developed a respect for the tough little "Jew boy" and soon reached an accommodation with him. He would act as their enforcer but could continue to freelance, as long as he did so outside of their territory.[23] Thus began Cohen's adult career in crime, though Hecht would quibble with such terminology. "Lawlessness," he mused, "is the debatable word in Mickey's early rise."

> He broke laws, but they were laws of an alien civilization; a civilization he had avoided from his first waking days. What made him successful, actually, was keeping and enforcing the laws of the only world he knew, the underworld. In this world cut throats were prime ministers and robbers were nobility. Like any Horatio Alger hero, Mickey aspired to a chummy nod from his betters. And Mickey's betters were finely dressed ex-killers now pot-bellied and flashing with diamonds, who bribed high police officials and politicians and put the screws on the town. And who sat "at the round table" where decisions were made on head breakings and "put outs." . . . Mickey carried out sentences against such undesirables.[24]

In 1934 Cohen's activities began to draw too much attention from the police. The mob stepped in to have an armed robbery charge reduced to embezzlement, and eventually dismissed, after Cohen was named in a cafeteria heist planned with the proprietor. But a shootout during another stickup had resulted in the arrest of one of his crew, and now investigators were closing in. As a result, Cohen fled to Chicago.[25]

Cohen claimed that shortly after arriving in Chicago, he met Capone at his headquarters. "I met him as a kid meets a hero," he told Hecht. "He ribbed me about some of my heists. But there was a piece of work I had done for him he kind of admired." However, Capone went to jail in 1931, three years before the embezzlement charge in Cleveland and Cohen's flight to Chicago. But Cohen had clearly spent time in Chicago before then. He knew Capone's brothers, Mattie and Ralph, whom he had met through former boxer Machine Gun Jack McGurn. A senior figure in the Chicago Outfit, McGurn was suspected in the Saint Valentine's Day Massacre and was assassinated on its seventh anniversary in 1936.[26]

Despite his respect for Capone, Cohen struck out on his own as he had in Cleveland, again creating friction with the mob. Unable to make do with a poker concession he had been allotted, he opened a "bust-out"—a less-than-reputable gambling joint—in the Loop, offering craps, a fast-money, highly volatile game that police and the Outfit had agreed to keep out of the downtown business district. "Greasy Thumb" Jack Guzik, treasurer for the syndicate, flew in from Miami and called Cohen to a round table. Guzik ordered the game terminated, but Cohen ignored the decree. On a wintry night a week later, Cohen was standing on the sidewalk outside his joint when a burst of machine-gun fire sprayed from a passing car. He hit the deck on the slush-covered pavement, ruining his fine clothes, but even this stern warning failed to deter him.[27]

It was nevertheless becoming clear that that the hot-headed young punk had outstayed his welcome in Chicago. During a clash in a drugstore soon thereafter, Cohen cracked a particularly truculent bruiser in the skull with a sugar dispenser and then the butt of the man's own pistol "till his head popped open like a melon and he bled like a hydrant." There again was that terrible temper. "It's a funny thing—while I'm talking about all those things I can hardly believe they happened to me," he told Hecht more than twenty years later. "It's like they happened to somebody else—a close friend or something. No, I don't feel any remorse or anything like that about those things, because, as I said, they weren't things I did. I mean, me who's sittin' here talkin'."[28] As before, Cohen's connections in the underworld—this time a Capone fixer—sorted the matter out with the police and courts. Cohen was then summoned to Cleveland, where Lou Rothkopf had a directive to pass along on behalf of the Italians in Cleveland and Lansky—the whole nationally organized Combination. They wanted him to join Siegel in Los Angeles and, Cohen said, "stand in for their end of the action."[29]

This was essentially a job opportunity offered by fellow Jews to a promising young boychick, though Cohen understood the Arnold Rothstein principle that mobsters, like rats, should be left free to scavenge for themselves. He recognized that Jews needed to stick together; the Italians had their power and organization, and "being Jews, Benny and me and even Meyer couldn't be a real part and parcel of that." However, he hadn't been told to put himself *fully* under Siegel's wing, and when he arrived home in Los Angeles in 1937, phoning up the senior mobster felt too much like reporting for work.[30]

"Actually we never even gave a fuck about Benny," he recalled. "We were just rooting, just taking off scores." Cohen decided that Siegel could make the first overture, and raiding bookie joints and brothels by the dozen did eventually catch Siegel's attention. When Cohen hit major bookmaker Morrie Orloff, he snatched $23,000 that belonged to the reigning Sicilian in Los Angeles, Jack Dragna. After that, Siegel sent Champ Segal, a well-respected boxing manager who had known Cohen as a boy, to bring him in.[31]

℞

At some point in the mid-1930s, Siegel had slipped into town unnoticed, having come West to establish the same kind of dominion he had built during the heyday of Prohibition back East. He intended to seize control of all the horse and dog tracks from Southern California to Mexico and take a cut of all gambling clubs, bookmaking operations, and brothels. But initially he faced resistance from the downtown syndicate, and while he built alliances and laid his plans, he maintained a low profile—to the extent that someone like him could manage. Locally Siegel was known as just "a wealthy sportsman," another flashy playboy hobnobbing with the rich and famous, until an unforeseen chain of events fortuitously wiped out the competition.[32]

Depression-era Los Angeles was controlled by a criminal cabal of elected officials, bosses, and police. "You know, in Chicago the gangsters paid off the police but the gangsters did the job," said one prominent defense attorney. "In Los Angeles, the police *were* the gangsters." When a reform-minded cafeteria owner and a former cop teamed up to expose the high-level corruption, the chief of the LAPD intelligence squad tried to silence them—with bombs. But both of his attempts were badly botched, leaving a trail of evidence that implicated Police Chief James ("Two-Gun") Davis and Mayor Frank Shaw. By the fall of 1938, LAPD Captain Earl Kynette had been convicted of attempted murder, Chief Davis had resigned, and Shaw was removed from office in an unprecedented recall election; the scandal swept clean the top ranks of the LAPD. The collapse of the Shaw administration and its LAPD cronies left a power vacuum that Siegel was poised to fill.[33]

℘

When he went to meet with Siegel in the summer of 1939, Cohen jammed a huge fifty-dollar Stetson hat onto his head and, "looking like a giant mushroom in motion," noted Jennings, trotted into the sweat room of the Hollywood YMCA. Siegel came out naked wrapped in a towel with a big smile on his face. *"For Christ sake,* Mickey thought, *he's almost pretty.* The eyes were baby blue beneath long dark lashes, the dark hair showed finger waves, and the mouth and chin were almost feminine."[34] In the version Cohen recounted to Hecht, Siegel said, "You were supposed to contact me when you got here." Cohen shrugged it off: "I hadn't gotten around to it yet." Siegel noted the big score Cohen had just made at Morrie Orloff's and asked him to kick back the money he had taken from Dragna's man.[35]

> "I don't know what you're talking about," I says. He looks at me confused for a minute. Them Eastern guys are used to giving an order only once. Then he smiles. "You're a good boy," he says, "but you're a little crazy. I want you to kick back that money."
>
> "I wouldn't kick back no money for my mother," I says. He looks at me cold and says, "You heard what I said." I says, "Go take a fuck for yourself." And walk out of that steam room before I start meltin'.[36]

Cohen survived and was even persuaded to return the money after Siegel gently urged him to at least give back a stickpin he had taken ("it was his family whoreloom"). Thus began a decade-long partnership and mentorship. Cohen served as a strong man in the conquest of Los Angeles, and, in return, Siegel made a *mensch* [man] out of him. "I found Benny a person with brilliant intelligence—he would look right through you," Cohen told Hecht. "He commanded 1,000 percent respect and got it. Also he was tough. He came out the hard way—muscle work, heists, killings. 'You little son-of-a-bitch,' he said to me. 'You reflect my younger days.'"[37]

Siegel more than just acted like guys Hecht made up. He was a ready-made American myth, a combination psychopath and starry-eyed dreamer possessed of the same "terrible innocence" as Tony Camonte. In the days of

Prohibition, he would break someone's bones for two dollars or kill them for less than fifty dollars. Running truckloads of bootleg liquor, Siegel never hesitated when danger threatened, recalled Joseph "Doc" Stacher. "While we tried to figure out what the best move was, Bugsy was already shooting," Stacher said. "When it came to action there was no one better. I've seen him charge ten men single-handed and they would all turn and run. I never knew a man who had more guts." The newspapers had taken to calling him Bugsy, a variation of *bugs*, slang for "crazy," a nickname Siegel couldn't stand. "His rages were so pure and incandescent, so very much the essence of Benny, that people who knew him did not take offense at them," observed Lansky biographer Robert Lacey.[38]

But the man the Federal Bureau of Investigation credited with thirty murders sealed his fate when he sank some $6 million of mob money into the Flamingo Hotel, a fabulous oasis on a lonely stretch of Clark County, Nevada, that would one day be the Las Vegas Strip. It had shimmered in the desert, beckoning Siegel, just as the neon billboard flashing "THE WORLD IS YOURS" had beckoned Hecht's fictional Camonte. Others had come before him, but Siegel could rightly claim credit for dreaming Las Vegas into existence. By then, however, he was laid out in his $5,000 bronze coffin lined with silk.[39]

Siegel paid his protégé handsomely to seize control of Los Angeles, which Cohen did over the next seven years. First to go was the gambling empire of Eddie Nealis. "Siegel was fixed on bringing Nealis to knees," Cohen told Hecht. "That Mexican son of a bitch thinks he's comin' in with me," said Siegel. "Keep on him." Cohen heisted Nealis's posh Clover Club (resulting in an embarrassing encounter with Betty Grable), wrecked five of his gambling joints, shot his tough Irish enforcer Jimmy Fox, and barked down his gun bulls with the Sheriff's Department. Finally, Cohen chased Nealis himself out of town.[40]

But the key to money and power, as Siegel well knew, was the racing wire, an essential service for bookies because it provided the nationwide racing results, as well as crucial information on track conditions, jockeys, and trainers. Since 1927 it had been the monopoly of the Nationwide News Service, owned by Moses Annenberg, the same man who, along with his brother, Max, had headed the circulation department for Hearst during Chicago's newspaper wars. Annenberg, who also owned the *Philadelphia Inquirer*, the *Miami Tribune*, and the *Daily Racing Form*, employed the same brutal methods to knock out nineteen competing wire services that he had used in the early days. "It was Annenberg's ruthless world that gave birth to Mickey Cohen," asserted Cohen biographer Tere Tereba. When Annenberg pleaded guilty to income tax evasion in 1939, control of the racing wire went to James Ragen, another veteran of the circulation wars, who renamed it Continental Press.

Siegel partnered with the Chicago Outfit two years later to set up the competing Phoenix-based Trans-America Service. The 1,800 Los Angeles bookmakers had remained with Continental, so he assigned Cohen to wrest control of them.[41] After Continental's West Coast representative, Russell Brophy, turned down a deal, Cohen and associate Joe Sica visited the competition's downtown headquarters. Marching past the receptionist, they tore out thirty phone lines, wrecked the office, and beat Brophy into semiconsciousness. When Cohen was asked about the incident years later at the Kefauver Committee hearings, he denied any assault; it had just been an argument. A senator noted that Sica had been fined $200 for hitting Brophy, while Cohen had been fined $100. "Then I must have hit him less," Cohen said.[42]

Cohen retreated to Phoenix for six months while Siegel fixed the charges; after he returned, he managed to bring five hundred bookmakers on board with Trans-America. Cohen later said that he was learning to use diplomacy rather than fists to reach his ends, but Jennings noted, "There is no existing record that shows how many cracked skulls or how many unsolved murders were a direct result of Siegel's western war on Continental Press." Ragen survived a shotgun blast in June 1946 but mysteriously succumbed at the hospital two months later from what was believed to be mercury poisoning.[43]

While waging the wire war during his work hours, Cohen sought to settle down to a life of domestic tranquility. In October 1940 he married LaVonne Norma Weaver, a beautiful, auburn-haired twenty-three-year-old shiksa whom he described as a dance instructor. Though seemingly as demure as a debutante, she had a record of her own for burglary and solicitation. They were married late at night in a chapel on Western Avenue, but the wedding almost didn't happen: the minister tried to bar the couple's bulldog, Tuffy, from attending, and Cohen refused to go through with the ceremony unless the dog could be present as a witness.

Like so many other young couples who flocked to the suburbs after the war, in 1947 the Cohens moved into a ranch-style home in the sleepy glen of Brentwood. Despite the house's modest outward appearance, Cohen had lavished tens of thousands on interior decoration and special modifications to accommodate his unique compulsions. A water-heating system large enough for a hotel allowed him to shower several times a day. His cedar-paneled walk-in closet contained hundreds of tailor-made, perfectly pressed monogrammed suits, well over sixty pairs of handmade shoes, sixteen hundred pairs of socks, and a breathtaking array of lotions and accessories.[44]

Hecht nevertheless understood Cohen as a primordial figure, a type that had remained unchanged throughout the eons, utterly uncorrupted by society. Paleontologists, Hecht wrote, had read the tale of armed robbery and murder "in the fractured fossil skulls of a million years ago. Heisters who had just learned to walk upright entered the caves of Spain and 'raised' missing links cooking dragon meat in the hills of Java. Hunting, sex and robbery were the three original occupations of *homo sapiens* when his jaw still held the monkey outline. I have felt, listening to Mickey, that he was obviously a throwback."[45]

Because criminals were "a part of man's soul, not his institutions," they remained immune to the high-flown political "jabberwock" of the McCarthy era, which seemed to be hurtling humankind toward the apocalypse. "In all my talks with Mickey Cohen, the word innocence has always haunted me," Hecht mused in his handwritten notes. Given the nature of the times, Hecht often confessed a certain admiration. "How harmless these crooks seem alongside today's honorables who are staunchly determined to blow up our planet so that the ideals of freedom shall not perish," he wrote in *Gaily, Gaily.* "Let us hope that the surviving insects will be smart enough to admire our recorded aspirations. *This way, ants and glow-worms, crawl up for a look at the highfalutin' print left behind by humanity.*"[46]

It may seem unfair and unfounded to suggest that Hecht likened his gangster to the ancient Maccabees or followers of Bar-Kochba and, by proxy, to the new Jew of Israel, or that he admired the latter for similar reasons. Certainly Hecht never drew a direct connection, but the parallels are obvious, as critics of his propaganda would have acknowledged. Meyer Levin, for example, had surmised in the 1940s that Hecht probably "thought he was echoing the brutal warriors and prophets of the early days of our people." Hecht was happy to point to the criminality of the so-called lawmakers, but he never tried to distinguish between the Irgun and the actual gangsters they were accused of being. Apparently, he never deemed it necessary to justify himself or his cause; also, his Romanticist worldview was less a conscious, clearly formulated philosophy than an intuitive way of thinking, a part of who he was. A creature of a certain milieu and era, Hecht hadn't consulted a textbook to discover that Romanticism was defined as "the rejection of civilized corruption, and a desire to return to natural primitivism and escape the spiritual destruction of urban life."[47]

Siegel was, in Cohen's own words, "trying to put some class in me, and trying to evolve me." Just as Hecht's Camonte had tried to train one thug as an administrative assistant and took his fellow hoods to the theater, both Siegel and Cohen scrambled to catch up with twentieth-century civilization. They were hardly alone in this in Hollywood—the land of self-transformation, despite what F. Scott Fitzgerald had claimed about second acts in American life. "The studios maintained in-house finishing schools to teach contract actors grammar, elocution, the social graces, and novel skills, like fencing," noted Tereba. "The publicity departments fabricated new names and birth dates, as well as 'proper,' even 'aristocratic,' backgrounds for the human assets. From waitress to Wellesley girl, from grease monkey to gent, the film city was a phony world replete with glittering surfaces. As the gag went, the men who owned the film factories had gone directly from Poland to polo, and early on, were caught up in self-improvement frenzies. With private tutors, they smoothed out their accents, and learned to handle cutlery and speak a smattering of French."[48]

Cohen hired Denny Morrison, the husband of *Los Angeles Mirror* columnist Florabel Muir, as a tutor to expand his vocabulary by teaching him a handful of "hundred-dollar words." He collected a library of more than a thousand volumes, all selected by his interior decorator. When he agreed to lend Muir a copy of *War and Peace* only for a short while, she asked if he was actually planning to read it. "Not in a thousand years," he said. "I got a war and peace of my own to worry about. Why should I worry about Tolstoy's? I want it back 'cause it leaves a hole on the shelf when it's gone. It matches the color of them other books."[49]

Cohen was taking after Siegel, who upon arriving in Los Angeles had enrolled his daughters in an elite girls' school and signed them up for riding lessons at the upscale Dubrock Riding Academy. Siegel smoked cigars, took the occasional snifter of brandy, and became a member of the exclusive Hillcrest Country Club. With the help of Countess Dorothy di Frasso and actor George Raft, who had starred opposite Paul Muni in *Scarface* and many other gangster pictures, Siegel cultivated contacts among Hollywood's aristocrats and celebrities. But he had long found

Los Angeles, with its patchwork of jurisdictions, a frustrating place to operate, and after a degrading petty arrest for bookmaking in May 1944, he decided he was fed up.[50]

Following the mob's playbook of using its profits from the wartime black market to expand into legitimate enterprises, Siegel looked to the wide-open territory of Las Vegas, where he soon became embroiled in entanglements that snowballed out of control. By 1946 he had led Lansky and other partners into investing in the Flamingo Casino Resort, the brain-child of Billy Wilkerson, founder of the *Hollywood Reporter*. Wilkerson had sought to duplicate the glamour and sophistication of his three nightclubs, which had given rise to the Sunset Strip, but his vision had outstripped his resources. Now a majority partner, Siegel took charge of the construction and set a Christmas 1946 deadline, but his own grandiose vision of a luxury resort knew no limits. Siegel demanded original designs, rare woods, and the finest marble—the plumbing alone cost $1 million—and fabulously expensive fixes to problems with the original layout and construction. To make matters worse, after he called director of the Federal Bureau of Investigation, J. Edgar Hoover, a cocksucker, the federal government shut down construction for weeks while it launched investigations into fraud, narcotics distribution, draft dodging, and tax evasion.[51]

Siegel's dream became a nightmare as costs soared to $3 million. Rushed to stick with the December deadline, his grand opening was an epic fiasco. None of the hotel rooms were finished; storms in Los Angeles grounded planes; the fountain didn't work; the lights went dark; and crooked croupiers and local gamblers took the casino's bank for tens of thousands. While Lansky and Costello provided the money to finish the hotel, a panicked Siegel flew into his infamous rages. Rumors circulated that Virginia Hill, his equally volatile and violent new girlfriend, was siphoning money into a Swiss bank account.[52]

When Siegel demanded $2 million from the Chicago Outfit to fold Trans-America now that Ragen's death had made it unnecessary, that was the final straw. The consensus among historians is that Luciano ordered Siegel's death, with Lansky's at least tacit approval. Most believe that Cohen, who had the most to gain, was also on board. "To be honest with you, his getting knocked in was not a bad break for me," Cohen later confessed. On the early morning of June 21, 1947, a gunman rested a .30-caliber army carbine into a notch of the garden latticework outside Virginia Hill's Beverly Hills mansion. Siegel was sitting on the living room couch when he was shot.[53]

While Siegel had been spiraling to his death, Cohen had taken care of the remaining few who openly challenged his reign as successor. After Hooky Rothman unceremoniously booted Joe Shaman out of the La Brea Club casino, Shaman's six-foot, 250-pound brother Max came to settle the score. Having enjoyed a reputation as a tough guy in the old Boyle Heights neighborhood, Max burst into Cohen's bookmaking headquarters, a dilapidated "paint store" on Beverly Boulevard. Cohen "banged him out," as he later recalled. Though police suspected that the gun found on Shaman had been planted there to support Cohen's claim of self-defense, they lacked the evidence to prosecute.[54]

Next to go, in 1946, were Bennie "the Meatball" Gamson and George Levinson, two Chicago hoods who had teamed up with local gambler Paulie Gibbons to knock Cohen off his perch. Following the fatal shooting of Gibbons at his Beverly Hills apartment, a drunken bum showed up at the funeral with a box and card that read "To my pal." The mortician gingerly lifted the lid, revealing a pile of horse manure. Five months later, Levinson and the round-faced Meatball were riddled with bullets at their hotel-room hideout. Cohen meanwhile delivered a message to longtime nemesis Jimmy Utley, who had recently "put on a heat campaign" using his police connections. Dressed casually in Hawaiian shirts, Cohen and an accomplice had entered Lucey's Restaurant, a fashionable lunch spot that Utley owned, and pistol-whipped him in front of dozens of studio executives, directors, and stars. They then tipped their hats to the crowd and waltzed out, leaving a trail of blood behind them.[55]

By the time Cohen and Hecht became friends in the summer of 1947, Siegel was in his grave and Los Angeles had a new king of the underworld. But Cohen found that his only reward was that he had become the biggest target of other mobsters and the police. Hecht recalled all-night rides along the Pacific Coast with the moody crime lord and his bodyguard, Neddie Herbert. "These were hard times for Mickey, and there was practically no diversion open to him," Hecht wrote. ". . . They tossed bombs into his Westwood home, killed several of his cronies, including his invaluable barrister, and eventually blew 'Neddie' Herbert's headfull of jokes off and sent most of Mickey's entourage into their caskets."[56]

"They" turned out to be Jack Dragna, who was secretly using "Happy" Harold Meltzer and Jimmy "the Weasel" Fratianno to infiltrate Cohen's gang. Two and a half months after the fund-raising dinner at Slapsy Maxie's, the Weasel set up a hit at Michael's Haberdashery, signaling

Dragna's gunmen as he left the store. But Fratianno had forgotten Cohen's obsession with germs and shook his hand when leaving; therefore, the lucky mob boss was in the bathroom when shotgun blasts rang out, claiming Rothman's life. "It sounded like a war broke out," Cohen told the press, which inspired them to dub these incidents "the Sunset Strip Wars."[57]

Herbert fell in the sixth assassination attempt, when Cohen and a phalanx of police and mobsters who were protecting him came under fire as they exited Sherry's nightclub at four in the morning on July 20, 1949. Bullets also struck a young woman and Special Agent Harry Cooper, who, in an extraordinary move by California's attorney general, had been assigned as police protection. Muir caught a ricochet bullet in the fanny. Wounded in the shoulder and barking commands, Cohen dragged the massive Special Agent Cooper into the back of a sedan that sped from the scene. After Herbert's funeral, Rabbi Baruch Rabinowitz told the newspapers, "I considered him a good boy" and recalled that he had been eager to help the underground in Palestine.[58]

Dragna's war came to a spectacular conclusion on February 9, 1950, when twenty-eight sticks of dynamite detonated under Cohen's home, blowing out windows throughout the neighborhood and sending shockwaves felt at a police station three miles away. Miraculously, Cohen, LaVonne, and even Tuffy escaped unscathed, because the bomb had been tossed into a crawlspace directly beneath Cohen's gargantuan cement-encased vault. The safe deflected the force of the explosion, which tore off the front of the house and blasted a crater twenty feet wide and six feet deep. Police and the press arrived to find Cohen staring in disbelief at his destroyed wardrobe.[59]

Angered by all the attention, the East Coast bosses pressured Dragna to cease and desist, but Cohen's luck had nevertheless run out. On June 20, 1951, he was convicted of three counts of income tax evasion and one count of making a false statement to the Internal Revenue Service. While he sat in county jail awaiting his sentence, reporters asked what he thought about comparisons people were now making to Al Capone. "That's the silliest thing in the world," he scoffed. "Me and Capone? Bfff!" Three weeks after his conviction, Judge Ben Harrison sentenced him to five years' imprisonment and charged him nearly $300,000 in fines, court costs, and unpaid debts to the government.[60]

"I am full of hair-raising information told me by an ex-underworld kingpin named Mickey Cohen," Hecht would begin his tale years later. "How he shot, slugged, gouged and swindled his way from rags to riches. How he preyed on society as a stick-up man and crooked gambler, how he corrupted its guardians and strutted for a time in the nation's headlines. In addition to facts, I have a knowledge of this disorderly man that may be a deep one. I know him as well as I know Macbeth or the blonde Borgia."[61]

Cohen's story would present Hecht with one last gangster epic for his final years. Hecht also plumbed his memories for tales of the underworld, but here was a fresh story packed with all of the myths and themes in which he was so well versed. In this story he could combine ideas that had percolated over a lifetime. The question remained, what would he make of it all? And there was one other unique element: Cohen was a man Hecht counted as a friend.

CHAPTER 18

The Old New Journalist

Memory is the worst of playwrights. Its ghosts have no time sense. They inter-mingle, overlap, pop up in the wrong places at the wrong time. And they even tell lies. But I welcome their mendacity and disorder without criticism. It is not easy to remember oneself.

—BEN HECHT, *GAILY, GAILY*[1]

Hecht could empathize with his many old friends and colleagues in Hollywood who found themselves out of work because of blacklisting, although he did not suffer so cruel a fate. "The cold war blew like an icy wind across the country to the Pacific Coast," remarked screenwriter John Howard Lawson, one of the so-called Hollywood Ten, fired for refusing to testify before the House Un-American Activities Committee. Hecht was no communist, but after the British boycotted his films, he returned west for "a chill Christmas week—there were no jobs or parties for me. The movie moguls, most of them Jews for whose pockets I had netted over a hundred million dollars in profits with my scenarios, were even nervous of answering my hellos, let alone hiring me." Nevertheless, he was much better off than those listed as subversives in the infamous *Red Channels* pamphlet. At one point he used the name of his chauffeur, Lester Barstow, as a pseudonym after the studios agreed to hire him for half his usual fee, which suggests that he was struggling to maintain his accustomed lifestyle with Rose and their daughter, Jenny—a large house-hold staff, homes in Nyack and Oceanside, and an apartment in Manhattan.[2]

Whether or not the British boycott encouraged Hecht to return to prose, this final phase was like the third act to one of his better scripts: in hindsight it would seem inevitable. He spent five years writing his massive autobiography, *A Child of the Century*, completing the 950-page manuscript in July 1953. In the meantime, he continued to churn out screen work at his usual pace and expanded into the new medium of television. In the fall of 1958, he hosted a weeknight television talk show on Manhattan's WABC-TV, inheriting Mike Wallace's production staff after Wallace interviewed Cohen, and the LAPD sued the network for libel. Although *The Mike Wallace Interview* departed from prime time, Hecht kept the pot boiling on local television. In addition to his caustic and colorful "Bedtime Stories" each night, he jousted over the merits of Hollywood with native son Budd Schulberg; swapped murder and gangster stories with crime photographer Weegee; sifted through the political dirt with columnist Drew Pearson; compared notes on writing, rebellion, and bohemianism with Jack Kerouac; and, in what proved to be the final straw for the station management, questioned Salvador Dalí about a newly invented form of sex.[3]

Yet in the conclusion to *A Child of the Century*, Hecht wrote that he inhabited a world full of ghosts. His parents were long dead, as were the indomitable Tante Chasha and his old newspaper buddies, Sherman Duffy and Wallace Smith. Herman Mankiewicz had just passed away, and Maxwell Bodenheim would soon be murdered in the Bowery. Even some who were still alive, like his first daughter, Teddy, now residing in Brazil, and the alcoholic Charles MacArthur, seemed more like wispy spirits than fellow living souls. Keenly aware of his own mortality, Hecht focused more than ever on his literary legacy.[4]

One of his last great films was *Where the Sidewalk Ends* (1950), director Otto Preminger's expressionistic noir thriller about a cop who becomes a killer. Haunted by his late father's criminality, Mark Dixon is a hard-bitten, brutal detective so obsessively driven to pin a murder on his dad's former crony, Tommy Scalise, that he goes too far interrogating a suspect. In trying to cover up the man's death by framing Scalise, Dixon spirals deeper into the abyss. Hecht was once again in his element, mixing up cops and criminals in a setting critic Boris Trbic described as "a doleful metropolis of crime and violence; a city with no limits, no values and absolutely no rules, inhabited by a series of disillusioned and insecure loners who are casualties of urban decline and decay."[5]

He script-doctored other films that became classics, such as Preminger's *Angel Face* (1953) and *The Man with the Golden Arm* (1955) and Alfred Hitchcock's *Strangers on a Train* (1951). He also authored a few gems, such as *Miracle in the Rain* (1956), an adaptation of his 1943 novella that has endured as a popular wartime romance. The posthumously produced *Seven Faces of Dr. Lao* (1964) is an astonishing, charmingly childlike comedy about an ancient Chinese sorcerer who brings a magical circus to a dusty town out West. Dr. Lao's troupe of chimerical creatures—an abominable snowman, Merlin the magician, Medusa, and, climactically, a Godzilla-like sea serpent—appear differently to each visitor to the circus tent and help set things right in a struggle between a crusading reporter and a corrupt local boss. While *Miracle* and *Seven Faces* could not appear more dissimilar on the surface, they both center around Hecht's signature character, a puckish young newspaperman, and in their warmhearted sunniness offer a retort to his cynicism that suggests a hidden continuity to his work. One hears, in Hecht's distinctive dialogue, a man carrying on a debate with himself.

The rest of his Hollywood output, such as *Trapeze* (1956), another circus film, and Dino de Laurentiis's *Ulysses* (1954), was generally mediocre; a few films were solid pieces of entertainment never meant to stand the test of time. "He didn't take the whole thing seriously," said Hugh Gray, one of his cowriters from those years. ". . . He was obviously good in the old tough style, the old Chicago newspaperman. He had a marvelous storytelling ability and was incredibly bright. I felt what he made of himself was a hack, a hack of genius."[6] Some movies were simply rehashes or adaptations of old work, like *Living It Up* (1954), a Dean Martin–Jerry Lewis vehicle that combined *Nothing Sacred* and *Hazel Flagg*, the Broadway musical based on the same material. *The Fiend Who Walked the West* (1958) was a western-horror remake of *Kiss of Death* that starred Robert Evans as "the kooky killer," trying to match Richard Widmark's famous performance as the psychotic Tommy Udo. Some films fell flat, like *Monkey Business* (1952), an attempted return to the screwball comedy, and *Actors and Sin* (1952), Hecht's third and final effort at directing after Astoria, which combined two short films adapted from satires of the film industry, *Actor's Blood* and *Concerning a Woman of Sin*. Others movies held promise, but either Hecht failed to come through with a great script, as in his collaboration with Howard Hawks and Charles Lederer on *The Thing from Another World* (1951), or the studio botched it, like when a producer tossed out Hecht's story for *Love Happy* (1949), a vehicle for his good friend Harpo that was the final Marx Brothers movie and one of the first speaking roles for Marilyn Monroe.[7]

The most tragic casualty of Hollywood's sausage making was Hecht's James Bond movie, *Casino Royale*, a project that had reawakened the old passion that had fueled his best film work of earlier years; the nearly complete final, polished version that he worked on just two days before his death on April 18, 1964, may have been one of the finest scripts he ever produced. The successive drafts of Hecht's screenplay, now collecting dust in his archive, "are a master-class in thriller writing, from the man who arguably perfected the form with *Notorious*," opined British spy novelist Jeremy Duns. "Hecht made vice central to the plot, with [the villain] Le Chiffre actively controlling a network of brothels and beautiful women who he is using to blackmail powerful people around the world. Just as the theme of Fleming's *Goldfinger* is avarice and power, the theme of Hecht's *Casino Royale* is sex and sin. It's an idea that seems obvious in hindsight, and Hecht used it both to raise the stakes of Fleming's plot and to deepen the story's emotional resonance."[8]

By 1964 the first two Bond films, *Dr. No* and *From Russia with Love*, had already been produced, though certain trademarks ("Vodka Martini, shaken not stirred," and "Bond. James Bond.") were not yet in the mix. Hecht sketched characters well suited to the emerging franchise, such as a ravishing Eurasian drug-addicted madam named Lili Wing and her lesbian girlfriend, Georgie, who has a black pussycat perched on her shoulder. The sinister wife of the colonel, Madam Chiffre, has a face torn apart by bullet wounds and rasps "metallically through a tube inserted in her ripped out larynx." She may be a classic Bond villain, but the spectacle of corruption envisioned in the pretitle sequence is classic Hecht: Central Intelligence Agency buddy Felix Lieter snatching senior United Nations diplomats from honey traps to which they have been lured by gorgeous call girls, moments before newspaper reporters arrive for the scoop. "Many of the scenes are darkly comic, and some of the sexual antics are politically incorrect even for the Sixties," Duns observed, "with references to politicians being attracted to children and a car chase through Hamburg's red light district ending with Bond drenched in mud disguised as a lesbian wrestler."[9]

Of the five drafts stored among Hecht's papers, the earliest, from 1957, hews closely to the novel with one significant exception: the hero is not Bond but Lucky Fortunato, "a rich, wisecracking American gangster who is an expert poker player." Perhaps because the draft is otherwise so faithful to the book, or because an article in *Time* mentions that Hecht "had three bashes" at it, Duns surmised that Hecht had not authored the Fortunato version, that the draft was sent to him as a starting point by producer Charles Feldman.[10] But Duns was not considering the script within the broader context of Hecht's published and unpublished material; if he had, he would have factored in Hecht's preoccupation with the gangster, arguably as much a signature of his work as his Huck Finn–like reporter.

Hecht enjoyed all criminals, and while the gangster was a favorite, he devoted attention to various types—wild outlaws like Teddy Webb and Tommy O'Connor, pretty murderesses like Roxie Hart (based on the real-life Beulah Annan), and cunning psychopaths like Henry Spencer. Starting with *A Guide for the Bedevilled*, Hecht spun tales from his crime-reporting days in *A Child of the Century*, *Charlie*, and *Gaily, Gaily*. He regularly published shorter pieces of memoir and fiction with titles like "Rehearsal for Murder" and "A Jackpot of Corpses" in *Ellery Queen's Mystery Magazine* and *Playboy*. Right up until his final days, he reworked drafts of a Runyonesque musical about the bootlegging wars between the Irish and Italians, with his old friend Deannie O'Banion as the hero and Al Capone as the villain; he gave it several possible titles: *Chicago, Chicago Days, Chicago Nights, Underworld*, and *Angel in the Underworld*.[11]

In January 1964 Hecht wrote to Feldman to update him on "our blissful *Casino Royale*," adding that he had "never had more fun writing a movie." His exuberance contrasts strikingly with the discontent he had expressed for years about writing for Hollywood, a measure of how little enthusiasm he'd had for work that otherwise only fed his insecurities. At some point in the 1950s, Hecht had complained about writing scripts for television, "the most completely infantile type of entertainment invented since the creation of the rattle." But there was nothing to be done. "I have never quite mastered the trick in books or theater of being both admired and 'bought,'" he wrote his sister-in-law. ". . . I was never meant to divert people and the fact that I have for thirty or forty years been tenaciously trying to do so is proof of my soft character and too vague ambition. I was never the gardener of my estate but always the handyman pushing wheelbarrows hither and yon."[12]

After Hecht died, the *Casino Royale* project fell apart in negotiations with Albert Broccoli and Harry Saltzman, the producers who owned the rest of the Ian Fleming properties, when Feldman demanded a bigger cut than they were willing to accept. The James Bond spoof that Feldman eventually brought to the screen in 1967 was an abysmal, incoherent mess. As for what could have been, Duns's verdict is that "all the pages in Hecht's papers are gripping, but the material from April 1964 is phenomenal. . . . It has all the excitement and glamour you would expect from a Bond film but is more suspenseful, and the violence is brutal rather than cartoonish. . . . *Casino Royale* might even have been regarded as not just a classic Bond film, but as a classic thriller." Hecht, however, had long understood that he could not control what became of such work—that was the nature of the Hollywood beast. And with movies, who really remembers the writer anyway?[13]

Clearly *A Child of the Century* (1954) was a determined effort to leave something substantial behind. Taking his title from Alfred de Musset's *La Confession d'un enfant du siècle*, Hecht drew on his experiences to write "inside history," offering an extraordinary window into his era. Biographer Doug Fetherling noted, "Hecht was truly, as he said, a child of the century: a member of that generation born close to 1900 and the first to come of age with the big-time gangster, the automobile, the world war, the skyscraper and the interior monologue. . . . In its depiction of one person's progress across the landscape of his time, it falls within the tradition of the best American autobiography that stretches from Benjamin Franklin through Henry Adams to Emma Goldman."[14] Like his historical pageants, it featured a giant cast of characters rendered in short, deft anecdotes, from Louis Brandeis to Groucho Marx, both Roosevelts, and dozens of the great writers, artists, and celebrities of his day. A final 115-page section that describes his partnership with the Bergson Group and the Irgun also made the book a powerful follow-through to his propaganda work. Historians ever since have found it difficult to write against the grain of Hecht's compelling narrative, to the great consternation of his political foes.

As for the book's critical reception, Hecht could hardly count on support from the great arbiters of literary taste of the day, the New York Intellectuals, particularly since he had launched a preemptive strike against them. In recalling New York City's wild fin de siècle party during the 1920s, he contrasted the old smart set with the current clique. Today's elite New Yorker "is as tame as a white mouse, and as given to running in circles. He is not a New Yorker unless you wish to insult him. He is a Citizen of the World with a grown-up soul. . . . With his second helping of ghoulash, my New Yorker takes up the problem of India. His small talk seldom embraces less than a continent."[15]

When the writers he was referring to, such as Irving Howe and Leslie Fiedler, thereafter acknowledged Hecht at all, it was with scorn, mostly as an example of the self-hating Jew depicted in his *A Jew in Love*. Somewhat typical of their antagonism was Louis Berg's slashing review of Hecht's memoir for the October 1954 issue of *Commentary*, "Brat of the Century," which described the author as "a word-slinger rather than stylist, master of invective rather than wit, poetaster rather than poet, crackpot philosopher and calculating crackpot, romantic cynic and cruel sentimentalist, third-rate Mencken and fifth-rate Rochefoucauld."[16]

Nevertheless, *Partisan Review* darling Saul Bellow proclaimed the book's importance in the *New York Times*. "Among the pussycats who write of social issues today," Bellow wrote, "he roars like an old-fashioned lion." Although Bellow hadn't picked up a copy of Hecht's early novels or the *Broken Necks* collection in twenty years, he still remembered the stories, the characters, and even some of the odd phrases, "the scribble of rooftops across the sky," "the greedy little half-dead." As a fellow Chicagoan and recipient that year of the National Book Award for *The Adventures of Auggie March*, Bellow graciously acknowledged the debt he owed Hecht and the other writers of the Renaissance: "What was marvelous was that people should have conceived of dignifying what we saw about us by writing of it, and that the gloom of Halstead Street, the dismal sights of the Back of the Yards and the speech of immigrants should be the materials of art." Four years later, Jack Kerouac would similarly tip his hat to Hecht as a guest on *The Ben Hecht Show*. Hecht gave Kerouac a friendly reception on the program, whereas most others who interviewed him about *On the Road* were hostile.[17]

A Child of the Century opened the floodgates in Hecht, unleashing a current that would flow into his later books, influencing in particular his biography of Mickey Cohen. Arguably, two major opposing trends were emerging in postwar literature. One, a backlash to the 1930s social realism of writers like John Dos Passos and James T. Farrell, eschewed a broader social and political landscape to focus on inner lives. In the brooding and paranoid atmosphere of the McCarthy era, the fiction of J. D. Salinger and Jewish writers such as Bellow and Bernard Malamud "set out on a course of self-examination," noted Mark Shechner, ". . . [T]hrown back on its own resources, it became more introspective and more literary." Starting in the 1940s, this became identifiable as the literature of *alienation*.[18]

The second trend was literary journalism, a resurgence of an old tradition kept alive after the war by Norman Mailer, John Hersey, and *New Yorker* writers A. J. Liebling, Lillian Ross, and Joseph Mitchell in the 1950s. After the phenomenal success of Truman Capote's "nonfiction novel" *In Cold Blood* in 1965, the New Journalism of the baby boom generation exploded with a wave of new talent—Tom Wolfe, Hunter S. Thompson, Joan Didion, Jimmy Breslin, Gay Talese, Michael Herr, and others.[19]

A year before Hecht's death, the University of Chicago Press acknowledged his place in literature with a backhanded compliment that made the occasion more bitter than sweet. The press had issued a new edition of *Erik Dorn* as part of its Chicago Renaissance series, without giving Hecht the opportunity to preview Nelson Algren's rather unusual introduction, which contained disparaging remarks about the author and the novel. Furious, Hecht refused the invitation to the publication party. "I have no hankering to pose in your local festivities as a literary patsy," he wired.[20]

Algren's introduction was itself a backhanded compliment. He credited *Erik Dorn* as an alienation novel decades ahead of its time, while at the same time suggesting that this was a dubious achievement. Since the book portrayed an empty, nihilistic "organization man," the whole enterprise was essentially a farce. "For no American yet has written a novel this good yet this bad," Algren asserted. "This is the one serious work of literature we have that by the same token stands a literary hoax." Ultimately, Algren didn't commend the book or the author: "For the value that is derived from the novel today is not within the novel itself, but from the curiously prophetic shadow that a book, written a half century ago, now casts across our own strange times." When Hecht retorted that this criticism displayed "a Beverly Hillbilly kind of intellectuality," Algren's comments were more unequivocally damning. "He hasn't done anything since *Erik Dorn*," Algren said. "He's made one or two good movies and some awful bad ones. . . . He won't take responsibility for his own talent."[21]

Since this assessment echoed the criticisms leveled against Hecht for many years, it became the conventional wisdom at the end of his life. Even his book editor at Doubleday, Margaret Cousins, who said she adored him, wrote ten years later, "Actually, I don't think he ever lived up to the brilliant promise forecast by his first book—the novel *Erik Dorn*—when he was hailed by critics as a Daniel-Come-to-Judgment, because he was more interested in living than in writing. Writing was his sometime mistress, but he was married to life." Hecht certainly had a reputation as a bon vivant, but this seems a curious conclusion to draw about so remarkably prolific an author.[22]

If Hecht can be credited as a pioneer of the alienation novel, then with hindsight it is likewise appropriate to acknowledge him as a forefather of New Journalism, a contribution that he made, *simultaneously*, in the early 1920s. Literary journalism had existed long before Hecht's time; it was a proud Chicago tradition during the late nineteenth-century heyday of George Ade, Finley Peter Dunne, Eugene Field, and the Whitechapel Club. But the four hundred sketches of Hecht's One Thousand and One Afternoons column revived this tradition and introduced it into the modern newspaper, reflecting the new crosscurrents shaping journalism: a rising skepticism about journalistic objectivity even as the American Society of Newspaper Editors codified objectivity as a professional standard. Fusing the factual data gathered by legmen with his own subjective impressions, psychological insights, and storytelling, Hecht forged a hybrid that Tom Wolfe would one day proclaim as a new literary form in his seminal 1973 anthology of baby boom journalists.[23]

The worst that can be said of *Erik Dorn* and Hecht's collected columns is that the prose was fitful and the stories lacked emotional depth; neither book added up to anything substantial enough to endure as a classic. This, however, had more to do with the author's relative youth and immaturity than with his discipline, craftsmanship, or storytelling talent. A lifetime of experience separated this author from the author of the cycle of books that started with *A Child of the Century*, a mellower and wiser man. As the stories of *Gaily, Gaily* demonstrate, the older Hecht possessed a command of narrative and a steady, natural rhythm that made his work more accessible. Fetherling noted that one striking aspect of *A Child of the Century* "is the verve with which Hecht invokes the environments of his past, as though he had never left them, while at the same time analysing and appraising them. The two actions are not distinct but take place simultaneously, giving the whole book an unusual quality of detached exuberance."[24]

Hecht had returned to prose, but with the minor exception of *The Sensualists* (1959), he no longer tried to write novels. Instead, his books proceeded from where he had started: his work as a journalist and columnist. Writing in the 1970s, Fetherling argued that "Hecht the Memoirist was the kind of writer their detractors accuse the present New Journalists of being. He shifted focus away from a careful analysis of the facts toward an impressionistic truth supported by a mesh of tiny detail. Much of the detail was certainly as he remembered it, but some was included because it sounded plausible. None of it was researched."[25]

The Cohen project was the closest Hecht would come to returning to journalism, the one book—with the exception of his ghostwritten 1954 "autobiography" of Marilyn Monroe—that wasn't populated by ghosts. A large excerpt finally appeared in the March 1970 premiere issue of *Scanlan's*, a groundbreaking monthly that showcased aggressive investigative reporting and slashing cultural criticism, launched by the maverick former *Ramparts* editor Warren Hinckle and Sidney Zion, a *New York Times* alum.[26] A latter-day Hecht champion, Zion provided an introduction to Hecht's piece that hailed his work for the Irgun and explained Cohen's role in the fight for a Jewish state. "Writing this tale, I am aware that it may sound a little crazy to a lot of people," Zion added. "What was a gangster doing helping Israel? . . . And the Irgun. Weren't they a bunch of right-wing Jewish terrorists?"

> The untold truth is that scores of Jewish outlaws were busy running guns around Mr. Truman's blockade while their liveried cousins shook their heads in shame or sat in those Frank Lloyd Wright temples rooting for the English.
>
> Those who had supped with Jewish mobsters will hardly be surprised by this. . . .Thus, the old Meyer Lansky mob on the Lower East Side of Manhattan was actively hustling guns for Palestine. And in Jersey City Harold (Kayo) Konigsberg, then breaking into the head breaking business, performed extraordinary tasks for the Irgun.[27]

Scanlan's made the connection between the old journalist and the New Journalists more than just theoretical. The magazine was "going to start Hecht's literary renaissance," Zion told the *New York Times* when asked about the Cohen excerpt. "Some kids read it and thought it was beautiful," he added. "There's closing the generation gap for you." "The Unfinished Life of Mickey Cohen" ran alongside a feature by a rising new talent named Hunter S. Thompson, who despite his success with *Hell's Angels* was still too much of a handful for the mainstream glossies. Thompson's profile of Olympic ski champion Jean-Claude Killy had originally been commissioned by *Playboy*, which recoiled in horror when he turned in an eleven-thousand-word exposé savaging the celebrity athlete as a mindless shill for Chevrolet. *Scanlan's Monthly* then published the piece alongside Hecht's, providing Thompson the opening he had been waiting for. As a follow-up, for their June issue, they teamed Thompson with a macabre British cartoonist named Ralph Steadman and sent the pair off to do their worst. The resulting story that surfaced out of an alcohol-poisoned delirium, "The Kentucky Derby Is Decadent and Depraved," immediately gained Thompson notoriety for a first-person style "so outrageous it needed its own name": gonzo journalism.[28]

News that Hecht was writing a book on Cohen came to light as Cohen was hitting the peak of his national celebrity, over a year after his October 1955 release from McNeil Island Federal Penitentiary. As the gangster had told the Kefauver Committee, he drew headlines every time he spat on the sidewalk, and this new development was treated with maximum fanfare. "Mickey Cohen's bizarre quest for publicity is easily understood when you hear that Ben Hecht is writing his biography—with a view toward the big movie money," Walter Winchell announced on May 31, 1957. Weeks earlier, the *Los Angeles Times* had reported that since the previous summer, United Artists had been considering a movie titled *The Mickey Cohen Story* or *The Poison Has Left Me*, to be written by Hecht, but no decision had yet been reached. Cohen's delivery of a 150-page manuscript at Oceanside two months after Winchell's announcement also garnered national attention. "He must have done it himself," Hecht told the press. "No one but Mickey uses words that way. It's a gold mine of facts—I haven't seen so many facts since I was a newspaper reporter."[29]

But Hecht had reservations from the start, which he mulled over months later as he waited for Cohen to emerge from a shower—his third of the day—at the Del Capri, an exclusive residential motel in Westwood. One the one hand, "it could be a fine shoot-'em-up story, with important sociological overtones," Hecht mused. ". . . Mickey leads me into an understanding of my time, and not a jolly one." But although Hecht was often nostalgic about his newspaper days, he had no desire to go "hopping around for data" like a cub reporter. Another source of concern was the ex-convict's new claim to be a changed man. He had identified himself as a florist, no less, the proprietor of Michael's Tropical Plants, operating out of a greenhouse on South Vermont Avenue, which actually sold plastic fakes. Having closed that, he would soon be opening the wholesome Carousel ice cream parlor. "I lost the crazy heat in my head," Cohen told Hecht, "even though I seen enough dirty crooked double-crosses to keep me mad for a hundred years." For the sake of the book, Hecht certainly hoped the new Cohen wasn't real: "Who wants to hear about a toothless tiger?" Then again, perhaps Cohen hadn't reformed permanently, which might make for a fabulous twist ending.[30]

"How to handle my biographic dynamite?" Hecht wondered. His years as a newspaperman had taught him the have-your-cake-and-eat-it-too approach to this kind of story. "You hold your subject up to scorn while titillating the reader with the details of his sadism, lechery and horrid misdeeds. . . . You identified your gangster as a vicious, rat-blooded character unworthy of human consideration, and then went on to consider every fascinating quirk of his being." It would be the safest approach, but Hecht couldn't summon any moral indignation about underworld criminals. "Unlike historical or political figures, they break laws on only a small scale," he reasoned. "They do not betray trusts, bankrupt widows and orphans, or invent hydrogen bombs—and drop them."[31]

At the same time, Hecht had no desire to be like the mob shysters he had watched tug a jury's heartstrings with sob stories about "extenuating circumstances"—a beloved wife and a hungry child to feed, a rough upbringing on the wrong side of the tracks. "I have an unquestionable record as an honest man," Hecht wrote. ". . . Having written many books as an honest man, I do not suddenly want to seem to be the mouthpiece of a criminal. And, perhaps, to have always been that."[32]

Cohen at last emerged from the bathroom at the Del Capri, naked except for green silk socks and maroon garters, covered from head to toe in talcum powder. Donning a fedora, he looked like one of those street performers who pose as a frozen statue or a snowman. Hecht watched in confusion as the pudgy mobster raced about, caroming from one wall of the tiny bedroom to the next. All Hecht could figure was that Cohen was trying to shake off the powder. Mad as this may seem, "it is no lunacy," Hecht wrote. "It is Mickey caught up in a mood so deep, tossed around on memories so violent, high diving into daydreams so vivid, that he has not the slightest awareness of darting around for an hour in a darkening room—naked and with a hat on."[33] Cohen was an unknown quantity—a Jack-in-the-Box that the old crime reporter did not completely understand.

Nor was Hecht even sure of his own point of view. "A thing baffles me which may well be baffling the reader," he confessed. "It is—what do I think of Mickey? And what do I feel about him and his infatuation with violence and lawlessness?" Other than for "outlandish fellows like the Marquis de Sade," in such matters a writer typically adopted the traditional view of society. But if Hecht was not altogether sympathetic with the law-abiding public, then what alternative did he offer?[34]

Six years later, Algren would conclude his contentious introduction to Hecht's first novel by observing: "It wasn't splendor that was lacking in Hecht, it wasn't gas he ran out of, and it surely wasn't brass. It was belief. For he came, too young, to a time when, like Dorn, he had to ask himself, 'What the hell am I talking about?' And heard no answer at all."[35]

CHAPTER 19

Time Out for Psychology

A horsefly on the rump of humanity.

—Television reporter George Puntam's
description of Mickey Cohen[1]

*The underworld is not a geographic area. Its trail runs thru slums, fine hotels,
swank residences and office buildings—cafés, theaters and the sanctums of
government.*

*... The corruption of government—the bribing of its large and little facto-
tums—is the perquisite of what Mickey calls "the higher echelon" of society. ...
Railroad, oil and manufacturing empires have been built in the Republic with
the aid of canny bribery.*

—Ben Hecht, notes for the Mickey Cohen biography[2]

Hecht may have resolved to write his book "without skittering about like
a cub reporter," but he trailed Mickey Cohen on several occasions in 1957
and 1958, capturing his companion's expressions and eccentricities with
the keen eye he had always possessed. After the gangster had performed
his bizarre talcum-powder dance, Hecht witnessed him finish preening
with more fussiness than a debutante primping for her coming-out party.
Cohen's vast wardrobe from Brentwood was long gone, but Hecht duly
noted the "thirty pressed and spotless suits crowded in the closet," along
with "twenty-five Chinese, Japanese and Persian robes of silk" and "thirty-
five pairs of glistening shoes" lined up neatly on the floor.[3]

Finally, the pair climbed into Cohen's newest customized Cadillac and headed out to the modest Hollywood bungalow of Fred Sica, one of the only bodyguards to have survived the 1940s. Sica had prepared a gourmet meal and greeted them at the door in a dainty apron. Eight fellow guests were already at the table. As storytelling was a favorite pastime in the underworld, each was eager to play Scheherazade, and they spun tales about many of Hecht's favorite characters from old Chicago, such as Teddy Webb, Blackie Weed, and Tommy O'Connor. He also heard about more recent legends, such as the Soldier, an ingenious con man who once collapsed in Reno from heart palpitations and then proceeded to scam his doctor. After dinner the hoods retired to the parlor, where their favorite movie, *Robin Hood*, hushed them into reverent silence. Hecht assured them that Errol Flynn was just as fine a drinker and fighter in real life.[4]

Aboard a chartered boat on a March 1958 fishing trip in La Paz, Mexico, Chicago mob attorney George Bieber provided Hecht and Cohen with a lesson on the ancient history of organized crime. In the time of the pharaohs, he said, as many as a hundred thousand slaves would die from whippings or hernias while building the pyramids—giant tombs for the rulers and their vast riches. After a pyramid was completed, hundreds of architects and artists who knew the secret location of the burial vaults would be poisoned or stabbed. Yet when archaeologists later uncovered the ruins, they discovered the storerooms had all been picked clean by heisters, who had schemed with the royal members of the pharaoh's court. This, Bieber explained, was the beginning of organized crime.

"If you was to ask me," Cohen remarked, "those monarchs stabbing and poisoning all those characters and putting all that wealth out of circulation were worse than the heisters."

"It's a point," Hecht agreed.[5]

Once Cohen's line hooked a marlin, all eyes were fixed on the crime lord locked in a thirty-minute tug-of-war with "the marine locomotive" off their stern. "His chin is tucked down," Hecht noted. "His left eye has become bloodshot. And he is addressing the lunging, thrashing, whooping marlin in a soft, lethal sort of voice. 'You dirty punk bastard, who d'ya think you are. I'll tear your goddam head off. Come on, you sonofabitch, or I'll jump in the water and pull your lousy fins off ya.'"[6]

Cohen brought Hecht's mind back to the days of Prohibition, and to himself as a young reporter. Hecht reflected that he had covered crime as though it was sports, without a thought for what it all meant. In the years leading up to the Volstead Act, he had witnessed a brash, noisy nation in the throes of late adolescence. His was an odd perspective—a nostalgia for the First Ward bosses and their gangsters' balls and blacklegs and ballot stuffers. "The pioneers were trying on their first frock coats and silk hats," he reminisced. "Ex-hobos and horse thieves and Ragged Dicks from city slums were in command of the million new factory chimneys. And the workers, without unions to guide them, were happily throwing bricks through windows and clubbing bosses on the street corners. I remember these Americans, despite the injustice, graft and filthy poverty, as a people childishly in love with themselves and the wonders of their democracy."[7]

All that had disappeared. Americans now were as obsessed with violence as ever, but they were the living dead, wandering shopping malls and gazing glassy-eyed at the cowboys and Indians, the cops and robbers, darting across their television screens like dim traces of memories not quite theirs any longer. "Crime . . . has become the only easy escape from the stupidity of laws, religions, economic problems, etc.," Hecht jotted in fragmentary notes. "It has become the last adventure open to the daring—taking the place of exploration and conquest. . . . Gangsterism is the only anarchic element left—it has taken the place of the arts in the U.S. Mass media—movies, radio, television—have hurried the process of regimenting the American mind and lowering it into docility. Lawlessness becomes more and more the only outlet for any social rebellion in the land."[8]

Hecht admired the heisters more than the politicians because at least the criminals were honest by comparison. In pursuing their own ends, they risked their own lives, rather than letting others do the dying for them. Yet a heister too grows old; loses his sharp, primitive instincts; and becomes "as full of nonsense as a Secretary of State." In Cohen's case, arriving in Al Capone's Chicago had changed him. Before that, he knew all about hooligans on the fringes of society. "He did not know, however, that there were ten times as many crooks in the respectable seats of government," Hecht wrote. "It was this vision that was to guide him to power and fortune."[9]

Like their fellow Americans, the mob had grown up and grown old over the decades. Back when East Coast crooks like Joe Adonis and Waxey Gordon had been "running beer," Hecht argued, Capone had figured out how to turn crime into big business. The suburb of Cicero became "an empire unto itself," where the Capone mob installed its own politicians and placed gunmen at all the polling places to ensure their election. On one occasion, upset over some trivial matter of municipal policy, Capone had slugged the mayor, Joseph Z. Klenha, knocking him down the steps of city hall while policemen stood by and watched.[10]

As these broader insights piled up, Hecht's book started to become something more than just Cohen's biography. The notes and drafts suggest an ambitious epic, an effort to expound on a whole philosophy. If Hecht was unable to do much legwork at his age, he could at least do the mental work to fit Cohen into some broader social and political context. He compiled research and wrote forty-two pithy essays on criminals and crime. Eschewing the old outlaw legends like Billy the Kid and Jesse James, he wrote profiles of a range of twentieth-century crooks and killers, from Albert Anastasia to Charles Ponzi, from John Dillinger to "The Ladies of Crime."[11]

An entry headlined "The New Criminal" described how the bosses now possessed major holdings in legitimate businesses, such as real estate and securities, while continuing to run the same old rackets in prostitution, narcotics, loan sharking, strikebreaking, gambling, and the rest. The existence of a national criminal cartel was famously exposed on November 17, 1957, when police stumbled on a summit near Apalachin, a hamlet in western New York. An alert state trooper had become suspicious when scores of expensive cars with out-of-state plates arrived at the estate of Joseph "Joe the Barber" Barbara, a local beer and soft drink vendor. Police arrested sixty of the Mafia dons in attendance, with $300,000 in their pockets.[12]

The episode drew increased scrutiny of Frank Costello, the "prime minister of the underworld," a close partner of Lucky Luciano, and one of the chieftains of the Combination, or National Crime Syndicate, as it was also called. Hecht noted that Costello owned a thirteen-story office building on Wall Street, as well as two others in the same neighborhood. Here and in other passages, he was already implying that by the late 1950s the financial industry was becoming a vast criminal empire. "Crime Pays" cited sixty-five financial interests of the delegates at Apalachin, including bakeries, law firms, textile manufacturers, food chains, consulting firms, power corporations, baseball clubs, and more. Initially, the rapid expansion into legitimacy had taken place after Prohibition and again after the war, when the mob took leases and concessions at the three major New York airports and bought into luxury hotels, such as the Beverly Wilshire in Los Angeles and New York's Waldorf-Astoria. But Hecht noted that the underworld had been buying up stocks and real estate since the days of Arnold Rothstein in the 1920s.[13]

Other essays questioned the distinction between criminals and respectable society. "We're All Crooks" listed numerous infractions that an average businessman might commit on a given day, such as fudging his taxes, bribing an elevator inspector, and accepting a kickback—in the form of a polite gift—for a client's contract. "Valentine for the Gunman" proposed a National Hall of Fame for crooks and killers, since crime was more popular in America than sports, "second only to our enthusiasm for saving the world." The televised Kefauver Committee hearings had been highly successful entertainment, he remarked, exhibiting "a catch of gila monsters and boa constrictors never before held." The senator had spent $300,000 on the investigation, "the cost of a B-movie," and "about as effective."[14]

Hecht's new book quickly began to draw nearly as much heat—at least on a personal level—as had his rather more public propaganda for the Irgun. Early on, revenue agents and police detectives appeared with a warrant to search his house and seize his manuscript as an asset belonging to the U.S. government. Hecht said he hadn't started writing yet and did not understand how his work could possibly be an asset before he'd had a chance to publish it. He'd had plenty of political opponents in the 1940s, but now his own friends were urging him to abandon the project and stay away from the gangster, which alienated him more from them than from Cohen.[15] But for the first time his own wife was objecting.

By the summer of 1958, Rose had invited her sister, the well-published psychoanalyst Dr. Minna Emch, into the discussion. An undated letter suggests that at first the three debated whether the book had been inspired by Hecht's work for the Jews. "When I came home last night Rose told me of your talk with her about me," he wrote Emch. "I was pleased and impressed by what you had to say, but had to shy away from your diagnosis of working the Jewish business out of my system. What neither you nor Rose appear to know is that my Jewish business was Rose. I contributed my logic, but Rose was the one who lived it emotionally and socially."[16]

Perhaps because Emch had no desire to argue with her brother-in-law, she ceded the point in her reply on July 3 and returned to the question of what had originally motivated the book. An artist hardly needs a reason for his choice of subject, she acknowledged, and indeed any reason he offers will likely be a self-deception covering an unconscious motivation. In this case, however, she had the impression that the idea had not origi-nated with Hecht at all, but with Cohen, and was rooted in the gangster's

need to fill "his own central psychic emptiness." Again, in a letter to both
Rose and Ben, she brought up the work the two friends did together for
the Jews:

> When Ben originally came to him and talked to him about the Irgun,
> Ben not only appeared as the master-mind of a bigger revolution than
> any of Mickey's, but I feel that a psychic love affair of a very deep kind
> began—a one-sided love affair to be sure—but generated by Ben with his
> genius for making people breathe more deeply in his presence. On that
> occasion Ben enlarged Mickey's concept of the little "Jew Boy" identity
> he had once worn, and made possible through this tag a primitive iden-
> tification with a "People" (not Mickey's bosses), and *with himself* (Ben).
> This Mickey obviously never let go of, for it is still his hoped-for ticket
> to an *acceptable* identity—*via Ben*.[17]

She argued, in effect, that in the process of using Hecht to fill a vacuum
inside himself, Cohen had encouraged Hecht to latch on just as tightly.
"To me it makes sense that this man could kill as he did," she concluded.
"For I have seen in the most swaggering of independent attitudes the utter
despair and the mad violence that the threat of separation arouses in these
swallowing ones."[18]

Two days later Hecht wrote back, thanking her for her letter, which
was "a big present." He agreed that Cohen wanted a new social existence,
recognition and status as something more than a hood. This in itself did
not interest Hecht, but what did was something about their relationship
that could prove elucidating, if he could ever put his finger on it:

> The thing that started me to writing tells me much about this relation-
> ship. It was my old literary friend—anger. The Government Revenue
> Agents and Narcotics Detectives questioning me about Cohen got me
> angry. A *Saturday Evening Post* writer named Jennings talking to me for
> hours about the Cohen articles he was going to write made me angrier.
> Jennings and the Govt. Agents (and nearly all who have spoken to
> me about Mickey) spoke out of such a goony sense of virtue, decency
> and nobility of soul (their own, all) that an old friend—iconoclastic
> me—was whistled out of his lair. I knew when I felt angry what my
> relation (in part) to my subject was. I have always questioned noisily
> the phony surfaces by which society binds itself to its own image. I

have always been a sort of pencil-outlaw. I felt in Mickey a fresh (and happily cockeyed) point of view against society. Mickey is the strayed wild dog wanting to get back into the kitchen warmth—the Lucifer spaniel. Peering into the kitchen, he becomes a remarkable and comic study in righteousness. . . . Mickey thus gives me a chance to attack the hypocrisies of society from a more primitive and gaudy point of view than psychologists (other than Dostoevsky) have usually taken. I am not sentimental about a gangster but my mind is pleased by the fact that a gangster can expose shams and stupidities with glaring light. I'll be frank. While seeming to present a vicious enemy of society (Mickey) it is my hope to present his brother—a vicious society. I am again poking around in my own plot—humanity debasing itself with pretenses and cowering pathetically behind its myths. Mickey, the criminal, is to me a small, half-clownish disturber of life alongside the cliché-maddened mindless idea-egomaniacs who are our political leaders (and there are no other leaders any more.)[19]

Hecht was in essence planning to do what he had done in much of his best work—present a protagonist who was the least unsympathetic of all the characters in the story. As for Cohen's psychology, Hecht had his own elegant theories, just as his sister-in-law had hers. He likened the gangster to a *gilgul*, a soul in transition in Kabbalistic terms, central to a conception of reincarnation within Jewish mysticism. In one passage of his most complete manuscript, Hecht described the gangster as stuck in a kind of purgatory, unable to complete the spiritual journey of his reform.[20]

Rose, however, had a simpler explanation for the man: he was no damn good. Apparently the tension between husband and wife escalated, because in August Emch wrote to her sister, "I do hope the 'problems' settle down to something that will allow you to stay in California for the present if that is what you want."[21] When Rose oversaw the archiving of her late husband's papers decades later, she inserted a typed, one-page record of her objections among his drafts: "Notes on what I think is a fallacy in Hecht's reasoning in the Mickey Cohen manuscript." She conceded that various officials in government and officers in law enforcement were on the take. But it seemed a false logic to therefore label all politics, or everyone else who is "tarred by the same brush of being in politics," as criminal. That, she said, "is a criminal's kind of reasoning, for purposes of self-justification."

But for an author to borrow this pattern when starting from the objective (vantage) of the criminal's psychology . . . makes the author seem dangerously infected by his character's point of view. I'll admit I think, as his wife, that it is unbecoming for Ben to rail at society like England's "angry young men," and when he says he was "always like that," I merely think it was less unbecoming in his youth, but not more sane.

In *The Untouchables* . . . the author speaks of Al Capone's evil talent for corruption. It is corrupting to buy officers who should be enforcing the law or threaten citizens by amply demonstrated death threats to join criminal enterprises. And it doesn't follow as a corollary that the "corrupter" is an innocent, because other classes join in through fear or greed.

. . . It is necessary for Mickey Cohen to convince himself now when he is at bay that "society" has no good, kind people. . . . It's Ben's attacking society from that vantage point that sticks in my craw. I don't say he shouldn't write about the Decline of Western Civilization. I just don't like Mickey Cohen as a Messiah.

What it amounts to in our present fight is that Ben and I are playing cops and robbers, with me naturally as cop. As a cop, I do abhor Mickey, and I know as papa's daughter what it might mean to a small legitimate businessman to become enmeshed, through fear, with a mob, as they did in Chicago.[22]

Rose was hardly alone in her judgment of Cohen. In 1959 Steve Stevens was a nineteen-year-old former Mouseketeer—a costar of Annette Funicello—struggling to become an adult actor when he fell in with the gangster's entourage. Cohen, a fan of Stevens's juvenile-delinquent roles on television, had reached out as if to a long-lost nephew. At first, the kingpin's world had been intoxicating, with the shining Cadillacs and access to nightspots like Earl Warren's and the Brown Derby, places so exclusive Stevens had only misted up their windows in the past, where celebrities, beautiful women, and obsequious attendants now hovered around him.[23]

But as Stevens recalled in his memoir *King of the Sunset Strip*, this seductive world soon turned ugly and dangerous. When Cohen overheard an insult from an adjacent table at the legendary Village Capri, he crashed a magnum bottle into the offending speaker's head and then returned to his meal while his goons carried the limp victim and his screaming date outside. Having reestablished his reign over the underworld, Cohen demonstrated his power by shooting Jack "the Enforcer" Whalen dead in the middle of Rondelli's Restaurant that December. The place had been full, but not a single witness would testify against him.[24]

During the same period, Stevens landed a role in *High School Caesar*, a B movie about a thug who runs protection rackets and cows the rest of his school into submission. Stevens played Cricket, the bully's sycophantic sidekick. When lead actor John Ashley described the main character as "a dyed-in-the-wool sociopath," Stevens asked what that meant. "He's a guy without a shred of conscience," said Ashley. "He's a user. He mistreats others who are close to him. He'll screw anybody, and yet while all his buddies know it, they still remain loyal to him, even as he gets them in deeper and deeper."

Stevens soon found himself Cohen's errand boy—a lowly but nevertheless treacherous occupation. Old friends began to avoid him. He witnessed the mobster beat one hood nearly to death, and after Stevens allegedly screwed up by getting arrested on a delivery, Cohen slugged and thrashed him into a bloody daze as well. "I couldn't admit, even to myself, that Mickey had done this—had beaten me," Stevens recalled. "Almost immediately I'd substituted his rationalization—that he'd done this 'for my own good,' so I'd 'pay attention'—for the blunt reality of his psychopathic behavior."[25]

Police were well acquainted with—and deeply frustrated by—Cohen's slipperiness. The LAPD continued to find him "a vexing enigma." The FBI decided he was useless as an informant: "These Agents report that Cohen has held back information, has been evasive, misleading, two-faced and ingratiating. Los Angeles suggests that Cohen may pretend to act as an informant simply to try to obtain information from the bureau." Another memo noted that he had been known to kill in the past and "can be considered armed and dangerous."[26]

Hecht, an early lay expert on psychopaths who had been writing about them since the 1920s, never seems to have considered that he was dealing with one. He evidently had forgotten what his old friend Sherman Duffy had advised about a killer they had encountered at the county jail, when Hecht had asked how people could seem so good and then appear to change so suddenly and dramatically. "You'll find that's easiest thing people can do," Duffy had said, "change into swine."[27]

Moreover, Hecht had a considerable reputation to uphold as the tough Chicago crime reporter who was nobody's fool. True, he had written many stories about himself as the naive and gullible cub reporter who would swagger into a brothel "playing the drunkard and whoremonger with all the vocabulary at my command," only to spend the evening clutching the hand of some fallen girl, imploring her to reform. But that was the boy reporter. He also told stories of the seasoned, jaded veteran who barely blinked at the sight of a workman being sawed in half by a locomotive. One reviewer called his memoir "a cry from the soul of an armored car."[28]

Hecht had long held to the Hobbesian view of humans as fundamentally barbaric and murderous. In *A Guide for the Bedevilled*, for example, he had in effect explained Nazism as mass psychopathy, likening Hitler's faithful to the killers he had met on death row. He had told many tales of the extraordinary cunning with which some murderers could convince you of their innocence. Yet somehow, when it came to Cohen, there was a blind spot.

He had noticed that Cohen had a trick: "It is that always . . . there are two Mickey Cohens talking. I have learned to listen to both at the same time." There was the wild young Cohen who ran around insensible as a beast, who could split a head like a melon, and there was the sensitive Cohen, who yearned to be a good, normal person—the one who served hot chocolate and cookies when he first met—and ostensibly sought the spiritual counsel of—the legendary evangelist Reverend Billy Graham. Hecht cautioned himself not to lapse into sentimentality, for gangsters have a talent for arousing in writers "a fellow sense of lawlessness—safe enough at the typewriter, or, worst of all, evoking in them a sort of boozy paternalism." Yet Hecht nonetheless concluded that the *real* Cohen who sat beside him was the gilgul, the soul waiting at the gateway of normal, decent life, seeking just to be let in.[29]

Although Hecht had assured his sister-in-law that he was not sentimental about gangsters, he nevertheless had concluded, "The odds are three to one that Mickey, if not stopped by a bullet, will wind up a Rotarian." Reinvoking the "terrible innocence" of his own celluloid creation, Tony Camonte, Hecht had, after all, observed that in all his talks with Cohen, "The word innocence has always haunted me. No matter how many killings, heists and other acts of violence and lawlessness Mickey related to me as part of his career, I came away from each confab with a curious feeling that there was something innocent about the man."[30]

And he sometimes forgot himself completely, launching into full-throated tributes to his friend: "He paid off on the dot and to the nickel. He fixed fights and let his pals in on the take. He operated hideaway gambling rendezvous where the dice, wheels and cards were as on the level as any operator could afford to have them. One the side he beat up Nazi propagandists, staked bums to binges, never overlooked the birthday of a policeman's kid, paid medical for all wounded supporters and was good for a touch to anybody who smiled and said, 'Hello, Mickey.'"[31]

These reveries were interrupted by Rose, and at least as consequentially, by Dean Jennings. The *Saturday Evening Post* writer had also noticed the two different Cohens, but he drew far different conclusions. He noted that Cohen had summed the matter up himself, in responding to syndicated columnist George Sokolsky, one of his fiercest critics: "I will not deny that at one time in my life, I was a pretty fair replica of the devil," Cohen wrote. "But today I am Michael Cohen, and every day I have to wrestle with Mickey Cohen." Jennings found the claim that the old villainous Mickey lay dead and buried somewhere to be "not quite compatible with the facts."[32]

"There is nothing in this world that shouldn't be done for a friend," Cohen later told the journalist, "and there is nothing in this world that shouldn't be done to an enemy." While Jennings's mind ran through all the pistol-whippings and murders that had been tied to his subject over the years, he asked just what should be done to an enemy. A small, sinister smile rippled across the gangster's face, but then Cohen just shrugged and replied that he had learned in recent years to be more of a diplomat. Jennings looked around the apartment, at the stocks of soap for washing and bottles of colognes for clearing up bad odors. Everywhere he looked, he felt that he saw the evidence of "the turbulent conflicts between Michael Cohen, the gentleman-diplomat, and Mickey Cohen, hoodlum—he once admitted he has to struggle with this Jekyll-Hyde problem every day."[33]

In September 1958, one month after Emch's last letter to Hecht, the first installment of Jennings's *Saturday Evening Post* series somewhat settled the debate over Cohen's character. Hecht and Cohen had agreed to a fifty-fifty split on the biography, but Cohen had gone behind Hecht's back to do the series for the *Post*, with its three million subscribers. Jennings's stories themselves revealed another betrayal: Cohen had been selling over $100,000 in shares for a nonexistent movie that Hecht was supposed to write.[34]

The *Saturday Evening Post* billed the series as "a revealing clinical study of a shameful American paradox," and Jennings's main thrust was that Cohen had manipulated the press and public, turning his celebrity into a jackpot. Figures for how much money he had taken Graham's supporters for have ranged, but according to W. J. Jones, a wealthy member of Graham's board of directors, $18,000 was the price tendered for Cohen's soul. The newly converted Jim Vaus had personally kicked in an additional $5,000. Naturally, the Graham camp was disappointed when Cohen did not come to Jesus—expected to declare himself saved before 17,500 people at Madison Square Garden on May 21, 1957, he had merely waved to the crowd instead. But as Cohen pointed out, they had profited from his big name—as had he.[35] All of this, however, along with an infamous appearance on *The Mike Wallace Interview* and thousands of newspaper headlines, had been mere stepping-stones to Cohen's big cash cow: Ben Hecht.

As Jennings pointed out, Cohen's scheme to use Hecht arguably originated in 1947, when the two men first partnered to raise money for the Irgun. Los Angeles businesswoman Ruth Fisher, who had invested $7,500 in the movie, told the journalist, "I first heard about Mickey when I was on a trip to Israel, and I'm one of the few people who can see his good side." A psychiatrist named Dr. Leonard Krause, as curious about Cohen's psychology as Hecht and Emch were, had invested more than $25,000. "I was very impressed by Mr. Cohen," he said. "He is a gentle and nice fellow." Underworld attorney Bieber had also dropped $25,000, as did retired Nashville shoe manufacturer Max Feigenbaum and a man in the appliance trade named David Krause. Smaller fish eager to get in on the action included jukebox dealer A. V. Stemler ($15,000) and a carhop, who was repaid $3,000 of the $10,000 he loaned.[36]

Back in March—the same month as the fishing trip—Cohen had approached Internal Revenue Service agent Guy McGowen with an offer. The U.S. government could get the first $50,000 from the book and movie deal, Cohen suggested, and he would keep the second $50,000. The feds could keep the rest of the money after that. But, in the meantime, Cohen's lavish lifestyle would be a necessary business expense. "I must keep up a front," he explained to McGowen. "My only asset is the motion picture. If I lowered my living standards it would take away my reputation. If I was to make myself unknown I'd be out of the picture." To Jennings, he commented, "You can't expect Mickey Cohen to go around like a three-dollar-a-day-bum." By late September Cohen was still pushing the movie, now appropriately titled *Flim Flam*.[37]

And this, in the end, was Jennings's point: Cohen had played everyone like a violin and used the media—journalists—to do it. Failing to recall any precedent for media manipulation that had been set decades earlier by

Capone, Jennings asserted, "Mickey Cohen—and this is what makes him stand alone in organized crime—shrewdly and deliberately courted the press." Now that Cohen was out of jail, he and the publicity-mad city of Los Angeles were stuck together "like two ends of a dumbbell."[38]

The series ended portentously with a quote from a revenue agent: "We have to move slowly. . . . Don't think that the Government isn't on top of the whole thing." Whether or not the articles pushed the impending prosecution of Cohen along or, as has been suggested, sealed his fate, Jennings certainly helped all he could to deliver the longest sentence ever given for tax evasion: fifteen years, three years longer than what had been given to Capone. "Dean Jennings may as well have been a federal agent," said *Post* columnist Al Aronowitz, "because his testimony later helped send Mickey to Alcatraz." If Cohen was indeed a manipulative psychopath who had long used journalists for his own ends, he had met his match. "That cocksucker," said Cohen, in the autobiography that he finally did publish. "I really believed Dean Jennings was my friend."[39]

The book and movie fiasco served as the central drama of Cohen's sensational, star-studded trial in 1961, which lasted forty-one days and included testimony from 194 witnesses. Hecht told the court he had first learned from Jennings that Cohen was selling shares in a movie. "I said to Cohen that Jennings had called up and that Jennings was no friend of his," Hecht testified. "And that he had got me angry, because he said to me that Mr. Cohen was out selling stocks or bonds or equities in this contract with the movies. And I said it couldn't be true, not that I couldn't imagine Mr. Cohen doing something like that, but I couldn't imagine anyone would be stupid enough to buy into a non-existent, non-extant piece of work. This I told Mr. Cohen."

Asked what Cohen had said in response, Hecht replied,

> I didn't ask him a question. . . . I just told him these things to wait to see what he would say. He didn't admit or deny, just went on talking about Jennings.
>
> May I say that I understood what the silence was.[40]

An appeals court was equally amazed that Cohen had been able to acquire such large sums from an extraordinary variety of people, rich and poor, famous and unknown. "The particular brand of magic that he used in obtaining these moneys does not always appear," the judgment said. "That there was fraud involved in many instances is plain." Perhaps it would have been unfair, but someone might have asked Hecht why *he too* had been stupid enough to invest so much—so many weeks or months of his life. The answer would have been no different for him than for the others: he had also been won over by Cohen's charm. He had described Cohen as "a small, half-clownish disturber of life" to his sister-in-law, but not only had he and Emch misread his buddy, he had underestimated Cohen as well.[41]

Two explanations have been given for why Hecht dropped his own book after the *Saturday Evening Post* stories. Rose told Sidney Zion that it was "partly because of a brilliant, questioning letter" Emch wrote to Hecht from her deathbed. The more popular explanation is that for legal or commercial reasons—it is never entirely clear which—the series rendered Hecht's story worthless, and the additional, obvious implication is that Cohen had violated the author's trust and friendship. Hecht did say that he returned a $2,500 publisher's advance to Henry Holt and Company after he learned of the Jennings interview. But Hecht never seems to have specifically affirmed either of these explanations—he continued to speak of the book as something he might want to finish, and he remained friends with Cohen.[42]

Neither explanation gives any weight to Rose's potential influence, nor does it consider two other possible factors—Hecht's pride and the pall that the whole episode cast on his prospective book. Jennings may have stopped short of openly deriding Hecht, but his narrative has Cohen playing all the reporters and media interests as pawns, leading up to his bamboozling of the biggest, most hardboiled reporter of them all. For the climax of the *Saturday Evening Post* series, Jennings suggested that all of Cohen's publicity making put the mobster in a position to turn the reputation of the tough old Chicago newsman and screenwriting legend into his own personal gold mine. Particularly after all the additional attention that Cohen's trial gave to his $100,000 fund-raising adventure, Hecht's attempt to use Cohen "as a fresh (and happily cockeyed) view against society" may not have played so well—especially since in the end it seemed that he was the one who had been used. Much of the reading public would likely see what his own wife had seen: an author "dangerously infected by his character's point of view."[43]

She had suggested, with her comments about England's angry young men and about Hecht's views on corruption, that her husband had been blinded by his own cynicism to what Cohen really was. Hecht was so caught up in railing against his democratically elected government that he let the wolf in through the front door. Yes, Hecht had always been like that, but it had never been sane. Back in the days of *Erik Dorn*, he had, in Nelson Algren's view, run out of belief. In the 1940s his liberal critics had called this lack of belief fascism.

∞

When he first set aside the Cohen biography in the fall of 1958, Hecht had plenty else to think about—his new television program was now on the air, putting him in contact on a nightly basis with some of the most iconic figures of the era. The evening with legendary crime photographer Weegee (Arthur Fellig) was like a meeting of two long-lost brothers. Reminiscing about what had endeared him to Murder Incorporated, Weegee said: "I was a freelance photographer and I had one stiff a night. I could live, with blintzes, coffee, hot tea with lemon." He recalled that after Dutch Schultz was gunned down, he had disguised himself as a doctor—"I had more uniforms than Willie Sutton"—to snap photos of the corpse. The two old newspapermen discussed the perfect murder, women killers, more gangsters, and, of course, Cohen.

W: Mickey Cohen? There you go name dropping again.

BH: I can't help it.

W: I tell you Mickey Cohen is the future of the murder business. Gangsters and so forth.

BH: Well I think he's the past. He's a very good boy now. He sells flowers.

W: Flowers? For funerals?

BH: No, for weddings.

W: All the gangster friends could get their flowers from him. They could open charge accounts. Hey, that's a new angle. . . .

BH: Now Weegee, tell me, what was the most vicious murder you ever ran into?

W: One of the early ones of Murder Incorporated, they took a guy in a lot in Brownsville, they tied him up with wires and poured kerosene on him and set him on fire. The guy was alive, mind you. As he tried to free himself, he would just strangle himself more.

BH: Why did they do that? They must have been sore at him.[44]

The program also gave Hecht the opportunity to connect with the new wave of writers. The major disagreement that was the beginning of the end for the show was WABC-TV's refusal to let Hecht interview Norman Mailer about his recently published essay, "The White Negro." The opening lines of Mailer's piece—"Probably we will never be able to determine the psychic havoc of the concentration camps and the atom bomb upon the unconscious mind of almost everyone alive in these years"—suggest the sweeping postwar context he would provide to explain the hipster, a new defining cultural figure, and the new cultural divide between the worlds of the hip and the straight.[45]

Like Hecht, Mailer argued that the criminal was the only true social rebel left in the land. But Mailer, taking his cue from a drift toward narcissism that he had observed in the rebels of the postwar era, focused specifically on the notion of the hipster as a psychopath. Unlike their predecessors from the 1930s, the new generation of rebels had no collectivist idealism, no socialist program to believe in. Mailer's essay explored this idea at length; he used the word *psychopath* forty-six times and quoted from Robert Lindner's book on the topic: "The psychopath is a rebel without a cause, an agitator without a slogan, a revolutionary without a program: in other words, his rebelliousness is aimed to achieve goals satisfactory to himself alone."[46]

Although Hecht didn't have a chance to discuss these ideas with Mailer, Jack Kerouac's appearance allowed Hecht to compare notes with the leading representative of the Beat Generation. Hecht started with a line from Kerouac's 1950 debut novel, *The Town and the City*: "Everyone feels like a Zombie, and somewhere at the ends of the night, the great magician, the great Dracula-figure of modern disintegration and madness . . . the Devil if you will . . . is running the whole thing." Hecht said the passage expressed how he had often felt about the world, but he wasn't sure if their devils were the same. Kerouac, however, was coy. He said only that the words belonged to one of his characters and did not reflect his own views at all.[47]

Their exchange was cordial, but Hecht struggled to find common ground with his mercurial guest. Finally, he asked, "What do you think about people who don't climb the mountain, don't have mysticism, people like me, on a treadmill, always trying to make a little money?" This elicited a surprising response. "No you lived a wonderful life," Kerouac said.

"I could write a book about the way you lived—newspaperman, traveling around writing scripts, plays, everyone throwing roses at you." With that last phrase, Hecht wondered whether he was once again being derided as a sellout, but Kerouac assured him this wasn't the case.

By 1964 Hecht's daughter Jenny was a twenty-one-year-old actress living on her own in Greenwich Village, a "wildly beautiful, stormy-looking blonde girl," as Doubleday editor Margaret Cousins remembered her. A member of the Living Theatre, she would die less than a decade later, on March 25, 1971, of either suicide or a drug overdose. "Ben was devoted to Jennie and liked to go to her apartment and hang around with her young friends," recalled Cousins. "He dug kids—who were just beginning to revolt and demonstrate—and acquire various other habits. What I mean is that he was not old in his mind or attitudes, although he did not entirely approve of the way the world was going."[48]

Meanwhile, Cohen's luck had finally run out. Having lost his appeals, he was sent to Alcatraz on May 15, 1962, and later transferred to a federal penitentiary in Atlanta, a month before Attorney General Robert F. Kennedy closed "the Rock" in March 1963. On August 14, fellow convict Burl Estes McDonald clubbed him with a three-foot iron pipe, splitting the back of his skull and driving fragments of bone into his brain. Cohen spent two weeks in a coma but somehow survived with his mental facilities intact; he was wheelchair bound for the rest of his life, however. When he sued the U.S. government for $10 million, prison authorities were hard pressed to explain how Estes had managed to escape his own maximum-security facility, scale a fence, and penetrate the building that housed the general population. Cohen was awarded $110,000, but the Internal Revenue Service immediately garnished the entire sum.[49]

Hecht mailed Cohen a copy of *Gaily, Gaily*. In reply, Cohen wrote on February 12, 1964, "I received your most appreciated book tonight, and the few words that you wrote to me on the inside of the book was better and done more for me then all the medicine and treatment that the doctors could possibly prescribe." In March he wrote at length of how much he and other prisoners had enjoyed reading *Gaily, Gaily*. "The more I think of it the harder I can kick myself in the rear end for not staying with you and for not nudging you more to get our book to an end," he added. "I would of stayed out of here, and wouldn't have wound up a cripple for the rest of my life. But I guess that is the way the ball bounces."[50]

Hecht had written to Cohen on March 17, "You are not in the only jail there is. There is another jail called 'old age' in which I am beginning to serve time." A month later, on April 18, 1964, he collapsed from a heart attack in his dressing room. Rose found him lying on the ground and held him. She tried to keep him breathing, but the color drained from his face. Shortly after he passed, she went downstairs and sat with Jenny, who had just arrived home with friends. "Every once in a while I went back to the room where he lay in our great bed and I kept on talking to him and telling him how dear he was, still in broken Yiddish," Rose recalled. "Except for a lullaby I used to sing to Jenny I had never spoken of love in the mother tongue. I felt these words would reach his soul. I guess that is what it means to be a Jew."[51]

The funeral service at Temple Rodeph Sholom on West Eighty-Third Street was packed. Peter Bergson delivered a eulogy, as did Menachem Begin, who came with a delegation from Israel. "I kept thinking how it would all have amused Ben," said Cousins. "And I kept hoping that wherever he had got to, he would find the rest of them—that his friends were waiting for him somewhere, with booze and nefarious plans. Something that much alive couldn't just disappear."[52]

Conclusion

In the opening pages of his biography, Hecht made light of a regret that haunted him for much of his life. "I can understand the literary critic's shyness towards me," he quipped. "It is difficult to praise a novelist or a thinker who keeps popping up as the author of innumerable movie melodramas. It is like writing about the virtues of a preacher who keeps carelessly getting himself arrested in bordellos."[1]

Hecht's literary merit has been disputed since the early days of his career. Biographer Doug Fetherling made an initial effort to salvage his reputation in 1977, explaining, "At the time of his first New York success (on stage) he was already a light in Hollywood, and it is difficult today to understand the harmful effect that had on his standing as a literary man. The common notion, that he had sold his creative soul to Hollywood . . . remained unchallenged until the 1960s, when his books were nearly all out of print and forgotten."[2]

While *Gone with the Wind* and Hecht's collaboration with Alfred Hitchcock, *Notorious*, stand as classics, and books like *1001 Afternoons in Chicago* go in and out of print, Hecht's best-remembered work remains *The Front Page*. Following the 1974 film version directed by Billy Wilder, starring Jack Lemmon and Walter Matthau, major stage revivals have included the 1986–87 run at the Vivian Beaumont Theater in Lincoln Center, and a 2016–17 run for 149 performances at the Broadhurst Theater. Starring Nathan Lane, John Slattery, and John Goodman among a cast packed with other Tony winners and well-known actors, the Broadhurst show earned nearly $5 million, the first production of the season to turn a profit. *Washington Post* critic Peter Marks compared the play to *Spotlight*, *All the*

President's Men, and *Absence of Malice*: "Even if some of them dexterously mined the irony of flawed people assigning themselves the elevated roles of society's truth seekers, none accomplished this with quite the depth and panache of 'The Front Page,' with characters who could seem at once so craven and so uproarious."[3]

It would not, however, be accurate to conclude that, other than *The Front Page*, Hecht has been forgotten. A ubiquitous, Zelig-like figure during his lifetime, he has continued to appear in a steady stream of articles and books on a variety of topics, from studies of screwball comedies and early gangster movies to histories of the Holocaust to biographies of Mickey Cohen. Indeed, judging by his frequent prominence in books published some fifty years after his death, there has been no slackening of interest in him.

As for comprehensive assessments, Hecht's extraordinary energy, rich experiences, and five careers—as journalist, novelist, screenwriter, propagandist, and memoirist—have presented writers with an embarrassment of riches, as well as a unique challenge. Jeffrey Brown Martin, author of *Ben Hecht: Hollywood Screenwriter*, contends, "So much wit, so many anecdotes, so many lives are there in a single man that his spirit threatens to overwhelm any study of his work, reducing it to a discursive meander through a witty man's life."[4]

Given the contempt for movies that Hecht shared with his contemporaries, he would likely be dismayed to find himself remembered chiefly as a screenwriter. Just as he passed away in 1964, he materialized as a central figure in a debate that established a new respect for film criticism and for film. The feud between Andrew Sarris and Pauline Kael became an examination, or what has been called an archaeological excavation, of Hecht's era, the seminal early years for movies with sound.[5] Writing first for the small but influential *Film Culture*, and soon thereafter for the *Village Voice* in the early 1960s, Sarris advanced the French auteur theory, the idea that "the director is king," the determining factor in a movie's artistic success or failure. Kael, a West Coast critic who found that theory more mystique than substance, retorted with a fourteen-page broadside in a 1963 issue of *Film Quarterly*.[6]

Kael ultimately fleshed out her own view in *The Citizen Kane Book: Raising Kane* (1971), which can be credited with establishing Hecht as a screenwriting legend. The story of how Orson Welles robbed the glory for *Citizen Kane* from its true author/auteur, screenwriter Herman

Mankiewicz, it is also Kael's tale of the great migration of writers that began with Mankiewicz's famous cable summoning Hecht West. What Kael continued to admire in Hecht was his breeziness, his ability to savage shallow people, corrupt politics, and a venal press with alacrity and glee, and without sanctimony.[7]

Yet Hecht's astounding output of film, fiction, memoir, journalism, and stage drama has itself been a favorite target of critics, who have pointed to it as evidence of his profligate waste of talent. Eight years after Kael's book on *Citizen Kane* appeared, Fetherling made the case for Hecht's broader literary significance, asserting that even those who had respected his prose had failed to appreciate the true nature of his genius. "They did feel that he published much too promiscuously even before he disgraced himself in their eyes by retiring to Hollywood," Fetherling wrote. "Yet . . . the fact that one man could write, near the start of his career, for *Mother Earth*, Emma Goldman's anarchist magazine, and later for the Marx Brothers, indicates a strength and not a weakness."[8]

It is worth considering the criteria we use to assess Hecht's significance as a twentieth-century writer. Hecht lived through an era when powerful new forms of storytelling—radio, film, and television—were just emerging. Contemporaries like Ernest Hemingway and F. Scott Fitzgerald became legends without ever mastering any of these. Hecht was unsurpassed in his versatility and has received little recognition for that achievement, despite his pioneering role. In a multimedia world, generations of writers since have faced the same challenge to adapt to forms that impose radically different demands. Yet our notions of great filmmakers and authors have remained fixed and stovepiped; our literary scholarship and criticism have yet to fully reflect the fundamental changes in the context of modern storytelling that occurred more than a century ago.

Moreover, Hecht cross-pollinated various cultural media with extraordinary wit and exuberance. A neo-Romanticist storyteller, he could weave Romantic tropes and styles into endless tales, blending the sensibilities of the decadents, symbolists, and expressionists of Europe with a gritty American realism drawn from urban newspaper work. His debut in fiction, *Erik Dorn*, was an alienation novel some twenty years ahead of its time. Simultaneously, the naturalistic sketches that he churned out daily for his newspaper column foreshadowed the New Journalism of the 1960s. In film he brought a new sophistication to popular culture, transforming it into something richer and more significant than it had been before.

Hecht also anticipated a trend that defined postwar writers, especially Jewish Americans: the casting aside of the old-guard, leftist collectivist spirit in favor of self-liberation and particularism. Modern literary histories like Mark Shechner's *After the Revolution: Studies in the Contemporary Jewish-American Imagination*, which focuses on postwar Jewish writers like Saul Bellow, Norman Mailer, Isaac Rosenfeld, Allen Ginsberg, and Philip Roth, are premised on the idea that the collapse of socialism after Stalin's purges and show trials was no less disorienting for these Jewish intellectuals than the collapse of traditional life under halakhah (Jewish law) had been for their grandparents. In terms of their own worldview, it had a more profound impact than the revelations about Hitler's death camps. Fans of these writers, and especially of Jewish bad boys like Roth and Lenny Bruce, may experience a sense of déjà vu in learning of Hecht's and Maxwell Bodenheim's antics.

In short, Hecht's literary legacy is due for a reassessment, but sensitive souls who admire him as a writer may find his political legacy troubling. In April 1977, confronted by controversy and scandal, Yitzhak Rabin stepped down as prime minister of Israel, opening the way for Hecht's old partner Menachem Begin to win election the following month. It was the first major transfer of power in Israeli history, the end of a Labor Zionist hegemony dating from the 1930s through the first Israeli elections in 1949. Begin's election was also a crucial victory for the budding settlement movement in the occupied territories, and thus for the original Revisionist dream of a Greater Israel. With the brief exceptions of Rabin's return to office and the tenures of Shimon Peres and Ehud Barak, the right-wing Likud Party has maintained power for more than forty years since then.[9]

The West Bank settlement population has since grown to more than 380,000 by 2017, while the world has watched Israel's slow drift from its liberal-humanist roots, with headlines that have proclaimed the death of the peace process and the two-state solution, the death of liberal Zionism, the death of a democratic Jewish state. "Liberal Zionists must now face the reality that the dissenters have recognized for years," observed British writer Antony Lerman in a 2014 op-ed for the *New York Times*. "A de facto single state already exists; in it, rights for Jews are guaranteed while rights for Palestinians are curtailed. Since liberal Zionists can't countenance anything but two states, this situation leaves them high and dry."[10]

During his era Hecht witnessed ignorance, xenophobia, and violent tribalism that rightly made him question the optimistic assumptions that were the bedrock of democratic theory. He understood the implications of his grim perceptions for war and peace, political institutions, law and order, the role of the press, and the democratic process itself. But if he had the personal distance, or the benefit of time and hindsight, perhaps he, of all people, would have been able to see his friendship with Cohen as an allegory for the blindness of tough-guy cynicism in politics, and the consequences.

It would be unfair, as well as inaccurate, however, to sum up Hecht as someone who pushed only a narrow view of the "soul of man." He is remembered for his movies precisely because he introduced complex, contradictory characters at a time when Hollywood had been offering only cardboard cutouts. He raised questions about basic contradictions in the world, questions that were crucial then just as they are now. Only Hecht could create a character like Cary Grant's Devlin in *Notorious*, an FBI agent who, seeking to infiltrate a Nazi spy ring and stop its leader's apocalyptic plot, was willing to convince a young woman to sleep with the enemy. When Alicia sneaks a meeting in a crowd to report back, grimly, that her work has begun, Devlin murmurs through a forced smile, under the watchful eye of her mark, "Dry your eyes, baby. It's out of character. . . . It's a tough job you're on."[11]

Selected Bibliography

I list here only key sources that have been the basis for my book. This bibliography is by no means a complete record of all the works and sources I have consulted. It indicates the content and breadth of reading upon which I have formed my ideas, and I offer it here as a resource for readers who wish to pursue further inquiry.

Alexander, Edward. *Irving Howe: Socialist, Critic, Jew.* Jewish Literature and Culture. Bloomington: Indiana University Press, 1998.

Allen, Frederick Lewis. *Only Yesterday: An Informal History of the 1920's.* New York: Perennial Classics, 2000.

American Psychiatric Association. *Diagnostic and Statistical Manual of Mental Disorders: DSM-IV.* 4th ed. Washington, D.C.: American Psychiatric Association, 1994.

Anderson, Margaret C. *My Thirty Years' War: An Autobiography.* New York: Covici, Friede, 1930.

Anderson, Sherwood. *Letters of Sherwood Anderson.* Edited by Howard Mumford Jones in association with Walter Rideout. New York: Kraus Reprint, 1969.

Anderson, Sherwood. *Sherwood Anderson's Memoirs.* New York: Harcourt, Brace, 1942.

Andrews, Wayne. *Battle for Chicago.* New York: Harcourt, 1946.

Antheil, George. *Bad Boy of Music.* Garden City, N.Y.: Doubleday, Doran, 1945.

Arendt, Hannah. *Eichmann in Jerusalem: A Report on the Banality of Evil.* Rev. and enlarged ed. Gloucester, Mass.: Peter Smith, 1986.

Aronoff, Myron J. "Establishing Authority: The Memorialization of Jabotinsky and the Burial of Bar Kochba Bones in Israel under the Likud." In *The Frailty of Authority,* edited by Myron J. Aronoff, 105–30. Political Anthropology 5. New Brunswick, N.J.: Transaction Books, 1986.

Avrich, Paul. *The Haymarket Tragedy*. Princeton, N.J.: Princeton University Press, 1984.

Baldick, Chris, and Oxford University Press. *The Oxford Dictionary of Literary Terms*. 3rd ed. Oxford: Oxford University Press, 2008.

Baran, Stanley J., and Dennis K. Davis. *Mass Communication Theory: Foundations, Ferment, and Future*. 2nd ed. Boston, Mass.: Wadsworth Cengage Learning, 2000.

Barri, Shoshana. "The Question of Kastner's Testimonies on Behalf of Nazi War Criminals." *Journal of Israeli History* 18, nos. 2–3 (1997): 139–65.

Bauer, Yehuda. *American Jewry and the Holocaust: The American Jewish Joint Distribution Committee, 1939–1945*. Jerusalem: Institute of Contemporary Jewry, Hebrew University; Detroit: Wayne State University Press, 1981.

Baumel-Schwartz, Judith Tydor. *The "Bergson Boys" and the Origins of Contemporary Zionist Militancy*. Modern Jewish History. Syracuse, N.Y.: Syracuse University Press, 2005.

Begin, Menachem. *The Revolt*. London: W. H. Allen, 1951.

Bekken, Jon. "Crumbs from the Publishers' Golden Tables: The Plight of the Chicago Newsboy." *Media History* 6, no. 1 (2000): 45–57.

Bell, J. Bowyer. *Terror out of Zion: Irgun Zvai Leumi, LEHI, and the Palestine Underground, 1929–1949*. New York: St. Martin's, 1977.

Benson, Michael T. *Harry S. Truman and the Founding of Israel*. Westport, Conn.: Praeger, 1997.

Berlin, Isaiah. *Freedom and Its Betrayal: Six Enemies of Human Liberty*. Princeton, N.J.: Princeton University Press, 2002.

Ben-Ami, Yitshaq. *Years of Wrath, Days of Glory: Memoirs from the Irgun*. New York: R. Speller, 1982.

Bender, John, Lucinda Davenport, Michael Drager, and Fred Fedler. *Reporting for the Media*. 10th ed. New York: Oxford University Press, 2005.

Bercovitch, Sacvan. *The American Jeremiad*. Madison: University of Wisconsin Press, 1978.

Berger, Charles R., and Steven H. Chaffee, eds. *Handbook of Communication Science*. Beverly Hills, Calif.: Sage, 1987.

Bethell, Nicholas. *The Palestine Triangle: The Struggle between the British, the Jews and the Arabs, 1935–48*. London: A. Deutsch, 1979.

Bilek, Arthur J. *The First Vice Lord: Big Jim Colosimo and the Ladies of the Levee*. Nashville, Tenn.: Cumberland House, 2008.

Black, Edwin. *The Transfer Agreement: The Dramatic Story of the Pact between the Third Reich and Jewish Palestine*. Cambridge, Mass.: Brookline Books, 1999.

Bodenheim, Maxwell. *Blackguard*. Chicago: Covici-McGee, 1923.

Bodenheim, Maxwell. *Duke Herring*. New York: H. Liveright, 1931.

Bodenheim, Maxwell. *My Life and Loves in Greenwich Village*. New York: Bridgehead Books, 1954.

Bodenheim, Maxwell. *Slow Vision*. New York: Macaulay, 1934.

Boettiger, John. *Jake Lingle; or, Chicago on the Spot.* New York: E. P. Dutton, 1931.

Bogdanovich, Peter, and the Film Library of the Museum of Modern Art. *The Cinema of Howard Hawks.* New York: Film Library of the Museum of Modern Art, 1962.

Boggs, Tom. *Millionaire Playboy: A Delirious and True Extravaganza of Inheriting a Fortune and Squandering It.* New York: Vanguard, 1933.

Borgwardt, Elizabeth. *A New Deal for the World: America's Vision for Human Rights.* Cambridge, Mass.: Belknap Press of Harvard University Press, 2005.

Brando, Marlon. *Brando: Songs My Mother Taught Me.* New York: Random House, 1994.

Brecher, Frank W. "'The Western Allies and the Holocaust': David Wyman and the Historiography of America's Response to the Holocaust: Counter-considerations," *Holocaust and Genocide Studies* 5, no. 4 (1990): 423–46.

Breitman, Richard. *FDR and the Jews.* Cambridge, Mass.: Belknap Press of Harvard University Press, 2013.

Breitman, Richard, and Shlomo Aronson. "The End of the Final Solution? Nazi Plans to Ransom Jews in 1944." *Central European History* 25, no. 2 (1992): 177–203.

Brenner, Lenni. *The Iron Wall: Zionist Revisionism from Jabotinsky to Shamir.* London: Zed; Totowa, N.J.: Biblio Distribution Center, 1984.

Buntin, John. *L.A. Noir: The Struggle for the Soul of America's Most Seductive City.* New York: Harmony Books, 2009.

Burrough, Bryan. *Public Enemies: America's Greatest Crime Wave and the Birth of the FBI, 1933–34.* New York: Penguin, 2004.

Butcher, Fanny. *Many Lives—One Love.* New York: Harper & Row, 1972.

Carey, James W. *James Carey: A Critical Reader.* Edited by Eve Stryker Munson and Catherine A. Warren. Minneapolis: University of Minnesota Press, 1997.

Carey, James W. "The Problem of Journalism History." *Journalism History* 1 (Spring 1974): 2–5, 27.

Childs, Peter, and Roger Fowler. *The Routledge Dictionary of Literary Terms.* London: Routledge, 2006.

Chipman, Bruce L. *Into America's Dream-Dump: A Postmodern Study of the Hollywood Novel.* Lanham, Md.: University Press of America, 1999.

Chisholm, Robert B. *Handbook on the Prophets: Isaiah, Jeremiah, Lamentations, Ezekiel, Daniel, Minor Prophets.* Grand Rapids, Mich.: Baker Academic, 2009.

Churchill, Allen. *The Improper Bohemians: A Re-creation of Greenwich Village in Its Heyday.* New York: Dutton, 1959.

Clarens, Carlos. *Crime Movies: From Griffith to* The Godfather *and Beyond.* New York: Norton, 1980.

Cochran, Molly, ed. *The Cambridge Companion to Dewey.* Cambridge: Cambridge University Press, 2010.

Cohen, Michael Joseph. *Truman and Israel.* Berkeley: University of California Press, 1990.

Cohen, Michael Mickey. *Mickey Cohen, in My Own Words: The Underworld Autobiography of Michael Mickey Cohen, as Told to John Peer Nugent.* Englewood Cliffs, N.J.: Prentice-Hall, 1975.

Cohen, Sarah Blacher, ed. *From Hester Street to Hollywood: The Jewish-American Stage and Screen.* Bloomington: Indiana University Press, 1983.

Cooney, John. *The Annenbergs.* New York: Simon and Schuster, 1982.

Corliss, Richard. *Talking Pictures: Screenwriters in the American Cinema, 1927–1973.* Woodstock, N.Y.: Overlook, 1974.

Corwin, Miles. *Homicide Special: A Year with the LAPD's Elite Detective Unit.* New York: Henry Holt, 2004.

Coser, Lewis A. *Men of Ideas: A Sociologist's View.* New York: Free Press, 1965.

Crane, Hart. *The Letters of Hart Crane, 1916–1932.* New York: Hermitage House, 1952.

Cruse, Harold. *The Crisis of the Negro Intellectual.* New York: Morrow, 1967.

Cuddon, J. A. *The Penguin Dictionary of Literary Terms and Literary Theory.* 3rd ed. London: Penguin, 1992.

Dardis, Tom. *Some Time in the Sun: The Hollywood Years of F. Scott Fitzgerald, William Faulkner, Nathanael West, Aldous Huxley and James Agee.* New York: Scribner, 1976.

Davis, David Brion. "Some Recent Directions in Cultural History." *American Historical Review* 73 (February 1968): 696–707.

Davis, Susan O'Connor. *Chicago's Historic Hyde Park.* Chicago: University of Chicago Press, 2013.

Dawidowicz, Lucy S. *The War against the Jews, 1933–1945.* 10th anniversary ed. New York: Bantam Books, 1986.

Dawidowicz, Lucy S. *What Is the Use of Jewish History? Essays.* New York: Schocken Books, 1992.

Deem, James M. *Kristallnacht: The Nazi Terror That Began the Holocaust.* The Holocaust through Primary Sources. Berkeley Heights, N.J.: Enslow, 2012.

Demaris, Ovid. *The Last Mafioso: The Treacherous World of Jimmy Fratianno.* New York: Times Books, 1981.

DiBattista, Maria. *Fast-Talking Dames.* New Haven, Conn.: Yale University Press, 2001.

Diner, Hasia R. *We Remember with Reverence and Love: American Jews and the Myth of Silence after the Holocaust, 1945–1962.* New York: New York University Press, 2009.

Dinnerstein, Leonard. Review of *Abandonment of the Jews*, by David Wyman. *Journal of American History* 72, no. 1 (June 1985): 186–87.

Doering, Bernard. "Madame Bovary and Flaubert's Romanticism." *College Literature* 8, no. 1 (1981): 1–11.

Doherty, Eddie. *Gall and Honey: The Story of a Newspaperman.* New York: Sheed & Ward, 1941.

Doherty, Thomas Patrick. *Hollywood and Hitler, 1933–1939.* New York: Columbia University Press, 2013.

Dornfeld, A. A. *Behind the Front Page: The Story of the City News Bureau of Chicago*. Chicago: Academy Chicago, 1983.

Dreiser, Theodore. *Newspaper Days*. Vol. 2 of *A Book about Myself*. 1st ed., New York: H. Liveright, 1922; 7th ed., New York: H. Liveright, 1931. Citations refer to the 7th edition.

Duffey, Bernard I. *The Chicago Renaissance in American Letters*. 2nd ed. East Lansing: Michigan State University Press, 1956.

Duncan, Hugh Dalziel. *The Rise of Chicago as a Literary Center from 1885 to 1920: A Sociological Essay in American Culture*. Totowa, N.J.: Bedminster, 1964.

Ehrlich, Matthew C. *Journalism in the Movies*. History of Communication. Urbana: University of Illinois Press, 2004.

Eig, Jonathan. *Get Capone: The Secret Plot That Captured America's Most Wanted Gangster*. New York: Simon and Schuster, 2010.

Eisenberg, Dennis, Uri Dan, and Eli Landau. *Meyer Lansky: Mogul of the Mob*. New York: Paddington, 1979.

Eisner, Lotte H. *The Haunted Screen: Expressionism in the German Cinema and the Influence of Max Reinhardt*. Berkeley: University of California Press, 1969.

Eliot, T. S. *The Letters of T. S. Eliot*. Rev. ed. New Haven, Conn.: Yale University Press, 2011.

Encyclopedia of World Biography. 2nd ed. Farmington Hills, Mich.: Cengage Gale, 2011.

Evans, Richard J. *The Coming of the Third Reich*. New York: Penguin, 2004.

Evans, Richard J. *In Defense of History*. New York: W. W. Norton, 1999.

Evans, Richard J. *The Third Reich at War, 1939–1945*. London: Allen Lane, 2008.

Fanon, Frantz. *The Wretched of the Earth*. Translated by Richard Philcox, with introductions by Jean-Paul Sartre and Homi K. Bhabha. New York: Grove, 2004.

Feingold, Henry L. *The Politics of Rescue: The Roosevelt Administration and the Holocaust, 1938–1945*. New Brunswick, N.J.: Rutgers University Press, 1970.

Feingold, Henry L. *Zion in America: The Jewish Experience from Colonial Times to the Present*. New York: Hippocrene Books, 1974.

Feinman, Jeffrey. *Hollywood Confidential*. Chicago: Playboy Press, 1976.

Fetherling, Doug. *The Five Lives of Ben Hecht*. Toronto: Lester and Orpen, 1977.

Fiedler, Leslie A. *The Collected Essays of Leslie Fiedler*. New York: Stein and Day, 1971.

Fisher, James Terence. *On the Irish Waterfront: The Crusader, the Movie, and the Soul of the Port of New York*. Cushwa Center Studies of Catholicism in Twentieth-Century America. Ithaca, N.Y.: Cornell University Press, 2009.

Fowler, Gene. *Skyline: A Reporter's Reminiscence of the 1920s*. New York: Viking, 1961.

Freeman, David. *A Hollywood Education: Tales of Movie Dreams and Easy Money*. New York: Putnam, 1986.

Friede, Donald. *The Mechanical Angel, His Adventures and Enterprises in the Glittering 1920's*. New York: A. A. Knopf, 1948.

Friedländer, Saul. *Nazi Germany and the Jews*. Vol. 1, *The Years of Persecution, 1933–1939*. New York: HarperCollins, 1997.

Friedländer, Saul. *The Years of Extermination: Nazi Germany and the Jews, 1939–1945*. New York: Harper Collins, 2007.

Friedman, Robert I. *The False Prophet: Rabbi Meir Kahane—from FBI Informant to Knesset Member*. Brooklyn, N.Y.: Lawrence Hill Books, 1990.

Fromm, Erich. *Escape from Freedom*. New York: Rinehart, 1941.

Gelb, Arthur, and Barbara Gelb. *O'Neill*. New York: Harper, 1962.

Gelber, Yoav. *Palestine, 1948: War, Escape and the Emergence of the Palestinian Refugee Problem*. Brighton, UK: Sussex Academic, 2001.

Gilbert, Martin. *Kristallnacht: Prelude to Destruction*. New York: HarperCollins, 2006.

Goldhagen, Daniel Jonah. *Hitler's Willing Executioners: Ordinary Germans and the Holocaust*. New York: Alfred A. Knopf, 1996.

Goldman, Emma. *Living My Life*. New York: Dover, 1970.

Goldman, Emma. *Nowhere at Home: Letters from Exile of Emma Goldman and Alexander Berkman*. New York: Schocken Books, 1975.

Goren, Arthur Aryeh. "Pageants of Sorrow, Celebration and Protest: The Public Culture of American Jews." In *Literary Strategies: Jewish Texts and Contexts*, edited by Ezra Mendelsohn, 202–18. Studies in Contemporary Jewry 12. Oxford: Oxford University Press, 1996.

Gottlieb, Polly Rose. *The Nine Lives of Billy Rose*. New York: Crown, 1968.

Greenwald, Richard A. *The Triangle Fire, the Protocols of Peace, and Industrial Democracy in Progressive Era New York*. Philadelphia: Temple University Press, 2005.

Haberski, Raymond J. *It's Only a Movie! Films and Critics in American Culture*. Lexington: University Press of Kentucky, 2001.

Hagemann, E. R. "*Scarface*: The Art of Hollywood, Not 'The Shame of a Nation.'" *Journal of Popular Culture* 18, no. 1 (June 1984): 30–42.

Halamish, Aviva. *The Exodus Affair: Holocaust Survivors and the Struggle for Palestine*. Syracuse, N.Y.: Syracuse University Press, 1998.

Halpern, Ben. "Herzl's Historic Gift: The Sense of Sovereignty." *Herzl Year Book* 3 (1960): 27–34.

Hansen, Harry. *Midwest Portraits: A Book of Memories and Friendships*. New York: Harcourt, Brace, 1923.

Harris, Jed. *A Dance on the High Wire: Recollections of a Time and a Temperament*. New York: Crown, 1979.

Hecht, Ben. *Actor's Blood*. New York: Covici, Friede, 1936.

Hecht, Ben. *The Ben Hecht Show: Impolitic Observations from the Freest Thinker of 1950s Television*. Edited and adapted by Bret Primack. Jefferson, N.C.: McFarland, 1993.

Hecht, Ben. *A Book of Miracles*. New York: Viking, 1937.

Hecht, Ben. *The Champion from Far Away*. New York: Covici, Friede, 1931.

Hecht, Ben. *Charlie: The Improbable Life and Times of Charles MacArthur.* New York: Harper, 1957.

Hecht, Ben. *A Child of the Century.* New York: Primus, 1985.

Hecht, Ben. *Count Bruga.* New York: Boni & Liveright, 1926.

Hecht, Ben. *Erik Dorn, a Novel.* Chicago in Fiction. Chicago: University of Chicago Press, 1963.

Hecht, Ben. *Fantazius Mallare: A Mysterious Oath.* Chicago: Covici-McGee, 1922.

Hecht, Ben. *Gaily, Gaily.* Garden City, N.Y.: Doubleday, 1963.

Hecht, Ben. *A Guide for the Bedevilled.* New York: Charles Scribner's Sons, 1944.

Hecht, Ben. *I Hate Actors!* New York: Crown, 1944.

Hecht, Ben. *A Jew in Love.* New York: Covici, Friede, 1931.

Hecht, Ben. *Letters from Bohemia.* Garden City, N.Y.: Doubleday, 1964.

Hecht, Ben. *Perfidy.* New York: Messner, 1961.

Hecht, Ben. *A Thousand and One Afternoons in Chicago.* New York: Covici Friede, 1922.

Hecht, Ben. *1001 Afternoons in New York.* New York: Viking, 1941.

Hecht, Ben. *To Quito and Back.* New York: Covici, Friede, 1937.

Hecht, Ben. *A Tribute to Gallantry,* in *The Best One-Act Plays of 1943.* New York: Dodd, Mead, 1944.

Hecht, Ben. *Underworld: An Original Story of Chicago.* [Chicago?]: Hecht, 1927.

Hecht, Ben, and Charles MacArthur. *The Front Page.* New York: Covici-Friede, 1928.

Heller, Joseph. *The Stern Gang: Ideology, Politics and Terror, 1940–1949.* London: Routledge, 2004

Hemingway, Ernest. *A Moveable Feast: The Restored Edition.* New York: Scribner, 2009.

Herf, Jeffrey. *The Jewish Enemy: Nazi Propaganda during World War II and the Holocaust.* Cambridge, Mass.: Belknap Press of Harvard University Press, 2006.

Higham, John. *Send These to Me: Immigrants in Urban America.* Rev. ed. Baltimore: Johns Hopkins University Press, 1984.

Hilberg, Raul. *The Destruction of the European Jews.* New York: Harper & Row, 1961.

Hillier, Jim, and Peter Wollen, eds. *Howard Hawks: American Artist.* London: British Film Institute, 1997.

Hilton, George W., ed. *The Front Page: From Theater to Reality.* The Art of Theater Series. Hanover, N.H.: Smith & Kraus, 2002.

Hoberman, J., and Jeffrey Shandler. *Entertaining America: Jews, Movies, and Broadcasting.* New York: Jewish Museum, under the auspices of the Jewish Theological Seminary of America, 2003.

Hochberg, Severin. Review of *Holocaust in American Life,* by Peter Novick. *Journal of American History* 87, no. 3 (December 2000): 1099–101.

Hoffmann, Hilmar. *The Triumph of Propaganda: Film and National Socialism, 1933–1945.* Providence, R.I.: Berghahn Books, 1996.

Holden, Henry M. *FBI 100 Years: An Unofficial History*. Minneapolis: Zenith, 2008.

Horkheimer, Max, and Theodor W. Adorno. *Dialectic of Enlightenment: Philosophical Fragments*. Cultural Memory in the Present. Stanford, Calif.: Stanford University Press, 2002.

Hovland, Carl Iver. *Experiments on Mass Communication*. Princeton, N.J.: Princeton University Press, 1949.

Howe, Irving. *Sherwood Anderson*. American Men of Letters Series. Stanford, Calif.: Stanford University Press, 1968.

Hume, Janice. "Press, Published History, Regional Lore: Shaping the Public Memory of a Revolutionary War Heroine." *Journalism History* 30, no. 4 (Winter 2005): 200–209.

Hume, Janice, and Noah Arceneaux. "Public Memory, Cultural Legacy, and Press Coverage of the Juneteenth Revival." *Journalism History* 34, no. 3 (Fall 2008): 155–62.

Jennings, Dean Southern. *We Only Kill Each Other: The Life and Bad Times of Bugsy Siegel*. Englewood Cliffs, N.J.: Prentice-Hall, 1967.

Jerome, Fred. *Einstein on Israel and Zionism: His Provocative Ideas about the Middle East*. New York: St. Martin's, 2009.

Johns, Elizabeth Dewey. "Chicago's Papers and the News." PhD diss., University of Chicago, 1942.

Johnston, Alva. *The Legendary Mizners*. New York: Farrar, Straus and Giroux, 1986.

Jowett, Garth, and Victoria O'Donnell. *Propaganda and Persuasion*. 5th ed. Thousand Oaks, Calif.: Sage, 2012.

Joyce, James. *A Portrait of the Artist as a Young Man*. Centennial ed. New York: Viking, 1982.

Kael, Pauline. *The Citizen Kane Book: Raising Kane*. Boston: Little, Brown, 1971.

Kael, Pauline. *5001 Nights at the Movies: A Guide from A to Z*. New York: Holt, Rinehart and Winston, 1982.

Kael, Pauline. *Kiss Kiss Bang Bang*. Boston: Little, Brown, 1968.

Kallis, Aristotle A. *Nazi Propaganda and the Second World War*. New York: Palgrave Macmillan, 2005.

Kammen, Michael G. *American Culture, American Tastes: Social Change and the 20th Century*. New York: Alfred A. Knopf, 1999.

Kaplan, Eran. *The Jewish Radical Right: Revisionist Zionism and Its Ideological Legacy*. Studies on Israel. Madison: University of Wisconsin Press, 2005.

Kaplan, Jeffrey S., ed. *Encyclopedia of White Power: A Sourcebook on the Radical Racist Right*. Walnut Creek, Calif.: AltaMira, 2000.

Katz, Elihu. "On Conceptualizing Media Effects." *Studies in Communication* 1 (1980): 119–39.

Katz, Elihu, and Paul Lazarsfeld. *Personal Influence: The Part Played by People in the Flow of Mass Communications*. Glencoe, Ill.: Free Press, 1955.

Kazin, Alfred. *On Native Grounds: An Interpretation of Modern American Prose Literature*. New York: Harcourt, Brace & World, 1942.

Keefe, Rose. *Guns and Roses: The Untold Story of Dean O'Banion, Chicago's Big Shot before Al Capone*. Nashville, Tenn.: Cumberland House, 2003.

Kefauver, Estes. *Crime in America*. New York: Greenwood, 1968.

Kerouac, Jack. *The Town and the City*. London: Penguin, 2000.

Klatt, Wayne. *Chicago Journalism: A History*. Jefferson, N.C.: McFarland, 2009.

Klinger, S., and Vladimir Jabotinsky. *The Ten-Year Plan for Palestine: A Brief Outline*. London: New Zionist Press, 1938.

Koestler, Arthur. *Promise and Fulfillment: Palestine, 1917–1949*. London: Macmillan, 1949.

Kollek, Teddy. *For Jerusalem: A Life*. New York: Random House, 1978.

Kook, Hillel [Peter Bergson]. "The Bergson Group, America, and the Holocaust: A Previously Unpublished Interview with Hillel Kook/Peter Bergson." By David S. Wyman. *American Jewish History* 89, no. 1 (2001): 3–34.

Koszarski, Richard. *Hollywood on the Hudson: Film and Television in New York from Griffith to Sarnoff*. New Brunswick, N.J.: Rutgers University Press, 2008.

Kotynek, Roy. *American Cultural Rebels: Avant-Garde and Bohemian Artists, Writers and Musicians from the 1850s through the 1960s*. Jefferson, N.C.: McFarland, 2008.

Kramer, Dale. *Chicago Renaissance: The Literary Life in the Midwest, 1900–1930*. New York: Appleton-Century, 1966.

Kreymborg, Alfred. *Troubadour: An American Autobiography*. American Century Series, S-22. New York: Sagamore, 1957.

Krivosheev, G. F. *Soviet Casualties and Combat Losses in the Twentieth Century*. London: Greenhill Books; Mechanicsburg, Pa.: Stackpole Books, 1997.

Lacey, Robert. *Little Man: Meyer Lansky and the Gangster Life*. Boston: Little, Brown, 1991.

Langner, Lawrence. *The Magic Curtain: The Story of a Life in Two Fields, Theatre and Invention, by the Founder of the Theatre Guild*. New York: Dutton, 1951.

Laqueur, Walter, ed., *Fascism: A Reader's Guide. Analyses, Interpretations, Bibliography*. Berkeley: University of California Press, 1978.

Laqueur, Walter. *A History of Zionism*. New York: Holt, Rinehart and Winston, 1972.

Lasch, Christopher. *The Culture of Narcissism: American Life in an Age of Diminishing Expectations*. New York: Norton, 1978.

Lasswell, Harold Dwight. *Propaganda Technique in the World War*. London: K. Paul, Trench, Trubner, 1927.

Lasswell, Harold Dwight. "The Strategy of Revolutionary and War Propaganda." In *Public Opinion and World-Politics* [Lectures on the Harris Foundation 1933], edited by Quincy Wright, 185–221. Chicago: University of Chicago Press, 1933.

Lasswell, Harold Dwight. "The Theory of Political Propaganda." *American Political Science Review* 21, no. 3 (1927): 627–31.

Lawrence, Jerome. *Actor: The Life and Times of Paul Muni*. New York: Putnam, 1974.

Leff, Laurel. *Buried by the Times: The Holocaust and America's Most Important Newspaper*. Cambridge: Cambridge University Press, 2005.

Lesy, Michael. *Murder City: The Bloody History of Chicago in the Twenties*. New York: W. W. Norton, 2007.

Levin, Meyer. *In Search: An Autobiography*. New York: Horizon, 1950.

Levine, Charles. *Propaganda Techniques of the Bergson Group, 1939–48*. Austin: University of Texas Press, 1974.

Levinson, Julian. *Exiles on Main Street: Jewish American Writers and American Literary Culture*. Jewish Literature and Culture. Bloomington: Indiana University Press, 2008.

Lieberman, Paul. *Gangster Squad: Covert Cops, the Mob, and the Battle for Los Angeles*. New York: Thomas Dunne Books/St. Martin's Griffin, 2012.

Lippmann, Walter. *Liberty and the News*. New York: Harcourt, Brace and Howe, 1920.

Lippmann, Walter. *The Phantom Public*. New York: Harcourt, Brace, 1925.

Lippmann, Walter. *Public Opinion*. New York: Harcourt, Brace, 1922.

Lipstadt, Deborah E. *Beyond Belief: The American Press and the Coming of the Holocaust, 1933–1945*. New York: Free Press, 1986 Reprint, New York: Touchstone, 1993.

Longstreet, Stephen. *Chicago, 1860–1919*. New York: McKay, 1973.

Luhan, Mabel Dodge. *Intimate Memories: The Autobiography of Mabel Dodge Luhan*. Albuquerque: University of New Mexico Press, 2014.

Lundberg, Ferdinand. *Imperial Hearst: A Social Biography*. New York: Modern Library, 1936.

MacAdams, William. *Ben Hecht: The Man behind the Legend*. New York: Scribner, 1990.

Mackay, Constance D'Arcy. *The Little Theatre in the United States*. New York: H. Holt, 1917.

Mailer, Norman. *Advertisements for Myself*. New York: Putnam, 1959.

Mailer, Norman. *Marilyn: A Biography*. New York: Grosset & Dunlap, 1973.

Mangione, Jerre. *The Dream and the Deal: The Federal Writers' Project, 1935–1943*. Boston: Little, Brown, 1972.

Manso, Peter. *Brando*. London: Weidenfeld and Nicolson, 1994.

Martin, Jeffrey Brown. *Ben Hecht, Hollywood Screenwriter*. Studies in Cinema 27. Ann Arbor, Mich.: UMI Research Press, 1985.

Mast, Gerald. *A Short History of the Movies*. 9th ed. New York: Pearson/Longman, 2006.

May, Henry Farnham. *The End of American Innocence: A Study of the First Years of Our Own Time, 1912–1917*. New York: Knopf, 1959; New York: Columbia University Press, 1992. Citations refer to the 1992 edition.

Mayer, Martin. *Making News*. Garden City, N.Y.: Doubleday, 1987.

McCarthy, Todd. *Howard Hawks: The Grey Fox of Hollywood*. New York: Grove, 1997.

McDonald, James G. *My Mission in Israel, 1948–1951*. New York: Simon and Schuster, 1951.

McGilligan, Patrick. *Alfred Hitchcock: A Life in Darkness and Light.* New York: Regan Books, 2003.

McPhaul, John J. *Deadlines and Monkeyshines: The Fabled World of Chicago Journalism.* Englewood Cliffs, N.J.: Prentice-Hall, 1962.

Medoff, Rafael. *Militant Zionism in America: The Rise and Impact of the Jabotinsky Movement in the United States, 1926–1948.* Tuscaloosa: University of Alabama Press, 2002.

Medovoi, Leerom. *Rebels: Youth and the Cold War Origins of Identity.* Durham, N.C.: Duke University Press, 2005.

Mencken, H. L. *My Life as Author and Editor.* New York: Knopf, 1993.

Mencken, H. L. *Notes on Democracy.* New York: Knopf, 1926.

Mendes-Flohr, Paul R. *Divided Passions: Jewish Intellectuals and the Experience of Modernity.* Culture of Jewish Modernity. Detroit: Wayne State University Press, 1991.

Merlin, Samuel. *Millions of Jews to Rescue: A Bergson Group Leader's Account of the Campaign to Save Jews from the Holocaust.* Washington, D.C.: David S. Wyman Institute for Holocaust Studies, 2011.

Miller, David. *The Blackwell Encyclopaedia of Political Thought.* Oxford: B. Blackwell, 1987.

Miller, Perry. *Errand into the Wilderness.* Cambridge, Mass.: Belknap Press of Harvard University Press, 1984.

Milton, Joyce. *The Yellow Kids: Foreign Correspondents in the Heyday of Yellow Journalism.* New York: Harper & Row, 1989.

Mindich, David T. Z. *Just the Facts: How "Objectivity" Came to Define American Journalism.* New York: New York University Press, 1998.

Moore, Jack B. *Maxwell Bodenheim.* New York: Twayne, 1970.

Moore, William T. *Dateline Chicago: A Veteran Newsman Recalls Its Heyday.* New York: Taplinger, 1973.

Morris, Benny. *The Birth of the Palestinian Refugee Problem Revisited.* 2nd ed. Cambridge: Cambridge University Press, 2004.

Morse, Arthur D. *While Six Million Died: A Chronicle of American Apathy.* New York: Random House, 1968.

Muir, Florabel. *Headline Happy.* New York: Holt, 1950.

Munby, Jonathan. *Public Enemies, Public Heroes: Screening the Gangster from Little Caesar to Touch of Evil.* Chicago: University of Chicago Press, 1999.

Murray, George. *The Madhouse on Madison Street.* Chicago: Follett, 1965.

Nasaw, David. *The Patriarch: The Remarkable Life and Turbulent Times of Joseph P. Kennedy.* New York: Penguin, 2012.

Nash, Jay Robert. *The Great Pictorial History of World Crime.* Wilmette, Ill.: History, 2004.

Newark, Timothy. *Mafia Allies: The True Story of America's Secret Alliance with the Mob in World War II.* St. Paul, Minn.: Zenith, 2007.

Newcomb, Horace, ed. *Television: The Critical View.* 3rd ed. New York: Oxford University Press, 1982.

Nord, David Paul. "James Carey and Journalism History: A Remembrance." *Journalism History* 32, no. 3 (Fall 2006): 122–27.

Nord, David Paul. "A Plea for Journalism History." *Journalism History* 15, no. 1 (Spring 1988): 8–15.

Novick, Peter. *The Holocaust in American Life*. Boston: Houghton Mifflin, 1999.

Nussbaum, Martha Craven. *Upheavals of Thought: The Intelligence of Emotions*. Cambridge: Cambridge University Press, 2001.

Ogden, Christopher. *Legacy: A Biography of Moses and Walter Annenberg*. Boston: Little, Brown, 1999.

Ophir, Ephraim. "Was the Transnistria Rescue Plan Achievable?" *Holocaust and Genocide Studies* 6, no. 1 (1991): 1–16.

Parry, Albert. *Garretts and Pretenders: A History of Bohemianism in America*. New York: Covici, Friede, 1933.

Payne, Stanley G. *Fascism: Comparison and Definition*. Madison: University of Wisconsin Press, 1980.

Pells, Richard H. *Radical Visions and American Dreams: Culture and Social Thought in the Depression Years*. Middletown, Conn.: Wesleyan University Press, 1984.

Penkower, Monty Noam. "Believe the Unbelievable!" *Midstream* 27, no. 4 (April 1981): 31–37.

Penkower, Monty Noam. "In Dramatic Dissent: The Bergson Boys." *American Jewish History* 70, no. 3 (March 1981): 281–309.

Perry, Douglas. *The Girls of Murder City: Fame, Lust, and the Beautiful Killers Who Inspired Chicago*. New York: Viking, 2010.

Poe, Edgar Allan. *Great Short Works of Edgar Allan Poe*. New York: Harper & Row, 1970.

Pound, Ezra. *The Letters of Ezra Pound, 1907–1941*. New York: Harcourt, Brace, 1950.

Prager, Ted, and Larry Craft. *Hoodlums: New York*. New York: Retail Distributors, 1959.

Presner, Todd Samuel. *Muscular Judaism: The Jewish Body and the Politics of Regeneration*. Routledge Jewish Studies. London: Routledge, 2007.

Rafaeli, Alex. *Dream and Action: The Story of My Life*. Jerusalem: A. Rafaeli, 1993.

Raider, Mark A. "'Irresponsible, Undisciplined Opposition': Ben Halpern on the Bergson Group and Jewish Terrorism in Pre-state Palestine." *American Jewish History* 92, no. 3 (September 2004): 313–60.

Rapoport, Louis. *Shake Heaven and Earth: Peter Bergson and the Struggle to Rescue the Jews of Europe*. Jerusalem: Gefen, 1999.

Ravitz, Abe C. "Ballyhoo, Gargoyles, and Firecrackers: Ben Hecht's Aesthetic Calliope." *Journal of Popular Culture* 1, no. 1 (June 1967): 37–51.

Redston, George. *The Conspiracy of Death*, with Kendell F. Crossen. Indianapolis: Bobbs-Merrill, 1965.

Rhodes, Chip. *Politics, Desire, and the Hollywood Novel*. Iowa City: University of Iowa Press, 2008.

Rideout, Walter B. *Sherwood Anderson: A Writer in America*. Madison: University of Wisconsin Press, 2006.

Robinson, Edward G. *All My Yesterdays: An Autobiography*. New York: Hawthorn Books, 1973.

Rockaway, Robert A. *But He Was Good to His Mother: The Lives and Crimes of Jewish Gangsters*. Jerusalem: Gefen, 2000.

Rollyson, Carl E. *Biography: A User's Guide*. Chicago: Ivan R. Dee, 2008.

Ronson, Jon. *The Psychopath Test: A Journey through the Madness Industry*. New York: Riverhead Books, 2011.

Rosemont, Franklin, ed. *The Rise and Fall of the Dil Pickle: Jazz-Age Chicago's Wildest and Most Outrageously Creative Hobohemian Nightspot*. Chicago: Charles H. Kerr, 2004.

Rosenbaum, Ron, ed. *The Secret Parts of Fortune: Three Decades of Intense Investigations and Edgy Enthusiasms*. New York: Random House, 2000.

Rosow, Eugene. *Born to Lose: The Gangster Film in America*. New York: Oxford University Press, 1978.

Roth, Jack J., ed. *World War I: A Turning Point in Modern History. Essays in the Significance of the War*. New York: Knopf, 1967.

Rubinstein, W. D. *The Myth of Rescue: Why the Democracies Could Not Have Saved More Jews from the Nazis*. London: Routledge, 1997.

Rudnick, Lois Palken. *Mabel Dodge Luhan: New Woman, New Worlds*. Albuquerque: University of New Mexico Press, 1984.

Ruth, David E. *Inventing the Public Enemy: The Gangster in American Culture, 1918–1934*. Chicago: University of Chicago Press, 1996.

Sachar, Howard Morley. *A History of Israel: From the Rise of Zionism to Our Time*. 3rd ed., rev. and updated. New York: Knopf, 2007.

Sand, George. *The George Sand-Gustave Flaubert Letters*. New York: Liveright, 1970.

Sandburg, Carl. *Chicago Poems*. New York: H. Holt, 1916.

Sayers, Michael, and Albert E. Kahn. *The Plot against the Peace: A Warning to the Nation!* New York: Dial, 1945.

Schudson, Michael. *Discovering the News: A Social History of American Newspapers*. New York: Basic Books, 1978.

Schumbacher, Claude, ed. *Staging the Holocaust: The Shoah in Drama and Performance*. Cambridge Studies in Modern Theatre. Cambridge: Cambridge University Press, 1998.

See, Carolyn Penelope. *The Hollywood Novel: An Historical and Critical Study*. Ann Arbor, Mich.: University Microfilms, 1976.

Segev, Tom. *One Palestine, Complete: Jews and Arabs under the British Mandate*. New York: Owl Books, 2001.

Seldes, Gilbert. *The Seven Lively Arts*. New York: Harper & Brothers, 1924.

Shechner, Mark. *After the Revolution: Studies in the Contemporary Jewish-American Imagination*. Bloomington: Indiana University Press, 1987.

Sherman, Stuart Pratt. *Critical Woodcuts*. New York: C. Scribner's Sons, 1926.

Shindler, Colin. *The Triumph of Military Zionism*. London: I. B. Tauris, 2006.

Skolnik, Fred, and Michael Berenbaum, eds. *Encyclopaedia Judaica*. 2nd ed. Detroit: Macmillan Reference USA in association with Keter, 2007.

Silver, Alain, and James Ursini, ed. *Gangster Film Reader*. Pompton Plains, N.J.: Limelight, 2007.

Simmel, Georg. *Sociology of Georg Simmel*. Edited and translated by Kurt H. Wolff. New York: Free Press, 1950.

Sims, Norman Howard. "The Chicago Style of Journalism." PhD diss., University of Illinois at Urbana-Champaign, 1979.

Sinclair, Upton. *The Brass Check: A Study of American Journalism*. Champaign: University of Illinois Press, 2002.

Sinyard, Neil. *Filming Literature: The Art of Screen Adaptation*. New York: St. Martin's, 1986.

Skloot, Robert. "*We Will Never Die*: The Success and Failure of a Holocaust Pageant." *Theatre Journal* 37, no. 2 (May 1985): 167–80.

Slater, Leonard. *The Pledge*. New York: Simon and Schuster, 1970.

Spinney, Robert G. *City of Big Shoulders: A History of Chicago*. DeKalb: Northern Illinois University Press, 2000.

Sproule, J. Michael. "Progressive Propaganda Critics and the Magic Bullet Myth." *Critical Studies in Mass Communication* 6, no. 3 (1989): 225–46.

Stansell, Christine. *American Moderns: Bohemian New York and the Creation of a New Century*. New York: Metropolitan Books, 2000.

Starrett, Vincent. *Born in a Bookshop: Chapters from the Chicago Renascence*. Norman: University of Oklahoma Press, 1965.

Steffens, Lincoln. *The Autobiography of Lincoln Steffens*. New York: Harcourt, Brace, 1931.

Sternhell, Ze'ev. *The Birth of Fascist Ideology: From Cultural Rebellion to Political Revolution*. Princeton, N.J.: Princeton University Press, 1994.

Stevens, Steve. *King of the Sunset Strip: Hangin' with Mickey Cohen and the Hollywood Mob*. With Craig Lockwood. Nashville, Tenn.: Cumberland House, 2006. Kindle.

Strausbaugh, John. *The Village: 400 Years of Beats and Bohemians, Radicals and Rogues, a History of Greenwich Village*. New York: Ecco, 2013.

Sullivan, Edward Dean. *Chicago Surrenders*. New York: Vanguard, 1930.

Sullivan, Edward Dean. *Rattling the Cup on Chicago Crime*. New York: Vanguard, 1929.

Sutton, Antony C. *Wall Street and the Rise of Hitler*. Seal Beach, Calif.: '76 Press, 1976.

Swanberg, W. A. *Citizen Hearst: A Biography of William Randolph Hearst*. New York: Scribner, 1961.

Teachout, Terry. *The Skeptic: A Life of H. L. Mencken*. New York: HarperCollins, 2002.

Tereba, Tere. *Mickey Cohen: The Life and Crimes of L.A.'s Notorious Mobster.* Toronto: ECW Press, 2012.

Trank, Richard, dir. *Against the Tide.* Written by Marvin Hier and Richard Trank. Los Angeles: Moriah Films, 2008.

Troy, Gilad E. "Ben Hecht: From Literary Gadfly to Political Activist." Bachelor's thesis, Harvard University, 1982.

Troy, Gilad E. "From Literary Gadfly to Political Activist: The Political Transformation of Ben Hecht." *Journal of Ecumenical Studies* 40, no. 4 (Fall 2003): 431–49.

Troy, William. "The Story of the Little Magazines." *Bookman* 70 (1930): 476–81.

Truffaut, François. *Hitchcock.* Rev. ed. New York: Simon and Schuster, 1985.

Urofsky, Melvin I. *American Zionism from Herzl to the Holocaust.* Garden City, N.Y.: Anchor, 1975.

Urofsky, Melvin I. *A Voice That Spoke for Justice: The Life and Times of Stephen S. Wise.* SUNY Series in Modern Jewish History. Albany: State University of New York Press, 1982.

Van Paassen, Pierre, and James Waterman Wise, eds. *Nazism: An Assault on Civilization.* New York: H. Smith and R. Haas, 1934.

Vorse, Mary Heaton. *A Footnote to Folly: Reminiscences of Mary Heaton Vorse.* Signal Lives. New York: Arno, 1980.

Wald, Alan M. *The New York Intellectuals: The Rise and Decline of the Anti-Stalinist Left from the 1930s to the 1980s.* Chapel Hill: University of North Carolina Press, 1987.

Ward, Nathan. *Dark Harbor: The War for the New York Waterfront.* New York: Farrar, Straus and Giroux, 2010.

Warshow, Robert. *The Immediate Experience; Movies, Comics, Theatre and Other Aspects of Popular Culture.* New York: Atheneum, 1971.

Watson, Bruce. *Bread and Roses: Mills, Migrants, and the Struggle for the American Dream.* New York: Viking, 2005.

Weber, Donald. *Haunted in the New World: Jewish American Culture from Cahan to the Goldbergs.* Jewish Literature and Culture. Bloomington: Indiana University Press, 2005.

Weinbaum, Laurence. *A Marriage of Convenience: The New Zionist Organization and the Polish Government, 1936–1939.* Boulder, Colo.: East European Monographs, 1993.

Weingarten, Marc. *The Gang That Wouldn't Write Straight: Wolfe, Thompson, Didion, and the New Journalism Revolution.* New York: Crown, 2006.

Weiss, Jeffrey, and Craig Weiss. *I Am My Brother's Keeper: American Volunteers in Israel's War for Independence, 1947–1949.* Atglen, Pa.: Schiffer Military History, 1998.

Weizmann, Chaim. *Trial and Error.* New York: Harper, 1949.

Wendt, Lloyd. *Lords of the Levee: The Story of Bathhouse John and Hinky Dink.* Indianapolis: Bobbs-Merrill, 1943.

Wetzsteon, Ross. *Republic of Dreams: Greenwich Village. The American Bohemia, 1910–1960*. New York: Simon and Schuster, 2002.

Whitfield, Stephen J. *In Search of American Jewish Culture*. Hanover, N.H.: University Press of New England for Brandeis University Press, 1999.

Whitfield, Stephen J. "The Politics of Pageantry, 1936–1946." *American Jewish History* 84, no. 3 (1996): 221–51.

Williams, William Carlos. *Imaginations*. New York: New Directions, 1971.

Williams, William Carlos. *The Selected Letters of William Carlos Williams*. New York: New Directions, 1984.

Wilson, Edmund. *Classics and Commercials: A Literary Chronicle of the Forties*. New York: Vintage Books, 1950.

Wise, Stephen S. *Challenging Years: The Autobiography of Stephen Wise*. New York: Putnam, 1949.

Wolfe, Tom. *The New Journalism*. New York: Harper & Row, 1973.

Wyman, David S. *The Abandonment of the Jews: America and the Holocaust, 1941–1945*. New York: Pantheon Books, 1984.

Wyman, David S., and Rafael Medoff. *A Race against Death: Peter Bergson, America, and the Holocaust*. New York: New Press, 2002.

Zaar, Isaac. *Rescue and Liberation: America's Part in the Birth of Israel*. New York: Bloch, 1954.

Zangwill, Israel. *The Melting-Pot: A Drama in Four Acts*. New York: Macmillan, 1909.

Zelizer, Barbie. "History and Journalism." In *Taking Journalism Seriously: News and the Academy*, 80–110. Thousand Oaks, Calif.: Sage, 2004.

Ziff, Larzer. *The American 1890s: Life and Times of a Lost Generation*. New York: Viking, 1968.

Notes

Introduction

1. E.g., Ben Hecht, "Letter to the Terrorists of Palestine," *New York Herald Tribune*, May 15, 1947, 17. Historian Rafael Medoff writes that the advertisement ran once in the *Herald Tribune* and twice in the *New York Post*. In his autobiography, Hecht reports that it ran in some fifteen newspapers and was reprinted as a news story in South America and Europe. Rafael Medoff, *Militant Zionism in America: The Rise and Impact of the Jabotinsky Movement in the United States, 1926–1948* (Tuscaloosa: University of Alabama Press, 2002), 197; and Hecht, *A Child of the Century* (New York: Simon and Schuster, 1954), 617. *A Child of the Century* was later republished by Primus in 1985.
2. For summaries of the response in the press, see Gilad E. Troy, "Ben Hecht: From Literary Gadfly to Political Activist" (bachelor's thesis, Harvard University, 1982), 111–15; Doug Fetherling, *The Five Lives of Ben Hecht* (Toronto: Lester and Orpen, 1977), 134; and Jeffrey Brown Martin, *Ben Hecht, Hollywood Screenwriter*, Studies in Cinema 27 (Ann Arbor, Mich.: UMI Research Press, 1985), 158–59.
3. Atay Citron describes large street rallies organized by Zionists in Philadelphia to picket Hecht's play *A Flag Is Born*. Citron, "Ben Hecht's Pageant-Drama: *A Flag Is Born*," in *Staging the Holocaust: The Shoah in Drama and Performance*, ed. Claude Schumacher, Cambridge Studies in Modern Theatre (Cambridge: Cambridge University Press, 1998), 91.
4. *Wikipedia*, s.v. "*The Front Page*," last updated November 25, 2010, http://en.wikipedia.org/wiki/The _Front_Page; Walter Kerr, "After 41 Years, It's Still Page One," *New York Times*, May 25, 1969; and Robert Schmuhl, "*The Front Page* Turns 75," *Poynter*, August 6, 2003, https://www.poynter.org/news/front-page-turns-75.

5. For Hecht's claim to have invented the gangster movie, see Hecht, *Child*, 479. On *Underworld* as the movie that created the gangster genre, see Carlos Clarens, *Crime Movies: From Griffith to* The Godfather *and Beyond* (New York: Norton, 1980), 15, 31–32, 34–38, 42–47, 51–53; and Eugene Rosow, *Born to Lose: The Gangster Film in America* (New York: Oxford University Press, 1978), 124. On *Scarface*, see Clarens, *Crime Movies*, 82–83. On the screwball comedy, see Andrew Sarris, "The Sex Comedy without Sex," *American Film* 3 (March 1978): 8, 14; William MacAdams, *Ben Hecht: The Man behind the Legend* (New York: Scribner, 1990), 7; and Martin, *Ben Hecht*. On writing *Gone with the Wind*, see Hecht, *Child*, 488–89; and MacAdams, *Man behind the Legend*, 7, 199–201.

6. Pauline Kael, "Bonnie and Clyde," *New Yorker*, October 21, 1967, 166–67.

7. William MacAdams offers the most careful estimate of Hecht's screen credits and actual contributions. See the interview with MacAdams in Ron Grossman, "Reporter, Film Writer, Spellbinder," *Chicago Tribune*, June 12, 1990, http://www.chicagotribune.com/news/ct-xpm-1990-06-12 -9002170872-story.html; and MacAdams's filmography and bibliography in *Man behind the Legend*, 299–357. See also see Robert Schmuhl, "History, Fantasy, Memory: Ben Hecht and a Chicago Hanging," *Illinois Historical Journal* 83 (Autumn 1990): 147.

8. Ben Hecht, "The Little Candle," in *A Book of Miracles* (New York: Viking), 23–53; and Hecht, *Child*, 380, 517–18. Isaac Deutscher may have coined the term "non-Jewish Jew" in his famous essay, but Hecht was writing about the "un-Jewish Jew" at least as early as *A Guide for the Bedevilled* in 1944. Isaac Deutscher, "The Non-Jewish Jew," in *The Non-Jewish and Other Essays* (New York: Oxford, 1968); and Hecht, *A Guide for the Bedevilled* (New York: Charles Scribner's Sons, 1944), 77, 158. Hecht used the exact same phrase a decade later in *A Child of the Century*, 380, 381, 577.

9. Elizabeth Borgwardt, *A New Deal for the World: America's Vision for Human Rights* (Cambridge, Mass.: Belknap Press of Harvard University Press, 2005), 53–56. Borgwardt observes that "'human rights' was not a new term born of World War II, but during this period it became a shorthand readily understood by educated readers and influential commentators, both in the United States and abroad" (53). She writes that it had previously been used as a variant of *rights of man*, and sometimes as a synonym for *civil rights*, but over the war years it came to apply to "the so-called fundamental freedoms" (53) denied by the totalitarian powers of the day. She traces its use and meaning and connects it with Roosevelt's New Deal. For a listing of the postwar institutions and tenets of international law that she sees as multilateralist expressions of the New Deal, see *New Deal*, 71. For her encapsulation of the fundamental philosophical linkages, see *New Deal*, 74–75.

10. Hecht, *Child*, 5.

11. Walter Lippmann, *Public Opinion* (New York: Harcourt, Brace, 1922); Walter Lippmann, *The Phantom Public* (New York: Harcourt, Brace, 1925); and H. L. Mencken, *Notes on Democracy* (New York: Knopf, 1926).

12. Walter Lippmann, *Liberty and the News* (New York: Harcourt, Brace and Howe, 1920), 47.
13. Isaiah Berlin, *Freedom and Its Betrayal: Six Enemies of Human Liberty* (Princeton, N.J.: Princeton University Press, 2002), 134.
14. Ben Hecht, "Champion in Chains," *Esquire*, October 1942, 36.
15. See, for example, Hecht, "Champion in Chains," 36, 168–69; and Hecht, "Letter to the Terrorists."
16. "Memorandum for Mr. Ladd: Information Furnished by Informants and Developed in Connection with the Crime Survey Program," Federal Bureau of Investigation, "Meyer Harris Cohen," file 62-HQ-89947, p. 88; and Steve Stevens, *King of the Sunset Strip: Hangin' with Mickey Cohen and the Hollywood Mob*, with Craig Lockwood (Nashville, Tenn.: Cumberland House, 2006), Kindle.
17. See, for example, Ben Halpern's accusations against the Irgun and the Stern Gang for "terrorism against the Jewish community," as well as for robbery. Mark A. Raider, "'Irresponsible, Undisciplined Opposition': Ben Halpern on the Bergson Group and Jewish Terrorism in Pre-state Palestine," *American Jewish History* 92, no. 3 (September 2004): 325–30. A December 1948 letter to the *New York Times* signed by Hannah Arendt, Albert Einstein, and other prominent Jews that protested Menachem Begin's visit to America accused the Irgun of persecuting the Jewish community of Palestine: "By gangster methods, beatings, window-smashing and wide-spread robberies, the terrorists intimidated the population and exacted a heavy tribute." "New Palestine Party Visit of Menachem Begin and Aims of Political Movement Discussed," *New York Times*, December 4, 1948; see also Tom Segev, *One Palestine, Complete: Jews and Arabs under the British Mandate* (New York: Owl Books, 2001), 456.
18. Robert A. Rockaway offers perhaps the most comprehensive account of the fund-raising and smuggling efforts by Cohen, Lansky, Siegel, and other underworld figures and has gone to the greatest lengths to sort out fact from fiction. See Rockaway, *But He Was Good to His Mother: The Lives and Crimes of Jewish Gangsters* (Jerusalem: Gefen, 2000), 244–52. See also Hecht, *Child*, 610–13; *Mickey Cohen, in My Own Words: The Underworld Autobiography of Michael Mickey Cohen, as Told to John Peer Nugent* (Englewood Cliffs, N.J.: Prentice-Hall, 1975), 92–93; and Medoff, *Militant Zionism*, 151. A seminal book on American arms smuggling for the Jews in Palestine is Leonard Slater's *The Pledge* (New York: Simon and Schuster, 1970).

Prelude

1. Hecht, *Guide for the Bedevilled*, 61.
2. Ben Hecht, "Go, Scholar-Gypsy!," in *1001 Afternoons in New York* (New York: Viking, 1941), 38, 39, 40.

3. Hecht, "Go, Scholar-Gypsy!," 40.
4. Ben Hecht, "U.S. World War I Draft Registration Cards, 1917–1918," Cook County, Illinois, Draft Board: 14, NARA microfilm publication M1509, Family History Library microfilm 1,439,759, National Archives and Records Administration (NARA), Washington, D.C.; Ben Hecht, "Passport Applications, January 2, 1906–March 31, 1925," roll 640—Certificates: 48250–48449, 23 November 1918–25 November 1918, NARA, Washington, D.C. (both records accessed via Ancestry.com, October 23, 2016); Peter Hecht to Stephen Fuller [aka William MacAdams], n.d., MacAdams Collection, folder 141, Ben Hecht Papers, Newberry Library (hereafter BHPNL), Chicago, pp. 1 and 4 of a ten-page letter; and "Ben Hecht, 70, Dies at His Home Here," *New York Times*, April 19, 1964, 1, 84. Accounts differ on the year of Hecht's birth. Although his *New York Times* obituary, Fetherling's *Five Lives* biography, and even Hecht's own headstone at the Oak Hill Cemetery in Nyack, New York, state that he was born in 1894, the 1917 draft registration card and 1918 passport application cited here, as well as his brother's letter, offer evidence that he was born the previous year. Peter Hecht estimates that the family arrived in Racine, Wisconsin, in 1903, but not all the dates and figures he gives seem to be accurate—for example, he states that his parents arrived in America in 1878, when his father was fourteen and his mother was twelve. The Hechts show up in *Wright's Racine City Directory* in 1906, when Joseph Hecht is listed as the proprietor of the Paris Fashion at 505 Main St., president of Ladies' Garment Manufacturing Co., and resident of 838 Lake Ave. It's possible Joseph provided this as his office address, but more likely the Lake Avenue address was also the site of his "factory." This is consistent with how production was done in the extremely tight spaces of the residences in the Lower East Side tenements. *Wright's Racine City Directory* (Milwaukee, Wis.: Alfred G. Wright, 1906), 247.
5. Hecht, *Guide for the Bedevilled*, 64.
6. Joseph Hecht, 1900 Census, Bronx, New York, New York, roll 1124, p. 13B, Enumeration District 0970, FHL microfilm 1241124, original source: T623, 1854 rolls, U.S. Bureau of the Census, *Twelfth Census of the United States*, NARA, Washington, D.C.; Joseph Hecht, 1920 Census, Chicago Ward 25, Illinois, roll T625_342, p. 15A, Enumeration District 1451, image 341, original source: T625, 2076 rolls, U.S. Bureau of the Census, *Fourteenth Census of the United States*, NARA, Washington, D.C.; and Henry L. Feingold, *Zion in America: The Jewish Experience from Colonial Times to the Present* (New York: Hippocrene Books, 1974), 129–30. In the 1900 census, the Hechts reported that Sarah had arrived in 1885, and Joseph in 1886, but twenty years later they reported that she had arrived in 1883, and he in 1885. Hecht wrote in *A Guide for the Bedevilled* (p. 62) that he spoke Yiddish almost as fluently as English at eight years of age. Feingold, who observes that the Lower East Side was one of the most densely populated places in the world, characterized it as "the *shtetl* in macrocosm" (129).

7. Peter Hecht to Fuller [MacAdams], n.d., circa spring 1976, MacAdams Collection, BHPNL, p. 4 of a ten-page letter. Peter Hecht said his father was a cloth cutter, while according to Ben he worked at "lowly tailoring tasks" before becoming a designer. See Hecht, *Child*, 65. For the long workdays, see Feingold, *Zion in America*, 60.

8. Hecht, *Child*, 80–85.

9. Hecht, *Child*, 85.

10. Hecht, *Child*, 81–82, 85.

11. Sister Honor Murphy, "Former Classmates in Racine Recall Ben Hecht," *Racine (Wis.) Journal-Times*, February 4, 1973; Marjorie Oden, "In Racine's Hall of Fame," *Racine (Wis.) Journal-Times*, April 30, 1953, 10. An undated letter to the *Milwaukee Journal* from one of Hecht's high school English teachers, Lulu M. Dysart, quotes verse that he wrote as advertising copy: "It is better by far / to smoke a cigar / and smoke it today / than to lead a whole life / of virtuous strife / and then smoke it anyway." The articles were provided by the Racine Heritage Museum.

12. Hecht, *Child*, 64–66.

13. Peter Hecht to Fuller [MacAdams], n.d., circa spring 1976, MacAdams Collection, BHPNL, p. 1 of an eight-page letter.

14. Peter Hecht to Fuller [MacAdams], n.d., circa spring 1976, MacAdams Collection, BHPNL, p. 5 of a twelve-page letter; and Hecht, *Child*, 65.

15. Peter Hecht to Fuller [MacAdams], n.d., MacAdams Collection, BHPNL, p. 2 of an eight-page letter; Hecht, *Child*, 62; Dean Jensen, "W. C. Coup: The Brains behind Barnum," in *The Biggest, the Smallest, the Longest, the Shortest: A Chronicle of the American Circus from Its Heartland* (Madison, Wis.: Wisconsin House Book Publishers, 1975), 32–33; Stuart Thayer and William L. Slout, "Prelude to Barnum, the Coup and Castello Show, 1870," in *Grand Entree: The Birth of the Greatest Show on Earth, 1870–1875* (San Bernardino, Calif.: Borgo, 1998), 1–14; and John Springhall, "The Emergence of the Railroad Circus," in *The Genesis of Mass Culture: Show Business Live in America, 1840 to 1940* (New York: Palgrave Macmillan, 2008), 85–87.

16. Jensen, "W. C. Coup," 43–45; Thayer and Slout, "P. T. Barnum's Great Traveling Exposition and World's Fair," in *Grand Entrée*, 33; Dorothy Osborne, "827 Lake Avenue," *Preservation-Racine, Inc. Newsletter*, Summer 1986; and Hecht, *Child*, 62. It is unclear when Frances Castello sold the house at 827 Lake Avenue, but as early as 1884, the next owner, W. T. Bull, is reported hosting a party there: "Social and Personal," *Journal Times* (Racine, Wis.), April 23, 1884, 3. Accounts differ on when Castello died. Jensen says that he died in 1907, whereas Slout writes that Castello died of Bright's disease in Rochester, New York, on July 27, 1909. See William L. Slout, *Olympians of the Sawdust Circle: A Biographical Dictionary of the Nineteenth Century Circus* (San Bernardino, Calif.: Borgo, 1998), 46–47.

17. Hecht, *Child*, 62–63; "Will Put Circus on Road/Harry Castello Gets Response to 'Ad,'" *Journal Times* (Racine, Wis.), 3; "First Night Tents Were Dry/Harry

Castello Writes the Rainy Weather Has Been Constant Attendant," *Journal Times* (Racine, Wis.), June 4, 1907, 9; "This Has Been a Bad Season for Circuses/ Several of the Smaller Circuses, Including the Castello Show, Goes on Financial Rocks," *Appleton (Wis.) Post*, October 24, 1907, 4. See also Peter Hecht to Fuller [MacAdams], n.d., MacAdams Collection, BHPNL, pp. 2–3 of an eight-page letter. There is an advertisement for a "Colossal Circus!!! A Grand Thrilling, Throbbing Spectacle of More Than Oriental Splendor" in the 1909 Racine high school yearbook, to be held at the YWCA ("All Girls Invited").

18. Hecht, *Child*, 23. See also Peter Hecht to Fuller [MacAdams], n.d., MacAdams Collection, BHPNL, p. 4 of a twelve-page letter.
19. Peter Hecht to Fuller [MacAdams], n.d., MacAdams Collection, BHPNL, p. 4 of a twelve-page letter; and Hecht, *Child*, 23.
20. Hecht, *Guide for the Bedevilled*, 236–38.
21. Hecht, *Child*, 85–109.
22. Hecht, *Child*, 96.
23. Hecht, *Child*, 108.
24. Hecht, *Child*, 85–86.
25. Ben Hecht, "The Vanished World of Sholom Alecheim: Tales of Capering Laughter" (review of *The Old Country*, by Sholom Aleichem), *New York Times*, July 7, 1946, 5, 22.
26. Hecht, *Guide for the Bedevilled*, 5, 61; Meyer Levin, *In Search: An Autobiography* (New York: Horizon, 1950), 306; and Hecht, "Jewish Situation Less Complex," *Los Angeles Times*, March 11, 1943, 4.
27. Hecht, *Child*, 109; and Georg Simmel, "The Stranger," in *The Sociology of Georg Simmel*, ed. and trans. Kurt H. Wolff (New York: Free Press, 1950), 403–8.

Part I

1. Hecht, *Child*, 115–17.
2. Hecht, *Child*, 117, 119.
3. The phrase "born perversely," attributed to Hecht, comes from Harry Hansen, *Midwest Portraits: A Book of Memories and Friendships* (New York: Harcourt, Brace, 1923), 320. Hansen quotes it from his copy of a paragraph that Hecht wrote about himself, originally requested by another critic or editor.
4. Norman Howard Sims, "The Chicago Style of Journalism" (PhD diss., University of Illinois at Urbana-Champaign, 1979), 197, 24, 261–66; and Bruce J. Evensen, "Journalism's Struggle over Ethics and Professionalism during America's Jazz Age," *Journalism History* 16, nos. 3–4 (Autumn-Winter 1989): 54–63.
5. Ben Hecht and Charles MacArthur, *The Front Page* (New York: Covici-Friede, 1928), 28. Near the end of act 2, editor Walter Burns barks over the phone: "Duffy! Send down word to Butch McGuirk I want ten huskies from the circulation department to lam right over here."

6. Wayne Andrews, *Battle for Chicago* (New York: Harcourt, 1946), 232. The casualty figure comes from the 1921 testimony of *Chicago Tribune* publisher Robert Rutherford "The Colonel" McCormick, when his paper was sued by the *Journal of Commerce* for obstructing newsstand sales. Max Annenberg also gave vivid testimony. See *Battle for Chicago*, 333–34, citing *Transcript of Record, Journal of Commerce Publ'g Co. v. Tribune Co.*, 286 F.111 (7th Cir. 1922) (No. 3116). The *Daily Socialist* and *Daily World* offered the only immediate accounts of the violence, but none of their articles include a grand total of the deaths. John Cooney has pointed out that McCormick's figure refers to newsboys; there is no estimate of the number of street soldiers killed. Cooney, *The Annenbergs: The Salvaging of a Tainted Dynasty* (New York: Simon and Schuster, 1982), 37. After the scandal that erupted over the mob execution of *Tribune* reporter Jake Lingle, McCormick denied that his paper had been involved in the circulation war. Andrews, *Battle for Chicago*, 285. On Lingle and McCormick's denial, see George W. Hilton, ed., *The Front Page: From Theater to Reality*, The Art of Theater Series (Hanover, N.H.: Smith & Kraus, 2002), 68n26.

7. For the earliest and most detailed accounts, see Ferdinand Lundberg, *Imperial Hearst: A Social Biography* (New York: Modern Library, 1936), 151–64, 391; Elizabeth Dewey Johns, "Chicago's Papers and the News" (PhD diss., University of Chicago, 1942), 2–54; and Andrews, *Battle for Chicago*, 232–41, 262, 285–86. See also W. A. Swanberg, "The .38 Caliber Circulation Drive," in *Citizen Hearst: A Biography of William Randolph Hearst* (New York: Scribner, 1961), 270–71, 274; and Stephen Longstreet, *Chicago, 1860–1919* (New York: McKay, 1973), 240, 454–56. For accounts of the newspaper war in memoirs, see Burton Rascoe, *Before I Forget* (Garden City, N.Y.: Doubleday, Doran, 1937), 268–76; George Murray, *The Madhouse on Madison Street* (Chicago: Follett, 1965), 41–54; and Vincent Starrett, *Born in a Bookshop: Chapters from the Chicago Renascence* (Norman: University of Oklahoma Press, 1965), 78. Describing the growth of protection rackets after the end of the circulation war, Rascoe explains in detail how "out of the Hearst publishers hiring the Annenbergs and their gunmen and sluggers to cripple competition in the newspaper sales, grew the worst reign of lawlessness in Chicago that any city has ever known" (271). For a subsequent look back by a Chicago paper, see Steve Mills, "Vending Violence in a '.38-Caliber Circulation Drive,'" *Chicago Tribune*, June 8, 1997. *Tribune* editor James Keeley provided a detailed description of the circulation war to a Senate committee at hearings in Chicago on July 26, 1911. See "Election of William Lorimer, Senator from Illinois, hearings 9 vols.," S. Doc. No. 484, Committee on Privileges and Elections, 62nd Congress, 2nd session, April 12, 1912, S2054–6, 2072–74.

8. The quotation "reign of terror" is from Lundberg, *Imperial Hearst*, 154.

9. Dewey, in Molly Cochran, ed., *The Cambridge Companion to Dewey* (Cambridge: Cambridge University Press, 2010), 26, quoted in Matthew C. Ehrlich's

chapter on *The Front Page* in *Journalism in the Movies*, History of Communication (Urbana: University of Illinois Press, 2004), 24.

10. Ehrlich, *Journalism in the Movies*, 22; and Wayne Klatt, *Chicago Journalism: A History* (Jefferson, N.C.: McFarland, 2009), 77. With the launch of Hearst's *Chicago Morning American* on May 2, 1902, there were ten dailies in town. When the full-blown war erupted in 1910, there were eight papers. By the time it was over, there were only six.

11. Klatt, *Chicago Journalism*, 72–74, 83.

12. Fetherling, *Five Lives*, 21.

13. Hecht, *Child*, 156.

Chapter 1

1. Hecht and MacArthur, *Front Page*, 40–41.

2. Quoted in Eddie Doherty, *Gall and Honey: The Story of a Newspaperman* (New York: Sheed & Ward, 1941), 46, https://babel.hathitrust.org/cgi/pt?id=ucl .$b112728;view=1up;seq=50.

3. George Murray's *The Madhouse on Madison Street* is typical of these memoirs. In his brief acknowledgments, Murray explained, "Most of my material came by word of mouth, and was checked for dates and details against old files and various newspapers. It would be impossible to name all the storytellers, but Harry Romanoff, John Dienhart, and Edward (Dynamite) Sokol cannot be overlooked" (vi). In another memoir, William T. Moore introduces an anecdote by debating whom to credit as the original storyteller, Walter Howey or his protégé, Frank Carson. W. Moore, *Dateline Chicago: A Veteran Newsman Recalls Its Heyday* (New York: Taplinger, 1973), 116.

4. Hecht, *Child*, 123–29, 132–36; and Samuels, quoted in MacAdams, *Man behind the Legend*, 14.

5. *Wikipedia*, s.v. "Charles Samuels," last updated October 4, 2010, http://en.wiki pedia.org/wiki/Charles_Samuels.

6. Klatt, *Chicago Journalism*, 1. Hecht's flair for self-invention was evident at least as early as 1922, in the publicity for his first book, *Erik Dorn*. An interview with the New York *Morning Telegraph* seems to corroborate his accounts in *A Child of the Century* of early careers as a violinist, trapeze artist, and newspaper picture thief, except that he told the *Telegraph* that he had played the violin while standing on his head, shipped himself back by freight from his circus adventures, and later talked his way out of being shot at sunrise while a foreign correspondent in Berlin. Roy L. McCardell, "Ben Hecht—Literary Huck Finn," *Morning Telegraph* (New York), April 30, 1922, 1.

7. Theodore Dreiser, *Newspaper Days*, 7th ed. (New York: H. Liveright, 1931), 153–54; and Starrett, *Born in a Bookshop*, 75, 79–80. Starrett started as a picture chaser for *Inter-Ocean* in 1906. Further evidence that Hecht's account has a basis in fact is provided by a 1933 James Cagney film, *Picture Snatcher*,

adapted from a story by Danny Ahern (sometimes spelled Ahearn), a pulp writer and gangster who ran with Meyer Lansky and Bugsy Siegel. See "Picture Snatcher," moviediva, film curator at North Carolina Museum of Art, revised April 2005, http://www.moviediva.com/MD_root/review pages/MDPictureSnatcher.htm; and Jay Robert Nash, *The Great Pictorial History of World Crime* (Wilmette, Ill.: History, 2004), 571, 572.

8. Sims, "Chicago Style of Journalism," 34–39.

9. Klatt, *Chicago Journalism*, 4; Hecht, *Child*, 142–46; and Starrett, *Born in a Bookshop*, 73.

10. Michael Schudson, *Discovering the News: A Social History of American Newspapers* (New York: Basic Books, 1978), 69.

11. Sims, "Chicago Style of Journalism," 260.

12. Alfred Lawrence Lorenz, "The Whitechapel Club: Defining Chicago's Newspapermen in the 1890s," *American Journalism* 15, no. 1 (1998): 85. See also Sims, "Chicago Style of Journalism," 216–17, 219; and Richard Digby-Junger, "The Chicago Press Club: The Scoop behind the Front Page," *Chicago History* 27, no. 3 (Winter 1998–99): 42–53.

13. Lorenz, "Whitechapel Club," 85–86; see also Sims, "Chicago Style of Journalism," 220–21. There are some minor discrepancies between Lorenz's and Sims's accounts. According to Sims, the club was formed in 1887, not in the summer of 1889. Lorenz describes a pane of stained glass at the transom with a skull and crossbones and the legend: "I, too, have lived in Arcady." Sims relates that in later years there was a ceremonial goblet in the upstairs bar—the skull of a well-known prostitute who had worked the docks, engraved with the inscription, "I, too was born in Arcadia." Lorenz drew from "Whitechapel Nights," a thirty-part series by Charles H. Dennis, who was Hecht's supervisor when Hecht left the *Journal* for the *Daily News*. Dennis was not a member himself but had been city editor at the *Morning News* when the club started.

14. On Opie Read and the Whitechapel style, see Opie Read, *I Remember* (New York: Richard R. Smith, 1930), 207, quoted in Sims, "Chicago Style of Journalism," 217, 242–46; Ziff's words are from Larzer Ziff, *The American 1890s: Life and Times of a Lost Generation* (New York: Viking, 1968), 165.

15. Martin Mayer, *Making News* (Garden City, N.Y.: Doubleday, 1987), 46; and A. A. Dornfeld, *Behind the Front Page: The Story of the City News Bureau of Chicago* (Chicago: Academy Chicago, 1983), xiii.

16. On the commercial imperative of accuracy, see Dornfeld, *Behind the Front Page*, 51–52, 69–71; on twentieth-century challenges, pneumatic tubes, and legmen, see Dornfeld, *Behind the Front Page*, 27–28, 55–61, 74, 89, 90. *Tribune* writer Bill Granger vividly recalled that decades later, when he was a copy boy at the *Daily News*, violent summer thunderstorms would flood the tube system with river water, which would then gush into the city room, creating a soggy, chaotic mess. The City News Bureau finally stopped using the tubes in 1961. Granger, "Sitting on a Big Story at the Daily News," *Chicago*

Tribune, April 16, 1992, http://articles.chicagotribune.com/1992-04-16
/features/9202030927_1_chicago-tunnel-tube-chicago-river.

17. Dreiser, *Newspaper Days*, 148, 152–53.

18. On sending rival reporters on wild goose chases, see Dornfeld, *Behind the Front Page*, 39. On the Harry Romanoff anecdote and his fame in *Collier's*, see Dornfeld, *Behind the Front Page*, 119–20; and United Press International, "Harry J. Romanoff, Chicago Newsman," *New York Times*, December 19, 1970. On Frank Carson's staged collision and the Ruth Randall diary, see Murray, *Madhouse*, 189; and Klatt, *Chicago Journalism*, 125; for background on the Ruth Randall story, see Hilton, *From Theater to Reality*, 153–55n170.

19. On Wright's eavesdropping, see Dornfeld, *Behind the Front Page*, 137; and on Smith's method, see Klatt, *Chicago Journalism*, 68, 131–32.

20. Starrett, *Born in a Bookshop*, 101.

21. Jon Katz, "No News Is Good News," *Hotwired*, October 9, 1996, quoted in David T. Z. Mindich, *Just the Facts: How "Objectivity" Came to Define American Journalism* (New York: New York University Press, 1998), 1; Charles G. Ross, *The Writing of the News: A Handbook with Chapters on Newspaper Correspondence and Copy Reading* (New York: Henry Holt, 1911), 18, quoted in Mindich, *Just the Facts*, 116; and Fred Fedler, et al, *Reporting for the Media*, 10th ed. (New York: Oxford University Press, 2012), 56.

22. John J. McPhaul, *Deadlines and Monkeyshines: The Fabled World of Chicago Journalism* (Englewood Cliffs, N.J.: Prentice-Hall, 1962), 19; Murray, *Madhouse*, 105; on Buddy McHugh's career and reputation, see Dornfeld, *Behind the Front Page*, 133–34 (the quote from McHugh is on p. 134); on McHugh as the inspiration for Buddy McCue, see Hilton, *From Theater to Reality*, 43, 58–59n9; on Romanoff and the doll, see Hilton, *From Theater to Reality*, 152–53n169.

23. On the swearing in of reporter as deputies, see Dreiser, *Newspaper Days*, 77–78; on press cards provided by the police, see Klatt, *Chicago Journalism*, 119; on Carson and the arrest in Wisconsin, see May Mann, Going Hollywood, *Ogden (Utah) Standard-Examiner*, December 5, 1940, 9; "Muscle Journalist," obituary, *Time*, March 31, 1941, 40; and Murray, *Madhouse*, 194–201. According to May Mann's Going Hollywood column, Carson "kidnapped people, tapped wires . . . burglarized houses for evidence armed with phony warrants, strong-armed his way through impassable barriers by means of fake police badges, and generally practiced the type of headline-smashing journalism alongside of which Hecht and MacArthur's 'Front Page' seems like a vehicle for Donald Duck." True or not, Klatt, Murray, and others have relayed this information as history. Dreiser's first reporting job was with the *Globe*, owned by McDonald, who had established a gambling syndicate and kept the Democratic Party machine well oiled with graft. For the sake of a good story, reporters Finley Peter Dunne and George Weber got themselves sworn in as deputy sheriffs to raid McDonald's gambling joints. Since the *Globe* existed to maintain and protect McDonald's position, Dreiser and

other reporters were deployed to retaliate against the rival Republicans. Dreiser's target was the mock auction shops downtown, which operated with police collusion.

24. "Hearst's Howey," *Time*, June 17, 1935, 36; and E. Doherty, *Gall and Honey*, 65. Another Howey line was, "When a Hearst paper gets sick, they call me in, and I make it sicker."

25. Howey lost an eye when, according to Hecht, he passed out one evening while drunk at his desk and planted his face on a spindle. Howey himself boasted that he lost it in the circulation wars. It is more plausible that the injury occurred when some chemicals exploded during one of his experiments related to the news-related devices he invented, for which he secured several patents, including one for a system for transmitting images over the phone lines. Ben Hecht, *Charlie: The Improbable Life and Times of Charles MacArthur* (New York: Harper, 1957), 49–50; and Klatt, *Chicago Journalism*, 112. Hecht was supposed to have said you could always tell which eye was glass because it was the warmer of the two. Pauline Kael, *The Citizen Kane Book: Raising Kane* (Boston: Little, Brown, 1971), 19. A 1935 article in *Time* describes a handheld device with an electric eye on one side and a speaker on the other side. Once a photo was scanned by the eye, the device could be screwed onto a telephone receiver to transmit electronic signals, which could be turned into a printout. In other words, Howey invented the fax machine. "Hearst's Howey," *Time*, June 17, 1935, 36.

26. Quoted in "Walter C. Howey, Boston Editor, 72," *New York Times*, March 22, 1954. Hecht also describes Howey's blackmail in *Charlie*, 50.

27. Murray, *Madhouse*, 178.

28. Quoted in Murray, *Madhouse*, 3.

29. Christopher Ogden, *Legacy: A Biography of Moses and Walter Annenberg* (Boston: Little, Brown, 1999), 44–45; Lundberg, *Imperial Hearst*, 140; and Klatt, *Chicago Journalism*, 79. According to McPhaul, "figuratively, a *Journal* man would take a trolley to a crime scene and two Hearst men would pass him en route in a taxi." *Deadlines and Monkeyshines*, 113.

30. The number of Chicago dailies in 1900 is from Klatt, *Chicago Journalism*, 77, 83. On the rough handling of newsboys, see Joyce Milton, *The Yellow Kids: Foreign Correspondents in the Heyday of Yellow Journalism* (New York: Harper & Row, 1989), 43. Mickey Cohen's battles as a West Coast newsboy are discussed at the end of part 1 of this book and in more detail in part 4. An article on May 6, 1912, in the *Daily Socialist* noted Max Annenberg's "flaming red sweater" and "soft cap" pulled low over his brow; quoted in Lundberg, *Imperial Hearst*, 158–59.

31. Andrews, *Battle for Chicago*, 232–41; Lundberg, *Imperial Hearst*, 149–62; Murray, *Madhouse*, 41–54; and Ogden, *Legacy*, 41–56.

32. Quoted passages and summaries of the news stories from the *Daily Socialist* and *Daily World* appear in Lundberg, *Imperial Hearst*, 153–61; for the May 6, 1912, account of a newsdriver, see p. 158; for the fatal shooting of a streetcar

conductor and two passengers, quoted from the Chicago *World*, June 17, 1912, see p. 159; accounts of the July 29 Madison Street trolley shooting and the August 15 elevated train shooting (p. 161) also appear to be drawn from the *World*, though no dates for these reports are given. Other papers reported the violent incidents but attributed them to labor unrest. See, for example, "3 Shot, One Stabbed, in Strike Riot on Car," *Inter-Ocean* (Chicago, Ill.), June 16, 1912, 9. For the description of bloody newspapers and bodies in the river, see Rose Keefe, *Guns and Roses: The Untold Story of Dean O'Banion, Chicago's Big Shot before Al Capone* (Nashville, Tenn.: Cumberland House, 2003), 77.

33. *Illinois Crime Survey*, in Keefe, *Guns and Roses*, 118. See also Andrews, *Battle for Chicago*, 234, 238–39; Lundberg, *Imperial Hearst*, 153–54; Ogden, *Legacy*, 49; and Cooney, *Annenbergs*, 36. Max Annenberg testified that at the height of the circulation wars, the papers had a total of about sixty thugs on their payrolls. Both Enright and Stevens were referred to in the press as the "dean of Chicago gunmen." "Moss Enright Slain in Labor War, Tim Murphy Held for Quiz," *Chicago Tribune*, February 4, 1920, 1; and "Chicago Gangster Defies Tradition, Dies of Pneumonia," *Decatur (Ill.) Evening Herald*, February 16, 1931, 1. In *A Child of the Century*, Hecht recounts being confronted in the middle of the night by two of Al Capone's hoods about his script for *Scarface*. Hecht assured them, "I don't even know Al," and then warmed them up by telling them it was about some of the gangsters he knew from years back. "I also knew Mossy Enright and Pete Gentleman," he said. Hecht, *Child*, 486–87.

34. Lundberg, *Imperial Hearst*, 162–63. Lundberg relates that O'Banion worked as "chief circulation agent" from 1917 to 1922, whereas Keefe, in *Guns and Roses*, has him working as circulation agent from 1910 to 1920. Both Hecht and MacArthur considered O'Banion a friend and told many fond tales about him, and he remained a favorite subject of Hecht's: up until weeks before Hecht's death, he was writing a Runyonesque musical with O'Banion as the hero, *Chicago Days*. For anecdotes about O'Banion, see Hecht, *Charlie*, 12–13, 20, 76. *Herald and Examiner* reporter Edward Dean Sullivan related a famous tale of how "circulation slugger" O'Banion provided a motorcycle chaperone and gallant, life-saving protection for coverage of a July 1919 race riot. Sullivan, *Rattling the Cup on Chicago Crime* (Freeport, N.Y.: Books for Libraries Press, 1971), 1–7.

35. Robert J. Casey, *Bob Casey's Grand Slam* (Indianapolis: Bobbs-Merrill, 1962), 22; and Pegler, quoted in Hecht, *Child*, 144.

Chapter 2

1. Dornfeld, *Behind the Front Page*, 139.

2. Ernest Hemingway, *A Moveable Feast: The Restored Edition* (New York: Scribner, 2009), 61.

3. Hecht, *Child*, 137; Hecht, *Gaily, Gaily*, 74; Hecht, "What a Newspaper Reporter Remembers," *Chicago Literary Times* 1, no. 17 (November 1, 1923): 8; Starrett, *Born in a Bookshop*, 78–79; and Dreiser, *Newspaper Days*, 156–59. Hecht's litany is found in *Child*, 150–56. For more biographical information on Larry Malm, see Hilton, *From Theater to Reality*, 78–79n44.

4. Hecht, *Charlie*, 3, 19.

5. Hecht, *Child*, 269. On journalism exposing Hecht to life, see Robert Schmuhl, "History, Fantasy, Memory: Ben Hecht and a Chicago Hanging," *Illinois Historical Journal* 83 (Autumn 1990): 155.

6. Quoted in Hecht, *Child*, 537. In another passage, Hecht wrote, "As I grew older I fell away from Mencken. The pessimism at the bottom of his thinking was not in my nature. . . . No pessimism was ever more thorough and serene than Mencken's. . . . It was the pessimism of a surgeon with a steady hand who could not be seduced into admiring the disease he was attending—humanity. There came a time when Menckenian sanity deserted me. . . . I was unable to stay reasonable and to view unreason with contempt alone. Compassion came to me, compassion even for the stupid, the hypocritical and the ugly" (177–78).

7. Hecht, *Child*, 111–14, 152. *Playboy* published "The Fairy," and "Clara" (the story that included the resurrection anecdote) in 1962. Both appeared in *Gaily, Gaily* a year later.

8. Hecht, *Gaily, Gaily*, 209.

9. The phrase "finest political plum" is from Hecht, *Gaily, Gaily*, 211; for other details, see Arthur J. Bilek, *The First Vice Lord: Big Jim Colosimo and the Ladies of the Levee* (Nashville, Tenn.: Cumberland House, 2008), 44, 53.

10. Hecht, *Gaily, Gaily*, 211. On the span of Bathhouse John's and Hinky Dink's rule of the First Ward, see Bilek, *First Vice Lord*, 268. See also Robert G. Spinney, *City of Big Shoulders: A History of Chicago* (DeKalb: Northern Illinois University Press, 2000), 151; and *Electronic Encyclopedia of Chicago*, s.v. "Era of 'Hinky Dink' and 'Bathhouse John,'" 2005, http://www.encyclopedia .chicagohistory.org/pages/2408.html.

11. Hecht, *Gaily, Gaily*, 212.

12. Bilek provides a rich and well-documented account of the First Ward Ball's rise and fall. *First Vice Lord*, 67–77. See also Spinney, *City of Big Shoulders*, 156. In *Gaily, Gaily*, Hecht claims that he attended some of these balls and wrote about them for the newspapers, but since by all accounts they had been shut down in 1908, this would not have been possible.

13. Michael Lesy, *Murder City: The Bloody History of Chicago in the Twenties* (New York: W. W. Norton, 2007), 306–7. See also Lloyd Wendt, *Lords of the Levee: The Story of Bathhouse John and Hinky Dink* (Indianapolis: Bobbs-Merrill, 1943), 294.

14. Hecht, *Gaily, Gaily*, 213–14.

15. On the approach to vice, see, for example, Bilek, *First Vice Lord*, 52. For stories of Hecht's efforts at reform, see *Child*, 198–202; and *Gaily, Gaily*, 34–49.

16. Hecht, *Gaily, Gaily*, 186–87. The stories may be referring to the same woman, or he may have tried this with several women.

17. On renting a room in a brothel, see Hecht, *Child*, 136–40; on the brothers Ignace and Manow, see *Child*, 146–47.

18. Quoted in Hecht, *Child*, 147.

19. Hecht, *Child*, 142.

20. Hecht, *Gaily, Gaily*, 31–32.

21. Hecht, *Child*, 260.

22. Hecht, *Child*, 263, 267. Chicago reporter, literary critic, and editor Harry Hansen told MacAdams that he had arranged for Hecht to be hired at the *Daily News* in 1914. Harry Hansen, interview by William MacAdams, n.d., MacAdams Collection, BHPNL. According to MacAdams's biography, Hecht was "*replacing*" Hansen, who left in August 1914 to cover the war. MacAdams, *Man behind the Legend*, 25. Hansen makes no mention of this during the interview, and MacAdams provides no sourcing. However, the dates seem vaguely correct: Hansen did indeed sail for France that July, according to a 1977 letter from his wife, Ruth McLernon Hansen. Some rare *Journal* articles that carry Hecht's byline, on file at the Newberry Library, also help narrow down when Hecht took his job at the *Daily News*: the latest *Journal* story is dated December 29, 1913. "Newspaper Articles, Chicago Daily Journal, 1912–1913," Series 1: Works, 1908–1983, box 14, folder 383a, BHPNL. Regarding Hansen's departure for Europe, see William Roba, "Harry Hansen's Literary Career," University of Iowa Libraries, Special Collections, http://www.lib.uiowa.edu/spec-coll/bai/roba.htm.

23. "Divorces Ben Hecht: Wife Gets Decree in Chicago on Grounds of Desertion," *New York Times*, February 28, 1926; and Marie Armstrong, Benjamin Heckt [sic] marriage license, dated November 30, 1915, Cook County, Illinois, Marriages Index, 1871–1920 (online database of Ancestry.com, accessed October 31, 2016).

24. In the memoirs and roman à clef in which Hecht recounts his experiences in Germany, he never mentions that Marie accompanied him. MacAdams offers many specifics of the couple's travels together, but without citing sources, in *Man behind the Legend*, 46–48.

25. Peter Hecht to Stephen Fuller [William MacAdams], n.d., p. 6 of an eight-page letter, folder 141, MacAdams Collection, BHPNL.

26. Hecht, *Child*, 269.

27. Charles H. Dennis to Edgar Price Bell, January 27, 1919, Series 2: Incoming Correspondence, 1914–1979, box 56, folder 1183, BHPNL; and Ben Hecht to Charles H. Dennis, February 1, 1919, Series 5: Subject Files, box 77, folder 2339, BHPNL. Clearly Dennis and Hecht did not have an ideal working relationship. Dennis's letter to Bell begins, "I am sorry that Mr. Hecht has such difficulty in arriving anywhere," and continues in the same tone— indeed fretting about his general uselessness.

28. Charles H. Dennis to Hecht, February 7, 1919, pp. 1–2, Series 2: Incoming Correspondence, 1914–1979, box 56, folder 1183, BHPNL; and Hecht, *Child*, 285.

29. Hecht, *Child*, 274.

30. In 1920 Walter Lippmann and Charles Merz carefully examined the news coverage and events to determine why American foreign correspondents had utterly failed to provide accurate coverage of the Russian Revolution. They concluded that the reporters had relied too much on their own biases. Walter Lippmann and Charles Merz, "A Test of the News," special supplement, *New Republic*, August 4, 1920, 1–41.

31. See, for example, Richard J. Evans, *The Coming of the Third Reich* (New York: Penguin, 2004), 73–76. The German militarists began exploiting the threat of bolshevism, rolling that in with the stories of the "November criminals" and the "stabbed-in-the-back" legend. As early as the end of 1918, these ideas and intensely bitter sentiments were being championed by a nascent new political faction, which by 1920 would be known as the Nazis.

32. Hecht, "All Berlin's Dreams of Utopia Shattered," *Chicago Daily News*, February 15, 1919, 2; and *Child*, 275. Hecht recalled that he was snubbed by the foreign press, with their "high-class journalism." A British reporter named Rennick told Hecht that he had been dropped from the Berlin Foreign Correspondents' Club. He had not been aware of the existence of such a club, but the news nevertheless depressed him. Hecht, *Child*, 286–87.

33. Ben Hecht, "Lenin Beat Germany, Says Commander Who Signed Russ Peace/Army Became 'Rotten with Bolshevism,' Gen. Hoffmann Declares," *Chicago Daily News*, March 13, 1919, 1.

34. Ben Hecht, "Watches Reds Snipe Troops from Roofs," *Chicago Daily News*, March 11, 1919, 1; and "Spartacan Captives 'Fell like Dominoes,'" *Chicago Daily News*, March 15, 1919, 1. Hecht recounted the "White Terror" in *Guide for the Bedevilled* and *A Child of the Century*. He recalled that at the bar of the Adlon Hotel, he came upon a German guard slugging back one shot of brandy after another. After the guard explained that he had manned a machine gun at Moabit Prison for three hours, mowing down three hundred men, women, and children, Hecht had rushed out and climbed a tree with binoculars to witness the murder of the last of the two thousand prisoners. See also a newspaper report from fellow *Chicago Daily News* correspondent Junius B. Wood, who watched a young officer at the Adlon Hotel bar describe the killing to Hecht. "The records show that as many as 1,500 men, women and boys have been marched across the Moabit prison courtyard and mowed down by [the officer's] machine guns in the course of a week," he writes. Junius B. Wood, "War Wears Germany's Veneer Bare; Shows Savagery Beneath," *The (Portland) Oregon Daily Journal*, April 6, 1919. In *A Child of the Century*, Hecht also recounted the Spartacist uprising that had sparked this crackdown. His companion that day at Alexanderplatz, the

seasoned war correspondent Dick Little, had remarked that it was the strangest battle he had ever seen. Nine hundred rebels had surrendered to the army with hardly a shot fired. According to the historian Richard Evans, "once the attempted coup had been defeated by a general strike, the Red Army was put down by Free Corps units, backed by mainstream Social Democrats and supported by the regular army, in what amounted in effect to a regional civil war. Well over a thousand members of the Red Army were slaughtered, most of them prisoners 'shot while trying to escape.'" Hecht, *Guide for the Bedevilled*, 72–74; Hecht, *Child*, 290–91; and Evans, *Coming*, 74–75.

35. Hecht, *Child*, 282.

36. *Foreign Correspondent*, draft manuscript ("Release Dialogue Continuity"), property of Walter Wanger Productions, August 3, 1940, reel 1-A, pp. 1–5, Series 1: Works, 1908–1983, box 9, folder 272A, BHPNL. Hecht's politically charged contribution to this script is particularly significant given the censorship of Hollywood films at the time, and it has received little to no attention from scholars. See J. Hoberman and Jeffrey Shandler, "Hollywood's Jewish Question," in *Entertaining America: Jews, Movies, and Broadcasting* (New York: Jewish Museum, under the auspices of the Jewish Theological Seminary of America, 2003), 62. Hoberman and Shandler report that producer Walter Wanger abandoned an adaptation of Vincent Sheean's *Personal History* after the Hays Office warned that its "pro-Jewish" content was inflammatory. In fact, the story was transformed into *Foreign Correspondent*, which still conveyed an anti-Nazi message. Thomas Patrick Doherty notes that once Britain had gone to war against Germany and Hollywood became free to make films critical of the Nazis, Wanger was able to take advantage of the new atmosphere to finally make the film. See T. Doherty, *Hollywood and Hitler, 1933–1939* (New York: Columbia University Press, 2013), 357–58. Clearly there is evidence that Hecht wrote these five pages, as they are stored in the Newberry archive with a note in the finding aid: "Purchase, Society of Collectors, 2008." According to MacAdams, Hecht was the one who originally rewrote the script, though he went uncredited. His draft had focused on the Nazis' "intrigue in Europe." Wanger wanted a revision that focused entirely on the intrigue story line, but Hecht was already committed to another project with director Howard Hawks. He was, however, tapped by Wanger and Hitchcock for an ending when the film was being shot. The opening scene in particular is vintage Hecht. MacAdams, *Man behind the Legend*, 208. Pauline Kael cites the script as a graphic example of Hollywood's contempt for writers, noting that Wanger put twenty-seven writers to work in groups in succession on *Personal History*. Kael, *Citizen Kane Book*, 27.

37. Hecht, *Child*, 295–99. That Hecht repeated two versions of this tale in his fiction before writing his autobiography suggests there may be some essential truth to it, but the evidence appears to contradict the details he offers in *Child*. For the alternate versions of the suitcase story, see Hecht, *Erik Dorn* (Chicago: University of Chicago Press, 1963), 319–67; and *To Quito and Back*

(New York: Covici, Friede, 1937), 17–32. Nevertheless, in a dispatch from late February 1919, Hecht reports that a bombing plane was placed at his disposal by the new bolshevist government in Munich. He used it to travel to Coburg, Germany, in an unsuccessful quest to interview Ferdinand, the ex-king of Bulgaria. Hecht reported that the plane crashed and wrecked in a cabbage field just as it was landing, but neither he nor any of the other passengers were injured. Hecht, "Uses Bombing Plane in Hunt for Ex-King, Ben Hecht Fails to Borrow Ferdinand's Auto, but Has Thrilling Flight," *Chicago Daily News*, March 1, 1919. MacAdams offers no source information but writes that Hecht tried to use *Daily News* funds to buy a plane for coverage around Europe, but the newspaper turned him down. Hecht caught a train to Munich, MacAdams adds, and was able to scoop the rest of the press corps on the Bavarian revolution. See MacAdams, *Man behind the Legend*, 47. See also Hecht, "Munich Unruffled as Soviet Rule Impends," *Chicago Daily News*, April 8, 1919, 1; "Radicals in Munich Split on New Regime," *Chicago Daily News*, April 9, 1919, 1; "Bavaria for Peace on Entene's Terms," *Chicago Daily News*, April 11, 1919.

38. Hecht, *Child*, 299.
39. Hecht, *Child*, 289, 292–95.
40. Ron Rosenbaum, *The Secret Parts of Fortune: Three Decades of Intense Investigations and Edgy Enthusiasms* (New York: Random House, 2000), 655–56. Although Hecht never specifically refers to a "Big Lie" or "stabbed in the back," he does capitalize the *L* in referring to the "Lie" about the threat of bolshevism. See Hecht, *Child*, 275, 280. Hecht was not the only one to articulate this interwar conspiracy theory about the Germans. See also Michael Sayers and Albert E. Kahn, *The Plot against the Peace: A Warning to the Nation!* (New York: Dial, 1945).
41. Hecht, *Gaily, Gaily*, 210.
42. Hecht, *Child*, 270.

Chapter 3

1. Hecht, "Scarface/Dialogue-Continuity by Ben Hecht," 78, typescript with ms. corrections and emendations, Case folio PS3515.E18 S32, Special Collections, Newberry Library, Chicago. J. E. Smyth uses this quotation as an epigraph on her study of early gangster films but offers a different version, perhaps because she is drawing from a draft of the script discovered in her archival research. Her version of the quote is: "Sounds like a typewriter, eh? I'm goin' to write my name all over Chicago with this, in capital letters." Smyth, "Revisioning Modern American History in the Age of *Scarface* (1932)," *Historical Journal of Film, Radio and Television* 24, no. 4 (2004): 535–63.
2. Lesy, *Murder City*, 303–4.
3. Klatt, *Chicago Journalism*, 4, 125.

4. Frederick L. Allen, "Newspapers and the Truth," *Atlantic Monthly*, January 1922, 44–54, quoted in Bruce J. Evensen, "Journalism's Struggle over Ethics and Professionalism," 54–55.

5. Evensen, "Journalism's Struggle," 55.

6. New York, Passenger Lists, 1820–1957, accessed via Ancestry.com, September 14, 2016; MacAdams, *Man behind the Legend*, 47–48; and Hecht, *Child*, 267. Hecht left from Rotterdam for New York and, according to MacAdams, left for Chicago within a day of his arrival in the United States. Hecht recalled that he returned from Germany in early 1920, but in his autobiography he consistently gets dates wrong.

7. Peter J. Kitson, "Beyond the Enlightenment: The Philosophical, Scientific and Religious Inheritance," in *A Companion to Romanticism*, ed. Duncan Wu, Blackwell Companions to Literature and Culture 1 (Oxford: Blackwell, 1998), 35.

8. "The Press Agents' War," *New York Times*, September 9, 1914. Electric power tycoon Samuel Insull, for example, began advising the American branch of the British propaganda office in 1914, and contributed a quarter of a million dollars for slanted war stories to appear in newspapers. After the war, Insull's Illinois Publicity Utility Information Committee borrowed the propaganda machinery he had used during the war to churn out a massive volume of promotional material, a trend soon copied by utilities across the country. Schudson, *Discovering the News*, 142–43.

9. Hecht, *Child*, 321. "By the spring of 1921, "he had been divorced from our staff for some weeks," wrote *Daily News* editor Henry Justin Smith, "and had married an overdressed, blatant creature called Publicity." Smith, preface (July 1, 1922) to *A Thousand and One Afternoons in Chicago*, by Ben Hecht (New York: Covici Friede, 1922), n.p. Hecht writes that he partnered with Atlanta entrepreneur Grady Rutledge to do publicity drives for J. P. Morgan's China Famine Fund, Herbert Hoover's Near East Relief Fund, and a project to spread the Baptist faith called "The Northern Baptist Drive," which raised $25 million in the Midwest. "A Chinese Fair in June," in "News of Chicago Society," *Chicago Tribune*, May 8, 1920, 2; and Hecht, *Child*, 321–23. According to researcher Florice Whyte Kovan, Hecht also helped organized anti–Ku Klux Klan campaigns as a partner in the firm. The campaigns were underwritten by the National Unity League. Having established the drive in Chicago, Hecht and Rutledge expanded it to Milwaukee on October 21, 1922, where they announced a plan to expose Klan members. See Kovan, "Some Notes on Ben Hecht's Civil Rights Work, the Klan and Related Projects," A Web Site Devoted to Ben Hecht Biography and Works, Snickersnee Press and BenHechtBooks.net, n.d., accessed August 31, 2018, http://benhechtbooks.net/ben_hecht__human_rights.

10. Smith, preface, n.p.

11. Hecht, *A Thousand and One Afternoons*, "Fog Patterns," 27; "The Sybarite," 60–63; "Waterfront Fancies," 68–71; "Fantastic Lollypops," 97–100; "Pandora's Box," 273; and "Ripples," 265–68; Smith, preface, n.p.

12. On the sketch, see Sims, "Chicago Style of Journalism," 31–34, 41. On the resemblance between Hecht's columns and Ade's, see Fetherling, *Five Lives*, 29–30. For a good overview of the late nineteenth-century Chicago columnists, see Ziff, *American 1890s*, 157–61.

13. Hecht, *A Thousand and One Afternoons*, 285–89.

14. For "naïve empiricism," Schudson's phrase, see *Discovering the News*, 6; the Luce statement is quoted on p. 149. For cogent analyses of the evolution of "objectivity" during the 1920s and the deep skepticism that was arising about it just as it was being adopted as a professional standard for journalism, see Schudson, *Discovering the News*, 121–59; and *James Carey: A Critical Reader*, ed. Eve Stryker Munson and Catherine A. Warren (Minneapolis: University of Minnesota Press, 1997), 137–41, 162–63, 192–94.

15. Schudson, *Discovering the News*, 123 (on the spate of writing about crowds, see 122–28); Mencken, *Notes on Democracy*, 15–23, 55, 209, 211; Mencken, *My Life as Author and Editor* (New York: Knopf, 1993), 1081–82; and Lippmann, *Phantom Public*, 65.

16. Hecht, *A Thousand and One Afternoons*, 285. On the new lack of confidence in the knowability of the truth, see David Hollinger, "The Knower and the Artificer," in "Modernist Culture in America," spec. issue, *American Quarterly* 39, no. 1 (Spring 1987): 37–55. On the tie between the knowability of truth and journalistic objectivity, see Carey, *Reader*, 162–64.

17. Hecht, *Erik Dorn*, 19.

18. "Erik Dorn," *Vanity Fair*, November 1921; and Hecht, *Erik Dorn*, 380.

19. Algren, "*Erik Dorn*: A Thousand and One Afternoons in Nada," introduction to Hecht, *Erik Dorn*, xiii; and Hecht, *Erik Dorn*, 9.

20. Algren, "*Erik Dorn*," viii; and Fetherling, *Five Lives*, 35–40.

21. The claim that Mencken fed him plotlines is from Abe C. Ravitz, "Ballyhoo, Gargoyles, and Firecrackers: Ben Hecht's Aesthetic Calliope," *Journal of Popular Culture* 1, no. 1 (June 1967): 38. On *The Florentine Dagger*, see Hecht, *Child*, 343. In a 1931 newspaper profile, Hecht said that he had wagered $1,000 to another man's $2,000, that he had dictated *The Florentine Dagger* in nineteen hours with the aid of two stenographers, and that it had sold fifteen thousand copies. See Ruth Seinfel, "Author of 'A Jew in Love' Longed for Lost Unpopularity, but Now That He Has It He Confesses Remorse," *New York Post*, 1931, Series 6: Publicity, 1920–1979, box 79, folder 2411, BHPNL. Horace Liveright told MacAdams that the novel in fact took two months to write and was based on Sardou's play *La Tosca*. MacAdams, *Man behind the Legend*, 67. According to *Tribune* reporter and book reviewer Fanny Butcher, Charles MacArthur's older brother, Alfred, had offered a $2,500 wager that no one could write a successful book in one sitting, and Hecht took him up on it. Hecht told Butcher that the two stenographers helped write the book: at every twist he would ask them who they thought the murderer was and would then change the plot to keep it unpredictable. Fanny Butcher, *Many Lives—One Love* (New York: Harper & Row, 1972), 67.

22. Hecht, *Child*, 467.

23. Hecht, *Child*, 349. See also "Divorces Ben Hecht: Wife Gets Decree in Chicago on Grounds of Desertion," *New York Times*, February 28, 1926. In the article, Marie said Hecht deserted her when he left Chicago for New York City on February 15, 1924. Hecht later wrote that he was awaiting the divorce so that he could remarry. *Charlie*, 129. On Rose, falling in love, and her influence, see *Child*, 350–54.

24. The quotation is from Hecht, *Charlie*, 69. On New York's society of newspaper veterans and the literary crowd, see Ehrlich, *Journalism in the Movies*, 27; Hecht, *Child*, 384–86, 390–96; and, in greater depth, Hecht, *Charlie*, 73–112. MacAdams writes that the 1927 season saw 263 shows open, while that number had dropped to significantly less than 200 by 1933, and fewer than 100 by the late '30s. See MacAdams, *Man behind the Legend*, 106.

25. Kael, *Citizen Kane Book*, 25; and Smith, quoted in Sims, "Chicago Style of Journalism," 266.

26. The phrase "the Golden Age of press criticism" is from Robert W. McChesney and Ben Scott, introduction to Upton Sinclair, *The Brass Check: A Study of American Journalism* (University of Illinois Press, 2002), xx. On neither Dewey nor Lippmann holding out hope that journalism would come to the rescue, see Michael Schudson, "What Public Journalism Knows about Journalism but Doesn't Know about 'Public,'" in *The Idea of Public Journalism*, ed. Theodore L. Glasser (New York: Guilford, 1999), 124.

27. On the origins of mass communication research, propaganda studies, and the Chicago school of sociology, see Jesse Delia, "Communication Research: A History," in *Handbook of Communication Science*, ed. Charles R. Berger and Steven H. Chaffee (Beverly Hills, Calif.: Sage, 1987), 20–98. For a clear, straightforward explanation of Lasswell's ideas, see Stanley J. Baran and Dennis K. Davis, *Mass Communication Theory: Foundations, Ferment, and Future*, 2nd ed. (Boston, Mass.: Wadsworth Cengage Learning, 2000), 81–83. For a cogent discussion of this history and the ways it has been misrepresented, see J. Michael Sproule, "Progressive Propaganda Critics and the Magic Bullet Myth," *Critical Studies in Mass Communication* 6, no. 3 (September 1989): 225–46; and Carey, "The Chicago School and the History of Mass Communication Research," in *Reader*, 14–33. On Lasswell's life, see *Encyclopedia of World Biography*, 2nd ed. (Farmington Hills, Mich.: Cengage Gale, 2011), 218–19.

28. Hecht, *Charlie*, 82–84.

29. Hecht, *Child*, 446–65. Journalist Alva Johnston essentially confirms Hecht's tale in one of a series of articles about South Florida and in his biography of architect Addison Mizner, published before *A Child of the Century*. Referring to Hecht's pamphlets, Johnston wrote, "It is impossible even now to read his prose without feeling an urge to rush South and invest a couple of hundred thousand dollars in the tidal swamp that was once the town's Millionaire's Row." Johnston, *The Legendary Mizners* (1953; New York: Farrar, Straus and

Giroux, 1986), 297. See also Johnston, "The Palm Beach Architect," *New Yorker*, December 13, 1952, 43–44. Hecht's tale about buried treasure let him have fun with a favorite subject—pirates. But, in fact, a wave of treasure hunters would find hundreds of millions of dollars' worth of gold pieces of eight in sunken Spanish galleons off the Florida Keys over the succeeding decades.

30. Hecht, *Charlie*, 129, 134–35. The first 135 pages of *Charlie* trace both MacArthur's life and his friendship with Hecht up until they started writing *The Front Page* together. Just before Hecht and MacArthur started collaborating, MacArthur had scored a hit with *Lulu Belle*, which he had written with one of Broadway's most successful playwrights, Ned Sheldon. See *Charlie*, 88–91, 122.

31. Hecht, *Child*, 391. At a 1980 Newberry Library dinner, MacArthur's wife, Helen Hayes, gave a speech about "Ben and Charlie," saying, "Ben was never comfortable in the adult world. He spent his whole life trying to hang on to youth, its mindset, its wonderment, its carefree fizz." Quoted in Robert Schmuhl, "Sorting Out Ben Hecht," *Chicago Tribune*, March 31, 2002, http://articles.chicagotribune.com/2002-03-31 /entertainment/0203290370_1_ben-hecht-joseph-epstein-carl-sandburg.

32. Sidney E. Zion, "The Scoop from Helen Hayes," *New York Times*, November 16, 1986, sec. 2, p. 1. Stories vary as to where Hecht and MacArthur worked on the play: at the Rockland Female Institute, a girls' school they rented in South Nyack, New York, or at the Hechts' apartment on Beekman Place, in midtown on Manhattan's East Side. Sidney E. Zion, "Playwrights' Widows Remember First 'Front Page,'" *New York Times*, May 12, 1969, 52; Hecht, *Child*, 391; and Hecht, *Charlie*, 129, 134–35.

33. Schmuhl, "*Front Page* Turns 75"; and J. Brooks Atkinson, "The Play," *New York Times*, August 15, 1928, 28. "The best American comedy ever written" was the judgment of English theater critic Kenneth Tynan, quoted in Barry Norman, "Michael Blakemore: Setting in Motion a Dazzling Machine," *Times* (London), June 17, 1972, 11. According to producer Jed Harris, the ovation in Chicago at the end of act 1 "sounded like the roar of a herd of wild animals panicked by fire at the zoo." Jed Harris, *A Dance on the High Wire: Recollections of a Time and a Temperament* (New York: Crown, 1979), 119.

34. Fetherling, *Five Lives*, 69.

35. Helen Hayes recalled that Tennessee Williams once told her: "Your Charlie and Ben Hecht made it possible for me to write my plays. They paved the way for me. They took the corsets off American theater." Quoted in Carol Lawson, "Theater Hall of Fame Gets 10 New Members," *New York Times*, May 10, 1983.

36. On the pressroom, see Fetherling, *Five Lives*, 69. On Tommy O'Connor's pork chop sandwich, see June Sawyer, "Following the Trail of a 'Terrible' Killer," *Chicago Tribune*, August 28, 1988, 9. On Carol Frink, see Hilton, *From Theater to Reality*, 2, and 111–12n109. MacArthur and Frink divorced on June 26, 1926.

37. Hecht, *Charlie*, 139. On the real Hilding Johnson and the jury ballot incident, see Dornfeld, *Behind the Front Page*, 110–11. Hilton's exhaustively researched *From Theater to Reality* explains the connections between the actual characters and events and those represented in the play.

38. Martin, *Ben Hecht*, 47.

39. Hecht and MacArthur, *Front Page*, 31, 129. The phrase "little greedy half-dead" is from Hecht, "Nocturne," *Little Review* 1, no. 5 (May 1918): 45, 46, 48.

40. Hecht and MacArthur, *Front Page*, 132, 150, 176, 179.

41. George Gordon Battle, "Stage Profanity under Fire," *New York Times*, September 9, 1928, sec. 10, p. 2, quoted in Ehrlich, *Journalism in the Movies*, 38; Stanley Walker, *City Editor* (New York: Frederick A. Stokes, 1934), 37; and Fetherling, *Five Lives*, 81. See also Stephen Vaughn and Bruce Evensen, "Democracy's Guardians: Hollywood's Portrait of Reporters," *Journalism Quarterly* 68, no. 4 (Winter 1991): 832.

42. Hecht and MacArthur, epilogue, in Hilton, *From Theater to Reality*, 187–88; and Ehrlich, *Journalism in the Movies*, 32–34.

Chapter 4

1. *Filmfront* 1, no. 3 (January 28, 1935), quoted in MacAdams, *Man behind the Legend*, 301–2.

2. *Scarface*, written by Oliver Stone, directed by Brian De Palma (1983; Universal City, Calif.: Universal Studios Home Entertainment, 2006), DVD.

3. Hecht, "Scarface/Dialogue-Continuity," 251.

4. *Motion Picture Classic*, August 1928, 52, quoted in Rosow, *Born to Lose*, 124. See also Ben Hecht, *Underworld: An Original Story of Chicago* ([Chicago?]: Hecht, 1927); and Clarens, *Crime Movies*, 15, 31–32.

5. Hecht evidently wrote a detailed sixty-page treatment for the film at some point between January and March 1931, before passing it to his own new hire, John Lee Mahin, and Hawks's trusted collaborator and script doctor, Seton Miller. Hecht then did further work on the script. See Todd McCarthy, *Howard Hawks: The Grey Fox of Hollywood* (New York: Grove, 1997), 129–38.

6. Rosow, *Born to Lose*, 117, 118. Frederick Lewis Allen most famously referred to the changes in the 1920s as "a revolution in manners and morals." Allen, "The Revolution in Morals and Manners," in *Only Yesterday: An Informal History of the 1920's* (New York: Perennial Classics, 2000). 67–92. For discussions of how the gangster film reflected these changes, see Jonathan Munby, *Public Enemies, Public Heroes: Screening the Gangster from* Little Caesar *to* Touch of Evil (Chicago: University of Chicago Press, 1999); and David E. Ruth, *Inventing the Public Enemy: The Gangster in American Culture, 1918–1934* (Chicago: University of Chicago Press, 1996).

7. Hecht, "The Unfinished Life of Mickey Cohen," *Scanlan's Monthly*, March 1970, 74; and Hecht, *Child*, 479.

8. Clarens, *Crime Movies*, 32, 34, 42.

9. Clarens, *Crime Movies*, 40; and Hecht, *Child*, 479–80.

10. Clarens, *Crime Movies*, 42; Rosow, *Born to Lose*, 124; and McCarthy, *Howard Hawks*, 134. Hawks said on more than one occasion he had been centrally involved with *Underworld*. He claimed that he had bought the story from Hecht, that the two had worked on it, and that he had recruited his frequent collaborator Arthur Rosson to be the director. When Rosson allegedly got drunk and was fired from the project, Hawks said he gave *Underworld* to Sternberg. However, McCarthy points to a problem with these stories: during the period when Rosson worked on *Underworld* and Sternberg started shooting, from late 1926 to March 1927, the film was a Paramount production, and Hawks had been directing pictures for Fox for over a year. He hadn't worked for Paramount for three years. To be charitable, Hawks may well have been involved, but not precisely in the way that he described. See McCarthy, *Howard Hawks*, 76.

11. Smyth, "Revisioning Modern American History," 531, 551; Ruth, *Inventing the Public Enemy*, 118; and Tere Tereba, *Mickey Cohen: The Life and Crimes of L.A.'s Notorious Mobster* (Toronto: ECW Press, 2012), 24.

12. Ruth, *Inventing the Public Enemy*, 119. Ruth discusses the production of the Capone legend in popular books, pulp magazines, movies, and feature articles. "The most important group in the production of this material was big-city newspaper reporters," Ruth observes, "who not only churned out daily stories but wrote most of the more substantial accounts." One Capone biographer, Walter Noble Burns, worked for the *Tribune*. Another, Fred Pasley, had been a reporter for the *Chicago Daily News*, like Hecht and John Bright, whose story "Beer and Blood" was adapted into the movie *The Public Enemy*. An early history of the Chicago underworld during Prohibition was *Rattling the Cup on Chicago Crime*, written by *Herald and Examiner* reporter Edward Dean Sullivan just a few weeks after the Saint Valentine's Day Massacre. In 1930 he published another, *Chicago Surrenders*.

13. Ruth, *Inventing the Public Enemy*, 118, 125–31.

14. Clarens, *Crime Movies*, 34–38, 43–47.

15. Clarens, *Crime Movies*, 51–53.

16. Clarens, *Crime Movies*, 53.

17. Clarens, *Crime Movies*, 82–83.

18. Clarens, *Crime Movies*, 83, 84.

19. Asbjorn Gronstad, "Mean Streets: Death and Disfiguration in Hawks' *Scarface*," *Nordic Journal of English Studies* 2, no. 2 (2003): 389–90.

20. Hecht, *Child*, 486; and "Popular Arts Project: The Reminiscences of Ben Hecht," Oral History Research Office, Columbia University, 1959, p. 736, filed as "Oral History, Transcript, Columbia University, 1959," Series 12: Miscellaneous, 1885–1974, box 133, folder 3006, BHPNL. Hawks corroborated Hecht's story about the arrangement and said the script was written in eleven days, but Hawks's biographer Todd McCarthy argues that Hecht

really knew better than to believe Hughes wouldn't pay him, and the arrangement was likely a publicity stunt dreamed up by Hecht and his film agent, Myron Selznick, to burnish Hecht's legend as the most prolific and highest-paid writer in Hollywood. See McCarthy, *Howard Hawks*, 132. For the revision process and other key details, see McCarthy, *Howard Hawks*, 130–35; Howard Hawks, interview by William MacAdams, Palm Springs, Calif., February 9, 1972, MacAdams Collection, BHPNL; John Lee Mahin, interview William MacAdams, Malibu, Calif., 1972, MacAdams Collection, BHPNL; and Hawks, interview by Peter Bogdanovich, in Jim Hillier and Peter Wollen, eds., *Howard Hawks: American Artist* (British Film Institute, 1997), 52. Burnett, Pasley, and Walter Noble Burns all worked on the script, contributing their knowledge of Capone and recent underworld history. By all accounts, however, it was Hecht who really put the story together and produced a viable screenplay, or at least a sixty-page treatment. John Lee Mahin, a short story writer and former reporter who had been working as an advertising copywriter, polished the script, accompanying Hecht to Hollywood on the promise of a job doing screenplay work at $200 a week. Mahin had help from script doctor Seton I. Miller. See Smyth, "Revisioning Modern American History," 554; Hawks, interview by MacAdams; Mahin, interview, in MacAdams, *Man behind the Legend*, 144–45; and Rose Hecht, notes about Mahin in the margins of an letter from Charlie MacArthur to Ben Hecht, n.d., p. 2, Series 2: Incoming Correspondence, 1914–1979, box 59, folder 1431, BHPNL.

21. "Popular Arts Project: The Reminiscences of Ben Hecht," Oral History Research Office, Columbia University, 1959, p. 736, filed as "Oral History, Transcript, Columbia University, 1959," Series 12: Miscellaneous, 1885–1974, box 133, folder 3006, BHPNL.

22. Ruth, *Inventing the Public Enemy*, 123–24. Ruth's chapter "The Invention in the Flesh: Al Capone of Chicago" (118–43) notes that Capone was cast in a favorable light in pulp magazines and newspaper and magazine feature articles, ranging from *Master Detective* to *Collier's* to the *Outlook*. Examples of press accounts that emphasize the Horatio Alger–like aspects of Capone include the March 1930 issue of *Time* that featured him on the cover, grinning like a celebrity with a rose stuck in his lapel; R. L. Ruffus, "Happy Hunting Ground for Racketeers," *New York Times Magazine*, October 3, 1930, 3; Raymond Moley, "Behind the Menacing Racket," *New York Times Magazine*, November 23, 1930, 2; and Cornelius Vanderbilt Jr., "How Al Capone Would Run This Country," *Liberty* 8 (October 17, 1931): 18, 20–21. Ruth adds, "The most important group in the production of this material was big-city newspaper reporters, who not only churned out daily stories but wrote most of the more substantial accounts" (119). Ruth cites Alger-like elements in Fred Pasley, *Al Capone: Biography of a Self-Made Man* (New York: Ives, Washburn, 1930); and Sullivan, *Rattling the Cup*.

23. Ruth, *Inventing the Public Enemy*, 125–31.

24. Hecht, "Unfinished Life," 71.

25. Richard H. Pells, *Radical Visions and American Dreams: Culture and Social Thought in the Depression Years* (Middletown, Conn.: Wesleyan University Press, 1984), 271–72, quoted in Munby, *Public Enemies, Public Heroes*, 15; and Robert Warshow, "The Gangster as Tragic Hero," in *The Immediate Experience: Movies, Comics, Theatre and Other Aspects of Popular Culture* (New York: Atheneum, 1971) 85–88. On Pasley's view of Capone, see Smyth, "Revisioning Modern American History," 552. The comparison to *The Great Gatsby* is from Marilyn Roberts, "*Scarface, The Great Gatsby* and the American Dream," *Literature/Film Quarterly* 34, no. 1 (2006): 73.

26. *Scarface*, produced by Howard Hughes, directed by Howard Hawks, screenplay by Ben Hecht et al. (1932; Universal City, Calif.: Universal Studios Home Entertainment, 2007); and Hecht, "Scarface/Dialogue-Continuity," 6.

27. Smyth, "Revisioning Modern American History, 551, 553, 538, 547, 558.

28. Clarens, *Crime Movies*, 91. On Sternberg and expressionism, see Thomas Schatz, "Paramount and the Emergence of the Hollywood Studio System," Film Reference, n.d., accessed October 8, 2018, http://www.filmreference.com/encyclopedia/Independent-Film-Road-Movies/Paramount-PARAMOUNT-AND-THE-EMERGENCE-OF-THE-HOLLYWOOD-STUDIO-SYSTEM.html; Thomas Schatz, "Paramount and the Emergence of the Hollywood Studio System," in Barry Keith Grant, ed., and Gale Group, *Schirmer Encyclopedia of Film*, Gale Virtual Reference Library (Detroit, Mich.: Schirmer Reference, 2007), 3:250–51.

29. Clarens, *Crime Movies*, 85, 88–89. Clarens recounts a version of the anecdote that has Capone bashing a single guest of honor, but the legend is rooted in the May 7, 1929, murders of three Capone gunmen: Albert Anselmi, John Scalise, and Joseph "Hop Toad" Guinta. Capone biographer Jonathan Eig explains that because their badly beaten bodies were discovered in a back alley, Walter Noble Burns took literary license in his 1931 book *The One-Way Ride*, imagining a banquet at which they had first been drugged before being killed. See Burns, *The One-Way Ride: The Red Trail of Chicago Gangland from Prohibition to Jake Lingle* (Garden City, N.Y.: Doubleday, Doran and Company, Inc., 1931), 255–56. Then in 1975's *The Legacy of Al Capone*, George Murray described a banquet scene in which Capone suddenly brandished a pair of wooden clubs. See Murray, "Caesar Deals with the Ambitious," in *The Legacy of Al Capone* (New York: G. P. Putnam's Sons, 1975), 113–15. However, the story of the baseball bat was obviously circulating by the early 1930s, when columnist Howard Vincent O'Brien asked Capone whether it was true. See Jonathan Eig, citing O'Brien's papers archived at the Newberry Library, in *Get Capone: The Secret Plot That Captured America's Most Wanted Gangster* (New York: Simon and Schuster, 2010), 315–16. On Burns, Murray, O'Brien, and the banquet story, see Eig, *Get Capone*, 223–25, 315–16. A depiction of the incident also turned up in the 1958 film *Party Girl*, as well as

the 1987 movie starring Robert De Niro as Capone, *The Untouchables*. Eig, *Get Capone*, 223–25, 315–16. On *Scarface* and the Gatsby imagery, see E. R. Hagemann, "*Scarface*: The Art of Hollywood, Not 'The Shame of a Nation,'" *Journal of Popular Culture* 18, no. 1 (June 1984): 33; and Roberts, "*Scarface.*"

30. Hawks, interview by Bogdanovich, in Hillier and Wollen, *Howard Hawks*, 52. Hawks said, "When I asked Ben Hecht to write it, he said, 'Oh, we don't want to do a gangster picture.' And I said, 'Well this is a little different. I would like to do the Capone family as if they were the Borgias set down in Chicago.' And he said, 'We'll start tomorrow.' We took eleven days to write the story and dialogue. We were influenced a good deal by the incestuous elements in the story of the Borgias. We made the brother-sister relationship clearly incestuous. But the censors misunderstood our intention and objected to it because they thought the relationship between them was too beautiful to be attributed to a gangster."

31. Clarens, *Crime Movies*, 85, 88–89; and Robin Wood, "*Scarface*," in *Gangster Film Reader*, ed. Alain Silver and James Ursini (Pompton Plains, N.J.: Limelight, 2007), 25.

32. Hecht, "Scarface/Dialogue-Continuity," 147–48.

33. Hecht, "Scarface/Dialogue-Continuity," 52–54, 90, 124. In trying to explain the play himself, Camonte says, "There's a minister and a soldier fella and this girl, unnerstan'? This Sadie—she's a been—(he searches for a word) . . . what you call it . . . disillusion. (he smiles, happy at his verbal accomplishment.)" Hecht, "Scarface/Dialogue-Continuity," 87. The phrase "terrible innocence" is from Wood, "*Scarface*," 24.

34. Quoted from Wood, "*Scarface*," 20; also, for more on Camonte's "terrible innocence," see pp. 22 and 24.

Part II

1. Max Bodenheim to Ben and Rose Hecht, n.d., Series 2: Incoming Correspondence, 1914–1979, box 55, folder 1078, BHPNL.

2. Jack B. Moore, *Maxwell Bodenheim* (New York: Twayne, 1970), 158, 160–61, 168.

3. Ross Wetzsteon, *Republic of Dreams: Greenwich Village. The American Bohemia, 1910–1960* (New York: Simon and Schuster, 2002), 380–81; see also J. Moore, *Maxwell Bodenheim*, 168.

4. Albert Parry, in his classic 1933 history of American bohemianism, asserts, "Hecht and Bodenheim were the most colorful characters of Chicago's bohemia of 1913–1923. There were, of course, greater names in the circle. There were Carl Sandburg, Sherwood Anderson, Edgar Lee Masters, and others. . . . But Hecht and Bodenheim provided action, scandal, amours. They were the unlaced souls of the group, the starters of clubs and journals, the noisy bearers of flags." Parry, *Garretts and Pretenders: A History of Bohemianism in America* (New York: Covici, Friede, 1933), 191.

5. Ben Hecht, *Count Bruga* (New York: Boni & Liveright, 1926); and Maxwell Bodenheim, *Duke Herring* (New York: H. Liveright, 1931).
6. Ravitz, "Ballyhoo, Gargoyles and Firecrackers," 39 (for the description of Bodenheim); and Hecht, *Child*, 216.
7. Hecht related this encounter several times in his writings. See Hecht, *Child*, 215–18; Hecht, "A Poet out of Yesterday," in *1001 Afternoons in New York* (New York: Viking, 1941), 61–64; and Hecht, *Letters from Bohemia* (Garden City, N.Y.: Doubleday, 1964), 122–24.
8. Hecht, *Letters from Bohemia*, 123–24. Just about every letter from Bodenheim from this period in Hecht's archive refers to their arrangement—either to thank him for a recent check or to prod him for another payment. See Series 2: Incoming Correspondence, 1914–1979, box 55, folders 1078–1082, BHPNL.
9. Hecht, *Child*, 109.
10. Max Horkheimer and Theodor Adorno coined the term *culture industry* in a famous essay published in 1944. See Horkheimer and Adorno, "The Culture Industry: Enlightenment as Mass Deception," in *Dialectic of Enlightenment: Philosophical Fragments* (Stanford, Calif.: Stanford University Press, 2002), 94–136.

Chapter 5

1. Margaret C. Anderson, *My Thirty Years' War: An Autobiography* (New York: Covici, Friede, 1930), 35.
2. Dale Kramer, *Chicago Renaissance: The Literary Life in the Midwest, 1900–1930* (New York: Appleton-Century, 1966), 244–45. Fanny Butcher recalled Anderson from a small bookshop in the Fine Arts Building, from which Francis Fisher Browne published his conservative literary magazine, the *Dial*: "That shop's showpiece for a while was an objet d'art, a salesgirl, as beautiful as a dream come true, one of her admirers confided to me, with the graces of Marie Antoinette and the dedication of a missionary. Her name was Margaret Anderson. She was to go down in literary history." Butcher, *Many Lives*, 67.
3. M. Anderson, *My Thirty Years' War*, 35–36, 40–41.
4. Margaret Anderson, "Announcement," *Little Review* 1, no. 1 (March 1914): 2. On building a temple for art, see M. Anderson, *My Thirty Years' War*, 46–47.
5. Carl Sandburg, "Chicago," in *Chicago Poems* (New York: H. Holt, 1916); and May, *End of American Innocence*, 102–3, 106.
6. Henry L. Mencken, "Civilized Chicago," *Chicago Tribune*, October 28, 1917, 5. Three years later, on April 17, 1920, Mencken published an essay about Chicago in the London *Nation* titled "The Literary Capital of the United States." Hugh Dalziel Duncan, *The Rise of Chicago as a Literary Center from 1885 to 1920: A Sociological Essay in American Culture* (Totowa, N.J.:

Bedminster, 1964), viii. Hecht said that Mencken's dubbing of Chicago as the literary capital "was one of his best jokes—a slap at the complacency of New York." Quoted in Butcher, *Many Lives*, 407.

7. Rascoe, *Before I Forget*, 318–21; Poetry Foundation, "A History of the Magazine," n.d., http://www.poetryfoundation.org/poetrymagazine/history; and Constance D'Arcy Mackay, *The Little Theatre in the United States* (New York: H. Holt, 1917), 103.

8. Bernard I. Duffey, *The Chicago Renaissance in American Letters*, 2nd ed. (East Lansing: Michigan State University Press, 1956), 190; see also, for the broader context here, 189–93. See also the brief history of the journal provided by the Modernist Journals Project: "Modernism Began in the Magazines," Brown University and the University of Tulsa, http://www .modjourn.org/render.php?view=mjp_object&id=LittleReviewCollection. This project has made all issues of the *Little Review* available online.

9. Hecht, *Child*, 233.

10. Henry Farnham May, *The End of American Innocence: A Study of the First Years of Our Own Time, 1912–1917* (New York: Columbia University Press, 1992), xxiii–xxviii. May's argument has become seminal to studies of the history of twentieth-century American cultural rebellion.

11. Hecht, *Child*, 220.

12. On developing out of the ruins of the Columbian Exposition, see Susan O'Connor Davis, *Chicago's Historic Hyde Park* (Chicago: University of Chicago Press, 2013), 122–23. On Currey's studio as the converted retail storeroom where Hecht met the fellow members of the Renaissance, see *Sherwood Anderson's Memoirs* (New York: Harcourt, Brace, 1942), 248; and Irving Howe, *Sherwood Anderson*, American Men of Letters Series (Stanford, Calif.: Stanford University Press, 1968), 64. On the scene that developed at Dell's and Currey's studios, and the title for the magazine, see M. Anderson, *My Thirty Years' War*, 36–42; and Kramer, *Chicago Renaissance*, 232–37. Vincent Starrett also recounts the evening everyone tried to come up with a title; he notes that Hecht had been invited but for some reason was unable to attend. *Born in a Bookshop*, 174–75. Currey's name is sometimes given as Curry or Currie in different accounts, and Hecht spells her first name Marjy in *A Child of the Century*. However, in issues of the *Little Review*, it is spelled Margery Currey. See, for example, *Little Review* 2, no. 8 (November 1915).

13. Hecht, *Gaily, Gaily*, 162–63. See also Hecht, *Child*, 174–75. Both Starrett and Hecht were colleagues of Currey at the *Daily News*. Hecht, *Child*, 221–23.

14. Upon Hecht's death, Anderson wrote to Rose: "Ben was always my favorite of all the first contributors to the *Little Review*, and the only one who kept up a correspondence with me." Margaret Anderson to Rose Hecht, April 20, 1964, Series 2: Incoming Correspondence, 1914–1979, box 55, folder 1037, BHPNL. That Hecht had grown tired of writing formulaic prose for Mencken comes from MacAdams, *Man behind the Legend*, 43.

15. Lawrence Langner, *The Magic Curtain: The Story of a Life in Two Fields, Theatre and Invention, by the Founder of the Theatre Guild* (New York: Dutton, 1951), 85–86.

16. Harriet Monroe, "Comment, Maxwell Bodenheim," *Poetry* 25 (March 1925): 320–27; and Langner, *Magic Curtain*, 86. On Hecht as a habitué of Currey's studio, see also Langner, *Magic Curtain*, 81.

17. Hecht, *Child*, 221–24; Hecht, *Gaily, Gaily*, 167–69, 180; and Hecht, *Letters from Bohemia*, 111, 114. The phrases "Your face is an incense bowl . . ." and "Your hair is a tortured midnight" are from Hecht, *Child*, 223; and Hecht, *Count Bruga*, 9, 143. The quotations "But beneath the surface there lurked . . ." and "I have a malady of the soul . . ." are from Allen Churchill, *The Improper Bohemians: A Re-creation of Greenwich Village in Its Heyday* (New York: Dutton, 1959), 307. Hecht also describes a corncob with a "sewer-smelling" tobacco called "nigger weed"; Sherwood Anderson describes the same pipe, while Margaret Anderson mentions the odor. Hecht, *Count Bruga*, 12; Hecht, *Child*, 222; Hecht, *Gaily, Gaily*, 167; M. Anderson, *My Thirty Years' War*, 59; and S. Anderson, *Memoirs*, 199. "If Ben Hecht was the most prominent of the Covici-McGee [Bookshop] habitués, Bodenheim was the most spectacular," recalled former *Tribune* reporter and critic Fanny Butcher in 1972. "He was the original hippie in our town. His never-washed blond hair was long, his clothes bizarre, and he ostentatiously smoked what he said was opium in a pipe with a bowl the size of a thimble. He also smelled—of a mixture of whatever he smoked, an allergy to soap and water, and potently of Maxwell Bodenheim." Butcher, *Many Lives*, 67. Although, in *A Child of the Century*, Hecht recalls meeting Bodenheim at Sherwood Anderson's Cass Street apartment in the spring of 1913 (p. 221), Anderson did not actually move there until the fall of the following year. See Walter B. Rideout, *Sherwood Anderson: A Writer in America* (Madison: University of Wisconsin Press, 2006), 191. According to Harry Hansen, the two met at the office of the *Little Review*. Hansen, *Midwest Portraits*, 322.

18. J. Moore, *Maxwell Bodenheim*, 13–16. In his endnotes, Moore explains that in addition to information provided by Bodenheim's first wife, Minna Schein, "Floyd Dell was one of several to mention to me Bodenheim's self-destructive tendencies. Dell has never published on Bodenheim, but wrote me several letters" (178n1). Two important sources on Bodenheim, which I was not able to consult, are the collection of his papers archived at Columbia University (http://www.columbia.edu/cu/lweb/archival/collections /ldpd_9025181/) and a 1957 doctoral dissertation: Edward T. DeVoe, "A Soul in Gaudy Tatters" (PhD diss., Pennsylvania State University, 1957). Recent studies of Bodenheim attest to the continued interest in his life and work. See Jason Boog, "People's Libraries," *Los Angeles Review of Books*, November 12, 2011, https://lareviewofbooks.org/essay/peoples-libraries; and John Strausbaugh, *The Village: 400 Years of Beats and Bohemians, Radicals and Rogues, a History of Greenwich Village* (New York: Ecco, 2013). Strausbaugh

provides a biographical treatment of Bodenheim on the website The Chiseler: Forgotten Authors, Neglected Stars and Lost Languages Rediscovered: http://chiseler.org/post/38071308208/maxwell-bodenheim.

19. Hecht, *Letters from Bohemia*, 111; and J. Moore, *Maxwell Bodenheim*, 13–16.

20. Alfred Kreymborg, *Troubadour: An American Autobiography*, American Century Series, S-22 (New York: Sagamore, 1957), 251–52 (including the Bodenheim quote); and William Carlos Williams, *Imaginations* (New York: New Directions, 1971), 27–28. Kreymborg and his wife finally had to kick Bodenheim out.

21. *The Letters of Hart Crane, 1916–1932* (New York: Hermitage House, 1952), 9; and *The Selected Letters of William Carlos Williams* (New York: New Directions, 1984), 37. See also J. Moore, *Maxwell Bodenheim*, 21–25, citing William Troy, "The Story of the Little Magazines," *Bookman* 70 (1930): 659; and Arthur and Barbara Gelb, *O'Neill* (New York: Harper, 1960), 361.

22. Herbert S. Gorman, "Poets of Today and Yesterday," *New York Times*, December 26, 1920, 48.

23. Hecht, *Child*, 225–28; Hecht, *Gaily, Gaily*, 167; Hecht, "About Sherwood Anderson," in *Letters from Bohemia*, 88–99; Hansen, *Midwest Portraits*, 109–80; Rideout, *Sherwood Anderson*, 154–61, 191–92; Kramer, *Chicago Renaissance*, 167–73, 288–89; and Howe, *Sherwood Anderson*, 46–49, 64–68. Anderson refers to "We Little Children of the Arts," "the little children of the arts," and "Little Children of the Arts" in his memoirs. See S. Anderson, *Memoirs*, 317, 319, 347.

24. On Anderson's progress as the man Dell called "the great unpublished author," see Kramer, *Chicago Renaissance*, 240–43, 288–93. On Anderson as being surrounded by urchins half his age, see Howe, *Sherwood Anderson*, 64–68. The quotation "If we are a crude and childlike people . . ." is from Sherwood Anderson, "An Apology for Crudity," *Dial* 63, no. 753 (November 8, 1917): 437.

25. On Sandburg's background, see Hansen, *Midwest Portraits*, 30–44; Kramer, *Chicago Renaissance*, 52–60, 182–84, 243, 263; and Duffey, *Chicago Renaissance*, 209–15. On Sandburg's relationship with the *Chicago Daily News*, see Kramer, *Chicago Renaissance*, 312; Duffey, *Chicago Renaissance*, 221; and Hecht, *Child*, 243–55.

26. Kramer, *Chicago Renaissance*, 278, 283–85.

27. Kramer, *Chicago Renaissance*, 302–9, 353–54; and Duffey, *Chicago Renaissance*, 219–22. Although Anderson's *Winesburg, Ohio* collection was not published until 1919, slightly different versions of five of the stories had appeared in *Masses*, *The Little Review*, and *Seven Arts* between February and December 1916. Another five had been published by *Seven Arts* and *The Little Review* by December 1918. The book consists of twenty-two stories altogether.

28. Kramer, *Chicago Renaissance*, 309; Duffey, *Chicago Renaissance*, 241; Mackay, *Little Theatre*, 113, 114 117. Hecht's *An Idyll of the Shops*, *The Home Coming*, *The Wonder Hat*, and *The Hero of Santa Maria*, all of which he cowrote with Kenneth Sawyer Goodman, were performed at the Little Theater in 1916,

as was his controversial play *Dregs*. The following year the theater produced a play he cowrote with Bodenheim, *Mrs. Margaret Calhoun*. The Hull House Players performed Hecht and Goodman's *The Poem of David*.

29. Hecht, *Letters from Bohemia*, 113.

Chapter 6

1. Parry, *Garretts and Pretenders*, 190–91.
2. Lewis A. Coser, *Men of Ideas: A Sociologist's View* (New York: Free Press, 1965), viii, 117, 328.
3. Sacvan Bercovitch, *The American Jeremiad* (Madison: University of Wisconsin Press, 1978), 180.
4. M. Anderson, *My Thirty Years' War*, 54; and M. Anderson, "Toward Revolution," *Little Review* 2, no. 9 (December 1919): 5.
5. Hecht, *Gaily, Gaily*, 185–86.
6. Albert Parry noted, "In New York, in the same early 1910s, the Greenwich Villagers also quoted the Bible, but it was in support of their Socialist views. The contemporary intellectuals of New York waved their banners of revolt in politics; they were acutely conscious of social problems. For New York's tempo was more tearing and grinding than Chicago's; it made no favorite of native sons but exploited all. . . . The intellectual youngsters who came there to create art for art's sake soon developed an interest in Socialism, especially since New York was a natural port of first call for all the newest currents of European thought floating to America." Parry, *Garretts and Pretenders*, 190.
7. Mabel Dodge Luhan, *Movers and Shakers*, vol. 3 of *Intimate Memories* (New York: Harcourt, 1936), 36.
8. Emma Goldman, *Nowhere at Home: Letters from Exile of Emma Goldman and Alexander Berkman* (New York: Schocken Books, 1975); Wetzsteon, *Republic of Dreams*, 220–21, 315–17; and Christine Stansell, *American Moderns: Bohemian New York and the Creation of a New Century* (New York: Metropolitan Books, 2000), 323–26.
9. Quoted in Martha Craven Nussbaum, *Upheavals of Thought: The Intelligence of Emotions* (Cambridge: Cambridge University Press, 2001), 688; see also Stansell, *American Moderns*, 327–28.
10. Frank H. Simonds, "1914—the End of an Era," *New Republic*, January 2, 1915, 12–13; and May, *End of American Innocence*, 361–62.
11. See Hansen's introduction, "Of an Ancient Tavern on a Well-Traveled Highway," in *Midwest Portraits*, 3–12; Kramer, *Chicago Renaissance*, 331–34; and Duffey, *Chicago Renaissance*, 246–48.
12. Samuel Putnam, "A Deepening Discontent with American Values," in *The Rise and Fall of the Dil Pickle: Jazz-Age Chicago's Wildest and Most Outrageously Creative Hobohemian Nightspot*, ed. Franklin Rosemont (Chicago: Charles H. Kerr, 2004), 138–39; and Hecht, *Child*, 345.

13. Franklin Rosemont, introduction to *Dil Pickle*, 23–24.
14. Ben Reitman, "Chicago's Intellectual & Literary Center," in Rosemont, *Dil Pickle*, 63, 64; and Jones, quoted in S. Anderson, *Memoirs*, 270. On all-night jazz and Little Theater productions of Ibsen and Strindberg, as well as Triphammer Johnson, see excerpt from Kenneth Rexroth, "A Most Important Part of the Mythology of Chicago," in Rosemont, *Dil Pickle*, 93, 95, 98. On the then unheard-of topic of atomic energy, see "Yellow Kid" Weill, "Different from Any Other Institution That Ever Existed," in Rosemont, *Dil Pickle*, 111. On the antisocialist Sirfressor (F. M. Wilkesbarr, aka Malfew Seklew), see George Murray, "Reflections of Old Picklers," in Rosemont, *Dil Pickle*, 116.
15. Rexroth, "Mythology of Chicago," 94, 95.
16. On the reaction to *Dregs*, see Starrett, *Born in a Bookshop*, 198–99. On the literary debate, see Parry, *Garretts and Pretenders*, 191.
17. Hecht, *Gaily, Gaily*, 124–25.
18. Note from Hecht to Bodenheim, quoted in Hansen, *Midwest Portraits*, 353.
19. "Startling the Radicals," *New York Times*, July 29, 1923, sec. 2, p. 4. The phrase "gazette devoted to the Sacred Ballyhoo" is from Hecht, "Our First Issue: Salutation on the Saxophone," *Chicago Literary Times*, March 1, 1923, 1. On Covici's belief that the magazine would promote his concerns, see Hecht, *Child*, 338–39. In *Midwest Portraits*, Hansen recounts that Hecht wanted to launch the magazine with sandwich-board men and a parade of brass bands and half a mile of floats, so at the very least it was meant to generate publicity for itself and for Hecht (354–55). For the circulation figures, see Ravitz, "Ballyhoo, Gargoyles and Firecrackers," 40–41. Abe C. Ravitz remarked of a full-page illustration in the premiere issue: "The ultimate in this literary caricature was Hecht's vision as a derby-hatted cane-waving barker at a side-show carnival endeavoring to lure the parading customers into the big tent to see the scribbling freaks, much of whom were cartooned" (45).
20. Hecht, "Our First Issue"; and Hecht, "Concerning the Natl. Cemetery of Arts and Letters," *Chicago Literary Times*, March 1, 1923, 1.
21. Hecht, "Semi-idiot Broadcasting Programs Doom Radio as Charm for Civilized Homes," *Chicago Literary Times*, May 1, 1923, 1; Hecht, "Surveying Bumper High-Brow Crop of Little Magazines," *Chicago Literary Times*, May 1, 1923, 1; and Bodenheim, "Peeping Tom in Verbal Dressing Rooms of Bohemia," *Chicago Literary Times*, May 15, 1923, 2.
22. Bodenheim, "The Waste Land," *Chicago Literary Times*, May 1, 1923, 7; on Fitzgerald, see Hecht, "The Vegetable," *Chicago Literary Times*, June 1, 1923, 7; and Bodenheim, "Again the Bozarts Seem on the Way to the Bow-Wows," *Chicago Literary Times*, July 15, 1923, 6. "The Waste Land" and "The Vegetable" reviews are attributed to Rene D'Or, which was a pen name for Bodenheim. For background on the origins of this pen name, which was wrapped up in an elaborate hoax that became an inspiration for Hecht's *Count Bruga* novel, see Parry, *Garretts and Pretenders*, 192–93.

23. "Bodenheim Runs Amuck; 4 Dead, and 3 Wounded," *Chicago Literary Times*, July 1, 1923, 1.

24. In one letter, Anderson wrote, "The smartiness will perhaps defeat Ben. It may have already." *Letters of Sherwood Anderson*, ed. Howard Mumford Jones in association with Walter Rideout (New York: Kraus Reprint, 1969), 119.

25. On Yiddish theater, vaudeville, and Charlie Chaplin, see "Obeisance to the Wrinkled Thalia of Yiddish Theater," *Chicago Literary Times*, July 1, 1923, 5; Bodenheim, "Vodvil Vignettes," *Chicago Literary Times*, June 15, 1923, 8; and Hecht, "Charlie Chaplin's Greatest Picture: A Future Review," *Chicago Literary Times*, July 15, 1923, 3. The author of the "Wrinkled Thalia" review is not identified, but given the praise in it for Sholem Aleichem, it was likely written by Hecht. On *Ulysses*, see Hecht, "Editorial Notes," *Chicago Literary Times*, March 15, 1923, 1. On the closing of the *Little Review*, see Bodenheim, "New York Letter Closeups of the Literary Suburbs," *Chicago Literary Times*, June 15, 1923, 5. On the lost bohemia, see Hecht, "High-Hat Complex Corrupts Circus of the Days Gone By," *Chicago Literary Times*, May 15, 1923, 1, 5; and on disappointed straphangers returning home, see Bodenheim, "Coney Island Notes," *Chicago Literary Times*, July 15, 1923, 7.

26. Hecht, "Editorial Notes," *Chicago Literary Times*, July 15, 1923, 4.

27. Hecht, "Adante con Amore Face to Face with Artist Anderson," *Chicago Literary Times*, April 15, 1923, 1; and Hecht, *Letters from Bohemia*, 92.

28. According to biographer Walter Rideout, Anderson found Hecht's first novel too flashy. See Rideout, *Writer in America*, 437. For Hecht's claim that being enemies was Anderson's idea, see Hecht, "A Pair of Windows," *Chicago Literary Times*, March 1, 1923, 2; and Hecht, *Child*, 230.

29. Quoted in MacAdams, *Man behind the Legend*, 61–62. The location of this letter, which MacAdams quotes in its entirety, is a mystery. It is not with Hecht's papers, nor printed in *Letters from Bohemia*, nor compiled in the *Letters of Sherwood Anderson*. MacAdams cannot remember where he found it.

30. Hansen, *Midwest Portraits*, 310. On Hecht's literary influences, see Hansen, *Midwest Portraits*, 310–20; on discovering Hecht reading *Arabian Nights*, see Hansen, *Midwest Portraits*, 306.

31. Burton Rascoe, "An American Epithetician," *Bookman*, October 1921, 164–65; and Gilbert Seldes, "Arriviste and Aristocrat," *Dial* 71, no. 5 (November 1921): 597–600. *Erik Dorn* was, however, hailed by many as the debut of an important new voice. "When Ben Hecht gets himself well in hand," wrote a critic for the *New York Times*, "America will have another great realistic writer of novels." "Latest Works of Fiction," *New York Times*, October 9, 1921, 12, 18. In the *New Republic*, Francis Hackett argued that the novel put to bed the idea that clever men are also brittle. *Erik Dorn* had "the same glassy sharpness of line" as his short stories in the *Little Review*, "the same bitterness and mockery . . . the same moonlit inhospitality." But instead of being a firework that fizzles out in a rain of sparks, it "whizzes with cold and elaborate ardor through the full length of 409 pages." Francis Hackett, "Erik

Dorn," *New Republic*, August 31, 1921. Russell Gore in the *Detroit News* wrote that a novel with a style "so darkly beautiful and so irritatingly clever as Mr. Hecht's divides readers into opposing camps." Gore, "Erik Dorn, a Cataract of Bizarre Epigrams," *Detroit News*, September 21, 1921.

32. Clinton Simpson, "Some Recent Fiction, in the Byways," review of *The Champion from Far Away*, *Saturday Review*, September 19, 1931, 136.

33. For a thorough bibliography and filmography, see MacAdams, *Man behind the Legend*, 299–357. In *The Five Lives of Ben Hecht*, Doug Fetherling set out to correct the record on Hecht's literary reputation and largely succeeds with a perceptive survey of Hecht's books.

34. Ben Hecht, *Fantazius Mallare: A Mysterious Oath* (Chicago: Covici-McGee, 1922), 11–18; T. K. Hedrik, "Ben's Most Hechtic Book," *Arts Monthly*, October 22, 1922; and Ravitz, "Ballyhoo, Gargoyles and Firecrackers," 39.

35. Hecht, "My Last Park Bench," *Chicago Literary Times*, June 1, 1924, 16. See also "Hecht Fined for Mailing Obscene Book in Chicago," *Bridgeport (Conn.) Telegram*, May 2, 1924, 10; and Hecht, *Child*, 180. Hecht's last column for the *Daily News* was published on October 10, 1922. The earliest mention of Hecht being fired from the *Daily News* that I could find was in Fetherling, *Five Lives*, 54. See also the biography on the Newberry Library web page for Hecht's papers: "Inventory of the Ben Hecht Papers, 1879–1983," n.d., http://mms.newberry.org/html/hecht.html. Hecht joined the Committee for the Suppression of Irresponsible Censorship and contributed to an anthology of essays by Dorothy Parker, Alexander Woollcott, and others. Hecht, "Literature in the Bastinado," in *Nonsenseorship: Sundry Observations Concerning Prohibitions, Inhibitions and Illegalities*, ed. George P. Putnam (New York, 1922), 17–32.

36. Hecht, *Count Bruga*, 1–28.

37. Hecht, *Letters from Bohemia*, 118–20.

38. Bodenheim, *Duke Herring*, 35, 150.

39. Bodenheim, *Duke Herring*, 119.

40. *The Letters of T. S. Eliot*, rev. ed. (New Haven, Conn.: Yale University Press, 2011), 2:476. On the trip to England, see also J. Moore, *Maxwell Bodenheim*, 55–56.

41. Maxwell Bodenheim, "Jewish Writers in America," *Menorah Journal* 8, no. 2 (April 1922): 74–78 (the quote "exhibiting a surface Jewish tendency . . ." is on pp. 75–76).

42. Bodenheim, "Jewish Writers in America," 76, 77, 78.

43. Hecht, *Guide for the Bedevilled*, 77, 158.

44. Hecht, *Guide for the Bedevilled*, 159–60.

45. On the absence of any mention of their Jewish heritage, and its implications, see Harold Cruse, *The Crisis of the Negro Intellectual* (New York: Morrow, 1967). Cruse uses the Jewish question as an example of the Villagers' attitudes toward the topics of ethnicity and minority rights. On Dodge's insistence on using her limousine, see Wetzsteon, *Republic of Dreams*, 41.

46. Israel Zangwill, *The Melting-Pot: A Drama in Four Acts* (New York: Macmillan, 1909). On Zangwill's territorialism, see Melvin I. Urofsky, *American Zionism from Herzl to the Holocaust* (Garden City, N.Y.: Anchor, 1975), 28.

47. Horace M. Kallen, "Democracy versus the Melting Pot, Part One," *Nation*, February 18, 1915, 191–94; and "Democracy versus the Melting Pot, Part Two," *Nation*, February 25, 217–20.

48. Hecht, *Child*, 380; see also Alan M. Wald, *The New York Intellectuals: The Rise and Decline of the Anti-Stalinist Left from the 1930s to the 1980s* (Chapel Hill: University of North Carolina Press, 1987), 27–28.

49. On the conflicted ethos of cultural pluralism, see Wald, *New York Intellectuals*, 29, who draws from John Higham, *Send These to Me: Immigrants in Urban America*, rev. ed. (Baltimore: Johns Hopkins University Press, 1984), 196. On the *Menorah Journal*, see Wald, *New York Intellectuals*, 30.

50. Hecht, *Child*, 381–82.

51. Gilbert Seldes, "The Daemonic in the American Theatre," *Dial*, September 1923, 303–8. Raphaelson, quoted in Hoberman and Shandler, *Entertaining America*, 81–83. *Entertaining America* has a reproduction of the souvenir program.

Chapter 7

1. Hecht, *Charlie*, 164.

2. F. Scott Fitzgerald, *The Crack-Up* (New York: J. Laughlin, 1945).

3. Hecht, *Charlie*, 178–83. On the seventy-five-acre Youngworth Ranch, see MacAdams, *Man behind the Legend*, 123; and McCarthy, *Howard Hawks*, 130. Both biographers interviewed John Lee Mahin, who said, "They paid twelve hundred dollars a month for it [the ranch], which at the time was godawful rent." Quoted in MacAdams, *Man behind the Legend*, 123. Hecht said he was put up at the ranch and given a salary of two hundred and fifty a week. Hecht, *Charlie*, 179. Mahin apparently described it to MacAdams as an avocado farm, but Hecht said 250 turkeys were running around the place. *Charlie*, 174.

4. Hecht, *Charlie*, 163–64.

5. Quoted in Hecht, *Charlie*, 158. In *Charlie*, Hecht further explained, "The boss liked a superior writer to turn out his kindergarten truck—for a number of reasons, some of them mystic. It was a foolish waste of money, like hiring a cabinetmaker to put up a picket fence. But there was a certain pleasure in it for the boss. The higher the class of talent he could tell what to do and how to do it, the more giddily cultured he could feel himself. A good four-fifths of Hollywood's bosses were money-grabbing nitwits whom movie-making enabled to masquerade as Intellects and Creative Spirits. The boss who hired Dostoevsky to write like Horatio Alger somehow became Feodor's superior" (157–58). On the spiritual toll, Hecht quoted from F. Scott

Fitzgerald's memo of anguished protest to a producer who had tossed out all of Fitzgerald's dialogue on a script: "How could you do this to me? . . . How can you throw me away in this fashion?" Hecht concluded, "Signature—and crack-up" (161).

6. Quoted in Hecht, *Child*, 466.

7. Richard Meryman, *Mank: The Wit, World, and Life of Herman Mankiewicz* (New York: Morrow, 1978), 68, 96–97, 123–37.

8. Meryman, *Mank*, 138–39.

9. Kael, *Citizen Kane Book*, 9–10.

10. Hugh Gray, interview by William MacAdams, n.d., MacAdams Collection, BHPNL.

11. Gray, interview by MacAdams.

12. For Hecht's screen work and credits during these years, see MacAdams, *Man behind the Legend*, 116–24, 132–33, 144–60. Based on interviews and letters, people were referring to Hecht's "script writing factory" at least as early as the 1940s, but the first published reference to it appears to have been in Doug Fetherling's 1977 biography: "At length his benchmark became so much in demand that he created a factory of anonymous younger writers to block out and draft scripts which he then revised and signed. The members of this assembly line, who were called into action only when needed for a specific job, did not necessarily know one another's identity, a fact that distinguished them from the gallery of disciples and apprentices employed by artists as far back as Michelangelo's time and revived for iconoclastic effect by Andy Warhol." Fetherling, *Five Lives*, 142. According to MacAdams, who calculated that Hecht received screen credits on 65 films and worked on a total of 146, Hecht started his writing factory in the early 1930s with *Scarface*, subcontracting to writers who included Bartlett Cormack, Johnny Weaver, Gene Markey, old friends Wallace Smith and Gene Fowler, and new friend Charles Lederer. MacAdams suggested that "in his movie days, Hecht managed to re-create the boisterous atmosphere of a Chicago newsroom." Quoted from MacAdams, interview by Ron Grossman in "Reporter, Film Writer, Spellbinder," *Chicago Tribune*, June 12, 1990. The article also contains MacAdams's estimates of Hecht's screen credits and overall output. Hecht himself disliked Hollywood's factory-like operation, and though he wrote of the joys of screenwriting collaboration in *A Child of the Century* (281), it is unlikely that he would have claimed credit for a "writing factory." For Hecht's initial factory and references to it by director Henry Hathaway and producer David Selznick in the 1940s, see MacAdams, *Man behind the Legend*, 245.

13. Hawks, interview by MacAdams.

14. Hawks, interview by MacAdams.

15. Hawks, interview by MacAdams.

16. Kael, *5001 Nights at the Movies: A Guide from A to Z* (New York: Holt, Rinehart and Winston, 1982), 796; and Andrew Sarris, "The Sex Comedy without Sex," *American Film* 3 (March 1978): 8, 14.

17. Percy Hammond, "The Colossus of Rose," review of *Jumbo*, *New York Herald-Tribune*, November 18, 1935, 10. See also MacAdams, *Man behind the Legend*, 163–65.

18. "Books on Our Table," *New York Evening Post*, January 26, 1931. See "A Jew in Love, n.d., 1930–1932," Series 6: Publicity, 1920–1979, box 79, folder 2411, BHPNL.

19. Donald Friede, *The Mechanical Angel, His Adventures and Enterprises in the Glittering 1920's* (New York: A. A. Knopf, 1948), 116–19.

20. Bob Stafford, "Book Notes and Comment," *Akron Times*, February 8, 1931; "Ben Hecht's Novel Brutal Study of a Book Publisher," *Baltimore Evening Sun*, January 24, 1931; "Ben Hecht Dissects Mind of an Egoist," *Honolulu Star-Bulletin*, January 31, 1931; "Mr. Hecht Writes a Novel," *Milwaukee Journal*, January 31, 1931; "'Festival' and Some Other Recent Works of Fiction/Mr. Hecht's Mockery," *New York Times*, January 25, 1931; and Adelin Hohfield, "About Books," *Wisconsin State Journal*, February 15, 1931. These reviews can be found in Series 6: Publicity, 1920–1979, box 79, folder 2411, BHPNL.

21. "'A Jew in Love' by Ben Hecht," *Newark News*, February 21, 1931; *Buffalo Evening News*, February 7, 1931. The headline is missing from the Newberry Library clipping of the *Buffalo Evening News* story. Series 6: Publicity, 1920–1979, box 79, folder 2411, BHPNL. Rabbi Newman's comment is quoted in "Two Rabbis Assail Hecht and Nickerson," *New York Times*, February 16, 1931, 18. On the banning of the book and Hecht's comment that "the Jewish race will survive," see *News* (Dayton, Ohio), April 3, 1931.

22. Ben Hecht, *A Jew in Love* (New York: Covici, Friede, 1931), 3; and Leslie A. Fiedler, "The Jew in the American Novel," in *The Collected Essays of Leslie Fiedler* (New York: Stein and Day, 1971), 2:82.

23. Hecht, *Jew in Love*, 142, 217.

24. Fiedler, "Jew in the American Novel," 2:81, 82; and Fetherling, *Five Lives*, 118.

25. Ruth Seinfel, "Author of *A Jew in Love* Longed for Lost Unpopularity, but Now That He Has It He Confesses Remorse," *New York Evening Post*, 1931 (date deleted from copy of article on file), Series 6: Publicity, 1920–1979, box 79, folder 2411, BHPNL.

26. "Unintelligent Fascism," editorial, *New Masses* 10, no. 13 (27 March 1934): 6, quoted in Wald, *New York Intellectuals*, 63; see also Wald, *New York Intellectuals*, 56–57, 58, 62–63.

27. Note from Hecht to Bodenheim, quoted in Hansen, *Midwest Portraits*, 353.

28. Hecht, *Child*, 365. On Hecht's psychological explanation for the radicalism of the 1930s, see *Child*, 360–62.

29. Hecht, *Charlie*, 191. On the studio, see Richard Koszarski, *Hollywood on the Hudson: Film and Television in New York from Griffith to Sarnoff* (New Brunswick, N.J.: Rutgers University Press, 2008), 28, 29. Composer George Antheil recalled that when he first came to the studio to negotiate his salary,

Hecht and MacArthur had said all money matters were handled by their "executive producer": "I advanced to the desk, where a little pinhead gentleman in a high wing-collar was writing. I looked at what he was writing. He was doodling. He looked up, and then jumped right over the desk at me! He always jumped right over the desk at visitors, jabbering incoherently. Otherwise he was harmless." George Antheil, *Bad Boy of Music* (Garden City, N.Y.: Doubleday, Doran, 1945), 271, quoted in Koszarski, *Hollywood on the Hudson*, 291.

30. On the troubled history of Astoria, Paramount's great white elephant, see Koszarski, *Hollywood on the Hudson*, 12, 22, 26–32, 57, 158–59, 179, 203, 225–27. On the million-dollar offer. . . Hecht, *Charlie*, 183. A truer and better way than the corporate compartmentalization of the studio system. . . MacAdams, *Man behind the Legend*, 169.

31. Hecht, *Charlie*, 183–87.

32. Hecht, *Charlie*, 158–59.

33. Joseph Epstein, "The Great Hack Genius," *Commentary* 90, no. 6 (December 1990): 43–44. It was actually in the mid-1940s, not the mid-1930s, that Wilson wrote that, a decade earlier, writers had fallen easy prey "to the great enemies of literary talent in our time: Hollywood and Henry Luce." Edmund Wilson, "Thoughts on Being Bibliographed," in *Classics and Commercials: A Literary Chronicle of the Forties* (New York: Vintage Books, 1950), 105–8, originally published in *Princeton University Library Chronicle* 5, no. 2 (February 1944).

34. Hecht, *Charlie*, 190; and Hawks, quoted in MacAdams, *Man behind the Legend*, 169–70. On Rosson, Selznick, Garmes, and Vorkapich, see Koszarski, *Hollywood on the Hudson*, 286. (Richard and Diane Koszarski interviewed Garmes in 1976.) Rosson is credited as general manager of *Crime without Passion* and *The Scoundrel* in the Internet Movie Database: https://www.imdb .com/name/nm0744504/?ref_=nv_sr_1 (accessed September 3, 2018).

35. Koszarski, *Hollywood on the Hudson*, 284–85.

36. *The Scoundrel*, written and directed by Ben Hecht and Charles MacArthur, starring Noel Coward and Julie Haydon (Paramount, 1935; s.l.: Zeus, 2017).

37. Hecht, *Child*, 483–84; Koszarski, *Hollywood on the Hudson*, 293–94; and "*The Scoundrel*," *Time*, May 13, 1935.

38. The quotation from the film "A few years ago . . ." is quoted in Frank S. Nugent, "Thunder over Astoria," *New York Times*, October 27, 1935. Koszarski, *Hollywood on the Hudson*, 295–97; "*Soak the Rich*," *New York Sun*, February 7, 1936; and "Hits and Flops of '36," *Hollywood Reporter*, July 13, 1936, 1, quoted in Koszarski, *Hollywood on the Hudson*, 297.

39. Alfred Hayes, "The Pair from Paramount," *New Theatre*, March 1936, 15, quoted in Koszarski, *Hollywood on the Hudson*, 285.

Chapter 8

1. Hecht, "Four Rabbis Speak," in *1001 Afternoons in New York*, 67.
2. Hawks, interview by MacAdams; see also Koszarski, *Hollywood on the Hudson*, 295.
3. Henry Hathaway, interview by William MacAdams, at Hathaway's Universal Studios office, January 30, 1972, MacAdams Collection, BHPNL; Hawks, interview by MacAdams; and "Ben Hecht Acts in Play He Didn't Write," *Pittsburgh Press*, September 1, 1936, 18, http://news.google.com/newspapers?nid=1144&dat=19360901&id=uyUbAAAAIBAJ&sjid=30sEAAAAIBAJ&pg=2728,2613280. On Hecht taking Taylor to Quito, Ecuador, see MacAdams, *Man behind the Legend*, 188–89.
4. Hecht, *To Quito and Back*, 22, 142, 181.
5. Hecht, *To Quito and Back*, 56, 145, 140, 142–43, 69.
6. Hecht, *To Quito and Back*, 148, 58–59, 154–75, 185.
7. Hawks, interview by MacAdams.
8. Hawks, interview by MacAdams.
9. Otto Preminger, interview by William MacAdams, New York, n.d. [ca. 1972], MacAdams Collection, BHPNL; and Bruce Cook, *Dalton Trumbo* (New York: Scribner, 1977), 281–82. Preminger draws the same conclusion about Trumbo's legacy.
10. Hawks, interview by MacAdams.
11. Hathaway, interview by MacAdams. Preminger and Hawks also discussed Ferraday in their interviews with MacAdams.
12. Bosley Crowther, "Home Is the Hunter, Home from the Hills," *New York Times*, September 19, 1937; and Ben Hecht to Rose Hecht, n.d. [1937], Series 4: Family Correspondence, 1915–1976, box 72, folder 2250, BHPNL.
13. Hecht, guest contributor to Walter Winchell, On Broadway, *Daily Mirror*, July 31, 1935, Series 1: Works, 1908–1983, box 31, folder 790, BHPNL.
14. Hecht to Samuel Goldwyn, in Series 3: Outgoing Correspondence, 1931–1977, box 67, folder 1926, BHPNL.
15. Martin Gilbert, *Kristallnacht: Prelude to Destruction* (New York: HarperCollins, 2006), 13; and "World War II: Before the War," *Atlantic*, June 19, 2011, http://www.theatlantic.com/infocus/2011/06/world-war-ii-before-the-war/100089/. Though most historians have focused on the events of November 9 and 10, it was in fact a four-day pogrom that started on November 7 with rioting in Kassel, a city in north central Germany. James M. Deem, *Kristallnacht: The Nazi Terror That Began the Holocaust*, The Holocaust through Primary Sources (Berkeley Heights, N.J.: Enslow, 2012), 10.
16. Ben Hecht, *A Book of Miracles* (New York: Viking, 1937), 25.
17. Hecht, "Preface to Shylock," 3, Series 1: Works, 1908–1983, box 24, folder 635, BHPNL; and John Selby, *"Book of Miracles,"* The Literary Guidepost (syndicated through the Associated Press), *Billings (Mont.) Gazette*, June 18, 1939, 4.

18. Hecht, *Child*, 520; and Hecht, *1001 Afternoons in New York*, 33–36, 45–48, 196–99, 131–35. On the pay for the column versus his Hollywood income, see Leonard Lyons, "Hecht's 'Manhattan Montage,'" *Saturday Review*, November 22, 1941, 8.

19. Hecht, *1001 Afternoons in New York*, 16–17, 37–40.

20. Hecht, *1001 Afternoons in New York*, 61–64.

21. Hecht, *1001 Afternoons in New York*, 49–52, 99–102; and Groucho Marx, note, August 29, 1941, Series 2: Incoming Correspondence, 1914–1979, box 60, folder 1452, BHPNL.

22. Hecht, *1001 Afternoons in New York*, 25–28.

23. David Nasaw, *The Patriarch: The Remarkable Life and Turbulent Times of Joseph P. Kennedy* (New York: Penguin, 2012), 497–510. According to Nasaw's account: "Thinking he was among friends—after all, Lyons was a Boston reporter—and assuming he was speaking off the record and would not be quoted directly, Kennedy held court for the next ninety minutes. . . . But Lyons, knowing a big story when he saw one, wrote up what Kennedy had told him." To address the concern, Lyons put in a paragraph, subheaded "Reporter's Dilemma," explaining that he had planned to do a "soft" piece" but, given what he had heard, felt obligated to share it with his readers. Nasaw, *Patriarch*, 498, 499.

24. Quoted in Nasaw, *Patriarch*, 501–2. On December 16, 1940, Kennedy met with Breckinridge Long, the special assistant secretary of state, who was keeping the immigration of Jewish refugees well below the quota (see part III), with the justification that some of the asylum seekers might be Nazi spies. In a diary entry that evening, Kennedy wrote that Long was facing pressure from Supreme Court justice Felix Frankfurter, *Washington Post* publisher Eugene Meyer, and other powerful Jews who had conspired to receive special treatment for their people. "A greater fraud and well-engineered scheme was never perpetrated on the American public than that a thousand refugees have been taken into the United States," Kennedy wrote a friend in Boston. "Not one of them, I know, had ever been investigated by the F.B.I., and yet I don't suppose any newspaper in the United States would print the truth for fear of losing advertisers—and then we boast of freedom of the press. Nuts, I say." Quoted in Nasaw, *Patriarch*, 509. Within a week after Hecht's column on January 16, 1941, a speech by Kennedy over the radio and contemptuous, evasive testimony before Congress on Roosevelt's proposed Lend-Lease policy would end Kennedy's political career for good.

25. Hecht, *1001 Afternoons in New York*, 26.

26. Hoberman and Shandler, *Entertaining America*, 14–22, 47–66, 73–75. See also Neal Gabler, *An Empire of Their Own: How the Jews Invented Hollywood*, 1st ed. (New York: Crown, 1988).

27. T. Doherty, *Hollywood and Hitler*, 2–8.

28. Adolf Hitler, *Mein Kampf*, trans. Ralph Manheim [1925 and 1927] (Boston: Houghton Mifflin, 1943), 470; and Goebbels, quoted in T. Doherty, *Hollywood and Hitler*, 18–19.

29. The phrase "probably the scum of the earth" is quoted in Thomas Patrick Doherty, *Pre-Code Hollywood: Sex, Immorality, and Insurrection in American Cinema, 1930–1934* (New York: Columbia University Press, 1999), 98. On Aryanization policy, see T. Doherty, *Hollywood and Hitler*, 21. The story of Nazi pressure on Hollywood is told in Doherty's *Hollywood and Hitler* and Ben Urwand's *The Collaboration: Hollywood's Pact with Hitler* (Cambridge, Mass.: Belknap Press of Harvard University Press, 2013).

30. T. Doherty, "The Unmaking of *Mad Dog of Europe*," in *Hollywood and Hitler*, 53–59 (see also 356–57); Urwand, *Collaboration*, 63–71; and Meryman, *Mank*, 233.

31. Quoted in T. Doherty, *Hollywood and Hitler*, 58.

32. Steven Joseph Ross, "The Most Charming Nazi in Los Angeles," in *Hitler in Los Angeles: How Jews Foiled Nazi Plots against Hollywood and America* (New York: Bloomsbury USA, 2017), Kindle.

33. T. Doherty, *Hollywood and Hitler*, 95–102, 120–21.

34. T. Doherty, *Hollywood and Hitler*, 311, 344–50; Hoberman and Shandler, *Entertaining America*, 47–66, 73–75; and David Denby, "Hitler in Hollywood," *New Yorker*, September 16, 2013, https://www.newyorker.com /magazine/2013/09/16/hitler-in-hollywood.

35. Hoberman and Shandler, *Entertaining America*, 62. See also my earlier discussion of Hecht's role in the adaptation of *Personal History* into *Foreign Correspondent*.

36. Hollywood League for Democratic Action, quoted in T. Doherty, *Hollywood and Hitler*, 352 (see also 351–52); and Mankiewicz, quoted in Meryman, *Mank*, 234.

37. Hecht, *Child*, 517, 381. For *Fun to Be Free*, see Hecht, *Child*, 517–18; and the souvenir program in Series 6: Publicity, 1920–1979, box 79, folder 2396, BHPNL.

38. Hecht, *1001 Afternoons in Chicago*, 27–28.

39. Hecht, *1001 Afternoons in Chicago*, 164–67.

40. Hecht, *1001 Afternoons in Chicago*, 166.

41. Hecht, *I Hate Actors!* (New York: Crown, 1944); Hecht, *The Champion from Far Away* (New York: Covici, Friede, 1931); Hecht, *Actor's Blood* (New York: Covici, Friede, 1936); and Hecht, "Concerning a Woman of Sin," pts. 1 and 2, *Collier's*, March 27, 1943, 11, 30–38, and April 3, 1943, 24–30. On the Hollywood writers of the era and the genre of the Hollywood novel, see Tom Dardis, *Some Time in the Sun: The Hollywood Years of F. Scott Fitzgerald, William Faulkner, Nathanael West, Aldous Huxley and James Agee* (New York: Scribner, 1976); Bruce L. Chipman, *Into America's Dream-Dump: A Postmodern Study of the Hollywood Novel* (Lanham, Md.: University Press of America, 1999); and Carolyn Penelope See, *The Hollywood Novel: An Historical and Critical Study* (Ann Arbor, Mich.: University Microfilms, 1976).

42. Hecht, *Book of Miracles*, 55–112. For an excellent summary and appraisal of the book, see Fred T. Marsh, "Miracles by Hecht," *New York Times*, June 18, 1939.

43. Hecht, *Book of Miracles*, 324.

44. Hecht, *Guide for the Bedevilled*, 161–99. On Yates turning the story down, see MacAdams, *Man behind the Legend*, 231–32.

45. Hecht, *Guide for the Bedevilled*, 202, 208; see also 207–10.

46. Popkin, in Hoberman and Shandler, *Entertaining America*, 136–37. The article by Henry Popkin, "The Vanishing Jew of Our Popular Culture: The Little Man Who Is No Longer There," *Commentary* 14, no. 1 (July 1952): 46–55, is reproduced in Hoberman and Shandler's book.

47. Hecht, *Guide for the Bedevilled*, 215–16.

48. Hecht, *Guide for the Bedevilled*, 216, 218, 219.

49. Hecht, *Child*, 219.

50. Mark Shechner, *After the Revolution: Studies in the Contemporary Jewish-American Imagination* (Bloomington: Indiana University Press, 1987), 7; Thomas Wolfe, "The 'Me' Decade and the Third Awakening," *New York Magazine*, August 23, 1976, 26–40; and Christopher Lasch, *The Culture of Narcissism: American Life in an Age of Diminishing Expectations* (New York: Norton, 1979). For more recent attention to this idea, see Kurt Anderson, "The Downside of Liberty," *New York Times*, July 3, 2012.

51. The phrase "strong note of inner drama" is from Epstein, "Great Hack Genius," 43.

52. Hecht, *Letters from Bohemia*, 122, 112.

53. For Hecht's sentiments, see, for example, "About Bodenheim," in *Letters from Bohemia*, 105–32; and *Winkelberg: A Play in Two Acts*, 1958, Series 1: Works, 1908–1983, box 31, folders 799–805, BHPNL.

54. Hecht, *Count Bruga*, 293.

55. Bodenheim to Ben and Rose Hecht, March 19, no year provided, Series 2: Incoming Correspondence, 1914–1979, box 55, folder 1078, BHPNL.

56. Hecht, quoted in Leonard Lyons, "Hecht Flooded by Calls," The Lyons Den, *Evening Standard* (Uniontown, Pa.), February 24, 1954, 11. On Bodenheim's death, see International News Service, "'Scar-Face' Hunted in Novelist Killing," *Los Angeles Herald-Express*, February 8, 1954, 1, 3, 12; "Indicted in Poet's Slaying," *New York Times*, March 3, 1954; and J. Moore, *Maxwell Bodenheim*, 172–73.

Part III

1. Deborah E. Lipstadt, *Beyond Belief: The American Press and the Coming of the Holocaust, 1933–1945* (New York: Free Press, 1993), 98–111; and Saul Friedländer, *The Years of Extermination: Nazi Germany and the Jews, 1939–1945* (New York: HarperCollins, 2007), 31, 187–88, 189, 237. The evolution and timing of the Nazis' extermination policy will be discussed in detail in chapter 12.

2. *Saturday Evening Post*, April 22, 1939, 104, quoted in Lipstadt, *Beyond Belief*, 103; and Roosevelt, quoted in Lipstadt, *Beyond Belief*, 105.

3. Lipstadt, *Beyond Belief*, 101–2; and Saul Friedländer, *Nazi Germany and the Jews*, vol. 1, *The Years of Persecution, 1933–1939* (New York: HarperCollins, 1997), 284–85.

4. "We Are Wanderers," *Time*, December 5, 1938, 19–20; and *Christian Science Monitor*, November 15, 1938, 1, discussed in Lipstadt, *Beyond Belief*, 107–11.

5. Hecht, *Book of Miracles*, 25.

6. Hecht, *Book of Miracles*, 25.

7. Walter Laqueur, *A History of Zionism* (New York: Holt, Rinehart and Winston, 1972), 523–27; and Nicholas Bethell, *The Palestine Triangle: The Struggle between the British, the Jews and the Arabs, 1935–48* (London: A. Deutsch, 1979), 59–68.

8. David Ben-Gurion, *Memoirs* [in Hebrew] (Tel Aviv: Am Oved, 1971), 6:200ff., quoted in Segev, *One Palestine, Complete*, 440; Chaim Weizmann, *Trial and Error* (New York: Harper, 1949), 410, quoted in Laqueur, *History of Zionism*, 527, 532–33. This session of the World Zionist Congress was held on August 24, 1939.

9. Ben-Gurion, comments to the Mapai Central Committee, September 12, 1939, paraphrased from Segev, *One Palestine, Complete*, 450; and Ben-Gurion, quoted in Segev, *One Palestine, Complete*, 461. On selectivity, see Segev, *One Palestine, Complete*, 393–96; and Laqueur, *History of Zionism*, 281, 315, 328–29, 351–53. Edwin Black provides a concise explanation and some additional sources. Black, *The Transfer Agreement: The Dramatic Story of the Pact between the Third Reich and Jewish Palestine* (Cambridge, Mass.: Brookline Books, 1999), 142.

10. Yitshaq Ben-Ami, *Years of Wrath, Days of Glory: Memoirs from the Irgun* (New York: R. Speller, 1982), 321. See also Judith Tydor Baumel, *The "Bergson Boys" and the Origins of Contemporary Zionist Militancy* (Syracuse, N.Y.: Syracuse University Press, 2005), 13, 75–76; S. Klinger and Vladimir Jabotinsky, *The Ten Year Plan for Palestine: A Brief Outline* (London: New Zionist Press, 1938); Laqueur, *History of Zionism*, 371; and Y. Ben-Ami, *Years of Wrath*, 122–30, 141–44, 157–58. Ben-Ami's activities are also summarized in Baumel, *"Bergson Boys,"* 5–7. The numbers smuggled by the World Zionist Organization are from Y. Ben-Ami, *Years of Wrath*, 321. According to Yehuda Bauer, who cites records from the Joint Distribution Committee Archives in New York, out of a total of 17,240 immigrants smuggled into Palestine illegally up until the war started in September 1939, "the Revisionists" claimed to have brought 9,460. Of that 17,240 total, 11,370 were seized by the British, meaning that only 5,861 made it through. Bauer, *American Jewry and the Holocaust: The American Jewish Joint Distribution Committee, 1939–1945* (Detroit: Wayne State University Press, 1981), 130. Ben-Ami, however, is clearly referring to a broader time frame than Bauer is. Baumel noted that documents in the Jabotinsky Archive in Tel Aviv and elsewhere substantiate Ben-Ami's narrative of his activities. In 2011 the memoir of fellow

delegation member Samuel Merlin was posthumously published; it offers a brief but vivid account of Ben-Ami's rescue of 2,400 refugees stuck on the icy Danube River. Samuel Merlin, *Millions of Jews to Rescue: A Bergson Group Leader's Account of the Campaign to Save Jews from the Holocaust* (Washington, D.C.: David S. Wyman Institute for Holocaust Studies, 2011), 29–30.

11. Segev, *One Palestine, Complete*, 459; Friedländer, *Years of Extermination*, 31, 188; and Y. Ben-Ami, *Years of Wrath*, 147, 152–53, 158, 184, 256–59, 274; the quote is from p. 209.

12. Henry Montor to Rabbi Baruch Rabinowitz, December 11, 1940, American Friends of the League for a Free Palestine, 11, Jabotinsky Archives, Jabotinsky Institute in Israel, quoted in Merlin, *Millions of Jews*, 30–31; and Baumel, *"Bergson Boys,"* 75. On the Emergency Committee for Zionist Affairs pamphlet, see Baumel, *"Bergson Boys,"* 76; and Y. Ben-Ami, *Years of Wrath*, 321. Henry Montor, active in Zionism since his adolescence, served with the United Palestine Appeal from 1930 until 1950, as executive vice president after 1939. According to the *Encyclopaedia Judaica*, "although Montor was an ardent Zionist, the prevailing Zionist aim at the time was for 'selective' immigration to build a Jewish state, not the rescue of Jewish refugees. Therefore in 1940 Montor . . . refused to intervene for a shipload of Jewish refugees stranded on the Danube. He wrote a letter to a rabbi in Maryland stating that 'Palestine cannot be flooded with . . . old people or with undesirables.' He circulated thousands of copies of the letter, which asked Jews not to support illegal immigration to Palestine." See *Jewish Virtual Library*, s.v. "Montor, Henry," n.d., http://www.jewishvirtuallibrary.org/jsource/judaica /ejud_0002_0014_0_14152.html.

13. Irving Howe, letter to the editor, in "American Jews and the Holocaust" letters section, *Commentary*, September 1983, http://www.commentarymagazine .com/article/american-jews-and-the-holocaust/. See also Lucy Dawidowicz, "Indicting American Jews," *Commentary* 75, no. 6 (June 1983): 36–44.

14. Jeremy Ben-Ami, afterword in Merlin, *Millions of Jews*, 195–99.

15. Jabotinsky, quoted in Laqueur, *History of Zionism*, 382; and Jabotinsky, quoted in Laurence Weinbaum, *A Marriage of Convenience: The New Zionist Organization and the Polish Government, 1936–1939* (Boulder, CO: East European Monographs, 1993), 21. See also Laqueur, *History of Zionism*, 347, 379.

16. Laqueur, *History of Zionism*, 381. On Revisionism as a broad umbrella for a variety of groups, see Joseph Heller, *The Stern Gang: Ideology, Politics and Terror, 1940–1949* (London: Routledge, 2004).

17. These are in fact Tom Segev's words summarizing how Haifa police chief Raymond Cafferata described Begin in an unpublished autobiography, although Cafferata may indeed have drawn the comparison to Capone—a high-profile figure in his day. Segev, *One Palestine, Complete*, 475.

18. J. Ben-Ami, afterword in *Millions of Jews*, 196–97.

19. Friedländer, *Years of Extermination*, xvii.

20. Historians have discussed and debated the alleged efficiency of the Final Solution, and the Reich as a modern, technocratic state gone mad, since Raul Hilberg published his 1961 classic, *The Destruction of the European Jews* (New York: Harper & Row, 1961). As David Wyman explained in "Managing the Death Machine," his review upon the release of a new edition of Hilberg's book in 1985, "early chapters define and analyze the 'destruction process' (definition of who the Jews are, expropriation of their property, concentration of the victims and then their annihilation) and the 'machinery of destruction.'" Christopher R. Browning noted, "It was not the chaos, anarchy, and internal competition of the Nazi regime that radicalized Jewish policy in Hilberg's view, but rather the 'fusion' of its four hierarchies into a single machinery of destruction that operated according to the inevitable logic of the destruction process. 'Consonance' and 'synchronization,' not chaos and internal competition—an 'inherent pattern,' not improvisation—hold center stage in Hilberg's view." The functionalist school of Holocaust historians, however, would later argue that the extermination developed in an unplanned and haphazard way and that "the Nazi regime was an inefficient machine out of control." But "for Hilberg it was a machine that was all too efficient and in control of both itself and its victims." David Wyman, "Managing the Death Machine," *New York Times*, August 11, 1985; and Christopher R. Browning, "The Revised Hilberg," *Simon Wiesenthal Annual* 3 (1986), http:// motlc.wiesenthal.com/site/pp.asp?c=gvKVLcMVIuG&b=395051.

21. Black, *Transfer Agreement*, 76–77; and Laqueur, *History of Zionism*, 371. Following two major waves of eastern European pogroms in the late nineteenth and early twentieth century, respectively, a third wave occurred between 1917 and 1921. The death toll peaked in the thousands in Ukraine and White Russia between 1918 and 1920, a number far higher than in the previous, pre–Great War pogroms, which nevertheless had drawn a much greater outcry around the world. See Laqueur, *History of Zionism*, 441–42.

22. Quoted in Berlin, *Freedom and Its Betrayal*, 137–38.

23. Hecht, "Preface to Shylock," 4, Series 1: Works, 1908–1983, box 23, folder 635, BHPNL; and Jabotinsky, quoted in Laqueur, *History of Zionism*, 372. and Hecht, *Child*, 531–32.

24. Merlin, *Millions of Jews*, 3–5. Jabotinsky's foresight should not, however, be exaggerated: he envisioned evacuation over a ten-year period and did not foresee the coming war. The second quote in the paragraph is from Melvin I. Urofsky, *A Voice That Spoke for Justice: The Life and Times of Stephen S. Wise*, SUNY Series in Modern Jewish History (Albany: State University of New York Press, 1982), 275. Urofsky in turn quotes from Feingold, "Who Shall Bear Guilt for the Holocaust: The Human Dilemma," *American Jewish History* 68, no. 3 (1979): 279.

25. James G. McDonald, *My Mission in Israel, 1948–1951* (New York: Simon and Schuster, 1951), 251, quoted in Weinbaum, *Marriage of Convenience*, 239; and

Alex Rafaeli, *Dream and Action: The Story of My Life* (Jerusalem: A. Rafaeli, 1993), 109.

26. Todd Samuel Presner, *Muscular Judaism: The Jewish Body and the Politics of Regeneration*, Routledge Jewish Studies (London: Routledge, 2007), 1–2; and Weizmann, *Trial and Error*, 63, quoted in Laqueur, *History of Zionism*, 378–79.

27. Weizmann, *Trial and Error*, 82, quoted in Laqueur, *History of Zionism*, 125–26.

28. *Kiss of Death*, written by Ben Hecht, Charles Lederer, Eleazar Lipsky, and Philip Dunne, starring Victor Mature and Richard Widmark, directed by Henry Hathaway (1947; Beverly Hills, Calif.: 20th Century Fox Home Entertainment, 2005), DVD; Stanley J. Baran, *Mass Communication Theory: Foundations, Ferment, and Future*, 6th ed. (Boston, Mass.: Wadsworth Cengage Learning, 2012), 94; and M. M. Cohen, *In My Own Words*, 91.

29. Hecht, *Child*, 515–16.

Chapter 9

1. Eran Kaplan, *The Jewish Radical Right: Revisionist Zionism and Its Ideological Legacy*, Studies on Israel (Madison: University of Wisconsin Press, 2005), xi.

2. Peter Bergson to Ben Hecht, August 28, 1941, Series 2: Incoming Correspondence, 1914–1979, box 55, folder 1069b, BHPNL. For Bergson's account of their first encounter, see David S. Wyman and Rafael Medoff, *A Race against Death: Peter Bergson, America, and the Holocaust* (New York: New Press, 2002), 89–90. For Hecht's account, see *Child*, 521–22. Hecht's column was originally published in *PM* on August 24, 1941 and later reprinted in *1001 Afternoons in New York*.

3. Ben-Ami, *Years of Wrath*, 238. See also Rafaeli, *Dream and Action*, 89–92, 93–99, 109–12; Y. Ben-Ami, *Years of Wrath*, 213–23, 238, 318–20; Merlin, *Millions of Jews*, 23–31; Rafael Medoff, introduction to Wyman and Medoff, *Race against Death*, 19–20; Peter Bergson, interviews by David Wyman, in Wyman and Medoff, *Race against Death*, 59; Baumel, *"Bergson Boys,"* 7–17, 28, 34–35, 38–43, 48–49, 51–52, 75–77; and Medoff, *Militant Zionism*, 33–44. The original organization was called the American Friends of a Jewish Palestine. The first three Revisionists dispatched to the United States in February 1938 were Colonel John Henry Patterson, who had commanded the Zion Mule Corps and Jewish Legion during World War I; Robert Briscoe, the sole Jewish member of the Irish parliament; and Haim Lubinsky, a young attorney and Irgunist. Ben-Ami joined them a month later. During the course of 1940, the remaining four of the six members of the Bergson Group joined Ben-Ami and Ben-Eliezer in the United States: Alexander Rafaeli, Hillel Kook (Peter Bergson), Samuel Merlin, and, finally, Eri Jabotinsky, Vladimir Jabotinsky's son.

4. Bergson used the expression "cutoff battalion" frequently in the interviews archived at the Oral History Division, Institute for Contemporary Jewry, Hebrew University, Jerusalem, 55 (b), cited in Baumel, *"Bergson Boys,"* 2, 284. Baumel's endnotes provide two dates for Kook's interviews with the Oral History Division: October 3 and November 7, 1968. No interviewer is named. On Jabotinsky's death, the campaign for a Jewish army, and Bergson's leadership, see Baumel, *"Bergson Boys,"* 46–47, 62–68, 82–87; Medoff, *Militant Zionism*, 45, 63, 65, 70–71; Y. Ben-Ami, *Years of Wrath*, 241–44, 249–50; and Merlin, *Millions of Jews*, 42–43. On quietly going hungry, see Hecht, *Child*, 516; Bergson, interview in Wyman and Medoff, *Race against Death*, 89–90; and Baumel, *"Bergson Boys,"* 49. Regarding Hecht's version of their first encounter, Bergson said, "It is all true except that we were hungry—physically hungry. That was also true, but not on that day. You know, a writer fuses these things."

5. Hecht, *Child*, 522, 523, 535, 536.

6. Hecht, *Child*, 536.

7. Quoted in Hoberman and Shandler, *Entertaining America*, 64–65. For the forceful response from Harry M. Warner (executive of Warner Brothers), Darryl F. Zanuck of Twentieth Century Fox, Arizona Democratic senator Ernest McFarland, and former Republican presidential candidate Wendell Willkie, who served as special counsel retained by the movie industry, see T. Doherty, *Hollywood and Hitler*, 361–62; and James E. McMillan, "The 1941 Senate Motion Picture Hearings," *Journal of Arizona History* 29, no. 3 (Autumn 1988): 277–302.

8. Souvenir program, Series 6: Publicity, 1920–1979, box 79, folder 2396, BHPNL. On the America First rally, see Robert Skloot, *"We Will Never Die:* Success and Failure of a Holocaust Pageant," *Theatre Journal* 37, no. 2 (May 1985): 173.

9. Ben Hecht to Rose Hecht, n.d., Series 4: Family Correspondence, 1915–1976, box 73, folder, 2255, BHPNL.

10. "Freedom Rally Thrills 17,000," *New York Times*, October 8, 1941, 1, 7.

11. Ben Hecht to Rose Hecht, December 12, 1941, Series 4: Family Correspondence, 1915–1976, box 73, folder, 2255, BHPNL. On his propaganda production, see Series 2: Incoming Correspondence, 1914–1979, specifically the files "American Red Cross, 1943," box 55, folder 1029; "Hollywood Victory Committee, 1942," box 58, folder 1339; "United States Treasury Department, 1944–1945," box 63, folder 1716; "United States War Department, 1942–1945," box 63, folder 1717. See also Series 1: Works, 1908–1983, specifically the files "Pageant of American Labor," box 11, folder 320; box 17, folder 436; and oversized box 54, 1942, BHPNL. See also G. Troy, "Ben Hecht," 53, 144n23.

12. Hecht, *Child*, 518; and G. Troy, "Ben Hecht," 54.

13. Hecht, *A Tribute to Gallantry*, in *The Best One-Act Plays of 1943* (New York: Dodd, Mead, 1944), 41–56; see also "War Fund Spectacle to Be Held Tonight," *New York Times*, November 15, 1943.

14. Hecht, *Miracle on the Pullman*, Series 1: Works, 1908–1983, box 89, folder 2583, BHPNL.

15. On *Samson*, see Lenni Brenner, *The Iron Wall: Zionist Revisionism from Jabotinsky to Shamir* (London: Zed; Totowa, N.J.: Biblio Distribution Center, 1984), 79–82. On Halperin, see Medoff, *Militant Zionism*, 48–49. Jabotinsky made far less use of the ancient Hebrew warriors than did the younger "maximalist" Revisionists who took charge of the movement in Palestine once Jabotinsky was barred from the country—the "historian-propagandist" Abba Achimeir, the "messianic prophet-poet" Uri Zvi Greenberg, and the "right-radical journalist" Yehoshua Heshel Yeivin. Avraham Stern and Israel Eldad would soon take up this imagery and mythmaking. See Eldad, *The First Tithe* (Tel Aviv: Jabotinsky Institute in Israel, 2008), 27–30; Heller, *Stern Gang*, 4–5, 11–20, 15, 39, 93–94; and Laqueur, *History of Zionism*, 361–65. For a quick summary of who the Maccabees, the *Sicarri*, the *Biryonim*, and Simon Bar-Kochba originally were and why diaspora Jews lionized the Maccabees but essentially buried the memory of the second rebellion, see Reuven Firestone, "Holy War in Modern Judaism? 'Mitzvah War' and the Problem of the 'Three Vows,'" *Journal of the American Academy of Religion* 74, no. 4 (2006): 957–58. Joseph Heller offers a cogent analysis of these myths and the Holocaust in Israeli collective memory and critiques their treatment by the "new historians." Heller, "Alternative Narratives and Collective Memories: Israel's New Historians and the Use of Historical Context," *Middle Eastern Studies* 42, no. 4 (July 2006): 571–86. On their use for publicity by the Bergson Group, see, for example, Baumel, *"Bergson Boys,"* 202; and Baumel, "Right-Wing Ideologies among American Jews: The Seductive Myth of Power in Crisis," *Nationalism and Ethnic Politics* 4, no. 4 (1998): 90–91. See also Myron J. Aronoff, "Establishing Authority: The Memorialization of Jabotinsky and the Burial of Bar-Kochba Bones in Israel under the Likud," in *The Frailty of Authority*, ed. Myron J. Aronoff, Political Anthropology 5 (New Brunswick, N.J.: Transaction Books, 1986), 105–30.

16. Laqueur, *History of Zionism*, 360–61, 380; and Kaplan, *Jewish Radical Right*, 24–27.

17. Hecht, "Champion in Chains," 36.

18. Hecht, "Champion in Chains," 168.

19. The estimate of 200,000 potential soldiers is from Bergson Group, report, series IV, box 4, folder 7, the Palestine Statehood Committee Papers, Yale University Library.

20. Hecht, "Champion in Chains," 36.

21. Hecht, "Champion in Chains," 168–69. On training the Jews of Palestine and the mission in Iraq, see Bethell, *Palestine Triangle*, 101–6, 134–35. Pierre Van Paassen's account of Raziel's mission in Iraq appears in *That Day Alone* (New York: Dial, 1941), 330–34. See also "Jewish Heroism at Tobruk Reported; Zionist Flag Ordered Removed," *Jewish Telegraphic Agency*, December 7,

1941, http://www.jta.org/1941/12/07/archive/jewish-heroism-at-tobruk
-reported-zionist-flag-ordered-removed. According to Yaacov Tarazi, one of
the three men Raziel led on the mission, the oil-field plan had been aborted
upon their arrival at Habbaniya, and they were en route to conduct recon-
naissance on Iraqi defenses in Pluga when their car was hit by a bomb from a
lone German scout plane. Interview with Tarazi by Daniel Levin, in "David
Raziel: The Man and His Times" (Doctor of Hebrew Letters diss., Yeshiva
University, 1969), 312.

Chapter 10

1. Heller, *Stern Gang*, 41. A lengthy excerpt from this speech appears in Colin
   Shindler, *The Triumph of Military Zionism* (London: I. B. Tauris, 2006),
   207–8.
2. Heller, *Stern Gang*, 53, quoting Eliezer Ben-Yair (a pen name for Avraham
   Stern), "Principles and Conclusions," *Omer La-Am* (Speaking to the People),
   July 29, 1939, n.p. *Omer La-Am* was an evening newspaper in Palestine.
3. M. Levin, *In Search*, 302–10. Levin is most famous as an early discoverer and
   champion of Anne Frank's diary whose later effort to bring it to the stage
   embroiled him in a bitter battle. His autobiography is scathingly critical of
   Hecht, who had once been his idol and had given him his first break. As
   a young man, Levin had brought an early attempt at a short-story collection straight to a small office on Clark Street, where Hecht and Maxwell
   Bodenheim were producing the *Chicago Literary Times*. Hecht had responded
   with a testimonial that won Levin a job as picture chaser at the *Chicago
   Daily News*. By the time "Ben Hecht had moved to New York, . . . I became
   the star feature reporter, feeling like the inheritor of an oversize mantle."
   M. Levin, *In Search*, 23–26.
4. Louis Rapoport, *Shake Heaven and Earth: Peter Bergson and the Struggle to Rescue
   the Jews of Europe* (Jerusalem: Gefen, 1999), 15 (see also 13–17).
5. The first quotation is from Brenner, *Iron Wall*, 104. The three types of Zionism
   are mentioned by Brenner as well as Heller, *Stern Gang*, 40–41; and Laqueur,
   History of Zionism, 164.
6. Hecht, *Child*, 535.
7. Quoted in Melvin Urofsky, *American Zionism*, 429.
8. Herzl, quoted in Ben Halpern, "Herzl's Historic Gift: The Sense of Sovereignty,"
   Herzl Year Book 3 (1960):29; and Segev, *One Palestine, Complete*, 5. See also
   Laqueur, *History of Zionism*, 104; and Segev, *One Palestine, Complete*, 33, 40,
   48, 50. The *Herzl Year Book* was an annual periodical edited by Raphael Patai
   that published studies about Zionism.
9. Heller, *Stern Gang*, 2; and Laqueur, *History of Zionism*, 346, 352, 495. Jabotinsky
   served in the World Zionist Organization's executive from March 1921 to
   January 1923; see Brenner, *Iron Wall*, 62, 64.

10. Quoted in Brenner, *Iron Wall*, 17. See also Brenner, *Iron Wall*, 13–17, 63–71; Laqueur, *History of Zionism*, 344; and Black, *Transfer Agreement*, 77.

11. Vladimir Jabotinsky, "O Zheleznoi Stene," *Rasswyet*, November 4, 1923, 2–4, excerpted in Brenner, *Iron Wall*, 72–78. On Weizmann's gradualist approach and the Lovers of Zion adage, see Laqueur, *History of Zionism*, 495.

12. Heller, *Stern Gang*, 6 (see also 4–7).

13. Tom Segev, "Words That Can't Be Retracted," *Haaretz*, April 20, 2012, http://www.haaretz.com/weekend/the-makings-of-history/words-that -can-t-be-retracted-1.425541.

14. Heller, *Stern Gang*, 21–22; see also Brenner, *Iron Wall*, 91–96. As prime minister in 1982, Begin appointed a former supreme court justice to conduct an official inquiry into the crime, but the investigation was inconclusive. David B. Green, "This Day in Jewish History/The Murder of Chaim Arlosoroff," *Haaretz*, June 16, 2013, http://www.haaretz.com/news/features/this-day -in-jewish-history/.premium-1.530046.

15. Heller, *Stern Gang*, 22–23, 30–32; and Laqueur, *History of Zionism*, 374.

16. Arthur Koestler, *Promise and Fulfillment: Palestine, 1917–1949* (London: Macmillan, 1949), 91; see also Rapoport, *Shake Heaven and Earth*, 19–23.

17. Heller, *Stern Gang*, 23, 31, 41; Brenner, *Iron Wall*, 99–100; and Rapoport, *Shake Heaven and Earth*, 28–29. Bergson was involved in setting up a retaliation unit upon the split in 1937. But he was physically slight, and he lacked Raziel's and Stern's charisma as a military leader. He was soon dispatched to Poland to serve as a contact with Jabotinsky.

18. Jabotinsky, quoted in Brenner, *Iron Wall*, 100. On Jabotinsky's hesitations, see Heller, *Stern Gang*, 30–32, 34–35, 37–40. On the attacks, see "Terror Strikes Haifa—23 Dead and 79 Wounded," *Palestine Post*, July 7, 1938, 1, 2; "Tension in Haifa as Death Toll Grows to 27," *Palestine Post*, July 8, 1938, 1, 2; "General Calm in Haifa/Arab Death Roll Now 53 from Monday's Bomb," *Palestine Post*, July 8, 1938, 2; "Ten Arabs Killed in Old City, Jerusalem/29 Others Wounded/Men, Women and Children in Panic; Market in Shambles," *Palestine Post*, July 17, 1938, 1, 2; "After the Bombs," editorial, *Palestine Post*, July 17, 1938, 8; "Hundred Arab Casualties in Haifa Bomb Explosion/Early Morning Outrage in Arab Melon Market in Kingsway; Curfew Imposed," *Palestine Post*, July 26, 1938 1; "The Haifa Disaster," editorial, *Palestine Post*, July 26, 1938, 6; "Palestinian Situation Again before House/Outrages in Haifa, Tel Aviv," *Palestine Post*, July 28, 1938, 1, 3; and "59 Arab Casualties in Jaffa Explosion/Bomb in Vegetable Market," *Palestine Post*, August 28, 1938, 1. For the numbers of those killed by the Irgun, see Heller, *Stern Gang*, 40; and Segev, *One Palestine, Complete*, 441.

19. Bethell, *Palestine Triangle*, 35–36, 52–55, 68; and Segev, *One Palestine, Complete*, 382–87, 398–400, 417–26.

20. Kaplan, *Jewish Radical Right*, 155–58.

21. Quoted in Weinbaum, *Marriage of Convenience*, 235. On Jabotinsky's attempts to broker an evacuation plan with the Polish government, see Weinbaum,

Marriage of Convenience, chs. 4 and 6.

22. Weinbaum, *Marriage of Convenience*, 136, 139–40.

23. Quoted in Weinbaum, *Marriage of Convenience*, 149–50 (see also 145–52).

24. Weinbaum, *Marriage of Convenience*, 130–31, 134–36, 150; and Heller, *Stern Gang*, 45–46.

25. Begin, quoted in Heller, *Stern Gang*, 41. See also Heller, *Stern Gang*, 7, 40–41; and Brenner, *Iron Wall*, 104.

26. Heller, *Stern Gang*, 53, quoting Stern, "Principles and Conclusions." See also Heller, *Stern Gang*, 41–45, 51–55; and Baumel, *"Bergson Boys,"* 8, 20.

27. The phrase "blood and the sword" is quoted in Heller, *Stern* Gang, 49; and Nimrodi is quoted in Nadav Man, "Germany in Pictures—Part V," *Ynetnews.com*, November 5, 2010, http://www.ynetnews.com/articles /0,7340,L-3971931,00.html. See also Heller, *Stern* Gang, 54–59; and J. Bowyer Bell, *Terror out of Zion: Irgun Zvai Leumi, LEHI, and the Palestine Underground, 1929–1949* (New York: St. Martin's, 1977), 49, 54–55.

28. Heller, *Stern Gang*, 61–62; and Bell, *Terror out of Zion*, 52.

Chapter 11

1. Rebecca Kook, interviewed by Marvin Hier and Richard Trank in *Against the Tide*, directed by Richard Trank, written by Marvin Hier and Richard Trank (Los Angeles: Moriah Films, the Jack and Pearl Resnick Division of the Simon Wiesenthal Center, 2009), DVD.

2. "JEWS FIGHT FOR THE RIGHT TO FIGHT," *New York Times* January 5, 1942.

3. Hecht, *Child*, 540. For details, see Hillel Kook [Peter Bergson], interviewed by Trank and Hier in *Against the Tide*; Wyman and Medoff, *Race against Death*, 23; Hillel Kook [Peter Bergson], "The Bergson Group, America, and the Holocaust: A Previously Unpublished Interview with Hillel Kook/Peter Bergson," by David S. Wyman, *American Jewish History* 89, no. 1 (2001): 14n9, http://muse .jhu.edu/journals/american_jewish_history/v089/89.1wyman.html.

4. Baumel, *"Bergson Boys,"* 87–88. Two years later, pioneering media scholar Paul Lazarsfeld would introduce "two-step flow theory," the notion that the public embraces ideas only after they are first championed by an elite group of "opinion leaders." Paul Felix Lazarsfeld, Bernard Berelson, and Hazel Gaudet, *The People's Choice: How the Voter Makes Up His Mind in a Presidential Campaign* (New York: Columbia University Press, 1944). See also Elihu Katz and Paul F. Lazarsfeld, *Personal Influence: The Part Played by People in the Flow of Mass Communications* (Glencoe, Ill.: Free Press, 1955).

5. Baumel, *"Bergson Boys,"* 85–86; and Medoff, *Militant Zionism*, 75.

6. Quoted in Baumel, *"Bergson Boys,"* 88.

7. Medoff, *Militant Zionism*, 70–71.

8. J. Ben-Ami, afterword in Merlin, *Millions of Jews*, 196–97; Baumel, *"Bergson Boys,"* 88, 148; Rapoport, *Shake Heaven and Earth*, 49, 57–58; Medoff,

Militant Zionism, 71–72, 112; and Wyman and Medoff, *Race against Death*, 124. Dr. Seuss's editorial cartoons for *PM* can be found on the University of California, San Diego Special Collections and Archives web page, "Dr. Seuss Went to War," http://libraries.ucsd.edu/speccoll/dswenttowar/.

9. Ben Hecht to David Selznick, n.d., Series 3: Outgoing Correspondence, 1913–1977, box 69, folder 2124, BHPNL.

10. Helperin, quoted in Heller, *Stern Gang*, 36. See also Baumel, *"Bergson Boys,"* 97.

11. Rapoport, *Shake Heaven and Earth*, 57; and Baumel, *"Bergson Boys,"* 91, 98, 105–6.

12. Hecht, *Child*, 537, 539–40. On Mayer's luncheon with Nazi editors, see Urwand, *Collaboration*, 198–200; and G. Troy, "Ben Hecht," 69. Hecht's papers offer few clues as to when the fund-raiser occurred, but the timing of the Jewish army campaign and other events suggest that it was in early 1942. This is also the time window according to Louis Rapoport's *Shake Heaven and Earth* (p. 53), which draws from interviews the author conducted with Bergson. William MacAdams dates the fund-raiser to February 1942 but provides no sourcing. MacAdams, *Man behind the Legend*, 225.

13. Ben Hecht to David Selznick, n.d., Series 3: Outgoing Correspondence, 1913–1977, box 69, folder 2124, BHPNL. See also Hecht, *Child*, 541–44; and G. Troy, "Ben Hecht," 69.

14. Baumel, *"Bergson Boys,"* 133; and Wyman and Medoff, *Race against Death*, 31.

15. Quoted in Baumel, *"Bergson Boys,"* 130 (see also 132–34).

16. Hecht, *Child*, 536; and Baumel, *"Bergson Boys,"* 132, 135.

Chapter 12

1. In *Against the Tide*.

2. Hecht, *Child*, 548–50.

3. Hillel Kook [Peter Bergson], interview by Trank and Hier, in *Against the Tide*. Some major dailies ran the story of Wise's announcement on their front pages, but most put it on an inside page. See Lipstadt, *Beyond Belief*, 181.

4. Elie Wiesel, "Telling the Tale," *Dimensions in American Judaism* 2 (Spring 1968): 11. See also David S. Wyman, *The Abandonment of the Jews: America and the Holocaust, 1941–1945* (New York: Pantheon Books, 1985), 42–45, 46–51, 54; Lipstadt, *Beyond Belief*, 159–96; and Rapoport, *Shake Heaven and Earth*, 235n44.

5. Although the Jewish press had been filled with stories of systematic extermination for weeks, Bergson said of Wise's announcement, "My first thought was disbelief. I hoped it was not true." According to Yitshaq Ben-Ami, "we became embroiled in a heated debate, some of us inadvertently repeating the arguments that Dr. Schiper had given to David Wdowinski in the Warsaw Ghetto: 'Germany will not dare kill millions of civilians because world opinion would not stand for it. Besides, it is physically impossible to

organize mass killings on such a scale.'" Bergson, interview, in Wyman and Medoff, *Race against Death*, 58; and Y. Ben-Ami, *Years of Wrath*, 281. On how the news had been leaking into the mainstream media since spring, see Lipstadt, *Beyond Belief*, 159–76.

6. Reams's phrase "avoid any implications" is quoted in Lipstadt, *Beyond Belief*, 183. For Roosevelt's pronouncements, see Richard Breitman, *FDR and the Jews* (Cambridge, Mass.: Belknap Press of Harvard University Press, 2013), 198, 223. See also Wyman, *Abandonment of the Jews*, 62, 65, 77–78; and Lipstadt, *Beyond Belief*, 185–86, 241–42.

7. The committee did run the ad nearly a year later: Hecht, "Ballad of the Doomed Jews of Europe," advertisement, *New York Times*, September 14, 1943, 12. On the decision not to publish Hecht's advertisement initially, see Bergson, interview, in Wyman and Medoff, *Race against Death*, 65–67.

8. Hecht, "Preface to Shylock," 10, Series 1: Works, 1908–1983, box 24, folder 635, BHPNL.

9. Lipstadt, *Beyond Belief*, 180 (see also 176–80).

10. "A Letter from Ben Hecht," *PM*, February 22, 1943 (this editorial was reprinted numerous times); and Ben Hecht, *Perfidy* (New York: Messner, 1961), 65.

11. Meyer, private letter to U.S. solicitor general Fowler Harper, n.d., quoted in Lipstadt, *Beyond Belief*, 228. See also Laurel Leff, *Buried by the Times: The Holocaust and America's Most Important Newspaper* (Cambridge: Cambridge University Press, 2005). Leff argues that because of Sulzberger's personal beliefs about what it meant to be Jewish—he regarded Judaism as a religion, not a peoplehood—"the *Times* never acknowledged that the mass murder of Jews *because they were Jews* was something its readers needed to know" (13–16).

12. Wyman, *Abandonment of the Jews*, 63; Hecht, "The Extermination of the Jews," *American Mercury*, February 1943, 194–99, http://www.unz.org/Pub /AmMercury-1943feb-00194; and Hecht, "Remember Us!," *Reader's Digest*, February 1943, 107–10.

13. Y. Ben-Ami, *Years of Wrath*, 281; Pierre Van Paassen, "A Proclamation on the Moral Rights of the Stateless and Palestinian Jews," advertisement, *New York Times*, December 7, 1942, 14; and "Action—Not Pity Can Save Millions Now!," advertisement, *New York Times*, February 8, 1943, 8.

14. Ben-Ami, apparently the only Bergsonite to mention when the pageant idea was hatched, said it happened on a January day when he and two friends with links to theater, Stella Joelson and Saul Collins, visited Hecht in Nyack. Also, Merlin wrote that Hecht invited some thirty Jewish leaders to discuss the pageant on January 26. The timing makes sense, because the pageant was performed early in March. Y. Ben-Ami, *Years of Wrath*, 284–85; and Merlin, letter to the editor, in "American Jews and the Holocaust" letters section, *Commentary*, September 1983, http://www.commentarymagazine .com/article/american-jews-and-the-holocaust. On pageants, see Arthur Aryeh Goren, "Pageants of Sorrow, Celebration and Protest: The Public

Culture of American Jews," in *Literary Strategies: Jewish Texts and Contexts*, ed. Ezra Mendelsohn, Studies in Contemporary Jewry 12 (Oxford: Oxford University Press, 1996), 202, 206–7; and Stephen J. Whitfield, "The Politics of Pageantry, 1936–1946," *American Jewish History* 84, no. 3 (1996): 221–34.

15. Whitfield, "Politics of Pageantry," 240–41. For details on the pageant, see *"We Will Never Die* Given in Washington," *New York Times*, April 13, 1943; Hecht, *Child*, 558–63; Skloot, *"We Will Never Die*," 172, 175; and Whitfield, "Politics of Pageantry," 240.

16. Garth S. Jowett and Victoria O'Donnell, *Propaganda and Persuasion*, 5th ed. (Thousand Oaks, Calif.: Sage, 2012), 247–48; and Hilmar Hoffmann, *The Triumph of Propaganda: Film and National Socialism, 1933–1945* (Providence, R.I.: Berghahn Books, 1996), 151, 176. Hitler and Goebbels's use of rallies to promote their anti-Semitic agenda is described in depth in Jeffrey Herf, *The Jewish Enemy: Nazi Propaganda during World War II and the Holocaust* (Cambridge, Mass.: Belknap Press of Harvard University Press, 2006).

17. Hecht, *Child*, 550–53.

18. Hecht, *Child*, 551.

19. Richard J. Evans, *The Third Reich at War, 1939–1945* (London: Allen Lane, 2008), 281. See also Aristotle A. Kallis, *Nazi Propaganda and the Second World War* (New York: Palgrave Macmillan, 2005), 67–68, 76, 82; and Herf, *Jewish Enemy*, 264–65 and throughout. Hecht and Menachem Begin were Holocaust "functionalists" of their day, each offering a variation on that theory. For Hecht, the idea that that Hitler was not some all-powerful leader carrying a grand plan to its inevitable conclusion offered hope that a public outcry might halt the killings. For Begin, the idea that the Nazis had conducted experiments to test the world's indifference to the murder of Jews would help justify the Irgun's Revolt. See Menachem Begin, *The Revolt* (London: W. H. Allen, 1951), 26–28.

20. Saul Friedländer, *Years of Extermination*, xviii–xix; see also Kallis, *Nazi Propaganda*, 84. On Hitler's talk of exterminating Jews, see Herf, *Jewish Enemy*, 5; and Evans, *Third Reich at War*, 245–47, 254–55, 263, 268, 280. On conspiracy theories, see Herf, *Jewish Enemy*, 264–65.

21. Hecht, *We Will Never Die*, 4–5, Series 1: Works, 1908–1983, box 31, folder 795, BHPNL. Audio of the Hollywood Bowl performance can be found at https://archive.org/details/WeWillNeverDieBenHechtKurtWeill.

22. Y. Ben-Ami, *Years of Wrath*, 285.

23. C. L. Sulzberger, "Romania Proposes Transfer of Jews," *New York Times*, February 13, 1943; Hecht, "For Sale to Humanity 70,000 Jews," *New York Times*, February 16, 1943, 11; and Welles, quoted in Wyman, *Abandonment of the Jews*, 83. See also Wyman, *Abandonment of the Jews*, 82–84; Robert Darst, "Guaranteed Human Beings for Sale: The Collaborative Relocation of Jews from Axis Europe, 1933–1945," *Journal of Human Rights* 1, no. 2 (June 2002): 207–30; and Ephraim Ophir, "Was the Transnistria Rescue Plan Achievable?," *Holocaust and Genocide Studies* 6, no. 1 (1991): 1–16.

24. Richard Breitman, "The Allied War Effort and the Jews, 1942–1943," *Journal of Contemporary History* 20, no. 1 (January 1985): 146, 152; and Hecht, *We Will Never Die*, 5.

25. Hecht, *Child*, 553–57. Merlin wrote that this took place on January 26. Merlin, letter to the editor, in "American Jews and the Holocaust" letters section.

26. Hillel Kook [Peter Bergson], Oral History Division interview, quoted in Baumel, *"Bergson Boys,"* 120–21 (see also 288n57–58).

27. Hecht, *Child*, 557. See also Hecht, *Child*, 563; Baumel, *"Bergson Boys,"* 120–22; Wyman, *Abandonment of the Jews*, 89–91; and Skloot, *"We Will Never Die,"* 173–74.

28. Hecht, *We Will Never Die*, 2. See also Skloot, *"We Will Never Die,"* 174; Lipstadt, *Beyond Belief*, 200–201; Wyman, *Abandonment of the Jews*, 90–91; and Whitfield, "Politics of Pageantry," 241.

29. Hecht, *We Will Never Die*, 6–19; and Skloot, *"We Will Never Die,"* 176–77.

30. Hecht, *We Will Never Die*, 25–26.

31. Hecht, *We Will Never Die*, 26–27.

32. Quoted in Wyman, *Abandonment of the Jews*, 91. See also Wyman, *Abandonment of the Jews*, 92; and Skloot, *"We Will Never Die,"* 171–73.

33. Hecht, "Preface to Shylock," 21. The White House had in fact been queasy about refusing Rose's request altogether. It had ordered the Office of War Information to formulate a response and was handed a bland statement condemning totalitarian brutality that mentioned neither Jews nor extermination. Even this, however, proved too strong for senior aides David Niles and Stephen Early, so the administration sent no message at all. Wyman, *Abandonment of the Jews*, 92.

34. Israel I. Taslitt, *Jewish News and Observer*, April 23, 1943, quoted in Wyman, *Abandonment of the Jews*, 92.

35. Hecht, *Child*, 576.

36. Anne O'Hare McCormick, "Two Acts in the Drama of the World," *New York Times*, March 3, 1943, 22; and "They Will Never Die," *New York Herald Tribune*, March 3, 1943, 18.

37. Hecht, *We Will Never Die*, 576; Whitfield, "Politics of Pageantry," 242–43; and Lipstadt, *Beyond Belief*, 201–2.

38. Quoted in Hecht, *Child*, 576.

39. Wyman, *Abandonment of the Jews*, xiv, 285–87, 328–29.

40. Kallis, *Nazi Propaganda*, 4–5, 74. On the trilogy of anti-Semitic films, see Hoffmann, *Triumph of Propaganda*, 173, 175, 176.

41. Hecht, *Child*, 587. See also Baran and David, *Mass Communication Theory*, 6th ed., 139, 149–51.

42. Darst, "Guaranteed Human Beings," 207.

Chapter 13

1. Alfred Kazin, "In Every Voice, in Every Ban," *New Republic*, January 10, 1944, 45.

2. See Evans, *Third Reich at War*, 419–20, 441–67, 479–83; Wyman, *Abandonment of the Jews*, 120–23; and Baumel, *"Bergson Boys,"* 136–37.

3. Hecht, "Jewish Situation Less Complex," *Los Angeles Times*, March 11, 1943.

4. Wyman, *Abandonment of the Jews*, 108–10, 113; and Baumel, *"Bergson Boys,"* 137.

5. Hecht, "Preface to Shylock," 12. Breckinridge Long was actually an assistant secretary of state, in charge of the visa division. On the conference, see also Wyman, *Abandonment of the Jews*, 116–19; Baumel, *"Bergson Boys,"* 137–38; and Breitman, *FDR and the Jews*, 224.

6. Quoted in Wyman, *Abandonment of the Jews*, 122–23.

7. Hecht, "Preface to Shylock," 14; Wise, quoted in Wyman, *Abandonment of the Jews*, 120; and, for the Bergson Group's advertisements, Wyman and Medoff, *Race against Death*, 37.

8. Lucas, quoted in Rapoport, *Shake Heaven and Earth*, 78; and Hecht, *Child*, 578. See also Baumel, *"Bergson Boys,"* 139; Y. Ben-Ami, *Years of Wrath*, 324–25; Medoff, *Militant Zionism*, 188–93; Wyman, *Abandonment of the Jews*, 149; and Medoff, "When the U.S. Government Spied on American Jews," David S. Wyman Institute for Holocaust Studies, January 2006, http://new.wyman institute.org/2006/01/when-the-u-s-government-spied-on-american-jews/.

9. "Hecht Flays Anti-Semites in His Stinging Philippic," *Chicago Tribune*, March 16, 1944; and Maxwell Perkins to Ben Hecht, January 25, 1944, Series 2: Incoming Correspondence, 1914–1979, box 61, folder 1533, BHPNL.

10. Scribner was quoted by Maxwell Perkins to Ben Hecht. Billy Rose to Ben Hecht, letters and telegrams, March 25, 1944; April 17, 1944; May 9, 1944; May 16, 1944; June 3, 1944; June 27, 1944; Whitney Darrow of Charles Scribner's Sons to Billy Rose, May 17, 1944, all found in Series 2: Incoming Correspondence, 1914–1979, box 61, folder 1586, BHPNL. Regarding Rose Caylor Hecht's suspicions of interference, see her notes on a June 27 letter from Billy Rose to Ben Hecht, found in Series 2: Incoming Correspondence, 1914–1979, box 61, folder 1586, BHPNL. See also G. Troy, "Ben Hecht," 86. "Pint-sized Barnum" and "Midget Maestro" were common nicknames for Billy Rose in the press. See, for example, United Press International, "Eleanor Files Suit against Billy Rose," *Wilmington (N.C.) News*, November 20, 1951, 20; and International News Service, "Price of Whoopee to Skyrocket," *Palm Beach Daily News*, March 18, 1944, 6.

11. Hecht, *Guide for the Bedevilled*, 1–7, 12–13.

12. Hecht, *Guide for the Bedevilled*, 11.

13. Norman MacDonald, "Hecht Makes Case for Jews," *Boston Herald*, March 30, 1944; and Selig Greenberg, "Nazi Concatenation," *Providence (R.I.) Journal*, April 30, 1944.

14. Stephen Wise, "The War upon World Jewry," in *Nazism: An Assault on Civilization*, ed. Pierre Van Paassen and James Waterman Wise (New York: H. Smith and R. Haas, 1934), 220.

15. Hecht, *Guide for the Bedevilled*, 20, 24.

16. Hecht, *Guide for the Bedevilled*, 27–29.

17. Hecht, *Guide for the Bedevilled*, 29.

18. Hecht, *Guide for the Bedevilled*, 29–31.

19. Hecht, *Guide for the Bedevilled*, 36–37.

20. Hecht, *Guide for the Bedevilled*, 71–75, 126, 150, 156.

21. Hecht, *Guide for the Bedevilled*, 11, 32–35, 73–75, 224–35; Elmer Rice, "A Prong at Both Ends," *Saturday Review of Literature*, March 25, 1944, 5–6, 20–21; and Harold Rosenberg, "The Possessed," *Contemporary Jewish Record*, June 1944, 309–11.

22. Hecht, *Guide for the Bedevilled*, 157; Stephen S. Wise, *Challenging Years: The Autobiography of Stephen Wise* (New York: Putnam, 1949), 293–94; and Daniel Jonah Goldhagen, *Hitler's Willing Executioners: Ordinary Germans and the Holocaust* (New York: Alfred A. Knopf, 1996).

23. Hecht, *Guide for the Bedevilled*, 149–50. See also Erich Fromm, *Escape from Freedom* (New York: Rinehart, 1941); and Hannah Arendt, *Eichmann in Jerusalem: A Report on the Banality of Evil*, rev. and enlarged ed. (Gloucester, Mass.: Peter Smith, 1986).

24. Hecht, *Guide for the Bedevilled*, 43; and Sam Roberts, "Declassified Papers Show U.S. Recruited Ex-Nazis," *New York Times*, December 11, 2010.

25. Hecht, "Dedication and Preface," in *Guide for the Bedevilled*, n.p.

26. Baumel, *"Bergson Boys,"* 142, 148–49; and Wyman, *Abandonment of the Jews*, 87–89, 144.

27. Rafaeli, *Dream and Action*, 104; and Baumel, *"Bergson Boys,"* 146–47.

28. Quoted in Baumel, *"Bergson Boys,"* 144.

29. Roosevelt, quoted in Wyman, *Abandonment of the Jews*, 148. See also Wyman, *Abandonment of the Jews*, 145–48; Baumel, *"Bergson Boys,"* 148; and Max Lerner, "What about the Jews, FDR?," *PM*, July 22, 1943, 2.

30. Hecht, *Child*, 572–73.

31. Goldstein's lament is cited in G. Troy, "Ben Hecht," 78. On the term "Jew Deal," see Wyman, *Abandonment of the Jews*, 15n, 107. On Roosevelt being greeted like Moses, see Michael T. Benson, *Harry S. Truman and the Founding of Israel* (Westport, Conn.: Praeger, 1997), 21.

32. Wyman, *Abandonment of the Jews*, 147; and Hecht, "Ballad of the Doomed Jews of Europe," advertisement, *New York Times*, September 14, 1943, 12.

33. "U.S. at War: Oil and the Rabbis," *Time*, October 18, 1943, 21; and Rosenman, quoted in Breitman, *FDR and the Jews*, 230. See also Breitman, *FDR and the Jews*, 229–31; and Rabbis Present Plea to Wallace," *New York Times*, October 7, 1943.

34. "Texts of Three-Power Conference Documents," *New York Times*, November 2, 1943.

35. Hecht, "My Uncle Abraham Reports . . . ," *New York Times*, November 5, 1943, 14.

36. Bergson, interview, in Wyman and Medoff, *Race against Death*, 139; Baumel, *"Bergson Boys,"* 153; and Hecht, *Child*, 574–75, 580–82. According to an interview quoted by Baumel, when Eleanor mentioned the ad, Bergson replied, "You know, Madam, I sometimes wonder where I find the strength to sit here with you and talk reasonably about these matters. If I were now to take two pistols and shoot you and anyone else who stood in my way and burst into the president's office and shoot him, it would not be overreacting. . . . How . . . can the president say that in a situation where five thousand people are being murdered daily . . . and we are simply trying to shout 'Help us' . . . that we are doing too much, how is it even possible to do too much?" Bergson, interview by the Oral History Division of Hebrew University, quoted in Baumel, *"Bergson Boys,"* 153.

37. Quoted in Breitman, *FDR and the Jews*, 227.

38. Roosevelt, quoted in Breitman, *FDR and the Jews*, 259; and Breitman, *FDR and the Jews*, 260 (see also 253–60).

39. Silver, quoted in Wyman, *Abandonment of the Jews*, 163 (see also 160–64).

40. Bergson, interview, in *Against the Tide*.

41. Quoted in Rapoport, *Shake Heaven and Earth*, 128, 138.

42. American Jewish Conference press release, quoted in "Relief Unit Scored by Jewish Group," *New York Times*, December 31, 1943; and Goldmann, in "Memorandum of conversation of E. M. Wilson, State Department, Near Eastern Division, with Nahum Goldman et al., May 19, 1944, regarding Peter Bergson," National Archives, State Department, 867N.01/2374, reprinted in the appendix to Wyman and Medoff, *Race against Death*, 229–32.

43. Wyman, *Abandonment of the Jews*, 160, 173.

44. Melvin I. Urofsky, *A Voice That Spoke for Justice: The Life and Times of Stephen S. Wise*, SUNY Series in Modern Jewish History (Albany: State University of New York Press, 1982), 261, 262; Breitman, *FDR and the Jews*, 78; and Black, *Transfer Agreement*, 33–46.

45. Urofsky, *Voice*, 264–66.

46. Wise, quoted in Wyman, *Abandonment of the Jews*, 71–72; and Urofsky, *Voice*, 315.

47. Hecht, *Child*, 547, 571; and Urofsky, *Voice*, 331.

48. Reinhold Niebuhr, "Jews after the War," pt. 1, *Nation*, February 21, 1942, 214; and Roosevelt, quoted in Lipstadt, *Beyond Belief*, 105.

49. Urofsky, *Voice*, 309–11.

50. Wise, *Challenging Years*, 311–12.

51. Wise, speech to Free Synagogue, March 10, 1935, quoted in Urofsky, *Voice*, 279; and Robert Silverberg, *If I Forget Thee, O Jerusalem: American Jews and the State of Israel* (New York: Morrow, 1970), 209.

52. Herbert Bentley to Ben Hecht, n.d., Series 2: Incoming Correspondence, 1914–1979, box 55, folder 1069, BHPNL; and Rapoport, *Shake Heaven and Earth*, 112.

53. Morgenthau and Winant are quoted in Wyman, *Abandonment of the Jews*, 181, 182 (see also 178–82).

54. Paul, quoted in Wyman, *Abandonment of the Jews*, 183; Morgenthau, quoted in Wyman, *Abandonment of the Jews*, 182; and Morgenthau, quoted in Breitman, *FDR and the Jews*, 233. See also Arthur D. Morse, *While Six Million Died: A Chronicle of American Apathy* (New York: Random House, 1968), 73–99.

55. On Breckinridge Long's characterization, see, for example, Wyman, *Abandonment of the Jews*, 190–91. On Long's influence on immigration, see Leibush Lehrer, president of the Yiddish Scientific Institute, "Refugee Figures Questioned," letter to the editor, *New York Times*, December 27, 1943. Lehrer's analysis is recited in Morse, *While Six Million Died*, 94.

56. Morse, *While Six Million Died*, 45; and Wyman, *Abandonment of the Jews*, 80–81.

57. Josiah DuBois, "Report to the Secretary on the Acquiescence of This Government in the Murder of the Jews," initialed by Randolph Paul, January 13, 1944, from the Franklin D. Roosevelt Presidential Library, *Morgenthau Diaries*, Series 1, vol. 693, 212–29. The *Morgenthau Diaries* archive is viewable online: http://www.fdrlibrary.marist.edu/_resources/images/morg/md0978.pdf. For the finding aid, go to http://www.fdrlibrary.marist.edu/archives/collections /franklin/index.php?p=collections/findingaid&id=535&q=&rootcontentid =188897#id188897 (accessed September 15, 2018).

58. Breitman, *FDR and the Jews*, 234–35.

59. Lucy Dawidowicz, "Indicting American Jews," *Commentary* 75, no. 6 (June 1983): 36–44. Dawidowicz was a brilliant and incisive writer, but in the midst of her polemics she often contradicted herself in ways she never satisfactorily addressed. For example, she originally championed the Bergson Group, before attacking them in print years later. When confronted about this by her major target, Samuel Merlin, she responded that her views had changed after she had learned more of the facts. What had changed her mind was learning of the crucial role Oscar Cox, general counsel of the Foreign Economic Administration, had played in creating the War Refugee Board. Cox was indeed instrumental, but that takes nothing away from the entirely different role played by the Bergsonites. The argument makes so little sense that it seems more like a tactical dodge, a deliberate use of obscurantism to throw people off her trail. See the letter from Merlin and her reply in "American Jews and the Holocaust" letters section, *Commentary*, September 1983. Another example is that she condemned the State Department as blatantly anti-Semitic but nevertheless defended Roosevelt against Wyman's *Abandonment of the Jews*. While there had been critics of Roosevelt, she wrote, "until now, no one has charged the United States and its people with complicity with the murder of the Jews." Lucy S. Dawidowicz, "Could America Have Rescued Europe's Jews?," in *What Is the Use of Jewish History? Essays* (New York: Schocken Books, 1992), 159–60. But that's exactly what Roosevelt's own people did, in an official document, as well as others such as Ziegelboim.

60. Dawidowicz, "Could America," 163.

61. Breitman, *FDR and the Jews*, 235.

62. Dawidowicz, "Could America," 166.

63. Dawidowicz, "Could America," 167.

64. W. D. Rubinstein, *The Myth of Rescue: Why the Democracies Could Not Have Saved More Jews from the Nazis* (London: Routledge, 1997); and Riegner, quoted in Saul S. Friedman, "Saving the Jews: Franklin D. Roosevelt and the Holocaust," Free Library, Farlex, September 1, 2007, http://www.thefreelibrary.com/Saving the Jews: Franklin D. Roosevelt and the Holocaust.-a0180029229.

65. Quoted in the *Morgenthau Diaries*, March 8, 1944, Series 1, vol. 707, 220–21.

66. Billy Rose to Ben Hecht, January 30, 1944, Series 2: Incoming Correspondence, 1914–1979, box 61, folder 1586, BHPNL. On Bernard Baruch as Rose's mentor, see Polly Rose Gottlieb, *The Nine Lives of Billy Rose* (New York: Crown, 1968), 212–13.

67. Dawidowicz, "Could America," 176–77.

Chapter 14

1. Quoted in Bell, *Terror out of Zion*, 184.

2. Quoted in Clifton Daniel, "Churchill Warns Jews to Oust Gangs," *New York Times*, November 18, 1944.

3. Quoted in Monty Noam Penkower, "The Kishinev Pogrom: A Turning Point in Jewish History," *Modern Judaism* 24, no. 3 (2004): 207.

4. Hecht, *Child*, 591.

5. Hecht, *Child*, 592.

6. Hecht, *Child*, 594.

7. Hecht, *Child*, 536.

8. Menachem Begin to William MacAdams, January 5, 1983, folder 373, MacAdams Collection, BHPNL.

9. Hecht to Samuel Merlin, early fall 1947, Series 2: Incoming Correspondence, 1914–1979, box 63, folder 1692, BHPNL. This letter appears to be misfiled. For one thing, it is outgoing correspondence from Hecht. For another, the "Sam" he is addressing is clearly Merlin, the acting head of the Bergson Group at the time, though Rose Caylor Hecht has written "Tamir?" on it. Tamir was an active Irgunist and later the attorney who defended Malchiel Greenwald in the Kastner trial; he worked with Hecht on *Perfidy*.

10. Wyman, *Abandonment of the Jews*, 149; Baumel, *"Bergson Boys,"* 175; Peter Bergson, interview, in Wyman and Medoff, *Race against Death*, 123; Medoff, *Militant Zionism*, 188–93; and Medoff, "When the U.S. Government Spied." The group's actual involvement in arms smuggling is discussed in chapter 15, "Only Thus."

11. Frederick R. Barkley, "New Group Sets Up a Hebrew Nation," *New York Times*, May 19, 1944; and Baumel, *"Bergson Boys,"* 201.

12. Grossman, Syrkin, and Goldstein are quoted in Rapoport, *Shake Heaven and Earth* (citing Meir Grossman, *Congress Weekly*, May 26, 1944; Marie Syrkin, "Liberation by Double Talk," *Congress Weekly*, August 11, 1944, 2–8; and Dr. Israel Goldstein, *Washington Post*, May 19, 1944); American Zionist Emergency Council, quoted in Frederick R. Barkley, "New Group Sets Up a Hebrew Nation," *New York Times*, May 19, 1944; and New Zionist Organization, quoted in G. Troy, "Ben Hecht," 93 (citing B. Netanyahu, "The Fiasco of the Hebrew Committee," *Zionews Magazine*, July 1944, 13). On Begin and the Bergson Group's opinion, see Y. Ben-Ami, *Years of Wrath*, 355–56; and Alexander Rafaeli, interview, in Baumel, *"Bergson Boys,"* 204.

13. Hecht, excerpt from personal message to Bergson published in *Answer* magazine, which Richard P. Gale inserted in the *Congressional Record*: Rep. Richard P. Gale, Extension of Remarks, June 15, 1944, 90 Cong. Rec. A3436–37 (1944).

14. Hecht, *Child*, 594.

15. Ben Hecht file, Series I, Palestine Statehood Committee Papers, cited in G. Troy, "Ben Hecht," 95; and Eldad, *First Tithe*, 155.

16. Hecht, *Child*, 597; Bell, *Terror out of Zion*, 65–66, 69; and Heller, *Stern Gang*, 89–90.

17. Bell, *Terror out of Zion*, 270–73; Heller, *Stern Gang*, 62, 68, 79, 85–89, 91–91, 96–97; "Gangsters Must Be Found and Punished," *Palestine Post*, January 25, 1942, 3; "Abraham Stern Wanted: Jewish Community Will Fight Terror," *Palestine Post*, January 27, 1942, 3; "Police to Offer L.P. 3,000 as Rewards," *Palestine Post*, January 27, 1942, 3; and "Leader of Stern Gang Shot Dead," *Palestine Post*, February 13, 1942, 3.

18. Bell, *Terror out of Zion*, 85; and Yellin-Mor, quoted in Bethell, *Palestine Triangle*, 181.

19. Clifton Daniel, "Churchill Warns Jews to Oust Gangs," *New York Times*, November 18, 1944.

20. Hecht, *Child*, 596; Bell, *Terror out of Zion*, 132–34; Segev, *One Palestine, Complete*, 451–58; Bethell, *Palestine Triangle*, 184–86; and Howard, "Duplicity and Prejudice," a review of *A Palestine Triangle*, *New York Times*, May 19, 1944. Hecht and his cohort considered partition to be scraps from Britain's table anyway and would hardly have been surprised, or impressed, that Churchill was considering the offer.

21. Jeremiah J. Berman, "Churchill Speech Protested," letter to the editor, *New York Times*, November 23, 1944.

22. Hecht, *Jewish Fairy Tale*, 1, in Series III, Subject File for Hecht, Palestine Statehood Committee Papers, Miller Nichols Library, University of Missouri-Kansas City. See also *"A Jewish Fairy Tale* at Carnegie Hall Tonight," *New York Post*, December 4, 1944, 22, FultonHistory.com.

23. Hecht, *Jewish Fairy Tale*, 1–6, 7, 9, 12.

24. Hecht, *Jewish Fairy Tale*, 13, 16, 17.

25. Hecht, *Jewish Fairy Tale*, 10; and G. Troy, "Ben Hecht," 96.

26. Hecht to the Earl of Halifax, February 26, 1945, Extension of Remarks, entered into the *Congressional Record* by Representative Andrew L. Somers, 91 Cong. Rec. A951 (1945).

27. Patrick McGilligan, *Alfred Hitchcock: A Life in Darkness and Light* (New York: Regan Books, 2003), 253, 366, 368.

28. Stettinius memo, quoted in McGilligan, *Alfred Hitchcock*, 368. See also McGilligan, *Alfred Hitchcock*, 369; and Hecht, *Child*, 583.

29. Hecht, *Child*, 583; *Watchtower over Tomorrow*, directed by John Cromwell and Hartold F. Kress (Washington, D.C.: U.S. Office of War Information, 1945); *Watch Tower for Tomorrow*, radio script, Series 1: Works, 1908–1983, box 31, folder 792, BHPNL; and "On Your Radio Dial," *San Bernardino County Sun*, April 25, 1945, 11. Hecht gets the title wrong in his autobiography, calling it *The World of Tomorrow*, an indication of his lack of pride in the film. The film is available online on Vimeo (http://vimeo.com/63510160).

30. Hecht, *Watch Tower for Tomorrow*, 3, 6, 18; and *Watchtower over Tomorrow*.

31. Hecht, *Watch Tower for Tomorrow*, 6, 18; and *Watchtower over Tomorrow*.

32. Hecht, *Watch Tower for Tomorrow*, 13; and *Watchtower over Tomorrow*.

33. Ben Hecht to Rose Hecht, April 2, 1945, Series 4: Family Correspondence, 1915–1976, box 73, folder 2257, BHPNL. See also Thomas W. Lippmann, "The Day FDR Met Saudi Arabia's Ibn Saud," *Link* 38, no. 2 (April–May 2005): 9, available at http://www.ameu.org/getattachment/51ee4866-95c 1-4603-b0dd-e16d2d49fcbc/The-Day-FDR-Met-Saudi-Arabia-Ibn-Saud .aspx.

34. Ben Hecht to Rose Hecht, April 2, 1945, Series 4: Family Correspondence, 1915–1976, box 73, folder 2257, BHPNL.

35. Ben Hecht to Rose Hecht, April 2, 1945, Series 4: Family Correspondence, 1915–1976, box 73, folder 2257, BHPNL.

36. Hecht, *Child*, 583.

37. Hecht, *Child*, 584. See also Irvine Douglas, "San Francisco Conference Opens with Short Session," *Sydney Morning Herald*, April 27, 1945, 1.

38. McGilligan, *Alfred Hitchcock*, 366; Kael, *5001 Nights*, 536; and *Notorious*, written by Ben Hecht, directed by Alfred Hitchcock, starring Cary Grant and Ingrid Bergman (RKO Radio Pictures, 1946; New York: Criterion Collection, Home Vision Entertainment, 2001), DVD.

39. François Truffaut, *Hitchcock*, rev. ed. (New York: Simon and Schuster, 1985), 168–69. See also Alfred Hitchcock, interview by François Truffaut, August 1962, "Part 19, "*Notorious* through to a Discussion about Success," the Alfred Hitchcock wiki, http://www.hitchcockwiki.com/wiki/Interview:_Alfred _Hitchcock_and_ Fran%C3%A7ois_Truffaut_(Aug/1962)#Audio. On IG Farben and Zyklon B, see Antony C. Sutton, *Wall Street and the Rise of Hitler* (Seal Beach, Calif.: '76 Press, 1976).

40. Leonard Maltin, interviewed in *Ben Hecht—the Shakespeare of Hollywood*, from *The Adventures of Young Indiana Jones Documentaries*, produced and written by David O'Dell (San Francisco: Lucasfilm, 2007), DVD set.

Chapter 15

1. M. Levin, *In Search*, 306–7.
2. Hecht, *A Flag Is Born*, 20, Series 1: Works, 1908–1983, box 9, folder 271, BHPNL.
3. Hecht to Peter Bergson, n.d. [fall 1946], Series 3: Outgoing Correspondence, 1931–1977, box 66, folder 1823, BHPNL; *Specter of the Rose*, written and directed by Ben Hecht (1946; Los Angeles: Republic Pictures, 1989), VHS; and MacAdams, *Man behind the Legend*, 239–40.
4. Hecht, quoted in Phineas Biron, Strictly Confidential, *Wisconsin Jewish Chronicle*, August 31, 1945, 10. On the fund-raising dinner, see G. Troy, "Ben Hecht," 97–98. On Hecht's film achievements of the mid- to late 1940s, see MacAdams, *Man behind the Legend*, 242–48.
5. Hecht, *Child*, 605–6.
6. Hecht, *Shake Heaven and Earth*, 204–5; and G. Troy, "Ben Hecht," 98.
7. "Hecht Claims Disputed," *New York Times*, April 16, 1946; Clifton Daniels, "Seizures Lift Costs in Smuggling Jews," *New York Times*, April 15, 1946; and "Britain Is Trying to Suppress This American Action," advertisement, *New York Evening Post*, August 28, 1946, 37.
8. Y. Ben-Ami, *Years of Wrath*, 357–58.
9. Y. Ben-Ami, *Years of Wrath*, 353; Bell, *Terror out of Zion*, 133, 136, 137–44; and Segev, *One Palestine, Complete*, 471–72.
10. Gene Currivan, "3 Terrorists Bands in Palestine Cited," *New York Times*, December 31, 1945; J. H. Nuemann, "Work of the Haganah Described," letter to the editor, *New York Times*, January 4, 1946; I. F. Stone, "Gangsters or Patriots?," *Nation*, January 12, 1946, 35; Nathan George Horwitt, "Gun-Moll Journalism," *Answer*, June 1946, 17, Series 5: Subject Files, 1919–1981, box 77, folder 2345, BHPNL; and Gene Currivan, "Palestine Breeds Teen-Age Gun Girl," *New York Times*, April 27, 1946, 6.
11. Hecht, *Perfidy*, 27–28; Begin, *Revolt*, 93–94; and Bell, *Terror out of Zion*, 150–67.
12. Bell, *Terror out of Zion*, 163.
13. Barker, quoted in Bethell, *Palestine Triangle*, 267; and Hecht, quoted in "Leading U.S. Jews Denounce Violence," *New York Times*, July 25, 1946. See also Bethell, *Palestine Triangle*, 257–68; and Bell, *Terror out of Zion*, 169–73.
14. On the report of the Anglo-American Committee, see Bethell, *Palestine Triangle*, 235–36. One the end of the Tenuat Hameri agreement, see Bell, *Terror out of Zion*, 173–74. The slogan is from Y. Ben-Ami, *Years of Wrath*, 384.
15. Hecht, "Tales of Capering, Rueful Laughter," *New York Times*, July 7, 1946, 100. On the Adlers, see Whitfield, "Politics of Pageantry," 247.
16. Peter Manso, *Brando* (London: Weidenfeld and Nicolson, 1994), 100–180 passim.

17. Marlon Brando, *Brando: Songs My Mother Taught Me* (New York: Random House, 1994), 105. On Brando's rise and the agreement to work for the equity minimum, see Manso, *Brando*, 176–77, 180–82. See also G. Troy, "Ben Hecht," 100.

18. Hecht, quoted in Jerome Lawrence, *Actor: The Life and Times of Paul Muni* (New York: Putnam, 1974), 292; and Luther Adler, quoted in Manso, *Brando*, 184. See also Manso, *Brando*, 183.

19. See Hasia R. Diner, *We Remember with Reverence and Love: American Jews and the Myth of Silence after the Holocaust, 1945–1962* (New York: New York University Press, 2009), 266–321.

20. Hecht, *Flag Is Born*, prologue, 1–5.

21. Hecht, *Flag Is Born*, 5–7.

22. Hecht, *Flag Is Born*, 7–17.

23. Hecht, *Flag Is Born*, 17–24.

24. Hecht, *Flag Is Born*, 24–26.

25. Bittner and Brando are quoted in Manso, *Brando*, 185. See also Brooks Atkinson, "The Play," *New York Times*, September 7, 1946, 10. For the audience reactions, see also Medoff, *Militant Zionism*, 155.

26. Quoted in Whitfield, "Politics of Pageantry," 247; G. Troy, "Ben Hecht," 104; and Citron, "Ben Staging Hecht's Pageant-Drama," 90.

27. "UN Men Feel at Home at New Hecht Play," *New York Times*, September 6, 1946; and Hecht, quoted in G. Troy, "Ben Hecht," 100.

28. Dr. Bernard Kahn, quoted in Citron, "Ben Hecht's Pageant-Drama," 91.

29. "A Flag Is Born," *Life*, September 30, 1946; Eliahu Epstein, quoted in G. Troy, "Ben Hecht," 103; and Medoff, *Militant Zionism*, 195–96.

30. Judah Magnes, "Magnes Says Play Supports Terror," *New York Times*, December 3, 1946, 41.

31. Quoted in Medoff, *Militant Zionism*, 159–60.

32. Quoted in G. Troy, "Ben Hecht," 104–5.

33. Quoted in G. Troy, "Ben Hecht," 109.

34. Whitfield, "Politics of Pageantry," 245; and Richard Watts Jr., "Koestler's Novel of Zionism," *New York Times* November 3, 1946, 158.

35. Brando, *Brando*, 109–11.

36. Jessie Zel Lurie, "Confusion Worse Confounded," *Congress Weekly*, February 7, 1947, 10; Medoff, *Militant Zionism*, 188–93; and Medoff, "When the U.S. Government Spied."

37. Hecht, *Child*, 609; Bergson, interview, in Wyman and Medoff, *Race against Death*, 123; Y. Ben-Ami, *Years of Wrath*, 424–25; Baumel, *"Bergson Boys,"* 237–38; Rapoport, *Shake Heaven and Earth*, 205–6; and Begin, *Revolt*, 63. Of Bergson's eventual departure from the group, Baumel notes, "Money matters continued to be an unfailing source for disagreements and harsh disputes between the Irgun and members of the Hebrew Committee" (237).

38. George Horne, "Mystery Ship Seen as Exiles' Haven," *New York Times*, January 18, 1947; and Aviva Halamish, *The Exodus Affair: Holocaust Survivors and the*

Struggle for Palestine (Syracuse, N.Y.: Syracuse University Press, 1998), 16. Rafael Medoff gives the same figures in *Militant Zionism*, 196.

39. Y. Ben-Ami, *Years of Wrath*, 395; and Baumel, *"Bergson Boys,"* 224.

40. Peter Bergson to Ben Hecht, October 10, 1946, Series 2: Incoming Correspondence, 1914–1979, box 55, folder 1069b, BHPNL.

41. Y. Ben-Ami, *Years of Wrath*, 356, 424.

42. Meir Zamir, "'Bid' for the *Altalena*: France's Covert Action in the 1948 War in Palestine," *Middle Eastern Studies* 46, no. 1 (2010): 17–58; and Hecht, *Child*, 621–25.

43. Ben Hecht to Samuel Merlin, early fall 1947, 1, Series 2: Incoming Correspondence, 1914–1979, box 63, folder 1692, BHPNL.

44. Ben Hecht to Samuel Merlin, early fall 1947, 2, Series 2: Incoming Correspondence, 1914–1979, box 63, folder 1692, BHPNL.

45. Ben Hecht to Samuel Merlin, early fall 1947, 2–3, Series 2: Incoming Correspondence, 1914–1979, box 63, folder 1692, BHPNL.

46. Hecht, *Perfidy*, 40; and Halamish, *Exodus Affair*, 16.

47. Raider, "'Irresponsible, Undisciplined Opposition,'" 322, 326, 327–28.

48. Raider, "'Irresponsible, Undisciplined Opposition,'" 330, 335–36, 341, 358.

49. Ze'ev Sternhell, "Fascist Ideology," in *Fascism: A Reader's Guide. Analyses, Interpretations, Bibliography*, ed. Walter Laqueur (Berkeley: University of California Press, 1978), 315. On fascism's start in Italy, see Stanley G. Payne, *Fascism: Comparison and Definition* (Madison: University of Wisconsin Press, 1980), 3–4.

50. Ernst Nolte, *Three Faces of Fascism: Action Française, Italian Fascism, National Socialism*, (New York: Holt, Rinehart and Winston, 1966);National Socialism.}, [1st ed.]. (New York: Holt, Rinehart and Winston, 1966 Ze'ev Sternhell, *The Birth of Fascist Ideology: From Cultural Rebellion to Political Revolution* (Princeton, N.J.: Princeton University Press, 1994), 4–5; and Payne, *Fascism*, 1–6.

51. Sternhell, *Birth of Fascist Ideology*, 6, 10.

52. Sternhell, *Birth of Fascist Ideology*, 10.

53. Y. Ben-Ami, *Years of Wrath*, 231; and Begin, *Revolt*, 164.

54. Yoav Gelber, "Propaganda as History: What Really Happened at Deir Yassin?," appendix 2 in *Palestine, 1948: War, Escape and the Emergence of the Palestinian Refugee Problem* (Brighton, UK: Sussex Academic, 2001), 307–90.

55. Hecht, "Unfinished Life," 72.

Part IV

1. Hecht, *Child*, 612. For the date of the event, see "Witness Tags Cohen as Debt Welsher," *Los Angeles Times*, June 8, 1951, 1,4. The journalist Dean Jennings also cites May 24, 1948, as the date. Dean Jennings, "Mickey Cohen: The

Private Life of a Hood," conclusion, *Saturday Evening Post*, October 11, 1958, 118.

2.	Ben Hecht, "Speeches: Delivered at Slapsie Maxie's (sic)—Financed by Mickey Cohen," Series 1: Works, 1908–1983, box 27, folder 683, BHPNL.

3.	Hecht, *Child*, 612.

4.	M. M. Cohen, *In My Own Words*, 89–91.

5.	Quoted in Hecht, *Child*, 610.

6.	Rockaway, *But He Was Good*, 221. On Lansky, Cohen, Morton, and Zelig, see Robert Lacey, *Little Man: Meyer Lansky and the Gangster Life* (Boston: Little, Brown, 1991), 10–11; M. M. Cohen, *In My Own Words*, 35; Rockaway, *But He Was Good*, 220–24; and Rose Keefe, "Big Jack Zelig, Lower East Side Gang Leader," J-Grit: The Internet Index of Tough Jews, n.d., http://www.j-grit.com/big-jack-zelig-lower-east-side-gangster.php.

7.	M. M. Cohen, *In My Own Words*, 67–68; FBI case file 92-HQ-3156, Part One, Criminal Record, pp. 11–14; "Accused of Libel on Gen. M'Arthur," *New York Times*, April 1, 1942; "Noble, Jones Face 3 Sets of Charges," *New York Times*, April 2, 1942; "Sentenced for Roosevelt Libel," *New York Times*, May 20, 1942; Louis Nizer, "What to Do When a Judge Is Put up against the Wall," *New York Times*, April 5, 1970; and Colin S. Hoffman, "Conspiratorial Politics: The Friends of Progress and California's Radicals of the Right during World War Two" (bachelor's thesis, University of California, Davis, 2004), 87. The declassified FBI documents come from an antiracketeering case file, dated October 8, 1960, that contains a table of contents and compiled research, including field office reports from over the years.

8.	M. M. Cohen, *In My Own Words*, 68; see also Hoffman, "Conspiratorial Politics."

9.	Dean Southern Jennings, *We Only Kill Each Other: The Life and Bad Times of Bugsy Siegel* (Englewood Cliffs, N.J.: Prentice-Hall, 1967), 74–76. Robert Lacey attributes Jennings's story to Siegel's friend George Raft, the movie actor. Lacey, *Little Man*, 112. Countess Dorothy di Frasso's niece was Mary "Mimsi" Taylor, the model and actress with whom Hecht was carrying on an affair. Hecht certainly knew di Frasso: in a 1960 article for *Playboy* about old Hollywood, he relates an anecdote she told him about Rudolph Valentino. Hecht and Siegel may therefore have been personally acquainted. Since they would have known each other through Hecht's mistress, it is unlikely that Hecht would have written of the connection. Mary Elizabeth Plummer, "'Winsome Bachelor' Girls of U.S. Await Right Man," Associated Press wire story, *Bee* (Danville, Va.), August 17, 1936, 2; and Hecht, "If Hollywood Is Dying as a Moviemaker, Perhaps the Following Are Some of the Reasons," *Playboy*, November 1960, 57.

10.	Jennings, *We Only Kill*, 77.

11.	Lacey, *Little Man*, 114–27; Timothy Newark, *Mafia Allies: The True Story of America's Secret Alliance with the Mob in World War II* (St. Paul, Minn.: Zenith, 2007), 89–111, 152–54; and Dennis Eisenberg, Uri Dan, and Eli

Landau, *Meyer Lansky: Mogul of the Mob* (New York: Paddington, 1979), 186–223. Much about this alliance was documented in the Herlands Report of 1954, commissioned by New York governor Thomas E. Dewey, who as a federal prosecutor had originally put Luciano away. *Meyer Lansky: Mogul of the Mob* quotes Lansky at length on ferreting out Nazi spies from West Side hotels, restaurants in Yorkville, and a gay brothel near the Brooklyn Navy Yard (pp. 195, 199). Lansky's recollections were first published in Uri Dan's three-part series "Meyer Lansky Breaks His Silence" in *Ma'ariv* in July 1971. Questions have been raised about the veracity of *Mogul of the Mob*, but the Herlands Report corroborates at least some of these accounts. See, for example, Newark, *Mafia Allies*, 105. For doubts about *Mogul of the Mob*, see Robert Rockaway, "American Jews and Crime," *American Studies International* 38, no. 1 (February 2000): 29.

12. Quoted in Eisenberg, Dan, and Landau, *Meyer Lansky*, 184.
13. Eisenberg, Dan, and Landau, *Meyer Lansky*, 184–85; Rockaway, *But He Was Good*, 228–29; and Lacey, *Little Man*, 113.
14. Luther Huston, "Bund Activities Widespread/Evidence Taken by Dies Committee Throws Light on Garden Rally," *New York Times*, February 26, 1939; "Nazi Secrets in U.S. Told by *Times* Men," *Chicago Daily Times*, September 9, 1937; and Lansky, quoted in Eisenberg, Dan, and Landau, *Meyer Lansky*, 185; see also Rockaway, *But He Was Good*, 229. On the Bund's activities, see Newark, *Mafia Allies*, 271.
15. Eisenberg, Dan, and Landau, *Meyer Lansky*, 185–86; "Seven Injured at Nazi Rally Here When Legionnaires Heckle Speaker," *New York Times*, April 21, 1938; and Newark, *Mafia Allies*, 74–75, citing "Veterans Fight Nazis on Hitler's Birthday," *New York Herald Tribune*, April 21, 1938, 1, 7.
16. Quoted in Eisenberg, Dan, and Landau, *Meyer Lansky*, 186.
17. Lansky, interview with Robert Rockaway, in Rockaway, *But He Was Good*, 230–31; and Eisenberg, Dan, and Landau, *Meyer Lansky*, 186.
18. Hecht, "Unfinished Life," 65. On challenging the distinction between lawmaker and lawbreaker, see, for example, Begin, *Revolt*, 37; and Eldad, *First Tithe*, 155. On urging the use of chemical weapons., see Rapoport, *Shake Heaven and Earth*, 91; and Baumel, *"Bergson Boys,"* 149–50, 213. Like Hecht and Bergson, Alex Rafaeli was also deeply concerned with the issue of war crimes. In his memoir *Dream and Action* he recounts that as an officer with the U.S. Army's Counter Intelligence Corps, he was responsible for the capture and indictment of Alfried Krupp, one of Germany's major munitions manufacturers. Krupp was convicted in 1948 of crimes against humanity for his participation in Germany's aggression, the plundering of occupied lands, and the barbaric treatment of concentration camp inmates, who were used for slave labor.
19. Richard Watts Jr., "Koestler's Novel of Zionism," November 3, 1946, 158; and Hecht, "Unfinished Life," 58.
20. Hecht, "All Day He Fell," labeled "First Draft, February 6, 1959," p. 1, Series 1: Works, 1908–1983, box 7, folder 220, BHPNL. All of the unpublished

documents cited in part IV from folders 216 through 229 are from Series 1: Works, 1908–1983, box 7, BHPNL. The dates for all these documents span from 1958 to 1959, except for Hecht's notes, which are undated. These folders include 216–25, "Cohen, Mickey, MS draft, 1958–1959"; folders 226–27, "Cohen, Mickey, Notes On, n.d."; and folders 228–29, "Cohen, Mickey, Research Notes on Crime and People, 1958–1959."

21. Hecht, *Charlie*, 23; Hecht, "Lament for a Lost Bohemia," *New York Times*, January 12, 1958; and Fetherling, *Five Lives*, 170–71.

22. Margaret Cousins, Hecht's editor at Doubleday for *Gaily, Gaily*, to Stephen Fuller, aka William MacAdams, February 4, 1976, p. 2 of 3, folder 378, MacAdams Collection; and Fetherling, *Five Lives*, 168.

23. Minna Emch to Ben Hecht, postmarked July 3, 1958, Series 4: Family Correspondence, 1915–1976, box 71, folder 2223, BHPNL. MacAdams reports that Hecht signed with Henry Holt in January 1958 to write *Soul of a Gunman*. MacAdams, *Man behind the Legend*, 270.

Chapter 16

1. Eisenberg, Dan, and Landau, *Meyer Lansky*, 10.

2. O'Dell, *Ben Hecht*, DVD.

3. Hecht, *Child*, 608–9; Hecht, "Speeches—[To the Crew of the *SS Ben Hecht*)—1947," Series 1: Works, 1908–1983, box 27, folder 689, BHPNL; and "Men of 'Ben Hecht' Get Hero Welcome," *New York Evening Post*, April 14, 1947, 20.

4. Hecht, "Letter to the Terrorists of Palestine," *New York Herald Tribune*, May 15, 1947, 17; Edward G. Robinson, *All My Yesterdays: An Autobiography* (New York: Hawthorn Books, 1973), 156; and Rapoport, *Shake Heaven and Earth*, 203.

5. "Halt in Palestine Agitation Here Requested by Truman," *New York Times*, June 6, 1947, 1; "Funds for Terror," *Newsweek*, June 16, 1947, 30, quoted in G. Troy, "Ben Hecht," 113; "Driving Backward," editorial, *Chicago Daily News*, May 21, 1947, 18; "The Latest Tragedy," editorial, *New York Herald Tribune*, May 20, 1947, 28; William A. Kirk, "Crime and Violence," and Alice E. Holden, "Sympathy Alienated," in "Ben Hecht's Letter on Palestine Terrorism Backfires," letters column, *New York Herald Tribune*, May 18, 1947, 7.

6. American Jewish Committee, quoted in "Hecht Views Decried by 2 Jewish Groups," *New York Times*, June 5, 1947, 17; Mardoqued Salomon, "Zionist Aims and Ideals," letter to the editor, *New York Herald Tribune*, 28; C. V. R. Thompson, "For a Year I've Wanted to Say This," editorial, *Daily Express* (London), March 20, 1947, 2; Gershon Agronsky, "A Zionist Answers Ben Hecht," *Daily Mail* (London), May 27, 1947; and George Lichteim, "Seeking an Easy Target," editorial, *Palestine Post*, November 2, 1948, 4.

7. "Winchell Calls Us Brutish," *Daily Express* (London), May 23, 1947, 1; G. Troy, "Ben Hecht," 112, 157n54; Rapoport, *Shake Heaven and Earth*, 203; J. M. Winnetka, "With Ben Hecht on Palestine," letters column, *Chicago Daily*

News, May 24, 1947, 14; and Marion Kuhn, "Why Irgun Fights," *New York Herald Tribune*, May 23, 1947, 24.

8. Hecht, "Speeches—[To the Crew of the *SS Ben Hecht*)—1947."

9. Hecht, "Speeches—[To the Crew of the *SS Ben Hecht*)—1947."

10. Hecht, quoted in "U.S. Zionists Fight Seizure of Vessel," *New York Times*, March 9, 1947; and "Britannia Waives the Rules/British Jail American Seamen in Palestine: Who Is Breaking What Law?," advertisement, *New York Evening Post*, March 19, 1947, 40. See also "U.S.-Manned Refugee Ship Seized at Haifa with Crew," *New York Times*, March 10, 1947; Medoff, *Militant Zionism*, 160–63; and "Men of 'Ben Hecht' Get Hero Welcome," *New York Evening Post*, April 14, 1947, 20; on the ship as a kind of Trojan-horse mission, see Hillel Kook, interview with Louis Rapoport, in *Shake Heaven and Earth*, 202.

11. Baumel, *"Bergson Boys,"* 223; "Hecht Ill," *Daily Express* (London), June 14, 1947; "Sundry Gleanings," in Sam Zolotow, "Lee, Huston to Do a Play on the Circus," *New York Times*, June 23, 1947; Hecht, *Child*, 615; Hecht, "Requiem for Three," *PM*, July 30, 1947, quoted in G. Troy, "Ben Hecht," 115; and Menachem Begin to Ben Hecht, Tammuz, 5707 (June–July 1947), Series 2: Incoming Correspondence, 1914–1979, box 55, folder 1059, BHPNL.

12. Hecht, *The Terrorist*, reprinted in the *Answer*, September 19, 1947, sec. 2, pp. 1–8, Series 5: Subject Files, 1919–1981, box 77, folder 2345, BHPNL.

13. Hecht, *Terrorist*; and "4 Dead in Police Raid on Ramat Gan," and "Official Communique," *Palestine Post*, April 25, 1946, 1.

14. Hecht, *Terrorist*, 4.

15. Hecht, *Terrorist*, 4–8.

16. Hecht, *Child*, 508. The Irgun launched dozens of attacks over the next three months; most notable were the Acre Prison jailbreak on May 4, 1947, and the hanging of the British sergeants Clifford Martin and Mervyn Paice. See, for example, Bell, *Terror out of Zion*, 199–238. On the "scathing letter," see Y. Ben-Ami, *Years of Wrath*, 424–25.

17. M. M. Cohen, *In My Own Words*, 89–91; and Hecht, *Child*, 610–11.

18. M. M. Cohen, *In My Own Words*, 91–92. See also Yitshaq Ben-Ami, "Gangsters Contributed $60,000 in Cash," *Jewish Week and the American Examiner*, January 18, 1981, 3.

19. Y. Ben-Ami, "Gangsters Contributed $60,000."

20. Benny Morris, "Lashing Back—Israel's 1947–1948 Civil War," *Military History Quarterly* 21, no. 3 (Spring 2009), http://www.historynet.com/lashing-back -israel-1947-1948-civil-war.htm; Benny Morris, *The Birth of the Palestinian Refugee Problem Revisited*, 2nd ed. (Cambridge: Cambridge University Press, 2004), 16–17, 36n7; Howard Morley Sachar, *A History of Israel: From the Rise of Zionism to Our Time*, 3rd ed., rev. and updated (New York: Knopf, 2007), 299–300; Slater, *Pledge*, 129, 132, 182–83, 208; and Samuel Merlin to Hecht, December 30, 1947, Series 2: Incoming Correspondence, 1914–1979, box 60, folder 1472, BHPNL.

21. M. M. Cohen, *In My Own Words*, 89, 92; and Sidney Zion, "Luciano a Genius? No, My Jews," *Daily News*, December 3, 1998, http://www.nydailynews .com/archives/opinions/ luciano-genius-jews-article-1.818998. See also Eisenberg, Dan, and Landau, *Meyer Lansky*, 295–96; and Lacey, *Little Man*, 163. On Charley "the Jew" Yanowsky, Albert Anastasia, Longy Zwillman, and the smuggling operations, see also Nathan Ward, *Dark Harbor: The War for the New York Waterfront* (New York: Farrar, Straus and Giroux, 2010), 169–71; James Terence Fisher, *On the Irish Waterfront: The Crusader, the Movie, and the Soul of the Port of New York*, Cushwa Center Studies of Catholicism in Twentieth-Century America (Ithaca, N.Y.: Cornell University Press, 2009), 145–46; Ginger Adams Otis, "Inside New York's 'Waterfront' Mob," *New York Post*, June 20, 2010; Rockaway, *But He Was Good*, 231, 246–47; and Ricky-Dale Calhoun, "Arming David: The Haganah's Illegal Arms Procurement Network in the United States, 1945–49," *Journal of Palestine Studies* 36, no. 4 (Summer 2007): 28.

22. M. M. Cohen, *In My Own Words*, 92–93. See also Eisenberg, Dan, and Landau, *Meyer Lansky*, 295–96; and Lacey, *Little Man*, 163.

23. Hecht, *Child*, 609. See also Robert I. Friedman, *The False Prophet: Rabbi Meir Kahane—from FBI Informant to Knesset Member* (Brooklyn, N.Y.: Lawrence Hill Books, 1990, 35–37). On the Zweibons, see Medoff, *Militant Zionism*, 202–5.

24. M. M. Cohen, *In My Own Words*, 92; Y. Ben-Ami, "Gangsters Contributed $60,000"; and Paul Gropman, interview with the author, August 2013. On the unpublished memoir of Rabbi Baruch Rabinowitz, see Rafael Medoff, "An Unorthodox Rabbi on Capitol Hill: The Legacy of Rabbi Baruch Rabinowitz," *Jewish Action*, Spring 2004, http://www.ou.org/publications /ja/5764/5764spr/PROFILE.PDF.

25. "Come and Salute the Colors of Hebrew Freedom," advertisement, *New York Evening Post*, May 3, 13; "U.S. to Deny Visas in Palestine Clash," *New York Times*, March 31, 1948; and G. Troy, "Ben Hecht," 117. See also Isaac Zaar, *Rescue and Liberation: America's Part in the Birth of Israel* (New York: Bloch, 1954); and Jeffrey Weiss and Craig Weiss, *I Am My Brother's Keeper: American Volunteers in Israel's War for Independence, 1947–1949* (Atglen, Pa.: Schiffer Military History, 1998).

26. Jeff Wheelwright, "How Punchy Was Slapsy Maxy?," *Sports Illustrated*, April 11, 1983, http://sportsillustrated.cnn.com/vault/article/magazine /MAG1120714/.

27. Hecht, *Child*, 611–13; and "Wellpott Heard Phone Recordings of Own Voice, He Tells Grand Jury," *Los Angeles Times*, August 10, 1949, 2–3.

28. "Witness Tags Cohen as Debt Welsher," *Los Angeles Times*, June 8, 1951, 1, 4; Ben Hecht, "Speeches: [Delivered at Slapsie Maxie's—Financed by Mickey Cohen], ca. 1943 (sic)," Series 1: Works, 1908–1983, box 27, folder 683, BHPNL; and Patrick Goldstein, "Did Mickey Cohen Really Own Slapsy Maxie's Nightclub?," *Big Picture* blog, *Los Angeles Times*, December 1, 2011,

http://latimesblogs.latimes.com/movies/2011/12/a-hollywood-history-lesson -did-mickey-cohen-really-own-slapsy-maxies-nightclub-.html. The date is also reported as May 24, 1948, in Dean Jennings's four-part 1958 series on Cohen. See Jennings, "Private Life," conclusion, 118.

29. Hecht, "Speeches: [Delivered at Slapsie Maxie's—Financed by Mickey Cohen] ca. 1943 (sic)."

30. Jimmy Fratianno, interview by Mike Wallace, *60 Minutes*, CBS, January 4, 1981, http://www. cbsnews.com/video/watch/?id=7405452n. See also Ovid Demaris, *The Last Mafioso: The Treacherous World of Jimmy Fratianno* (New York: Times Books, 1981). Fratianno and Demaris were slapped with a $110 million defamation suit in April 1981 for the claim that a story about a sunken ship had been planted in the press at Cohen's request. Agnes Underwood, the now-retired assistant managing editor of the *Los Angeles Herald-Examiner* whom Fratianno had named in his story, said she never even knew Cohen at the time and complained that the mobster had smeared her lifelong reputation as a journalist. Fratianno then tried to sue Demaris, claiming that the words attributed to him in the book "were not [his] words or statements"—though this would do little to explain what he had told Wallace on television. A judge ultimately dismissed Underwood's libel case, concluding that the Fratianno's statement was mere opinion and could not be construed as fact. Myrna Oliver, "Retired Newspaper Editor Claims Book Defamed Her," *Los Angeles Times*, April 23, 1981, A9; Myrna Oliver, "Ex-Hit Man Takes Aim at Author," *Los Angeles Times*, November 25, 1981, A16; and Myrna Oliver, "4 Dropped from $110-Million Libel Suit," March 19, 1982, D3.

31. Y. Ben-Ami, "Gangsters Contributed $60,000."

32. Rafaeli, *Dream and Action*, 160–62.

33. Morris, "Lashing Back"; and Slater, *Pledge*, 133.

34. Arazi, quoted in Slater, *Pledge*, 133; and Teddy Kollek, *For Jerusalem: A Life* (New York: Random House, 1978), 68–69. See also Slater, *Pledge*, 81–85, 127, 133, 196; and Eisenberg, Dan, and Landau, *Meyer Lansky*, 296. On Dafni, see Rockaway, *But He Was Good*, 246–48.

35. Slater, *Pledge*, 63–65, 181–82; and Eisenberg, Dan, and Landau, *Meyer Lansky*, 296.

36. "Arab Aides in U.N. Hail TNT Seizure," *New York Times*, January 10, 1948; Slater, *Pledge*, 132, 171–72, 192, 321; and Medoff, *Militant Zionism*, 207–9, 210–11.

37. M. M. Cohen, *In My Own Words*, 92; and Benson, *Harry S. Truman*, 113. On Truman's sympathies and motivations, see also Michael Joseph Cohen, *Truman and Israel* (Berkeley: University of California Press, 1990).

38. Calhoun, "Arming David," 31.

39. Hecht, quoted in C. V. R. Thompson, "Bernadotte Was an Ass, Hecht Says," *Daily Express* (London), September 25, 1948, 1; "Hecht's Films under Ban," *New York Times*, October 14, 1948; Thomas F. Brady, "Britain Objects," *New*

York Times, October 24, 1948; Peter Bergson to Ben Hecht, July 12, 1951, and September 15, 1951, Series 2: Incoming Correspondence, 1914–1979, box 55, folder 1069b, BHPNL; Ben Hecht to Peter Bergson, December 26, 1952, Series 3: Outgoing Correspondence, 1931–1977, box 66, folder 1823, BHPNL; and G. Troy, "Ben Hecht," 118.

40. Hecht, "Speeches: [Menachem Begin Welcome], n.d.," Series 1: Works, 1908–1983, box 27, folder 687, BHPNL. See also "Former Irgun Leader Sees Palestine Unity with Brotherhood among Jews and Arabs," *New York Times*, November 30, 1948; and "£12-A-Head Banquet Served with Hate," *Daily Express* (London), November 30, 1948, 1.

41. Hannah Arendt et al., "New Palestine Party/Visit of Menachen [sic] Begin and Aims of Political Movement Discussed," letter to the editor, *New York Times*, December 4, 1948. According to Benny Morris, between 110 and 120 villagers were killed at Deir Yassin. On the death toll, the motivation and orders for the operation against the village, and the reverberations, see Morris, *Palestine Refugee Problem*, 233–40.

Chapter 17

1. *A Street with No Name*, screenplay by Harry Kleiner and Samuel G. Engel, directed by William Keighley, starring Mark Stevens and Richard Widmark (Los Angeles: 20th Century Fox, 1948). The trailer is featured on Ben Hecht, Charles Lederer, Eleazar Lipsky, and Philip Dunne, *Kiss of Death*, directed by Henry Hathaway, starring Richard Widmark and Victor Mature (Los Angeles: 20th Century Fox, 1947), DVD.

2. Frank Tashlin, interview with William MacAdams, n.d., ca. 1972, MacAdams Collection. Also see MacAdams, *Man behind the Legend*, 270. Tashlin was a screenwriter who cowrote *Love Happy* with Hecht. In the finding aid, MacAdams notes that this was the last interview Tashlin gave before he died on May 5, 1972.

3. Quoted from Tereba, *Mickey Cohen*, 22. See also Estes Kefauver, *Crime in America* (New York: Greenwood, 1968), 249; Hecht, "About Me, First," 19, folders 216, 219; and Hecht, "Unfinished Life," 62.

4. Paul Lieberman, *Gangster Squad: Covert Cops, the Mob, and the Battle for Los Angeles* (New York: Thomas Dunne Books/St. Martin's Griffin, 2012), 180, 202, 495; and Jennings, "Private Life," pt. 2, *Saturday Evening Post*, September 27, 1958, 110. *Life* published photos of him on numerous occasions, most famously a photo essay titled "Trouble in Los Angeles," *Life*, January 16, 1950, 75–85. Alas, the doggie bed photo is not included in the set *Life* has posted on the Internet: http://life.time.com/crime/mickey-cohen-photos-of-a-legendary-los-angeles-mobster-1949/#1.

5. Tereba, *Mickey Cohen*, 65–69, 85. See also Mickey Cohen, "Own Story," n.d., Series 1: Works, 1908–1983, box 51, folder 976, BHPNL; Hecht,

drafts titled "About Me, First," 9–10, folder 219, BHPNL; "Some Notes for Cohen Movie," 3–5, Series 5: Subject Files, 1919–1981, box 77, folder 2341, BHPNL; and A. Rose to Mr. D.M. Ladd from, office memorandum, "Michael 'Mickey' Cohen, information concerning," July 21, 1949, FBI file 62-HQ-89947, pp. 2–3.

6. The phrase "miniature colossus" is from Ted Prager and Larry Craft, *Hoodlums: New York* (New York: Retail Distributors, 1959), 95. Hecht's quote is from *Child*, 611. On Cohen's headquarters, the store, and the surroundings, see M. M. Cohen, "Own Story," n.p.; Lieberman, *Gangster Squad*, 93, 121; John Buntin, *L.A. Noir: The Struggle for the Soul of America's Most Seductive City* (New York: Harmony Books, 2009), 129; and Tereba, *Mickey Cohen*, 86.

7. Quoted from Tereba, *Mickey Cohen*, 86. See also Tereba, *Mickey Cohen*, 87–88; and Hecht, "Unfinished Life," 66, 72.

8. George Redston, *The Conspiracy of Death*, with Kendell F. Crossen (Indianapolis: Bobbs-Merrill, 1965), 87. On the fleet of Cadillacs, see Jennings, "Private Life," conclusion, 114; Prager and Craft, *Hoodlums*, 95–96; and Tereba, *Mickey Cohen*, 88–89.

9. M. M. Cohen, "Own Story," n.p.; Jennings, "Private Life," pt. 3, *Saturday Evening Post*, October 4, 1958, 120; and office memo to FBI director from Special Agent in Charge (SAC), Los Angeles, October 30, 1950, FBI file 62-HQ-89947, 226–27.

10. M. M. Cohen, "Own Story"; M. M. Cohen, *In My Own Words*, 2; and Hecht, "Unfinished Life," 60. There's a slight discrepancy here. On page 2 of Cohen's unpublished biography, "Own Story," on file in the Hecht archive at the Newberry Library, he recalls that when his mother "moved Lillian and me to Los Angeles she opened a small grocery store." But page 2 of *In My Own Words*, cowritten with Peer Nugent, recounts that his mother moved the whole family from Brownsville, Brooklyn, to Boyle Heights, Los Angeles.

11. Hecht, "About Me, First," 5, folder 219; Hecht, "Unfinished Life," 60; Florabel Muir, *Headline Happy* (New York: Holt, 1950), 215–16; M. M. Cohen, *In My Own Words*, 6; and M. M. Cohen, "Own Story."

12. Quoted from Hecht, "About Me, First," 5, folder 219; and Hecht, "Unfinished Life," 60. See also M. M. Cohen, *In My Own Words*, 2–6. For the story of Cohen trying to hold up a downtown movie theater, see Tereba, *Mickey Cohen*, 10–11, citing Jeffrey Feinman, *Hollywood Confidential* (Chicago: Playboy Press, 1976), 86.

13. M. M. Cohen, *In My Own Words*, 8. See also M. M. Cohen, *In My Own Words*, 64; Hecht, "About Me, First," 5, folder 219; and Hecht, "Unfinished Life," 60.

14. Rockaway, *But He Was Good*, 44–47; Tereba, *Mickey Cohen*, 14–16; Hecht, "About Me, First," 7, 8, folder 216; untitled manuscript, 3, folder 217; and Hecht, "Unfinished Life," 60, 61. Salerno's statement is the opening epigraph in M. M. Cohen, *In My Own Words*.

15. Hecht, "About Me, First," 37, folder 216; and Hecht, "Unfinished Life," 66.

16. Alva Johnston, "The Cauliflower King-I," *New Yorker*, April 8, 1933, 24, quoted in Buntin, *L.A. Noir*, 45; see also M. M. Cohen, *In My Own Words*, 11–14; and Tereba, *Mickey Cohen*, 15.

17. Hecht, "The Philoolooloo Bird," *New Yorker*, November 3, 1928; and Hecht, *1001 Afternoons in New York*, 367. An article in the *Jewish Criterion* reported that Hecht had been recruited by the *Morning Telegraph* to cover prize fights, joining Ring Lardner on the payroll. "The Money Lure," *Jewish Criterion*, January 4, 1929, 42. See, for example, Hecht, "The Rights That Failed," *Morning Telegraph*, January 19, 1929. On Hecht's coverage for the *Morning Telegraph*, see also MacAdams, *Man behind the Legend*, 114. Hecht wrote that every morning at eight for twenty years he "punched the bag, did mat work and grunted lifting weights" under the eye of trainer Elmer Cole. See Hecht, *Child*, 300.

18. Hecht, "Letter to the Terrorists of Palestine," *New York Herald Tribune*, May 15, 1947, 17; and Rob Edelman, "Boxing Writer Learned His Love of the Gloves as a Child," *Jewish Daily Forward*, May 23, 2003, http://forward.com /articles/8860/boxing-writer-learned-his-love-of-the-gloves-as-a/. The article also reports that Schulberg was about to be inducted into the Boxing Hall of Fame and Museum on June 8, 2003. Max Baer was only half Jewish—his father was Jewish—but he came into the ring with Schmelling wearing a Star of David emblazoned on his boxers. *On the Waterfront*, written by Budd Schulberg, starring Marlon Brando, directed by Eliah Kazan (1954; Culver City, Calif.: Columbia Tristar Home Entertainment, 2001). A year later, Schulberg released the acclaimed novel based on the material, though he rejected the idea that the book was a "novelization" of the film. Schulberg, *Waterfront: A Novel* (New York: D. I. Fine, 1955).

19. Hecht, "Unfinished Life," 60; and M. M. Cohen, *In My Own Words*, 13–14. Cohen told Senator Estes Kefauver's committee investigating organized crime that he had fought in thirty-two main events. See "Investigation of Organized Crime in Interstate Commerce, Hearings before a Special Committee to Investigate Organized Crime in Interstate Commerce, United States Senate, Eighty-First Congress, Second Session, Pursuant to S. Res. 202" (Washington, D.C.: Government Printing Office, 1951), http://archive.org/stream/investig ationofo10unit/investigationofo10unit_djvu.txt. The claim to seventy-nine bouts is found in John Hall, "The Old Fighter," *Los Angeles Times*, November 13, 1974, E3. The most credible source is "Mickey Cohen," BoxRec, n.d., accessed September 22, 2018, http://boxrec.com/en/boxer/166332. The record on the site appears to be relatively accurate and complete, consistent with what I could find reported in newspapers. One source of confusion is that a welterweight from Denver at the time was also named Mickey Cohen—a far more successful boxer. "Decision Stuns California Boy," Cohen bout with Ollie Bartlett, *Los Angeles Times*, December 11, 1930; "Chalky Wright to Meet Cohan," *Los Angeles Times*, April 6, 1933; and Associated Press, "Arizmendi Stops Cohen," *Los Angeles Times*, May 15, 1933, 11.

20. Hecht, "About Me, First," 6, folder 216; Hecht, "Unfinished Life," 60; and Jennings, "Private Life," pt. 1, *Saturday Evening Post*, September 20, 1958, 86.

21. Hecht, "About Me, First," 35, folder 216; untitled manuscript, folder 217; and Hecht, "Unfinished Life," 66.

22. M. M. Cohen, *In My Own Words*, 16. See also Buntin, *L.A. Noir*, 45; and Hecht, "Unfinished Life," 61.

23. Hecht, "About Me, First," 8, folders 216, 219; and Hecht, "Unfinished Life," 61. See also Bryan Burrough, *Public Enemies: America's Greatest Crime Wave and the Birth of the FBI, 1933–34* (New York: Penguin, 2004), xi–xii, 16. Hecht asked Cohen how he had managed to commit so many robberies without getting arrested and received several different explanations. Of these, he eventually decided the most illuminating was that Cohen was "right for it." Hecht noted, "There are hard luck heisters who walk into a sheriff's posse if they so much as make a pass at a candy store. And there are heisters who can blow up a safe at high noon without attracting attention." "About Me, First," 41, folder 216.

24. Hecht, "About Me, First," 7, folder 219; and Hecht, "Unfinished Life," 60–61.

25. Hecht, "About Me, First," 44–46, folder 216; Hecht, "Unfinished Life," 69–70; M. M. Cohen, "Own Story," 11–12; and M. M. Cohen, *In My Own Words*, 18.

26. Hecht, "About Me, First," 61, folder 216; and Hecht, "Unfinished Life," 73–74. On Mattie and Ralph Capone and Machine Gun McGurn, see Hecht, "About Me, First," 54, folder 216; Hecht, "Unfinished Life," 71–72; M. M. Cohen, *In My Own Words*, 24–26; and "'Machine Gun' McGurn Is Slain in Chicago; Linked to St. Valentine's Day 'Massacre' of 1929," *New York Times*, February 15, 1936.

27. Hecht, "About Me, First," 8, 60–61, folder 216; Hecht, "Unfinished Life," 73–74; and M. M. Cohen, "Own Story."

28. The first quotation is from "About Me, First," 70, folder 216; untitled manuscript, 70, folder 217; and Hecht, "Unfinished Life," 76. For slight variations on the phrasing, see M. M. Cohen, "Own Story," 22–23; and M. M. Cohen *In My Own Words*, 32. The second quotation is from Hecht, untitled manuscript, 9, folder 217. In other drafts, Cohen is quoted as saying, "And now when I'm telling you these things it's like they happened to somebody else—a close friend or somebody. I feel ashamed over lots of them happening. Maybe it's just a way of coverin' up but, so help me—they didn't happen to me. And they never will." Hecht, "About Me, First," 14, folders 216, 219.

29. Hecht, untitled manuscript, 70, folder 217; Hecht, "Unfinished Life," 76; and M. M. Cohen, *In My Own Words*, 34.

30. On the Arnold Rothstein principle, see Lacey, *Little Man*, 50, 60–61, 66. On Lansky, Rothkopf, Jewish fellowship, and phoning Siegel, see M. M. Cohen, *In My Own Words*, 35–36. Cohen said, "If you want to know the truth about it, I didn't even want to go to work, and that's what being with Benny would be like."

31. Hecht, untitled manuscript, 82–84, folder 217; Hecht, "Unfinished Life," 80; M. M. Cohen, *In My Own Words*, 36–38; and Jennings, *We Only Kill*, 69–71.

32. A. Rose to Mr. D.M. Ladd, office memorandum, "Michael 'Mickey' Cohen, information concerning," July 21, 1949, FBI file 62-HQ-89947, p. 2; and Jennings, *We Only Kill*, 36, 38, 46, 243. On Siegel's plans, see Jennings, *We Only Kill*, 42–46, 80, 106–7; and Tereba, *Mickey Cohen*, 33–35, 44–45.

33. Lieberman, *Gangster Squad*, 44–48; and Buntin, *L.A. Noir*, 70–76.

34. Cohen, quoted in Jennings, *We Only Kill*, 71. See also Jennings, *We Only Kill*, 70, 72–73.

35. Hecht, untitled manuscript, 83–84, folder 217; and Hecht, "Unfinished Life," 80.

36. Hecht, untitled manuscript, 83–84, folder 217; and Hecht, "Unfinished Life," 80.

37. M. M. Cohen, *In My Own Words*, 39; and Hecht, "Mickey notes," 1, folder 216.

38. Stacher, quoted in Eisenberg, Dan, and Landau, *Meyer Lansky*, 57; and Lacey, *Little Man*, 157. See also Eisenberg, Dan, and Landau, *Meyer Lansky*, 56; and Rockaway, *But He Was Good*, 22.

39. Henry M. Holden, *FBI 100 Years: An Unofficial History* (Minneapolis: Zenith, 2008), 76; Muir, *Headline Happy*, 189; and Jennings, *We Only Kill*, 176. On Siegel's $5,000 coffin, see Lieberman, *Gangster Squad*, 83; and United Press International, "Brief Siegel Service Held," *Tucson Daily Citizen*, June 27, 1947, 2.

40. Hecht, "Mickey notes," 3, folder 216.

41. Jennings, *We Only Kill*, 80; Lieberman, *Gangster Squad*, 79, 184; Buntin, *L.A. Noir*, 91–92, 115–16; and Tereba, *Mickey Cohen*, 63–64. See also Ogden, *Legacy*, 92–112; and Cooney, *Annenbergs*.

42. Cohen, quoted in "Investigation of Organized Crime," 201. See also Hecht, "Mickey notes," 9, folder 216; M. M. Cohen, *In My Own Words*, 61–62; and Tereba, *Mickey Cohen*, 64.

43. Jennings, *We Only Kill*, 80. See also Drew Pearson, "Chicago Gangland Songbird Murdered for His 'Singing,'" Washington Merry-Go-Round, *Morning Herald* (Hagerston, Md.), October 26, 1963, 5; and Tereba, *Mickey Cohen*, 80.

44. M. M. Cohen, "Own Story," n.p.; Tereba, *Mickey Cohen*, 51–52, 92, 133–34; and Jennings, "Private Life," pt. 2, 110.

45. Hecht, untitled draft, 79, folder 217; and Hecht, "Unfinished Life," 78.

46. The quotations about political "jabberwock" and "a part of man's soul" are from Hecht, draft titled "Why I Write This Book," 1, 3, folder 216; and Hecht, "Unfinished Life," 58, 59. The next quote is from Hecht, handwritten notes, folder 221. The final quote is from Hecht, *Gaily, Gaily*, 87.

47. M. Levin, *In Search*, 306–7; and L. Kip Wheeler, *Literary Terms and Definitions*, s.v. "Romanticism," n.d., http://web.cn.edu/kwheeler/lit_terms_R.html.

48. M. M. Cohen, *In My Own Words*, 43; and Tereba, *Mickey Cohen*, 104. See also Jennings, *We Only Kill*, 124. On second acts in life, see F. Scott Fitzgerald, "My Lost City," in *My Lost City: Personal Essays, 1920–1940*, ed. James L. West III (New York: Cambridge University Press, 2005), 114. The line also appears in notes for his unfinished 1941 novel *The Last Tycoon*. But actually,

here in its original use, the full line is "I once thought that there were no second acts in American lives, but there was certainly to be a second act to New York's boom days." This suggests that he did indeed believe in second acts in American life and that he has been routinely misquoted. My apologies to Mr. Fitzgerald for compounding the error.

49. Quoted in Muir, *Headline Happy*, 220.

50. Jennings, *We Only Kill*, 38, 48, 124, 142–43; and Muir, *Headline Happy*, 193–95.

51. Muir, *Headline Happy*, 188–90; Jennings, *We Only Kill*, 148–52, 176; Rockaway, *But He Was Good*, 167–68; and Tereba, *Mickey Cohen*, 76–78.

52. Jennings, *We Only Kill*, 160–63, 180–81; Eisenberg, Dan, and Landau, *Meyer Lansky*, 153–54; Rockaway, *But He Was Good*, 168; and Tereba, *Mickey Cohen*, 78–79.

53. On Siegel's demand for $2 million, see Jennings, *We Only Kill*, 191–92; and Buntin, *L.A. Noir*, 116. On Siegel's death and its results for Cohen, see, for example, Tereba, *Mickey Cohen*, 80; M. M. Cohen, *In My Own Words*, 81; Jennings, *We Only Kill*, 203–4; and Los Angeles SAC R. B. Hood to J. Edgar Hoover, FBI director, July 1, 1947, pp. 3, 4, 7, FBI file 62-81518, http://vault.fbi.gov/Bugsy%20Siegel%20/Bugsy%20Siegel%20Part%2030%20of%2032.

54. M. M. Cohen, "Own Story," 22; and M. M. Cohen, *In My Own Words*, 71–73.

55. M. M. Cohen, *In My Own Words*, 51–52; Lieberman, *Gangster Squad*, 55–58; Buntin, *L.A. Noir*, 112–13; and Tereba, *Mickey Cohen*, 73–74.

56. Hecht, *Child*, 611.

57. "Mickey Cohen Associate Slain, Gang Warfare Revival Seen," *Los Angeles Times*, August 19, 1948, 1, 2; Lieberman, *Gangster Squad*, 120–23; and Tereba, *Mickey Cohen*, 99, 172–75.

58. Rabinowitz, quoted in "Cohen Fails to Fly East as Planned," *Los Angeles Times*, July 30, 1949, 1, 3. See also "Gang Guns Wound Cohen and 3 Aides," *Los Angeles Times*, July 20, 1949, 1; and Muir, *Headline Happy*, 202–10. Assigning Special Agent Cooper to Cohen was just one of many favors that Attorney General Fred N. Howser bestowed upon the underworld. Cohen was scheduled to appear before a grand jury about corruption. Howser argued that there was a price on Cohen's head and that he deserved the right of public protection.

59. Tereba, *Mickey Cohen*, 144–47; and Buntin, *L.A. Noir*, 152.

60. "Mickey Cohen's Splendor Fades like Frayed Jail Garb He Wears," *Los Angeles Times*, June 22, 1951, 2.

61. Hecht, "Why I Write This Book," 1, folder 216; and Hecht, "Unfinished Life," 58.

Chapter 18

1. Hecht, *Gaily, Gaily*, 197.

2. Lawson, quoted in MacAdams, *Man behind the Legend*, 255; and Hecht, *Child*, 607.

3. MacAdams, *Man behind the Legend*, 255, 260–61; Mike Wallace, foreword to *The Ben Hecht Show: Impolitic Observations from the Freest Thinker of 1950s Television*, by Ben Hecht, adapt. and ed. Bret Primack (Jefferson, N.C.: McFarland, 1993), xi–xii; Bret Primack, introduction to Hecht, *Ben Hecht Show*; and Bret Primack, "Ben Hecht, Television Performer," in Hecht, *Ben Hecht Show*, 1–4, 5–17, and throughout.

4. Hecht, *Child*, 631; and Fetherling, *Five Lives*, 148.

5. Boris Trbic, "Where the Sidewalk Ends," *Senses of Cinema*, no. 8 (July 2000), http://sensesofcinema.com/2000/cteq/sidewalk/.

6. Hugh Gray, interview by William MacAdams, n.d., MacAdams Collection, BHPNL; and MacAdams, *Man behind the Legend*, 260.

7. On the "kooky killer," see the 1958 trailer for *The Fiend Who Walked the West*, video, 2:14, posted by lasbugas on December 27, 2011, http://www.youtube.com/watch?v=6HpvhW8o0sQ; and *The Fiend Who Walked the West*, screenplay by Harry Brown, Phillip Yordan, Ben Hecht, and Charles Lederer, from a story by Eleazar Lipsky, directed by Gordon Douglas, and starring Robert Evans (Los Angeles: 20th Century Fox, 1958). On what happened to *Love Happy*, see MacAdams, *Man behind the Legend*, 256–57.

8. Jeremy Duns, "Casino Royale: Discovering the Lost Script," *Telegraph*, March 2, 2011, http://www.telegraph.co.uk/culture/film/jamesbond/8345119/Casino-Royale-discovering-the-lost-script.html.

9. Duns, "Casino Royale."

10. Duns, "Casino Royale."

11. Hecht, "Rehearsal for Murder," *Ellery Queen's Mystery Magazine*, January 1955, 134–46; "A Jackpot of Corpses," *Playboy*, March 1961, 51, 132–33; and "Chicago Days, 1959," title page, Series 1: Works, 1908–1983, box 4, folder 152, BHPNL.

12. Hecht to Charles Feldman, January 13, 1964, Series 3: Outgoing Correspondence, 1931–1977, box 66, folder 1888, BHPNL; and Ben Hecht to Minna Emch, n.d., Series 4: Family Correspondence, 1915–1976, box 71, folder 2234, BHPNL.

13. Duns, "Casino Royale."

14. MacAdams, *Man behind the Legend*, 255; and Fetherling, *Five Lives*, 157.

15. Hecht, *Child*, 359.

16. Louis Berg, "Brat of the Century," *Commentary*, October 1954, 374–78. See also Edward Alexander, *Irving Howe: Socialist, Critic, Jew*, Jewish Literature and Culture (Bloomington: Indiana University Press, 1998), 53; and Fiedler, "Jew in the American Novel." Because of *A Jew in Love*, Howe characterized Hecht as "the first to attack Jewish group existence from a standpoint close to fashionable Bohemian anti-Semitism" (53).

17. Saul Bellow, "The 1,001 Afternoons of Ben Hecht," review of *A Child of the Century*, *New York Times*, June 13, 1954.

18. Shechner, *After the Revolution*, 16, 42.

19. Marc Weingarten, *The Gang That Wouldn't Write Straight: Wolfe, Thompson, Didion, and the New Journalism Revolution* (New York: Crown, 2006), 1–34.

20. Austin C. Wehrwein, "Hecht Attacks Algren Preface," *New York Times*, November 21, 1963.

21. Algren, *"Erik Dorn,"* x, xiii, xvii; Hecht's and Algren's subsequent comments are quoted from Wehrwein, "Hecht Attacks Algren Preface."

22. Margaret Cousins, Hecht's editor at Doubleday for *Gaily, Gaily*, to Stephen Fuller, aka William MacAdams, February 4, 1976, p. 2 of 3, folder 378, MacAdams Collection, BHPNL.

23. Tom Wolfe, *The New Journalism* (New York: Harper & Row, 1973), preface; and Tom Wolfe, "The Birth of 'the New Journalism': Eyewitness Report," *New York*, February 14, 1972, http://nymag.com/news/media/47353/.

24. Fetherling, *Five Lives*, 157.

25. Fetherling, *Five Lives*, 167.

26. Weingarten, *Gang*, 228.

27. Sidney Zion, "On Ben Hecht," preface to Hecht, "Unfinished Life."

28. Henry Raymont, *"Scanlan's*, a Monthly Magazine, Promises to 'Vilify' Institutions," *New York Times*, February 25, 1970; Weingarten, *Gang*, 228–35; and Hunter S. Thompson, "The Kentucky Derby Is Decadent and Depraved," *Scanlan's Monthly*, June 1970, 1–12. Weingarten is quoting from a letter to Thompson from Bill Cardoso, who was editor of the *Boston Globe Sunday Magazine*.

29. Walter Winchell, On Broadway, *Humboldt (Calif.) Standard*, May 31, 1957, 4; "Bandsman with Welk Turns Cinema Villain," Movieland Events, *Los Angeles Times*, April 10, 1957; and Hecht, quoted in "Cohen Takes Manuscript to Author," *Los Angeles Times*, August 4, 1957, 34.

30. Hecht, "About Me, First," 1, 2, 13, folders 216, 219; and United Press International, "One-Time Mobster Takes Up New Life in Greenhouse," *Salina (Kans.) Journal*, July 30, 1956, 19.

31. Hecht, "About Me, First," 3, folders 216, 219.

32. Hecht, "Author Confessions," 2–3, folders 216, 222.

33. Hecht, "About Me, First," 18, folders 216, 219. Two informants advised the Federal Bureau of Investigation, "in the beginning of 1958 while he was residing at the Del Capri Hotel, that Cohen in his showers will 'air dry' himself rather than as he expressed it have a rough towel possibly injure his skin. [Redacted] advised from their personal observation this process of 'air drying' Cohen has after a shower takes approximately forty-five minutes." "Personal Habits and Peculiarities," October 8, 1960, FBI case file 92-HQ-3156, Part One, 252.

34. Hecht, "Author Confessions," 1, folders 216, 222.

35. Algren, *"Erik Dorn,"* xvii.

Chapter 19

1. Quoted in Redston, *Conspiracy of Death*, 69.
2. Hecht, "Mickey notes," handwritten and unnumbered, folder 226.
3. Hecht, loose page of untitled draft, p. 18, folder 219; Hecht, "About Me, First," 19, folders 216, 219; and Hecht, "Unfinished Life," 62.
4. Hecht, "About Me, First," 19–26, folder 216; 19–24, folder 219; and Hecht, "Unfinished Life," 62–64.
5. Hecht and Cohen's conversation is quoted from Hecht, "About Me, First," 33–34, folder 216; and Hecht, "Unfinished Life," 65. On the trip to La Paz and its timing, see also "Cohen Departs for Mexico to Finish His Book," *Los Angeles Times*, March 13, 1958.
6. Hecht, "About Me, First," 47, folder 216; and Hecht, "Unfinished Life," 70.
7. Hecht, "About Me, First," 64–65, 66, folder 216, 217; and Hecht, "Unfinished Life," 74–75.
8. Hecht, "About Me, First," 65–68, folder 216, 217; Hecht, "Unfinished Life," 74–75; and Hecht, "Mickey Notes," 1, folder 226.
9. The first quote is from "Why I Write This Book," 4, 216; Hecht, "Unfinished Life," 59. The second is from Hecht, "About Me, First," 49, folder 216; and Hecht, "Unfinished Life," 70. See also Hecht, "About Me, First," 3–4, folders 216, 219.
10. Hecht, "Al Capone," n.p., in "Cohen, Mickey—Research Notes on Crime and People, 1958–59," folder 229; and Eig, *Get Capone*, 28.
11. Hecht, "Mickey—Research Notes on Crime and People, 1958–59," folders 228–29.
12. Hecht, "The New Criminal," folder 228; Buntin, *L.A. Noir*, 242–43; and Lieberman, *Gangster Squad*, 368–70.
13. Hecht, "The New Criminal" and "Crime Pays," folder 228; and Tereba, *Mickey Cohen*, 73.
14. Hecht, "We're All Crooks" and "Valentine for a Gunman," folder 228.
15. On the revenue agents, see Hecht, "About Me, First," 21–22, folders 216, 219; Hecht, "I Set the Stage," 4–5, folders 223, 224; and Ben Hecht to Minna Emch, July 5, 1958, Series 4: Family Correspondence, 1915–1976, box 71, folder 2234, BHPNL. On his friends' reactions, see Hecht, "About Me, First," 2, folders 216, 219.
16. Ben Hecht to Minna Emch, n.d., box 71, folder 2234.
17. Minna Emch to Ben and Rose Hecht, July 3, 1958, box 71, folder 2223.
18. Minna Emch to Ben and Rose Hecht, July 3, 1958, box 71, folder 2223.
19. Ben Hecht to Minna Emch, July 5, 1958, box 71, folder 2234.
20. Hecht, "About Me, First," 68–72A, folder 216; and Hecht, "Unfinished Life," 75–76.
21. Minna Emch to Rose Hecht, August 13, 1958, box 71, folder 2228.
22. Rose Hecht, "Notes on What I Think Is a Fallacy in Hecht's Reasoning in the Mickey Cohen Manuscript," Series 5: Subject Files, 1919–1981, box 77, folder 2341, BHPNL.

23. Stevens, *King of the Sunset Strip*.
24. Stevens, *King of the Sunset Strip*, n.p.; and Walter Ames, "Locigno Indicted in Whalen Murder," *Los Angeles Times*, December 11, 1959, 2. On the Whalen murder and trial of Cohen associate Sam Locigno, see also Lieberman, *Gangster Squad*; Buntin, *L.A. Noir*; and Tereba, *Mickey Cohen*.
25. Stevens, *King of the Sunset Strip*, ch. 28.
26. A. Rosen to Mr. Ladd, office memo, April 24, 1951, FBI file 62-HQ-89947; and "Personal Habits and Peculiarities," FBI field office file, 92-106, October 8, 1960, pp. 253–54, FBI file 92-HQ-3156, 250–51.
27. Hecht, *Child*, 147.
28. Hecht, *Child*, 182; and "In Rusty Armor," review of *A Child of the Century*, *Time*, June 21, 1954.
29. Hecht, "About Me, First," folder 216, 69–70; and Hecht, "Unfinished Life," 76. Columnist Florabel Muir noted about her relationship with Cohen, "And so gradually with him, as with hundreds of others in trouble, I've come to assume a sort of mother-confessor role." Muir, *Headline Happy*, 219.
30. Hecht, "About Me, First," 1, folders 216, 219; and Hecht, "All Day He Fell, 1958–1959," 4, folder 221.
31. Hecht, "About Me, First," 11, folders 216, 219; and Hecht, "Unfinished Life," 61.
32. Jennings, "Private Life," pt. 1, 25.
33. Jennings, "Private Life," pt. 2, 110.
34. On the fifty-fifty split, see United Press International, "Hecht Discovers Little Interest in Life of Cohen," *Terre Haute (Ind.) Star*, May 18, 1961, 33. On the movie shares, see Jennings, "Private Life," conclusion, 118.
35. Jennings, "Private Life," pt. 1, 23, and conclusion, 118.
36. Jennings, "Private Life," conclusion, 118; and Tereba, *Mickey Cohen*, 256–57.
37. Cohen, quoted in Lieberman, *Gangster Squad*, 355–56; and Cohen, quoted in Jennings, "Private Life," pt. 1, 86. The new title, *Flim Flam*, is noted in FBI field office file, 92-106, October 8, 1960, on Meyer Harris Cohen, p. 237, in FBI file 92-HQ-3156, Part One, 234.
38. Jennings, "Private Life," pt. 1, 25, 85.
39. Jennings, "Private Life," conclusion, 118; Al Aronowitz, "The Gift," The Blacklisted Journalist website, Column Seven: March 1, 1996, sect. 2, http://www.blacklistedjournalist.com/column7a.html; and M. M. Cohen, *In My Own Words*, 116–17. Aronowitz was a rock music journalist who covered the major stars of the 1960s, including Bob Dylan and the Beatles, for the *New York Post*, the *Saturday Evening Post*, and other publications. The website is a compilation of his work dating back to 1995.
40. Ben Hecht's testimony in Transcript of Record, *United States v. Meyer Harris Cohen, also known as Michael "Mickey" Cohen*, No. 28991-CD (S.D. Cal. August 28, 1961), National Archives and Records Administration, the National Archives at Riverside, California, Record Group 21, Records of District Courts of the United States, Criminal Case Files, 1907–1999, folder 28991, box 2505, pp. 2336–2337.

41. The appeals court judgment is quoted in Lieberman, *Gangster Squad*, 495. Hecht's description is from Hecht to Emch, July 5, 1958, box 71, folder 2234.

42. Both of these explanations can, in fact, be found in Zion, "On Ben Hecht," 56–57.

43. Rose Hecht, "Notes on What I Think Is a Fallacy in Hecht's Reasoning in the Mickey Cohen Manuscript," box 77, folder 2341.

44. Hecht, *Ben Hecht Show*, 51–58.

45. Norman Mailer, "The White Negro," in *Advertisements for Myself* (New York: Putnam, 1959), 338, originally published in *Dissent*, Summer 1957. See also Primack, "Ben Hecht, Television Performer," 14–15.

46. Quoted in Mailer, "White Negro," 309.

47. Jack Kerouac, *The Town and the City* (London: Penguin, 2000), 370; and "Jack Kerouac Interview by Ben Hecht," October 17, 1958, pts. 1 and 2, aired on WABC-TV, video, 8:19 and 7:11, posted by Clarice Douglas Waill on May 22, 2009, http://www.youtube.com/watch?v=uK39vf4otrg (part 1) and http://www.youtube.com/watch?v=rcsUW _LBJlk (part 2).

48. Margaret Cousins, Hecht's editor at Doubleday for *Gaily, Gaily*, to Stephen Fuller, aka William MacAdams, February 4, 1976, folder 378, MacAdams Collection.

49. Tereba, *Mickey Cohen*, 258–59, 262–64, 266–67.

50. Mickey Cohen to Ben Hecht, February 12, 1964, and March 22, 1964, Series 2: Incoming Correspondence, 1914–1979, box 56, folder 1133, BHPNL.

51. Ben Hecht to Mickey Cohen, March 17, 1964, Series 3: Outgoing Correspondence, 1931–1977, box 66, folder 1852, BHPNL; and Rose Hecht, quoted in MacAdams, *Man behind the Legend*, 283.

52. MacAdams, *Man behind the Legend*, 284; and Margaret Cousins to Stephen Fuller, aka William MacAdams, February 4, 1976.

Conclusion

1. Hecht, *Child*, 2.

2. Fetherling, *Five Lives*, 16–17.

3. Peter Marks, "Why 'The Front Page' Is the Best Newspaper Comedy of All Time," *Washington Post*, October 15, 2016. See also the Internet Broadway Database, s.v. *The Front Page* 1986, accessed June 16, 2018, https://www.ibdb.com/broadway-production/the-front-page-4432; and Andrew Gans, "Broadway Revival of *The Front Page* Closes Jan. 29," *Playbill*, January 29, 2017.

4. Martin, *Ben Hecht*, 4.

5. Raymond J. Haberski writes that Sarris and Kael would "move quite a bit beyond their predecessors in popularizing the notion of movies as art." Haberski, *It's Only a Movie! Films and Critics in American Culture* (Lexington: University Press of Kentucky, 2001), 123–24.

6. See Andrew Sarris, "Notes on the Auteur Theory in 1962," *Film Culture* 27, no. 27 (Winter 1962/63): 1–8; Pauline Kael, "Circles and Squares," *Film Quarterly* 16, no. 3 (Spring 1963): 12–26; Martin, *Ben Hecht*, xi; Fetherling, *Five Lives*, 17; Haberski, *It's Only a Movie!*, 122–43; and David Kipen, "Auteurism's Great Snow Job," *SFGate*, April 22, 2001, http://articles.sfgate .com/2001-04-22/living/17595246_1_auteur-theory-auteurist-andrew-sarris. Hecht was not just at the center of an argument about movies as art: Haberski explains how the Kael-Sarris exchanges became deeply intertwined with broader debates on the merits of popular culture, which reflected changes well under way by the mid-1960s, as the old divisions between highbrow and lowbrow blurred. Dwight MacDonald, taking aim at Sarris, jumped into the fray with arguments about Masscult and Midcult; Sarris, for his part, incorporated Susan Sontag's advocacy for the democratization of art in her essays "Against Interpretation" and "One Culture and the New Sensibility." For MacDonald on Sarris, see "The Birds," in *Dwight MacDonald on the Movies* (Englewood Cliffs, N.J.: Prentice Hall, 1969), 305–7. For Sontag, see "Against Interpretation" and "One Culture and the New Sensibility," in *Against Interpretation and Other Essays*, 4th ed. (New York: Farrar, Straus & Giroux, 1969), 3–14, 293–304.

7. Kael, *Citizen Kane Book*. See also the reviews in Kael, *Kiss Kiss Bang Bang* (Boston: Little, Brown, 1968), 33, 59, 319–20; and in Kael, *5001 Nights*, 310–11, 335, 399, 629, 657, 758, 796.

8. Fetherling, *Five Lives*, 186.

9. Itamar Rabinovich, *Yitzhak Rabin: Soldier, Leader, Statesman*, Jewish Lives (New Haven, Conn.: Yale University Press, 2017), 138–40.

10. Antony Lerman, "The End of Liberal Zionism," *New York Times*, August 22, 2014. For population figures for the settlements, see Yotam Berger, "How Many Settlers Really Live in the West Bank?," *Haaretz*, June 15, 2017.

11. Hecht, *Notorious*.

Index

About the Author

Julien Gorbach spent most of his ten years as a daily newspaper reporter on the police beat, covering drive-by shootings and murder trials, and publishing an investigative series on killings that remained unsolved because gangs had intimidated witnesses into silence. As a freelancer, he contributed to the *Boston Phoenix*, *Time Out New York*, the *San Francisco Bay Guardian*, and the *New Orleans Gambit*, among other publications. He covered Hurricane Katrina for the *Boston Globe*. Gorbach earned a doctorate in media history at the University of Missouri-Columbia in 2013 and is now an assistant professor in the School of Communications at the University of Hawaii at Manoa.